HOMETOWN

Do your little bit of good where you are; it's those little
bits of good put together that overwhelm the world.

– Desmond Tutu

Support for this publication comes from

Library of Congress Cataloging-in-Publication Data

Names: Bullard, John K. (John Kilburn), author.
Title: Hometown / John K Bullard.

Identifiers: LCCN 2022058237 | ISBN 9780932027436 (cloth)
Subjects: LCSH: Bullard, John K. (John Kilburn) | Historic
  districts--Conservation and restoration--Massachusetts--New Bedford. |
  Historic buildings--Conservation and restoration--Massachusetts--New
  Bedford. | Waterfront Historic Area League (New Bedford, Mass.) |
  Waterfronts--Massachusetts--New Bedford--History--20th century. | New
  Bedford (Mass.)--Buildings, structures, etc. | New Bedford
  (Mass.)--Biography.
Classification: LCC F74.N5 B855 2024 | DDC 974.4/850092
  [B]--dc23/eng/20221207
LC record available at https://lccn.loc.gov/2022058237

HOMETOWN

To Roy
who I have admired and
respected for many, many
years

J.K. Bullard

John K. Bullard

Spinner Publications, Inc.
New Bedford, Massachusetts

for

Laurie

Foreword by Ken Hartnett

British-born Joseph Rotch was the pre-industrial age visionary who transformed New Bedford from a sleepy farm and fishing village to the global center of the whaling industry that endured for more than a century, shaping the city and region into the 20th century. With foresight and imagination, he bought ten acres of New Bedford waterfront from fellow Quaker and whaling enthusiast Joseph Russell III in 1765. With this purchase, Rotch had the right winds, the right harbor, the right timber—and none of the limitations crimping his earlier operations on Nantucket Island.

Mission-bent, Rotch built a family home an easy walk from the harbor, and he got down to work, milling timbers to build ships broad-beamed and ample enough to carry cargo across the Atlantic. Before long, he was building the iconic whaling ship, with a barrel perched atop the mainmast that would position an eagle-eyed lookout aloft to scour the sea for prey. Tryworks were constructed on deck to melt down whale blubber, and oared pursuit boats were clamped to sturdy rails for easy dispatch of harpoon-darting crews after a whale sighting.

A vertical integrationist ahead of his time, Rotch would also add banking and accounting arms to his ocean freight, shipbuilding, and whaling operations. He struck gold. Within ten years, some 90 ships would be operating out of New Bedford's harbor. The city competed with rivals near and far in producing fine candles and other byproducts of the spermaceti oils deemed vital as industrialization spread throughout the Western world.

Henceforth, a Rotch or a Rotch descendant has almost always been present—be their names Rotch or Gardner or Morgan or Bullard—whenever decisions of great weight have been made in New Bedford.

John K. Bullard, the author of *Hometown*, grew up under the weight of all those ancestral expectations. He was, after all, the 13th in a succession of John Bullards. All had gone to Harvard College. Along with their names, all inherited certain responsibilities to their family and community—carrying forward the burden and bounty of those who had gone before. How our contemporary John Bullard has handled the weight of his inheritance is a subtheme of this book.

In one sense, *Hometown* is Bullard's personal story. But the book is also about New Bedford and the richness and diversity of its people. As a history book, it tells the tale of two cities: the New Bedford that was and the New Bedford that is now becoming as we move through the 21st century.

Way back when, favorable winds and a deep harbor played a considerable role in Joseph Rotch's decision to bet his fortune on New Bedford. Today, it seems that the winds off New Bedford will likely play a key role in the city's future as the world struggles to cope with profound climate change. And right in the middle stands a Joseph Rotch descendant, John Bullard, as head of the Ocean Cluster team of advisors helping guide the city to manage the changes ahead in an economy that may well be wind driven.

I am a friend and longtime neighbor. I know how deeply the man cares about the earth and its protection, especially the sea and its fisheries. As a federal fisheries official he always sought to be fair while remaining relentlessly fearless and independent. It's not surprising to find Bullard once more in a central role. A major combat of ideas and understanding is unfolding in his hometown. Where else would the man be?

Smack in the middle of every fight worth having, you'll find John Bullard, a towering, robust, sea-loving bear of a man with a vigorous mind and a generous spirit who genuinely cares about the principles at stake in this often-muddled world. Preservationist, planner, and politician, Bullard has been head of heritage-saving WHALE and was New Bedford's mayor. He helped rescue the Rotch-Jones-Duff house, the Zeiterion Theater, and the historic district. He forced, at the risk of his budding political career, a reluctant city to build a modern sewage treatment plant and create the park at Fort Taber. He's made enemies, a few, while forging countless friendships.

In *Hometown*, Bullard piles on the details of hundreds of players in his narrative as if fearful their contributions to key planning or executive decisions might get overlooked in the story or lost to history. The author is serious about sharing the credit and/or the blame for the assorted outcomes. Conveniently, an index is provided.

One name repeatedly occurs, Sarah Delano. Bullard writes about this "graceful woman with the will of steel," a Rotch descendent, by the way: "Sarah…brought an appreciation of New Bedford's history, an eye for beauty and the significance of what WHALE was trying to save, and the courage, vision, and entrepreneurship of her whaling ancestors… She would work hard to avoid a battle, but if a battle was to be joined, she was always at the head of the pack, urging everyone on."

He recalls the showdown within the WHALE executive committee when it faced a decision to outbid a would-be restaurant developer for the Rotch-Jones-Duff House or lose the historic home. The developer would remodel the interior and pave over the magnificent gardens for a parking lot unless WHALE met his bidding price. The board wrestled with the costs, seemingly wildly beyond its means.

According to Bullard, Sarah had the last word with this declaration to the more timid officers: "No one is going to remember what we paid for this building. People will only remember whether we saved it."

John K. Bullard was talking about the mind and spirit of Sarah Delano. He was reminding me a lot of the mind and spirit of John K. Bullard.

Ken Hartnett is a veteran newsman, retired editor of the Standard-Times *newspaper, and founding president of the* New Bedford Light, *a nonprofit, nonpartisan digital news outlet.*

Contents

Introduction: Horizon Line

In the fall of 1969, I was sailing off the coast of Vigo, Spain, more than 3,000 miles from my hometown of New Bedford, Massachusetts. Fresh out of college and far from everything I knew, I was searching for a way to save the world.

I was determined to make a difference. So much needed changing, and I wanted to be part of that change. War was raging in Vietnam. The battle for civil rights was moving into the North. Consciousness-raising events had unleashed a powerful environmental movement.

As a college undergraduate, I focused on architectural sciences and physical design, and those fields attracted me as I considered the future. How could I use this for change? What occurred to me so far from home was that the best way to save the world was to focus on just one piece of it. And the best way for me to do that would be to work to make my hometown a better place. As I look back on my life more than a half-century later, I believe that decision has served me well. Saving the world can feel like an overwhelming task. But focusing on a place I know and love has made that work more joyful, effective, and achievable.

In those early years, two books shaped my journey. Saul Alinsky, a community organizer in Chicago in the 1960s and 1970s, wrote a very influential book. His *Rules for Radicals: A Pragmatic Primer for Realistic Radicals* offered practical advice for those seeking to lead others in creating change. His advice was profound and obvious: communicate through your audience's experience and value system. If you want to change the system, you must start with the system you want to change. "Look homeward," he advised his readers, likely mostly middle-class activists, who were perhaps not quite as privileged as I was in some ways. I doubt many of them would have had the means to sail halfway around the world after college. Despite my particular advantages in life—including a well-off family whose even wealthier ancestors played a significant role in American maritime history—I felt connected to these activists and was inspired along with them. Alinsky's advice struck a chord with me: "We must start from where we are if we are to build power for change."

The second book was Viktor Frankl's *Man's Search for Meaning*. The Nazis stripped nearly everything from Frankl in the Holocaust. The one thing they could not take was his attitude. Frankl said the key to happiness is for one's life to have meaning. The search for meaning must be directed outward. That is, you cannot make yourself happy by trying to make yourself happy.

I had traveled far from home and been through tumultuous times to understand place and purpose. The recent riots at Harvard awakened and alerted me. Storms at sea made me realize that every day is precious. Those weeks on that sailing trip, where the only constant was the level line of the horizon, made some things simple. The weeks alone in Vigo and later in Lisbon allowed for soul searching. I was able to dig deep because I had the time.

As I sailed, a strange thing happened. With distance and thought, what I had always seen as a confining pressure-packed prison of family expectation evolved into an opportunity. What I had thought of as a path that someone else had laid out for me suddenly became my path. I knew I needed to go home to make a difference and find meaning.

While this purpose became clear in my early twenties, the seeds were planted much earlier. From childhood, I had been caught in a spider web. On Christmas Eve each year, my parents, younger brother, younger sisters, and I would leave our farm in Dartmouth to visit my paternal grandparents nearby in New Bedford. I considered both places home. My grandparents resided in the 1845 ancestral home where my wife Laurie and I later would live with our family. Part of these Christmas Eve celebrations involved a spider web made of string that wound all over the house and led from one ancestor portrait to another. Some paths led to a bookshelf full of history books, several written by my grandfather John Morgan Bullard, who had extensively researched our ancestors. Not very exciting Christmas presents for young children, but fortunately, other fun gifts were sprinkled in along the way.

Still, the history and the family stories seeped into my consciousness. During those Christmas Eves, in those books, and in many conversations, my grandparents instilled in me a heritage to be aware of, to be proud of, and, make no mistake, to carry on. I am the 13th John Bullard in succession. All before me had gone to Harvard except one, who had been otherwise busy fighting in the Revolutionary War. My Rotch ancestors had brought their whaling business from Nantucket to New Bedford, setting my hometown on its course to become the whaling capital of the world. Joseph Rotch's business acumen outfoxed rival John Hancock for supremacy in the whaling business before the revolution. William Rotch Jr. was the first president of the New Bedford Abolitionist Society and a friend and business partner of possibly the wealthiest and most well-known man of color of his time, Captain Paul Cuffe, the free-born son of Cuff Slocum, a formerly enslaved West African, and Ruth Moses, a Wampanoag woman. Two of the Rotches had been New Bedford mayors. Two other ancestors were congressmen. One ancestor, Edmund Gardner, was badly injured by a sperm whale off Peru as a 23-year-old captain of a whaleship, yet he managed to have a successful voyage and career. Another ancestor, Charles W. Morgan, owned a vessel still visited today by millions at Mystic, Connecticut.

These stories and others shaped me. They created a tremendous bond to New Bedford, where many of these people had lived, were buried, and I was born. They showed that public service was a path that could take many directions. They also set a seemingly impossible level of achievement that somehow, I, among my siblings, felt I was supposed to carry forward. While that pressure had its good points, I often found myself resisting it, like when my first child was born. We broke family tradition and named him Matthew.

For me, it was always clear that I was expected to follow the path that others had walked before me. Growing up, I could map it forward and back. Certainly, I could go off on my own and blaze a new trail, but family expectations were clear, and they set out a definite course for me to follow. I remember a couple of preordained decision points along the way. For example, where would I go to high school? My grandfather insisted I go to St. George's School in Newport, Rhode Island, where he and, later, my father had gone. It was a fine New England preparatory school, but as soon as my grandfather spoke the words "St. George's," that was the last place on earth I wanted to go. He said if I chose otherwise, he would cease to be my grandfather. My parents acquiesced. I went and pretty much disliked every minute of my experience there, even though I made many very good friends.

The second fork in the road came my senior year in high school when I was choosing a college. I had defied the football coach and the headmaster by quitting football and playing soccer instead, and my grades miraculously rose. This meant I was a good candidate for Harvard University, the family alma mater in Cambridge, Massachusetts. Exercising my independence, I also decided to apply to Stanford University. I felt determined to get off the long family path of attending East Coast institutions and instead pursue my education on the West Coast. I wanted escape, was absolutely set on escape. As my family and I waited for the decisions to arrive in the mail, I visualized my life in Palo Alto, far away from the Ivy and my grandfather. I refused to be entangled.

Then two letters came—both Stanford and Harvard accepted me. I stared at the letters and their respective letterheads. And, for some reason, which I still do not fully understand, I abandoned my California dream and moved forward on the well-worn family path.

When the Strike of '69 happened during my senior year at Harvard, I woke to the outside world. During the protests, students expressed their collective anger against the Vietnam War, the lack of civil rights for minorities, and even Harvard's rampant expansion into Cambridge. We shut down the university for several weeks. There were confrontations with police, but all in all, for me, it was a very creative and thought-provoking time.

Aware of the draft, opposed to the war, and wanting to find a way to fulfill my service "requirement," I tried to enlist in the US Navy and the US Coast Guard. When I received a medical deferment because of my asthma, I decided to hitchhike by sailboat around the world to discover what I was meant to do. Significant time at sea is an excellent way to learn humility. It is spiritual. It can clear your mind, make you ready for new ways of thinking. Nurtured by role models, stoked by tumult and fury, and cleared and calmed by the vastness and solitude of the sea, a seed was planted that took root and anchored my life. I knew I needed to go home.

A half-century later, we don't have Nixon as president, but we are still in tumult. We are reeling from the aftereffects of a Trump presidency. Our environmental crisis is worsening. A dramatic assault on civil liberties is gaining strength. And despite the work that has been done, the content of a person's character still sometimes may not mean as much as their skin color, birthplace, gender, or religion. Indeed, as in my youth, "saving the world" remains an intimidating prospect.

There is, of course, no single right answer to the question, "How can I make a difference?" There are hundreds of thousands of right answers. For me, I knew I needed to start in my hometown, my community.

My definition of community started out as a physical space. Later in my career, when I returned to Harvard as a fellow at the Kennedy School's Institute of Politics, I had many conversations with my friend the late John Perry Barlow, a lyricist for the legendary rock band Grateful Dead. We talked about how community could mean a physical place, like my hometown of New Bedford or John's of Pinedale, Wyoming, which he referred to as "meatspace." He was an early adopter of the term, which in its simplest sense means the physical space where people interact. He also considered the definition of community to include "virtual" communities in cyberspace, where people gather online to communicate shared interests. I have discovered over the years that we were both right—an individual can find a home and a community in many kinds of places and spaces.

When I ended my sailing trip, I went back to my hometown, determined to make it a better place. I put down roots, got to know the people and the issues, helped to raise a family, and slowly but steadily made a difference. The issues changed over time. My job changed over time. My definition of hometown changed over time. But I always stayed rooted in a sense of place. What follows are stories of my journey over 50 years. Stories are stories. Mine are true to the best of my imperfect memory. I haven't changed any names or facts, but I don't proclaim this to be a history book. It's just a grandfather's collection of stories about caring for my hometown based on my sometimes-faltering recollections. As my friend Donald Gomes said, "Well, John, your memory of something might be very different than my memory of the very same thing." Inaccuracies or differences in memories or interpretations are, therefore, solely my responsibility.

These are *my* stories.

What is New Bedford? I've asked myself that so many times, and I've been asked that a million times by others. I've whittled my answer down to a word: seaport. The city of New Bedford is a seaport. We send our people to sea. We always have. I hope we always will. The port is 60 miles south of Boston, but at times, New Bedford could be in Rhode Island or on the Moon as far as the good people of greater Boston are concerned. It is 13 miles long and a mile-and-a-half wide.

It shares its harbor with Fairhaven. It is located in Bristol County and bordered by Fairhaven, Dartmouth, Acushnet, and Freetown. New Bedford is a tough, working-class town that struggles through each day. The public schools struggle to provide an adequate education. The police and non-profit sector struggle to cope with a drug culture borne of too little hope. The port has been the top-dollar port in the entire country for the last two decades, but a rougher, more dangerous job than fishing is hard to find. Many jobs that descend from the city's once-famous textile industry still exist in the city's apparel industry, but like fishing, these are not for the faint of heart or the weak of back.

Regardless of other industries and issues that may come or go, the character of New Bedford, in my eyes, is tied to the sea and the relationships it has forged because of these ties. Crews of whaling ships established early ties to the Azores, Madeira, and Cabo Verde (known earlier as Cape Verde), as well as pre-statehood California, Hawaii, and Alaska.

Even Japan, isolated for more than 200 years, was opened up in part by the whalers. As predicted by Herman Melville in *Moby-Dick*, "If that double-bolted land, Japan, is ever to become hospitable, it is the whale-ship alone to whom the credit will be due; for already she is on the threshold."

Before Melville inked those words while cruising the Pacific in 1841 on a whaling voyage out of Fairhaven, he likely crisscrossed the wake of the New Bedford whaleship *John J. Howland* which had on board a young Japanese castaway named Manjiro, who had been rescued from a desolate Pacific island. The captain brought the 15-year-old to his home in Fairhaven, where the young man lived for 11 years and obtained an education. He later returned to Japan and was instrumental in opening it up to the West, thus fulfilling Melville's prophesy. In 1987, when Japan's Crown Prince Akihito, who has since become emperor, visited the United States to see President Ronald Reagan, he made a special trip to Fairhaven to see the home and environs of Japan's pioneer of the West, Manjiro Nakahama, one of the first Japanese citizens to come to the United States.

This is what "Gateway City" means. New Bedford has been the gateway to America—and the American Dream—for tens of thousands of people. Some arrived on ships like the *Ernestina*, the sailing schooner that brought immigrants from Cabo Verde to New Bedford. Before and since, the city has welcomed others as well, such as Frederick Douglass, who escaped slavery via the Underground Railroad. Through their triumphs and challenges, these newcomers have helped build New Bedford and worked to build good lives for themselves and their families. Success was not guaranteed, and life was frequently a struggle, but one often full of meaning, purpose, dignity, and results.

New Bedford's economy reached phenomenal heights with whaling in the 1850s. The industry's geniuses took some of their profits and invested in textiles, beginning in 1848 with the Wamsutta Mill. The city's population grew from about 20,000 at whaling's pinnacle to about 130,000 when textiles peaked before the factory workers' Strike of 1928. The city's textile industry suffered from labor issues and competition from the South, but the factory magnates had no transition plan to keep the city's economy healthy. New Bedford lost population and jobs and eventually hope as an economic depression became a social depression, and the city's unemployment rate rose to 32 percent, the second highest in the nation. Instead of coming to New Bedford for opportunity, people looked to escape the city.

In the fall of 1969, as I considered my hometown from half a world away, I felt an enormous pull, both intellectual and emotional, to return. Intellectually, I could see New Bedford needed help. The city had problems every bit as complex as anywhere else in America, if not more so. It had about the lowest educational attainment anywhere, a high dropout rate, a struggling manufacturing economy, and a high unemployment rate. Suburban malls had emptied out its downtown. The poverty level was high, and a large population of non-English-speaking residents had little access to resources. Many major banks and corporations had fled. The population had dropped to about 100,000, and there were few big "movers and shakers" left to get things done. Students who managed to get into college after graduating from the city's substandard public school system often went away, never looking back. New Bedford's challenges were as tough as or tougher than any small city in America, and it didn't have the resources to tackle them.

Urban planners and other professionals wanted to work in places like Boston, Washington, and New York, where there was more "excitement." But unless you were a uniquely innovative city planner like Robert Moses, you weren't going to make much of an impact in a place as big as New York. This was an intellectual reason to work in New Bedford—it was a place where I might really make a difference.

Still for me, the emotional pull was the strongest. This was my hometown. My ancestors were laid to rest in the soil of New Bedford. I had a connection here that I didn't have anywhere else. I had a past and present here that connected to a future and made a path I could understand. There was continuity here that made sense to me. Just as I saw history in the cenotaphs at the Seamen's Bethel, I saw sense in keeping my connection to this seaport. I was from here. One's own concept of "where I come from" is personal. Everyone will describe it differently; there isn't a right or wrong perception of it, just what you feel in your heart. And for some reason—maybe my grandparents' crazy spider webs—I felt a strong tie to New Bedford, where I come from. If there was any place I was going to try to fix up, it was going to be here—my hometown.

I have always been very aware that while my roots in New Bedford go back to 1765, much of New Bedford is very different than I am. I am a White male Yankee with all the advantages that a privileged upbringing bestowed upon me. "Entitled" is an apt description. New Bedford today is definitely *not* all those things.

Whenever I confronted that dichotomy over the years, two questions would always come to mind: How can I live up to those advantages? Why should New Bedford trust me? Those questions motivated me. Every day, I worked as hard as I could to make those advantages work for the city I love. And every day, I worked as hard as I could to earn the trust of the people of New Bedford. It is only my hometown if I earn it, and I hope I have.

The back of my grandfather's gravestone says, "He loved New Bedford, Past and Present." I'll be happy if someone writes on the back of mine, "He loved New Bedford, too."

I. CHARTING A COURSE

Sintra, Portugal, 1969

CHAPTER 1

Coming Around

Running Before the Wind

Chance encounters or offhand comments can have lasting impacts. Perhaps it is like the famed "butterfly effect," where, in theory, a butterfly flapping its wings may change the course or timing of a distant tornado. While planning has been important, chance too has been key in shaping my life.

Before attending Harvard, my then-girlfriend Lynne Mace told me I should read *The Fountainhead*. I did. Thinking the protagonist Howard Roark was pretty cool, I decided to major in architectural sciences. A couple of years later, I read a book about Frank Lloyd Wright for an architectural class and realized his story was, essentially, the same as *The Fountainhead*. Lynne's comment set me off on a path of physical design that shaped my life.

While an undergraduate, I found summer work at Turner Construction Company. One summer, I worked as a low-level laborer on the IM Pei-designed Polaroid plant in Waltham. To this day, I feel a little jolt of pleasure whenever I drive by it.

Another summer, I was part of the engineering team that designed the Mather House for Harvard, also a Turner project. This work was physically easier but more mathematically taxing. Once, we laid out where a huge hole was to be drilled into bedrock for one of the elevators. After the elevator pit had been dug at great expense, our head engineer checked his measurements and found we were off by about a dozen feet. I learned several new swear words that day!

When I wasn't studying in the Swiss French architect Le Corbusier's fantastic and unique Carpenter Center at Harvard, I was racing small boats in the fall and spring with the varsity sailing team. We got to race bigger boats twice each year at the Naval Academy, but we needed a big boat for practicing. Fortunately, we had a loyal alumnus, Richard M. Burnes, who had sent several sons to the college and owned a 45-foot yawl named *Adele*. We practiced on it, and I got to know the "Burnes Boys."

When I graduated in 1969 and wanted to hitchhike around the world by sailboat while figuring out what to do with my life, I called Richard Burnes. Even though I had never raced more than 100 miles, he took a chance on me in the upcoming 1969 transatlantic race from Newport to Cork, Ireland, which covered several thousand miles. That would be my first leg around the world.

During a 100-mile tune-up race with the Burnes family aboard the *Adele*, I was hit in the head with a winch handle, and Danny Burnes, who would go on to become a fine doctor, put ten stitches over my eye as we continued racing. It was a good way to get to know the family and what they were capable of as mates and people.

One night off the Canadian province of Nova Scotia, just as I was about to come on watch, the skipper Mr. Burnes (everyone called him "Bunny") shouted up to his son James (everyone called him "Bear") at the helm.

"What's it like up there, Bear?"

"We've got the bullet-proof spinnaker up. It's blowing 45 knots. We've been out of control for ten minutes," Bear shouted back.

Back home in Buzzards Bay, where I had learned to sail, if it was blowing 45 knots, you didn't go sailing—you stayed home under your bed! Yet, here I was, nearly in the middle of the ocean and a very long way from any help, racing with a spinnaker up. In the middle of the night.

Captain "Bunny" Burnes

Aboard the Adele, *1969*

Bunny sat back from his chart table, stubbed out his Carlton cigarette, and closed the trashy novel he was reading. He put away his reading glasses. He slowly got up and yelled over the maelstrom topsides to Bear.

"Well, I guess we should take in the spinnaker."

To me, the skipper's calm was somewhat reassuring. I got my foul-weather gear on and went topsides. I couldn't believe the scene. It was a nightmare come to life. Waves crashed into us, and we crashed into the waves. Everyone shouted instructions at the top of their lungs. The noise was deafening between the wind itself and the wind rushing through the rigging. But it wasn't just the noise. It was the blackness of the night against the intense whiteness of the wave crests, the foam, and the sails. Even at night in the blackness, I could appreciate the majesty of the waves and how insignificant they made me feel as if I could be crushed at any moment, on a whim.

We were on a big, heavy boat, but running before the wind under a spinnaker and surfing down these waves at twice her usual speed, the *Adele* was moving like a light dinghy, wildly careening from crest to crest. I tried to reconcile my sense of terror with the skipper's sense of calm. Finally, we managed to blanket the spinnaker under the lee of the mainsail and lower it to the deck. We set a jib and made our way through the storm.

I don't remember how we did in the race, but I do remember these three weeks at sea, the storms and the calms, and the being away from land. I remember that before we saw Ireland, we could smell the land. In those weeks, I learned that going to sea was powerful and that it changed a person. It was impossible to be at sea and not believe you could only exist with the permission of a far greater power.

"Remember," the ocean cries, "you are incredibly small, and you have a lot to be humble about."

After the *Adele*, I sailed on a different American boat for the Cowes Week regatta, a major international race week with hundreds of boats from dozens of countries in waters between Great Britain and the Isle of Wight. I sailed with the crew in the 600-mile Fastnet Race, named for the Fastnet Rock off southern Ireland, which the racecourse rounds. Next, I joined a Dutch boat crew to race from Plymouth, England, down to La Rochelle, France. That's when I discovered that the Aussie boats were not being sailed back to Australia; they were being shipped back "down under."

My hopes to circumnavigate the globe were dashed.

I rejoined the *Adele* to cruise south and then back across the Atlantic. We made our way "south until the butter melts" to warmer seas and then turned east in the trade winds to Barbados and Grenada.

Our last stop before turning east was the then-Portuguese colony of Cape Verde, an island chain off the northwest coast of Africa. We put into Mindelo, São Vicente, needing repairs to our refrigeration. All our meat had gone bad, and we had a three-week voyage in front of us.

We tied up astern of a beat-up schooner named *Ernestina*. While Bunny was off trying to get our refrigeration repaired, I wandered over to the schooner. The man on deck didn't speak much English, and I didn't speak Portuguese, but somehow, we communicated anyway. He definitely understood when I said I was from New Bedford. His eyes lit up. He told me the *Ernestina* had made many trips to New Bedford. Little did I know then how involved I would later become with this storied schooner. At the time, the wooden sailing ship was badly hogged with a sagging bow and stern and could no longer even make inter-island passages.

We had put in here along the trade winds for repairs and provisions, just as New Bedford whaleships had regularly done a century before. Whalers also picked up crew and continued on their multi-year voyages, and in this way, many Cape Verdeans came to settle in New Bedford and become American citizens. As a result, there is a robust population of Cape Verdeans in New Bedford and a healthy ongoing relationship between New Bedford and Cabo Verde.

As we were waiting for repairs, an inter-island packet, the *Maria Sony*, pulled in with chickens, goats, and other animals. We bought a goat and asked the crew of a Chinese fishing boat to put the meat in their freezer while ours was getting fixed. The request was not understood, and when we left the dock for our three-week passage, our only meat was one spoiled goat. Fortunately, there were many dolphin fish along the way, so we had fresh fish for the entire passage.

After we arrived in Barbados, most of the crew departed, leaving Bunny, Nick King, and myself to bring the *Adele* to Grenada, where they departed. I lived alone aboard the boat for three months, interrupted now and then by various visitors.

One afternoon, I was sitting in the cockpit taking apart a winch to re-grease when a man walked over and started a conversation. There weren't many visitors, so conversation was very welcome. I asked his name.

"Howard Turner."

"You aren't by any chance related to Turner Construction Company, are you?" said I, the wise ass. What were the chances I would run into a Turner in Grenada from Turner Construction in Massachusetts? It turned out, pretty good.

"Why yes, I am Turner Construction Company."

"You probably don't remember me. I worked for you for two summers," I said, pressing my luck. With that, he came aboard, and we talked for a while. He asked what I studied, what my interests were, where I was headed. After a few hours, he got up to leave and gave me his card.

"John, if you ever get off this boat and find yourself in New York, come by my office, and let's talk."

We said goodbye, and I didn't think much of it. By March of 1970, I had figured out what I needed to figure out, and it was time to get to work and move on to graduate school. I departed the *Adele* and Grenada and flew into New York before going home to New Bedford. I still had Howard Turner's card, and on a whim, I called his number, figuring he would never remember me. Boy, was I wrong. He immediately made time for me and asked if I had decided on graduate schools yet. I hadn't.

"Why don't we get IM Pei on the phone and see what he has to say."

"What?!?"

And for the next 45 minutes, I talked to the most famous architect in the world about graduate school. Why? Because Howard Turner took an interest in an ordinary college student.

Howard Turner   *Bonney Street Playground*

Next, he picked up the phone and put me on with a top executive at the architectural and urban planning firm Skidmore, Owings & Merrill. Mr. Turner spent most of that afternoon listening to the entirety of both those conversations, and he discussed them with me afterward.

What did I learn from that? Howard Turner was the CEO of one of the most prominent construction firms in the country. I was a nothing. But he made time for me. I learned that influential people make time for young people to guide them along. He showed me there are people out there who care about you, who root for you, and that you aren't alone in this. I have always tried to be like Howard Turner whenever a young person asks for my time.

Selling a Protection Plan for the Waterfront Historic District

Home from sea in 1970, I applied to the New Bedford Planning Department for a job to fill the time before beginning graduate school. I had the immense good fortune to be hired by City Planner Benjamin B. Baker. He was old-school and wise in the ways of the street. I couldn't have found a better person with whom to begin my real-world studies.

Ben immediately put me to work helping his assistant planner, Doug Bell, design and build playgrounds in New Bedford's South End. We created an adventure playground on Bonney Street and a soccer field and tennis court behind the hurricane barrier by Cove Road. None of these survive today, but for me, they were a way to learn about the city and to make parts of it better with my own hands. Ben had assembled a good and diverse staff. Ben Watkins, Peter Espinola, Paul Fernandes, and Bruce Rose formed my post-graduate course in New Bedford as we shared the back room. Years later, I am still working with Bruce Rose, a former chair of the NAACP, as we find ways to diversify the emerging offshore wind industry.

The planning department was my real introduction to the workings of New Bedford City Hall. George Rogers was mayor. He served many roles at different times—among them city councilor, state senator, and convicted felon. He was a colorful and controversial politician, the kind you find sprinkled throughout history, and he gave me my first job.

At the time, the waterfront historic district that had been the city center during the days of whaling had fallen into terrible decline. The issues were complex. The district encompassed 15 city blocks of about 70 buildings between the waterfront and the downtown district, but a divided highway separated it. It met every definition of urban blight. Most buildings failed to meet the building code and were vacant above the first floor. Utilities were above ground. There were numerous bookie joints and bars.

However, the area was also the support base for the city's dominant and defining industry—fishing. Chandleries, settlement houses, union halls, electronics stores, and other businesses supported the fishing fleet just as those same buildings had equipped and outfitted whaleships a century before.

New Bedford from the Regency Tower on Pleasant Street

The New Bedford Whaling Museum sat in the heart of the district, bringing tourists from far and wide to see the half-scale model of the whaling bark *Lagoda*, the largest ship model in the world. Across the street from the museum, the New Bedford Port Society operated the Seamen's Bethel, where mariners since before Herman Melville's time had come in the days ahead of venturing into the unforgiving waters of the Atlantic and beyond. A new historic preservation organization founded in 1960, the Waterfront Historic Area LeaguE (WHALE), had started work in the area, inventorying historic buildings and working with—and sometimes against—the New Bedford Redevelopment Authority to protect the district.

The ocean connects us—to other countries, to opportunity, to our past, and to our future. Although there are exceptions, it is hard to think of a city that has not developed around the water, be it an ocean, a river, or a lake. The water's edge is the most valuable real estate because it provides opportunity, whether for those stepping ashore for the first time or those going out to sea for food, commerce, or exploration. That explains why the first settlers of New Bedford lengthened the water's edge by building piers, docks, and bulkheads. And that is why the New Bedford Redevelopment Authority (NBRA) decided to modernize the waterfront when urban renewal started.

While most redevelopment agencies in America focused on residential blight with a strategy that tore neighborhoods down in order to "save" them, the city's redevelopment authority decided to focus on New Bedford's major asset—the harbor. First, they tackled the South Terminal, then the North Terminal, and with that, the redevelopment authority rebuilt nearly the entire New Bedford waterfront, laying a foundation for marine-based economic expansion for the next several generations. It was great foresight.

After revitalizing the harborfront, the New Bedford Redevelopment Authority looked to the waterfront historic district. With City Planner Richard Wengraf's assistance, WHALE was to be a key partner. Robert Kerr from Newport and his Corinthian Conservation Company produced the "orange book," an urban renewal plan for the district so groundbreaking it was featured in the *New York Times*. The book set restoration requirements that owners would have to meet to be consistent with federal historic preservation standards. The plan included designs for a "water-form" that would bring an inlet of water into the district near Centre Street. It also reintroduced mixed-use. It called for massive federal investment that would transform the district in a matter of a few years. At a time when redevelopment agencies were destroying neighborhoods all over America, this was revolutionary.

There was only one little problem with the plan—almost none of the people would be left.

Under the rules of eminent domain and urban renewal, a property owner would have to bring their building up to standard, or the New Bedford Redevelopment Authority would take ownership for fair market value, then sell the building at a reduced value so someone else could afford to restore the property. An economic analysis showed that it would make sense for only seven property owners to stay; the rest would have to leave. If the authority had gone ahead with the "orange book" plan, all the physical structures in the district would have been restored, but the social structures would have been destroyed. Continuity of use would be gone. We would have risked losing our real connection to the water. We would have risked becoming a cute tourist town or a one-dimensional museum village. Pretty, but pretty dull.

Benjamin Baker

During the late 1960s and early 1970s, unrest seemed to be everywhere, and New Bedford was no exception. A tragedy in 1970 refocused the authority's attention, and plans shifted. A 17-year-old Black youth, Lester Lima, was shot and killed in the city's West End during growing protests about discrimination, poor education, high unemployment, and substandard housing. As the authority reexamined its priorities, the "orange book" was put on the shelf, and most of the businesses and people stayed in place. It abandoned its plan for the waterfront historic district and focused on the West End instead. When historic preservationists and city officials realized that the restoration was not going to move forward, they took steps to protect it with historic district legislation.

The shift meant the future for the district was going to be messier, but not necessarily worse. It also meant that a holding action was necessary to prevent further blight. The City looked to Massachusetts Chapter 40(c), a state law that allowed a city to enact controls over what changes could be made to the exteriors of buildings in a defined historic district. Owners wanting to change something like the type of a sign, the color of a door, or the material covering a building would have to get approval from a historic district commission, whose members would be appointed by the mayor and deemed qualified to determine "appropriate" design.

You can imagine how easy it would be to convince New Englanders they needed permission from the government about what color to paint their door!

My job at the planning department was to talk with people in the district to explain the advantages of working with city officials and WHALE to create a plan and to describe to them how other communities had enacted similar laws. I got to know the people and the law. I started drafting the ordinance and working with the committee planning its enactment. It was a laborious process and took a long time to pass the New Bedford City Council. But it did eventually pass.

The historic district legislation is still in effect and has served a valuable purpose for the district. No one wants to remove it. But attempts to expand it have failed on several occasions. The ordinance was the right remedy for the right place at the right time. Credit goes to City Planner Ben Baker and WHALE for seeing that.

Police raid the Black Panthers headquarters, Kempton and Cedar Streets, July 1970.

The West End Comes Apart

In the early 1970s, I joined the New Bedford chapter of the civil rights organization NAACP, called the NBAACP, and became a life member. Bill do Carmo was president, and meetings went on forever because an activist named Jack Custodio protested every motion made at every meeting.

The redevelopment authority had done a good job on the harborfront, but in the West End, the authority sadly followed the country's urban renewal patterns that displaced minority and Black families, patterns that the author and activist James Baldwin famously called "Negro Removal." The agency demolished hundreds of buildings, effectively destroying a once viable neighborhood. And the West End came apart.

The redevelopment wasn't the only cause. Far from it. Everett Allen wrote a 40-part series for the local paper, the *Standard-Times*, entitled "Unemployment: New Bedford's Greatest Problem." It could have been called "Unemployment: New Bedford's Greatest Symptom." Allen detailed everything from New Bedford's average educational attainment of only eight years—the nation's

Kempton Street community members fighting fire

lowest—to language barriers, crime- and drug-related issues, lack of affordable housing, and on and on.

These problems were not evenly distributed by race, and in 1970, things boiled over.

The Black Panthers, a national civil rights activist group, organized in the West End. One of the organization's original purposes was to protect residents from police brutality, and the group also advocated better housing, better employment, and a fairer justice system. They were among many groups that gathered in the neighborhood to protest inequities. Although the Panthers ran food programs for students in

NAACP meeting at Ash Street headquarters with Charlie and Bill do Carmo, and Manny Costa, 1968

the city, their militant reputation also caused friction in the community.

Unrest simmered and boiled over. Several buildings burned down in New Bedford that summer, including the Model Cities headquarters in the historic district. And on July 15, 1970, on a stiflingly hot evening, a car carrying three White men drove through a crowd in the West End, firing guns.

Young Lester Lima, 17, was shot and killed. The investigation into his murder went nowhere, and many felt betrayed.

"I went to school with Lester Lima. I went to school with those three White guys. We all knew each other. We knew who killed Lester Lima," Lee Blake, who now leads the New Bedford Historical Society, told me.

Despite this, no one went to jail.

Senator Edward Brooke on Kempton Street, July 12, 1970

Earle M. Carter and Shirley A. Magnett (left), Ruby Dottin at center, and Mary Barros

How was this possible in New Bedford, the city that welcomed Frederick Douglass and provided him his first home and wages as a free man? How could this happen in New Bedford, a destination along the Underground Railroad? On a whaleship, it wasn't the color of your skin that mattered; it was how well you threw a harpoon. How had that changed? New Bedford was a diverse city built by immigrants. The city's Quaker founders had championed the abolitionist cause. How could this happen here?

I wanted to do what I could, so I worked with Westerly Associates, a housing offshoot of the NBA ACP led by Earl Carter. We represented the neighborhood as Ed Fish and Peabody Properties designed two housing projects near where Lester Lima had been shot. One was Bedford Townhouses, and the other was King Village. Both projects bordered the new elementary school, Carney Academy, named for city resident Sgt. William Carney, the country's first Black Medal of Honor winner. Both projects, one a low-rise and one a high-rise, were well built and, more importantly, well managed.

Pushing back against racism has been a constant battle for Black and minority communities, an exhausting weight to carry. We need to step up as a community if we are to help, and over the years, I have tried to be part of plans and movements that bring us together, not tear us apart.

In 1976, Dr. Margery "Ruby" Dottin decided to run for the New Bedford School Committee to break the color barrier. No person of color had been elected to the school committee before,

Jack Custodio

Bedford Townhouses are under contruction near the intersection (left center) of Kempton and Cottage Streets, 1979. Carney Academy is visible at top.

and well, it was about time. I joined her campaign. It was there I made my first political speech. I delivered it to a packed hall at the Verdean Vets Hall, following Dr. Melvin "Mel" King, an activist, state legislator, and MIT professor. He was a tall man with a shaved head and an imposing beard. He wore a bright dashiki and completely commanded the room. About 400 people, mostly Cape Verdeans, filled the hall to support Ruby.

Was I nervous? Yes.

I don't know what I said in that first political speech of mine, but I do remember the energy in the room seemed to shake the building. I must have survived because I'm still here. Ruby got elected. She was a great school committee member and paved the way for others to follow. But somebody had to go first.

Nearly a decade later, in 1984, because of my work in the minority community, the planning committee organizing the 10th anniversary of New Bedford's celebration of Martin Luther King Jr. Day asked me to be the first White person to give the keynote address. This created quite a stir. Activists Jack Custodio and Mary Barros decided to boycott. Despite our many arguments, I considered Jack a dear friend and precisely the sort of witness that New Bedford (and every city) needs to stay the course for justice. The same is true of Mary, who later was elected to be a city councilor.

As weeks passed, the boycott caused pressure to build. I figured my speech had better be good if the event went on. The afternoon came, and as I and others approached what was then the YWCA building on Spring Street, we passed Jack and Mary standing in the middle of the street, firm in their call for a boycott.

But people wanted to celebrate, and they came out anyway. After prayers, songs, and essays from schoolchildren, I approached the podium, looking out at 400 people crammed into every nook and cranny in that old gym.

"Well," I began, "if they are going to continue to boycott this great celebration, we are going to have to get a bigger gym."

MIT Architecture Studio class, early 1970s

MIT: Vibrant and Complicated and Busy

I worked for the planning department during the day and with the NBAACP in my spare time. After several months, I decided it was time to apply to graduate school. I wasn't sure what skills were needed to fix up New Bedford, but my background and interests were in architecture, so I felt I should start there. By the time I was ready to apply though, I had missed all the application deadlines. A childhood friend, Woody Underwood, was at the Massachusetts Institute of Technology in Cambridge and spoke very highly of it. *Why not pay a visit?*

The women in the MIT office explained I was months late, but they conferred and decided it would be okay if I applied anyway. They said I had to interview with the head of admissions, Professor Chester Sprague. They directed me to his office. When I walked in, he was lying on his desk looking at the ceiling. He said his back hurt.

I wasn't exactly sure how to do an interview with a man lying on his desk. *How am I supposed to make eye contact? Get a ladder?* I circled the desk a few times. We discussed my suitability for MIT. He was friendly enough and left me with a feeling that MIT is a quirky place. I decided it was worth thinking about.

I enjoyed my undergraduate time at Harvard. Still, I really didn't like how the faculty and administrators at Harvard ingrained their students with a sense of superiority and the feeling they have everything figured out. As I wandered around the studios and halls of MIT and talked some more with Woody, I got a sense of confusion and ambiguity. *Maybe this is closer to the truth I'm looking for?*

MIT accepted me to its Master of Architecture program beginning in the fall of 1970. I majored in architecture as an undergraduate, and this would be another four-year program, with half of the coursework in design studios. If I wanted to go on to become a practicing architect, I would have to work an additional three years for a licensed architect after graduating and then pass a five-day licensing exam. It would be quicker to become a physician.

I jumped right in.

Because I knew exactly why I was there, I worked harder than ever before. I wanted to get all the tools necessary to fix up my hometown. If I had to write a paper on zoning, I did it on zoning in New Bedford.

The studios were the center of learning, and my first professor, Maurice Smith, was quite unusual. He had come to America from New Zealand either to teach architecture or play professional table tennis, or both. He challenged his students—if anyone could beat him in a game, he would give them an "A." And he would spot the aspiring students 15 points out of 21. No one ever came close!

Maurice's designs were vibrant and complicated and busy. No "less is more" for Maurice Smith and his disciples at MIT. We all constructed wood workstations according to that philosophy. Fortunately, the Cambridge fire marshal never set foot in the place.

Design requires many intense hours, so people would be in the studios at all times of the day and night. We would take breaks to practice at the ping-pong table, hoping to sharpen our skills against the professor. The table was also used for "juries" to present and defend our designs.

My workstation was against a wall of the studio. I would often venture to the other side of the wall to the embryonic "Architecture Machine" set up by Nick Negroponte. He was making tiny robots that assembled two-inch cubes into structures. But there was a hitch. Inside his villages, Nick introduced mice, and the mice would move the cubes. The robots had to figure out how the cubes had been moved and react to that development. This little creation of Nick's evolved into the now famous Media Lab with its own building and a mission that has transformed how we think and use machines. Amazing what mice can get into!

Three professors were influential in helping me develop my thinking about participatory design. Robert Goodman, Jan Wampler, and Hans Harms all stressed the importance of involving the people who would eventually use the environment—at the outset of the design process. They also focused on people who were not usually served by the design profession.

This philosophy of involving people in the decisions that shaped their environment complemented a book I had read as an undergrad. In *Notes on the Synthesis of Form*, Christopher Alexander posits that some of the best designs, whether adobe villages or Indian tapestries, result from an unselfconscious process shaped over generations. Although unsophisticated in design, people keep choosing a slightly better design over a slightly worse one. Over time, this process produces beauty and sophistication far superior to what the conscious designer can produce in a single attempt to make all the right choices.

Nick Negroponte's mice and robots

Unlike Ayn Rand and Frank Lloyd Wright, I felt that good design was based on participation and incrementalism. To me, the best designs were the result of a flexible, gradational process that started with a general vision or goal that clients were working toward and allowed for adaptation as the situation or people changed.

I knew this approach would produce a messy result.

When I worked as an undergraduate in Le Corbusier's Carpenter Center at Harvard, the soft drink dispenser was hidden in the basement because the great man had not accounted for thirst in his design, which was all about clean lines. The studios at MIT were a rabbit warren of spaces that changed daily as students modified them to meet their own changing needs or those of their neighbors.

Le Corbusier's environment seemed to say, "I am the master. You exist and will do your work in MY space. But it is *mine*." The space was beautiful. It was sublime. It was a work of art. But it certainly wasn't yours.

It is said we shape our spaces, and then they shape us. This is what happened to me at MIT.

Graduate Studies: Avenue Arches and Collective Private Urban Renewal

There was, of course, a requirement for the master's program in architectural history. I went to Professor Stanford Anderson to discuss that. I had already talked with New Bedford City Planner Ben Baker about an independent study, and he had agreed to serve as my advisor.

I proposed a one-year project to look at a single street in my hometown. Not the entire street, just part of it. When I think of it now, this request seems a bit audacious. But one of the great things about MIT is its flexibility in tailoring resources to meet the needs of diverse students.

I explained to Dr. Anderson that Acushnet Avenue in the compact North End of New Bedford served two contradictory purposes. I wanted to analyze that contradiction and make suitable recommendations. Since the time when Native Americans had occupied the area, Acushnet Avenue has been a linear transportation path. Known as "The Avenue," the street also serves as the center of the North End, a densely populated section that grew rapidly as textiles attracted tens of thousands of immigrants. Something that is the "center" of anything usually isn't linear.

I mapped out the stretch from Coggeshall Street, the first street north of Route 195, which forms a natural southern boundary, to up past Brooklawn Park, where poet, naturalist, and historian Daniel Ricketson once entertained Transcendentalists Henry David Thoreau and Ralph Waldo Emerson in his modest homestead.

I then walked The Avenue, interviewing every store owner to understand how they viewed it, where their customers came from, and what issues were uppermost in their minds. I got to know the store owners who saw themselves as the center of the North End. They ran the coffee shops, restaurants, jewelry stores, and gift shops. They were the bakers and shoe repairers and police officers and firefighters and librarians who made up the North End. After work, they frequented the bars, social clubs, and restaurants that advertised the heritage of the French-Canadians, Polish, Madeiran, and several Azorean islands.

As I walked up and down The Avenue, I could sense that the strength of the district was its international flavor. The street was home to the *Portuguese Times* newspaper and the Madeira Feast, and many of the families there spoke a language other than English when they were at home at night. The dense population created a market within easy walking distance for businesses, but the linear layout created traffic backups and made getting around difficult for pedestrians. Solutions were not easy because, fundamentally, the street needed to serve as a center for the North End while maintaining its function as a transportation path. Those purposes are as hard to reconcile as a circle and a line.

This slice of Acushnet Avenue (left center) snakes through the city's North End between Coggeshall Street and Brooklawn Park, 1938. Visible is St. Anthony of Padua church and hundreds of three- and four-decker wooden buildings sandwiched between mills (upper right) along the riverfront and the railroad (out of view at left).

Working with the New Bedford Planning Department, the best we could come up with in the end was a proposal to treat The Avenue as a "pearl necklace" and develop the area accordingly. City officials, going forward, would try to identify key intersections to build up as mini centers with more pedestrian amenities. This would break up the commercial strip characteristic and ease automobile and pedestrian movement.

I even hazarded a recommendation that arches be constructed at key intersections. The designs could be created in cooperation with the various ethnic groups who lived and worked near and along The Avenue so that each would be unique and connect social clubs to their respective arches. That way, traveling along the street would feel like a procession, much as the annual parade of the Feast of the Blessed Sacrament (the Madeira Feast) proceeds through arches of fresh bayberry flowers harvested from Gooseberry Island in Westport. In the following years, however, New Bedford moved only somewhat in this direction. The Avenue is now called the International Marketplace. The

Along the Avenue, 1981

entrance at Coggeshall Street is elaborately designed to be pedestrian friendly. New Bedford has identified other key intersections further north to turn into friendly pearls in this historic necklace. Who knows, maybe arches are in the future!

As I was working on Acushnet Avenue, I was also taking courses in MIT's Department of City Planning. I went to Bill Porter, dean of the School of Architecture and Planning, and told

Looking north on Acushnet Avenue from Marvin Street, one block south of Coggeshall Street, 1950s

him I was interested in pursuing a joint degree. His first response was that they didn't offer one. Case closed. Despite his initial reaction and to his credit, we continued to talk.

I explained that I wanted to merge the disciplines of architecture and city planning to make my hometown a better place. Bill responded that the traditional merger of the two disciplines is called environmental design, that is, the design of large spaces. I understood that, but I wanted to approach the profession from the opposite axis. Most design professionals, whether in architecture or city planning,

Bill Porter

narrow their specialties. For example, they become designers of low-income housing or hospitals, and then they go wherever they need to practice their specialty.

I told Bill I wanted to hold my location constant to New Bedford and vary my technical profession, depending on what my hometown needed. To do that, I needed a joint degree in architecture and planning. He agreed to support my proposal.

Again, MIT went out on a limb. They agreed to do what hadn't been done before and allow a joint degree. While so many people at MIT and Harvard were justifiably working on problems that confronted the globe, MIT was willing to let me drill down to my hometown, allowing me to be the first to pursue a joint degree in the departments of Architecture and Urban Studies and Planning.

I had argued that small cities like New Bedford have problems as complex as anywhere—poverty, low educational attainment, language barriers, crime, environmental injustice—but larger cities have more resources to help them solve those problems. One of the tragedies of smaller communities like New Bedford or Fall River or Lynn or Fitchburg—it is a long list—is that often when a young person with promise comes along, they leave the area for opportunity elsewhere. In addition to all the other challenges, smaller cities must add "brain drain" to the list of disadvantages.

For Bill Porter to allow me to focus on my hometown was a huge decision, I think, for small cities. I wish more had been made of it.

I focused on the 15-block waterfront historic district that I had worked on four years earlier during my time in the planning department. This blighted area between the downtown and the waterfront was politically powerless but had strategic importance as the support base for the fishing industry and potentially as a center for development based on the tourism attracted by the Whaling Museum and many historic structures.

With this thesis, I wanted to test two hypotheses. The first was whether we could achieve the subtitle of my thesis, "Collective Private Urban Renewal." In 1973, President Richard Nixon was eliminating all federal urban renewal programs. Without these programs, could we reach people through their social groups and organizations and get them behind a collective vision to renew their shared district? Could they do together what it did not make financial sense for them to do individually?

The second hypothesis was whether one could be a "location-oriented change-maker." This was less important to the people in the district than it was to me, but I had been thinking about it since Vigo, Spain. Could I specialize in a place and adapt my professional skills to what the place needed? There weren't many professional role models for this, so there was some risk in choosing this as a potential career path.

I asked Professor Tunney Lee of the Urban Studies faculty to be my thesis advisor. Tunney had deep experience working with community groups, and I was fortunate to have him as my advisor. He was born in China, and his approach was more about empowering people than building buildings. He stressed the process of how a community engages in design. With Tunney, the designer was anything but elite. Plus, Tunney had an ever-present smile that made it impossible for anyone not to like him. With him as my mentor in Cambridge and Ben Baker as my mentor in New Bedford, I had very positive influences at the start of my career.

As I had with my Acushnet Avenue project, I started banging on doors, this time in the waterfront historic district, getting to know the people there and listening to their concerns and dreams. I knew many of them from my time working on the historic district legislation, and as I talked with them, an interesting thing happened. People told me the truth. I was just a graduate student. I had no power over them. I had no agenda. I wasn't on anyone's "side." I was just there to listen, and I had time for each and every one of them.

The people in this neighborhood were separated into different organizations with different missions, outlooks, value systems, and personalities. The groups didn't much like each other, but they would all talk to me, and over time, I discovered they all wanted pretty much the same thing for the neighborhood. There was, in fact, a shared vision if they could get past the barriers of personality and other conflicts.

During the nine months it took to write my thesis, I got to know everyone, and they got to know me. They all wanted a working waterfront and a real connection to the harbor. They didn't want to become a museum village focused only on the past. They were proud of their historic buildings and wanted to see them restored, but they also wanted to see more economic activity, mixed-use, better utilities, safer streets, higher property values, and more tourism.

People thought at the time that government would probably not be able to help them, so they were prepared to explore "collective private urban renewal." We decided we would work together to pursue this vision by hiring a director or an agent to achieve goals on their behalf.

Tunney Lee, at center rear

CHAPTER 2

Agent for Change

Putting It to Work: Ten-Acre Revival

In June 1974, I left MIT and moved to New Bedford with my young family. During graduate school, I married Judith Havens, and in January 1974, we had a baby boy, Matthew. I was excited to come back to the city and begin full-time employment. I wanted to get to work.

One of the first actions I took was to propose the Ten-Acre Development Committee, named for the ten-acre purchase my ancestor made in 1765 and that now made up the waterfront historic district. This committee would be made up of groups wanting to work toward the neighborhood's revival. Drawing from my graduate thesis, I laid out goals expressed to me in the many interviews I had conducted in the district.

All except the Port Society agreed. Being a religious organization, the society supported our goals but felt the committee would ultimately be involved in political work, so it declined direct involvement. The other three groups—the Old Dartmouth Historical Society, which runs the Whaling Museum, the Waterfront Historic Area LeaguE (WHALE), and the Bedford Landing Taxpayers Association—signed two agreements setting us on our way. The first was a pledge to work together toward those broad goals. The second was cooperatively to retain my services at the princely sum of $10,000 per year. I was fortunate enough to have family income to supplement this salary, so I could take the job and pursue the work I wanted to do. The group assigned me an office in one of the buildings owned by WHALE. I would work only on projects that all three organizations unanimously approved.

"If you can agree on only one thing today, that is what I'll work on," I told them. "Maybe tomorrow you will agree on something else."

We discussed my title. I wasn't going to be an executive director because I would be working for three organizations. I suggested that I should be the committee's agent. That word had several meanings that I liked. One was the chemical definition of an agent as a catalyst that mixes with other elements to speed a reaction. Another was the waterfront definition of the person who represents owners as I would be doing, like a shipping agent. But I found the best description of an agent in a John Irving book, *The Hotel New Hampshire*:

> It's what all the great agents do: they make the most incredible and illogical advice
> sound reasonable, they make you go ahead without fear, and that way you get it, you
> get more or less what you want, or you get something, anyway; at least you don't end
> up with nothing when you go ahead without fear, when you lunge into the darkness
> as if you were operating on the soundest advice in the world.

The goals revolved around realizing a shared vision of a working waterfront historic district—a district whose buildings were from many eras and where history continued to be made each day by people who were proud of their heritage but didn't want to be contained by it.

The real connection to the fishing industry had to be protected and strengthened, and the physical barrier of the highway had to be addressed. People and goods needed to flow back and forth from the district to the waterfront.

Historical buildings, largely empty and in disrepair, were to be restored appropriately and occupied. While the district was zoned for industrial use, people knew that commercial and

State Fruit Company *New Bedford Ship Supply*

residential uses were better suited for the district and that, along with fishing-related uses, we would aim to develop places to support the tourists the Whaling Museum attracted.

There was also the practical matter of the infrastructure. The streets were in terrible shape, with asphalt, concrete, paving block, and potholes all over the place. Sidewalks were hard to navigate. High-speed through-traffic made walking dangerous. Overhead telephone and electric lines on wooden poles were a visual blight, and the few "cobra-head" type streetlights left the district dark at night.

Our vision was that the people in the district, working cooperatively, would fix these problems and bring economic vitality back in a way that respected history, continued the relationship with the sea, and created new uses around a developing cultural market—all while maintaining control within the district itself.

As I drove to work the first day, I passed North Water Street, which had housed most of the banks—and therefore the wealth—of the richest city per capita in the country during the days of whaling. By 1974, the banks had moved up the hill as the downtown had retreated further from the waterfront, but there were other businesses there. Bob Hathaway in Northeast Marine Electronics served the fishing fleet, and two stores away, Loring Weeks was doing the same. Myron Marder had his headquarters for the famous Marder fleet of eastern-rigged, wooden scallopers close to Union and South Water Streets. State Fruit, Tropicana Banana, and Union Tobacco all landed imported fruit on nearby State Pier.

In the Double Bank Building on North Water Street at the foot of William Street sat the Teamsters Union, where Umberto "Battle" Cruz and Robert C. "Porky" Viera represented the fishing crews and managed the union's pension and health care funds. Around the corner, on Rodman and Front Streets, sat New Bedford Ship Supply run by Rasmus Tonnessen, among the many ship suppliers in the neighborhood. Not far away was Kruger Brothers Ship Supply run by Billy Kruger and Skip's Marine run by Ray Drouin. These businesses outfitted fishing boats with everything from groceries to foul-weather gear.

Closer to the waterfront were related businesses such as settlement houses where fishermen got paid after their trips and many bars where that pay sometimes quickly got spent. Settlement houses function the way counting houses did in the days of whaling. Basically, they do the accounting.

Perhaps the most remarkable invention that the whaling industry offered was not the tryworks that rendered whale blubber into oil or Lewis Temple's game-changing toggle harpoon but the profit-sharing payment system, which kept every member of the crew invested in voyages that stretched from three to five years and at times could be life-threateningly dangerous and at other

Ray Drouin, Skip's Marine

"Battle" Cruz, president Teamsters Local 59

times maddeningly boring. What was this invention? It was called the "lay system." American whalers likely adopted it from Dutch whalers who were using it in the early part of the 17th century. At the outset of each trip, each crew member was assigned a "lay," or a set share of the proceeds, based on their skills. In this way, if the voyage was successful, every whaling crew member felt it in their pocketbook. And if it wasn't, they felt that as well. Similarly, fishermen are paid a lay, or a share, and at the end of a trip, the crew heads to a settlement house to settle up. After a seven- to ten-day fishing trip—the hardest, most dangerous working stint there is today outside of the military—when you have fresh money in your pocket, the next business to visit might be a bar, so there are several bars located near the settlement houses, right on the waterfront.

As I continued on my drive to work that first morning, I turned from Water Street onto Centre Street and headed down the hill. Behind Bob Hathaway's shop, on the left, Arthur Hathaway kept his carpentry shop. Arthur was in his seventies and held court with a few other old-timers

This panoramic view looking north on North Water Street is composed from two photos taken at different times.

Arthur Hathaway

Rasmus Tonnessen, New Bedford Ship Supply

around a potbellied stove on the first floor. The wood-framed, gambrel-roofed building was quite a structure. I'm not sure it ever could have passed a building inspection, and I gave up trying to figure out how the loads were passed down from the roof to the ground. I just surmised that the building was supported by memories.

The next building on the left was the John Harrison Warehouse, home of Harry Kaller's Beef and Provisions. Made of brick and stone, it was a substantial building but had its oddities like every building in the district. Besides all the frozen carcasses of premium beef being wheeled in and out of the building and the gorgeous gold-plated sign of two steers hanging outside, one of the building's middle floors was only four feet high and had concrete floors, which made future development of the property somewhat problematic.

Left page view is from head of Rose Alley, 1965; right page view is from head of Centre Street, 1970.

On the right or south side of Centre Street stood four vacant or little-used buildings. The first was a handsome brick-and-random-stone warehouse used by DeWolf and Vincent Hardware for storage. It was four stories of potential, but it wasn't an active business, and its run-down condition contributed to the blight in the district.

Then came two modest but historically significant wood-frame buildings that WHALE had saved and moved into the district from urban renewal areas to fill a large empty lot. WHALE had purchased the Caleb Spooner House and the Henry Beetle House from demolition contractors who had planned to tear them down as part of the redevelopment authority's plans to "improve" other neighborhoods. These houses on their new foundations stood vacant, awaiting courageous pioneers to fix them up and live there.

The last building on the right, at the foot of the street and across from my office, wasn't technically even a building. It had four walls—well, most of four walls—but it didn't have a roof or any floors. What it did have inside was a large ailanthus tree. This "tree of heaven" reached up from the basement over the three stories of the ruin and was the sturdiest part of the structure. As I looked at this building, something else grabbed my eye. In the open lot where I was about to park my car, three gentlemen reclined against the stonewall of the ruin. Wine bottles surrounded them.

I parked, got out of my car, and locked the door. I started walking toward my office.

"Hey, why did you lock your car?" yelled one of the men, whose first name I later learned was Gary.

"Well, basically, because of you guys."

"Your car is safe with us. If anything happens to it, the cops will come down and give us a hard time. We like it here. We don't want to have to move. We'll look after it."

I locked it anyway.

I walked to my office on the second floor of the William Tallman warehouse, built at the corner of Front and Centre Streets in 1790, and began my first day of work for the people of the Waterfront Historic District. From my window, I looked directly across the swath of land cleared for the highway and, beyond the highway, a dock separating State Pier from Piers 3 and 4. I could see the fishing boats surrounding these piers and a small brick building, the Wharfinger Building. At the time, inside this building, every morning, the fleet's daily catch of scallops and groundfish was auctioned off in two ten-minute bursts of frenetic activity that set the market price for seafood around the country.

I thought back to 1765 when my ancestor Joseph Rotch had landed on this pier from his home on Nantucket. The ten-acre name of the committee harkened back to when he settled in New Bedford. He had moved his considerable whaling business from Nantucket, an island constrained by sandbars, to this deepwater port. By doing so, he set New Bedford on a course that would make the seaport an international powerhouse for more than a century. He had purchased a ten-acre tract of land that

Going to work at WHALE, Front and Centre Streets

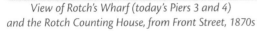
View of Rotch's Wharf (today's Piers 3 and 4)
and the Rotch Counting House, from Front Street, 1870s

Razing the Rotch Counting House, 1972

stretched from the harbor up both sides of what would later be known as William Street (named for his grandson) almost to what is now City Hall and the New Bedford Library—the very heart of the city. I was now tasked with helping revive the area, which despite its historical significance, had fallen on such hard times that it had become one of the most blighted sections in the entire city.

This city, my city, the city where my ancestors were buried, mattered to me not just because I was trained in architecture and city planning. It had a place not just in my head but also in my heart. As if to drive the point home, the first act of destruction I witnessed out my office window was the demolition of the Rotch Counting House, which had been sitting empty in the path of the waterfront highway that the redevelopment authority needed to complete. This simple Quaker stone building with its Dutch cap roof had been where the Rotch fortunes—riches that had been "harpooned and dragged up hither from the bottom of the sea," as Herman Melville put it in *Moby-Dick*—had been counted and paid out to crewmen and caulkers, shipbuilders and cask makers and all the different tradesmen involved in the constructing, outfitting, and sailing of a whaleship, the processing of its oil and baleen and bone, and the worldwide marketing of its products.

To me, despite the gut-wrenching destruction of this building and others, New Bedford's architecture and waterfront economy remained authentic, connected to the past, the present, and the future. History is a continuum. New Bedford, in a word, is a seaport. Our people go to sea. You don't have to dress people up in old clothes to explain the ancient relationship we have with the oceans. The docks that were home to whaleships are now home to fishing boats, but people still go to sea. The counting houses may be gone, but the settlement houses and other working waterfront businesses still perform the same or similar functions as they did long ago. If Melville were to magically reappear on the waterfront, he would not get lost. He would feel at home.

As I looked out my window at this view that had such a personal meaning to me, I recognized that, while the buildings were in terrible condition and there were many vacant spaces, the essential uses still supported a working waterfront. For the committee, this was a major building block and point of consensus. The streets showed disrepair everywhere you looked. Still, this district was real, its history was real, the relationship to the water was real, and most importantly, the people in the district—well, they were very real.

This was my first day of a career that had no model. I was 26 years old with a wife and a 6-month-old child. I had granny glasses and a beard and was fresh out of a fancy Cambridge graduate school, working in a gritty seaport in an office that overlooked the working waterfront from one window and Gary and his friends from another. I couldn't wait to get to work.

Cenotaphs on Bethel Walls: The Port Society and Richard Paull Sr.

Four organizations comprised the bulk of the social structure of the district. The oldest was and still is the New Bedford Port Society. Founded in 1830 by New Bedford's leading citizens—including Charles W. Morgan, Samuel Rodman Jr., John Howland Jr., and James Arnold—its mission was "the moral improvement of seamen."

The founders were concerned that prostitution and other ills were present in New Bedford. Befitting a whaling port, houses of prostitution worked out of "arks," old whaleship hulls abandoned on the shoreline. In the first "ark riot," an outraged crowd burned down one of these derelict hulks of ill repute, but another soon replaced it. A second "ark riot" also failed to stamp out the brothels. It was then that some citizens thought a church for sailors might be a better solution, and so the Port Society was formed.

Two years later, the Seamen's Bethel was built for $5,000. The first preacher was Reverend Enoch Mudge, who served until 1843 and is believed to have been the model for Father Mapple in *Moby-Dick*. We do know that Herman Melville, like most whalers, visited the Bethel before heading out on his whaling voyage on the *Acushnet* in 1841. Sailors often felt it wise to make their peace with God before departing for the unknown.

In 1833, the Ladies Branch of the Port Society was founded with Sarah Rotch Arnold as its first president. In 1851, a year after the death of her father, William Rotch Jr., Sarah gave his original home to the Port Society. The house had been constructed at the corner of William and Water Streets in 1787, 22 years after William's grandfather made his ten-acre purchase. (William Jr. had lived in this house before moving up the hill in 1835 to the house now known as the Rotch-Jones-Duff House and Garden Museum, which he built after losing his first wife and remarrying.) The Ladies Branch raised funds to furnish the donated house, and it was moved up Johnny Cake Hill to where it sits today, next to the Bethel.

Seamen's Bethel (left) and Mariner's Home on Johnny Cake Hill, circa 1930

Until recently, the house provided low-cost lodging for active seamen. This is one of the many ways both branches of the Port Society reflect the continuing relationship between New Bedford and the sea. When I first started going to Port Society meetings, I thought I had stepped back in time. The way meetings were conducted, from the reading of the minutes to the way people spoke, seemed from another age. Richard Paull Sr. was president when I presented my Ten-Acre Development Committee plan. A lawyer in town, he lived a few towns over in Westport and was a man of few words. Polio had left him with a limp. He always dressed in gray. The general effect was one of understatement and humility. You leaned over to hear what he said because he was always worth listening to—not a word was wasted.

Richard Paull

Other members of the board of managers had similar demeanors, contributing to my sense of being in another age. Formal in their manner, conservative in their dress, and sparing in their language, Port Society members were still about the "moral improvement of seamen." Bibles were given out to newly commissioned fishing vessels.

Every Memorial Day, members hoist the Bethel's old organ into a wooden wheelbarrow and wheel it down to Pier 3, where people sing hymns, listen to moving words from clergy and local officials, and toll a ship's bell while reading each name of those who had gone to sea, never to return. This service has been repeated in New Bedford and other seaports for as long as seafaring folk have gone down to the sea. All those who live in fishing communities know the words of the hymn, "For Those in Peril on the Sea":

Eternal Father strong to save   *Its own appointed limits keep*
Whose arm has bound the restless wave   *O hear us when we cry to Thee*
Who bids the mighty ocean deep   *For those in Peril on the sea*

Ceremony at the Seamen's Bethel

Tourists learn about the Seamen's Bethel.

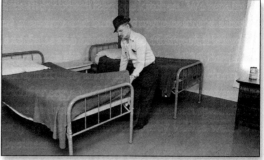
Inside the Mariner's Home

I have told many a person contemplating a visit to New Bedford that if they have time to visit only one place, they need to find their way, as Herman Melville did, to the Bethel. They need to sit quietly in the pews, gaze upward to the cenotaphs on the Bethel walls and read the stories of those who left these shores in search of whales or fish, definitely in search of opportunity, only to be lost in the loneliest abyss. The story is the same, whether the seafarers lost their lives two centuries ago from a whaleship in the Indian Ocean or two years ago from a fishing vessel on Georges Bank. It is the story of a husband who will never again come home, a parent who will never again attend a child's birthday party, a relative who will never again toast at a family wedding.

The cenotaph is what you have when there is no grave to visit. The marble slabs hang silently on the Bethel walls, testifying to New Bedford's continuous relationship with the sea. They tell of a city that, from the earliest times, has been connected by the ocean to the entire world. As a result, its people grew as diverse as the planet itself. The cenotaphs speak of strength and perseverance and sacrifice to build a better life for those left behind and those who found themselves here—and in so doing built the city itself.

When I sit in the Bethel surrounded by these cenotaphs, I hear the message that the past has relevance for the future. The ocean has always defined us and been the source of opportunity. It connects us to all places, all people, and all possibilities. It is powerful, unforgiving, and demanding of great skill, respect, and humility. There is dignity and honor in the work that has brought us this far. That must be respected. Excellence has always been the standard. We must find a way to be up to the task.

Three of the many cenotaphs that grace the walls of the Seamen's Bethel

In Memory of
CAPT. WM. SWAIN,
Associate
Master of the Christopher
Mitchell of Nantucket.
This worthy man,
after fastning to a whale,
was carried overboard by
the line, and drowned
May 19ᵗ 1844.
in the 49ᵗ Year of his age.

Be ye also ready: for in such an hour as ye
think not, the Son of man cometh.

Erected by
AMELIA NANSETT TRASK
in loving memory of
her sister
LAURA M. LEWIS
her niece
DOROTHY L. LEWIS
and her brother-in-law
CAPTAIN JOSEPH LEWIS
and the crew
of the whaling brig
"VIOLA"
Left New Bedford Sept. 4, 1917
Lost at sea

This Tablet was erected by
the Capt. Officers & Crew of
the Ship Huntress
of New Bedford.
In memory of
WILLIAM C. J. KIRKWOOD,
of Boston Mass. aged 25 y'rs,
who fell from aloft, off
Cape Horn, Feb. 10, 1850.
and was drowned.

The Sea curls o'er him, and the foaming billow,
As his head now rests upon a watery pillow;
But the spirit divine has ascended to rest,
To mingle with those who are ransomed and blest.

Dueling Missions: Old Dartmouth and Richard Kugler

The next oldest organization in the district is the Old Dartmouth Historical Society, which operates the Whaling Museum.
It was founded in 1903 "to create and foster an interest in the
history of Old Dartmouth." (Old Dartmouth was later divided
into the city of New Bedford, and the towns of Acushnet, Dartmouth, Fairhaven, and Westport.) At the turn of the century,
whaling was in decline, and logbooks, artifacts, and other documents were being lost. One hundred founding members selected
my ancestor and former Congressman William W. Crapo to be the
first president of the society, which soon grew to 700 members in
its offices at the Masonic Lodge at Pleasant and Union Streets. In
1906, Henry Huttleson Rogers donated the Bank of Commerce
building on Water Street to the society, and a year later, it opened
as the New Bedford Whaling Museum. Since then, the museum

*Museum director Richard Kugler,
right, assists a New Zealand author.*

has had dueling missions of being both an international Whaling Museum and a local historical
society. It has carried out these sometimes contradictory roles extremely well.

When I became the committee agent, I had been long familiar with the museum. My parents
and grandparents had taken me there many times to see its exhibits. My grandfather had schooled
me in the history of New Bedford, dating back to its beginnings. He had written a 583-page book,
The Rotches, which became the ultimate reference on the family responsible for so much of the
whaling-related development of New Bedford. Let me tell you what an impression a 583-page
family history book makes on a young boy. It's quite a weight to carry around. And it wasn't his
only book, just the heaviest.

The New Bedford Whaling Museum on Johnny Cake Hill

But my most fascinating exposure to the museum came when a high school history teacher suggested I write a paper on "The Great Stone Fleet." This was a fleet of 24 mostly New Bedford whaleships purchased by the federal government in 1861 to blockade the ports of Charleston and Savannah. Petroleum had been discovered a couple of years before, putting the writing on the wall as to the future of whale oil. Many whaleships lay idle or underused. When an offer came to buy ships to carry a final load of stones for the cause of the Union Army during the Civil War, there were many takers. Unfortunately, the blockade did little good. The ships were scuttled down South, sank into the mud, and kept sinking, so much so that the blockade was fruitless since opposing ships could sail right over or through them.

What I remember most about the assignment is that no one before had ever written a paper on the Great Stone Fleet. I was working from original materials and firsthand accounts. All I had to go on were the logbooks from the ships themselves and newspaper accounts from those days. As I poured over those logbooks, trying to adjust my eyes to the writing style of the various captains, I realized that I was likely the first person to read those pages since the whalers had closed the books. For a 16-year-old boy to be thus transported back into the captain's cabin of a whaleship traveling to Charleston Harbor during the Civil War, this was a very powerful experience. It drove home the points that history is real and tangible and that you can touch it and be affected by it. New Bedford's ships connect us to important events, places, and people. And these connections are important to honor.

When I started work in the historic district, the director of the Whaling Museum was Richard Kugler. A handsome man with a fine mind, he was a gifted writer, and I wish he had written more because he knew so much about our history. I was taken by one lecture he gave on the international competition and business practices of whaling before the American Revolution. There were three power centers at the time in the whaling business: Boston, Newport, and Nantucket. Thomas and John Hancock in Boston were merchants who sold oil in England. Jacob Rodriguez Rivera, Aaron Lopez, and other Jewish merchants manufactured candles in Newport from spermaceti. And the Rotch family operated out of Nantucket and later New Bedford.

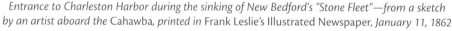

Entrance to Charleston Harbor during the sinking of New Bedford's "Stone Fleet"—from a sketch by an artist aboard the Cahawba, *printed in* Frank Leslie's Illustrated Newspaper, *January 11, 1862*

According to the talk, which later became an Old Dartmouth Historical Sketch, the Hancocks and the Newport merchants felt that horizontal integration—monopoly, in other words—would be the winning business strategy. Richard Kugler described how, before the American Revolution, John Hancock bought up all the whale oil, paying a steep price for it, so he could control the price. Or so he thought would happen when he was ready to put it on the English market.

But unknown to Hancock, Joseph Rotch had been stockpiling oil on Nantucket and in Europe, and he strategically dumped it on the English market just before Hancock got there, dropping the price, and driving Hancock out of the whaling business. Rotch's business model was vertical integration, not horizontal. He wanted to have a piece of every part of the whaling business, from building the ship to outfitting it, to insuring it, to owning it, to sailing it, to processing the products of the voyage, and to marketing the products domestically and overseas. He had a hand in every aspect of the business, and that model proved successful.

On the one hand, the museum was a window to the excitement and relevance of New Bedford's history, a window open to anyone willing to read through the museum's pages, look through its exhibits, or listen to its lectures. On the other hand, the Old Dartmouth Historical Society was an incredibly conservative group. It had custody of remarkable artifacts from the world's most extensive collection of logbooks to the world's largest model of a whaleship, the one-half scale model of whaling magnate Jonathan Bourne's most successful ship, the bark *Lagoda*. Having a responsibility to protect things forever means you must conserve them from harm or destruction. The museum's mission required its members, literally, to be conservative in their nature.

When I came along suggesting that we were going to change the district, even for the better, the Old Dartmouth Historical Society was extremely cautious. "Change" is not a word that goes well with "conservative."

Half life-size model of the Lagoda *on display in the Bourne Building of the Whaling Museum*

There was a history of ill feelings between the organizations that signed the committee contract. The Old Dartmouth Historical Society was supported primarily by people from South Dartmouth, many from the town's coastal neighborhood of Nonquitt. The society's board was chaired by Merchants Bank President Elliot Knowles, who lived in Nonquitt. Board members were devoted to their mission, but, at the time, they did not have much interest in historic buildings in the district, nor did they have a positive relationship with their city neighbors. They were content to run the museum, deal with the tourists, and foster the scholarship of people like historian Richard Kugler and Arctic historian and archaeologist Dr. John Bockstoce.

Clearly, though, the Whaling Museum would have to be a player in the revitalization. It was the major institution in the district, owning virtually an entire city block. If we were going to build an economy around cultural development and the expansion of tourism, the museum would have to take a leading role. It had an international reputation and drew people to New Bedford to spend time and money. We could build on that. The museum set a standard of excellence that had to be our hallmark. It had recently completed an auditorium addition to the museum designed by the world-renowned Cambridge Seven architectural firm and built on the original site of William Rotch Jr.'s mansion at William and Water Streets. The auditorium was a windowless modern brick building that still respected the historical architecture around it. Responding to the title of Kevin Lynch's masterpiece on city planning, *What Time Is This Place?*, the new construction said forthrightly, "This city of New Bedford is honest. We are not fake; we are not trying to be something we are not. We are respectful of our past but not prisoners of it." Like the rest of the district, it let people discover for themselves that history is not frozen in New Bedford but is constantly being made.

As you walk around the district, if you pay attention, you can see architecture from many centuries.

If we wanted to revitalize the waterfront historic district, we needed to know from whence it came. We needed to understand the economic history, the social history, the political history, the architectural history, the immigration history, and the civil rights history. New Bedford is a diverse and multi-dimensional place, and that is why it is so interesting. The Old Dartmouth Historical Society had the key to the past, which could help us unlock our future.

Construction of the Whaling Museum auditorium on North Water Street

Leading the Charge: The Waterfront Historic Area LeaguE and Sarah Delano

In the late 1950s, several citizens became concerned about the fate of historic buildings around the Whaling Museum. New Bedford attorney George Perkins, along with Peter Grinnell of Fairhaven, Stephen Delano of Westport, and the Port Society's Richard Paull Sr., had grown increasingly alarmed over the fact that while the Whaling Museum was focused on paintings and other artifacts within its walls, outside those walls the very buildings

George Perkins   Peter Grinnell   Stephen Delano

that were the center of New Bedford's whaling heritage were crumbling. These men had served on a Whaling Museum committee that worked with a consultant on a report that judged it to be both significant and feasible to restore the buildings in the surrounding neighborhood. And yet, the museum declined to take on the job.

Angry at this response and encouraged by New Bedford City Planner Richard Wengraf, these men formed the Historic Area Committee. They asked renowned Rhode Island historian and preservationist Antoinette Downing to survey the district. Mrs. Downing's report identified 39 buildings as historically significant, laying the groundwork for the district's designation as a National Landmark District by the federal government several decades later. The committee used this "stamp of approval" from a recognized outside expert to persuade others in the New Bedford business community to join them in preserving the neighborhood's buildings. A small, committed core of businesspeople agreed to do so.

These farsighted individuals created the nonprofit Waterfront Historic Area LeaguE, known as WHALE, in October 1960. George Perkins became its first president. Its vision from the outset was remarkable. WHALE envisioned a living working waterfront thriving among restored

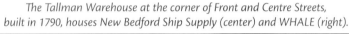

The Tallman Warehouse at the corner of Front and Centre Streets,
built in 1790, houses New Bedford Ship Supply (center) and WHALE (right).

historic structures. Its members were committed to the people who already worked in the district and along the waterfront and to cooperating with the local government to achieve their goals. They wanted the historic buildings to come alive, imagining a place where history continues, and the relationship to the sea is ongoing.

Sarah Delano

Despite this encompassing concept, WHALE had complicated relationships with others in the district. While everyone at WHALE recognized the importance and value of the museum—they attended its functions and supported its mission— they were annoyed at the museum for disrespecting the neighborhood in which it existed by declining to take on the task of saving its buildings. In the end though, for New Bedford, this disinterest turned out to be fortunate.

In most communities, the local historical society and the historic preservation organization are one and the same. One role requires a conservative mission of protecting treasures forever. The other requires a role where leaders must assume significant risk. This can tear an organization apart or prevent it from achieving its missions completely. Because WHALE essentially split off from the Old Dartmouth Historical Society, it was free of this burden. Throughout its history, whenever a decision came before WHALE about whether to take on a project, WHALE's board invariably put saving the building ahead of saving itself. And the more they did that, the more the public supported them.

Another relationship issue for WHALE was that few of its leaders came from the district. Steve Delano owned a building in the district, and George Steele operated an international cotton brokerage business in the Double Bank Building. Aside from them, everyone else was from the outside. The people inside the district were always suspicious that WHALE was there to tell them what color to paint their front door, force them to sell their building, or meddle with their business in some other way, no matter what WHALE said about a working waterfront.

That relationship wasn't helped by the work WHALE did with the New Bedford Redevelopment Authority in the mid-1960s. This established a culture within WHALE of cooperation with the government as a preferred option, in contrast to many preservation organizations whose first stance was often to oppose government authorities.

WHALE acquired the William Tallman Warehouse, or more accurately the east half of it, at the corner of Front and Centre Streets. This brick warehouse, surrounded by New Bedford Ship Supply, an outfitter to the fishing fleet, had been built in 1790. It stood empty but was in fair condition.

To fill in some of the empty lots in the district, WHALE also bought two wood-frame buildings from contractors who had been hired by the redevelopment authority to demolish certain neighborhoods as part of the agency's "improvement" plan. The first was the Henry Beetle House, which stood in the way of the "Octopus" intersection where Route 6 intersects Purchase and Pleasant Streets. The two-and-a-half-story building had been home to the builder of Beetle Boats, which carried countless whalemen as they rowed after leviathans. The other house was from the same period and was built in 1806 by Caleb Spooner. It was a one-and-a-half-story Federal-style structure. WHALE moved both to new foundations on a lot that had been empty for decades except for the remains of a warehouse similar to the Tallman Warehouse.

The Caleb Spooner House on Pleasant Street, 1972

Henry Beetle House, N. Second and Kempton Streets

In 1966, WHALE turned from George Perkins to Sarah Delano for leadership, and a new chapter began. WHALE had accomplished much in its short tenure, documenting the significance of the neighborhood locally and all the way to the federal government. It adopted a strategy of leveraging government power instead of employing a knee-jerk opposition, which can prove much less effective. The group also established a revolving fund by acquiring and reselling some threatened, significant properties.

Into a world where power and influence were wielded by men stepped this graceful lady with gray hair, a pleasant smile, and a will of steel. Sarah Ashley Delano was a descendant of the founding family of Rotches and had been married earlier to the late Clifford Ashley, one of the city's long line of famous painters. She brought an appreciation of New Bedford's history, an eye for the beauty and significance of what WHALE was trying to save, and the courage, vision, and entrepreneurship of her whaling ancestors.

An inspirational leader, she would work hard to avoid a battle, but if a battle were to be joined, she would always be leading the charge and urging everyone on. It was said of the historic preservation movement that it was led by "little old ladies in tennis shoes." Sarah may have worn tennis shoes, but in them, she could leap tall buildings! And save old ones.

The Caleb Spooner House on delivery to Centre Street by George Church of Rochester

Business Voices: Bedford Landing Taxpayers' Association and Wilbur Johnson

The final major community group in the district was the Bedford Landing Taxpayers' Association, founded in the late 1960s in response to the redevelopment authority's plan to build a highway, Route 18, through the district. The highway was intended to more efficiently connect the newly created South Terminal Redevelopment Area with Route 195, which would then connect the city's seafood industry to markets in New York City and elsewhere. The New Bedford Redevelopment Authority considered this critical to the economic success of the fishing industry and a central plank in the economic future of the city. They called this stretch of road the Downtown Connector because they saw it as connecting the downtown to the seven million people traveling on Route 195 every year.

Wilbur and Bea Johnson

Local businesses saw the proposed highway in quite another way. Many of them served the fishing vessels tied up on the docks just a few feet away from the waterfront historic district. The chandleries, settlement houses, electronics stores, machine shops, restaurants and bars, and other fishing-related businesses relied on the easy ability to go back and forth between their companies and the boats many times a day. For them, the proposed highway wasn't a connector; it was a disconnector. And they were livid.

The original highway plan was to march straight down from Route 195 to the west of North Terminal and plow through the heart of the historic district along North Second Street. This would have resulted in the demolition of the Robert Mills-designed Custom House (still in federal service today), the old New Bedford Institution for Savings (now the National Park Visitors Center), the Benjamin Rodman House, the Citizens Bank Building (now Freestones City Grill), and other important historic buildings. WHALE protested vigorously, and the redevelopment authority relented, agreeing to move the highway eastward and closer to the harbor.

Many years later, I was driving to a fishing meeting with a good friend, Howard Nickerson. Besides a long career representing fishermen, Howard had once chaired the board of directors of the New Bedford Redevelopment Authority. We got to talking about the historic district, the highway,

Johnson's Auto Parts in the original New Bedford Institution for Savings, circa 1960

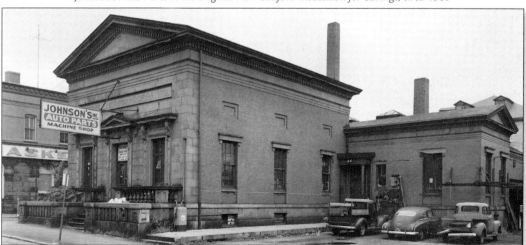

and the various personalities involved. He recalled that the authority's director during this time had been a large, imposing man named Howard Baptista. He was tough. You couldn't be in that job without being tough. You had to make difficult decisions. There were lots of controversies. People were angry with you all the time, yelling at you all the time. Baptista wasn't shy; he would yell back. But Howard Nickerson told me there was one person who could unnerve Howard Baptista.

"John, there was only one person Howard Baptista was afraid of. That was Sarah Delano."

Must have been the tennis shoes!

Moving the highway east created a different set of problems. It put the Rotch Counting House square in the path of

Henry Horn and Howard Baptista, 1967

the highway. This simple, Dutch-capped building had been the nerve center of the world's most famous whaling business, one that operated successfully on all oceans and most continents for the family that had outfoxed the likes of John Hancock and other international merchants.

More importantly, the highway would now separate every single waterfront-related business from the vessels they served. While the highway would not be a visual barrier the way FDR Drive is in New York, it would be six highway lanes, including the service road, to negotiate. Pedestrian traffic would become close to impossible, and vehicle traffic would be much more congested and inefficient.

The affected businesses formed the Bedford Landing Taxpayers' Association, and it sued the New Bedford Redevelopment Authority. The chair of the association's board was Wilbur Johnson. Bill and his wife Bea lived in the back of their auto parts store in the original New Bedford Institution for Savings building on the northeast corner of William and North Second Streets. The district was zoned "Industrial A" for some reason, so the Johnsons' residence wasn't strictly legal, but nobody seemed to mind. Historically, the district had had a number of mansion houses in it, so Bill and Bea were carrying on a historical use, I suppose. Bill's business didn't really relate to the fishing industry, and it didn't relate to tourism. It just happened to be there,

New Bedford's central waterfront before urban renewal, 1960

probably because the district was low-value space. When the district picked up a bit, Bill and Bea saw the potential of tourism and switched from Johnson's Auto Parts to Johnson's Antiques. They were no dummies!

The association had several other board members. Bob Hathaway was a quiet man who operated Northeast Marine Electronics in the Seth Russell House on North Water Street. He serviced the fishing industry with navigational and communication equipment out of a building that was the only structure to survive the British invasion of 1778.

Myron Marder worked nearby on the southeast corner of Union and Water Streets. In an industry dominated by those of Norwegian and Portuguese heritage, Myron was a Jewish businessman who owned and managed a substantial fleet of wooden eastern-rigged scallopers, distinctively dark green and black vessels. The boats were beauties and successful, as well.

Bill Carter ran Carter's Clothing at William Street and Acushnet Avenue. His office was in the basement. He was gruff, tough, and intimidating to me, just a young man fresh out of grad school. But he proved a great man to work with. He and his son, Steve, have contributed much to the district over the generations.

Roland Poitras ran Electric Service and Sales out of the Bourne Warehouse at 47 North Second Street, right near both Bill Johnson and Bill Carter. Roland sold a lot of fluorescent light bulbs and, like Bill Johnson, had no special reason to be in the district other than low-cost storage space.

The Bedford Landing Taxpayers' Association hired a young lawyer, Martin Lipman, to fight the redevelopment authority's plan to build the highway. Marty was familiar with the district, as his family's Mt. Royal Realty owned property there, including the building that housed the The National Club, a popular waterfront bar. Marty's first move was to put the Rotch Counting House on the National Register of Historic Places, not necessarily out of a desire to save historic buildings but as a strategy to stop the federally funded highway project. WHALE had declined that move and instead told the redevelopment authority they would try to raise money to move the counting house.

These different approaches reflected the conflict pointedly inherent in the very name Taxpayers' Association. It was not lost on anyone that the other organizations were not taxpayers.

Bill Carter near his store on William Street and Acushnet Avenue, 1965

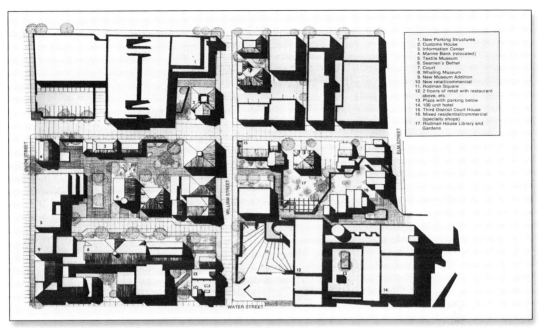

Site plan in the "orange book" urban renewal plan

While Bill's group was proud to be conducting business out of historic buildings and happy to name the committee after the original name for the district, they did not want any suburban do-gooders telling them what to do.

The lawsuit failed, and Marty only was able to extract a commitment to build an overpass over the highway at the foot of Elm Street. The New Bedford Redevelopment Authority demolished the counting house, and the highway proceeded. The overpass was rarely used. But the Taxpayers' Association had been formed, and it had come together in battle—laying the foundation for its later work toward the betterment of the district.

Shared Vision: Building on Block Grants and Sidewalk Conversations

While I had included many pages of data in my thesis, as well as a shared vision developed through dozens of interviews and even some drawings (as Professor Tunney Lee admonished, "It's a thesis for a master's in architecture, John. You have to have some drawings!"), and while I was working under a contract with the three groups that specified written goals to work toward, the reality was that our "master plan" was a lot looser than that.

The committee groups had a broadly shared vision of a working waterfront with, among other things, improved infrastructure, restored historic buildings, more tourism, mixed uses, and greater economic activity. But the specifics were left to be worked out and needed to be negotiated among parties that were still very wary of each other.

I had told them that I would work only on tasks that they all agreed on, and that is the way we proceeded. To help figure out these areas of agreement, I walked the streets to learn the specific concerns and hopes in the district. I wanted to know what they liked, what their dreams were, and what bothered them. I wanted to know how they were different from their neighbors and for them to tell me how they were part of this unique community. I wanted them to know me and, perhaps, to trust me. I wanted each person to know I didn't work for WHALE or for the Whaling Museum or for the Taxpayers' Association. And I certainly didn't work for City Hall. I worked for everyone and each of them, *together*.

I wasn't sure how we were going to finance the improvements. In my thesis, I called for "collective private urban renewal." I assumed that under President Nixon, there would be no more federal funding, and that if we were to fix up the district, it would have to be by ourselves. I had the kind of impractical idea that students put forth in papers: citizens would contribute their properties to a joint development corporation to secure financing the way a major real estate developer would. Only in this case, the developer would be the community itself. The benefits would accrue to the community, and the community would control the process. It might work in a student paper. It was never going to work in real life.

So, it was a good thing that President Nixon destroyed my assumption. He combined several federal programs, such as Model Cities and Urban Renewal, into the Community Development Block Grant Program (CDBG). This opened up funding. These block grants would go to cities based on a formula, but at the beginning, cities had very few rules about how to spend the grants other than they had to be used in income-eligible or blighted neighborhoods. The waterfront historic district qualified.

Under the formula, New Bedford's fair share was calculated to be three million. One provision in the grant process looked at how much federal money had been invested into each city over previous years; if that number was very high, those cities had their block grant allocation increased so as to ease their withdrawal from dependency on federal dollars. Kind of like a methadone maintenance program for addicted cities!

This meant that New Bedford, with its very aggressive redevelopment authority, was in line for $10.1 million in its first year and over $9 million in the second and third years. That was a lot of money with very few restrictions.

We agreed to approach Mayor John A. Markey to make the case that the waterfront historic district was a neighborhood worth investing in and that he should steer a significant amount of the grant funding to get the revitalization started. We wanted to send a message about partnership—that public investment would spur private investment—and that we would work with the city as a team.

It was important that everyone in the district be united behind the vision of a working waterfront with restored historic buildings and businesses that supported the fishing industry and a developing tourist-based economy. Our groups agreed that pedestrian traffic and mixed use were to be encouraged, public utilities needed upgrading, trees needed to be planted, and the district needed to look as if it was cared for and maintained. It was also critical that everyone firmly agree that I, fresh out of graduate school, was speaking for them as their agent.

I went to see Mayor Markey to tell him that the 15-block district just down the hill from his office could be revitalized into a center of activity that would attract young people into the city after 5 p.m., instill pride in the city, foster private investment and new businesses, and create momentum that would lead to activity in other neighborhoods. This message came from a young man in granny glasses, long hair, and a beard talking about a district that was one of the most decrepit, run-down parts of the city.

"Can you imagine? That kid thinks we can fix up the historic district!" Markey said to an aide when I left his office.

While I didn't learn of that remark until many years later, even at the time, we knew we had some persuading to do. I was a good friend of Richard Pline, who was head of the Community Development Program for Mayor Markey and earlier had been the head of the Model Cities program. Richard is a man of tremendous intellect and vision, and I felt he understood the district's potential. But it was also clear that he served the mayor. Richard was very good at explaining the decision-making process to me.

Mayor Markey was a fiscally conservative person, and he wasn't sure how long this block grant program would be around. He wasn't going to spend any money on operating funds for social programs, no matter how worthy, because he didn't want to build up a dependency on a program that might disappear. He wanted to consider only projects that made capital improvements in eligible districts.

To help decide how to spend the federal funds, Mayor Markey set up a broad-based Citizens Advisory Committee (CAC) chaired by former state Representative Theophile Desroches. The advisory committee conducted hearings all over the city to listen to citizens' ideas on how the money would be best spent. I went to every meeting and made our presentation at the last one. I wanted our message to be the last thing the CAC heard before final deliberations. That way, I was a familiar face, and my argument could reflect everything they had heard before. The strategy must have helped our pitch. We were among the projects the committee recommended for funding.

An Audience of One: Mayor Markey

Mayor Markey still made the final decisions, and we wanted to make the strongest possible case to him. I turned to Bill Hart, regional director of the National Trust for Historic Preservation. We had several excellent examples of historic preservation transforming American cities. We decided that the trust would hold a small conference in the Whaling Museum auditorium, showcasing three cases. We invited Tim Anderson, an architect from Boston. Tim had done the Prince Spaghetti building, which helped start the rejuvenation of that city's North End. Tyler Smith came from Hartford to talk about their center-city work. And all the way from Seattle came Arthur Skolnick, who had done Pioneer Square and Pike Market.

The auditorium was packed. Many people from the district, WHALE members, and other interested folks came. But this whole presentation was put on for an audience of one, and he was sitting in the front row paying rapt attention: Mayor John Markey.

Mayor Jack Markey, 1979

The message from all three was that historic preservation created jobs and made cities cool, vibrant, and successful. Many before-and-after pictures of buildings and districts made it possible to envision how a community in as bad a condition as ours could be transformed. It had happened elsewhere with great results. Why couldn't it happen here? All three outside experts, who had toured New Bedford earlier, were lavish in their praise of what we had to work with.

Mayor Markey saw the presentations and absorbed the lessons from Seattle, Hartford, and Boston. He understood that preserving old buildings could bring jobs, vigor, and life to a city, and he certainly realized that New Bedford had neighborhoods full of historic buildings. He made a substantial bet on historic preservation—a $1.3 million bet—from his Community Development Block Grant allocation, $900,000 of which would be spent in the waterfront historic district.

To put that in perspective, only one federal program for funding historic preservation was running at the time. A National Park Service program issued grants to states to fund important projects. States were awarded varying amounts based on relative need and how many historic properties they had. Massachusetts, one of the original 13 colonies with a very active preservation program, always got a top-level grant from the park service. That year's grant for the entire state of Massachusetts was $800,000. Mayor Markey was allocating 62 percent more for preservation in New Bedford than was being spent in any state in the country!

Once the decision on the amount was reached, the next step was to figure out what to do. Mayor Markey assembled a great team that brought seasoned professionals together with bright young talent who were full of energy, open to new ideas, and mission driven. The combination was potent. And in a very unusual move, Markey made me part of that team. Nothing was "you" and "us." Everything was "we." Jack Markey wanted to solve problems and get work done. He didn't care about being in the limelight. He was quiet, courageous, funny, and as honest as the day is long.

Richard Pline and Ed Lopes in the Community Development office were the cerebral members of the team. They connected us to the federal funding source and the guidelines to follow. They were ably assisted by Peter Rioux, one of the young rock stars that Mayor Markey had a way of attracting. It was (and is) a fact of life that a mayor cannot afford to pay for the talent needed to fill jobs that are high stress, highly technical, and involve long hours. You either have to have committed people who rise through the ranks earning seniority pay and benefits, or you have to identify young, talented people at the beginning of their careers and keep them for as long as you can. Peter worked and learned under Pline and Mayor Markey and stayed for a decade, then went on to a very successful career in real estate development. While he worked for New Bedford, the citizens got a great service, and Pete got a great education. He was joined by Steve Roberts, who did the same thing except for spending a few years as my chief of staff in the Mayor's Office before rejoining Pete at Claremont Company. John Whelan also worked for Mayor Markey before going off to a very successful career in real estate development.

Markey set up an Office of Historic Preservation and brought in two young stars to lead the way. Tenney Lantz ran the office. A great administrator, she got the office off to a perfect start, coordinating with city departments, state agencies, and federal grant programs. The mayor also hired Tony Souza to work with Tenney. Tony became one of the nation's foremost experts in historic preservation and provided the best advice possible to homeowners and store owners. Tony's eye was perfect, and his knowledge of how buildings should be brought back to life was encyclopedic. An owner listening to Tony would see a picture of what could be, and sooner or later, Tony was helping turn a grant or a loan into reality. Tenney and Tony showed that just as blight can be contagious, so can revitalization.

New Bedford's Planning Department was another critical element. My mentor Ben Baker had moved away from planning to manage his creation, the Southeastern Regional Transit Authority,

| *Tony Souza* | *Richard Pline* | *Hugh Murray* | *Richard Walega* |

bringing public transportation to the people of New Bedford, Fall River, and surrounding towns. But he left a protégé, Richard Walega, who was both a young idealist and an old-school kind of guy. He became another instrument in Mayor Markey's well-tuned orchestra.

George Brightman was head of public works. Talk about old school! He knew where every pipe and catch basin was located. He knew how to get every job on every street done. Just as importantly, because street work always involved the telephone and electric companies, he had everyday relationships with important people in those utilities. He was down to earth in a very literal way. No baloney. Somebody you definitely wanted on your side. One of his young assistants, Kathy Burns, learned enough working with him that I appointed her the first female head of the New Bedford Department of Public Works when I became mayor.

George Brightman's counterpart was Ed Peters, who ran the New Bedford Water Department. Mr. Peters' water lines lay near Mr. Brightman's sewer lines, so they were used to working together. Once they opened a street up, they got the job done quickly and successfully.

New Bedford Building Inspector Paul Landreville was another "up through the ranks" guy who knew the city inside out, knew the building codes, and knew what kind of challenges we faced in a district where no one had paid any attention to buildings in half a century.

Lastly was Hugh Murray, the city wire inspector. He was responsible for street lighting and electrical codes, but unlike Brightman and Peters, Hughie Murray had an oversized charismatic personality. He was always smiling, was a massive fan of history, and was just pure enthusiasm. In time, he found a beautiful four-faced Victorian clock on an 8-foot pedestal and installed it in front of City Hall. He also found a huge bell, restored it, and installed it next door in front of the library. He discovered a turn-of-the-century sleigh, had it restored by his crew, and displayed it in front of City Hall during the winter. Hughie also made sure every meeting included laughter.

These people had hundreds of requests land on their desks every day from all over the city. They had far more problems to solve than they had people and resources. Every citizen was quick to criticize, and rare was the compliment for a job well done. Just keeping the status quo was a tall order.

Meanwhile, on behalf of the citizens in the waterfront historic district, I was proposing to take 15 city blocks in one of the worst parts of town and concentrate city resources so that we could turn it around. And exactly two voters lived there!

Mayor Markey had assembled a formidable team and promised that by working with me and the people in the historic district we could succeed. I don't know whether he believed it at first, but he got everyone else to believe it. And that made all the difference.

We were underway.

CHAPTER 3

Optimism Takes Root

Public Money in the Public Way: Dynamite!

We had money to work with—$900,000 was a lot of money in 1974—but it certainly wasn't enough to fix the district. We had to figure out how best to use the city resources. I listened to people's concerns, needs, wants, and aspirations in day-to-day sidewalk conversations. The conversations were constant, and I was never more than a few blocks away, so everyone always felt engaged in the process. And we didn't have absentee owners, so even though there was diversity of background and business and opinion, we were all right there every day. I could efficiently communicate the district's views to City Hall so that we could figure out a workable approach. No one wanted to impose a solution, and the work was collaborative.

The most visible improvements would be made to buildings, but if we put public money into private buildings, how would we get the streets and public infrastructure fixed? We agreed to begin with the public space and repair everything underground first. Water lines and sewer lines were over 100 years old and leaked badly. Some of the oldest telephone conduit was wooden. All would be replaced.

We also looked at the streets and found a patchwork of paving blocks. Paving blocks are the rectangle pieces of granite that replaced the rounded cobblestones that first replaced mud as a paving material. Some of our paving blocks were covered in asphalt. Where trenches had been dug to repair water or sewer lines, the paving had been replaced with asphalt or cement. The result was an unsightly conglomeration of materials that shouted, "Nobody cares about this place!"

Neighbors in the district wanted to get rid of through traffic. People using the district as a shortcut between the North End and the South End drove fast. We wanted to encourage pedestrian movement, but not the kind that happens when an 18-wheeler hits a pedestrian.

DPW crew laying paving blocks on Johnny Cake Hill, 1977

We decided to cover all the streets with paving blocks when we finished with the utilities. This would reflect the period when most of the buildings had been built and would be consistent with being a "historic" district. Just as important, if more subtle—no one who wanted to keep all their teeth in place would travel through the district at more than 20 mph.

City officials approached the utility companies. Gas lines were underground but needed attention. Electric and telephone lines were above ground, strung on unsightly poles. Here and there, high "cobra head" streetlamps designed for highways lit the tops of pedestrians' heads, not their faces. The City announced that it would dig up all the streets to do its work and then cover the streets with paving blocks. The utilities were on notice that if they waited, every time they opened up a street, they would be in for the very costly project of replacing the paving blocks. *Or,* they could work alongside the City, burying their cables and modernizing their gas lines as the City went along, street by street. The utilities simply couldn't turn down this reasonable offer. As a result, the district bene-

Tom Hauck

fited from at least a couple of million dollars of additional investment in utility work.

To strengthen the partnership between the district and the City, WHALE hired an architect. Letting WHALE and its partners assume this control was extraordinary for Mayor Markey and his team. It was certainly not the way things usually worked. WHALE had hired architects before to work on smaller restoration projects. Bill Devlin and Carolyn Hendrie had done exemplary work in the early years but had moved on to Boston. We were lucky to find Tom Hauck, a gifted, gentle, young architect from Cleveland, for this ambitious partnership.

Tom was tall, handsome, and had a perpetual smile. He was a great listener. We asked Tom first to design the sidewalks. The vocabulary would be bluestone, cobblestone, paving block, brick, and grass. There would be trees, streetlights, curb cuts, and ramps for the disabled across the intersections. Every owner had to approve the sidewalk design in front of their property: no grass or planting bed unless the owner agreed to care for it!

Tom and I reviewed old pictures of the district. We found two streetlight poles still in existence that matched the photos from the mid-19th century. One was on Ocean Street in the West End, and the other was in front of the Water Department on Shawmut Avenue. Tom made drawings from these poles so replicas could be cast. As in the case of the paving-block streets, our design was serving two purposes. One was to recreate the period style consistent with most of the buildings in the district. But the other, more subtle purpose was increased illumination. The plan called for these 8-foot-tall lights to be placed closer together to provide more even light throughout the neighborhood. Light from these lamps would shine horizontally, thus illuminating people's faces as they approached someone on the sidewalk, important from a security standpoint.

Tom also worked with city engineers on tree selection. Unmistakable in the old photos were the majestic trees throughout the city. American elms were ideal because of their vase-like shape, narrow at the base and widening as they soared over the rooftops to meet at the center of the street in a Gothic arch. Unfortunately, when we were planting, there still wasn't an ironclad cure for Dutch elm disease, so we planted the closest variety we could find, a Zelkova species, along both sides of William Street.

While Tom was busy consulting with every owner in the district about what they wanted to see, I was busy talking with them about their business needs. When we opened a street for repairs, we had to make sure everybody's business access was considered. We had to know when deliveries were made and what days were busy days. And we looked for more money. Dick Walega showed me a three-inch-thick Economic Development Administration application he had prepared to get the work done on North Second Street. He was very proud of it, as he should have been, and it stretched the block grant dollars even further.

When the work started, we discovered why Johnny Cake Hill is a hill. There was a whole lot of granite bedrock everywhere we wanted to dig. And so, it wasn't long before the sounds of dynamite were heard in the district. I love the smell of nitroglycerin in the morning! If you want to convince people that change is coming, dynamite is a good way to do that. When people's buildings started to tremble, they knew it was a new day. Fortunately, the old lime mortars that held the buildings together were more resilient than today's cement mixtures, so the buildings absorbed the shocks. But it did shake people up, and it put a premium on communication.

As street work continued, traffic routes changed every day, a definite hardship on businesses. One morning, I was walking to work down William Street, and I spotted Leon Halle, an engineer for the city's Department of Public Works, half a block ahead of me. Tom Hauck, Leon, and I worked very closely together, coordinating all that needed to be done and interacting with property owners so that deliveries could get through. Street closures had to respect the needs of businesses. We could try to minimize impact, but there were still going to be impacts. And I mean *impacts*.

While I watched, the head of CP Brodeur stopped his Jeep and motioned Leon to climb in. As he continued driving down William Street with his left hand on the steering wheel, he was punching poor Leon in the head with his right hand. I assume he was communicating his thoughts on how he felt the street work was affecting his ability to conduct his business! As I said, *impacts*.

This was the nature of the district for a couple of years. Constant communication. Tom Hauck, Leon Halle, and I were on the streets every day, talking with business and property owners about everything from what kind of a tree they wanted (or didn't want), to how their water and sewer line would tie in, to how deliveries would be made the next day, to what their evolving dreams for the district were. It was a climate of change and excitement. Anything was possible. We also wanted to make sure that everyone knew they were part of the picture. This was their neighborhood.

It is interesting how different materials age. When I walk through the district now, more than four decades later, I can see what time has done. The trees, which were 3½ inches in diameter when we planted them, have reached maturity and, in some cases, have trunks larger than a foot in diameter. The paving blocks, bluestone, bricks, and cobblestones have shifted with frost heaves and weather but have taken on the patina of age. The places where cracks have formed don't detract in most cases. In other cases, there have been inappropriate patches, but the maintenance has been excellent for the most part. The streetlights, benches, and grass have been well maintained.

Tom Hauck died far too young of AIDS. His younger brother, Chuck, attracted to the area by Tom, continues Tom's genius as the founder and creative force behind Gallery X. I remember Tom every time I walk the district's sidewalks. I look at every piece of bluestone and every brick and cobblestone and know that the placement of that stone resulted from a thoughtful conversation between the property owner and Tom. A legacy of listening, etched in stone.

Carl Caivano: The First Artist Arrives

While Mayor Markey assembled his team and undertook all the planning around the community development process, I was trying to help WHALE get its revolving fund going. I don't think WHALE ever formally said that it would operate a revolving fund in so many words. Still, its practice was to acquire threatened historically significant properties, make necessary improvements to stabilize them, and then market and sell the properties to parties who would carry out the restorations. The proceeds of the sale could go into the next project. Hence, funds could be "revolved," and donated dollars could impact more than one building.

WHALE had rescued several buildings and stabilized them by making minimal repairs or moving them onto new foundations. Moving usually accomplished two objectives: it kept a historic building from being demolished and filled a hole left by the loss of another old building. Some might criticize the moving of historic buildings as destroying the context, but moving buildings was often done in the past. If the alternative was a total loss, then WHALE usually felt moving was the better choice.

The WHALE office was in one of those rescued buildings, the William Tallman Warehouse. We had empty office space downstairs and storage space on the third and fourth floors. On the second floor, I occupied a quarter of the space, and there was a small toilet. The rest was unfinished. As in many old warehouses, there was a large wooden wheel in the fourth-floor attic. From the protruding ridge beam, a rope lift allowed heavy objects to be lifted to any of the floors. A long loop of rope attached to the wheel went through openings on every floor. As long as you knew how to tie knots, you had a freight elevator.

William Tallman built this warehouse in 1790, 25 years after Joseph Rotch's purchase of the land underneath. The building had a commanding view of the harbor, the fishing boats at Piers 3 and 4, and the north side of State Pier. We were surrounded on two sides by New Bedford Ship Supply, owned by a titan of the fishing industry, Rasmus Tonnessen. Fishermen constantly streamed in and out of his store. This was New Bedford's business to the core and had been for

Carl Caivano in his Bourne Warehouse studio on North Second Street, 1976

hundreds of years—the outfitting of ships and the men who sailed them. Rasmus sold fishermen all the clothing they would need and the foul-weather gear to keep the clothing dry. Fishermen and scallopers could get fillet knives, shucking knives, rubber gloves, sou'wester hats, and all manner of safety equipment, although, considering the dangerousness of the job, it was scandalous how little of that was used. The store also provided food and provisions, lines, and other gear for vessels. And I suspect on several occasions, when a fisherman needed an advance, Mr. Tonnessen, though outwardly a gruff Norwegian, would help a family out.

As full and active as Ship Supply was, most of the Tallman Warehouse was empty and devoid of activity. It seemed to me that there must be a couple of uses for it that would make sense in the district. All groups wanted to maintain the connection to fishing, so anything related would be encouraged. Tourism-related businesses, too, were an option. Everyone viewed the Whaling Museum as an "anchor tenant" that could attract businesses that might serve tourists visiting the museum. We knew that the longer visitors spent in New Bedford, the more money they would spend in the city exponentially. Retail shops, restaurants, and at some point, a downtown hotel would encourage longer stays.

The first tenant we got for the warehouse was a marine broker named Nelson Long. Nelson and his partner, Bill Daniels, set up their commercial fishing boat brokerage business on the first floor. This was right about the time the Magnuson Act extended the US maritime boundary from 12 miles off the coast to 200 miles, creating a tremendous amount of activity among people buying and selling fishing boats. Nelson and Bill were at the center of it, Front and Centre (Streets), to be exact!

The next person to express interest in WHALE's building was Carl Caivano, an artist from western Massachusetts. Carl walked into my office one day and sat down. He was in his twenties, like me. He had long curly hair, inquisitive eyes, and an engaging smile. New Bedford Public Schools had hired him as their artist-in-residence. We talked about that for a while, and then Carl got around to the purpose of his visit. He needed a place to live. He had looked all over New Bedford and decided that the third and fourth floors of the WHALE building would be perfect.

"No, Carl."

"Why not?"

"It would be illegal. This area is zoned industrial. Residences are not allowed. Plus, there isn't an apartment up there."

"But…"

"Not going to happen, Carl."

On that note, Carl left. But he kept returning.

"What is it about 'No' that is hard to understand?" I would ask him, but I respected his tenacity. *Damn artists. So impractical. And full of good ideas.*

As I relayed these encounters to my several bosses, our incremental plan for the district started to shift. Bill and Bea Johnson lived in the district, after all. Even if they weren't there legally, they certainly understood the appeal. And it made sense, after all, that the upper floors of many of these buildings could support residential use. It would mean there would be people here 24 hours a day, which would be better for security. The business climate would benefit as well.

Bill took the idea to the board of the Taxpayers' Association and came back to WHALE with a deal. They would support any appeal for a zoning variance for residential use if WHALE didn't try to change the whole zoning. This compromise wouldn't please a purist, but it would do the job.

The next time Carl wandered into my office (he never gave up), we worked out an arrangement where we would apply for a zoning variance. If we succeeded, he would build the apartment for himself and his cat, Jasper, in exchange for a certain number of months' rent.

I talked with a lawyer, Davis Howes, who had a lot of experience before the Zoning Board. He explained that variances on the legal merits were almost impossible to justify and were granted only if there was no or minimal opposition. I prepared my argument, not knowing what to expect. I arrived at 7 p.m., the appointed time for the meeting. I was nervous and not sure what to do.

The chair of the board was Donald Gomes. I later learned he had been one of the Black activists during the "riots" in the West End in the 1960s, but when I first faced the board, I didn't know him. He looked at me with great skepticism. He was loud and brash, and I was more than a little intimidated. John Harrison, Dick Fontaine, and Joe Kolbeck were members along with one other. I needed four of the five to vote in my favor. I told them I worked for everyone in the district and that everyone thought it would be a good idea if we had some of the upper floors used for residences. I explained that we thought it would be best to take this on a case-by-case basis and not change the whole district's zoning at once. We should move slowly and see how it went. If it went well, I expected to be back in front of them again. They peppered me with questions, but I survived. Rather than focusing on the four legal requirements of a zoning variance, we discussed whether this was good for the district. In the end, we won the vote. Nearly 50 years later, I still run into Donald Gomes, who now works in a well-known funeral parlor. He is still loud and brash, and I consider him a good friend. He has contributed much to New Bedford and has found many ways to serve the city.

With that variance in hand, we had set two important precedents. One was that people could live in the waterfront historic district legally, and two, that artists would lead the way.

Donald Gomes, with hand raised high, makes a demonstrative point during an Onboard meeting at its headquarters on Union and South Water Streets. Other attendees include (left to right) Ronnie Cruz, Jim Magnett, Bill do Carmo (seated), Tim Bargasse, John Monteiro, Zoe Fabio, Charlie do Carmo, Arthur Lopes, Marlene Tavares, Julio "Skippy" Alves, Bumpy Lopes, Regina Henderson, and Rose Tavares Pinto.

The Truth of Old Buildings: Mary Scott Magnan and the Spooner House

The next people to move into the district were also artists. Allen and Mary Scott bought the Caleb Spooner House from WHALE in 1976. The simple one-and-a-half-story Federal-style house was built in 1806 in what is called the Foster Hill neighborhood. But it was in the way of the realignment of Routes 18 and 6 into an intersection, an intersection not-so-fondly referred to as the "Octopus." WHALE bought the building before the Octopus could devour this simple and historic house. The group had George Church move it to a vacant lot on Centre Street, where it was placed on a new foundation constructed by Ed Medeiros.

There, Allen and Mary spied it. With winos inhabiting the next lot and the site surrounded by empty buildings, what did they see? They saw what artists see and what WHALE saw, which is the beauty and the truth of old buildings. Like Carl Caivano, Allen and Mary saw the authenticity of the past and were willing to bet their future on it. Other artists would follow. Many years later, the visionary (and infamously corrupt) Providence Mayor Buddy Cianci spoke at a talk in New Bedford.

"We use artists like Marines. We send them into questionable neighborhoods. And they make them safe. And they make them cool. And then others follow."

Artists are leaders; they see what others cannot. They see the beauty of the architecture and are drawn by the history of the buildings and the district. The working waterfront has always exerted a powerful attraction, with an energy you can feel and hear and smell. And Allen was a scrimshander. He carved drawings into the teeth, tusks, and bones of whales and other animals procured before the passage of the Marine Mammal Protection Act, which made trade in those goods illegal. Allen and Mary saw the potential of being located near the biggest museum devoted to whaling, a place where people from around the world would visit, people who were interested in Allen's craft.

Without question, artists are also drawn to "questionable neighborhoods" because those are the neighborhoods they can afford. And it is a sad fact that in Mayor Cianci's scenario, after artists succeed in turning around neighborhoods and making them cool, they often get priced out because the wealthy folks "discover" the joys of living in the city.

Most of New Bedford in the mid-70s was available at bargain-basement prices. Allen and Mary could have bought a house anywhere. On the street where I lived in the West End, between the downtown and the city's hospital—considered one of the "better" neighborhoods—every house had been purchased for $20,000–$30,000. And we didn't have winos peeing in our backyard!

But Allen and Mary were drawn to the history, the roughness, the authenticity of the district, and its potential. As work activity increased and sidewalks and building projects grew, the momentum and energy grew.

Mary thought the time was right for more. In 1976, she and Allen organized a juried craft fair and invited folk musicians to play for two days on Centre Street. They called it the Centre Street Summer Festival, and they aimed high. New Bedford had organized the Whaling City Festival earlier that summer in Buttonwood Park, but it was essentially a flea market with amusement rides.

Mary and Allen partnered with the New Bedford Preservation Society for the Center Street Summer Festival. They wanted to set a new standard for New Bedford: we could produce the best and expect the best. They wanted only the highest-quality crafts and musicians. They were betting that people would turn out if you offered the best. Their bet was risky because New Bedford had an image of discounted goods and lower-quality offerings.

Well, on the weekend of the festival, you couldn't find space on Centre Street. It was packed. Allen and Mary had clearly touched a nerve and satisfied an unfulfilled need. People celebrated the change. It was the nation's bicentennial year, and Mayor Markey had many additional activities underway—hot air balloon rides, Coors-sponsored professional bike races, and Black history walking trails, to name a few. He asked me to chair the bicentennial commission. There was a budget to get a lot of stuff done, and we had many people involved in doing it.

The Centre Street Summer Festival came at a perfect time. There was genuine joy in the waterfront district that summer, and it was the result of a mix of courageous leadership under Mayor Markey, the united neighborhood effort, and the special sauce added when artists take lead positions in neighborhood revitalization efforts.

In 1987, Allen, a Vietnam War veteran, died a very sad death in part from Agent-Orange-related cancer. The Scotts' son, Travis, picked up stakes and sailed around the world in a small boat, settling finally in Key West, Florida. But Mary remained in the Spooner House and found happiness with another artist, John Magnan. They married and continued bringing life and interest to the neighborhood.

Centre Street Festival, 1988

John had spent his career working as a mathematician and Russian codebreaker for the top-secret National Security Agency in Maryland. When he decided to give that up, he brought his woodworking hobby to UMass Dartmouth and received a Master's in Fine Arts in sculpture. John established a studio on the first floor of what had been the Kaller Beef Building across from the Spooner House and gained an enthusiastic national following. Mary and John continued to be an anchor for the neighborhood. They were there 24/7, adding eyes on the street and voices in meetings. They looked out for their neighbors.

Neighbor is one of my favorite words because it defines relationships. You can't be a neighbor by yourself. And you can't have a neighborhood without neighbors. Neighbors care for each other. They seek each other out to make sure everything is okay. They take in the paper or look after the cat if someone is away. They share information or help with difficult tasks.

Mary was one of the earliest neighbors in the district. In 1999, she was diagnosed with ovarian cancer. John grieved through his art. As Mary fought, John's art tried to explain ovarian cancer to the world. He had showings across the country and on national television. A street in Georgia was named for Mary. Her fight and the way he told her story touched millions. But it was a battle she ultimately had to lose, and she died in 2006.

John carried on and continued to develop his art. He forged a partnership with his next-door neighbor, acclaimed realist painter Bob Duff to create some startling joint pieces. Eventually, as the district got more popular and crowded, and fishermen's bars gave way to a hipper, younger, and definitely louder crowd, John picked up stakes and left the district behind.

But the Spooner House is still home to first-rate artists. Dora Milliken and her husband, Tripp, now have a home and studio there. Dora is an accomplished oil painter who exhibits at the Whaling Museum and other galleries. The artist baton—originally fashioned by local painters like Albert Bierstadt, Albert Pinkham Ryder, Benjamin Russell, Clifford Ashley, and Caleb Purrington and passed on to Centre Street artists such as Caivano, Scott, Magnan, and Duff—is now carried by Milliken and other creative people. Like waves on a beach—they follow one after the other.

The Candleworks: Leading the Banks Toward the Waterfront

The excitement in New Bedford was drawing attention from Boston. A daring and farsighted preservationist named Roger Webb in Boston's Old City Hall took notice. Roger was familiar with New Bedford. In the early 1960s, he worked with my grandmother, Catherine Crapo Bullard, to restore the exterior of the Elizabeth Rotch Rodman House, later known as the Benjamin Rodman House, the first major preservation job in the district. The idea was to return the Wing's Department Store warehouse to the elegant 1820s mansion it had once been. The hope was that if the exterior was fixed up, someone would buy it and continue the interior work. Perhaps, that would jump start the district. Alas, the re-ignition didn't take at the time, and the restored shell waited for years for the its moment.

Roger returned to Boston and worked on a concept that James Rouse would later develop into Quincy Market. Having lost out to Rouse, Roger developed Old Boston City Hall with L'Espalier as a first-rate restaurant on the first floor and offices above. It was clear to him that preservation paid off, and cities across Massachusetts could benefit from the lessons learned and shared. Roger gathered knowledgeable people like lawyer John Bok and real estate developer Bob Kuehne to form a statewide preservation group called Architectural Conservation Trust (ACT) for Massachusetts with headquarters in the basement of Boston's Old City Hall. I joined the board. The group hired a brilliant and tenacious young man named Andy Burnes as its first full-time staffer. Andy was my former classmate at Harvard and shipmate aboard the *Adele*. As an undergraduate, he had learned real estate development working with housing activist Rudy Waker in Roxbury at Low Cost Housing Corp.

The group looked around the state for a project outside of Boston to begin its business model of a statewide historic preservation revolving loan fund. They wanted to identify a project, raise the money, develop it, and use the completed project to springboard into another. In other words, the organization wanted to be a nonprofit real estate developer focusing on historic properties. The question was where to find a challenging enough project to earn recognition but one where they wouldn't lose their shirt right out of the gate?

The members liked all the activity in New Bedford and the commitment shown by Mayor Markey. The group saw a good preservation partner in WHALE. And Andy and I had a mutual trust from sailing across an ocean together, and we could work well together. We were going to have each other's back no matter what.

We decided that the Rodman Candleworks building would be a good project. Located at the corner of Water and Rodman Streets, the three-and-a-half-story building stood sentry at

Rodman Candleworks Building, built 1810   *Meeting with city council members to discuss its re-use*

the district's edge and faced people entering from the highway. Prominent and very visible, the building was owned by the New Bedford Redevelopment Authority and had been vacant for almost 100 years. Built by Samuel Rodman in 1810 to render spermaceti whale oil into candles, the Candleworks had been one of the most noxious businesses on the waterfront. That it was located across the street from William Rotch Jr.'s mansion on William and Water Streets (now the Mariner's Home) shows what a mixed-use neighborhood the district once was and how closely merchants kept tabs on the making of money.

The two walls of the building that faced the streets had mortar that covered the rubble stone. The mortar was etched to make the building look as if it was made of cut granite. The mortar fit into granite quoins on the building's corners and around the windows. The back two sides were not designed to be seen and had no adornment.

In developing real estate, the most crucial element is figuring out the use and, therefore, the income that will support debt servicing. Picking architects, building materials, and design concepts are important, but those elements pale compared to the building's use. After forming the partnership between WHALE and the architectural trust and securing an agreement from the redevelopment authority to develop the building, Andy and I focused on that question. At the height of whaling, Water Street had been America's Wall Street, with many banks lining the street to finance and profit from the country's most profitable energy business. With the discovery of petroleum in 1859 and the transition to textiles, the banks moved away from the waterfront and up the hill into New Bedford's downtown. Andy and I wondered if we might entice them to a return. Banks at the time were locally controlled, profitable, and community minded. Because some banks had practiced "redlining," where they literally drew red lines on maps around inner-city areas where they would not make loans, Congress had passed the Community Reinvestment Act in 1977 to require commercial and savings institutions to invest in low- and moderate-income neighborhoods.

First, we approached Karl Goodwin at New Bedford Five Cents Savings Bank. One of its vice presidents, John Kelleher, was on WHALE's board and was a firm believer in our work and the district's potential. We showed Karl the building and suggested that the bank open the first branch in the district by leasing the first two floors of the Candleworks.

Try to imagine walking through a warehouse that hasn't been occupied for 100 years and looking at dust and cobwebs and heavy beams, one of which still had "Chas. W. Morgan" written

New Bedford Five Cents Savings Bank

in chalk. I don't know what their decision-making process was at the bank, but they decided to go forward with us, opening a branch that didn't even have a drive-through! And with a lead tenant as strong as New Bedford Five, we had also secured our major lender.

The bank referred us to an out-of-town law firm, Karns and Fairbanks. We talked with Bob Karns and George Fairbanks. Sure enough, they were interested in opening an office in New Bedford, and especially interested in our third floor right next to a major client, the bank. Now we had the three main floors rented to substantial tenants. We then hired a Boston architectural firm, Childs Bertman Tseckares, which had much experience in this emerging field of historic preservation. They got to work designing the transformation of a candle factory into offices.

Andy and I then examined the four-foot-high dirt basement. If we dug it out, could it be a restaurant? It was structurally feasible. We targeted a local restaurant called The London Grille. Emile Kasafi owned the restaurant and operated out of a nondescript place off King's Highway in the North End. Emile was an incredible chef and had an underground following that stretched far and wide. When we approached him, he was interested and brought in a partner, a Belgian man named Maurice Jospé. Maurice was a gold broker from Wall Street with no restaurant experience.

Negotiations were proceeding. We were about to sign a lease to start excavating the basement to ready the restaurant space when we saw Emile running away from us down Purchase Street. As far as we could learn, he headed back to Lebanon, never to be seen again in the New Bedford area.

Back to square one. But Maurice Jospé came to us saying he wanted to open the restaurant.

"Maurice, what do you know about restaurants? You're a gold broker with no money and no restaurant experience. What do you have to offer?" we said.

Maurice was not easily dissuaded.

"Look, it is going to take you a year to get this place ready," he said. "I'm going to Boston to work for L'Espalier. Then I'm going to return with experience and a partner in the restaurant business."

I don't know why, but we went ahead. When the restaurant was ready, so was Maurice. He had done a great job at L'Espalier, and he had gotten the backing of David Friedman, a substantial restaurant supplier from Providence.

Rodman Candleworks restored

Maurice opened The Candleworks Restaurant, creating "A World Away from the Everyday." Maurice, Dave, Andy, and I enjoyed our first lunch there, but the meal took three hours!

Maurice Jospé

"Maurice, you *cannot* take three hours to serve people lunch. They don't have that much time!" I said.

"John, you don't understand. This is fine dining. It is different. People want to experience the ambiance of the surroundings. They want to savor the food and the wine. That takes time. They don't want to rush,".

Dave Friedman, who had bankrolled many a restaurant, weighed in.

"Look, Maurice, there are five-star hotels in New York that get you in and out in an hour. You can do it."Andy and I looked at Dave gratefully.

Restaurants are a very risky business. The great majority fail within three years. Maurice Jospé ensured that every customer who came would experience dining as a special treat. As a result, he was successful until he decided it was time for him to retire to a life of painting and quiet evenings with his wife Suzanne.

There were other happy results from this project. Having the successful development of The Candleworks, the Architectural Conservation Trust for Massachusetts garnered national attention and published a book on the incredibly complex financing required to put the project together. Next, the group took on a second and much more extensive project in Fall River. The Durfee Union Mill complex kept Andy busy for several more years as he transformed about nine major mill buildings in the Spindle City.

The Candleworks has evolved, but it still houses a bank branch on its main floors and a wonderful restaurant below. For me, the happiest result is that it was in this romantic dining room that I proposed to Laurie Miller, who became my wife. Like the building, we're still growing strong!

Candleworks Restaurant—"A World Away from the Everyday."

Distinct Layers: NBIS, Mitch Miller, and Freestones

New Bedford Five's move down the hill created an impact. If anyone thought the neighborhood was just for fishermen and tourists, this major bank showed them it could attract other heavy hitters. It gave the district *gravitas* and stamped it as a good business risk. It also generated a lot of publicity and excellent public relations for the bank.

This did not go unnoticed by Bob McCarter. He was president of the largest savings bank in town, the New Bedford Institution for Savings, known as NBIS. It was founded in 1825 by William Rotch Jr. While Karl Goodwin of New Bedford Five was a quiet and understated man, Bob McCarter was…not. He was tall and engaging, with a ready laugh and a larger-than-life personality. He had come to New Bedford from western Massachusetts, where he ran the Springfield Institution for Savings. Bob could not stand New Bedford Five getting the spotlight.

He discovered that an earlier home for NBIS was still standing in the historic district on the northeast corner of William and Second Streets. Designed by noted architect Russell Warren, that building was constructed in 1853 of brownstone, brick, and granite.

Whaling had been at its peak in 1853, and NBIS had been at the heart of the district, close to the harbor, kitty-corner to the US Custom House, and neighbor to several other banks. NBIS stayed in its William Street building until, needing larger headquarters, it moved to a grander building at Union and Fourth (now Purchase) Streets. The bank occupied this building until deciding to "go public" to cash out.

After the bank moved uphill into the downtown, the William Street building was transformed into the Third District Court of Bristol County, complete with new etching in the soft brownstone front and new government seals in the interior lobby. When the courthouse decided that it, too, needed larger quarters around the turn of the century, this once-grand institutional building transitioned to more pedestrian uses. Or should I say, automotive uses, because that's when Bill and Bea Johnson opened Johnson's Auto Parts in the front of the building and turned the back into their living quarters.

I frequently visited to talk to Bill in his role as head of the Bedford Landing Taxpayers' Association, and I always marveled at the history evident in the building. As you entered, you were confronted by the grand seal of the Commonwealth of Massachusetts in full *bas relief* painted with gold leaf, while on the side wall hung all manner of alternator belts, hub caps, windshield wiper assemblies, and other auto parts.

As we pursued our initial plans for the district, Bill and Bea exchanged their Johnson's Auto Parts sign for Johnson's Antiques. Eventually, they realized that even better than selling antiques to tourists was selling a beautiful historic building to the bank. With the sale, NBIS returned to its roots in the waterfront historic district, and Bill and Bea got to retire.

Before moving in, the bank needed to do some necessary restoration. The front had been built of brownstone, a sedimentary rock. Granite is igneous, or volcanic, which means it is stable in all directions and therefore a good building material. Brownstone was made over time by layers

Wilbur Johnson and Bob McCarter

of earth compressing into stone. It, therefore, has distinct layers. The adage for builders is, "You lay it the way you find it." In other words, keep the layers horizontal. Unfortunately, even with the great Russell Warren as the architect, almost every piece of brownstone had been laid with the grain vertical, facing out, which meant that when water inevitably penetrated behind the outside layer and froze in the winter, that layer would be popped off, exposing more layers to spalling, a complicated problem to fix. But NBIS stayed the course and was committed to doing a first-rate job for their

Mitch Miller

new, old branch. They had the resources, so the building got a needed new life.

Bob McCarter didn't just arrive in the district. He took out full-page ads in regional editions of *TIME, Newsweek, Sports Illustrated,* and other mainstream magazines promoting NBIS's role in revitalizing the waterfront historic district. For me, I confess, it was a lot of fun watching two big banks compete to see which could outdo the other in accomplishing more for the district. I wanted them both to win!

Winter rolled around, and Bob McCarter brought television personality Mitch Miller to the district for one of his famous Sing-Alongs. By that time, we had installed the replica streetlights on the bluestone, brick, and cobblestone sidewalks. We got volunteers to wrap the lampposts with laurel boughs and red ribbons. From the steps of the new old NBIS building, Mitch Miller led hundreds of excited citizens, including many children, in singing Christmas carols into the crisp night air. This became an annual tradition for many years and was one of many events that invigorated the city.

Not all was so bright and cheery at the bank's new location, though. Bob took special note of the bar across Second Street from his bank, the Pequod Lounge. It was a notorious hangout, and not because it was named for the vessel in Herman Melville's literary masterpiece. It had beds in the basement, contraband goods alongside the liquor, and large windows almost completely covered with plywood so that no patrons could be thrown through the glass. I was told that the police let things go on there and at certain other bars—free-fire zones as they were called—because if they needed to find someone, they would know where to look.

Bob McCarter wasn't bothered by the Pequod when he was a couple of blocks away, but when it was across the street from the bank branch, he felt he had to act. And act he did. He went back to his connections in western Massachusetts. He contacted Kerry Mitchell, Debbie Sequin, and Mike Galusha, the managers of a very popular "fern bar" called Fitzwilly's in Northampton, where Bob had come from. Fitzwilly's featured lots of exposed brick and ersatz furnishings in a restored building and catered to a young crowd in a college town. It was very successful. Bob's pitch to Kerry, Debbie, and Mike was that they could replicate that success in New Bedford and be owners instead of managers. He would lend them the money to do it.

What he failed to tell them was that in downtown New Bedford even the McDonald's closed at 5 p.m. All the offices and stores shut their doors early and there wasn't much night life. Nobody lived downtown. And everyone knew that nobody went out to eat in New Bedford.

But Kerry, Debbie, and Mike, being from far away, didn't know what everyone in New Bedford knew, so they took Bob's money and started removing from the Pequod Lounge with their sweat equity whatever didn't look like a historic building. They uncovered the remains of an old bank that, when constructed, had been part of the largest commercial building in New Bedford. It

Citizens National Bank, later Freestones Restaurant

Kerry Mitchell and Debbie Seguin

originally had been three floors tall and connected to what is now the Carter's Clothing Building by a one-and-a-half-story building.

The new owners spent hours scraping away the linoleum at the entrance to reveal beautiful marble. They removed the plywood from the windows to discover the historic leaded glass. Venturing beyond the Pequod, they discovered an old church that was removing its pews, so they bought them for seats. Gradually, the Pequod Lounge evolved into Freestones. Then it was time to find out if anyone in New Bedford went out to dinner.

When Freestones opened its doors, there was a line around the block. The place was popular from the very start. And the owners discovered why no one went out to dinner in the downtown: there was no place to go. In the beginning, Debbie and Kerry lived upstairs and worked downstairs. Mike eventually went off to Plymouth to start another restaurant. Debbie and Kerry moved to the West End when things got more stable. They employed each of our kids at

Freestones Restaurant interior, 1979

Visitors' Center at the Whaling National Park *Exhibits inside the Visitors' Center*

one time and were mainstays of the community for decades until eventually retiring from an all-consuming business. Other owners eventually drove the life out of Freestones until it closed in 2021. However, the restaurant was purchased and reopened in 2023.

Meanwhile, the NBIS bank building had one more chapter to write. WHALE and New Bedford, led by district residents Jean and Arthur Bennett and with great help from Senator Edward Kennedy and Congressman Barney Frank, successfully petitioned the US Department of Interior to create a Whaling National Historical Park in New Bedford in 1996. The park is unusual in that while it encompasses 34 acres, there is only one park building—the Visitor Center. People now come from around the world to the National Park to get their first orientation to New Bedford where NBIS once received the deposits from whaling voyages, where civil actions were settled in Third District Court, where Bill and Bea Johnson would sell you a belt for your alternator or a piece of scrimshaw or tell you a story that would leave you laughing. Those brownstone and brick walls have seen and heard it all.

I should point out that to do my job as agent for the committee, I had to become skilled at what was then the very new profession of historic preservationist. There were probably about 20 of us around the country at the time, and we would get together when the National Trust for Historic Preservation held its annual national conferences. We would share stories, learn from each other, and serve as a mutual support group. We deliberated on what this "profession" entailed. Should there be formal training and standards? We needed to be experts in architectural history. We needed to understand the many variations of American architecture styles, why they arose, who the architects were, and what motivated them. Of course, we also needed to know the history of our localities and how our community fit in with regional and national (and sometimes international) history.

We needed to know about building technology through the ages, so we could examine a building and deduce its age by such things as whether the nails were cut or wrought or how the wood was sawn. We joined organizations like the Association for Preservation Technology and attended lectures by experts like Morgan Phillips or Max Ferro at the Society for the Preservation of New England Antiquities. We learned about trees, dendrochronology, and lime mortars. And we learned how to be real estate developers. Just because we worked for nonprofit organizations didn't mean we weren't business oriented. As our movement grew and the benefits of preservation became more widespread, Boston University, Columbia University, Roger Williams University, and other schools offered majors in historic preservation. Ours was indeed a profession.

Moving Heaven and Earth: The Robeson House and Other Moves

When I was writing my thesis and interviewing property and business owners in the district, I met Roland Poitras, who owned Electric Service and Sales at 47 North Second Street, a very nice 1880s four-story brick commercial building located across the street from the 1820 Benjamin Rodman House. Roland sold all manner of light bulbs, fixtures, and supplies for electricians. His business had no connection to either the fishing industry or a budding tourist industry and no real reason to be located near the downtown. His was an industrial use that needed good access to the highway, but Roland had chosen the district years ago because property values were low and there was a lot of cheap space. He ran a good business.

While we were talking, I looked over Roland's shoulder as he stood behind the long counter at the back of the building. I couldn't help noticing a set of granite steps leading up to what looked like the front door of another building.

"Roland, where do those steps go?"

"Come on, I'll show you."

I went behind the counter, and Roland led me up the steps. He unlocked what looked to me like the front door of a large building jammed right up next to the back of his building.

We entered. My jaw dropped.

I had just walked back 150 years in time to the front entrance of an 1820 mansion house, almost exactly like the Benjamin Rodman House across the street. Roland's building, the Bourne Warehouse, had been constructed smack dab in front of another building in 1887. There it was, frozen in time: central hall, four main rooms on the first floor with their original wallpaper and fireplaces. It was filled with fluorescent tubes in storage. I don't think I breathed for several minutes. I felt the same amazement as we ascended the grand central staircase to a central hall leading to four bedrooms on each corner of the building. Each bedroom still had its original wallpaper, and each room had two windows recessed into each wall with wooden shutters you could close from the inside. Virtually all the glass was intact with the wavy imperfections characteristic of glass from that period. Each bedroom had a small closet, and there was an ell in the back with a second set of stairs.

The Andrew Robeson House, west side of North Second Street, north of William Street, circa 1870

Here was a building I hadn't known about, hiding in the middle of the district: The Andrew Robeson House. Robeson, a prosperous merchant and Quaker abolitionist from Pennsylvania, built this mansion on what is now two city blocks across from his brother-in-law, Benjamin Rodman. While also Federal in design, Andrew's house was built of rubble stone faced with expensive pressed bricks made in Robeson's native Philadelphia and individually wrapped in paper for shipment to New Bedford. The portico that framed the front door had been supported by two full and two engaged Doric columns that were unusually slender and made for a very graceful entranceway. Originally, gardens and stately elm trees had surrounded the property and gave it the appearance of quiet wealth. It must have been quite a sight to have these two elegant mansions facing each other just a block away from the activity of the odoriferous Candleworks, the banks, and the waterfront.

As whaling generated vast fortunes, its wealthy moved their homes up the hill to the County Street area and left their smaller mansions behind. The buildings were absorbed into the neighborhood. For example, the Benjamin Rodman House turned into Wing's warehouse and was surrounded by one-story warehouses. For easier storage of furniture, parts of its beautiful granite walls had been removed.

Likewise, the neighborhood was built up around the Robeson mansion, so it was hidden from view. After Robeson vacated, the largest commercial building in New Bedford, the Corson Block, was built around the mansion in 1880. The four-story Bourne Warehouse slammed up against the front wall to the east. The Corson Block filled the entire side of William Street from Second to Acushnet Avenue, passing close by the Robeson House on the south. Another four-story brick commercial building was built right behind the mansion on the west. An alley, Dover Street, ran close by to the north, and the entire block north of that was taken up by the telephone company in its four-story commercial brick building. Until the central part of the Corson Block burned down and exposed the south side of the Robeson House, you pretty much needed a helicopter to see this magnificent mansion in the heart of the historic district!

In 1978, we went to Mayor Markey with an idea for this building. With the City's help, WHALE would move it across Bill Carter's parking lot and down William Street to an empty lot that WHALE owned across from the Custom House. This lot was where the Model Cities office

The Andrew Robeson House being moved onto the Carter's Clothing parking lot

had burned down, and the loss of that historic wooden building had left a hole at a very important intersection.

Before talking with Mayor Markey, I wedged myself between the Bourne Warehouse and the Robeson front wall to measure the width. Then, I measured the distance between the Custom House and the Pequod Lounge. I figured the Robeson House would just fit. I had also talked with Bill Carter, who gave me a hard time as he always did, but eventually said we could move the building across his parking lot as long as we didn't block the street "any time between Thanksgiving and Christmas, which is when I do all of my business." I readily agreed. Once we got the building to the new location, we would rotate it counterclockwise, put it on a new foundation and offer it for sale to someone who would restore the building for a new use. That was the plan. WHALE had moved smaller wooden buildings, so we felt somewhat confident.

Although moving historic buildings removes them from their original context, it seemed clear to us that the context was already gone. The gardens now contained very late-19th-century commercial buildings. To us, it didn't make sense to tear them down, destroying the businesses inside in an attempt to capture an earlier time. We needed more activity, not less. And moving buildings was something people did in the "old days" when resources were scarce. The Port Society had moved William Rotch Jr.'s first home from William and Water Streets up Johnny Cake Hill, and that house had brick end walls and had had to go up a hill.

If we had a preservation philosophy, it might have been captured in the previously mentioned book by an MIT professor of mine, Kevin Lynch, titled, *What Time Is This Place?* He felt you should be able to walk through a city looking at its architecture and know from what time each place originated. If each building is honest about when it is built, you can do that. George Stephen from the US Department of Interior codified this in a set of Historic Building Standards that encouraged people to respect things like building material, fenestration, setbacks, and roofline heights while discouraging the copying of particular styles of architecture. Federal style means something was built around 1820 or so. It shouldn't mean something else. When you see a Federal-style building in New Bedford, you can be confident it was built between the beginning of

The Robeson House being moved onto William Street, 1978

our country and the election of Andrew Jackson in 1829. Jackson's election caused an increased focus on democracy and brought into vogue the Greek Revival style, which harkened back to the country that had shaped democratic values. New Bedford is very fortunate to have many excellent examples of Federal and Greek Revival styles.

Mayor Markey agreed to our plan and funded the move with Community Development Block Grant funds. Before we moved the building, there were things in it that we wanted to remove. Emptying the building wouldn't appreciably lighten the load of this monster, but we wanted bare bones so we could see exactly what we were dealing with.

We thought the things in the building that we weren't going to use in the restoration might as well be auctioned off to raise a little money. Then we thought, as long as we are going to go to the work of having an auction, let's ask our board and supporters if they have any interesting stuff they want to contribute.

And so, the first WHALE Auction was born. We received a lot of fabulous and exciting donations. People bid knowing their bids were supporting a good cause. We raised a significant amount of money, and importantly, everybody had a tremendous amount of fun.

Naturally, we decided to do it again. And again. For more than 20 years. The second year, we approached Peter DeWalt at Reynolds DeWalt Printing to do a poster for us. He had his extremely talented designer, Tom Corey, design a two-foot-by-three-foot, four-color, high-gloss poster that showed off what his company could produce. Peter gave us enough copies to paper the city—a remarkable donation. And he and Tom did this for every year's auction.

But, back to the move. New Bedford put the job out to bid, and Metropolitan Building movers won. They got under the Robeson foundation and braced it with heavy timbers going in both directions. They put monstrous jacks under the timbers and lifted them.

Richard Pline came down to see the move, and we stood talking on the sidewalk. We discussed how the building looked as if it was made of brick but was really rubble stone covered with brick, held together with 150-year-old lime-based mortar.

"John, what do you think the odds are we don't get this building moved ten feet before it ends up just a big pile of bricks and stones?" Richard asked.

"Richard, don't even talk like that! Not a whisper!"

The Robeson House being moved down William Street, 1978

The movers jacked it up, and we found out the Robeson House weighed 550 tons, a piece of trivia that might come in handy someday. As they inched the house away from the neighboring Bourne Warehouse, I was able to get in and re-measure its width—51 feet—a foot wider than I had initially calculated. I wasn't sure we had a foot to spare between the Pequod Lounge and the Custom House. When I looked up, I realized that the problem wasn't down where I could measure. The roof overhangs would narrow the gap even more. But we were on our way, so it was time to cross our fingers and hope.

The movers laid tracks across Bill Carter's parking lot and started to pull the Robeson House across. Then we ran into another surprise. The lot was constructed over the Corson Building basement, and it appeared that whatever they had filled the basement with before applying asphalt was strong enough to support cars, but not a 550-ton building. The movers would pull the Robeson House two feet south during the day. It was a slow process. Then they would quit for the night. When they returned in the morning, whatever part of the building was over the parking lot had sunk up to a foot into the ground. So now the movers had to pull the house *uphill*, dragging it out of a perpetual hole to get it across the parking lot. The house went down into the hole, then up out of the hole, twisting and being tugged at.

And all the while, I was thinking of Richard Pline's "big pile of bricks."

The move proceeded much slower than expected, but it proceeded. Remarkably, the house stayed in one piece. By Thanksgiving of 1977, we had gotten it all the way across the parking lot so that the building was standing right in the middle of William Street. While we were relieved because William Street was stronger than the parking lot and the house would stop sinking, Bill Carter was irate.

"John, what was the one thing I said you couldn't do when I gave you permission to use my parking lot?"

"Mr. Carter, you said we couldn't block William Street between Thanksgiving and Christmas when you do all your business."

"And what day is it?"

"The day after Thanksgiving."

"And with that damn house where it is, water couldn't run down William Street!"

Of course, Mr. Carter was basically right, although I think water would have found its way down the street. The Robeson House blocked pretty much anything but water from going down this major downtown street, making it very hard for patrons to get to Carter's store. From a practical standpoint, there was little we could do about the problem other than keep moving as fast as we could, which was about one or two feet a day.

One day, I stopped to watch the move. It was so nerve-racking for me, convinced as I was that Richard Pline's vision was just a moment away, that I decided that I would look at the building only first thing in the morning and then on the way home at night. I couldn't take seeing this 1820 antique house being tugged and pushed all day by massive hydraulic jacks.

When the house approached the Pequod Lounge and the Custom House, we faced another moment of truth. Would it fit? The movers lined it up and pushed. The Robeson roof shingles on the south side scraped the underside of the soffit of the Custom House as the building squeezed by. But squeeze by it did. With not an inch to spare.

As if this weren't difficult enough, as we entered the intersection with Second Street, Mother Nature decided to get into the act, delivering us the famed Blizzard of '78. The storm blanketed the city with 26 inches of snow and left five-foot drifts that required the National Guard to assist with getting stranded people to hospitals. *Was anything about moving the Robeson House going to go as planned or be easy?*

Somewhere during this process, the original moving company went bankrupt, and another moving company took over, so the quick answer was, "No."

When the house was positioned opposite its new foundation, the movers rotated it 90 degrees counterclockwise and pushed it south onto the site of the old Reynolds Building. They had built a new concrete foundation with a full basement to support the house, and once the front wall of the house was lined up, I went inside and looked around before they lowered it down. I noticed two problems. One was that

The Robeson House at its current location, southeast corner of William and North Second Streets

the interior doors wouldn't close as they had before. Something was out of line. Then I went down to the basement and saw that while the front wall lined up over the foundation, the back wall was pushed about a foot to the east. The move had turned what was essentially a square building into a parallelogram. If they lowered it as it was, the east wall would be hanging out over the foundation. I told the movers that this was not acceptable, that masonry walls are not designed to be hung. They don't do well in tension; they are compression elements. I told the movers they would need to build additions to the foundation to support both sidewalls. The movers said that would cost a lot of money, and they would think about it overnight.

I went home. They didn't just think; they acted. They positioned a bunch of hydraulic jacks crosswise under the building and, like some mad building chiropractors, jacked the building back into square. That the house did not fall apart at the corners and collapse in a ton, or 550 tons, of bricks is a testament to the plasticity of the old lime mortar that held everything together.

When I returned the next morning, I could not believe my eyes. The house lined up perfectly on the foundation. I went inside, and all the doors fit perfectly into their jambs. The house sat securely on its new foundation, ready for a new chapter.

We had a party at the Pequod Lounge to raise money for Freddie Almeida, whose business we had essentially ended by parking the house six inches in front of his door for a couple of months. It was very difficult to get in or out. He would later sell his building to the people who would create Freestones, so that had a very happy ending.

WHALE raised money to restore the exterior of the Robeson House so that we could establish the standard of restoration from the start. Kit Wise was the architect. Restoration would also give us a better chance of marketing the property, which still looked pretty gruesome.

After completing the exterior in about 1984, WHALE sold the Robeson House to Ken Alves, John Holmes, and Ray Lantz, who hired Max Ferro as their architect to restore the interior. To take advantage of historic tax credits, they had to follow the US Secretary of Interior's rigorous guidelines for historic preservation. They kept the original doors, windows, and fireplaces and replicated the moldings while replacing the plaster and the ell at the back.

They kept the house for about ten years before selling it to a well-known local lawyer and close friend of mine, Philip Beauregard, for his law office, Beauregard, Burke, and Franco. As I walked through the mansion's front door to talk with Phil and to see the entryway that I had first entered almost 50 years earlier, there to greet me were two beautiful William Allen Wall portraits of Andrew Robeson and his wife, Anna Rodman Robeson. The home had a new use and a new location, but it was elegant and alive with voices. The people and the place were still setting a standard of excellence for New Bedford as the home celebrated its 200-year birthday.

Fire and Ice: The District Blows Up!

It was Tuesday, January 18, 1977. A little before 5 a.m., the phone rang. It was Mayor Jack Markey.

"John, you better get down here right away. Your building on Union Street has blown up."

The winter had been bitterly cold. Snow and ice covered the streets, sidewalks, and yards. As I hurried the few blocks from our house down to the district, I could see an orange glow in the sky. Nothing could have prepared me for what I saw when I got there.

The mayor was already there. A ladder truck was parked in front of Union Tobacco. A pumper was in front of the Sundial Building. The huge Palladian windows in the Whaling Museum at the top of the hill were blown out. There were flames everywhere. The combination of fire and ice in the darkness was surreal.

Our Macomber-Sylvia Building on Union Street was gone. It had been an 1820s wood-frame building, modified in the 1870s with a Victorian gable on the front. Vacant for many years, it had been in terrible shape but formed part of a beautiful three-building assemblage facing Union Street, with the three-and-one-half-story O'Malley's Tavern in the middle and the stately brick Sundial Building on the corner. Except for O'Malley's Tavern, every other space had been vacant and in need of major work.

WHALE purchased the Macomber-Sylvia Building to do just that. Anne "Pete" Baker from Westport knew how to tackle historic wooden buildings. She was also a very talented potter and a very good friend of Sarah Delano's. Her small crew included Doug Keffer from Vermont, who knew his way around historic wooden buildings.

There is an old joke that says one way to draw an elephant is to cover a piece of paper with gray from a pencil and then just erase what doesn't look like an elephant. Similarly, Pete and Doug began by erasing what didn't look like the original 1820 building or its Victorian modification. When they got down to its roots, we could see the structure's beauty. We scoured old photographs for what the missing pieces might have looked like, and Doug and Pete filled in those pieces. Our goal was to meet the modern building code and restore the exterior. This they had done, completing work on January 14, 1977, a Friday. The building had been transformed. It was beautiful. WHALE had spent $41,000 on the work, emptying its account.

Looking north toward Union Street and Johnny Cake Hill before the gas explosion, circa 1970

While Pete and Doug were busy with the restoration, I was trying to find a buyer for the property. I found two prospective developers, each willing to buy the building, finish the interior work, and use the building in a way that would benefit the district. WHALE was to set to decide which buyer to select at its regularly scheduled board meeting at noon, January 18, 1977, at the Wamsutta Club. Because of the quick turnaround between finishing the project and selling the building, WHALE decided not to increase the insurance on the building to cover their investment.

The noon meeting did not go off as planned. WHALE did not sell the building because there was no building to sell. We couldn't find even a few pieces of it. Pete and Doug's handiwork and 150 years of history were blown to smithereens.

As I said, it had been a freezing winter. The frost had driven deep into the ground. Although the gas company had replaced many gas lines, it had not replaced a 19-inch diameter feeder line that went over Johnny Cake Hill and across Union Street. Where the gas line made that bend from downhill to level, the pipe got close enough to the surface to be above that year's unusually low frost line. A weld in the cast-iron feeder pipe cracked. Gas started to leak to the surface. But instead of dissipating into the air, where eventually it would have been noticed, it was blocked by the ice that covered everything. The gas had no choice; it migrated under the surface until it found Mr. O'Malley's tavern. And perhaps the Macomber-Sylvia Building. The gas seeped into the tavern until 4:43 a.m., when the furnace kicked on.

And that was the end of Mr. O'Malley's building. And WHALE's building.

Fortunately, nobody was inside either one. Things got scarier still as we were trying to grasp what we had lost and how it had happened.

Union Tobacco was a one-story, concrete-and-brick building on the northwest corner of Union Street and Johnny Cake Hill. It was built sometime after World War II. Like several nearby buildings, it was used to sell food and tobacco products befitting a seaport.

The ladder truck had pulled up in front of it to fight the fire raging on the next block. Suddenly, Union Tobacco also blew up, slamming a four-foot-high I-beam, 20 feet in length, into the ladder truck. The blast had enough force to suck the north wall of the brick YMCA across the street seven inches toward the explosion. We were extremely lucky that no firefighters or bystanders were in the way of the I-beam. But another building had been lost, as well as a valuable piece of firefighting equipment. We realized the danger wasn't over. The gas was moving.

What is going to blow up next?

We didn't have long to wait.

At 7:08 a.m., the Eggers Building blew up on the other side of the Whaling Museum. It was a tidy two-and-a-half-story wood-frame building next to the massive brick museum auditorium annex. It had a gable front and Greek Revival detailing. Once a bookie joint with hundreds of telephone lines coming out of the roof, it was now home to Crowell's Fine Art Gallery on the first floor and Tim Sylvia's commercial photography studio upstairs. The explosion lifted the roof into the air, blew out the gable front and back, and the roof settled back onto the first floor, making it flat as a pancake.

The Whaling Museum's officials had begun examining the damage. I went in with Richard Kugler. Inside the museum's Bourne Building, all the windows had been blown out, and the sails on the half-scale ship model, *Lagoda*, were filling with wind. It looked as if she were straining from her permanent berth in the floor to escape the carnage, which didn't seem like a bad idea.

More worrisome was the report that gas was filling the Hirst Building, which housed the museum's library. The implications were clear and ominous. The entire museum was at stake. Richard Kugler reported this to the authorities. They succeeded in shutting off the gas, venting the building, and avoiding another catastrophe.

Other reports came in. Three blocks away on Purchase Street, Saltmarsh's store had gas inside. At the top of the hill on County Street, the Unitarian Church reported gas. In the "fog of war," the firefighters, the gas company workers, and other emergency personnel weren't sure of the extent of the problem. Early national news reports stated that New Bedford's entire downtown had been lost to the explosions.

When all the gas had been shut off and all the fires put out, we took stock. By some miracle, no lives had been lost. We felt very fortunate about that. Four businesses had been wiped out. Mr. O'Malley never reopened his tavern. He retired, and his son, John, took a job at a funeral parlor. The business, a long-time gathering spot in the district, was gone forever.

Union Tobacco disappeared. Sid Wainer decided to leave the district he had been a part of for many years. His son, Henry, transformed the business into a specialty food business in the city's

Union Street and Johnny Cake Hill, January 18, 1977

North End. Today, Sid Wainer & Son trucks can be seen on our nation's highways bringing the best foods, many locally grown, to the finest restaurants all over the country.

Barbara and Ed Bushell moved their frame shop, Crowell's Gallery, for the second time. They had come into the district from a historic Catholic church building on Pleasant and School Streets—torn down for a parking lot. After the explosion, they decided to expand to a brick building in the district, on Acushnet Avenue, right behind Carter's Clothing. It was

The Eggers Building on William Street, next door to the Whaling Museum—after the explosion

owned by the Electrical Workers Union and provided more space than the Eggers Building. They would enjoy a successful run in that location until deciding to retire many years later.

Photographer Tim Sylvia also decided to stay in the district, relocating his business to a brick industrial building owned by Thornton Klaren one block north of the Whaling Museum. Many businesses and organizations suffered major damage—including the Whaling Museum, the YMCA, and the New Bedford Fire Department—and several others had burst and broken windows. Every one of these got quickly to work repairing the damage that cold winter.

The Whaling Museum insisted that the Eggers Building be removed from its property. They claimed it was a fire hazard and a threat to the auditorium. I tried to persuade them that it had already blown up and caught fire and hadn't caused a nickel's worth of damage to the auditorium, but what I thought was a logical argument wasn't persuasive. They would give the building away, but it had to go.

Aftermath of gas explosion, Union Street and Johnny Cake Hill

I found a developer from Newport, Rad Romeyn, who was interested in doing something in New Bedford. He bought the Union Tobacco Company site from Sid Wainer at One Johnny Cake Hill, took possession of the Eggers Building, and bought the Wing Carriage House in Westport. He tried to put them all together in one development on the corner. He received approval for the design, but moving the Carriage House proved too costly, so he built a new building that looked like the Carriage House and rebuilt the Eggers Building after moving it to the site. It became the Baggywrinkle Restaurant with a specialty retail store and offices.

Eggers Building at new location, Union Street and Johnny Cake Hill

While Rad was doing the site work, he pulled up the concrete floor of Union Tobacco and discovered a well right at the intersection of Union Street and Johnny Cake Hill. When he called me to look at it, we noticed a couple of things right away. When most historic wells go out of use, they get filled up with garbage of the times. They are excellent places for archeological digs. This well was empty down to the bottom, about 20 feet below. And it appeared to be fed from a spring that was coming down from the direction of the Bethel. We lowered a bucket and tasted the water. Delicious! Then we looked at the several versions of the William Allen Wall painting, *New Bedford 50 Years Ago*, which depicts the Corner of Union and Water Streets in 1820. There, at the intersection of Johnny Cake Hill, you can see people gathered around a well.

Many of these post-fire stories took time to play out. But there was a more immediate story that unfolded in the days after the explosion, a building that would require quick and decisive action after the fires or else be demolished. It hadn't taken long that "explosive" morning for the gas-and-wood-fired flames coming from O'Malley's Tavern to blow onto the roof of the adjacent Sundial Building. This three-and-one-half-story, granite-and-brick building had been built in 1820 by Charles and Seth Russell Jr., great-nephews of Joseph Russell, who had founded New Bedford. It had once been a dry goods store and then home for the *Evening Standard*. It also had been the building where clocks and chronometers were manufactured, which explained the sundial attached to the southern face of the building. It is an excellent example of Federal-style architecture, one of the district's best and most important buildings.

At the time of the fire, the Karalekas family owned the building and had used it for their State Fruit Company. Nearby was the State Pier, and it had been common for fruit and lumber to be unloaded in New Bedford. Diagonally across from State Fruit was Tropicana Banana, both waterfront-related businesses in the hurly-burly of the port. But by the time of the fire, these landings at State Pier had trickled to almost nothing, and the Karalekas family had abandoned the building and put it up for sale for the outrageous price of $98,000. Nobody was interested.

On the day of the gas explosions, its roof caught fire before 7 a.m., and soon after, it collapsed, pushing out the third story of brick wall toward Water Street, endangering anyone who might walk by on the sidewalk. The building was covered in ice from the firefighters, and its roof was gone. It had been vacant for quite a while and was, indeed, a very sorry sight. Paul Landreville, the building inspector, pronounced it a hazard to public safety. He said it had to be demolished.

I talked with Mayor Markey about the value of the building and the need to save it. We discussed this with Paul, who agreed to demolish only down to the third-floor windowsills. We got to work.

I went first to the Whaling Museum. The Sundial Building sat on their block, and their long-term master plan called for them to acquire it at some point. I argued with Richard Kugler that now would be a good time. He went to his board and took until Friday after the Tuesday fires to decline. The Whaling Museum, technically the Old Dartmouth Historical Society, has a mission to protect items of historic importance forever. This is a long time and forces you to be conservative in many senses of the word. It means you avoid risk at all costs. And the ice-covered, fire-damaged Sundial Building with an unknown cost of acquisition and restoration represented RISK in capital letters. They did not want to assume this risk. It was unfortunate that they took from Tuesday to Friday to tell me this because we had a building in a very vulnerable condition with the fallen roof pressing out on the walls, but this was the case.

I turned to WHALE. WHALE was not afraid of risk. Its founders had created it precisely because the Old Dartmouth's conservative philosophy and priority placed on smaller objects resulted in lost historic structures. This difference caused friction between the two groups, but it was an advantage for New Bedford. It meant the city had two organizations with separate missions and separate skill sets.

WHALE wanted to save the building. The problems were that we had $2,000 in bills and only $500 in the bank, we had just lost a building that we had invested $41,000 in, and we had not increased the insurance. WHALE wasn't in an ideal position to buy anything.

The directors met in an emergency session Saturday morning in George Perkins' law office on Orchard Street. Each of the 21 directors personally pledged to guarantee $3,000 toward a loan to buy the building. We got the three Karalekas brothers to come to the office to see what they wanted for the building. After two hours of bargaining, they agreed to lower the price to $68,000 and a case of beer if we would agree to place a plaque about their family on the building once it was finished. We shook hands and signed a Purchase and Sale Agreement. We immediately let Mayor Markey know that we owned the building and needed his help.

On Monday, we hired a contractor, and by Tuesday, he had removed the roof and temporarily stabilized the walls—one week to the day from the explosion. This was the essence of WHALE, ordinary people who did extraordinary things. They cared more about the preservation of historic buildings than about self-preservation. They took risks and acted fast. And they delivered time after time.

Sundial Building after gas explosion, and after restoration

Solving Problems in Different Ways: Phoenix Rises

WHALE had not let its coffers empty without planning to replenish them. They had planned a fund drive, and Bob Saltmarsh had agreed to chair it. Bob and his wife, Maura, owned and operated Saltmarsh's department store on Purchase Street. He was a leader of the downtown merchants, always among the first to do anything to support increased activity in the downtown area. He had taken the former Hutchinson's Bookstore and turned it into a four-story department store that sold everything from greeting cards and office supplies to souvenirs of New Bedford. Bob was also a world-class laser sailor, so he was competitive and always wanted to win. It was good knowing he was on your side. He was confident, and his optimism spread easily to those around him.

WHALE had set the fund drive's goal at $275,000, about $100,000 more than we had ever raised. The campaign's purpose was to restore the Robeson House and undertake other smaller projects. On the Wednesday following the removal of the roof, several of us met in Bob's office atop his store. We discussed the relationship between WHALE and the community.

"When WHALE goes way out on a limb to save a building like the Sundial Building, people know we are acting on their behalf," Bob said.

Sarah Delano was confident in the community's support.

"They have never let that limb get sawn off while we are out there. They will support our action. They will back us up."

Others in the room who would have to go out and raise the money concurred. We increased the goal to $425,000 that day. We went into the community for support, and they did indeed back us up. Before long, we had raised $426,000 to replenish our revolving loan fund. We were back off the limb.

We researched what the Sundial had looked like. To our surprise, it had not been a Spartan Quaker building devoid of ornament, but one sporting an ornate wooden balustrade along the roofline and wooden shutters for every window. We included those in the specifications. Mayor Markey put the building in his Community Development Block Grant plans, and, with an emergency grant from the Massachusetts Historical Commission, we restored the exterior to its 1850 appearance, complete with the wooden shutters and balustrade. Now that the building was fully restored on the outside and represented zero risk, we again approached the Whaling Museum.

Robert Saltmarsh

Café inside Saltmarsh's store

Blowing glass at New Bedford Glassworks in a newly-built adjunct to the Bourne Warehouse

Robert Bryden, CEO of Pairpoint, inspects decorative antique glass once manufactured in New Bedford.

A sale was quickly negotiated, and the museum has used and maintained the building ever since. Unfortunately, they removed the shutters and the balustrade, and the Karalekas brothers got their case of beer but not their plaque.

There was much else going on at that time. Once the Robeson House was cleared of the site behind the Bourne Warehouse, I reached out to Pairpoint Glassworks. This famous glass company had once employed hundreds in the South End of New Bedford to manufacture the highest quality high-lead-content art glass. The company had moved and was manufacturing out of a plant in Sandwich near the Cape Cod Canal. I visited with CEO Robert Bryden and asked if he would like to return to New Bedford. I suggested he could expand into the first floor of the Bourne Warehouse and a new building to be built where the Robeson House had been. After much discussion that entailed my learning a lot about the manufacture of glass, he agreed. They constructed the new factory, and Pairpoint candlesticks, vases, and famous cup plates once again were made in New Bedford.

WHALE bought an empty lot across the street north of the New Bedford Glass Museum in the Benjamin Rodman House. We identified two small wooden Greek Revival homes in the city's South Central neighborhood that the redevelopment authority had contracted out to demolish. To save the buildings, we acquired the houses from the demolition contractors. We hired George Church, a farmer whose family had raised crops in Rochester for several hundred years, to move the structures. Soon the Abijah Hathaway House and the Haile Luther House had new sites on

Haile Luther House, after being moved to North Second and Elm Streets—and restored

Second Street. This secured an important corner, as the Elm Street Parking Garage entrance was right across the street. Visitors to the district would see these two houses as their first impression of the community after they disembarked from their cars. Bob and Maura Saltmarsh restored the Haile Luther House as a small adjunct store, Salt-Fen Pottery, and put an apartment on the second floor. Penry and Dorothy Warr restored the Abijah Hathaway House next door for their Coracle Clothes, made with fine Irish wools. While their uses have changed over time, these two buildings continue to greet visitors. To me, they seem like a couple of good friends, holding forth on that corner, keeping each other company through the seasons.

Another building move illustrates the benefits accrued from the cooperation and trust among the district's varied groups. The Whaling Museum needed a new library for its extensive collection of whaling logbooks, documents, books, and paintings that could not be displayed. Quite naturally, they wanted this building to be on their block. If they nestled it among their other buildings, they could, with one elevator, make all of their buildings, including the Sundial Building, handicapped accessible. Cambridge Seven, the firm that had designed the auditorium building, designed the library and the central spine to link all the structures. Their design was brilliant. And like the auditorium, it was unabashedly modern but still respectful of its historic surroundings in terms of building material, roofline, fenestration, setback, and color.

There was only one problem. It would require the acquisition of Northeast Marine Electronics from Bob Hathaway. Bob conducted his fishing-related business in the Seth Russell House on Water Street, a two-and-one-half-story wooden structure that might be the oldest building in New Bedford. Seth Russell was the father of the men who built the Sundial Building and the nephew of Joseph Russell, the founder of New Bedford. While the building had a Water Street address and was Greek Revival in appearance with its gable front to the east, when Seth Russell built it in 1765, it would have been a Federal-style house set back from Union (then King) Street (before the Sundial Building was there).

Thirteen years later, in 1778, British Major General Charles Grey landed a force of 4,000 men halfway up the west side of what is now West Rodney French Boulevard. They marched up what is now Brock Avenue, then along County Street and down Union Street burning everything in their path. There are many stories about why the only house to survive was Seth Russell's. The one most fascinating to me is that as the British were burning houses, they lit fire to Seth Russell's house, and a woman, likely his wife, Keziah Walker Russell, put it out with a broom. The soldiers lit it again. Again, she put it out. A third time they tried, and a third time she extinguished it. Pressed for time, perhaps, they gave up and marched to the waterfront, where they burned ships and wharves. They then marched north to Acushnet, across the river, and down to Fairhaven, the true object of their anger.

Seth Russell House, North Water Street, before moving

I climbed all around the attic of the Seth Russell House and saw timbers held together with wrought nails. These nails, individually made by a blacksmith who hammered them to a point over a flame, stopped being used for buildings for anything other than window sashes in 1790 when nails started to be cut from a single sheet of iron. So, the house was certainly earlier than 1790.

Seth Russell House, after being moved to Union and Front Streets

In the days before our Ten-Acre Agreement with other organizations in the district, this problem would have been solved one way. The Whaling Museum would have approached Bob Hathaway to buy his building. Bob would not have wanted to sell and would have resented the suggestion. He would have put an outrageous price on his building. The museum would have paid it. Bob would have moved out of the district. The museum would have torn the building down. Ill feelings, already high, would have ratcheted even higher, and the cost of the library would have been inflated by the cost of the acquisition. And the district would have lost a fishing-related business. The oldest building in New Bedford would have been destroyed by the Historical Society, or possibly sent out of the region to a maritime museum such as in Mystic, Connecticut.

Instead, we devised a plan that would yield a different outcome. The museum owned two wood-frame buildings almost directly across Water Street. One, at the corner of Water and Centre Streets, was similar in size to Bob's building but in better condition. We persuaded the museum's leadership to offer it in trade so that no one had to put a price on their building, which often involves people's egos. Bob agreed because he would get a better building in essentially the same location. The museum gave the Seth Russell House to WHALE, which moved it down Union Street to an empty lot it owned on the northwest corner of Union and Front Streets. The Whaling Museum then built its library on the land acquired in the trade from Bob Hathaway.

WHALE recruited Kevin Dawson, who operated a settlement house, to buy the Seth Russell House and occupy the first floor. We went to the Zoning Board of Appeals, as we had done with every other building we had developed. Not only did we need variances for setback and parking requirements, but also, again, we wanted to have a residence on the second floor. At this hearing, we encountered something we hadn't faced before.

As the meeting proceeded under Donald Gomes's firm grip, things seemed to be going along well. We had been through this many times. They knew us and had never denied us. While Donald liked to give me a hard time, we had always gotten what we came for and did not anticipate any problems. But, when the chairman asked if anyone objected, Dick Alcobia raised his hand.

Dick Alcobia ran the National Club across Union Street, a bar that catered to the people of the waterfront. It was a tough joint, just what you would expect on a working waterfront.

I vividly remember one evening, shortly after I had started work in the district, looking out my window up Front Street. I glanced toward Union Street and saw a man running as fast as he could down Front Street and away from the National Club. Fifty yards behind him came Dick Alcobia, his long ponytail flying. Dick was holding his stomach, and blood was spurting out. They raced by the WHALE building, and I ran downstairs as they rounded New Bedford Ship Supply and up Hamilton Street. The guy got away, and I caught up with Dick. He had been stabbed breaking up a fight in one of his restrooms. We got him to the hospital, and he was okay. Stabbings were not a normal occurrence at the National Club, but breaking up fights was part of Dick Alcobia's job.

Dick Alcobia

"State your objection," Chairman Gomes declared.

"Mr. Chairman, we were here first," Dick said. "I run the National Club. It is a bar. It can be loud, and we don't let out until one o'clock in the morning. Our patrons can be noisy. Now, even though someone moving into an apartment across the street from us may know there is a bar next door, they are still not going to like it when they are woken up at one o'clock in the morning. So, they are going to call the police. And the police are going to give us a hard time. And we were here first. We don't have any objection to the building being there or the business on the first floor. Just somebody living upstairs. We have never objected to people living elsewhere in the district. Just across the street from us. It is going to cause us trouble, and we were here first."

Dick sat down.

Donald Gomes looked at me.

"What do you think, Mr. Bullard? Does Mr. Alcobia have a point?"

I knew he did, and I could see he was painting an accurate picture of the future of a gentrifying district. How could I argue with his right to exist?

"Mr. Chairman, would it be all right if we modified our petition for a variance in order to delete the request for a second-floor residence?"

"It would, Mr. Bullard. It would."

And with that, the Seth Russell House was moved, and sold to Kevin and Sandra Dawson, who restored the building and carried on the business of settling the harvest of a ship's catch—a task that has been going on for centuries.

National Club and Skip's Marine Supply, Union Street, early 1960s

Authentic Design: Into the Neighborhoods

Revitalization can be as contagious as blight. When people see good things happening in one part of their city, the energy spreads. People in New Bedford were hungry; they wanted more. There are academic theories related to this. On the negative side, there is the "broken windows" theory of policing that sprang from a 1982 paper by James Q. Wilson and George L. Kelling and was put most famously into practice by New York City Police Commissioner William Bratton. If you saw one broken window, you fixed it quickly, communicating that you cared about the neighborhood. If you failed to fix the first broken window, then pretty soon there would be two, then three. Then, the building would be broken into, and then there'd be a fire. That is the way blight spreads. It starts with the message that people don't care.

Promoting New Bedford, circa 1980

The positive side was best expressed in a book by architect Christopher Alexander, *Notes on the Synthesis of Form*. I first encountered this book as an undergraduate, and as I have said, it shaped my philosophy on design. Alexander describes designs that have evolved over generations, as people who did not consider themselves designers compared two examples and picked the better solution. He posited that, given two choices, people did not have to be sophisticated designers to choose the more beautiful or, the more effective. Over hundreds of years, this system would produce designs that were both functional and beautiful. Very different from starting with a blank sheet of paper and trying to get every possible relationship correct on the first try. Alexander's theory is backed up by the fact that so many architects who taught and practiced self-conscious design were attracted to or lived or worked in environments created by the incremental process of unselfconscious design.

Coors International Cycling Race, 1987

In New Bedford's case, people from all around the city saw old buildings coming back to life in the waterfront historic district. They saw new paint, new businesses, new people moving in, and new energy. With the Centre Street Summer Festival and Mayor Markey setting off hot air balloon rides from downtown and getting Coors to sponsor a major bicycle race through the downtown and historic district (cobblestones and all), you couldn't help but notice that there was a spirit of optimism taking root in a city that had been down on itself since the textile Strike of 1928.

Mayor Markey facilitated this with his Office of Historic Preservation. Tenney Lantz and Tony Souza were out in the neighborhoods consulting with property owners. They handed out mini-grants if you wanted to fix your storefront. They helped arrange loans if you wanted to paint your house. Tony would help you figure out a color scheme to make the architectural style of your building sing. It was remarkable to watch. You would look at a block of drab and run-down houses and see one brave homeowner go first. The asbestos shingles or aluminum siding would come off. The clapboards would be repaired and sanded. Trim would be patched or replaced. Windows were re-glazed. And then, painters would use four or five contrasting colors to high-light the intricate wooden detailing. Add a few touches with period hardware, and the house was a marvel! Suddenly, every other owner on that street wanted to talk to Tony or his assistant, Peter Jacobsen, to figure out how to do something similar.

New Bedford had an advantage in part because it had been through many economic ups and downs. Neighborhoods are made up of buildings, and buildings are like men's ties. They go in and out of fashion. In cities that maintain a constant level of prosperity, people tend to destroy the buildings that go out of fashion. When fashion finally changes, as it always does, there aren't many old houses left. New Bedford went into a deep economic freeze beginning with the textile Strike of 1928, followed by the Great Depression. When Greek Revival and Victorian houses went out of fashion, they could have been replaced by bungalows and homes from a Sears catalog, but New Bedford's people didn't have the capital to tear down their buildings; they just let them stand—unpainted and unloved. As a result, the city has thousands of historic structures built in the 19th and early 20th centuries. These are clustered in the South Central neighborhood, the West End, and Foster Hill neighborhoods that grew up around whaling. Later, when the city's

Farmers Market, Purchase Street Pedestrian Mall, 1981

population peaked in the 1920s, three- and four-deckers built to house mill workers filled the North and South Ends.

Merchants in the downtown organized the Downtown Action Committee and hired me to expand the magic of the waterfront historic district. Leaders like Elaine Lima, Bob Saltmarsh, Leo Kavanaugh, Joel Karten, Karl Goodwin, and Bob McCarter helped organize new advertising and a farmer's market. New Bedford replaced sidewalks and installed streetlights with replicas of 19th-century streetlights. It was a good effort but suffered because it was reliant on voluntary contributions and actions. Our competition was the malls, which had a different business model.

I remember a conversation with Joel "Buzzy" Karten, whose original jewelry store was on Union Street. He was opening several new stores in different malls. We were talking in his Union Street store when Buzzy described a disagreement over a sign he wanted to put at his Braintree Mall location.

"John, it's a beautiful sign. I paid $3,000 for it. I hung it, and the mall manager came over and measured it and told me it was two inches too tall. Two inches! Can you believe that!?! She ordered me to get rid of the sign and replace it! Two inches! I can't believe it!"

Buzzy's voice was getting louder and louder. I tried to imagine a similar conversation about our downtown. If someone had put up a new sign here, we would have been thrilled. The New Bedford City Council would have given him a citation.

"Buzzy, what are you going to do?" I asked.

"I'm going to take it down, throw it away, and build another one, two inches smaller."

"Jeez, Buzzy, how does that make you feel about the mall where you are about to open?"

"John, it makes me feel like I'm going to make an awful lot of money there."

Buzzy was a great businessman, and he did make a lot of money there. He knew that malls worked because they have strict rules. Everybody opens on time, closes on time, adheres to a standard marketing policy, and contributes to common cleaning, security, parking, landscaping, tenant mix, and other beneficial management measures. Nothing is voluntary. No one is a freeloader. And this is the case whether your store is in an obvious mall like a shopping center or a mall pretending to be a city like Quincy Market in Boston. The mall can require businesses to open at night and on Saturdays when many people like to shop.

In many downtowns, everybody makes their own decisions. Shops tend to close at 5 p.m., and people park in front of their stores because nobody wants to be the only one to sacrifice in order to

Looking north on Purchase Street from Union Street, 1971

William Tallman Russell House on Russell Street   *Elizabeth G. Leonard House, 99 Madison Street*

benefit everyone else. Getting people to stay open late, open up parking, and contribute to maintenance, for instance, will work only if everybody follows the rules, and that won't happen unless the rules are part of a lease or another mandatory measure like a Business Improvement District.

But there was a role for WHALE in the neighborhoods surrounding the downtown. We learned that the William Tallman Russell House on Russell Street in the South Central neighborhood was threatened after a fire badly damaged the back of the building. This Greek Revival building was historically and architecturally significant, an important part of this Cape Verdean neighborhood. We bought the building, made emergency repairs, and found a wonderful couple, Joe and Arlene Davis, who had moved down from Boston. With help from New Bedford and a lot of sweat equity, Joe and Arlene brought this building back to its former glory. Just as important, they became valuable contributing members of the South Central neighborhood.

WHALE responded to another threat at 99 Madison Street in the West End. In 1881, Mrs. Elizabeth G. Leonard built a beautiful Queen Anne House at the corner of Madison and Orchard Streets. While Federal and Greek Revival had been somewhat disciplined architecture, styles and colors loosened up quite a bit as people moved into the Victorian age. When it was built, Mrs. Leonard's house featured hints of the Shingle Style, in which the structural elements of a building didn't matter at all. Posts and beams, square corners, and symmetry gave way to an emphasis on volume and the continuous skin of a building, almost as if you had inflated the skin like a balloon. The architect or builder could emphasize the skin by varying textures with shingle patterns and windows.

Mrs. Leonard's building was a large house and an excellent example of early Victorian architecture, and it was on a prominent corner. It once had a famous owner, Andrew Pierce Jr., one of the titans of the textile industry back when New Bedford was producing "a mile of cloth a minute." Mr. Pierce was also president of Pairpoint Glass for 27 years, a director of several banks, and a wealthy man.

But time had passed, and Mrs. Leonard's big house had fallen into different hands. What brought WHALE to the building was that its current owner, possibly not well, was systematically destroying the house from the inside out. He was burning ornate wooden parts of the building in the fireplaces for heat. We had to act fast, and we did. We acquired the house. The owner had been in the furniture business, and we removed dozens of stored mattresses and other junk. We held a Halloween party to raise some money but mainly to raise interest in the property. We were able to get the place developed as three condominiums that could financially support the restoration. As with other properties WHALE bought and sold, we attached conservation restrictions to the deeds so that future changes to the building exterior would have to be approved by WHALE.

The biggest neighborhood project that WHALE got involved in was the Hatch properties. Millie Hatch was a wonderful lady who lived in a beautiful Italianate building on the corner of Pleasant and Hillman Streets. Not only did she keep her own house up perfectly, but she was also the major supporter of the First Baptist Church next to City Hall, a significant landmark that, as a wooden church built in 1829, required constant care. Millie also owned and rented out six wood-frame houses just north of her on Pleasant Street. The buildings varied in age, one possibly dating back to the 18th century and others to the mid-19th

Hatch properties, looking north on Pleasant Street from Hillman Street, before restoration

century. The rental properties were in deplorable condition, and Millie wanted to tear them down and build a large commercial building like the one on the other side of Pleasant Street.

I had many conversations with Millie. She lived on the very edge of the Foster Hill neighborhood. This neighborhood was filled with historic houses, but the widening of Route 6 and the construction of the enormous intersection known as the "Octopus" had cut it off from the nearby downtown. High-rise housing developments and new commercial buildings faced it on the east, as did the headquarters of the New Bedford Fire Department.

WHALE felt that the Foster Hill neighborhood could not afford to lose another row of houses. The Hatch properties became a beachhead where we had to stand our ground for the neighborhood. Finally, we talked Millie into selling the properties to WHALE. Again, with help from the city, we fixed up the exteriors and sold each property to individuals who agreed to finish the restoration.

As we did so, more owners in the neighborhood started fixing up their homes. The New Bedford Preservation Society held several "holiday house tours" in the neighborhood. We successfully showcased the architectural wonders in what had been the city's northern edge during the whaling era and one of the first neighborhoods to house the people who powered the early and nearby mills. More importantly, these tours spotlighted the care that New Bedford's residents were putting into their homes and the pride they took in the results of research and hard work.

Restored Hatch house, Pleasant and Maxfield Streets   *Restored Hatch house, Pleasant and Hillman Streets*

Nowhere in All America: The Rotch-Jones-Duff House

In 1981, another threat loomed. A mansion house at 396 County Street, the grandest example of what the wealth of whaling produced, was under threat.

County Street follows the crest of a hill, and it was here that the whaling merchants eventually decided to build their homes. When Herman Melville came to the city in 1841 before shipping out on the *Acushnet*, he became familiar with the city and described the scene in *Moby-Dick*:

> *Nowhere in all America will you find more patrician-like houses, parks, and gardens more opulent, than in New Bedford. Whence came they? How planted upon this once scraggy scoria of a country? Go and gaze upon the iron emblematical harpoons round yonder lofty mansion, and your question will be answered. Yes, all these brave houses and flowery gardens came from the Atlantic, Pacific, and Indian oceans. One and all, they were harpooned and dragged up hither from the bottom of the sea.*

William Rotch Jr. built his house at 396 County Street after the death of his first wife, Elizabeth Rodman. His second wife, Lydia Scott, wanted to move up the hill. As we know, William's daughter, Sarah Arnold, gave his first house at William and Water Streets to the New Bedford Port Society, which moved it up to Johnny Cake Hill and used it as the Mariner's Home.

It is hard to overstate William Rotch Jr.'s impact on New Bedford. He ran the world's largest whaling business from the city, while his father and brother ran the French side of the business. Rotch's Wharf was where Piers 3 and 4 now extend, and their Counting House, destroyed when Route 18 was built, was next to it. Rotch was the first president of the New Bedford Abolition Society and a friend and business partner of Paul Cuffe. Rotch was the first president of the New Bedford Institution for Savings, and the largest funder for creating Friends Academy.

When he, at age 75, and Lydia moved up the hill and built their house, they had William's son-in-law, James Arnold, lay out the gardens. Gardening was serious business for the whaling merchants, who often brought exotic plants back from distant ports. James Arnold's will broke down into two parts. He left the first portion for "the poor and needy of New Bedford who may be deserving," which my brother, Peter, and I help administer through the Community Foundation. The remaining half went to Harvard University, which used it to create the Arnold Arboretum in Boston.

The property at 396 County Street was significant for several reasons besides being the home of New Bedford's leading whaling merchant. When William died at 91 in 1850, Edward Coffin Jones bought the house and lived there with his family until his death in 1880. Edward was involved in the whaling and ship chandlery businesses. After he died, his daughter, Amelia Hickling Jones, lived in the mansion until she died in 1935. Like the rest of her family, Amelia was a significant contributor to New Bedford.

When Amelia died, Mr. and Mrs. Mark Duff bought the house. Mark Duff had been involved in whaling but had diversified into petroleum and coal as whaling died out. When he died in 1967, his wife Beatrice took over. She maintained the house, the gardens with their large gazebo, the greenhouse, and the outbuilding in the back until they became too much for her. By this time, the property was the only estate left in New Bedford that still comprised its original landscape, occupying an entire city block with a formal boxwood and a rose parterre garden.

Richard Upjohn had designed this house for William Rotch Jr. It was the first commission for the architect, who would later gain fame as the designer of New York's Trinity Church and become the first president of the American Institute of Architects. The property, without question, has historical significance because of the three families who lived there and because it

William Rotch Jr., 1850 *Amelia Jones, circa 1900* *Beatrice and Mark Duff, circa 1950*

uniquely remained in context, complete with gardens and outbuildings. It also had architectural importance because of its designer and because it had not been significantly altered.

In 1982, Mrs. Duff could no longer afford to maintain the property. Her children had grown up and left home, and the mansion was simply more than she wanted to care for. She reached an agreement with a developer who would buy the entire property and put a restaurant in the home. He would need parking for the restaurant, but that could go where the gardens were. No doubt it would be a beautiful restaurant, but when WHALE and others found out about the plan, we were aghast.

The developer needed a zoning variance to go ahead with his plan. Attorneys for Mrs. Duff and the developer put forth their plan and made their case for hardship to Chairman Donald Gomes and the zoning board members. The room was packed with people opposing the variance and talking about the property's significance. There was much passion. Many people had opinions on how Mrs. Duff ought to proceed with her building.

Chairman Gomes let everyone talk, and then he concluded the meeting. I'm pretty sure he was looking straight at me as he spoke because I had been before him more than anyone else in the room when it came to historic buildings.

"Well, we listened to a lot of testimony about why this building is so important," the chairman said. "But that doesn't get away from the fact that Mrs. Duff has a right to sell it, and she has a reasonable buyer here. And her hardship is real. I don't want to say to Mrs. Duff that you can't sell your building. So, you have 90 days to come back here and tell us what you are going to do about that!"

The chairman had given us a reprieve to find an alternative to the restaurant. It wasn't much time, but it was some time. The developer was willing to pay Mrs. Duff somewhere between $135,000 and $150,000. A lot of money in those days and not a lot of time. But at least Donald Gomes had given us a chance.

The first question was who should act. The New Bedford Preservation Society had formed around the issue of widening County Street and the resulting loss of trees. This was their neighborhood. They had a regular series of County Street walking tours, and many of their leaders lived and worked nearby. But they were an educational organization, so if something was going to be done to avoid the restaurant fate, it would undoubtedly be up to WHALE.

The second question revolved around real estate development: What is the best use of a property? The knee-jerk answer for many threatened historic properties is to make them into museums. That is almost always a terrible idea. But as we considered different uses and the significance and attributes of this property, we kept circling back to the museum idea. There is no question in anyone's mind that the Old Dartmouth Historical Society is an excellent museum. It conveys much of the history of Old Dartmouth better than any place else could. Trying to duplicate their resources would be foolhardy. But what they don't do, and in fact cannot do, is educate people about domestic life in a domestic setting. They can set up a room and put out the tea plates, but they can't set up an entire home. They have individual pieces of furniture, but they can't place them in context. And they certainly can't tie indoor life to outdoor life as befits a city where horticulture was so important. We felt that a house and garden museum was the highest and best use in this particular case.

We began negotiations with Mrs. Duff. We appealed to her sense of history and legacy, saying we wanted to tell the story of the three families who lived there. We explained that we were a nonprofit and that gifts made to WHALE were tax-deductible. We talked about mutual friends. We tried everything we could. Mrs. Duff wasn't moved. She may have been angry at our interceding in her sale. She knew there was a three-month window. At any rate, she said her price was a firm $150,000. She wasn't going to budge.

Next came a WHALE board meeting. We usually met in the Sunroom of the Wamsutta Club, which is in the James Arnold mansion. WHALE met monthly on the third Tuesday at noon for lunch, and Sarah Delano chaired the meeting from the head of the table. I sat next to her. There were about 20 directors, including a clerk, who took the minutes, a treasurer, who kept the books, and a vice president. The directors got along well with each other. They didn't take themselves too seriously, but they took WHALE's work very seriously.

When we met, Sarah and I explained what had transpired at the zoning board and in the negotiations with Mrs. Duff. Some members grumbled about the high price, saying we should be able to buy the property for $135,000. Others worried about what it would look like if we overpaid.

At the time we were considering this project, we were also well into saving the Zeiterion Theatre, the biggest endeavor we had ever undertaken. The Rotch-Jones-Duff project would come at a time when we were already extremely stressed financially. Everyone understood this property was unique and believed a restaurant with a parking lot was unacceptable. Members

Rotch-Jones-Duff Garden

also realized that there really wasn't any other organization except WHALE to help save the mansion. The real question was, when is a project finally more than you can handle? When do you finally have to say, "Enough! This is beyond our resources."

I looked at Sarah. I looked around the table as the sun shone through the windows onto the white tablecloth, the plates of food, glasses of water, and people's faces. Everyone was looking at Sarah. What I saw was a transfusion, almost like a blood transfusion. Call it a courage transfusion. It emanated from Sarah and went down each side of the table to the end through each and every person. Their expressions changed. Sarah was calm. Her face had a firm look to it. She wasn't stern or animated, just clear and calm.

"No one is going to remember what we paid for the building. People will only remember whether we saved it."

After Sarah said that, there was no further debate. There was no need of a vote, though one was taken. Once again, ordinary people did the extraordinary and committed themselves to a task, not knowing exactly how we would succeed but knowing we would.

When the zoning board reconvened a few months later to conclude the drama of Mrs. Duff's decision, the room was again filled with people anxious to know the mansion's fate. Chairman Gomes wanted to know what solution we proposed.

"Well, WHALE, you have had your 90 days to decide what to do. Mrs. Duff has a hardship and deserves an answer. The zoning board is ready to make a decision."

Sarah Delano rose.

"WHALE has agreed to buy the building."

I would say her words brought the house down, except that isn't the right analogy when talking about saving buildings!

We bought the house and started work immediately on several fronts. Knowing how important the gardens were, we reached out to the Buzzards Bay Garden Club. Suzanne Underwood was on WHALE's board and was a landscape architect and member of the Garden Club. My mother was also a Garden Club member, so I talked with her. We toured the parterre garden, the wildflower walk, the greenhouse, the rest of the grounds, and the house.

We told the Garden Club we were planning a house and garden museum, and we thought that a partnership with them would be ideal. They could restore the gardens, use the greenhouse, and utilize the facility for educational programming. The club supported the idea and has been an active and beneficial partner from the beginning.

One of the club members, Betsy McBratney, brought an added dimension. Her husband, Dr. Greer McBratney, raised bees, and so we were able to bring back beekeeping to the gardens. Through the club, we also connected with Allen Haskell, whose landscape business up on Shawmut Avenue in the near North End was famous all over America. Allen served clients like Martha Stewart and won prestigious awards at the Boston Flower Show year after year. He joined the effort and helped decorate the house during the holidays every year until his death.

We realized we would have to set up a separate governance structure. We established the Rotch-Jones-Duff House and Garden Museum as a separate nonprofit organization with a separate mission and a separate board of directors. Unlike WHALE, this organization would need to be around forever and would have a very different kind of mission. Through the museum, we wanted to tell the story of New Bedford through the eyes of the three families who had occupied the house. To help us do that, we also set out to find members of the three families.

Sarah Delano and I were both Rotch descendants, and others still lived in the region, so we set out to inform them of the plans for the house and recruit them. One early recruit was my cousin, Francis "Frank" Gray, who became an early and longtime treasurer. We also knew members of the Duff family because we had bought the house from them, but there were far fewer of them, and their interest seemed weaker, at least at the outset. The Jones family had lived in the house the longest but was hardest to reach. I finally reached a wonderful woman named Marjorie Forbes Elias, who was related to the Jones family through the Forbes connection. She lived in Cambridge. When I told her about our efforts to save the house, she became very interested and was helpful in locating her relatives, many of whom still have connections to the nearby Elizabeth Islands. As a result, we have usually been able to have representatives of all three families on the board as we govern the house and gardens of their ancestors.

Sarah Delano and Anne Brengle

The next big step was hiring an executive director. We chose Anne Brengle, who had worked with me as membership director at WHALE. She had also worked at the Whaling Museum for several years, so she knew the museum world. She was the ideal person to get the Rotch-Jones-Duff House and Garden Museum off the ground and running. She was familiar with New Bedford and all the people who would need to be involved. Everyone knew and respected her. She was organized, calm under pressure, and optimistic. And she was engaging. People just jumped in to help her with projects that needed doing.

Anne started organizing the interior exhibits to tell the stories of the three families and working with the families to see what might be available from them to display. She also stayed in touch with the Garden Club as they researched what the gardens had looked like and figured out the best way to bring the grounds back to mid-19th-century times. She worked with the board on fundraising to restore the exterior and build restrooms and an office for museum use.

One challenge was how to get people to visit a house museum more than once. Because of my involvement in certifying museums for the Massachusetts Council on Arts and Humanities, I had to visit many museums. On one of my visits to a house museum on the Connecticut

Overview of entire property of Rotch-Jones-Duff House and Garden Museum

River, I saw how they solved this problem. They had concerts out on a field overlooking the river. No one had to enter the historic building, which meant no damage to wooden thresholds or floors. And people returned to the museum, again and again, to hear music in an idyllic setting. I suggested to Anne that if the R-J-D Museum had concerts in the garden, they could also attract repeat customers. Anne started summer concerts in the gardens, and the experiences have been breathtaking. Here we were in the middle of the city, sitting on a chair or on the lawn surrounded by tall trees, roses, and flowering bushes, serenely listening to great music that transported us away from the hustle and bustle of the day. The concerts were an immediate hit.

Interior of Rotch-Jones-Duff House

The Rotch-Jones-Duff House and Garden Museum is still going strong more than 40 years after WHALE took that fateful vote. Anne Brengle set the stage for Kate Corkum, who led the museum from 1994 until 2018. Dawn Salerno has now taken over the reins of an institution that continues to personalize New Bedford's history through the lives of the families who lived there.

Were William Rotch Jr. to return somehow to this city that lit the world and wander past this brave house and flowery garden, even after two centuries, he would encounter a view that would strike him as quite familiar. And as the first president of the New Bedford Abolition Society, I think he would look on with approval the R-J-D sponsorship of the annual Black in Business Outdoor Market that is put on each year by BuyBlackNB.

Rotch-Jones-Duff House, 2021

At Home in a Rotch House

In 1845, William Rotch Jr.'s grandson, William J. Rotch, and his wife, Emily, decided to build a house nearby. They knew New York architect Alexander Jackson Davis, either because Davis had assisted on the First Unitarian Church or because they had visited an area around the Hudson River on their honeymoon and seen some of his work, or both. At any rate, they contacted him in 1845 to design a home. The design was radical for New Bedford, which

William J. Rotch   Emily Morgan Rotch

William and Emily had to have known. Their home was an early example of Gothic Revival and would have caused quite a stir in a city that had known only Federal and Greek Revival.

One rendering by Davis shows the house to be constructed of cut granite. Another rendering housed at the Metropolitan Museum and dated 1838 shows it to be built of random stone. The earlier date suggests to me that Davis had conceived this design much earlier, and when Rotch wrote to him, he decided this was the client for this design. It later became Design No. XXIII in Andrew Jackson Downing's book *The Architecture of Country Houses*. Downing was an influential tastemaker of the time, similar to Martha Stewart today. He told you what colors were appropriate, what styles of architecture you should like, and what plantings went where. His stamp

William J. Rotch (in back with hat) watches a family croquet game at his Orchard Street home, circa 1880s.

of approval was highly sought after. Alexander Jackson Davis was one of his favorite architects. There is no question that William J. Rotch had selected the hottest architect on the planet.

Rotch was a leading businessman in New Bedford. He founded the New Bedford Cordage Company and was on the board of many businesses, among them the Howland Mills, Wamsutta Mills, Rotch Spinning Company, Pairpoint Glass, New Bedford Institution for Savings, and the Rotch Wharf. At 33, he was elected the city's second mayor.

In written correspondence with Davis, he wrestled with modifications to the house design. Rotch, a Quaker, wanted the house to look like stone, but he wanted it made of wood, so it is flush board painted an ochre color. He wanted interior shutters so you could open the windows and close the shutters. Later on, to admit more light into the upstairs bedrooms, additional windows with Gothic dormers were installed on each side of the main gable, facing the front. The couple chose to build their home in a country setting, west of County Street, on

Sarah Tappan Crapo   *William W. Crapo*

Drawing by Alex J. Davis, 1838

aptly named Orchard Street. It boasted a fruit orchard and a large front yard. When heat was added, the delicate, engaged chimneys needed more flues, so they became blockier. And an acorn replaced the fleur-de-lis at the top of the main gable. Because William and Emily had eight children, they built a house-sized addition on the back, designed by William Emerson.

The William J. Rotch House is among the finest examples of Gothic Revival architecture in America. It is featured in architectural history books everywhere, and bus tours of architecture buffs occasionally draw up outside, get out of the bus, and just applaud.

By accident of marriage, this house had always been in my family. As described in the formidable genealogy, *The Rotches*, which my grandfather wrote, William and Emily Rotch and their large family lived in the house beginning in 1845. Emily died after giving birth to her eighth child. Even with the addition, the house was crowded. In 1866, William married Emily's younger sister, Clara. William's uncle, James Arnold, died two years later, leaving his estate on County and Union Streets to William and Clara. They spent a few years enlarging that house with a mansard roof and moved to that mansion in 1871.

They then rented the Orchard Street property to William W. Crapo and his wife, Sarah Tappan Crapo, who loved the house and wanted to buy it. William was a prominent attorney and was elected to Congress in 1875, where he served three terms. Among other things, he was the founding president of the Old Dartmouth Historical Society and donated the Whaleman's Statue to the City of New Bedford. The Rotches would not sell to the Crapos, and when William J. Rotch's son, Morgan, married in 1879, he moved back to Orchard Street, evicting the Crapos, who moved a block away west onto Hawthorne Street. Sarah Tappan Crapo wrote a poignant poem about her nine years in the house, watching friends come and go from the Oriel window.

Irving Street hallway, 1960   *Irving Street library, 1960*

And every day in all these nine glad years
From the same window, I have seen the gate
Swung to and fro by loving hands, and friendly
Coming feet have changed to precious jewels
Every well worn stone along the pathway
And I fain would come even like the faithful bird
It may not be. The Oriel closes now;
And ne'er again shall I with eager hands
Turn back the diamond panes, view from this nook
The varied beauty of the seasons change, nor see
The dear familiar forms glide up the winding path,
Then blame me not—if for a while I grieve.

Morgan Rotch and his wife, Josephine Grinnell, moved into the house in 1879. They had just two children. Morgan was in the insurance business, but he also was elected mayor of New Bedford and served from 1885 to 1888. Perhaps because the family wealth had been divided among so many children, Morgan carved up the property. He moved the house back, extended Irving Court and Maple Street, subtracted the addition, and made it a separate house on Cottage Street. Now the house had an Irving Street address. Morgan died in 1910, and when Josephine decided to sell in 1928, Henry Crapo bought the house that he had lived in as a child.

In 1945, my grandparents bought the house. John Morgan Bullard was a Rotch descendant, the grandson of William J. Rotch, who had built the house. My grandmother, Catherine Crapo Bullard, was the granddaughter of William W. Crapo. So now, through their marriage, one could say that the house has always been in one family.

My grandparents lived at Irving Street in the colder months and, when the weather was warmer, in the summer colony of Nonquitt in Dartmouth. The Irving Street house was formal, with lots of antiques inside. Their Nonquitt house had extensive gardens, but the landscaping at Irving Street was not designed for outside living. Huge shrubs, bushes, and prickly barberry surrounded the front and sides, and the driveway to the garage took up the back.

When my grandfather died in 1965, my grandmother decided to move to a new house in Nonquitt. She lent the Irving Street house to the Swain School of Design, an excellent college of art located in several historic buildings nearby to the east, which used the house as the home for its president. My parents sold the farm I had grown up on in Dartmouth and moved to my grandparents' former summer house, which they modified into a year-round house. I had loved the farm with its herd of Crapo cattle brought back from Michigan and the hundreds of chickens and other odd animals that had been part of most of the first 18 years of my life. But I was going off to college, so it didn't matter all that much.

When I returned to the area with my young family after graduating from MIT, I knew I wanted to live in the family home on Irving Street as I worked to make New Bedford a better place.

My grandmother agreed to sell it to me for the appraised value. We got an appraisal and found that almost every house within a block that had been sold within the last five years had gone for under $30,000. Such was the state of New Bedford. Nobody wanted to live there. The appraiser valued our house at $35,000 because it was bigger and on a corner. The fact that it was an architectural masterpiece was seen neither as something of value nor as a negative. Just something to maintain!

Siblings Morgan Rotch and Emily Morgan Rotch

I called William J. Finn, the Swain School president, and explained the situation. Bill was very nice about it. He said that Swain appreciated the gift for as long as it had been made and understood completely. Then he resigned as president. That was very unfortunate, but Swain moved on and eventually merged with UMass Dartmouth.

Morgan Rotch at Orchard Street before the property was subdivided and the house moved

Judi, Matthew, and I tore out all the heavy bushes and modernized the kitchen. We repainted the inside, respecting the significant architectural elements but not trying to make the house into a museum. As Matthew grew older, he had a train set up on the third floor, which had no heat or plumbing. It had been used for bedrooms when the Rotches and their many children occupied the house.

Meanwhile, I was putting an enormous amount of energy and thought into my work saving buildings. It was consuming work. And one of the things it consumed was our marriage. After a few years, I was alone in the house, with visits from Matthew.

But perhaps, I wasn't completely alone.

Several people over many decades have described to me how they encountered a woman dressed in Victorian clothes in and around my house. Usually, they would see her in the bedroom by the Oriel window. Sometimes they would be outside the house looking in and see her. Other times they would be in the room and see her there with them. Sometimes this woman would speak to them, occasionally calling them by name. Everyone described her as friendly.

Of course, I'm quite sure this is the ghost of Sarah Tappan Crapo, returning to her favorite room. If one person tells you such a thing, you wonder about that person. But if 20 people independently describe the same phenomenon, then I say, "Why not?" Her presence certainly made itself known—to some. I only wish she would have sat down and talked with me, her great-something grandson. But she never did appear to me.

In August 1980, I visited my brother Peter and his wife Tia in Vermont, where Peter was in law school. At 3 a.m., August 12, the phone rang. My father was on the line. Never a good sign.

"Your house is on fire. I'll call you back."

I waited. I paced. I imagined. I waited some more. Finally, an hour or so later, he called back.

"How bad is it, Dad?"

"Just a small hole in the roof."

"Thank God. What does it look like inside?"

"You can't go inside. It's too bad."

"I'll get there as fast as I can."

I said goodbye to Peter and Tia and drove four hours south, trying to reconcile the conflicting images in my mind of my father's two messages. *Just a small hole in the roof. Too bad to go inside.* I tried to imagine the scene. I knew the roof shingles were the old asbestos type of shingle. They wouldn't have burned, but they would have contained the fire like a kiln. I wondered what had caused it; nobody was in the house.

When I finally got there at about eight in the morning, my house was quite a sight. I saw the small opening in the roof where the New Bedford firefighters from Station #3 had punched a hole to vent the fire.

My neighbor Nancy Crosby told me that there had been a ferocious thunderstorm the previous evening. "It felt like bombs were going off in the neighborhood. The flashes were so bright and so frequent. The noise was deafening. A lightning bolt must have hit your chimney and started a fire."

Nancy said the fire must have had quite a head start. The fire alarms had gone off inside the house, but they couldn't hear them because of all the thunder. It wasn't until they smelled smoke that they knew something was wrong and called the fire department.

My house sat on top of a hill. I knew that from the jogs I would take in the neighborhood. There was no downhill way home. And the two tall and massive chimneys provided an inviting target for lightning to reach the ground.

When I arrived, I saw almost everything I owned out on the front lawn. My neighbors, my parents, Laurie Miller, her parents, and others were all there helping. I had been seriously dating

Laurie Miller for a few years by this time. She and her two kids, Lexie and Toby, were living in Dartmouth, and we had been spending a lot of time together. It was a comfort to see Laurie and my friends and family, but I was shocked to see the house.

The crew had carefully removed as much as they could from the house. It seemed as if every towel within a mile of the house had been deployed to soak up all the water the firefighters had used to extinguish the blaze. Carol Nelson, an architect and friend, had procured a half-dozen industrial fans, and they were hard at work inside the house, blowing air out the open windows in an attempt to dry out the wet plaster.

The first floor was extremely wet, with the wallpaper in the front hall peeling off the walls and water stains already coming through the paint on the walls and ceilings. A six-foot length of plaster crown molding in the library had crashed to the floor.

As I walked up the central stairway, I looked to the Oriel window. The ceiling to the third floor had burned through to that second-floor bedroom. Water damage was everywhere. I proceeded up the narrow stairway to the third floor and attic. Everything was black char. Practically every roof rafter was burned through. I walked toward the front of the house, where Matthew had his train set. It was a melted mess. The smell, as anyone who has had the misfortune of losing a home to a fire knows, is unforgettable.

More bad news came when I called my insurance agent, Charlie Toomey, who sat on WHALE's board. I had insured the house for what it was worth. It took Charlie about two days to declare the house a total loss and get me a check for the full amount. But when I talked to a contractor about what it would take to fix the place up, the number was *three times* as much. That was an expensive lesson about the need to insure a property for what it will cost to replace, not what it is worth, especially in a city like New Bedford, where beautiful buildings were still undervalued.

I moved back to my parents' house, which I know is what every parent wants to see! I engaged my neighbor Max Ferro of Preservation Partnership to help with the design and specifications

With Matthew, Toby, Laurie, and Lexie on the back steps at Irving Street, 1989

as we repaired my house. Max was one of the most knowledgeable and well-known preservation experts in the country. He had relocated to New Bedford because of all the preservation activity in the city. He was a hugely entertaining speaker and much in demand. But he lived right next door, so perhaps I had an advantage!

This was an opportunity to design everything with Laurie. I didn't want this to be *my house*. I wanted it to be *our home*.

We got local contractor Edward Martins to do the work, signing a contract in December 1980. The most common phrase in Ed's vocabulary is "No problem." I love working with contractors like that. Over the course of the job, Ed and his wife Elaine became good friends. They were so positive. There wasn't an obstacle Ed couldn't overcome. That included on Sunday mornings when we both played basketball in the over-35 league at the Boys Club a few years later!

The biggest job was the roof. Not only did it have to be totally reconstructed, but we needed to decide the big question of what kind of material to use. We went with special fireproof wooden shingles because they were historically accurate and met the building code, which did not allow plain wooden shingles. They were quite a bit more expensive, and the cost of restoring the house was already emptying my bank account, so we secured a modest grant from the Massachusetts Historical Commission in exchange for giving them a five-year preservation restriction on the property. Before finishing with the roof, we made sure to attach lightning rods!

The lightning strike had also fried all the electrical wiring, so we replaced and upgraded it. Ed rebuilt the floor that had burned through between the second and third floors, but we did not rebuild the third-floor bedrooms, leaving painted outlines on a plywood floor for future reference.

19 Irving Street

The rest of the work was surface treatment. Master mason Carmino Arena repaired the cornice molding and other plaster that was too water-damaged to save. Varnished wood floors that had curled a bit because of the water were lightly sanded and re-varnished. The front entry floor, which had been covered with linoleum, was first painted with a historic stencil pattern and, when that gave way to the heavy traffic, we installed a Marmoleum covering. For the two front rooms, we obtained Wilton wall-to-wall carpeting of the type manufactured when the house was built. We painted all the rooms in a way that highlighted the Gothic trim moldings around the doors and windows. We also painted the outside, maintaining the distinctive ochre

The WHALE agent at work, 1985

color for the body of the house offset with warm off-white trim and black doors and sash. We did a scraping of the paint colors and thought these were the original colors, although it is hard to tell for sure about the trim. It might have been deep brown.

Finally, we got G. Bourne Knowles with my cousin Peter Bullard to redo the landscaping, building a large terrace off the southern sunroom and a pergola that wrapped around the giant ash tree and attached to the garage. As they were ripping up the asphalt driveway to lay two lanes of paving block, we discovered a 20-foot-deep cistern that had connected to the roof drains, so we installed a pump so we could use it for the garden.

But the best news was that I proposed marriage to Laurie Miller during this project, and she accepted! Then it became a race to get everything finished before the celebration. On June 27, 1981, we married and had our reception in the garden outside the restored house. The mortar and paint might have still been wet, but the day was spectacular.

As I reflect on the lightning bolt that targeted my house, I think about its impact. Before it hit, I'd felt like I was the latest in a line of Rotches and Crapos to live in this family house, doing what Rotches and Crapos do. After the lightning strike, I felt as if we were living our own lives and not somebody else's. Ed Martins and all the other skilled craftsmen made the house habitable. Laurie moved in with me, and with her came her daughter, Lexie, and son, Toby. They joined Matthew and me together with a wonderful German Shepherd, Kata, and a succession of cats, many of whom walked up to our front door demanding to join us. We became a family, and the house became our home.

It didn't take long for our new family to fit in. Mayor Markey, who lived a few blocks from us, saw me a few weeks after Laurie, Lexie, and Toby had moved in. His daughter, Jen, was a close friend of Lexie's.

"John, Jen came in to tell me the other day that she was going to visit her friend Lexie at the Miller house. I said, 'Jen, where's the Miller house?' She told me it was the fancy one on the corner of Irving and Maple. I busted a gut laughing. I said, 'Jen, that house has been in John Bullard's family for 150 years. The Millers moved in two weeks ago, and it's already the Miller House!'"

Lexie took over Sarah Tappan Crapo's room and made it hers. She would spend hours sitting in the Oriel window talking on the phone with her friends or watching for them to walk up the street and then up our walk, just as Sarah had done more than a century before. Now Lexie lives in Pittsfield and has Sarah's poem framed by her bed. One of her favorite memories is sitting in her favorite window with her daughter, Caroline, looking through the diamond windows to the garden below as the sun played on the leaves of the maple trees.

Ushering in the Zeiterion

Before the Great Depression, New Bedford boasted 23 theatres, 17 in the downtown alone. By 1980, we were down to three in the city. The Orpheum was vacant in the South End, the Strand languished in the North End, and the State Theatre was in trouble downtown.

The Penler brothers—John, Jim, and Bob—ran Paragon Travel, a very successful travel agency and bus tour company out of the State Theatre's front portion. Tom Shire operated a movie theater in the back. The last movie Tom had shown was *Caligula*. But the movie business had declined to a point that the Penlers

The State or Zeiterion Theatre, 1933

felt the space would be more valuable as parking. They came to me with their dilemma. They couldn't afford to save the theater, but they wanted to know if WHALE was interested.

We had never done a project this big or tackled a theater before. I thanked them for coming to us and said I would check with my boss, meaning Sarah Delano.

The Zeitz family had built the building in 1923. The front was three stories, with the lobby in the center on the first floor and Paragon Travel occupying the rest. The theater itself was in the back. It wasn't the best of the downtown theaters. The Empire and the Olympia, with their grand balconies, were more stunning architecturally. The State just happened to be the last. The Zeitz family had held a contest to name the theater, and the winner miraculously had come up with the name Zeiterion! It was named that for a short time before becoming State Theatre. As for us, we liked the sound of "The Zeiterion Theater" and thought it would be a great name.

Sarah and I met the Penlers in the lobby, and they let us into the darkened auditorium. We stood there by ourselves at the rail behind the seating that occupied the back two-thirds of the house. The original seating had been ripped out, and the front third of the house was bare concrete.

The damask panels on the walls were badly ripped and hanging in shreds. There was a chandelier above, but it was so grimy and full of cobwebs that it was hard to ascertain any beauty. Paint was peeling everywhere. Water stains dotted the walls and ceiling. The cove was painted flat black, hiding what we would later discover there.

The orchestra pit rail also was painted black, hiding gumwood underneath. The theater was cavernous and dark, and if you strained, you could hear the echoes of applause for the many shows, from vaudeville to the World Premiere of *Moby Dick*.

Sarah and I took in the sight. We were quiet for a while as we thought about the possibilities and risks. She turned to me.

"John, we are going to have such *fun* fixing up this theater."

I wasn't so sure. *Fun?*

That was my cousin Sarah Delano in a nutshell. She had vision. In the words of Robert Kennedy, "Some men see things as they are and say, why; I dream things that never were and say, why not." Sarah had more than vision; she had courage—and the optimism and confidence that are essential parts of courage. When confronted with a challenge, she didn't get flustered and never panicked.

But it was the word "fun" that revealed another essential ingredient in the unofficial master class on leadership that I was fortunate to be enrolled in with Sarah Delano. She taught me that solving problems is best approached with a sense of joy. Certainly, hard work will be involved. We will encounter setbacks, frustrations, and disappointments. But we are privileged to be engaged in this fight. It is a worthy mission, and the people with whom we join hands are the best of folk. In the end, we are going to be successful, so let us have fun along the way and see how it plays out. These qualities made Sarah an exceptional leader and me a tremendously lucky young man to learn from her so early in my career.

After our visit to the theater, we went back to WHALE's Board of Directors and presented the situation. On the plus side, we had successfully restored about two dozen buildings, and working in partnership with the city and the other groups in the district, had generated tremendous momentum in the waterfront historic district.

On the negative side, this was a huge building, and the costs would be much greater than anything we had done before. The more critical issue, as we all knew about saving old buildings, was the use. This building was clearly a theater, and we didn't know *anything* about running a theater.

Under Sarah's guidance, the board made an interim decision. They knew that the project would require a lot of financial support; how much, we didn't know. We set a somewhat arbitrary goal. We said if we could raise $200,000 in a month from four parties, we would know there was sufficient support to go forward with the project, and we would accept the challenge. If not, we would reconcile ourselves to the fact that some projects are beyond us, and the Penlers would have themselves a parking lot.

Sarah led here as well. She was the first person to pledge $50,000.

I visited my friend Charlie Dana at his farm in Dartmouth, which he had bought from my family. Charlie had grown up in New Jersey and had known Laurie since childhood. In fact, he and his wife, Posy, had introduced me to Laurie, so I was deep in his debt already! He was on WHALE's board and familiar with our work. Having spent a lot of time in New York City, he could understand the potential value of having a theater downtown. Charlie told us he would make a $50,000 gift if we got three others.

World premiere opening for Down to the Sea in Ships, *State Theatre, 1949*

I've spent a lot of time raising money, and I think there are two essential ingredients to fundraising. You need a purpose that resonates with the person or people you are approaching. And you need the right person doing the asking, someone the potential donor likes and respects.

With Sarah's gift, we were halfway there. Sarah and I next met with Karen Lloyd. Karen had given her house and property in Dartmouth to start an environmental organization called the Lloyd Center for the Environment.

Robert Foreman conducts community feedback session for proposed theater restoration.

She had moved into downtown New Bedford, a few blocks away from me. Her husband had died, and she had a daughter who was an artist in another part of the country. The Lloyd family was well known in the region. The family owned large amounts of land around Buzzards Bay and the Slocum River and had done much to preserve the coastal and estuarine environment of the area. This included, most notably, donating the Demarest Lloyd State Park along the Slocum's River.

Sarah and I explained the situation to Karen, who also served on WHALE's board. We said if we didn't meet our goal, we would have to pass on the project, and the theater would become a parking lot. Sarah said she was making one of the gifts, and we had one other pledged, but we needed two more. Karen quickly agreed to be the third.

I then went out to see Karen's sister, Angelica Lloyd Claggett, at her home in the Barneys Joy section of Dartmouth. As quiet as Karen was, Angelica was vivacious. She had two sons, Peter and Lloyd, and three daughters, Kissy, Dedee, and Vicky. I was closest in age to Kissy, but I knew them all. We had all attended Friends Academy in Dartmouth, and I had spent many hours at their beautiful Barneys Joy farm. A wonderful couple named Manny and Mary Sylvia worked for them, and Manny had taken me goose hunting when I was a boy. I had a deep personal connection with Angelica. I explained the situation. Angelica and her relatively new husband, Tom Claggett, agreed to split the commitment for $50,000.

We had met our internal challenge and went back to the board with the news. We were buying a theater. It should be known that without these people stepping forward when the risk was highest and the unknowns were greatest, we would not have the Zeiterion Performing Arts Center today. We owe them our deep thanks every time we see a show at "The Z," as it has come to be familiarly known. Without them, it would be just another parking lot.

Given that we were doing both the theater and the Rotch-Jones-Duff House at the same time, we were going to need much more than $200,000. So, WHALE also set out on a $1.2 million capital campaign led by our treasurer, John G. Hodgson, a prominent city accountant.

The next step was to learn how to operate a theater. We did two things quickly. First, we hired a theater expert to do a feasibility study. As luck would have it, Ted Stevens, considered a leading expert in bringing historic theaters back to life, was working nearby. He had led the rebirth of the historic Fox Theatre in Atlanta and had come to the region to work his magic at the Ocean State Performing Arts Center, now the Providence Performing Arts Center. We paid him a relatively small amount to look at the Zeiterion, tell us what we were getting into, and advise us how to proceed.

The second thing I did was join the League of Historic American Theatres. I attended a conference that took the attendees to several historic theatres in Ohio, Kentucky, and Indiana over a week's time. I listened to experts, saw amazing theatres, and met people doing what I was going to attempt to do.

Refinishing the stage

City leaders inspect restoration

I remember sitting in an atmospheric theatre where you sat down inside the make-believe walls of a castle, looking up to a ceiling of stars sparkling through the deep blue sky with a few wispy clouds. The effect transported you back through time to the Middle Ages and a faraway land. And this was before anything appeared on the stage. These types of theaters were palaces for the people. The trip made a deep impression on me. I learned that a good theater in a city like New Bedford performs a function like a great public park. It provides a space and an experience where, no matter how little money you have, no matter how many troubles you have at home, while you are in this space, you have everything that the richest person in the world can have. You are in a palace listening to Yo-Yo Ma or watching the Washington Ballet or whatever it is that you came to see. You leave your troubles at the door. It is a profoundly egalitarian experience that would be so important in the city of New Bedford.

Ted Stevens delivered his report to WHALE's board. He was enthusiastic about the prospects for the Zeiterion. He studied our market area and told us the nearest competition was Providence and Boston, so we had all of Southeastern Massachusetts and the Cape to ourselves. Based on his considerable experience, he said that we would have to subsidize the theater for three years while we developed an audience. After that, the theater would support itself through ticket sales and program ads.

This gave the WHALE board further encouragement, and we proceeded with fundraising and initial work on the building. We knew we could talk to people about the benefits of having a theater downtown, but if we could put on a performance and get people into the theater, that would be the best argument possible.

Ted Stevens knew two wonderful young men who masterminded the restoration of the Ocean State, and we brought them to the Zeiterion. Rob Foreman was working at the Brooklyn Academy of Music but joined us as our technical director while Ted stayed on as our first executive consulting director. Rob brought his assistant, Mike Guy. They immediately started work on the stage house, which hadn't been used for anything other than movies in more than 50 years.

And we started fundraising. I remember four conversations with business leaders that revealed the situation at the time.

I met with Cliff Tuttle, the CEO of Aerovox, a large company in the North End that manufactured electric capacitors. Cliff was a big man and a leader in the business community. I sat down with him in his office and explained how downtown was in danger of losing its last remaining theater and how WHALE had plans for rescuing it and returning it to a performing arts center. I said we could do so only if we got significant support from the business community, and that would include a substantial gift from Aerovox.

Staging the house

Cleaning every piece of crystal

"John, I understand what you're saying. I understand how important a performing arts center would be to downtown New Bedford. Right now, I just don't see how it can work. I don't think there is a market to support it."

He paused.

"But John. I've watched what you and WHALE have done. I didn't think a lot of those things would work either. And you've been right every time. So, I'm going to bet on you."

We got a significant donation from Aerovox.

I also met with Jack Wilkens, who ran the Polaroid plant in the Industrial Park. Polaroid was very highly regarded in New Bedford, and, like Cliff, Jack was a community leader, though he had not been in the city for very long. I made my pitch.

"John, we are going to support the Zeiterion, and I'm going to tell you why. Before coming to run the plant in New Bedford, my wife and I were living in New York. When I got the offer, I brought her up here to see the city. She cried. We need the Zeiterion to succeed in New Bedford. It is very important, and we will do everything we can to help."

Jack Wilkens and Polaroid became great supporters of the Zeiterion.

In my fundraising efforts, I also took Jack Ludes to lunch at the Rodman Candleworks. Jack was the CEO of Titleist. If there is an iconic company in New Bedford, it is Titleist, the makers of the number one ball in golf. It had plants in Acushnet, New Bedford, and Dartmouth at the time and is known worldwide for setting the standard of continued excellence. Jack was also a progressive community leader. I once attended a Chamber of Commerce breakfast where he stood up and said that everyone should find it unacceptable that people were going hungry in our city. Out of that meeting came the Greater New Bedford Food Bank.

I laid out the situation and our plans to Jack and asked for a gift from Titleist and his parent company, the Acushnet Company. Like Cliff, he had his doubts.

"I'm not sure whether the performing arts center idea is feasible, John, but I think it will say more about us if we don't try than if we do."

Acushnet and Titleist were on board.

Matthew, 8, helps his dad with restoration

I had also heard that there was a new stockbroker in town. New Bedford was a very sleepy town with a reputation as being very poor. There was only one brokerage house, Tucker Anthony. In the banking world, nobody rocked the boat until a hairdresser named Gus LaStaiti started a new bank called Southeastern Bank and Trust and shook up the old, established order of things.

When Merrill Lynch opened an office on Union Street, I went up to see the guy in charge, Joe Barry. He said he had worked in the Providence office, and the head guy asked for a volunteer to go to New Bedford. Everyone laughed, saying there was no money here. He volunteered. When we met, I gave him $2,000, said it was time for me to start saving for retirement, and asked if he would start an IRA for me. He did.

Then I asked him if Merrill Lynch would donate $10,000 for marketing the Zeiterion. He laughed and called me crazy but investigated and found that Merrill Lynch did have such a community support program. He pushed hard for it, and before long, Merrill Lynch became our first presenting sponsor.

I also told Joe that we would need to set up a separate board of directors to manage the Zeiterion. The project was big enough and different enough to warrant its own board. I told him that the nature of WHALE was to go from project to project, assuming significant initial risks, and get projects to a point where they could be passed on to others. The nature of the Zeiterion was to grow into something that would be a mainstay of the community for as long as we could imagine. The board would need an entirely different mission and culture.

I knew that because Joe was new to the community, he had not committed to other organizations. That was a reason I wanted to get to him early before others had a chance. I don't know why Joe said yes. The sensible thing would be to put me off and tell me he needed time to get his feet on the ground. But Joe is a remarkable person. With a smile, he agreed to take the risk of chairing the board into the unknown.

Restoring and painting bas reliefs and plaster ceiling

With Joe as chair, we recruited Joseph Tomlinson, a retired businessman from Marion, to be our treasurer. He soon earned the nickname "velvet hammer" for the soft and diplomatic way he controlled costs. During the first few years, it seemed as if Joe Tomlinson would tell me every few weeks, "I think this is the week we go out of business." Somehow, it never happened—the two Joes, the staff, and the directors kept the lights on.

Before setting up the new board, we had to get a show on. With Ted Stevens' guidance, we hired a great young executive director from Wisconsin named Dan Kirsch. Dan was young and had theater experience. He could work for us at an affordable price and grow with us. He was a real find. He booked Shirley Jones to take the stage for our first show on September 25, 1982.

We got to work on the priorities to put on a stage performance. We focused on the lobby, the proscenium, the stage, the dressing room, and the auditorium floor. There was an awful lot that we would have to leave for Phase II, but we needed to get people into the house to see and hear a live performance.

The work was feverish. I remember one Saturday, I was in the lobby with our son, Matthew. We were removing the ugly paneling from the walls. As we pry-barred the paneling off the north wall near the doors to the auditorium, we gasped at what was underneath. There were two ornately carved marble ticket windows hidden from view for decades. What a wonderful surprise!

Speaking of surprises, the cove where the walls curved up to the ceiling had been painted a flat black. There was a molding just below it that held lights. As Rob oversaw the restoration of the proscenium, we realized that the curved cove contained life-sized muses in bas relief in the plaster in about a half-dozen different poses.

We didn't have time to do the whole auditorium before the first show, but we did the front of the house so that the audience would see what we had and know that these Greek artistic spirits were looking down on us and helping us along. Jimmy Leal, a master mason, did an amazing job restoring these lovely "ladies of the Zeiterion."

Rob and Mike also alerted us to an old theater in Providence that had been converted into a travel agency, where the balcony seating had been hidden away above the dropped ceiling. They were willing to give us the seats if we came and took them. We rented a convoy of trucks. My friend Carl Cruz, Rob, Mike, some volunteers, and I unbolted several hundred theater seats from the balcony above the dropped ceiling, loaded them into trucks, brought them to the Zeiterion, bolted them into the concrete floor in front of the modern rocker seats, and painted them red to match the upholstered seats. We figured they would last about five years until we reseated the entire theatre. They are still in use 40 years later! They almost doubled the seating capacity, which was very important not only from an economic standpoint but also because it created a better feeling of energy, as only a full house can.

We started scraping the thick black paint on the rail that surrounded the orchestra pit and found a rich brown gumwood underneath that was brought to a beautiful luster with lots of elbow grease and wood oil. We lowered the Czechoslovakian chandelier, cleaned off the cobwebs, and polished the hundreds of pieces of cut glass. We replaced the light bulbs so that people could see the beauty of what had cost the Zeitz family $7,000 in 1923.

A member of SENETOS, the Southern New England Theater Organ Society, learned about our efforts and called.

"I have your original Wurlitzer organ in pieces all over my basement floor in Newport," the member said.

Not long after that phone call, they reassembled it near the proscenium arch, where it had provided the sound for silent movies many years before. It remains a thing of beauty!

Class Acts: Performing at "The Z"

Finally, we were ready for our reopening gala on September 25, 1982. Shirley Jones came to Laurie's and my house for a reception before the show. People, many in black tie, lined up around the block to get into the Zeiterion for the show. Restaurants were packed beforehand. Downtown was alive.

Shirley Jones did not disappoint. And from then on, we did not have to explain why we needed to save the Zeiterion. Anyone who was there that night or on subsequent nights knew. We ran a short season and then closed for Phase II to complete the renovations.

Sarah Delano with Director Dan Kirsch

During this time, Governor Ed King was worried about his re-election and sought support around the state. There was a fund set up to help the Hynes Auditorium in Boston with state money, but for it to get passed legally, it had to make other places in Massachusetts technically eligible. If other cities had civic centers or exhibition halls, they also were eligible. I went to Mayor Markey with an idea. I suggested we make the building two condominiums and turn the theatre into an "exhibition hall" so it would be eligible for state funding. The Penlers would keep the front, except for the lobby, for their travel agency. WHALE would transfer the second one to the city, which would accept it and then create an "exhibit hall commission" to oversee it. The commission would turn around and contract with WHALE to run the theater. Nothing would really change except that we would be eligible for the state money, which I thought might amount to $1.1 million for Phase II. Even though I am sure Mayor Markey had doubts about owning a historic theater, he agreed.

Tom Bucar, our vice chairman and a good lawyer, created the first condominium in New Bedford. Mayor Markey set up the commission. We received $1.1 million from the state, which funded the restoration of the auditorium, the roof, bathrooms, utilities, and more, all designed by the architectural firm of Dyer Brown of Boston. Dyer Brown was getting so much preservation

Cutting the ribbon, officially marking the theater's opening, 1982

Governor Michael Dukakis visits the Zeiterion   *Big band and folk music come to the "Z"*

work in New Bedford that they opened an office on William Street and Acushnet Avenue. In his spare time, architect Joe Booth built a bar off the lobby, which became known as the Booth Booth.

A few vignettes stand out that illustrate the theater's meaning and power to me.

In the first program book, Mayor Markey had a letter to the audience. In it, he wrote, "It is not possible to define exactly where the line is that separates the efforts of WHALE from the efforts of government. It is the opinion of this administration that this melding of private effort and public efforts is the lesson to be learned here. Without one, the other would not operate well. This partnership, which is working, stands as testament to the ideal in government."

The second is when Yo-Yo Ma came to perform. The afternoon before his performance, he was on stage, and a group of kids had gathered around him. I was off to the side, watching him interact with our students. Now, you might think that Yo-Yo Ma is a cellist, and, of course, you would be right. But he is also Santa Claus and the Ice Cream Man rolled into one. These kids were all over him. He had laid a few of his cellos on the stage, and he was just letting the kids play with them. I was aghast! These instruments are really *valuable*.

We didn't need lights on in the auditorium. Yo-Yo Ma's smile and those of the kids were 1,000-watt smiles. The laughter and joy were transcendent. How do you get a young person to *love* music? What a gift he gave. It wasn't part of his contract. It wasn't part of his act. There was no press there. It was just joy and love of music.

The third happened later in my last month as mayor in December 1991. I was in St. Petersburg, Russia, at the American Consulate, as a reception was held for Isaac Stern, the great American violinist born in Poland. Soviet President Mikhail Gorbachev had invited several elected officials from all levels of government to Moscow to talk to them about federalism. We got there the day the Soviet Union dissolved, so it was an exciting time.

I went up to Stern and introduced myself as the mayor of New Bedford.

"New Bedford! I just played the Zeiterion Theatre. It's a great theater. Wonderful acoustics. And a very appreciative audience." Stern couldn't have been more animated or sincere.

"I know you played the Zeiterion, Mr. Stern. I was there. What you might not have realized is that about a third of the people in the audience were young people. It is why we saved the Zeiterion. Because once our young people hear you play the violin, Mr. Stern, they will know what excellence is. And having experienced it, they will look for it always. They will look for it in their leaders. In their teachers. In their parents. And they will look for it in themselves. That is the gift you gave to New Bedford, Mr. Stern."

Scott Lang's Suggestion

As we were putting together the board for the Zeiterion in 1982, I knew we needed a lawyer. I had heard that a young man named Scott Lang had experience in entertainment and sports, so I paid him a visit at his office at 401 County Street. He practiced with John Xifaras, and they both also specialized in labor law.

Scott was a fascinating guy with a breadth of talent and experience that was hard to believe, considering how young he was. He lived in the West End with his wife, Gig, and their three kids, Nate, Andy, and Sarah. He had gone to Marquette College in Wisconsin, earned his law degree at Georgetown University, worked on Jimmy Carter's Presidential campaign, and served in his administration for a few days before deciding it wasn't for him.

He had represented several NBA basketball players and served on the Rules Committee of the Democratic National Committee. Close to the Kennedys, he had worked with Senator Ted Kennedy in his unsuccessful presidential bid in 1980.

Scott has a droll sense of humor. You can see his jokes coming like a big slow curveball. But like curveballs that can't be hit, they are effective just the same and right on target.

When we met at his office, we started talking about the Zeiterion, the board, and needing someone with his skills to serve on it. He listened for a while.

"John, have you ever thought about running for mayor?"

"What!"

"Mayor Jack Markey is going to be made a judge, and there will be a special election. Have you ever thought about running?"

"Scott, we're here to talk about you joining the board of the Zeiterion. Don't go turning this around."

But turn it around, he did. Scott wasn't interested in joining the board.

I had never run for anything since elementary school. I grew up in Dartmouth, not New Bedford. I was an old-time Yankee who had gone to prep school, not the local high school, and then Harvard. I had more strikes against me than I could count.

Scott pointed out that I had a record that no one else in the city had, except the man retiring to become a judge. He pointed out that I had led the revitalization of the very visible waterfront historic district in partnership with the mayor. He said that such work had created a spirit in New Bedford that touched people all over the city. He suspected many of the people who supported Mayor Markey, valuing that partnership, might support my candidacy.

He then made another argument. He said I had done a lot for New Bedford, working with WHALE and other groups in the historic district. He said I could do a lot more for New Bedford if I were the mayor, and there was a lot that needed to be done. I couldn't argue with that. We talked for a while longer in the bay window overlooking County Street. I told him I would need to think about it and talk with Laurie.

"One more thing, Scott," I said when I got up to leave. "I'm not running for mayor unless you are my campaign chairman."

Attorney Scott W. Lang, 1982

111

II. Dropping Anchor

Danger zone

CHAPTER 4

Mayor of New Bedford

First Run

I discussed the decision with Laurie, Lexie, Toby, and Matt. Running for mayor would change our lives completely. It would be a very public process that would intrude into our lives, all of our lives. We talked about how it would require a total commitment from me, including nights and weekends. That would mean less family time. We discussed how politics could be nasty. Opponents can say mean things that aren't true. They would certainly criticize me, but they might criticize my family too. People in politics don't necessarily fight fairly.

I don't know how much of this sank in as a warning, but my family was clearly supportive of the campaign because they knew I wanted to do it. We were in, all in. We weren't sure how this adventure would unfold, but we expected it would test us and hoped it would teach us.

With my family behind me, I now had to put a campaign team together. With Scott Lang as my campaign chair, I had someone with tremendous experience to guide a novice like myself. True, I had worked on Gerry Studds's first unsuccessful campaign for Congress in 1971, and I had supported Mayor Markey's campaigns by doing odd jobs, selling tickets to fundraisers, and working on "visibility" to get the candidate's name out there.

But I had never been in the inner circle, and now I was as far inside as anyone could get.

When Markey agreed to become a judge, he had to step aside as mayor. That triggered a special election in the midst of his term. Following Mayor Markey would not be easy, but there was a pent-up demand for someone new after a decade of one administration. Nineteen people stepped forward to run in the non-partisan preliminary special election, which was held in February 1983. The preliminary would narrow the race to two candidates for the final election in March 1983. This meant the campaign would begin around Thanksgiving of 1982 and run through the winter, an unusual season for politicking. This special election would decide who would be mayor for the six months remaining of Markey's term, which ended with the regular election in November 1983.

Tryne Costa, Peter Bullard, and Walter Ramos join the candidate on a walk the length of New Bedford—13 miles.

The general gist of a campaign is that you put together an organization made up mainly of volunteers who accomplish a series of tasks that reach a crescendo on Election Day. If you win, a very small percentage of those volunteers might transition into your administration, but most go back to their normal routine until the next campaign. People's motivations vary, but the great majority give their time, money, and good ideas for the same reason you do—they want to make their community a better place for themselves, their children, and their grandchildren. It sounds corny, but you realize how many people are idealistic when you work on campaigns.

Campaign work gets divided into various areas. One of the most critical is raising money. For a mayor's race in New Bedford in 1983, we figured we needed about $100,000. I started making personal phone calls to neighbors, close friends, and relatives, and of course, I donated myself. With this initial funding, we were in business.

I called my brother, Peter, who was out of law school and looking for a job in Boston, to ask him if he would take several months off from his job search and join the campaign. Not knowing if it was true or not, I argued that no one in the Boston law community would be making hiring decisions between Thanksgiving and the election anyway. I don't know whether Peter bought that argument, but being the great brother he is, he and his wife, Tia, relocated to New Bedford to help out.

Growing up, I had watched Peter be scrupulously thrifty with a dollar. While I was and am a liberal Democrat, he is a fiscally conservative Republican. He is also my brother and has my absolute trust. With those two qualities in mind, I asked him to be my campaign treasurer. Politics can get very sticky around money. Sometimes people give you money expecting something other than good government in return. Laws have been enacted to discourage this, requiring disclosure of names and occupations and limiting donations, but I think someone can give you $1,000 for the right reason and $25 for the wrong reason. You need to know the intent. I wanted my brother in charge to ensure we weren't accepting any donations unless we were 100 percent certain they were being made for the right reasons.

Another important part of the campaign is issue development. Everyone says they want to run on the issues. We were determined that I be known as the candidate most knowledgeable on issues. We also knew that the media tends to write about issues in politics. We figured if we put out two meaty issue position papers a week, the media would be forced to write a substantial story on each one, guaranteeing us two free stories a week. In a race with 19 candidates, that would set us apart. To get newspaper coverage every Wednesday and Sunday, we set a goal of releasing substantial position papers every Tuesday and Saturday.

To help hone our positions, we set up a policy group that included Ben Baker, Tony Souza, Steve Roberts, and Peter Rioux, another key member of Markey's administration. Several others also weighed in. The group assigned people to write drafts about crime, education, environment, housing, historic preservation, drug abuse, economic development, government, and other issues. We would then come together to debate the issues to ensure we thoroughly vetted and properly articulated sensitive issues such as community policing. Then we started rolling the papers out. This operation was good preparation for the candidate debates that would follow, and it helped us boil down the main message.

We fine-tuned our message with polling and public relations. We retained the services of New Bedford-based marketing and public relations firm Moore & Isherwood Communications. John Moore and Liz Isherwood were local. They knew New Bedford like the backs of their hands, had worked many successful political campaigns, including Jack Markey's, and had many clients in the business community. They also had an advanced sense of marketing. As an added benefit for us, one of our oldest and dearest friends, Clara Stites, worked there as a writer.

We also needed good polling, so we hired Irwin "Tubby" Harrison from Cambridge, who was nationally known for his expertise. Polling would help us understand where we were in the horse race and what would resonate with the electorate. Tubby told me at one meeting in Liz and John's office that consistency in a campaign was paramount.

"John, when we boil down all this data into a single message, you will *never* depart from it. Understand? Never! The speeches you give and the coffee hours you attend are not for your entertainment. I don't care how bored you get. I will consider it a victory when Laurie throws you out of the house because she is so damned sick of you saying the same thing over and over again."

And that is what is so hard and smart about political communication—boiling down so much information to the essential message that will put more people on your side than your opponent's. Henry David Thoreau once wrote, "Not that the story need be long, but it will take a long while to make it short." The challenge is distilling a massive amount of material to its absolute essence. Getting that part right is beautiful and sublime in a political campaign. If you get that part right, you run downhill. If you get it wrong, you run uphill. You can still win, but it is harder.

We also needed a field operation that would focus on identifying our voters and how best to get them to the polls on Election Day. These Voter ID and GOTV (Get Out the Vote) efforts would require hundreds of volunteers to make phone calls, do mailings, hold signs on street corners, go door-to-door, hand out leaflets, register voters, collect signatures, pass out bumper stickers, host coffee hours, plan and hold $5 ham-and-bean fundraisers, staff the polls on Election Day, staff the office 16 hours a day, and much more.

We had tremendous expertise in how to organize this from both Scott Lang and Mardee Xifaras. I met Mardee in 1971 when she was running Gerry Studds's campaign field office in New Bedford. She had organized field operations for local, state, and federal campaigns for many years. I couldn't get better advice.

Scott also advised me that we would have to hire staff, something my frugal treasurer brother did *not* want to hear. But Scott prevailed and recommended Walter Ramos, a young Cape Verdean man who had done some work for Ted Kennedy.

I'll never forget our first meeting, held in somebody's office in the old First National Bank Building. When Walter came in and saw Scott, Peter, and me, the look on his face was priceless. Looking at Peter and me, he was confronted with these two tall, dorky-looking Yankee types. I'm sure the first thing he wanted to do was an about-face and walk right out the door. The difference in height, skin color, background, and at that moment, attitude was a chasm. We shook hands and somehow managed to bridge that gap. Walter agreed to come aboard. As head of operations, he brought experience, professionalism, and the organizational skills we desperately needed. And as an unforeseen benefit, Walter became such a close friend he is like a member of the family.

The Bullard campaign set up an office downtown on Union Street. The rent was low because the one-story office building didn't have heat. We bought several space heaters powered by some kind of fuel that smelled but didn't fill the place with carbon monoxide.

We assigned ward captains to organize efforts throughout the city's six wards and corresponding 57 precincts. With that, we had unmatched experience and local knowledge on our team. Add to that our volunteer corps, powered by the idealistic energy of friends and family who had supported me through my work at WHALE and new supporters, many of whom were new to politics but not hard work and tough tasks. They pitched in wherever and whenever we needed.

One morning, I remember coming into the headquarters and seeing my mother sitting next to Mary Maciel, a fiery Australian lady from Fair Street. Mary shares my same birthday but had a couple of decades on me. She and my mother were sitting with several others at a long table doing mailings. They had the radio set to "Open Line," and the moderator was stoking anti-Bullard commentary as he did most mornings. Mary and my mother were fuming. They were yelling at the radio and getting worked up at the unfairness of it.

"Mom, you know you don't have to listen to the radio."

My mother didn't miss a beat.

"What fun would that be?"

Campaigning: A Sewer System Runs Through It

Now that we had a mission, a team, and money to start, we ramped up the campaign to full speed. While there were 19 candidates, there were only two heavyweights. Brian Lawler was a city councilor from Ward 1 in the North End. He was popular, and his father, Francis J. Lawler, had been mayor in the 1950s. Brian had almost beaten Markey in 1979, so there was no question he would be tough. David Nelson was a state representative and had also been a popular city councilor. He seemed to have the endorsement of Governor Michael Dukakis, and as a result, it seemed to me that he carried himself with an arrogant sense of entitlement, almost as if the election was just a formality.

There were also a few characters in the bunch. Michael Zarritt, for one, was a very intelligent man who marched to the beat of a different drummer. He once mentioned to me that he was having problems getting his mother's vote because she wanted to vote for me. He told me that if I got elected, he wanted to be the "night mayor."

One of our first outreach events was during a New Bedford High School football game at Walsh Field. Scott and I arrived and spotted David Nelson at the entrance with a half dozen henchmen, all in suits. Besides his own suit, David wore a smirk of over-confidence as he greeted people. Scott and I bought tickets and went inside dressed in our regular football-watching clothes. We worked the crowd while enjoying the game. As we walked out after the game, Scott and I said to each other, "Boy, it is going to be great to beat that guy."

We also arranged coffee hours in people's homes. A supporter would invite 10 to 20 friends for refreshments, and I would come by to meet them. I would give a 15- to 20-minute talk and answer questions. Because of the relaxed setting and the small groups, coffee hours offered a very personal way to meet people and enlist their support. We tried to do five or six a week, sometimes two in an evening. My talk emphasized how my love of New Bedford inspired the work I had done already and the work I hoped to do in the future. On many occasions, I heard back that my love of New Bedford was the reason people supported me.

Each weekday morning, we started by swinging by manufacturing plants for about 30 minutes before the opening shift. Peter picked me up in his green Volkswagen bug, which for some reason, didn't have a passenger seat. I had to climb over campaign signs, bumper stickers, and stacks of leaflets and squeeze myself onto the bench seat in the back. There was a "Bullard for Mayor" roof rack on top of the car and bumper stickers on the front and the back. Whether Peter was picking me up at 4:30 a.m. or 5 a.m., the conversation usually went something like this at the beginning of the campaign:

"Hi, Pete. Where are we headed?"

"Goodyear, then Chamberlain, and then Aerovox."

"Great. How do we get there?"

Michael Zarritt	Brian Lawler	David Nelson

"I haven't the faintest idea!"

At first, we were the blind leading the blind, but we soon became familiar with every neighborhood in the city.

Every morning as I dressed, the thought of getting up so early and sticking my hand in strangers' faces to ask for a vote just turned me cold. And as fall turned to winter, it did get cold. People were bundled up and in a rush to get inside. It seemed like even more of an imposition to go up to someone, shake their hand, and ask them to support me.

Meeting workers at plant gate before dawn

But when Pete and I got to each plant gate, something unexpected happened. Everyone coming to work would smile and say, "Hello." There would be easy banter. We could feel the energy from all the people headed to work.

Like much of campaigning, the abstract idea of working plant gates in the early morning conjured up negative feelings. Once I got there, though, it was fun and exciting because the people we encountered were so upbeat. That didn't mean they were all going to vote for me. It just meant that the New Bedford people who had good jobs at these plants were positive people.

I spent many afternoons going door to door in different neighborhoods. I carried a printed list of registered voters. If someone was home, I introduced myself and tried to engage them in conversation by asking them to tell me about the top issues in their neighborhood. Eventually, I asked if they might support me. After we met, I would rate them from "1," for strongly pro-Bullard, to "5," for strongly pro-opponent, and keep track of these ratings on paper. Others were also acquiring similar information by phone calling and knocking on doors so we could identify our voters. Come Election Day, this knowledge would be important in our efforts to get our voters out to the polls.

I always found going door to door to be very enjoyable. I would head back to campaign headquarters with my rating sheets filled out, saying, "We should get about 90 percent of the vote in that neighborhood!" Most people are by and large very nice and polite. They never want to tell you to your face that they aren't going to vote for you. I always had a great time chatting with people, but I would come back with a totally unrealistic view of the world!

As a campaign tactic, David Nelson tried to paint me as aloof and removed from the people. His campaign was circulating the message that "They don't know Bullard on Bullard Street." To counter this, we figured I would knock on every single door on Bullard Street, which was in a North End neighborhood of mostly three- and four-deckers constructed at the turn of the century when the mills attracted thousands of new residents to the city. While the neighborhood today has many absentee landlords and more than its fair share of drug-related crime, in the mid-1980s, it was a healthy center of the Portuguese community. As I walked up the backstairs of the tenements each afternoon, the aromas coming down the stairways would welcome me. The backyards usually had grape arbors and gardens, and if the weather was good, laundry drying in the sun.

During these days, I climbed a lot of stairs and heard a lot of Portuguese, and it was a great way to learn about our city, where more than 50 percent of the people had Portuguese ancestry. We had one English newspaper, two Portuguese newspapers, and one Cape Verdean newspaper. There were two AM radio stations and two Portuguese-language radio stations. As I met the residents on Bullard Street, I learned more about this city of immigrants. Three or four generations often lived under one roof, perhaps in the same apartment. Family support from across the generations often helped with the problems of daycare, elder care, and a myriad of other challenges, such as trying to make ends meet.

This was one of the major benefits of running for mayor—getting a deeper understanding of the people. I met and listened to residents at factory gates, on the docks, in coffee shops and diners, at their back doors or kitchen tables in many different neighborhoods, and at coffee hours in people's homes. As I was introducing myself to them, they and the city were introducing themselves to me.

The great Speaker of the House of Representatives Thomas P. "Tip" O'Neill, famously said, "All politics is local." I believe that. Even more, I believe all politics is personal. Politics is about the personal information people entrust to you because they believe you will do something with their story.

The second major benefit of running for mayor was meeting an amazing group of people through the campaign who cared deeply about the city. As our campaign built momentum, our organization grew. We attracted people to the cause of improving our city—the city we loved. Every day we looked around, there were more of us, from every part of New Bedford, people Laurie and I would never have met had we not decided that I should run for mayor. And these people gave of themselves, not for political favors or to get a job, but because they wanted a better city. Each was a distinct personality who added something to the campaign.

We needed hundreds of visibility signs so volunteers could stand on street corners and wave at people driving by. These had to be assembled with wood furring strips, thin plywood, and Bullard signs front and back. Nothing fancy, just quick. Nate Bekemeier, who had worked with me at WHALE, and some other folks set up a shop to manufacture signs. One day, Nate came into headquarters to give me my own special sign, a two-foot by three-foot campaign sign in a chamfered frame that was bejeweled with fancy upholstery tacks. It still hangs in my office.

I wanted to go door to door in the old New Bedford Hotel, which had been converted to housing apartments for the elderly, but I needed a resident to take me around. Bill Peters volunteered. He knocked on every door with me, delivering a similar through-the-door opener at every apartment.

"Hello, Mabel. It's me, Bill. Bill, the blind man. I'm here with John Bullard. John is running for mayor. If he's elected, he's going to make me his driver."

With that, the door would usually open, and we would have a good conversation. Bill was one of a kind, another terrific person I would never have met if I hadn't run for mayor.

With Brian Lawler at a community function

One day, we decided to walk from one end of the city to the other. Now, New Bedford is 13 miles long, running south to north, and about two miles wide, east to west, so the easy thing to do would be to walk the width of the city. We didn't do easy. We started early in the morning at the South End as the sun came up and finished with a coffee hour in the Far North End that night long after sunset. My brother Peter, Walter Ramos, Tryne Costa, who was a friend from the Unitarian Church, and I walked from Fort Rodman and then north along East Rodney French Boulevard.

We timed our march to pass Rodney Metals to greet the workers on the first shift. We then headed for breakfast at Hazelwood Diner on Brock Avenue to chat with people at this South End landmark. Behind the counter, Mary Souza had a gruff personality that made her a city legend. I would stop at her place as often as I could for the food and the banter. We continued our march up County Street toward downtown, where we visited some stores to hear what merchants and customers had to say. Then, we walked down to the waterfront historic district and the waterfront itself, where we talked with fishermen and others working on the boats that maintained New Bedford's relationship to the sea.

We reached Acushnet Avenue in the Near-North End by lunchtime, stopping for food and conversation, then made our way past the bustling shops in the "International Marketplace." We, of course, had to stop at Ma's Donuts near Brooklawn Park for coffee and donuts in the afternoon. Then we did some door-to-door work as the commercial neighborhood gave way to residential homes.

We had dinner at Pa Raffa's, again introducing ourselves to guests. We ended the day at a coffee hour near the Acushnet line, where we talked with voters for several hours about issues that concerned them. I shared with them what I hoped to achieve as mayor. It was a long day, but we met many people and generated favorable publicity. We wanted to let people see that our campaign was full of ideas and energy.

We also did a lot of debating. We had one very large debate, with all 19 candidates or close to it, which doesn't leave much airtime for each candidate. The hall was packed with each candidate's supporters, who weren't likely to be swayed by any amount of rational "debate" in the room. I treated debates as a chance to reward our volunteers by firing up the crowd with passion and going for the

The candidates interview with host Ray Delgado.

jugular whenever there was an opportunity. The more raucous the debate, the more entertaining the evening would be for everybody putting in long hours for the candidates they supported. What was the point of having a dull evening?

Reporter Jim Phillips gets a quote while City Councilor Tom Kennedy looks on.

Primary election night finally came around. We surprised everyone with a pretty comfortable victory, beating Brian Lawler by a few thousand votes. David Nelson, who had assumed he would win, came in third and was out of the running. The final election would be in a month, and now it was Lawler versus Bullard, which many saw as a Markey/Lawler rematch. Lawler's camp accused us of being part of the Markey machine. We printed buttons that said, "I'm part of the Bullard machine."

For the first week, we focused on the everyday issues of jobs, crime, and housing. Then during a press conference, a reporter asked a question way, way out of left field on a subject that had never been part of the campaign or the civic discussion up to that point.

"Mr. Bullard, should New Bedford have a sewer-use fee?"

The world, or at least the campaign, seemed to shift.

Several of my campaign aides were in the room. I could tell from the panicked looks on their faces that they wanted me to steer clear. I'm not sure if they put their heads between their knees, but looking back, it felt that way to me and that's what their body language screamed: "DO NOT TOUCH THAT QUESTION WITH A TEN-FOOT POLE! DECLARE AN EMERGENCY. LEAVE THE BUILDING BUT UNDER NO CIRCUMSTANCES ANSWER THAT QUESTION!"

It must be very trying to work for me as a candidate or in any other capacity because faced with that sage counsel, I responded exactly in a way they would have not recommended.

"Federal law requires that we have a sewer fee in New Bedford. We are a part of the United States, so, yes, we should have a sewer fee in New Bedford."

During the last three weeks of the campaign, nobody talked about crime or the ravages of the drug problems in New Bedford. Nobody talked about creating jobs or affordable housing. For the run-up to the election in 1983, all anyone talked about was whether there should be a sewer-use fee in New Bedford.

Brian Lawler was no dummy. He saw my answer as a gift that he gladly accepted. He said with conviction that under no circumstances would there be a sewer-use fee if the voters elected him mayor. Experts came down from Boston and up from Washington to testify on both sides of the issue, leaving the voters no clear answer. The Lawler campaign grabbed on to ill-advised interpretations of the law that said New Bedford might be able to get out of the sewer fee, but we knew it was clear that the City would eventually have to address the sewer issues whether it wanted to or not.

Voters went to the polls, scratching their heads. After months of campaigning, all they were left with was, "If I vote for Bullard, I'm getting a sewer fee. If I vote for Lawler, I'm not."

The election wasn't close. Lawler beat me by a greater margin than I had beaten him in the primary, all on a single issue, one on which I thought he had basically lied to and misled the people.

We gathered on election night at the Madeira Club in the North End. Madeira is a beautiful Portuguese island located 600 miles southwest of Lisbon in the Atlantic Ocean, off the northwest coast of Africa. I had sailed there after graduating college. I remember approaching the lush green volcanic coast of the main island and the capital of Funchal and seeing four or five waterspouts lurking just outside the entrance to the harbor. As in Greek mythology, one could not enter a place this beautiful without going through a test. We navigated through these water tornadoes and found a land known for wine, lace, and industrious people, many of whom made their way to New Bedford to find a new home over the years.

Anibal Moniz was president of the Madeira Club. He and his wife, Gabriela, were good friends of Laurie's and mine, and they made the Madeira Club available for what we all had hoped would be a celebration.

Instead, when I walked in with my family, there were a lot of tears. Laurie's mom was crying. Our kids were crying. Many of our supporters were crying. As good as Madeira wine is, it could not salve these wounds. We had poured our hearts into the campaign, and they seemed broken.

I got up to speak. I may have had some notes, but I didn't look at them. I focused on those gathered before me. I had to congratulate Brian Lawler and concede the election. I tried to be gracious, and I think I succeeded. But all the while, what was running through my head were lyrics from a song by the Police that was popular then:

> *Every move you make*
> *Every bond you break*
> *Every step you take*
> *I'll be watching you*

I pushed the song out of my head and directed myself to the people in the room. I don't remember exactly what I said. I just remember I said it with abandon and emotion. I gave myself to them the way they had given themselves to me. I didn't hold back on what we had done together, on what it had meant for New Bedford, or on the friendships we had formed. I told them we ran a campaign with honor, and we could be proud of the way we ran, despite the outcome.

We might not have won this time, I told them, but we had shown everyone we were a formidable force. This wasn't over. We would be back.

And next time, we would win.

A defeated candidate addresses supporters at the Madeira Club.

A Second Run and Victory: Exhilarating and Humbling

After cleaning up from the campaign and saying a lot of thank yous, I went back to work for WHALE and the other groups in the historic district, spending time on the Zeiterion Theatre and the Rotch-Jones-Duff House and Garden Museum.

Brian Lawler served the half-year of the special term and then ran for re-election. We felt that was not enough time for him to demonstrate whether he could be a good mayor, so we did not challenge him in the race in the fall of 1983.

But by spring of 1985, we felt the city needed a change, and we gathered our team together for a run. It was most important to define our central issue. While we benefited from Tubby Harrison's polling for this, I also relied on about a dozen people whose advice was based on a thorough knowledge of the people of New Bedford, political experience born of many campaigns, integrity, street smarts, and an idealistic vision for our city. Their ideas were sometimes different from poll results, and we argued that knowledge on the ground was the team's strength. We trusted each other, so the arguments produced better decisions that everybody got behind. We were loyal to each other and the cause.

Scott Lang led this group, which included my brother, Peter, who, in one of the happy accidents of the first campaign, decided not to become a Boston lawyer but rather to join Scott and Mardee in starting a law firm in New Bedford. Ben Baker, Pete Rioux, Steve Roberts, and Dick Walega were key players. Elsie Souza, a New Bedford teacher, and her husband Tony contributed significantly, as did Ed Girard, a retired teacher. Maria Tomasia, who was working for Congressman Gerry Studds, and her husband, John, introduced me to many influential people in the Portuguese community. Jeannie Duval, who headed the teachers' union, was a vital volunteer. Liz Isherwood and her husband, John Moore, again provided invaluable advice and services, from buying ad space to creating leaflets. Walter Ramos again added wisdom and professionalism. Robert Alves, head of the Longshoremen's Association—the only union to support me in 1983—was a key labor advisor. This time around, he was joined by Umberto "Battle" Cruz, who headed the Teamsters.

Announcing a second run, Spring 1985

Laurie was the sounding board for all of this and allowed me to process things at the end of the day. She is an excellent judge of people and can spot BS a mile away. Having a perceptive judge of people on your side is incredibly valuable when so many folks come at you each day with their many agendas.

As we sifted through the many possible issues that might define the upcoming race, we looked at the usual major issues such as the economy, crime, housing, and the like. But another even more significant issue seemed to stand out, bigger than all those others—trust. Many things were going on that called into question whether the citizens of New Bedford should trust Brian Lawler. He had, after all, beaten me in 1983 by promising that he would not impose a sewer fee, while I had said it was federal law and we needed to have one. He eventually had to admit it was the law. Subsequently, he stalled as much as possible, costing the City $390,000 in court settlements and pumping equipment. He was finally forced to impose the fee. I had told the truth. He hadn't.

Then there was the issue of Foster Herman, who owned a lot of real estate in New Bedford and was delinquent in his property taxes by about $300,000. Despite being the biggest tax delinquent in the city, Herman received preferential treatment from Mayor Lawler, who gave him assistance in renting his properties. We also discovered a school milk contract that the City awarded to a Lawler campaign contributor who was not the low bidder. Once that company won the contract, it promptly subcontracted to the low bidder. Finally, there was the case of police officer Stanley Webb, who was brought before a rare joint meeting of the New Bedford City Council and Mayor Lawler on charges that he was associated with gambling machines in bars. He was eventually fired, but Lawler switched his vote and kept him on the force after being reminded that Webb had contributed $500 to his campaign.

Police raid removes gambling machines from a neighborhood bar.

These shady acts formed the basis of our campaign's tagline, "A Man You Can Trust." With that, we set up the organization the same way we had in our first campaign, with ward captains organizing activities in their neighborhoods. We did plant gates in the mornings, door-to-door visits in the neighborhoods in the afternoons, and coffee hours at night. Volunteers made phone calls to identify our voters. And we had visibility days to register voters and ask people if we could put bumper stickers on their cars. We stood waving signs at busy intersections. The campaign was

Campaigning in the North End

additive. Every event brought in more volunteers. We ended up with about 1,000 volunteers working on Election Day. We held a few fundraisers where the ticket price was $100, so we could pay for the advertising and brochures and everything else. We also had ham-and-bean dinners with $5 tickets to maximize the number of people invested in the campaign.

At one fundraiser at Thad's Restaurant in the North End, Scott got young Patrick Kennedy to come. Before I had even had a chance to meet Patrick, he gave a rousing speech on my behalf that would have convinced anyone in the room that we had known each other for years! I have known a number of the Kennedy family members, Patrick's dad best of all, and their commitment to public service and their unwavering adherence to core democratic values is something that has always inspired me. Patrick's visit is one example of how Kennedy family members go out of their way to help other like-minded people standing for election.

There were not 19 people in this race, only 4, I think. But that meant there would be a preliminary election in October, which we thought was good for us. Every election ends up being essentially about the incumbent. People either vote for the incumbent or against them. Only the challenger's family and close friends are voting *for* the challenger. The incumbent has many advantages. Name recognition is one. But power is the biggest. All cautious people—and that includes business CEOs, most labor unions, and anybody at risk of losing something—will stick with the incumbent, figuring they can easily make friends with the challenger if the challenger wins by making a campaign donation right after the election.

Our goal for the preliminary was to be close enough to Lawler to show everyone that he could be beaten. We figured that would open the door and let people know they could vote for us without throwing their vote away. The other two candidates were marginal competitors, so this election was basically a rematch of 1983: Bullard versus Lawler.

When I went door to door in the neighborhoods, people remembered the '83 campaign. It was not uncommon for people to say to me, "Oh, you were the guy who told us the truth. I'll give you a vote this time."

We ran an aggressive campaign. We went after Lawler and didn't pull punches. The debates were the best. One debate was at St. Martin's Church on Rivet Street, and the tiny hall was filled to overflowing with partisans of both sides. The room was hot and noisy, with campaign signs everywhere. The atmosphere was raucous, with not an undecided voter in sight. Brian and I went back and forth, hammering away at each other as we answered questions from the news media and rebutted each other's answers. As the end approached, I stood up at the table on stage with one of Brian's full-page newspaper attacks and rebutted each of its charges. Then I ripped it into shreds and threw it into the crowd, which went wild. It was great entertainment, which all the volunteers on both sides enjoyed.

We hired Peter Fenn from Washington, DC, to do our radio ads on Scott's advice. Scott had known Peter from his work with the Democratic National Committee and the Kennedy Presidential Campaign in 1980. Peter had actually grown up in nearby Westport, and his mom still lived there. He usually worked on national and statewide races, but he was willing to work on ours as a favor to Scott and because he could visit his mom. Peter has become a very close friend. He produced an unforgettable radio ad that listed Lawler's false or questionable claims followed by the comical sound of a slide whistle. The sound was the perfect reaction to falsehood, and it really hit the bull's eye.

Lawler won the preliminary election but only by 68 votes. We had shown the electorate that he could be beaten. If you factored in votes for the other two candidates, more people had voted against him than had voted for him.

There was no sewer fee surprise in the four-week sprint to the finish. We just poured it on, energized by the preliminary result. We had identified our voters. We had two volunteers at every one of the 57 precincts for the entire time the polls were open. Their job was to listen to people give their names as they voted so we would know when our voters had checked in. We had volunteers driving our voters to the polls. We had people at headquarters and other phone banks after 5 p.m. calling our voters who had not already voted, reminding them to vote, offering them rides, and telling them where their polling place was. We had volunteers delivering snacks to our volunteers during the day.

All in all, we had assembled a trained volunteer corps of almost 1,000 dedicated people for this single day, people motivated only by the chance to improve their city. It was both humbling and awe-inspiring. Even though it rained on Election Day, 72 percent of the registered voters voted! If you got half of registered voters to come to the polls, you were doing well. To get nearly 75 percent—that was amazing.

Celebrating victory at the Fishermen's Club

On election night, I was home with Laurie and the kids while our team gathered at the United Fishermen's Club for what would prove to be a long night. Paper ballots were counted in blocks of 50, and Pete Rioux and Steve Roberts had calculated what we needed to win based on the first three blocks from each precinct. By 10 p.m., they had projected we would win by between 900 and 1,000 votes. But at the time, the radio was reporting that Lawler was ahead, and that's what we were listening to at home. You would think maybe Pete and Steve might clue the candidate in. But, no! Best to keep him in the dark!

Finally, a little after midnight, the last precinct came in—the large precinct in the western part of Ward 3, Precinct 3J. The predictions had proved right. We won by 960 votes. Brian won the two wards north of Route 195 by just shy of 1,000 votes—he lived in the Far North End, so this was his home territory. But then we won the four wards south of Route 195 by 2,000 votes, and that carried the day.

My feelings were all over the place. I was physically exhausted from six months of 19-hour days and seven-day weeks. I had lost weight and needed to recharge. I knew the campaign had taken it out of my family too and that I owed them some time. I was thrilled that we had won and earned the trust of the people of New Bedford. Winning was especially meaningful to me because, in so many ways, I was different from many of the voters, yet they were willing to take a chance on me. I was a Yankee from a relatively wealthy family and had been educated outside the public school system. My opponents had tried very hard to paint me as an outsider despite the seven generations that my family had been here. But by winning, the voters said I belonged. To earn the trust of people in every nook and cranny of New Bedford was both exhilarating and humbling. I realized I would have to work very hard to measure up and keep that trust.

People say many things after elections that seem trite. They seem trite because they are true, and unless you have put your name out there before the people and been in the arena where people can put their thumbs up or down for you, you won't know that experience. But I had lost an election, and now I had won one. I learned some things in the process. One is that winning is definitely much better than losing! Another is that winning is a humbling experience. You put your fate before the people and give them the right to reject you publicly. There is nothing quite like losing on the paper's front page to give you a sense of humility. Even when you win, you realize that the people have the power, and they have only allowed you to use it. If you are smart, you keep close to mind that they can take the power away. You are there to serve the public's interest, so to say it is humbling may be trite, but it is also profound.

The difference between winning and losing may be only a few hundred votes, but when you walk down the aisle at the supermarket, it is the difference between the victor and the vanquished. And that is a chasm.

With the win, we were euphoric and exhausted, and it hit us that we had only two months before we needed to have an administration in place to govern the commonwealth's fourth-largest city. There was no time to waste. Scott arranged for a quick trip to Washington to introduce myself to our delegation and another to Boston to meet with the governor and our state delegation. Meanwhile, we had an administration to assemble.

The Making of an Administration: Reflecting the City

The two months before the inauguration were busy. I had to put together a team. I had to educate myself. I had to introduce myself. And over the holidays with my family, I had to rest and recharge. And reflect.

White men had dominated the senior management at City Hall forever. This was true of practically every institution in New Bedford and elsewhere in 1985. Still, I felt that if we were

Walter Ramos   *Carol Pimentel*   *Robert Alves*

going to successfully govern a city as diverse as New Bedford, we would need our administration to reflect the people we served.

I asked Walter Ramos to come on board as head of Community Development. While sitting in the next pew at the First Unitarian Church, I asked Carol Pimentel, an active member in the Cape Verdean community, to leave her job at Peabody Construction to manage our budget office. I persuaded Robert Alves to leave his long-time job running the largely Cape Verdean Longshoreman's Association to work in our human relations area. Later, we got Jackie Custodio Whyte, the daughter of one of New Bedford's most famous and outspoken minority critics, Jack Custodio, to lead our IT department. Jackie's father had never been afraid of telling me when he thought I was headed in the wrong direction, and Jackie turned out to be a loyal and perceptive member of our team.

We had six positions to fill in the mayor's office. I knew I needed experience and trust. I was very aware that I was moving from WHALE, an organization with three employees and a $100,000 budget, to an organization of 3,000 employees and a $100 million budget. While I felt I was as capable as previous mayors, I had a more than healthy respect for the demands of a job I had not done before.

I decided that the three top positions under me in the office would be focused in this way: inside, outside, and on constituents. We would then have two administrative positions to manage what would be an enormous amount of paper and telephone work. This was before the days of email. Even a fax machine was a new-fangled gadget.

I turned to Ben Baker to be Mr. Inside. Every decision and piece of paper would go through Ben. He would be the chief of staff. I said to him, somewhat tongue in cheek, "Ben, if the answer is 'No,' you give it. If the answer is 'Yes,' I give it."

Ben got an ample supply of green pens. He never signed his name to anything, but everything I saw was marked up with green ink, so I always knew what Ben thought. Ben had a tiny office right next to mine, made tinier because Ben collected mountains of paper. However big his office was, it would have filled up with paper, so we minimized the fire hazard by keeping the office small. Despite the towering piles, Ben could find any document in an instant. He had a magical power.

Ben had the perfect old-school cranky attitude that you needed in that job, and it didn't take long before everyone in the building lovingly called him "Dr. No." He was invaluable to me because he knew everything about city government—the budgets, the laws, the people, and the history. He could smell bullshit approaching a mile down the road before it presented itself in our office. Another quality that made Ben perfect for the job and someone who will always rank high in my hall of fame is that he never talked to the press. They couldn't get a quote out of him on the record or off the record, even with the Jaws of Life.

For Mr. Outside, I turned to one of my campaign co-chairs, Ed Girard, a retired New Bedford teacher. Ed was gregarious, organized, unflappable, optimistic, and very approachable. His job would be to connect the administration to the outside world. That certainly meant telling our story through the press, but it meant much more than that. New Bedford is a diverse city made up of many social organizations. If we wanted to stay connected to the city we would lead, we needed to reach people wherever they were. That could be at a Little League field, at the Feast of the Blessed Sacrament, at the Cape Verdean Band Club, at the swearing-in of officers of an Elks Lodge, or visiting with people at Ma's Donuts in the North End. Another

Edward R. Girard

way to think of it is that many people have normal working hours during the day, but they gather together during the evenings and weekends. Those gatherings are opportunities for connecting. While Ben made sure my days were efficiently organized with the business of running the City as its CEO, Ed made sure my evenings and weekends were scheduled to attend the many events and functions where New Bedford's "Head of State" was expected to show up. This would keep me in touch with people.

The third element, constituency, I learned from observing Congressman Gerry Studds. He was known not just for being smart on policy but also for being excellent at constituent services. When citizens called his office needing help, they got it. They weren't ignored or given the run-around. Whatever the problem, if it could be solved, it was solved, and someone from the congressman's staff made sure to respond promptly and respectfully. I knew we needed that kind of operation.

I went to the person who ran that operation for Gerry, Maria Tomasia. She was immensely respected in the Portuguese community. I knew if we had Maria in the office handling constituent services, this critical element that can make or break an administration would be in the very best of hands. I didn't really think she would want to leave a congressman to work for a mayor, but I had to try. Maria said, "Yes!" and made my day.

City Hall can be an intimidating place. The slogan, "You can't fight City Hall," exists for a reason. The monumental architecture is designed to intimidate. If you want a pothole fixed on your street, answers about your tax bill, or relief from your neighbor's barking dog keeping you up at night, you come to City Hall for help. Those might seem like minor problems to the outside world, but they are big issues to you. You want them taken care of. If you are nervous about government or perhaps not comfortable with English or unfamiliar with which part of city government you should deal with, your problem can seem overwhelming. Our office was on the first floor, right near the front door, and Maria Tomasia was one of the first people you would see when you came in. And Maria could put anyone at ease. And she could get problems solved.

I asked Rosalind Poll Brooker to serve as city solicitor. Roz was a Republican and the first woman elected to be a city councilor, and then, the first woman elected as council chair. When she agreed to the city solicitor post, she became the first woman to hold that job. She was sharp, enormously respected, and known for overcoming obstacles, whether physical or gender-based, to make her community better. A lawyer like Roz could make substantially more money in the

Rosalind Poll Brooker at City Hall

private sector. By saying yes to the City of New Bedford and to me, she was making a significant financial sacrifice.

I wasn't the only one who loved New Bedford. Roz and the others did, too. And because municipal law is fascinating in the types of issues you deal with, there can be professional rewards. In any case, it was good to have Roz on board and to see the glass ceiling crack a little more.

Another appointment was Tony Souza. I had worked closely with Tony to fix up the waterfront historic district, and now I asked him to head a newly created Office of Neighborhoods and Historic Preservation. I thought Tony was probably among the top ten people in the country in historic preservation, and his knowledge of New Bedford's neighborhoods was unmatched. He had a wonderful way of working with people to teach them about their property's potential, listen to their hopes, and help them realize their dreams. I was elected in part because people yearned to see the excitement and change in the waterfront historic district spread throughout the city. Tony would be a big part of that effort.

As hiring continued, I did some more serious damage to the glass ceiling. I promoted Kathy Burns to head the Department of Public Works, the first woman to do so. Having a female department head in a field in the building trades made a statement: City Hall would be an inclusive environment. Kathy had spent her career in the department and had worked her way up through the engineering division. She had the full support of George Brightman, who had retired. And she had earned the support of all the people in the department through her knowledge, work ethic, and the way she managed people and projects.

Because of a retirement, we also needed a treasurer for our $100 million operation. Ben came to me and said we would have a problem recruiting because the job paid only $20,000 a year, so we requested the New Bedford City Council to double the salary. My own ward councilor, Nelson Macedo, came up to me to complain.

"Why do you need $40,000? There are plenty of people in the unemployment line that would take that job for $20,000."

"Nelson, is that where you think we should get a treasurer for a $100 million public institution? Is that where you go for medical or legal advice?"

We got the raise. It didn't make us competitive, but it gave us a chance. We hired a whip-smart young lawyer named Irene Schall, who came in and did a bang-up job.

Another difficult task was human relations. The City has about 3,000 employees, most of them in the school department. Most come in at a young age, learn their jobs by doing them, belong to one of nine unions, advance through seniority or promotion, and retire decades later. An enormous percentage of the budget is devoted to the workforce, either as pay, benefits, or retirement. The financial investment in our people is very significant. Yet the human resources department had only three people who stayed busy handling civil service complaints. They didn't have much time for proactive measures like training, which meant we weren't investing in our most critical resource. People were our most important asset, but we were doing nothing to build their capacity or help them be better at their jobs.

For many years, Angela Natho had labored in this department under the watchful eye of labor negotiator Arthur Caron. Arthur came to me and told me that he saw something in Angela that set her apart. We promoted Angela to the top position. She worked miracles with a very limited budget and turned a personnel office into the "Human Relations Department." Like many people we hired, Angela was so good that future mayors saw the wisdom of keeping her at City Hall for many years to come.

While I was putting together the team that would form the Bullard administration, I also had to educate myself further about the city, its issues, and how to govern. This happened on many fronts, all in the space of the two months between the election and inauguration.

Peter Rioux had worked in City Hall under Mayor Markey. He contacted all the department heads and asked them to prepare briefing books on their departments. I had cleared this with Mayor Lawler, and he had graciously promised a smooth transition, on which he delivered. The briefing books contained material about budget, personnel, work items, pertinent legislation, short- and long-term issues, and other items we would need to know about if we were to hit the ground running. Department heads had a few weeks to prepare these books so we could analyze them well before the inauguration.

I also set up a 66-member advisory panel of community leaders that met twice before the inauguration. As a message that I intended to be mayor of the whole city, I included two leaders from the Lawler team, Phil Paleologos and Beverly Souza. Advisory panel meetings were designed to collect ideas and priorities and to show people that I wanted their input then and, in the future, and that we could be successful if we worked together. We rented a big room and had lots of paper taped to the walls to get people's ideas down and get a discussion flowing. The meetings were animated with a sense of empowerment and hope in the room.

I also had an off-the-record meeting with the New Bedford City Council. There has been a long history of the mayor and the council not getting along, and I wanted to see if we could get off on the right foot. I called it a social meeting and closed it to the press to minimize the grandstanding. That earned me several negative stories and editorials from the *Standard-Times*, a strong defender of the Open Meeting Law. Bristol County District Attorney Ron Pina ruled that the meeting was legal but cautioned the council that such gatherings were temptations to break the law.

At any rate, we had an opportunity to get to know each other and for me to get across the message that if I knew each of their priorities, I could try to make them successful as we advanced an agenda for the city. I also told them that I needed frequent communication with them; if any of them had an issue, I hoped they would pick up the phone or walk into my office.

Advice for Newly Elected Mayors

I took time to attend a three-day session at the Kennedy School of Government for newly elected mayors from around the country, organized in partnership with the US Conference of Mayors. There were lectures on everything from labor negotiations to the newest theories in policing. I met several mayors who became longtime friends. Jerry Abramson was the mayor of Louisville, Kentucky, and later, when it merged with Jefferson County, he became the mayor of the consolidated jurisdictions. Jim Moran was the mayor of Alexandria, Virginia, and later represented that city in Congress. Dirk Kempthorne came from Boise, Idaho, and after serving there as mayor, went on to serve as governor, senator, and secretary of the Interior under President George W. Bush.

The speakers included Governor Michael Dukakis, who kept everyone alert as he peppered us with questions and took us through a case study of Boston's Park Plaza. That Saturday morning, after many of the mayors had spent a late night playing poker, he proved to me he was as good a teacher as he was a governor, which is to say, he was excellent. Nobody nodded off. We also heard from retired New York City Police Chief Pat Murphy and several Kennedy School faculty.

Henry Cisneros, the very popular mayor of San Antonio, Texas, talked to us about the job's demands. He advised us not to think in terms of work time and family time. He said that separation would not exist. We would be going all the time. There would be no time off. But he also communicated that the mayor's job is great because you are working on the problems that people care about the most—safe neighborhoods, good schools, and clean water. He said, "In Washington, these may be considered 'local problems,' but life is lived at the local level." He warned us to accept that this would be a very demanding job: "If you want to be the mayor, be the mayor."

This advice from Mayor Cisneros was reinforced by one of the many messages waiting for me when I got home. People often called and wrote letters and sent articles for me to read. (Laurie and I briefly considered getting an unlisted phone number, but we never found the number of phone calls we received to be burdensome or trivial.) One note that I received at this time described an opera singer's exchange with a friend, telling her that after performances, she would spend a half-hour signing autographs for fans.

"My God, you *have* to do that?"

"No, I *get* to do that."

That attitude between "have to" and "get to" would be the difference between whether I would eat this job up or whether it would eat me up. And that attitude was something I would decide every morning. Totally under my control.

I went down to Washington to meet with our delegation. My message was simple: I would need their help to address many of our city's problems, and I wanted a strong relationship with them.

Talking with Congressman Studds was easy. I had worked on his first campaign in the 1970s and knew him well. I knew his staff and had poached one of his top aides, Maria Tomasia. I also knew previous staff members, and Mardee Xifaras was a very close friend to both of us.

Studds was influential in national maritime and fisheries issues and had co-authored the 1976 Magnuson Act, which at the outset had been called the Studds-Magnuson Act, creating the 200-mile limit. This law was the greatest advancement ever for the fishing industry, so he needed to maintain a good relationship with New Bedford. Our meeting went well.

My meeting with Congressman Barney Frank was unusual. His district bordered New Bedford. Barney, who later became a good friend, never looked up from his desk at this new mayor. The only way to describe his behavior was rude, and that would not have been the first time that adjective would have been used about Barney. But that was his personality, and I got a good dose of it on my first meeting.

Next, Walter Ramos and I walked over to the Senate to meet with his old boss Ted Kennedy. Again, there were many connections. Walter wasn't the only one in my circle who knew Senator Kennedy. Scott Lang was also very close to him, and Mardee Xifaras was another link. So that meeting was very warm. I felt that the people of New Bedford couldn't have a stronger fighter on their side than Senator Edward M. Kennedy.

Senator John Kerry, the junior senator, was a different story, and I approached him with a bit of caution. I had met him when he was Governor Dukakis' lieutenant governor. He had supported Brian Lawler against me, which was the safe thing to do. What would this meeting be like? Well, Senator Kerry took care of that. Instead of a short meeting in his office, he invited me to dinner with several of his senior aides. We spent three hours putting the last campaign behind us and talking about how we would go forward. It was a gracious move on his part, and I certainly appreciated it.

Walking with Maria and John Tomasia in the Feast of the Blessed Sacrament Parade, 1986

Four Priorities and a Fish Strike

Finally, there was time for some rest with the family around the holidays. After the campaign's intensity, Laurie and I looked forward to a week of uninterrupted family time. We had earned it.

A few years earlier, at a WHALE auction, we had bought a one-week timeshare on Captiva Island, off the southwest coast of Florida. Captiva was very relaxing, with a beautiful beach and unbelievable wildlife. Former Wimbledon champion Virginia Wade was the tennis pro at the resort. I would always get to play a few sets with her, and our most significant decisions would be what to put in our rum drinks. We went to Captiva that year for the week between Christmas and New Year's, so the kids were on vacation. The weather was great. We swam with dolphins. Our one-week timeshare neighbors were all there. So relaxing. Except for one thing. The national media was reporting a violent fish strike going on in New Bedford. And my inauguration was only ten days away.

On Monday, January 6, 1986, in New Bedford High School's Bonspiegel Auditorium, inaugural exercises commenced at 10:30 a.m. with the high school marching band playing Aaron Copland's *Fanfare for the Common Man*. The Charles Ashley School glee club sang the *Star-Spangled Banner*, and Joseph Theodore Jr. led everyone in the Pledge of Allegiance. Joe was the long-time Americanism officer for American Legion Post #1. During the Vietnam War, he had persuaded the City to fly the American flag at night fully lit as a show of support for our troops. When New Bedford agreed to do that, Joe took his campaign successfully to the Commonwealth of Massachusetts and then to the entire country. He always called himself my twin because of our height difference. He may have been short of stature, but he was long on impact.

Reverend Lawrence Van Heerden of the Interchurch Council gave the invocation, and City Clerk Janice Davidian read the certificates of election for mayor, assessor, school committee members, and city councilors. Superior Court Justice George Jacobs then swore me in with Laurie

Judge George Jacobs swears in the new mayor on Mayor Rotch's family bible.

The inauguration, 1986: at left, Carl Cruz sings; at right Rabbi Bernard Glassman leads prayer.

by my side. I put my hand on two Bibles owned by William J. and Morgan Rotch, ancestors who had lived in our house and been the City's second and 19th mayors, respectively. Carl Cruz sang *Precious Lord*, a prayer I had said to Matthew every night when we were the only ones living at 19 Irving Street. Carl later gave me a framed version of the poem, which I keep close by.

Rabbi Bernard Glassman of Tifereth Israel Synagogue offered a prayer, as did Reverend Manuel Chavier, pastor of the International Church of the Nazarene, and Reverend Constantine Bebis of the Greek Orthodox Church in the North End. Janice Davidian swore in everyone else. Finally, it was time for my inaugural address.

A speech can be important both for what you say and for the tone you set. I have given hundreds of speeches, maybe more. Some were formal, as this one was; many have been off-the-cuff. Many were delivered to just a few people. Others I made before over a thousand people, as in my inaugural speech. Some were from prepared remarks, others from talking points.

I shared with the audience how I felt. This wasn't an obvious way to begin. I have often joked with people that, as a New Englander, I was brought up not to have feelings, and if I did have feelings, then certainly I was never to share them with anyone! That was a joke, but as the saying goes, "Many a truth is said in jest."

I began: "I stand before you today, filled with feelings of humility, honor, awe, and hope."

I went on to say that I was humbled by the act of submitting my name before the people for a public vote of approval or rejection. I would never forget the source of the power I exercised. It came from the people. I was honored because of the thousands of individuals who shared with me their love of New Bedford and who stepped forward to join this effort for our city. This

At left, City Clerk Janice Davidian swears in the City Council. At right, front row guests—Dick Walega, Steve Roberts, Peter Rioux, Peter Bullard, Tia Bullard, and Chris Souza (behind Tia)—settle in to hear the inaugural address.

sense of shared purpose would be necessary to meet the challenges ahead, and I believed it would be a great honor to work alongside such people toward a common goal.

I told the audience that I was in awe of the responsibility I was about to shoulder. Up until that day, I had only been responsible for the well-being of my family of five. Now I was responsible for a city of 100,000 people. I had run a non-profit business with a budget of under $1 million. Now I would run a city with a budget 100 times greater. Yes, I was in awe of the job I was stepping into.

I let them know we would be powered by hope. We would face many challenges and deal with various problems on a day-to-day basis, but four priorities would guide us. These priorities were distilled from thousands of conversations during the campaign and from the transition reports and the task forces we had set up. I felt these priorities represented the major challenges the city would wrestle with for the rest of the century. One of a chief executive's subtle powers is laying out an agenda. What you include may be obvious. What you leave out is not as obvious, yet the omissions are as important as the pauses in music that accentuate the notes. The combination is like figure and ground in a painting, with the relationship between a composition's foreground and background defining the work. I emphasized that we would focus on economic development, housing, drug abuse, and the environment.

I didn't mention taxes, although we quickly started a task force to look at ways to manage municipal government efficiently, and I didn't mention the fishing industry, which was in crisis, but I felt they both were encompassed under economic development. I didn't mention crime, but I felt most of that fell under the umbrella of drug abuse as one of its symptoms. Another topic that I didn't focus on was education, in particular, public schools. If I had to do it all over again, I would definitely raise education as an area that the city needed to raise its citizens to their potential, and I regret that I didn't focus more on it at the time.

Regarding economic development, I said our approach to economic development that had worked in the past was not going to work for the future. For many, the ticket to the American dream had been to leave school early, work hard and long (often at more than one job), and invest in real estate. And when you "made it," you could move to the suburbs where your kids would enjoy better schools and living conditions. But jobs in the mills and manufacturing plants were declining, and new jobs required an education. We would need to build a partnership with the local university. Southeastern Massachusetts University, now UMass Dartmouth, was headed by a dynamic young chancellor, Dr. John Brazil, who was enthusiastic about being an active partner with New Bedford. I also said that we would need all city sectors engaged in this effort.

Regarding housing, I pointed out that we were fortunate to have many distinct neighborhoods of well-built, historic housing stock. We had once housed a population of over 120,000 people, so we had ample supply. But families were smaller now. Our population was getting older, and we had many people with special housing needs.

It would have been easy to describe the third priority as crime and talk about the role of the police. That makes the solution somebody else's responsibility. Instead, I decided to define the issue as drug abuse with external and internal forces putting pressure on the city. Externally, we are part of an international crime network being used without our permission by drug cartels. This is a fight our police force, working with law enforcement at the state and national levels, faced. There is also the internal component of drug abuse when drugs become a substitute for hope—hope that is lost because a person sees no opportunity, and addiction follows. These are our citizens' lives that get wasted, our children's lives. This is where we must be accountable and play a role. This is too big just for the police.

The first three issues were familiar to my audience. City councilors and former mayors had spent many hours debating the best ways to tackle these challenges. I came at them differently, but the terrain was familiar.

The fourth issue, though, was completely foreign territory. I elevated the issue of the environment, the first mayor to do so directly in an inaugural address. I made a few general points. One was the issue of intergenerational equity. I said that our collective decision to pollute comes at the expense of our children and grandchildren. They have no role in making these decisions, but they will live with the consequences of our actions and judge us for what we have done or failed to do.

I argued that if we assume that cleaning the environment comes at the expense of the economy, we are making a false choice. That is unfair to our people. Historically, people have come to this "gateway city" looking for a better life. That better life includes attending better schools, owning your own home in a nice neighborhood, and having clean air and water. People have sought to achieve these goals by working hard, saving money, and moving to the suburbs. But that is not right. We can have a clean environment here in our city, right here for our people. Aren't we just as deserving as everyone else?

I pointed out some specific problems we were going to tackle. I mentioned the two known Superfund sites: the New Bedford Harbor and Sullivan's Ledge. I mentioned the unlined landfill at Shawmut Avenue and how the modern regional landfill at Crapo Hill in Dartmouth was behind schedule. And I mentioned the third major environmental issue: our primary treatment plant at Fort Rodman, whose condition may have us in violation of the Clean Water Act.

After talking about these four great challenges, I acknowledged the reality that confronting them would cost money. The people of the commonwealth had recently passed Proposition 2½, limiting how much communities could raise through property tax, which was the major source of local revenue.

Years later, Rep. Frank wisely summed up human nature on the subject of taxes by saying that people "support spending decreases in general and spending increases in particular." That's why tax limits like Prop 2½ pass by large margins. But people need and still want the increased services that the government provides.

Quoting the Irish-born British statesman Edmund Burke, I told my audience that "Mere parsimony is not economy." I went on to say that if I thought investments were necessary to meet challenges ahead and put the city in a better position in the future, I would recommend those investments.

My address ended on an optimistic note. I talked about the feeling of hope. I mentioned the people I had gotten to know over the campaign and their stories of meeting individual challenges. I described how I had seen neighbors and community groups coming together time and time again to meet civic goals. I quoted the lyrics in one of the hymns of our Unitarian Church.

> *What makes a city great and strong*
> *Not architecture's graceful strength,*
> *Not factories extended length,*
> *But men who see the civic wrong,*
> *And give their lives to make it right,*
> *And turn the darkness into light.*

I finished by saying that while our challenges were great, our people, working together, have always been up to the task and that I was eager to get started.

A Seething Waterfront

In the early 1980s, New Bedford was still a leading fishing port, but it was feeling the strain from several fronts. About 250 boats from New Bedford and Fairhaven fished out of the port. Scallops and groundfish made up the bulk of the catch, with lobster and highly migratory species like tuna and swordfish also contributing. The Magnuson Act, passed in 1976, extended the US jurisdiction from 12 miles offshore to 200 miles, Americanizing fishing areas and creating a bonanza for the fleet. The benefit was short-term. We soon found out that we could overfish as easily as the Russians and the Japanese.

Two weeks after inauguration, pickets demand the private auction house be shut down.

Then, in 1983, the World Court in The Hague, Netherlands, settled a dispute between the US and Canada over where the border should be drawn between the two countries. The court awarded Canada the northeast part of Georges Bank, home to some of the most productive fishing areas in the world. The creation of "The Hague Line" had two adverse consequences for the American fleet. The first was obvious—we lost access to precious fishing grounds that our people had fished for over 100 years. The second was less obvious—overfishing the areas we were left with. New capital had been pumped into the New Bedford fleet after the Magnuson Act passed. This larger, newer, more powerful fleet now was forced to fish in a smaller area, guaranteeing that the remaining grounds would be overfished at an even more destructive rate than in years past.

By the winter of 1985-86, the port of New Bedford was feeling the economic strain of collapsing fisheries. Profits were running low, and tensions were running high. Half the fleet was unionized, and those crews abandoned the Teamsters and switched to the Seafarers International. But the boat owners didn't want to deal with either union. Instead, the owners wanted more and demanded that crews take a lesser share of the revenues from the trips.

In January, about 500 fishermen marched on City Hall. This is what awaited me on the day I was inaugurated. As I vacationed with my family in Florida trying to gather my thoughts and the priorities for my administration, I read in the national press about a fishing strike in New Bedford that had violent overtones. Anger was high, and a couple of buildings had been torched. I had been hoping for a grace period, but that looked less and less likely.

Strikers fight for better wages and pension and health benefits.

Right after I was inaugurated at New Bedford High School at noon on January 6, 1986, I took my son Matthew and went for my first ride in the mayor's car, a big black Buick with the blue municipal license plate "M 4." I asked Sergeant Ed Craig to drive us down to Conway Street in the South Terminal.

When we arrived at Conway and MacArthur Drive, we saw about 200 angry fishermen on one side of the intersection and about 100 police officers with shields and a few dogs on

Strikers take their fight to City Hall

the other side. I asked Matthew to stay in the car with Sergeant Craig while I got out and went over to the fishermen to listen to what they had to say. I was immediately surrounded. The men talked and yelled, and their frustration was evident. They were angry at the boat owners. They were angry that the fishing wasn't any good, and they were angry that they weren't making money. They were angry that their benefits were being cut back. They were angry that I wasn't helping them.

I listened for a while and then went over to the police and talked and listened to them. I told them they had a difficult job to maintain peace in such a highly charged arena, but I knew they were up to the task. I returned to the car, and as we drove away, one of the fishermen threw a huge rock in our direction. It missed, but the message was unmistakable. This was a volatile situation that could be dangerous. It seemed clear to me that the boat owners wanted to bust the union, but there was more at play in this conflict than just the boat owners and the union. To make matters more complicated, the seafood dealers decided to get into the act. When a fishing boat lands, seafood dealers buy the catch at auction and then process the seafood and send it to market.

For decades the auction had been held in the city-owned Wharfinger Building on Pier 3. The scallop auction took place at 7 a.m. and lasted about ten minutes. An hour later, the groundfish draggers would list their catches on the blackboard broken down by species. Each boat's entire catch would be sold to the highest bidding dealer, and after the auction, the captain would steam over to the dealer's fish house and unload. What upset the boat owners and fishermen was that as a catch was being unloaded, a dealer might decide to renegotiate the price, at which point the boat was at a disadvantage.

The dealers may have competed at the auction, but during this time, when boat owners and crews were distracted battling each other, the dealers banded together and planned a coup. They deserted the Wharfinger Building and set up shop at a warehouse used by Yellowbird Trucking on Conway Street in the South Terminal. Then they informed all boats, union and non-union, that they would only buy catches at their new private facility.

The waterfront was seething. A few days into my new administration, the phone rang. It was Harvey Mickelson, whom I had known for years. Among other things, Harvey had always gathered all the fishing industry members together to raise money for Gerry Studds, Ted Kennedy, John Kerry, and other politicians who could be helpful to the industry. He said his offices were under siege.

"Mr. Mayor, my building is surrounded by hundreds of angry fishermen," Harvey said. "They are throwing rocks at the windows. I am worried they may storm the building. Right now, I am crouched under my desk, calling you. Your job is to protect lives and property. You need to send police down here immediately."

"Harvey, we'll get right on it, but what did you think would happen when you set up that private auction?" I said, trying to convince the dealers to back down. "You brought this on yourself. Why don't you have your guys return to the public auction where it is supposed to be."

"Not going to happen. This is a much better facility," Harvey countered.

"Says the guy crouched under his desk," I said. "We'll send the police, Harvey."

The situation was heating up. I conferred with Ben Baker and Roz Brooker. The public auction was important to maintain because it was one more right being taken away from fishermen. If the auction were public, there was some transparency. If it was a private enterprise, deals and prices were confidential. We knew there was a city law requiring boats to sell at the Wharfinger Building, and we wondered what would happen if we decided to enforce it. I called Superior Court Judge George Jacobs, who had sworn me in just days before, and explained the situation.

"Mayor, I know the law well," the judge said. "As it happens, I wrote that law when I was city solicitor for a previous mayor. Having written it, I know it is unconstitutional! We did it just for show. If you arrest some unfortunate captain and bring him before my court, I'm going to throw that case out so fast your head will spin."

"Judge Jacobs, that's very helpful to know upfront," I said with a laugh.

George certainly hadn't made our position any stronger, but at least we knew what we were looking at.

Ben, Roz, and I discussed the issue with Police Chief Arthur Oliveira and decided, despite what George had told us, we would ask the police to enforce the law against the first captain who sold at Yellowbird. That happened to be Joe Avila. The fine was $50. I don't know whether he paid it. The New Bedford City Council raised the fine to $300 to put more teeth in the law, but I didn't want to make any changes until the courts could get us a definitive answer.

Protesters angry about the private auction face-off against police, creating a volatile situation.

The fish strike wore on. Boat owner Bob Bruno's truck went up in flames, and there were other incidents. Despite the anger and the resistance, the union boats never got a contract, and the auction never returned to the Wharfinger Building. The owners busted the union, and the dealers privatized the auction. In my opinion, that was two steps back for the industry.

Six years later, after I had left City Hall and was working for the New Bedford Seafood Co-Op, I was driving three people to a fisheries meeting in Portland, Maine. Fisherman and boat owner Rodney Avila was in the front passenger seat of my VW Rabbit. Howard Nickerson, a long-time organizer for the Offshore Mariners, sat in the back behind me. Behind Rodney was his cousin, Joe. We had a three-hour drive ahead of us.

"So, John, you remember when you were mayor?" Joe started the conversation off.

"Yea, Joe, I remember that," I said.

"So, John, you remember right at the beginning there was a fish strike?"

"Yea, Joe, I remember that too."

"So, John, you remember how they moved the auction?"

"Yea, Joe, I remember about the auction."

"And John, you remember how you went and arrested a captain?"

"Yea, Joe, I remember that, but I don't remember who it was."

"Well, that captain was me!"

"Oh, well, I guess this is going to be a *long* ride to Portland, Joe."

We talked about the strike, what had happened to the industry since the strike, and touched on other topics. Rodney was a great storyteller, and so was Howard, so the drive went quickly. Along the way, Joe mentioned he had lost his house recently in a fire. I told him about the fire in my house, and we shared our experiences. When you lose a home to fire, you lose more than just the physical structure. You lose all the items inside connected to your memories.

Joe said one of the things he missed the most was his collection of Brother Dave Gardner albums. Brother Dave was a comedian from Tennessee with a real Southern sense of humor. My college roommate was from Louisville, and he loved Brother Dave. I had acquired two Brother Dave records, which is the *last* thing you would expect a New England Yankee to own. When I told Joe I would give him my Brother Dave records, the arrest from the strike days was officially forgiven.

Striking fishermen were a constant presence on the waterfront.

Chief and Police

In addition to the fish strike, the first 100 days of the administration were filled with activity. I continued adding great people to my administration, such as Barbara Fernandes, a Cape Verdean and sharp banker, as chair of the Election Commission, and Jerry Messier, a French Canadian from the North End, as head of Civil Defense.

Sadly, we also lost some good people in the transition. My good friend Richard Pline left as head of Community Development to pursue a career in law. His responsibilities and salary were out of line with the rest of the team, and he, naturally, did not want to

Police Chief Richard Benoit

accept a pay cut. His departure was unavoidable, but I was very sad to lose someone I admired so much. We had worked closely together to advance the waterfront historic district, and he had served the City at the highest level possible.

There were other losses in these early days. I picked a battle with school committee members over my candidate to fill a vacancy during a special election. We lost 9-8, which isn't advisable for a new mayor who doesn't want to show weakness. And I fought and lost to the Airport Commission over their support for a past-his-prime director, Isidor Eisner.

On a brighter note, during this time, we succeeded in getting a $900,000 state grant to rip up the Purchase Street pedestrian mall, which was hurting business downtown. The downtown businesses complained that the mall had eliminated parking and prevented people in cars from seeing their stores. It had not increased pedestrian traffic as had been hoped.

Selecting a new police chief to replace retiring Chief Arthur Oliveira may have been the decision of the most consequence that I made that spring. Under our local form of government, the mayor is the chief appointing authority, making me responsible for the police force. That is a responsibility unlike any other.

In many ways, police officers hold the most difficult and the most powerful jobs. A police officer has the right to take your life away in certain circumstances. With that right comes a tremendous responsibility to know the law, protect a person's rights, protect public safety, and use excellent judgment—all of which must come together in seconds when an officer might be under high stress from an attack or threat of an attack. As an officer, you do the job knowing that your actions can be dissected after the fact in a court of law and put under scrutiny by highly paid lawyers interrogating every move you made. Your decisions can be questioned by the press, the public, and your superiors, who might wonder if you could have done something differently. If this second-guessing finds you at fault, it could mean the end of your career. That is what police officers sign up for.

Firefighters, too, have a tough job. They put out raging fires and pull people to safety. It takes a special kind of person to run *toward* a fire. Everyone seems to love firefighters. But the public has a more complicated relationship with the police. People tend not to like the police. They don't like to see them coming. It's never a good thing. And the reverse is true. Police can become suspicious of the public.

Friedrich Nietzsche said, "Whoever fights monsters should see to it that in the process he does not become a monster. And if you gaze long enough into an abyss, the abyss will gaze back into you."

In their efforts to protect, police officers can spend their careers looking at monsters. When they find the monsters among us, the police are heroes. When they see monsters where they don't exist, or when some in the ranks turn away from their core mission, the police can become the monster. That is what they deal with every day. It is an occupational hazard to ward off the abyss.

By requirement, I had to choose the new chief from the three candidates who scored highest on the civil service chief exam. All the candidates were smart, experienced captains on the force. Each was 44 years old, which meant that the next chief would, likely, hold that post for quite a while.

As I looked over their qualifications, I was highly aware that I, not the chief, was ultimately responsible for every action of the 242 members of our police force. The person I chose would be leading officers in the most difficult assignments, with the greatest responsibility, and at the highest stakes, often with little training.

The head of the police union Leonard "Lenny" Baillargeon and the union's executive board met with me before the exam scores became public. They said they wanted to stress how important it was to remove "politics" from the process and just go with the highest scorer.

The police union was very powerful in the department. Only the chief and deputy chief were not members. Even captains were members of the bargaining unit, which made managing the membership a challenge. As I considered this aspect, I recalled the observation former New York City Police Commissioner Patrick Murphy made at a Kennedy School session. Pat said that while he came from several generations of police, he had never run into a group that was more resistant to change. He said the unofficial motto of police is, "But that's the way we have always done it."

Richard Benoit scored 97 out of 100 on the civil service test, the highest score of the three candidates. He was a training officer, had an advanced degree, and was studying for a law degree. Robert Vital scored a 94, also a very high score, and one I would think certainly qualified him to be an excellent chief. In his public comments during the process, Bob said he believed that the high scorer should be selected. Carl Moniz scored a 91, which was also an excellent score. As the only Portuguese candidate in a city over 50 percent Portuguese, Carl had a substantial following.

Each candidate submitted a written statement of his goals for the department and the steps he would take to achieve them. I interviewed each man. I remember having serious reservations about Richard Benoit because he seemed to have a tough time looking me in the eye during the interview.

I talked the choice over with Ben Baker and a few others. Benoit had the best education. His background as a training officer was appropriate. He had submitted a very good written statement. And most important, Benoit had the highest score. I thought all the scores were very good, but there was no question that if I picked anyone else, people would scream, "politics." Benoit seemed the top choice.

The only thing wrong was my nagging concern about no eye contact. If I had been in the office longer and had more confidence in my intuition or "gut," perhaps I would have made a different decision. But I made what I thought was the best decision. It was certainly the safe political decision. I chose Richard Benoit. We had a good relationship through the years, but when I needed him to step up at a few critical moments, he fell short.

One of my goals as mayor was to introduce community policing. This was a fundamental shift from a policy of prioritizing "response to calls for service" to one that integrates officers into the neighborhoods where they can head off problems before they happen. It is proactive instead of reactive. To use a stereotype, when an officer is in a car, the car is one barrier between the officer and the people. The uniform can be another. If the officer chooses to wear reflective sunglasses, that is another barrier. If the officer lives out of town and doesn't know the people, that is yet another barrier. Community policing tries to break down barriers by getting officers out of their cars and into neighborhoods where they can get to know the people and their issues. It makes officers a part of the community, not apart from the community.

Chief Benoit selected Lt. Guy Oliveira to lead the community policing effort. Oliveira was well respected, a pillar of the Cape Verdean community, and a good person for the job. He did his best, but the "that's-not-the-way-we've-always-done-it" camp did not make it easy. The rank and file didn't support the new policy, and the chief never really pushed for it. Sadly, it never achieved more than demonstration status.

Toward the end of my time in office, the relationship with the police blew up during contract renewal negotiations. During the previous contract, I had allowed binding arbitration to settle any contract issues when the two sides could not agree. What I hadn't realized was that the arbitration process has a history of leaning toward the union. I did not want binding arbitration for this contract. The police did not want to give it up.

My labor negotiator Arthur Caron characterized the position of unions in general as, "What's mine is mine; what's yours is negotiable." A great lawyer who had represented mayors going back to Markey, Arthur had earned the respect of even those he negotiated against. There were money and other issues to be hammered out in this negotiation, but the real sticking point was binding arbitration. The argument became very bitter, with charges flying back and forth. It came to a head one night during a political fundraiser for my election campaign at the Skipper Motor Inn in Fairhaven. The union thought this would be a great time to show their strength. It was no accident that they chose an event in Fairhaven because they would not be required to act like police since they were not inside city limits. It turned very ugly very fast.

More than 100 members of the police union set up a picket line, illegally blocking access to the parking lots at the Skipper. When people tried to drive in, the police stopped them, even arresting some. They put Aerovox CEO Cliff Tuttle in handcuffs, a picture of which appeared on the paper's front page the next day. Cliff hadn't broken any laws, so he was never formally charged.

When another guest tried to park, an officer stood in front of his car. A second officer opened the car door to drag the driver out, and the first officer jumped on top of the hood, yelling and screaming at the driver. As the driver was being pulled out of the car, his foot came off the brake,

Aerovox President Clifford Tuttle Jr. is handcuffed outside a Bullard fundraiser during police picket.

and the car lurched. The officer on the hood lost his footing, fell in front of the vehicle, and was run over, breaking his back. He recovered but only after many surgeries and a long convalescence.

It was a nasty night. As my family entered the Skipper, New Bedford police officers screamed at them. They hurled F-bombs at my daughter, Lexie, and my mother-in-law. They were shaken up. The fundraiser was a disaster. The worst day of my six years as mayor ended that night when Lexie, who was in her early twenties at the time, came into our bedroom.

"I thought policemen were supposed to protect us. What were they doing?"

I had no reasonable explanation.

While several laws were clearly broken, from malicious destruction of property (the keying of several cars) to blocking legal access to private property—all of which was captured on television—the fraternity of law enforcement seemed to hold firm. Fairhaven police were nowhere to be seen. State police were invisible. No one would charge or prosecute these lawbreakers for what they had done.

The year of the police riot turned out to be my final year in office.

The following summer, as private citizens, Laurie and I enjoyed a visit to the Feast of the Blessed Sacrament, a four-day celebration in the city's North End that attracts several hundred thousand people annually. The feast was initiated in 1915 by four Madeirans in honor of their safe passage to America and in memory of their homeland—the Madeira Islands. We were skewering *carne de spit* by the barbecue pit and enjoying some Madeira wine when an off-duty police officer came up to us.

"Mayor Bullard, I want you to meet some relatives who are visiting from out of town for the feast," he said.

He introduced me.

"This man was the greatest mayor the city ever had!"

After a bit of small talk, we parted company.

"When you are out of power, and you can't impact people anymore, you become a great statesman!" I said to Laurie. "It's like the fiasco at the Skipper never existed."

The Skipper riot was not the only police problem during my time as mayor. There was another incident that occurred, but to my regret, I did not register its significance until I was out of office.

In 1990, during one of my many meetings with Chief Benoit, he mentioned in passing that a prisoner in the downtown jail had died. I asked him the cause. He told me it was a cocaine overdose, that the man had ingested 10,000 times the "normal" dose. I asked how that was possible. He said the prisoner swallowed the plastic bags of cocaine when police officers confronted him. The bags burst in his stomach later.

"It happens," the chief said. He seemed dismissive.

The conversation took five minutes. I'm not sure if I asked the prisoner's name, why he was arrested, or who the arresting officers were. I trusted the chief to alert me to events needing my scrutiny and attention, even if these situations might be difficult for me to hear about. His report and manner suggested nothing out of the ordinary.

But the death of 32-year-old Morris Pina Jr. was not ordinary.

The environment in which my conversation with the chief took place was a day, like most days, jam-packed and broken up into very small increments. I would always carry an index card in my shirt pocket with a minute-by-minute schedule. This was before cell phones and calendar apps. I lived by that daily index card, moving from meeting to meeting as it dictated. It might be a ten-minute meeting to decide on something. It might be a two-hour briefing on a complex topic that required reading the night before. It might be in my office or somewhere else. But every minute was scheduled, every minute was important, and I had to be "on" all the time. Sometimes, it seemed as if I was developing an addiction to adrenaline and reverting to the attention span of a seven-year-old. I often had only a few minutes to make serious decisions before moving on to the next topic. There was so much going on, I could not adopt a leisurely pace.

In that high-stakes, hurry-up atmosphere, Chief Benoit said, "It happens."

And I let it slide.

A year or so later, after I was out of office and working in the Clinton administration in Washington, I got a notice that I would be deposed in the civil rights case of the family of Morris Pina Jr. vs. the City of New Bedford, et al. When I contacted the City Solicitor's office, they said that Assistant City Solicitor Patrick Walsh would defend me as I was one of the parties being sued along with Chief Benoit, arresting Officer Leonard Baillargeon, and other city officials and police officers. I asked Pat what the case was about, and he said the family alleged that Baillargeon and other police officers had used excessive force contributing to Morris Pina's death. He said I would have to testify in federal court in Boston.

I flew from Washington and took the witness stand. The lawyer for Mr. Pina's family showed me several pictures of the young Black man's body on the jail cell floor. He was surrounded by a pool of blood and looked as if he had been badly beaten. I was shocked. The case concluded and awarded Pina's estate about $500,000, which I was told was low for such an outcome. The findings determined that Mr. Pina had been beaten and that the incident had been covered up.

I thought back to my misgivings during Benoit's job interview. He looked away then and, in another significant moment, looked away again. It seemed to me that he chose to tell me something he thought I wanted to hear instead of something that I needed to hear. He was a training officer whose officers had not been properly trained to follow the most basic rules of proper use of force. If Baillargeon, as head of the union, behaved this way, I wondered who else was acting this way? When you make errors with people who carry guns and batons, those errors can be tragically serious and even fatal. When leadership doesn't address problems, they are allowed to continue.

I had made many excellent choices of people to serve. But I do have some regrets. Clearly, I had not done enough to set expectations about department heads' responsibilities to me, each other, and the people we served.

Environmental Issues

The environment was one of the four priorities I set out in my inaugural address after I was first elected. The people of New Bedford deserved clean air and water just as much as the people in the wealthier suburbs. Whenever I said that it always generated applause. Getting results proved more complicated. The task before us was daunting on so many fronts. New Bedford had dirty air, dirty water, and run-down parks, in part because we are a poor city with industries that will pollute if allowed.

I get sick and tired of corporate titans like GE's Jack Welch being lionized as great examples of how the private sector works and how corporate America is so much more efficient than government. They brag so much about the benefits of capitalism. But then, you see how GE disposes of PCBs (polychlorinated biphenyls) that cause cancer and are endocrine disruptors in the Hudson River and around Pittsfield, MA. They leave their waste for others to clean up at a cost of hundreds of millions of taxpayer dollars. This is what is known as "privatizing profits and socializing costs." And it makes Jack Welch and his ilk among the biggest hypocrites you can find. He should be a role model for no one.

New Bedford had its own companies that dumped their trash and pollutants in our public places for other people to clean up. To be fair, when PCBs were declared illegal, the companies

Introducing new recycling program

Tires dumped at Sullivan's Ledge

stopped dumping, and when the Environmental Protection Agency sued them, they paid a portion of the cleanup costs. Still, these amounts did not come close to the overall cost of cleanup, and it seemed these penalties were simply absorbed by the companies as the cost of doing business.

For residents of this impoverished city, the costs were higher. They paid with higher health care costs and a lower quality of life. The factories spewed smoke into the air, breathed in mostly by people in the tenements and not by the CEOs in the tonier suburbs. The PCBs were discharged by Aerovox, Cornell Dubilier, and Revere Copper into the Acushnet River and New Bedford Harbor, not into the harbors of more affluent towns and neighborhoods such as Marion or Padanaram. And more chemicals were dumped into Sullivan's Ledge on Hathaway Road, Morse Cutting Tools in South Central, and other sites in and around New Bedford. The people and leaders of New Bedford knew this and accepted it as our fate as a poor city. We felt jobs were more important than a clean environment, and we assumed it was a choice we had to make. In my first inaugural address, I had said that this had to change.

We started on multiple fronts. Just next door was the town of Dartmouth, where a regional landfill at Crapo Hill was planned to replace unlined landfills in the region. The project was moving very slowly. We pushed for the regional landfill to move forward since we wanted to close the older, leaky landfills that were leaching pollutants.

US Army Corps of Engineers testing for PCBs on the Acushnet River

I remember meeting in my office with Camp Dresser & McKee of Cambridge, the engineering firm working with New Bedford on many projects. Several town and city officials were there. I was sitting next to one of the out-of-town engineers, listening while a local guy described where the landfill would be located in his very local accent.

"It's going to be right here in Dakmuth," he said, pointing to a spot on a map.

I watched the engineer write "Dakmuth" in his notes. I wondered how long he would spend looking at maps when he got back to his Cambridge office, trying to find where to put our landfill!

I also worked with Kathy Burns at our Department of Public Works to hire a recycling coordinator to launch a new recycling program at the Shawmut Avenue landfill. At first, it was modest, with cardboard, some plastics, glass, metal, and white goods such as washing machines and refrigerators. But it was a beginning.

I visited all the towns surrounding New Bedford, which I was told no mayor had done before, at least not in anyone's memory. I did this so we could coordinate the protection of the tremendous freshwater resources that New Bedford owned in Middleboro, Lakeville, and Freetown. New Bedford has an excellent source of freshwater from five ponds, second only to New York City in terms of quantity and water quality per capita.

The problem was the distribution system. Pond water is pumped, treated, and then travels through more than 250 miles of pipes to get to city homes and businesses. But the pipes, many put in about a century ago at the urging of my ancestor William W. Crapo as a measure to fight tuberculosis, had lead solder joints. Even a tiny amount of lead in drinking water is extremely dangerous to the development of children's brains. There were also numerous leaks, causing significant inflow and outflow along the way. Many of the cast iron pipes had rusted, so their inside diameters are a small fraction of what they used to be. This reduces water pressure and can be a safety hazard with fire hydrants. We needed to upgrade the system.

The unlined Shawmut Avenue landfill near the end of its useful life, 1983

CLF Is on the Phone: We Will Sue You

Among all these environmental issues, perhaps the one with the greatest impact on the environment and the greatest potential risk to the city was our primary wastewater treatment plant at Fort Rodman in the extreme South End. Primary treatment adds chlorine to the sewage before it is discharged into Buzzards Bay. This process does not remove solids. While we weren't transmitting disease, we were spreading what is known in the trade as "floatables." These would pop up and wash onto area beaches depending on wind direction. Floatables made swimming very undesirable, to say the least.

Our wastewater plant also made New Bedford the target of the entire region's ire when it came to the quality of life in the marine environment. The Coalition for Buzzards Bay was formed about this time, headquartered in Bourne, with the express purpose of ridding the bay of the primary plant in New Bedford, which they identified as the largest source of pollution in the bay.

Not only was the primary plant an affront to the bay, but it was also out of step with federal law. New Bedford was in serious violation of the 1972 Clean Water Act, which required that cities provide secondary treatment to remove solids. When this act was passed along with so much other environmental legislation in the early 1970s, federal and state grants were rolled out to help cities and towns comply. The programs covered 90 percent of a community's costs. With that type of carrot, practically every city had invested in clean water. But a handful didn't. Boston didn't. San Diego didn't. New Bedford didn't. It seemed that we, the proud people of New Bedford, wouldn't let the federal government tell us what to do.

So now it is 1986, I'm mayor, and we are 14 years out of compliance. The grant program was long expired. There was no money for us to tap. It was a problem without a simple solution.

Then, the phone rang.

It was Cleve Livingston, a college classmate of mine from Harvard. Cleve had rowed with a good friend of mine, Fritz Hobbs. They went to the 1968 Olympics in Mexico City and then

By 1984, the primary wastewater treatment plant was a dozen years out of compliance.

won a silver medal at the 1972 Olympics in Munich, both in eight-oared shells. In Munich, they were joined by Mike Livingston and Bill Hobbs, so the crew became known as "the brothers and the others." During my first year at MIT, I had roomed with Fritz and another rower, Charlie Hamlin, while they were attending Harvard Business School in the early 1970s.

When Cleve called, I thought it was old home week or something. I was happy to take a few minutes to catch up. We exchanged pleasantries, reminisced about college, and talked about what we had done since graduation. Cleve told me he worked for the Conservation Law Foundation, known as CLF, in Boston.

"That sounds great, Cleve! What do you do there?"

"Well, actually, John, that's the purpose of my call. We're going to sue you. I wanted to give you a heads up."

"Sue me! What for?"

"For violations of the Clean Water Act."

"Jesus, Cleve, we've been in violation of the Clean Water Act for 14 years! Why are you suing me now? I am actually trying to bring us into compliance."

"We know that, John. And we think our lawsuit may be just what you need to get the job done."

"Thanks a lot, Cleve. I'll try to remember that."

In Search of the Urban Gurgle

The lawsuit did move the situation to the urgent pile. New Bedford could be in for some severe penalties. We needed to mobilize fast. We divided the problem into components: legal, engineering, financial, and political.

Legally, this had many aspects and involved local, state, and federal levels of government. This was going to be a high-stakes, high-profile case, and it would blow the fuses of our City Solicitor's office. To compound matters, just before the phone call, Roz Brooker had decided to leave her post as city solicitor to take a job that paid a lot more with many fewer headaches.

I selected Armand Fernandes to succeed her. Armand is a rare gem of a person. He was willing to sacrifice substantial private income from his very successful law practice to come down the hill to work for the people of New Bedford. He had honed his skills in the public arena working for former Bristol County District Attorney Edmund Dinis. Armand wasn't afraid of controversy or the pressure of the spotlight. He relished it. He had an easygoing personality. As I write this, he is still competing in national track meets and playing soccer, well into his eighties. He is competitive and likes to win. You want him on your side. But even with someone of Armand's talent, the complexity of the case meant we also needed the resources of a large Boston firm, so we retained Palmer & Dodge to help us out on the legal front.

Engineering expertise would be crucial. We felt comfortable with Camp Dresser & McKee, the city's engineering firm already on board. Steve Hickox, who later became CEO, was the lead for this project. With their help, we would determine the best available technology, estimate costs, analyze siting and piping, and work on many other issues.

We also had the challenge of finances. We knew that this project was totally out of reach without federal and state funding. Somehow, we had to create new financing mechanisms to afford what we needed to do.

Finally, there needed to be a political strategy. At the outset, I knew that building a sewer treatment plant was a political loser of an issue. I knew that, ultimately, it might cost me my job. I knew that it wasn't just NIMBY—Not In My Back Yard—that prevented projects like this from happening. A more powerful force was at play: NIMTOFF—Not In My Term of Office. It had caused many mayors to simply do nothing. This is what happens with so many important but difficult decisions in politics. "Yes, we have to balance the budget, just not this term." "We have to reform immigration laws, just not before this election."

To get a new wastewater treatment plant built, we would need support from the city councilors. And no one had ever accused them of being courageous. Some of the issues required a majority vote, so we had to get six out of 11 votes for those. If we put forth a zoning change or some other approval, we would need eight votes. We had to reverse opinion on an issue that had 14 years of resistance baked into it.

I did a few things right away. One was total immersion. Literally.

I wanted to see for myself the impact the primary plant was having on the environment. I had learned scuba diving from Bob Mercer Sr. at Whaling City Sea and Ski, so I asked if he would take me on a dive to the end of the sewer outfall pipe where the sewage was released after primary treatment. Bob said he didn't get that request every day. We could do it, but the dive would require special dry suits impermeable to water instead of wet suits that let water through to warm next to your skin.

The two of us donned our dive suits and headed out in Bob's boat.

About a half-mile south of Fort Rodman in about 30 feet of water, we located the outfall by the bulge in the water's surface. Sailors and fishermen sometimes called this the "bubbler" or the "urban gurgle." Its color changed day to day, depending on what dyes the textile plants were using on any day. On the day of our dive, the water was murky. The gurgle was a purplish brown.

We dove in and followed the anchor line to the bottom. Visibility was limited to about two feet maximum. The bottom was barren. It looked like a desert. No eelgrass, no fish, just flat sediment. And one live horseshoe crab! We surveyed the area for 20 minutes or so, never seeing the actual pipe, but we knew we were in the right spot because it was marked by lack of life and the sedimentation that the waste stream had produced.

We surfaced and climbed back onto the boat. I was feeling very grateful I had the dry suit on to protect me from the sewage spewing out of the pipe, but then I realized that the area around

The mayor sees for himself what comes out of the outfall pipe.

my mouth where the regulator fits in to supply air was totally unprotected. Well, it was too late to do anything about it. I don't seem to have suffered any ill effects other than the queasy feeling of the moment, so we chalked that up to good fortune.

With the lawsuit hanging over our heads, we got all the legal players around a table in Boston to sort out what we were going to do. The tool we were using to help resolve the lawsuit was called a "consent decree." That meant that all parties had to negotiate until they all *consented* to everything from technology, siting, schedule, and other details. The premise is that if all stakeholders are doing their job, then any agreement consented to by all parties *must* be a good one. And when agreement is reached, a plan would be presented to a federal judge who would approve it, superseding the law that had been violated by his decree.

Around the table were representatives from federal, state, and municipal government—folks from the EPA, the US Attorney's office, the state Attorney General's office, the secretary of Environmental Affairs' office, CLF, and New Bedford. To say that it was daunting looking at all that firepower would be an understatement.

I told the group we could not undo the mistakes of past administrations, but we wanted to come into compliance using the best available technology. I pointed out that we were not a wealthy city. We were not even a middle-class city. I mentioned the political realities I would face with our City Council. I pledged my commitment to work as hard as I could and gave as evidence that I had already been willing to lose one election over the issue of telling the truth about the need for a sewer use fee.

I knew Secretary of Environmental Affairs Jamie Hoyte and Massachusetts Attorney General Jim Shannon from past political campaigns, so I felt that I had a relationship of trust with them. US Attorney Frank McNamara was a friend and college classmate of mine, and while our politics were very different, we had a long-time friendship.

The primary treatment plant was located at the extreme south end of Clarks Point.

Even though he lived in Marion, I didn't know EPA New England Regional Director Mike Deland. So, we both set out to get acquainted, knowing this would be a long and difficult fight. Mike was a renowned Shields Class sailor, and he invited me to go racing with him. He and his wife, Jane, became friends of Laurie and mine and remained so well after we had both gone on to other things. After his service in the Navy, Mike developed a debilitating disease that landed him in a wheelchair. As I got to know him, it became evident that the wheelchair was more of a launching pad in the manner of Franklin Delano Roosevelt. We would go out in his beautiful boat, *Rebel*, and it didn't take long to realize that Mike was tough as nails, wily, smart, and **did not** like to lose—all important information to know when you are negotiating with someone about clean water. Although we represented different institutions in the wastewater treatment issue, we shared the same goal of cleaning up Buzzards Bay.

Another thing I did was to try and get the public involved by forming a Citizens Advisory Committee, but I miscalculated by making it open to anyone. We got about 15 people willing to advise me on the project. One of them was Dr. Bob Bowen, a neighbor in the West End and professor in Marine Policy at UMass Boston. Bob saw this as a marine policy case study in his home city and a way to give back. This was a noble gesture, and he was a great resource for the city. Every other person came from the Fort Rodman neighborhood near the existing plant and gelled into a group that seemed to have one agenda item and one agenda item only—they did not want the new plant in their neighborhood. So, from the start, my citizens committee was going to be of limited effectiveness, but there it was.

And I had a city to run with other issues that also needed attending.

A Working Waterfront Works

In a city defined as a seaport where we send our people to sea, the water's edge is a critical landscape. Waterfront development needed to be thoughtfully managed and new projects carefully vetted to ensure the vision of a working waterfront was not overshadowed. During my time in office, I found several instances where I could help shape the landscape so New Bedford would not lose its working and recreational connections with the river, the harbor, the bay, and the ocean.

As I was taking office, a developer proposed building residential and office condominiums along Steamship and Coal Pocket Piers—two relatively small piers located just south of the State Pier. There is no question the piers would have been an attractive housing site with the waterfront historic district catching fire—literally, then figuratively—and an active harbor providing a backdrop attractive to tourists.

But the piers provided dockage for the small day boats and inshore fishing boats that couldn't find space along piers serving the larger fishing boats that made longer trips. There was a real concern that the smaller boats would be displaced with no other place to go.

We leveraged state law in our favor. Under Chapter 91, the Massachusetts Public Water Act, licensing priority is given to water-dependent uses over water-enhanced uses, and condominiums clearly fit in the latter category. In the end, not only did we reject the condominium project, but we also extended Steamship Pier to accommodate more vessels.

We also combined Piers 3 and 4, two busy but run-down piers to the north of the State Pier, into a single, much larger New Bedford Fish Pier. This project had special meaning for me as it was the original site of Rotch's Wharf, where my ancestor Joseph Rotch centered his whaling business in 1765.

Another interesting waterfront proposal came my way when Walter Hughes and Bob McCarter came to my office with an idea for a hotel. Hughes was a real estate developer and insurance salesman from the North End. He had been a long-time city councilor, was immensely popular, and I considered him a good friend. McCarter was president of the New Bedford Institution for Savings, the largest bank in the region, and another good friend. He was incredibly supportive of the work in the waterfront historic district. There wasn't any doubt in my mind that this dynamic duo could carry out any idea they wanted to propose.

After pleasantries, they laid out their plan for a Sheraton Hotel on the east end of State Pier at the water's edge. They had schematic drawings of a high-rise building of over ten stories. They told me how much downtown New Bedford missed a first-class hotel since the old New Bedford Hotel was converted to senior housing in 1969. They enumerated the economic benefits, explaining that tourist spending goes up logarithmically with time spent in a place. The key to visitors spending more time in New Bedford was a hotel where they could spend the night.

They asked me to imagine myself up on the hotel's tenth floor looking out on the harbor.

"Isn't it an incredible view? You'll be able to see all the way up north to the end of the river," Walter painted the picture. "You'll be able to see out to the south to the Elizabeth Islands and the Vineyard!"

I love a good water view, but I had reservations.

"There's no question from a hotel's point of view this would be a great location. I couldn't agree more with you," I told them. "What I have to think about is whether a hotel is the best use for the water's edge of our working waterfront."

This needed more thought.

"I'll tell you what I'll do," I said. "I'll put a committee together to explore this issue. I'll ask Jim Mathes from the Chamber of Commerce to be on it and have them give me their thoughts in a couple of weeks. I really appreciate you bringing this idea in to discuss."

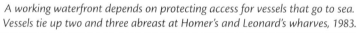

A working waterfront depends on protecting access for vessels that go to sea.
Vessels tie up two and three abreast at Homer's and Leonard's wharves, 1983.

Jim Mathes and I had a very good relationship over the years, agreeing on many things and disagreeing on a few. We trusted each other and never minced words. Once, when Jim was introducing me at a State of the City event, he pretended to hit me over the head with a large Nerf baseball bat to get my attention on some issue. We worked well together, enjoying lots of laughs.

Later, I heard Jim describe the hotel committee process.

"The mayor appointed this committee to study the hotel and asked me to be on it. I readily agreed," he said. "I went to the first meeting in his office on the first floor of City Hall. I looked around the room and saw myself and 20 longshoremen. That was the committee! I knew there wasn't going to be a hotel on State Pier."

I felt it was critical to keep water-dependent uses on the waterfront. There was no question that the arguments Walter and Bob made about the economic benefits of the hotel were valid, but I felt the downtown hotel would happen anyway. It shouldn't come at the expense of the working waterfront.

We had to wait for the hotel—much, much longer than I would have expected or wanted. But finally, the LaFrance family, who had operated White's of Westport for many years and were expanding into the hotel business in partnership with Marriott, built a Fairfield Inn and Suites just inside Route 18 and across from Coal Pocket Pier and Homer's Wharf. They added a conference center in the historic Baker Oil Works next door and, in 2019, acquired the old Louie's on the Wharf restaurant and renamed it Merrill's on the Waterfront.

The right uses ended up in the right places; it just took some time. If you lose public access to the waterfront for water-dependent uses, it is nearly impossible ever to regain that access.

While commercial fishing and other industrial uses dominate New Bedford's harbor, we thought there was still room and opportunity to expand into the recreational boating sector that supported communities like Newport and nearby harbors such as Padanaram, Mattapoisett, and Marion. The challenge was to do it in a way that took advantage of the vitality of the New Bedford waterfront, the attractiveness of New Bedford as a destination, and the

Marty Manley's office at the Pope's Island marina

world-class reputation of Buzzards Bay as a sailing venue, while also being careful to eliminate conflict with the working uses of the harbor.

We identified Pope's Island as an ideal location for recreational development. With help from the state and under the guidance of our Harbor Development Commission, led by Marty Manley, we got the state to build a 200-slip marina off the southern side of Pope's Island, complete with parking and a building that contained offices, showers, laundry, and restrooms for visiting boaters.

After I left office, this became the foundation for continuing efforts to increase recreational boating. New Bedford now boasts 2,000 recreational slips and moorings in a harbor that is still visually and in every other way dominated by fishing and maritime industrial uses. There are as many yachts now in New Bedford Harbor as in any other harbor on Buzzards Bay, but the character of the port remains a working port.

Recreational boating got a major boost years later, in 2007, when Laurie convinced Jim Mattingly to consider New Bedford Harbor for the annual cruise of the International Yacht Restoration School, which stopped in several ports. Jim was on the school board, which had its headquarters in Newport. Scott Lang, my former campaign chair, was mayor at the time. Laurie and I loved sailing our 1965 wooden, Concordia yawl, *Captiva*, and we occasionally participated in the annual "Classic Yacht Cruise."

One evening at a cocktail party at Lisa and Joel Alvord's house in Westport, Jim tried to recruit Laurie to help organize the cruise.

"Where are you planning to go, Jim?" Laurie asked.

"The usual itinerary, Laurie. We'll start in Nantucket, then go to Edgartown, Padanaram, and finish with a party in Newport."

"Not interested."

"What! Why not?"

"How about coming to New Bedford, Jim?"

"New Bedford! That's a fishing port. No one would want to go to New Bedford."

Laurie took the challenge. She and Matt Morrissey, head of the Mayor's Economic Development Corporation, went to Newport to pitch New Bedford to James Russell, the CEO of IYRS.

"Have you ever been to New Bedford, James?" Laurie asked.

"Well, actually, no."

"Great, come on over. We'll show you around."

To James's great credit, he accepted the invitation. Laurie and Matt showcased the historic district, the waterfront, the Whaling Museum, and downtown restaurants. They brought him to Pope's Island Marina. They pointed out the harbor's various mooring fields. They sang the praises of Jeff Pontiff's tour boat and harbor launch.

James was blown away. That year, New Bedford was added as a cruise stop in place of Padanaram.

More than 30 classic yachts came through the hurricane barrier under perfect skies. Both sail and powerboats, some as old as 100 years, cruised into the harbor, breath-taking in their beauty. Mayor Lang sent a boat with a photographer to greet each one. Visiting yachts received a gift bag filled with visitor information highlighting local attractions, mooring and launch instructions, and local products such as Titleist golf balls and AHEAD ball caps. Each vessel also got locally manufactured Crystal Ice—the clearest, best ice on the East Coast. Welcoming festivities included cocktails at the Whaling Museum and dinner at Cork, a nearby restaurant.

That evening, the positive buzz about the warm welcome was exciting to hear for those of us from New Bedford. We knew we were fighting prejudices about the city.

As Laurie and I sailed in with the parade of boats, we overheard a conversation on the boat radio between two parties not on the cruise. One said she was headed to New Bedford.

"Really, you are going to New Bedford! I can't believe you would go there," said the other, disdain dripping from her voice.

"Oh, I don't mean New Bedford. I mean the New Bedford Yacht Club in Padanaram."

That was the attitude we were fighting. It was prevalent whether you were talking about the boating community in Buzzards Bay, the ferry service to Nantucket, or getting rail service to Boston. Many folks looked down very long noses when it came to New Bedford. It is a toxic combination of racism and economic snobbery that people from New Bedford have long dealt with as we encounter the outside world.

The city's hospitality extended into the next morning. As the sun came up, Jeff Pontiff stopped by every boat mooring. Onto each deck, he placed a Dunkin Donuts "Box of Joe" coffee. He also delivered a copy of the *Standard-Times* with a full-color picture of the fleet coming through the hurricane barrier, top of the fold, page one. And because Jeff noticed there was an Irish boat in the fleet, he delivered the crew a new copy of the *Irish Times* as well!

The morning activities offered a tour of a scallop vessel and a tour of the Joseph Abboud factory a mile away with its world-famous suits. As a parting gift, everyone got a bag of fresh scallops from the nation's number one fishing port, fresh from Eastern Fisheries.

We listened to the chatter during the remainder of the cruise and heard the members saying they had never been treated that way in any port. We loved listening to the accolades. They vowed to bring their home yacht clubs back to New Bedford in the future.

James Russell was so taken with New Bedford that he later took a job as head of the New Bedford Whaling Museum, where his dynamic leadership led them to new heights.

Laurie continued working with the Harbor Development Commission on the city's welcome program and its recreational services for yachts. In 2010, the *Boston Globe* put her on the cover of their magazine for the work she did bringing a "sea change" that turned the "gritty port" into a "yachting haven." New Bedford continues to build on recreational opportunities. In 2019, it hosted 95 vessels from the fabled New York Yacht Club. That hadn't happened since 1856.

New Bedford Harbor is proving that with patience and proper planning, a diversity of uses can live and work along the waterfront without destroying the working nature of the port. As in whaling days, New Bedford today is still home to all that is needed for a fishing voyage. We can build a fishing vessel and outfit it with gear, electronics, nets, and everything to make it seaworthy. We can supply it with food, ice, and diesel. We can finance and insure the boat. We can outfit the crew with clothing before they leave, and when the vessel returns, we can process the catch and market it around the world. There are settlement houses for issuing paychecks and paying bills, and we have churches for giving thanks and praying for a safe return. In short, everything a fishing vessel and the people who fish need is right here. This is why New Bedford will always send its people to sea.

And the fishery is diverse. Dollar-wise, the port is dominated by scallops, accounting for a half a billion dollars off the boats before the multipliers kick in. But there are also significant landings of surf clams and ocean quahogs, fisheries that used to be based in Cape May, New Jersey. We also have boats bringing in offshore lobster, red crab, Jonah crab and groundfish.

Other maritime uses include some short sea shipping and barge traffic. Fast ferries take people from New Bedford to the islands of Martha's Vineyard and Nantucket. Cruise ships now call on New Bedford. And a major offshore wind support terminal hosts research vessels for the offshore wind companies and later will support the construction and servicing of this new industry.

Row, Row, Row Your Whaleboat

You can also spot a few whaleboats out on the water. There are two whaleboat rowing clubs that began with an innocent challenge when I was mayor. James Ragsdale was the longtime editor of the *Standard-Times*. He said the press could beat City Hall in an old-fashioned whaleboat race like the whalers used to have in the harbor in the 1800s. The *Standard-Times* and City Hall, at the time located almost across the street from one another, viewed each other with necessary mutual suspicion. Jim Ragsdale said we should take a day off from our professional rivalry and get out on the water with a friendly contest.

Everyone was game, but we didn't have any whaleboats. So, we borrowed two lifeboats from Massachusetts Maritime Academy in Bourne and brought them to New Bedford Harbor. Anne Eisenmenger, the Sunday editor at the newspaper, was instrumental in organizing the race.

Each team had a few days to practice before the event that would be part of the Fourth of July festivities. The three-legged course was about a mile or so. On the day of the race, the rowers piled into the whaleboats. The start was even, and there was much shouting and huffing and puffing as the gender-mixed crews raced the boats around the course. Gradually, the power of City Hall, under the expert leadership of the mayor, showed its mettle. We crossed the finish line well ahead of our rivals. The members of the press accused us of going around the wrong buoy.

"It wasn't an official part of the course," they protested.

We had a different take.

"Whichever buoy the mayor goes around is an official part of the course," we countered.

The next day, we read, to our chagrin, that the press had won the first whaleboat race, proving once again that real power is held by those who write the history!

The following year, we added a race between police and fire, which for years seemed to be won by the Fire Department. The highlight that year was Carol Pimentel, our city auditor, commandeering a fire hose on top of one of the trucks and getting everyone within 200 yards soaking wet.

After several years of fun, people wanted to get serious and train all year long, so the Whaling City Rowing Club was born. Thanks to funding from local businesses such as Acushnet Company and Compass Bank, the club paid for four Edey & Duff whaleboats based on the original Beetle

Whaleboats, gigs, and Olympic shells are an increasing presence in New Bedford Harbor.

design but made with modern materials. A few years later, Gail Isaksen of Fairhaven started a rival club, the Buzzards Bay Rowing Club, so now there are dozens of people out at all times of day enjoying the vitality of this diverse, exciting port of New Bedford.

Joining in the fun, a group of athletes formed the New Bedford Rowing Club, headquartered on Popes Island. Led by D'Arcy MacMahon, longtime founding director of the famous Head of the Charles Regatta, the Rowing Club introduces people to Olympic-type rowing in shells, a very different experience from rowing a whaleboat. But it is still a great way to get out and enjoy New Bedford's fantastic working harbor.

Into the Classrooms: Quizzing the Kids and Schooling the Mayor

As I look back on my time as mayor, I can see accomplishments, but I also can see some mistakes I made where I wish I had had better vision. It's useful to learn from those hits and misses.

More than half the budget goes to the school department. As mayor, I chaired the school committee, so I had a significant role in setting school policy. We had very bright superintendents during my time, first Constantine "Charlie" Nanopoulos and then Dr. Joe Silva.

We also had a persistent drug problem in the city, and I wanted to find a role to play. I conferred with school personnel and police Lieutenant Don Cook. We decided that I could have the most impact by reaching out to children in the third grade and later the second grade to build their self-esteem and fortify their decision-making skills.

At the time, First Lady Nancy Reagan was promoting "Just Say No." We thought we could build off that with a campaign to "Say No, Tell Somebody." I started by going into every third grade—about 40 different classrooms.

We worked out a plan. I would talk about New Bedford's history and mention how good the fishing industry is, how companies like Titleist, Calvin Clothing, and Polaroid produce the very best products in the world, how New Bedford has always aspired to be the best, and how people who work at companies like those—people like their parents and neighbors—routinely deliver excellence. I wanted the message to be that we can compete with anyone, anywhere. Then, I would ask how many wanted to go to college and stress the importance of staying in school. I'd

Kids take a break on City Hall steps during Youth Council parade, 1989.

say we have a really good college right nearby: UMass Dartmouth. Next, I would ask if they knew anything about drugs to find out what they knew about them. After that conversation, I would get into what to do if someone approached them to take drugs. The plan seemed good to me.

The first school I went to was the Hathaway School on Union Street, not far from our home. Everything was going according to plan. I asked them who wanted to go to college. Every hand shot up. I knew the statistics were that 40 percent would not graduate from high school, let alone go to college. I was devastated that they all had the dream of going to college in the third grade, but somewhere along the line, that dream would be taken away from many of them.

As I visited these classrooms, I was surprised that the third graders could tell me about every drug. They knew the name, what it looked like, and how it was taken. They told me about marijuana, cocaine, crack, and heroin. They also told me about meth, short for methamphetamine, a powerful, highly addictive drug that affects the central nervous system. I knew about meth but did not realize it was in New Bedford, and I was running the city. Later, I talked with Don Cook, and he said the police were just starting to see it.

At this point in my talk with the students, I would tell them that someone would likely approach them to take one of these drugs at some point in their lives. I would ask them what they should do.

"*Say no!*" they would immediately yell back.

"And then what would you do?"

"I'd tell someone," a student would offer.

"Right! Who would you tell?"

Several kids would answer.

"My teacher."

"A policeman."

"My mom."

I would agree.

"Right!" I would say. "You would tell someone you trust."

A girl in the back wearing a pretty pink dress tentatively raised her hand. She looked like a little angel.

Youth Council parade along Union Street, 1989

"What if it is your mother who is asking you to take the drugs?" she asked.

I felt as if I had been hit by a truck. I tried to catch my breath. I looked at the principal, who was looking at me with concern. I looked over at Don. Clearly, they were not as surprised at this question as I was. How I was still standing, I don't know.

"Oh, you poor sweet girl. You still must say 'No,' and it is very important that you tell someone like your teacher."

After the class broke up, the principal told me the school was aware of the situation. The girl's mother was a prostitute, and her father was long gone. I wondered what kind of chance this child had. The hours she spent in school were the safest time in her life, and every moment at home, after school, or on weekends, she was in danger. And this was only a few blocks from our house.

I met with classes about every week for two years during the school year. In the second year, we decided I should talk to second graders to reach kids a year younger. I also would occasionally talk to other classes.

I remember a sixth-grade class at Gomes School. The class had a subscription to the *New York Times*, which they read every day. I quizzed them on current events in Washington and was blown away by their knowledge of who the players were and what was happening in our nation's capital. I would have wagered that their knowledge of national politics exceeded that of almost any of our city council members.

These classroom visits gave me tremendous respect for our teachers who did this all day, every day. I saw firsthand the diversity of backgrounds of students who came together to be educated in our public school system. I witnessed the variety of our schools, from small schools built over 100 years ago to more modern, larger facilities, complete with gymnasiums and cafeterias. I discovered that "modern" doesn't necessarily mean "good." Students in some of the more recently built schools studied in rooms without windows that you could see out of because planners thought students should not be able to view outside lest their attention be diverted by the changing light—for example, if the sun got obscured by a cloud. Where there were windows, plastic had been used instead of glass, and it had clouded to the point of opaqueness.

Here is where I think I let these kids down. I listened to our superintendents tell me how our system did well compared to schools in our "urban cohort." Instead of probing, I went along with this argument that we should be measured against other schools that taught students from similar social and economic backgrounds. In this way, our poor performance tended to be measured against other poor performers rather than top school systems.

Even though in the classes I had taught, I had preached that we could compete with anyone in the world and that we should aspire to excellence, I accepted the idea that we should set a lower bar for ourselves. When I asked how many students wanted to go to college, every hand went up. Despite that, I accepted from our school leaders that it was okay that 40 percent of our students would not graduate high school on time, let alone attend college.

This was a serious sin of omission. I went along, and I didn't challenge this thinking. I didn't challenge the superintendents. I didn't challenge the teachers' union. I didn't challenge other members of the school committee. I just accepted mediocrity, and in so doing, I let a generation of students down.

It fell to a later mayor, Jon Mitchell, elected in 2012, to take on the establishment and bring in a dynamic agent of change in Superintendent Dr. Pia Durkin, who believed in educating every child. Mayor Mitchell, who was in high school when I was mayor, built a majority of support among the members of the school committee, so when Dr. Durkin started making change, Mayor Mitchell and that coalition could back her up.

Dr. Durkin recognized that principals are the most influential leaders in creating the culture in each school. When she started reassigning principals to get higher performance, many people started screaming. But these and other changes produced results. Attendance rates increased. Test scores went up, and graduation rates climbed. Importantly, the philosophy changed to one in which the school system was geared to help every child succeed, not just those from the advantaged families.

I wish I had the wisdom to see what was going on and force the issue the way Mayor Mitchell and Pia Durkin did. We could have brought about that change a whole lot earlier. Thomas Anderson followed Pia Durkin, and the reforms took hold. Recently, the four-year graduation rate at the high school was 88 percent.

Parks and Recreation

I think I did some things well in terms of the quality of life in the city. I had been elected because of my work in the waterfront historic district and in saving the Zeiterion Theatre, so I knew that design excellence meant something to people beyond just the districts where we had worked. Everyone took pride in those accomplishments, and we wanted to build on that.

Tony Souza ran the Office of Neighborhoods and Historic Preservation, which was funded with Community Development Block Grants. He had an able staff of young people, including Rick Bennett and Peter Jacobsen. They fanned out into the neighborhoods encouraging people and small business owners to fix up their properties. They showed people historical photos and coaxed them through the process of financing, grant writing, dealing with contractors, and doing their own work.

They showed time and time again that revitalization is as contagious as blight. One restored house on a city block leads to another and leads to yet another until a neighborhood is transformed. Tony's office successfully got National Register listings for more than 1,000 buildings in New Bedford.

We also took steps that eventually led to the waterfront historic district and surrounding area being designated as a national park. The effort actually started with failure. Initially, we tried to join the state's Heritage Park system, which included parks such as Battleship Cove in Fall River. When we struck out there, I asked a group led by Jean Bennett and Robert Alves to plan a strategy to become a national park. Jean had been one of the founders of the Friends of Buttonwood Park and was a longtime activist for downtown and the waterfront historic district. Robert had been the business agent for the International Longshoremen's Association, a Cape Verdean-led union with historic ties to the waterfront. In June 1990, Senators Edward Kennedy and John Kerry wrote the Senate Appropriations Committee, suggesting New Bedford become a national park.

At the time, I described our vision as "a park without boundaries." Its purpose was to "connect people of New Bedford with the sea—to try to form a connection from downtown through the historic district, across the highway, to the harbor's edge, to the harbor islands, down to Fort Rodman, and with the schooner *Ernestina*, out into the Atlantic."

The proposal took many twists and turns, but in 1996, well after I left office, the New Bedford Whaling National Historic Park was finally established. During my administration, we also made strides in renovating and creating public spaces for residents to enjoy. Dana Souza, no relation to Tony, was head of our Parks Department. He was as caring and innovative a person as one could find. When Hurricane Hugo hit Charleston, Dana drove down with a crew. There he learned how toppled trees with intact roots could be saved by tipping them back up and securing them with guy wires. With proper care and watering, Charleston was able to rescue more than half its fallen trees. This lesson came in useful when we were hit in 1991 by Hurricane Bob, which took down many of our big trees in Buttonwood and Hazelwood Parks. Dana increased the maintenance in all the parks and helped other departments. He reached out to the Cemetery Department and then to Larry Worden in Public Works.

"Larry, if Al Santos in the Cemetery Department and I retrofit our pickup trucks with snowplows, we could help you out on smaller streets after we finish clearing our own roads come wintertime," Dana said.

Larry thought that was a great idea. He even put snowplows on garbage trucks. This meant more plows out during a snowstorm, resulting in much quicker street clearing. Dana set an example for department heads to consider themselves part of a team working for the good of the city, not just their own fiefdoms. He was great for morale and was always looking for ways to do things better. And he was a beast on the court during our pick-up basketball games.

Governor Dukakis created a $15 million Olmsted Park grant program for old parks that could be connected to the famous landscape architect Frederick Law Olmsted, who had designed Central Park in New York and the Emerald Necklace string of parks in Boston. Many Olmsted parks had not been identified as such, and that was a requirement for the grants. Working with the newly created Friends of Buttonwood Park, Dana discovered a drawing showing that Buttonwood Park had been designed by Charles Eliot of the firm Olmsted, Olmsted & Eliot. We qualified for a $1.5-million-dollar grant to restore the park to its natural state as envisioned when passive recreation was the goal. We relocated some facilities out of the park's center to emphasize the pastoral nature of parks that, in Olmsted's words, acted as "the lungs of the city."

Great public parks like Buttonwood are examples of democracy at its best, just as great theaters like the Zeiterion are. They offer superior public spaces that everyone has a right to enjoy. While you are there, it doesn't matter the quality of the house you will return to or the troubles that keep you up at night. You can enjoy the best the region has to offer.

While Olmsted advocated for passive rather than active recreation, I noticed in Eliot's plan that he had included a few tennis courts. I mentioned this to Dana, who knew I was an avid tennis player. He also knew that the tennis courts at Buttonwood were in horrible condition. After consulting with Jean Bennett, Frank Farrell, Richard Leary, and other Friends of Buttonwood Park members, we decided the courts should be rehabilitated as part of the project.

A day at Buttonwood Park, 1980s

At the time, Alex Pavao was leading the Whaling City Tennis Association, which had over 1,100 members. Tennis was big time in New Bedford—the association ran several tournaments a year. It also sponsored a junior excellence program, and, as bad as the courts were, they were used all the time by players of all ages and abilities. When the courts were fixed up, Tim Dyer, the vice president for marketing at Compass Bank (formerly the New Bedford Five Cents Savings Bank) and an excellent tennis player, came to me with an idea to sponsor a tennis tournament. The Compass Classic was born with hundreds of players and coverage over local cable.

As a sidelight, I played some friendly matches with Tim's brother-in-law, television and radio personality Geraldo Rivera, who had a summer home in Marion. When I ran for mayor in 1985, Geraldo had given me $200 for my campaign. He was working for Roone Arledge in ABC's news division at the time, but they did not get along. When Arledge found out about Geraldo's donation, he fired Geraldo, saying that as a newsman, he shouldn't donate to a political candidate. Every time I saw Geraldo after that, I joked that I set him on his path to fame and fortune. In 1987, he started his popular and long-running talk show "Geraldo."

While I am proud of what Dana, the Friends of Buttonwood Park, and so many others accomplished, I failed to see the potential for the Buttonwood Park Zoo. The zoo had well-known elephants, Emily and Ruth, but its exhibits lacked coherence and were not maintained to a high standard. After I left office, others saw the opportunity to remake the zoo into a facility that now attracts more people than any other institution in the city and whose exhibits educate about where we humans fit into the natural ecosystem.

Downtown Ups and Downs: Economic Development

During my days as mayor, Tim brought me another great idea. When he came bouncing into my office one day, I could tell he was not going to be able to contain his enthusiasm. Tim has so much energy that when I say he *bounced* into my office, that is only a mild overstatement.

"I've got a great idea, John."

"I'm sure you do, Tim. What is it this time?"

"You know First Night in Boston?"

"I do."

"We should do it here in New Bedford. Grucci Brothers fireworks. Ice sculptures. New Bedford High Marching Band. Sing-alongs. Zeiterion puts something on. Restaurants open late. Family entertainment. Crowds downtown. Toe Jam Puppet Band. Funky White Honkies. You get the picture!"

I did. Outwardly, I was smiling and looking enthused. Inwardly, I was thinking about losing my family vacation.

I had been looking forward to going to Florida with the kids to our Captiva timeshare. We bought it at a fundraiser years ago for the week between Christmas and New Year's, thinking this would be a safe bet for schedules. "Nothing ever happens between Christmas and New Year's," we had told ourselves. Now, here was Tim ruining my annual retreat. We absolutely loved Captiva. The beach looks out on the Gulf of Mexico, and the sunsets are spectacular. The birdlife is magnificent, from eagles to ospreys to skimmers, herons, egrets, and sandpipers. *Oh well, maybe not this year.*

"Tim, this is an awesome idea. Let's get started right away planning it and lining up sponsors," I said.

Tim, as usual, was right. First Night was a blast. I attended the first one and everyone during my years as mayor. It was a great way to start off the year and celebrate the arts, which were so important to the city's resurgence. Laurie and the kids still enjoyed the full week at Captiva, and I got there for part of the time, but I wasn't going to miss First Night.

I think I missed the boat, however, on the downtown district. I focused a lot of attention on the ground floor retail and worked hard with the small business community. One of our first projects was tearing up the Purchase Street Mall and getting traffic moving again. We arranged storefront improvement grants, sidewalk improvements, and farmers' markets. I thought if we could get the retail sector going on the ground floors, then residential uses would follow on the upper floors.

I'm afraid I got it backward. If we had focused more attention on bringing housing downtown, we could have created a stronger 24-hour district. We did have some success with projects like Regency Towers, but we could have done more.

Developer Pat Carney did a lot for New Bedford at this time. He invested in buildings downtown, and instead of playing to the lowest common denominator by offering B-Class office space, he restored the buildings perfectly. He took advantage of historic tax credits and rented the space at A-Class rates. No one thought the market could support such rates, but Pat proved that if you aim high, you can hit the target. Pat's work was great for New Bedford and for his company, Claremont.

Before I came into office, only a few architectural firms had offices in the city. Max Ferro had come down from Boston, where he had been one of the resident experts at the Society for the Preservation of New England Antiquities. While Max's credentials were unsurpassed in the field, from architectural history to preservation technology, the thing I liked most about him was that he was a consummate showman. He proved that you didn't have to be a stuffed shirt to know your stuff. He consulted on many buildings, wrote a book about preservation in New Bedford, fell in love with the city, and moved here.

Other firms followed because of the dynamic energy in the city. Architectural firm Dyer Brown & Associates came down from Boston and set up shop above Hayes Hardware store

First Night proved a great success.

on William Street and Acushnet Avenue. They got a contract to work with the New Bedford Housing Authority and, over time, transformed our public housing stock into some of the finest housing in the city.

I moved our Economic Development Office into City Hall so the director would be near me and have easy access to the department heads issuing permits for businesses. In that way, we could bring into reality the concept of "one-stop shopping" for business attraction and expansion.

I also started a business roundtable with about 15 industrial leaders that met about once every four to five months to discuss areas where they might find cost savings. I asked Glen Johnson, the retired head of Goodyear Tire & Rubber, to chair the group. The idea was that they would focus on a city service such as water or solid waste. They would bring their concerns, and we would explain how we priced services and offer our thoughts for savings and investments. We invited a few city councilors to the meetings to comply with the Open Meeting Law and left plenty of time for questions and suggestions about how we could do a better job. The business leaders appreciated our transparency and made some recommendations that led to significant savings. Our meetings created much greater acceptance overall about what went into their sewer and water bills. We worked with them to reduce costs, and we had some successes.

Still, I was a skeptic about the adage that the private sector was a paragon of efficiency. Goodyear, for example, used a million gallons of pure, fresh water each year to cool their boilers, and then they drained this pure, fresh water into our wastewater plant to treat! They did this because the cost of buying the water and the cost of treatment were so incredibly low—to them! We worked out an arrangement to lend them money to build a recirculating system that cut their water use by 90 percent, financing the project with future savings in their water and sewer bills. It was a win-win and done cooperatively. The problem only existed because our billing system made it possible to benefit by wasting fresh water because we charged so little for it.

An example of a savings success that wasn't so cooperative involved Frionor, a large Norwegian fish processor. Frionor made breaded fish sticks, battered fish, and other value-added fish products for institutional and commercial markets. The process involved frying, and the fat would go down the drain into our wastewater treatment system. As a result, our workers had to cover themselves in protective gear, climb down the maintenance holes, and remove all the grease from the city's pipes. We instituted a new charge in our sewer fee that set a lower rate for gray water and a higher rate for "suspended solids."

Making breaded fish sticks at Frionor, 1980s

I could almost hear the reaction from Oslo when the $2 million bill hit their desk! In a heartbeat, Frionor's local accountant Ray Eisenberg was in the office of Ron LaBelle, DPW head. Ron's guys were the ones cleaning out the grease, so Ray didn't get much sympathy. Before long, these smart Norwegians figured out an engineering solution that removed the grease before it entered our system. If we hadn't made pollution cost them money, they wouldn't have changed their behavior. You have to make polluters pay.

Constant Vigilance

I am very proud of the team we assembled during our administration. It was characterized by diversity of background, integrity, teamwork, high energy, loyalty to the city, support, creativity, and passion. We reached for the highest performance, but sometimes we fell short. When we did, we tried to learn from our faults.

Marty Manley was an excellent leader of the Harbor Development Commission. Marty knew his way around the waterfront and was respected by all the players there, even though they are a tough bunch. He knew how to resolve conflict and how to get along with city councilors and folks in the State House. But one day, he used a racial epithet when talking with a union official. That was unacceptable behavior, so I formally reprimanded him.

Since its earliest days, New Bedford as a community has struggled with and fought racism and other forms of discrimination. We welcomed Paul Cuffe, Frederick Douglass, and Lewis Temple. We honored Sergeant William Carney, the first African American to win the Medal of Honor, who lived in the city for many years. But no one should ever think that racism or other forms of bigotry have been defeated in any place or in anyone. It can sit just beneath the surface, waiting for an opportunity to rise up, like pus out of a boil. As with any infection, it needs constant vigilance to ensure it doesn't spread.

I gathered our department heads together for a diversity training day at the Buttonwood Library. Angela Natho, who headed our Office of Human Relations, brought in Dr. Wilbert "Skeeter" McClure from Harvard University to work with us. Besides having two doctorates and teaching at Harvard, Skeeter had won a gold medal in boxing at the 1959 Pan Am Games and an Olympic gold medal in Rome in 1960. His teammate and fellow gold medal Olympian, Cassius Clay, would become known as "The Greatest" Muhammad Ali. Ali remained friends with Skeeter throughout his life. Dr. McClure's background had everyone's attention for the day! It was important for all of us to spend the day discussing our biases. We should have done more of it.

At lunchtime, Angela arranged for Skeeter to give me one-on-one leadership coaching at the Orchid Diner.

"Mr. Mayor, Angela tells me you have a hard time going up to people at a diner like this and introducing yourself," Skeeter said.

John "Buddy" Andrade (pointing) has been teaching us about environmental justice for 40 years.

"I do, Skeeter," I admitted. "I don't want to interrupt their lunch. I think it's rude to just barge into the conversation they are having and stick my hand in their face."

He set me straight.

"This is what I learned from Ali, John," Skeeter said. "You are the mayor. When you go up and say, 'Hello,' you are giving them a gift that they will appreciate. You represent the city, and they know you are here, and if you don't stop by and say 'Hello,' they will be hurt and feel disconnected from you and their city. You aren't being rude by going up to them. You are showing love."

This was an important lesson. I wish I had had that lunch before my first campaign instead of toward the end of my administration. As I said, people sometimes saw me as distant. I managed to overcome some of my reserve in three elections, but the criticism stuck to me.

A Mussel Adheres Itself to a Rock: Links to Higher Education and Scientific Research

In October 1990, UMass Dartmouth Chancellor John Brazil designated Fort Rodman as the site for the new Coastal Zone Resource Laboratory. We had competed with Fall River and Bourne to host this facility and won the competition because of our commitment to the sewer plant. This lab evolved into CMAST, the Center for Marine Science and Technology, and later SMAST, the School for Marine Science and Technology. It was the first step into the city that the university had taken since moving to Dartmouth in the 1960s.

Reflecting on my time in office, bringing SMAST to New Bedford may be one of my most significant accomplishments. It connects New Bedford to the university and its people to higher education. As I have mentioned, the biggest vulnerability the city has is its level of educational attainment. Roughly 10 percent of city residents have college degrees compared to about 25 percent nationwide and 33 percent in Massachusetts.

Perhaps that worked for some when factories lined our neighborhoods, and one might manage to achieve the American dream by leaving school early, working one or two union jobs, saving money, investing in real estate, and moving to the suburbs. It was never an easy road. But that formula has even less chance of working when there aren't union jobs, and a high school diploma gets you fast-food wages in an industry whose business model is to keep turnover high to keep pay low. While a few of our students will go to colleges in Boston or beyond, the best answer to moving the needle on how many of our people have college degrees and a shot at better-paying jobs is UMass Dartmouth.

Getting the university to locate a facility in New Bedford made higher education more visible and more accessible. Robert Alves, who worked in my administration and graduated from UMass Dartmouth back when it was SMU (Southeastern Massachusetts University), started a "Sport-O-Rama" summer program that also made connections. Kids from the projects were bused to the Dartmouth campus for a couple of weeks in the summer for athletic games.

At the end of the program, six students were awarded four-year full scholarships. While that was incredibly important to the recipients, the program impacted every child who participated. They knew in their heads that they wanted to go to college, but "college" was some kind of abstract concept to them. For all they knew, college might have been on the Moon. It was inaccessible. But by participating in "Sport-O-Rama," they saw the buildings; they went to the gym; they learned that college was just a bus ride away. They could get there. And now they had a fixed image of these dramatic Paul Rudolph buildings to keep in their heads as they thought about college.

Siting SMAST in New Bedford had a snowball effect on achievement in the region. As competitive as New Bedford and Fall River are, Fall River had to get something as soon as we got SMAST. The Advanced Technology and Manufacturing Center was built there. When that happened, well, we had to get something. Thanks to state Senator Mark Montigny, we got the university to move its consolidated arts programs into the vacant Star Store Building in downtown New Bedford, right next to the Zeiterion Theatre. This brought hundreds of art students and 24-hour usage into the downtown. UMass Dartmouth's arts program had absorbed the Swain School of Design, which had earlier absorbed Boston University's Program in Artisanry. The powerhouse of arts assembled under Swain's late President Bruce Yenawine was now being guided by UMass Dartmouth Dean John Laughton of the College of Visual and Performing Arts. Artists have led the resurgence of New Bedford for decades, and the side-by-side development of the Star Store and the Zeiterion provided a powerful engine that stoked many other enterprises.

SMAST has also given New Bedford a competitive advantage by continuing to connect us to the potential offered by the ocean. The sea can provide more than the harvest of fish and mammals. Eleven miles to the east (as the seagull flies) is Woods Hole, one of the world's largest aggregations of marine scientists. They study the two-thirds of the blue planet that is wet, all of which supports life, and SMAST connects us to that. Also, just as whaling made New Bedford a city of great wealth and diversity, and fishing maintained that connection to the sea, the prospect of offshore wind promises another chapter, continuing the energy business that began with whaling.

It is a truism that we know more about the Moon's surface than the seafloor. We learned how to go down to the sea for fish about 10,000 years ago, and other than shipping goods, we haven't really figured out how else the oceans may benefit humanity.

A mussel adheres itself to a rock with an adhesive that is incredibly strong, water-resistant, flexible, and biodegradable. Could we learn something valuable from that for internal surgery? A sea star can re-grow a limb that has been severed. This is a "lower" life form, but we can't do that. How might we harness the immense energy of ocean currents or thermoclines or waves? Are there pharmaceuticals that could help cure Ebola or cancer? Can seawater replace scarce freshwater and turn parched deserts into arable fields? Are there rare minerals that could be economically harvested? Could algae be grown as a source of carbon sequestration or fuel? These questions and many more can be studied and answered if people choose to look down at the ocean depths as well as up toward the stars. And as people make discoveries, manufacturing opportunities will follow.

I feel SMAST could be a link between UMass Dartmouth and the incredible, unmatched intellectual infrastructure in Woods Hole. In providing this link, New Bedford may be able to take advantage of the ocean in many more ways than fishing. And I think this will be important for our future.

School for Marine Science and Technology (SMAST) at Clarks Point in New Bedford.

CHAPTER 5

Meeting of the Minds and the Mayors

Mayor as Ambassador

When I chose to be active in Boston, Washington, and other cities, my work raised the visibility of New Bedford and awareness of the problems we faced. Still, it also served to further the distance between me and a city that, though once a global leader in innovation and ideas, had in many ways grown very parochial.

I felt the work I did as an ambassador was well spent. I went to Boston often for the Massachusetts Municipal Association and the Massachusetts Mayors Association. I also served on the state Joint Labor Management Committee for Police and Fire under Professor John Dunlop of Harvard. While there were many good reasons for devoting time to these endeavors, a few stand out above the rest.

First, we needed to be on the minds of state officials, especially during budget time. Roughly 60 percent of New Bedford's budget came from local aid in the state budget. I needed to know my way around the governor's office, his administration, and the legislature because we were highly dependent on them.

Second, if we were going to be successful in funding a secondary wastewater treatment plant in an amount that would keep it affordable, we would need help creating a funding mechanism where none had existed before.

Third, the Dunlop Commission was the final stop in resolving labor disputes in police and fire contracts. Public safety is an area where, for obvious reasons, you cannot afford work stoppages. Investment in this labor-relations tool was critical, and to learn from a former secretary of Labor was an opportunity not to be missed.

As president of the Massachusetts Mayors Association, I campaigned around the state with Jim Braude, then the leader of the Tax Equity Alliance formed to oppose Barbara Anderson's Citizens for Limited Taxation (CLT). The group had successfully passed Proposition 2½, which limited property taxes to 2½ percent of total valuation with increases of no more than 2½ percent each year. This puts a real constraint on the local government's ability to raise funds to provide services. Barbara then pushed for ballot measures to reduce income tax surcharges and other ways for local government to raise money.

Nothing stops the electorate from demanding both lower taxes and more services. I felt it was necessary to invest time at various events that helped pay for the services we provided at the local level. Local government is generally more trusted than other levels of government, but you still have to educate people. I wanted citizens to know what their police officers did, what their firefighters and DPW workers did, how the libraries functioned, what happened at senior centers, how the parks were maintained, and so on.

It is not lost on governors and state budget makers that they can help bring a state budget into balance by cutting local aid. When the mayors and selectpeople are forced to close a fire station or lay off teachers, the public will be angry at the local officials making the cuts and not at the state officials who cut their budgets.

I also participated in the National League of Cities and was very involved with the US Conference of Mayors. For the League of Cities, I chaired the Committee on Water. I testified before Congress on the need to fund communities trying to eliminate combined sewer overflows, which were built as part of collection systems to carry both sewage and stormwater in the same pipes. The overflow sewers act like a relief valve during rainstorms, allowing stormwater and raw sewage to discharge into waterways. This design prevents backups into homes and businesses, but it is a major pollution source and needs to be addressed.

Mayor David Dinkins of New York City

New Bedford had over 60 overflow pipes. Although they were out of sight, they carried millions of gallons of untreated sewage into the harbor and Clarks Cove during heavy rains. This was happening all over the country. The national bill for this was immense, and, unlike celebrations for schools or aircraft carriers, you couldn't cut a ribbon to dramatize a sewer pipe. It was a difficult sales pitch, to say the least.

For the Conference of Mayors, I chaired the Urban Economic Policy Committee, which Lance Simmens staffed. We brought in influential congressional leaders like House Budget Committee Chairman Leon Panetta to give the mayors insight into priorities on the Hill. We brought in well-known economists to help us shape our political positions, and we had government officials talk to us about programs that affected cities.

When we testified in Congress, we were primarily pushing for a "peace dividend," given that the Cold War was coming to an end. We argued that there was a reason to spend significantly less on guns and more on infrastructure at home.

I found going to meetings of the Conference of Mayors stimulating. Only other mayors understood the demands of the job. They were great sources of support, practical advice, and inspiration. Mayors are creative people. Every meeting was a showcase for ideas being tried out in other cities, free for the taking if your city might benefit. Meeting with other mayors was an easy way to stay abreast of the best thinking in everything from community policing to waste management. The conferences were cooperative and not marred by partisanship. While the membership is made up of Republican and Democratic mayors, I always found it challenging to tell which was which just by listening to what they said.

These gatherings were also a good place to make friends with no agenda concerning my city. When I first met David Dinkins, the mayor of New York City, he shouted to me from an escalator, "John Bullard, you're the tennis player. I want to meet you." We teamed up to play other mayors during our spare time, and we never lost! I assisted him with an issue that came up in my committee about economic incentives for Puerto Rico. When I was hoping to work in the Clinton administration, he put in a call to Commerce Secretary Ron Brown on my behalf.

One of the last times I saw Dave was when the plane carrying the bodies of Secretary Brown and my other colleagues from the Commerce Department landed at Dover Air Force Base after they lost their lives on a mission to Croatia. Dave and I sat next to each other to mourn our friend.

The Color of Mortar: Designing Mayors

In 1987, I was invited to attend the second annual Mayor's Institute of City Design at the University of Virginia. I jumped at the chance. The institute was founded in 1986 by Charleston Mayor Joe Riley, who served 40 years and is a professional hero of mine. I count Joe as one of the world's best mayors of the last century, along with Jerusalem Mayor Teddy Kollek.

Joe established the program with help from Jacque Robertson, a dean at the University of Virginia School of Architecture; Adele Chatfield-Taylor, director of design at the National Endowment of the Arts; and Bob Campbell, architecture critic for The *Boston Globe*. The institute's mission was to educate mayors and build their confidence so they could play a more influential role in the design of their cities.

The format was intimate and intense. Ten mayors and ten world-class design professionals met on campus for three days without staff. Each mayor brought a design problem they were wrestling with and presented it to the group. I brought the problem of reconnecting the down town and historic district to the waterfront across the barrier of Route 18. The location of

Mayor Joe Riley of Charleston, SC

the meeting was important. The University of Virginia, designed by Thomas Jefferson when he was 78 years old, is considered by some to be among the top ten works of architecture in the country.

Mayors don't tend to be bashful people. They don't hesitate to weigh in on subjects, even if they know little about the topic at hand. But a curious phenomenon occurs when mayors confront architecture and urban design. They retreat. Too many of these city leaders let developers and architects walk all over them—even though they have a lot of power to influence outcomes. In today's world of complicated finance, it is nearly impossible to build anything without the mayor's support.

Mayor Riley recognized that mayors weren't leveraging their power to shape and design their cities. And, unlike some areas where they might be lacking in expertise, mayors have an innate understanding of the potential of their cities in a way developers may not. With mayors not weighing in, a lot of terrible design was happening, and cities were suffering as a result. Bad developments and urban plans would last for many years. At the time, only two mayors in the country had architectural backgrounds—Harvey Gantt of Charlotte and me. Joe wanted to give more mayors the tools to better stand up for their communities.

I first met Joe Riley at a Conference of Mayors meeting in Charleston. I was excited to visit Charleston in part because of my high school project about the Stone Fleet. When I got to Joe's office, I gave him a map of where about 25 New Bedford ships lay in the mud in his harbor, part of the failed blockade during the Civil War. I joked that he had more of our maritime heritage than we did. I also told him that there was probably not much left but the stones given the warm water, worms, and wood. He hadn't known about the Stone Fleet and kept the map for display. We became good friends, and he helped me rise through the conference ranks to become chair of the Urban Economic Policy Committee, in charge of our positions on major economic issues.

I remember a few things from the institute. One was the campus itself. It is impossible not to be overwhelmed by Jefferson's skill and intellect. He designed something beautiful and profound, organizing a system of education in a village atmosphere of collegiality while simultaneously anchoring people to the classical origins of Greece and the future opportunities of the American West. He also found the time to write a Declaration of Independence, serve as a diplomat and president, advance agricultural innovations, and more. The mind boggles. If a mayor responded to the institute invitation by saying they were too busy to take time to talk about design, a good rejoinder might be, "Are you busier than Thomas Jefferson? Do you have more on your plate than he did?" Spending a few days on his campus lets Jefferson's genius sink in, and that alone is worth the visit.

Another highlight was Bob Campbell's two rules for cities.

"The first rule is the faster you make it possible for people to drive, the longer it will take them to get to work. See Los Angeles as an example for Rule #1," he told us. The more highways you build, the more you encourage people to use cars and the more time they will spend in cars.

"Rule #2 is the harder you make it for people to build in your city, the more they will want to do so," he said. "Now, this takes some explaining. Most developers already own property in your city, so a tight zoning ordinance, for example, makes their existing property more valuable. They are going to like you for that. If you force them to build something really good with consistent written rules, they may not like that, but what you are assuring them is that the developer who comes in after them is not going to devalue their property by building something terrible right next to them. They will appreciate that."

Cities like Boston or San Francisco, where regulations are strict, and the real estate market is extremely hot, seem to confirm Bob's theory. It might be harder to verify in softer markets like New Bedford. But his point was valid and worth hearing.

Also memorable was Mayor Riley delivering what became his famous talk on how he led the creation of a public waterfront revitalization in Charleston. He offered us many detailed anecdotes. One involved persuading a bank to sacrifice parking spaces for landscaping. This included saving a large tree right where the bank president wanted to park his car. Not satisfied that the agreement would survive after he left office, Joe had the Charleston City Council declare the tree a memorial to fallen soldiers so it would be protected in perpetuity!

The message from Joe's talk was that he, trained as a lawyer and as busy as any other mayor, paid attention to the details of what was going on in his city as far as design was concerned. As a result, when you visit, you can see the attention to detail in everything from the city's architectural planning to beautiful landscaping.

A few years later, after I attended the institute, Laurie and I went to a "New Urbanism" conference in Toronto. I got to talking with the developer building the Omni Hotel in Charleston. He didn't know I knew Joe.

"John, you wouldn't believe it," he said. "I'm in an argument with the mayor of Charleston over the color of mortar between the bricks of the hotel I'm building in the downtown of his city. The color of mortar! Can you believe it? And do you know what? He's going to win!"

Joe did. And the city did. If you go to Charleston, you will notice that the mortar at the Omni Belmond is a subtle pink that complements the purple bricks far better than the standard light gray of Portland cement.

Paying attention to details such as that, no matter how busy you are, whether you are Mayor Joe Riley of Charleston or President Thomas Jefferson of Virginia, determines whether you leave a legacy of excellence for future generations. That was a point I tried to make when Massachusetts Governor Michael Dukakis invited me to address his cabinet secretaries and division heads on the design of public structures. He had assembled officials who dealt with the built environment. We met in central Massachusetts. There were people in charge of highways, prisons, schools, universities, parks, health centers, courthouses, environmental facilities, and others, all gathered in one room for a day. Dukakis asked me to do a one-hour talk.

During my presentation, I put up a picture of the Hastings Keith Federal Building in downtown New Bedford. I didn't want to critique a state-owned building in front of state officials,

Hastings Keith Federal Building, downtown New Bedford

but a federal building seemed fair game. I discussed the many ways this structure did **not** fit in with its surroundings. It had the wrong orientation to the street. The wrong setback. The wrong building material. The wrong height. The wrong window shapes. The wrong roof design. The wrong color. The wrong art in front. It intimidated people instead of welcoming them. I went on and on about how incongruous this building was and how insulting it was to the people and character of our city. I said the developers should have spent a portion of their 1 percent for the art budget to have artists Christo and Jeanne-Claude wrap the building so we wouldn't have to look at it.

After a half-hour on the topic, I moved on to general design principles but left the slide up. Five minutes later, someone raised their hand.

"John, you're not talking about the federal building anymore?"

"Correct."

"Could you take the slide down?"

"No, I'm going to leave it up because when someone builds something this bad, we have to look at it for 100 years. So, you are going to look at it for an hour."

I have done several talks on design over the years. Another that stands out is when Joe Riley called me in September 1989 after Hurricane Hugo hit and asked me to deliver his keynote address to begin a meeting for him. I readily agreed and prepared a talk on how we had revitalized the waterfront historic district in New Bedford.

"I stand before you with great trepidation," I addressed the crowd. "I am going to attempt to give you a talk on the role of mayors in design, standing in for Joe Riley, the greatest mayor ever to think or talk on the subject. I am going to talk to you about design standing here in Jefferson's Rotunda on the University of Virginia campus, one of the greatest designs in the history of architecture. If I am not struck by lightning right now for the audacity of trying to do this, I will consider myself very lucky."

Somehow, I made it through the lecture and the rest of the meeting.

Mayor's Job Description: Liberating Art and Riding Garbage Trucks

I also learned a lot from Mayor Kollek of Jerusalem. He taught me about stretching the boundaries of a mayor's job description. In 1990, I was part of a group of 30 mayors from around the world to travel to Jerusalem for 10 days. My trip was generously funded by one of our local synagogues, Tifereth Israel, along with the American Jewish Congress. It was organized on the American side by the US Conference of Mayors.

We gathered in the Knesset, and Mayor Kollek welcomed us. He was 75 and had been mayor for 25 years. He spoke to us for about an hour about the history of the Jewish state and the City of Jerusalem, which is simultaneously the center of Judaism and Christianity and the third holiest site in the Islamic world after Mecca and Medina. His wisdom and passion were immediately evident. He turned the podium over to the mayor of Enschede in the Netherlands, who spoke on behalf of all of us. The Dutch mayor wasn't five minutes into his remarks when Teddy fell fast asleep right next to him. *This is what you can do when you are 75 years old and you have been mayor for 25 years!*

During the mayor of Enschede's remarks, he mentioned that the Nazis had occupied his city during World War II. He said the Allied troops that liberated his community were led by Chaim Herzog, who was now sitting a few seats over and was the acting president of Israel. What a small world, and what a message that freedom was never taken for granted by the people in this room.

President Herzog added levity to this solemn occasion by exclaiming, "We thought we were liberating a different town. We came into your city by mistake!"

Later, I had the chance to meet Shimon Peres, who had just lost a very close vote for prime minister to the leader of Likud, Yitzhak Shamir. I presented Mr. Peres with one of the commemorative plates etched with our city seal that New Bedford had commissioned to give as gifts.

"I wish this plate were the 41 votes you needed," I told him.

While I was there, Tim Phelps, a foreign correspondent for *Newsday*, called me. We had gone to high school at St. George's together. He was also in Jerusalem and had heard I was there.

"John, you know you're just getting Jewish propaganda on this trip."

Mayor Teddy Kollek of Jerusalem

"I do, Tim. What are you going to do about it?"

"Well, if you give me an evening, I'll take you to the Palestinian parts of town."

Tim and I went off one evening so he could balance what I was learning about Jerusalem and Israel. I already knew that the city was a flashpoint for history, politics, and religion. Being surrounded by machine-gun-toting soldiers in many places during our visit underscored that. Tim's accounts were informative and helpful.

"Tim, what do the Palestinians think of Mayor Kollek?"

"They love him."

"They love him! Do they know he's Jewish?" I deadpanned.

"Oh, yeah. But he provides housing. Keeps the streets safe. There's public transportation. The schools are good."

There, in a nutshell, is the value of mayors and local government. Mayors deal with the problems people really care about. They can't afford to be ideologues. The famous Republican New York City Mayor Fiorello La Guardia once said, "There isn't a Republican nor a Democratic way to pick up garbage."

What Teddy taught me about the mayor's role was that, yes, this 75-year-old man did nap through part of our opening ceremony, but he also got up before dawn on many days to ride garbage trucks around the city, making sure the streets were clean.

During our visit, Kollek went entirely missing for about four days. When he returned, it was with paintings the Germans had stolen during World War II. He had smuggled guns during that war, and now he had "liberated" these paintings and brought them back to the Israel Museum collections. I had never considered smuggling art to be part of my job description, but mayors like Teddy Kollek and Joe Riley show you that it is grand vision, great daring, persistence over time, and attention to detail that make a city great.

Cracks in the Cold War

On January 6, 1991, I joined Mayor David Dinkins of New York, Sharpe James of Newark, Ted Mann of Newton, and Juanita Crabb of Binghamton at a meeting at the United Nations. We met with four Soviet mayors and one Soviet governor. They came from Baku, Kazan, Kuybyshev (now Samara), Murmansk, Ust-Kamenogorsk, and Semipalatinsk. At the beginning, Carl Sagan from Cornell University addressed our small group, which had gathered to discuss changing priorities with the ending of the Cold War and the banning of nuclear testing.

As I listened to our Soviet counterparts, I heard them criticize their federal government for spending too much money on missiles and national defense. I heard them advocate for more federal spending on local schools, housing, and roads. And it dawned on me. Not only can I not tell apart a Democratic mayor from a Republican mayor, but I cannot tell apart a socialist mayor from a capitalist mayor! We all just want to fix our cities for our people, so they are safe, with good housing, good jobs, and good schools. Maybe mayors should be in charge!

I had another opportunity to learn about the differences and similarities between our country and the Soviet Union before I left office. In 1991, Mikhail Gorbachev was president of the Soviet Union and was liberalizing its policies through *glasnost* (openness) and *perestroika* (decentralization). He invited a small delegation from the United States to visit and educate his government on our federalist system. Three mayors spoke about local government: Colorado Springs Mayor Bob Isaac, who was also the president of the Conference of Mayors, Newton Mayor Teddy Mann, and me. US Senators Paul Wellstone of Minnesota and Slade Gorton of Washington represented the federal legislative branch. Supreme Court Justice Antonin Scalia came from the federal judicial branch. Missouri Governor

John Ashcroft represented state government. We also had about a dozen academics. Lance Simmens assisted us from the Conference of Mayors, and we had a student from Holy Cross College, Heather Parrish, who spoke Russian.

We arrived on December 26, 1991, to find that Russia had lowered the Soviet flag. President Gorbachev had resigned the day before. The Soviet Union had dissolved. We didn't even know what to call the country we were in. We met in a two-city-block academic center in Moscow called the Foundation for Political and Social Research. It had meeting rooms, dormitories, hotel-style bedrooms, and cafeterias. A few years before, it had been called the Institute of the Communist Party and had been used to train missionaries from places like Cuba, China, South America, and Angola in ways to promote communism. Now it was being used to understand and spread the ways of democracy—with many of the same teachers!

It was an exciting time. As we interacted with the Russians, we realized how much we had in common and the potential if they were successful on the road they were exploring. Around the city, statues of past dictators were toppled and smashed.

A few of us met with Moscow Deputy Mayor Sergey Stankevich, one of a young band of reformers working with Gorbachev and later with Boris Yeltsin. Speaking to us in English, he admonished us to keep our expectations reasonable.

"You think we should achieve a democratic state in a year or two when it took your own country from 1776 to 1788, and you had 13 states with a common language, a common heritage, and no history of trying to invade each other," he said. "We don't have any of those advantages."

I wondered to myself how many of our elected leaders spoke Russian or knew Russian history as well as this young leader knew our language and history.

As we shopped in their town square, called the Arbat, or relaxed in a hard currency bar during the evening, we could see that Russians knew how the free market worked. I also learned that despite a Grand Canyon of differences in political views, it was fun to go drinking with Antonin Scalia. I would never say the same about John Ashcroft.

When the working session was over, we had an unscheduled day. Lance Simmens always had a plan, and this day was no different. He knew of a shipment of food being airlifted from one of our bases in Germany to St. Petersburg for an orphanage. He suggested we participate. Lance, Teddy Mann, Heather Parrish, and I got on the midnight train from Moscow to St. Petersburg.

When we arrived, the contrast in cities could not have been greater. Moscow struck me as dark and dreary. Moscow in December struck me as dark and dreary. The architecture and the dirt on the buildings left me feeling that the whole city, except for Red Square, should be steam cleaned. On the other hand, St. Petersburg seemed light and airy, even though it was farther north. Although life under the czars could not have been easy, the architecture connoted joy. This was the city that had resisted Adolf Hitler's Nazi forces for 900 days. I asked our hosts why, given how much the people seemed to hate the czars, so much money was being spent restoring the czarist castles and monuments harmed by the Nazis. The response was, "Sure, we hated the czars, but we hated the Nazis even more, and we aren't going to let them take our history away from us."

We caught a cab out to the airfield and saw two huge US Air Force cargo planes on the tarmac—a C-5A and a C-141. They were carrying food and emergency rations that had been stored in Italy originally for Operation Desert Storm. Now the rations were being sent to the largest orphanage in the region, in Pavlovsk, just outside St. Petersburg. We knew there had been criticism that the food would be stolen along the way and would never reach the intended destination.

At the airport, more than 100 young Soviet troops in brand-new uniforms stood in formation, looking very uncomfortable. I tried to imagine what thoughts were going through their mind as their country accepted charity from the United States. They had been trained to fight against us as an equal opposing superpower, and now, here we were, bringing them food. It couldn't have been easy for them. Then things got stranger. The Air Force crew started to unload the planes. Driving the forklift was a woman. She was expert. She was fast. The Soviets were non-plussed!

But there was work to be done. For the next three hours, the four of us worked with the Soviet soldiers and about 20 others from the Air Force crew and the US Consul's office transferring pallets of food to waiting army trucks. Our shared task broke down the barriers. When the work was complete, we posed for pictures, exchanged cigarettes (even if we didn't smoke), and felt the Cold War melt before our eyes.

We followed the trucks to the orphanage and spent time with the kids in an unheated building. On our way back to St. Petersburg, we passed the Alexander Palace just as it was getting dark. We jammed on the breaks and entered this museum where Czar Nicholas II, the last emperor of Russia, had lived before the 1917 Russian Revolution when he abdicated and was exiled to Siberia. We did the quickest tour of the museum that we could, got back in our car, and returned to St. Petersburg. We attended a party for American violinist Isaac Stern at the US Consulate that evening before boarding the midnight train to Moscow.

When I returned home, I wrote an op-ed for the *Boston Globe* about the promise of the end of the Cold War. At the time, I felt we had so much in common. If we could focus on that and if Russia continued a path of liberal reform, we could beat our swords into plowshares. With the 2000 election of Vladimir Putin, this proved to be very naïve. As this cold-blooded KGB murderer seeks to destroy Ukraine, committing hundreds of war crimes in the process, it shows the depths that Russia has traveled in 30 years.

But I had seen those soldiers feeding cold and hungry children with American food, and it wasn't hard to translate the smiles on their faces. And I had heard the entreaties of Soviet mayors who wanted only to care for the needs of their own citizens. When we visited a school in Moscow, I looked at the children and realized that with their clothing and music and how their faces lit up, they could be our kids in our schools.

Since that trip, I have thought about our respective countries' civic leaders on many occasions. It seemed to me that mayors—in Russia, Israel, America, and wherever I went—were non-ideological problem-solvers. As a group, we tended to focus on the people we served because we were very close to them. And the problems we dealt with—quality of schools, safe neighborhoods, clean water to drink, emergency services, public libraries, and parks—these weren't jazzy public policy issues that would get the attention of the Kennedy School, but they were what people thought about.

They were local issues, and life is lived at the local level.

On another international front, New Bedford also enjoys a strong Sister City relationship between Fairhaven and Tosashimizu, Japan, a fishing port not too far from Kyoto. I have visited Tosashimizu to bring greetings, and many Japanese delegations have visited Fairhaven.

At one gathering in Fairhaven, I spoke about 1841, when Manjiro, who came from Tosashimizu, was rescued by a New Bedford whaleship and brought to Fairhaven. I also spoke about 1941, when the Japanese bombed Pearl Harbor, and about 1945, when the US bombed Hiroshima and Nagasaki. I said that these seem to me to represent the best and the worst of what we humans are capable of doing.

I said that if there is a lesson from these extremes, it might be that when we look at each other as fellow fishermen, we see what we have in common, what unites us, and what brings out the best in us. Together we can do great things. When we look at each other as nations, we focus on what makes us different. That separates us and creates a distance, like looking through the wrong end of a telescope. It makes it easier to attack the other.

Closer is better, and that may be why mayors of every nationality have something to offer.

Mayor and Mentor: Carl Viveiros

The mayor who was closest to me in every way and taught me the most was Carlton Viveiros of Fall River. Carl is a little older than me and was elected to office before me. He was good friends with Jack Markey, and in many ways, he is very different from me. He is Portuguese; I am Yankee. I had advanced degrees; he didn't. I was outspoken; Carl was quiet. I was book smart; Carl was street smart. But Carl saw in me someone who had potential and the right motives. I will always be grateful that he mentored me and became a lifelong friend. He would bust my chops mercilessly, but he taught me with kindness and love about politics.

Fall River and New Bedford are arch-rivals on the playing fields. Still, they are very similar cities with large Portuguese populations, low educational attainment, heavy manufacturing, aging populations, and housing stock, and more than their fair share of problems. Both cities suffer from being ignored by the powers in "greater" Boston. We worked with Taunton Mayor Dick Johnson, UMass Dartmouth Chancellor John Brazil, and CEOs of the region to develop a strategy by which we could gain strength through unity. It was clear that everyone saw Carl as the region's leader.

We enjoyed each other's company. In the winter, we had a ski team called "Bullard's Bombers" that raised money for charity. Brenda Viveiros, Carl's wife, was hardly 5 feet tall, but she could get down the mountain like a rocket ship. With her "Bomber" knit hat, Brenda provided laughter and stories that lasted the rest of the year.

Toward the end of Carl's mayoral career, federal, state, and municipal officials honored him at a huge party in Boston. There must have been a thousand people in attendance. The governor, as well as politicians from Beacon Hill and Capitol Hill, spoke glowingly about Carl. The applause was frequent, loud, and heartfelt.

Finally, it was Carl's turn at the mic. He seemed a little uncomfortable with all the attention. I don't remember much of what he said, but I will never forget the way he ended. He looked at all these people from Boston, Washington, and elsewhere.

"I just want to say, as I finish, that for me, what is most important is—I come from Fall River," Carl said.

I got goosebumps. I still do. He felt exactly the same as I did. Hometown is everything.

Mayor Carlton Viveiros of Fall River

Chapter 6

Clean Water and Falling Out

Hard Circumstances

While I dealt with many issues, the issue that defined my time in office, and ultimately ended it, was the wastewater issue. It was a financial, technological, and political minefield. Making progress was incredibly frustrating.

The Citizens Advisory Committee was dominated by Fort Rodman area residents who seemed more interested in keeping it out of their neighborhood than analyzing potential sites and finding the best overall choice for the city. They worked with Camp Dresser and McKee (CDM) in the site selection process, but I wouldn't describe them as an impartial group.

In addition to siting, we also examined the requirement for "best available technology" and what that meant from an engineering standpoint. A local lawyer recommended a lawyer from the Washington, DC area with expertise in alternative technologies. Wanting to make sure we looked at everything that might work, we brought that person on board as a consultant.

CDM advocated for a standard secondary treatment plant design for our wastewater flow in an urban system with aging pipes and remnants of PCBs and other contaminants. The legal consultant was arguing for a more natural system, utilizing plant life. It sounded good, but unfortunately, it didn't meet the required water quality goals because of the PCBs and heavy metals in our waste stream. In a discussion around the table in my office, the consultant kept pushing and started holding forth about our obligation to advance new technologies.

I had finally had enough.

"Look, we brought you in here as a lawyer to give the City of New Bedford advice on how to meet the terms of the consent decree. This decree has, as you know, severe financial penalties for failure by the City to meet deadlines or standards set forth."

I continued, my voice rising to a level that could be heard outside the room's closed doors.

"And yet, knowing this, you come here and offer us advice that you know does not meet those water quality standards. I sure hope your legal malpractice insurance is paid up because we are engaged in serious business here. This is not some kind of game!"

With that, I slammed my hand on the table to emphasize the point. We didn't hear much from the consultant after that. I very rarely lost my temper as mayor (or in other jobs), but it is useful for people to know that you have one.

The technology issue was nowhere near as difficult as the siting. Starting with about 44 sites, we eventually got the list down to four: Fort Rodman, where the existing plant was located; the Standard-Times Field, a privately-owned vacant site located on the waterfront just inside the hurricane barrier; the railroad yard near the North Terminal; and the landfill on Shawmut Avenue, which was ruled out by the state because there were too many adjacent wetlands. So, we added an additional site near the airport.

Costs were estimated for each, with Fort Rodman the least expensive at $166 million. The Standard-Times Field, named after the newspaper that once owned the property, came in at $168 million, the North Terminal at $199 million, and the airport at around $241 million because of the length of piping that would have to be installed.

Predictably, the Citizens Advisory Committee voted 14-1 to recommend the airport. They voted to eliminate Fort Rodman and Standard-Times Field from consideration. This was in

December 1988. Professor Bob Bowen, the one dissenting vote, came into my office, describing with dismay the biased process, the lack of objective criteria, and how he considered the whole effort a sham. He was distraught.

I reassured him.

"Don't worry, Bob. You and me, that's a majority."

The committee could only recommend. I knew what the committee would do, and I did not take their work seriously. However, I did take the site selection process seriously.

I gathered about a dozen members of my administration and divided them into two teams. I assigned one to make the case for Fort Rodman and the other to make the case for the Standard-Times Field. I gave them a couple of weeks. Each made a 45-minute presentation, and we had a full discussion and debate. I didn't think that selecting the better site was an obvious decision. But we made the decision to site the plant at Fort Rodman and got everyone in the administration on board.

We scheduled the auditorium at New Bedford High School, knowing that the announcement would be controversial either way and hoping any crowd would look small in that huge auditorium. As I drove to the meeting, I listened to WBSM radio.

"John Bullard doesn't have the guts to make the right choice and put the plant at Fort Rodman," talk show host Henry Carreiro said. "It belongs there, but he doesn't have the courage to stand up to the people in the South End."

From the stage in the auditorium, I announced that the preferred site would be Fort Rodman. Immediately, booing filled the room, and it was hard to explain the decision over the noise, but I went on. I said that Fort Rodman was public land and that we should only take private land if absolutely necessary. I said it was the least costly, although not by a significant

South Enders demonstrate against the sewer plant. *The mayor's vision of Fort Rodman*

amount over the Standard-Times Field. I mentioned that I had promised that whatever site hosted the plant would receive $7 million in neighborhood improvements. With that money, we could accomplish much of what the Save Fort Rodman group had advocated, such as creating a waterfront park, providing a home for the Low Tide Yacht Club, restoring Fort Taber and Battery Milliken, and making other improvements to what was then a run-down and inaccessible part of the city.

I also mentioned that while the Standard-Times Field was vacant, it would not be so forever. It was valuable land and could be developed in a way that could eventually create significant jobs and tax revenue. If we located the plant at the Standard-Times Field, that parcel would never be privately developed.

I said quite clearly that we simply could not afford the pipe dream of putting the plant at the airport. Locating the plant at Fort Rodman was the only choice that allowed us to fix up Fort Rodman. We did not have surplus money in the budget to create an extra park except through this mechanism.

Driving home that night, I heard Henry Carreiro praising my decision on his radio show, saying what a wise man I was. That didn't last long. Talk radio feeds on opposition, and by the next day, Henry had switched his position and was castigating me for choosing Fort Rodman and hurting all those long-suffering citizens of the South End. He was relentless.

My decision in 1989 to locate the plant at Fort Rodman became a major issue in the next mayoral race. I was running against Dave Williford, whom I had beaten handily in 1987. Dave had been a city councilor and had a country and Western show on the radio in which he used the stage name "Cousin Dave." He was originally from Oklahoma and was a likable guy.

Politically, I had always done very well in the far South End of the city, winning two-thirds of the vote in my first three elections, better than any part of the city except my home neighborhood.

But when I selected Fort Rodman as the site for the sewer plant, everything changed dramatically. People had *very* strong feelings. The Fontaine family was a perfect case in point. They were a large family, well known in the South End. Dick Fontaine was on the Zoning Board of Appeals and was a commodore of the Low Tide Yacht Club. For Dick and his wife, Ellie, to strongly support me, given their iconic status in the neighborhood, took real courage. It was a gift I never will forget. John and Natalie Arnett, Ellie's sister, were the Save Fort Rodman group leaders that picketed me wherever I went, including visits to other cities! The Fontaine and Arnett sisters stopped talking to each other over this issue. Their Thanksgiving dinners became a thing of the past. It was a real shame. It took years after I left office for this family to mend the rift that this polarizing decision had caused. The South End was filled with similar stories.

It was also true that by 1989, the wheels were starting to come off the "Massachusetts Miracle" that had catapulted Michael Dukakis into the national spotlight of a presidential race. Local aid cuts were causing us to make tough local budget cuts. Manufacturing plants were closing their doors. The result of all this was a very close election in 1989. I beat "Cousin Dave" Williford by 874 votes. He beat me by more than two to one in the South End. He was not considered a strong candidate, and I had almost lost. There was a lesson to be learned.

People again brought up my aloofness, saying I needed to spend less time in City Hall. I needed to get out more, be more "political" and less "professional." I tried, but I was never comfortable as a glad-handing, back-slapping old-time pol. I watched them in action and respected the connection they made with people when it was genuine, which it was with the best of them, but something about my Yankee reserve kept getting in my way.

Not only that, but I had to solve some serious problems that would not make me popular. With state budget reductions, I would have to make some painful cuts in city services.

Business Agent Rod Poineau addresses United Electrical union workers at Morse Cutting Tools.

The economy continued to worsen. Morse Cutting Tools, which I had helped to save at one point, closed its doors. Chamberlain Manufacturing, makers of artillery shells and ammunition, closed its doors. Goodyear Tire & Rubber was bought by a liquidator, which shuttered the plant. Elco Dress sent its workers home, as did several other plants in the needle trades. We lost about 10,000 jobs in a few short years.

The city was hurting.

When military bases close, much is made about the impact those closures have on the local economy, and it can truly be devastating. But when a military base closes, the people leave. They still have jobs; they just move. The businesses supported by those people bear the brunt. When factories close as they did in New Bedford and other manufacturing cities, the people lose their jobs, and they are still here. The plant didn't close because of any fault of the workers. Often, the workers have already made one wage concession after another. Yet now, they are unemployed, and the businesses they supported when they were working are also suffering.

During tough economic times, thousands of families have a prime wage earner out of work and are supported by unemployment compensation for a finite period while they try to get retrained and placed in an economy that is bleeding jobs. Along with rising unemployment rates, incidences of abuse in all forms—alcohol, drug, domestic—also rise.

This was explained to me by Agnes "Posa" Raposa, who ran the Schwartz Center for Children in New Bedford, and once gave me a tour of the facility. As I looked into the faces of the little children she cared for, my heart broke over and over again, knowing that child abuse was so closely linked to our sagging economy.

Some people, without thinking much, might say we should run city government like a business. But in a private business, when there is less demand, you make less product and reduce expenses. When an economic downturn causes local aid to shrink by several million dollars, we can't simply reduce expenses. People still expect us to pick up all the garbage, catch all the crooks, put out all the fires, and educate all the kids. There is no lessening of demand for social services.

But we had to cut, so we did. I closed a fire station—the one that had been the first to respond when my house had caught on fire. But the chief felt its closure would be easiest to cover. We drastically reduced library hours, and we made other cuts. While we explained that these were due to cuts the governor had made to our budget, the citizens of New Bedford weren't interested. The mayor runs the City, so I got the blame.

In this unfavorable climate, I also had to advance the wastewater treatment plant. In March 1990, the 11-member New Bedford City Council took a vote on whether to back my decision of Fort Rodman. I got support from Mary Barros, Danny Hayes, Fred Kalisz, John Saunders, and Jim Sullivan. That was five. Another five supported the Standard-Times Field: David Alves, Nelson Macedo, George Rogers, Steve Sharek, and Ralph Saulnier, the councilor from the South End. Cynthia Kruger, a professor at UMass Dartmouth, proved to me that having a PhD didn't mean you were intelligent. She couldn't make up her mind.

Fearing that the easiest thing for the council to do was what it always did when faced with a difficult issue—nothing—I challenged them to make a decision, to vote for the increase in sewer fees necessary to fund New Bedford's share of the costs, and to promise not to instigate any lawsuits. If they could do that, I promised to support whatever decision they made. This caught the councilors off guard. I think some were uncomfortable being given responsibility, while others seemed to appreciate that I had enough respect for them to give them a potential role.

As they deliberated, progress happened on other environmental fronts. The EPA announced it would begin dredging the harbor Superfund site with $14.3 million as an initial cost. The planned disposal method was incineration, which became controversial as the project got closer to implementation. The EPA later went to a safer method.

We also secured $74 million in funding for the Crapo Hill landfill, a modern, lined landfill that would add decades to the region's solid waste capacity while protecting the environment. It meant we could close down the unlined Shawmut Avenue landfill, which was leaking into nearby wetlands.

Then in May 1990, my campaign to link New Bedford's wastewater needs to Boston Harbor paid dividends. Thanks in large part to Representative Emmet Hayes, we had a State Revolving Fund. It committed a $134 million, 0 percent interest loan to New Bedford to construct the plant. We had now gone from unaffordable to barely affordable.

That month, city councilors voted to support the Fort Rodman site. Professor Kruger from Ward 3 finally had made up her mind, siding with Fort Rodman to give us a 6-5 majority. That's what we needed to go forward with the financing. But we also had to lift some deed restrictions on the land, and for that, we needed eight votes. We got them in December when Steve Sharek and David Alves joined the majority, realizing that the project had to go forward.

The relationship between the mayor and the New Bedford City Council has always been strained. The City has a "strong mayor" form of government. The council has the power to cut the mayor's budget but not much else, so there is a tendency to act in a disruptive, sometimes juvenile way from time to time.

On more than one occasion, whoever was council president couldn't wait for me to be out of town so they could drive the mayor's car. That's what I mean by juvenile. But on other occasions, councilors are the eyes and ears of the neighborhoods. Helping them look good can be good for the city. Residents tell councilors about problems in their neighborhoods that need fixing. They can bring those needs to the administration, and we can see if we have the resources to fix them. It can be a good partnership.

Perhaps the best city council president I ever worked with was John Saunders. He was an old-school politician through and through. We were different, but we had a good relationship. He would walk into my office, and we would chat.

"What do you want?" he'd ask.

I'd tell him. He would tell me what he wanted. If the plan was doable and good for the city, we would agree.

"I'll try to round up the votes," he would say.

He was very good at that. When John told you something, he was true to his word. The sewer plant wouldn't be at Fort Rodman without John. I think it hurt him politically, but we got the votes. While there were heated arguments and sore feelings between the mayor's office and city councilors, we could work together for the good of the city.

As I kept telling the EPA and others, New Bedford had a limited ability to pay. At one point, the EPA said we should extend the outfall pipe seven miles into the middle of Buzzards Bay. The EPA said cost was no object. Of course, they felt that way because they weren't paying—the City of New Bedford was.

We estimated the cost would be $70 million. We argued against the idea on two points. First, we couldn't afford it. Second, introducing effluent into the center of the bay, where it was pristine, was guaranteed to degrade the environment, while improving the effluent coming out of the existing outfall was guaranteed to improve the environment.

In July, the *Boston Globe* ran a story pointing out that compared to more affluent cities, the council and I were investing more in sewer fees, solid waste fees, water fees, and commitments for the wastewater plant. And CLF went to bat for us, even though they had brought the suit against us in the first place.

"What is inspirational is that the City appears willing and able to accomplish the project despite the very hard circumstances the City finds itself in," CLF attorney Peter Shelley (who was born the same exact day I was) wrote in the *Globe* article. While it was certainly nice for our efforts to be appreciated, Peter and CLF didn't vote in New Bedford. He was correct in saying these were "hard circumstances." I had promised that whatever neighborhood hosted the plant would receive $7 million in mitigation. In August 1990, City Planner Richard Bohn reached out to South End residents to develop a plan. As much as they did not want to participate because they felt participation would be interpreted as acceptance of the decision to locate the plant in their neighborhood, we still managed to create a plan with their input.

We would spend practically all the money creating a park at Fort Rodman. Because the new treatment plant had to be moved north to a higher elevation away from the water, it freed up the most desirable land at the very tip of the peninsula where the old plant had been. We emphasized recreation on the east side of the park and nature on the west side with nature trails and a bike path. We made the southern tip a grassy area for picnics and concerts, with plenty of benches so people could enjoy the view of Buzzards Bay.

We restored the pier that jutted out toward the entrance to New Bedford harbor and repaired buildings for the Low Tide Yacht Club and a community sailing school. We added more picnic spots near the southern end of East Beach and built a playground. We spent about $350,000 to upgrade East Beach just north of the Fort and $450,000 to do the same to West Beach (aka Municipal Beach) near Hazelwood Park. Finally, we spent $500,000 to partially restore Fort Taber, which had been designed under the leadership of Captain Robert E. Lee— the future Confederate general—when he was with the Army Corps of Engineers in 1842. Fort Taber is also where Colonel Henry Robert was stationed when he wrote *Robert's Rules of Order*, guidelines on the parliamentary procedure still used for most governing meetings.

The Final Campaign: Losing the Battle, Winning the War

With SMAST and the new wastewater treatment plant located in the far South End—one providing clean water and the other providing a research link to the oceans—we had laid a base for the city's long-term health. But 1991 was an election year, and there was blood in the water. My blood. And it was centered in that same South End.

People were still up in arms over my decision to locate the plant there. Many feared the plant would smell. It would make noise. Trucks carrying sludge away from the plant would tip over into their yards. Their property values would go down. No one could be mollified with promises of clean water, clean beaches, nice parks, or a restored fort. They were afraid of the unknown, and someone from the government—me!—wasn't going to reassure them.

On top of that, the economy was in a full recession. Unemployment in the city surpassed 12 percent, and major plants were closing their doors. In 1989, I had barely beaten Dave Williford, who'd been considered a weak opponent. I was weak. With blood in the water, the sharks were out.

Six opponents jumped into the race that summer. Dave Williford wanted a rematch. Newcomer Steve Beauregard threw his hat in the ring and looked like he had potential. Former state Representative Tom Lopes, publisher of the *Cape Verdean News*, joined the fray. Eileen Marum-Gomes and perennial candidate and character Michael Zarritt also entered.

But the heavyweight in the group was Rosemary Tierney, who lived close to us on Maple Street. Rosemary was 15 years older than me, had a long political career, and had a good reputation. She had been a member of the school committee and the Governor's Council. I had supported her in all her races. She was a very popular old-style Irish politician who had grown up in Boston and moved to New Bedford early on with her husband, Jack, a well-regarded lawyer and later a judge. Rosemary called herself "Tenement Tess" (I'm not sure of the origin of the term) and fashioned herself as a woman of the people even though she lived in the same well-to-do neighborhood that we did. She knew how to work a crowd. It was clear from the outset that she would be very hard to beat.

We assembled our usual team for another try. And we picked up new talent. My cousin Sally Bullard and her husband, Bob Steck, lived in Washington, DC. He wrote speeches for corporate CEOs and some politicians and offered to help us. I told him I was about to announce my reelection campaign and needed assistance writing a speech.

Debating Rosemary Tierney

"Sure, John. Which one do you want?"

"What do you mean, Bob? 'Which one?'"

"Well, John, there are only two political speeches. One is the 'Viewing with Alarm' speech. The other is the 'Pointing with Pride' speech."

"Jesus, Bob, when I ran to knock out the incumbent Lawler, I could have used the 'Viewing with Alarm,' but now I'm running for reelection, so I better get the 'Pointing with Pride.'"

"Okay, have someone send me what you've done, and I'll put something together."

Bob correctly pointed out that every election is really about the incumbent. People either vote for the incumbent or against them. Very few people are really voting for the challenger. Challengers can disqualify themselves by not having the right qualifications or personality, but the election is still really about the incumbent when there is one. I was the incumbent in this race, and I had several strikes against me. The economy was horrible. I had to make unpopular cuts. And I had antagonized the people in the South End, where folks had formerly supported me.

The October 2 preliminary cut the field to two. I won with 6,584 votes to Rosemary's 5,674. Williford got 4,223, and Steve Beauregard pulled in 2,152. The other candidates trailed far behind. It was nice to win, but it was also clear that almost two-thirds of the people had voted for change. We had our work cut out for us. We campaigned as if we were behind, calling for many debates. Rosemary agreed to just one. She ran as if she were ahead, which probably made sense. She played it smart. One of her campaign ads was devastating—she listed the plants that had closed on my watch: Goodyear, Chamberlain, Cornell Dubilier, Nabisco, Carol Cable, Morse Cutting Tools, and Elco Dress.

We earned the endorsement of the *Standard-Times*, major labor unions, and the Minority Action Coalition. We ran our own campaign ads, one signed by women leaders of the community saying they had appreciated what my administration had done to advance women's rights.

While she didn't run ads about the sewer plant, Rosemary allowed the people in the South End to think she would reverse my decision and move the plant to the Standard-Times Field if she were elected. She was their champion.

Debating Rosemary Tierney

On November 5, 1991, the people of New Bedford spoke.

When the votes were finally counted at 12:35 a.m. the next morning, Rosemary Tierney had beaten me by a mere 390 votes. She had earned 12,804 to my 12,414. In precincts 6A and 6B, the South End peninsula, she trounced me 1,147 to 578, a margin of 569. In the newspaper's analysis the next day, the sewer plant had cost me the election—the political price of clean water.

I was bone tired and profoundly sad.

We had assembled a first-rate team inside City Hall and organized dedicated volunteers for the campaign. I felt I had let them down. When you lose an election by only 390 votes, you second-guess every move you made. You know you could have won it. Our people had been working so hard for the city of New Bedford. They shared our idealism, values, and optimism. I didn't want to disappoint them and have those resources end up on the sidelines. It seemed like such a waste.

Adding to my anguish, I heard we had been betrayed by some people very close to us who were secretly working for Rosemary. That just devastated me. I couldn't believe people I had trusted could turn on us that way. That was a knife. *How could people do that?*

Transition: The Basis of Democracy

We did our best to pull ourselves together and prepare the city for a transition. The basis of our democracy is that no matter how you feel about your opponent, you owe it to the people you serve to provide an efficient, informative transition that helps your opponent get off to a good start.

One meeting that I remember distinctly concerned the wastewater plant. Rosemary came in with one of her closest advisors, Jimmy Sylvia, for a full briefing. We had assembled our team of engineers, lawyers, financial analysts, and others involved in this most complicated, most expensive project the City of New Bedford had ever undertaken. I told Rosemary this was a complex project from a legal, financial, engineering, and political aspect, and I wanted her to hear from experts on all those dimensions. We went through them one at a time. Rosemary and Jimmy seemed to be paying some attention, though they didn't ask many questions. Near the end, we got to the issue of siting.

"Rosemary, when I made the decision to site the plant at Fort Rodman, we laid out the pros and cons between that site and Standard-Times Field. It was a close call, but we chose Fort Rodman," I said. "Obviously, you feel differently and based your campaign on reversing that decision. The people have spoken. I want to assure you that there is plenty of time to shift course and move the plant to Standard-Times Field."

"I'm not moving the plant."

"Come again?"

"I'm not moving the plant. It's going to be located at Fort Rodman."

"Okay, well, then, I guess that concludes the briefing."

After she left, my team and I sat there stunned. I could not believe that before Rosemary Tierney had even sworn an oath to serve the people of New Bedford, she had sold out the voters who elected her. It amazed me. The brazenness of it amazed me.

Later, I reflected on why her decision made sense. Rosemary was nothing if not a very shrewd politician. She went on to serve three terms as mayor. She knew that a sewer plant wasn't anything that anybody wanted. As an issue, it was a political loser. If it stayed at Fort Rodman, the sewer plant would always be associated with me. If she moved it to the Standard-Times Field, it would become *her* sewer plant, and any opponents, and there would be opponents—the fishing industry, for one—would be *her* opponents. She was a savvy politician. But I still couldn't fathom how she could so ruthlessly sell out the people who put her in office just a couple of weeks earlier. Nor how they didn't seem to hold it against her. Tenement Tess.

Removing the Source of the Injury and Moving On

My feelings about the loss began to change. I gradually moved from the anger of the moment to reflect on what we had been able to accomplish with the time we had.

I'm a pretty competitive person, and until I reached 50 or so, I was never very good at losing. When I was a kid, and Debby Clark beat me at tennis, I walked over 100 yards away, taking my tennis racket and smashing it into a thousand pieces. Later, when we lived in New Bedford, Toby and I used to play basketball in the back driveway. I had installed a backboard on the roof of our garage. When Toby was young, I always beat him because I was taller and could post him up. Inevitably because he, like Matthew, is a better athlete than I am, there came a time when the torch got passed. He was just too good, and he beat me. That was the day I took the backboard off the roof.

"Jeez, John, you are one sore loser," Toby said.

Truer words were never spoken. I did not like to lose. Not a good role model, I admit. I got much better at losing, which is lucky because in sports and everything else, I did some winning and some losing. I learned from both—definitely learned more from losing. But this loss was really hard. I had done what I thought was right, made the tough decisions, and now I was out of office. It seemed to me that Rosemary had basically conned the people of the South End. And now she was the mayor. It didn't seem right. But there it was.

Losing an election is a very public rejection. It occurs on the front page of the paper. The reality may be that whether you win or lose, about a third of the people like you, a third don't like you, and a third don't care. Many don't vote. But what plays out in the public eye is if you win even by one vote, you are king of the world, and if you lose by one vote, or in my case 390 votes, you feel as if everybody in the city has personally rejected you. The electorate had rejected me in a very public way. I had no job. My self-esteem took a huge hit. I second-guessed campaign strategies. I worried about what my kids were thinking. I wondered what was next. But I didn't think that choosing Fort Rodman was wrong. I had known it would probably hurt me, but I knew it was still the right decision.

Rosemary knew it too. She built the plant at Fort Rodman.

Park and recreational facilities at Fort Rodman

189

The surrounding waters immediately started to improve because of the cleaner discharge but also because of the work of Ron Labelle. I had hired Ron to run the wastewater department. He also worked diligently to eliminate the dry weather overflows and the combined sewer overflows, which made a big difference. Sludge trucks did *not* tip over, and property values remain among the highest in the city. The swimming off East and West Rodney French Boulevards became much better. With better water quality, eelgrass began to grow again. The state lifted the ban on harvesting shellfish, creating about 200 shellfishing jobs. Now Clarks Cove has some of the cleanest water in Buzzards Bay next to Quissett Harbor on the Cape side. It never ceases to amaze me that if you remove the source of an injury, Mother Nature will work to heal herself. And sometimes, she will do that with remarkable speed.

Later, when I worked at the National Oceanic and Atmospheric Administration, I became a trustee of the Harbor Superfund Trust Fund and was able to steer several million dollars toward the creation of the park at Fort Taber, honoring my commitment to building a park that is used routinely by hundreds of people on a pleasant day. Weddings, concerts, kite flying contests, and other events take place within feet of the wastewater treatment plant that people thought would be a detriment to the neighborhood. Historic Fort Rodman, once a blighted, inaccessible embarrassment, is now a city crown jewel.

And what of the Standard-Times Field? It took a little while, but businesses eventually located there, bringing in jobs and tax revenue. Then the big shoe dropped. At the urging of Mayor Lang, Massachusetts invested over $100 million to create a shore base for offshore wind on the site. This heavy-lift terminal positions New Bedford to be the support base for the fast-developing wind energy industry that Mayor Mitchell envisions, could have the same long-term boost for the city that whaling, textiles, and fishing have had. If I had located the wastewater plant at the Standard-Times Field, the offshore wind terminal would not have been able to take advantage of this spot. That opportunity for New Bedford would have gone to another community.

In August 2020, the state signed multi-year lease agreements worth $32.5 million with Vineyard Wind and Mayflower Wind to use the terminal to stage projects south of Nantucket. This lease positioned New Bedford to become home to the first port terminal in North America built specifically for the staging and installation of offshore wind projects.

By the 2020s, Standard-Times Field would be transformed to become the support base for offshore wind as the Massachusetts Clean Energy Center.

"These are the two first projects that Massachusetts is involved in, and they're going to stage their construction project from New Bedford," New Bedford Port Authority Director Edward Anthes-Washburn said. "Hundreds if not thousands of jobs and dozens of vessels, and all of those vessels will need supplies and fuel and everything else that you need in order to stage a marine operation. That's what we're great at here in New Bedford."

Whether at sea or on land, we come from a long line of people who figure out what needs to be done, determine the means and resources we have to do it, and then find a way to make it happen. I'm proud to be part of this community and that tradition. As a young man, I set out to work to make my hometown a better place, knowing that there were several roles I could play in achieving that goal. I was a community organizer and historic preservationist while I worked to improve the waterfront historic district. I had to learn the skills necessary to perform those roles. During ten elections and six years as mayor, I was a politician and navigated that role to serve my hometown. I introduced many programs, including community policing, recycling, AIDS prevention, SMAST, and a state-of-the-art landfill. I brought more women and minorities into government than ever before.

As I left office, I was proud of the work of my administration, and I remain proud. But what I am proudest of is that I confronted NIMTOFF (not in my term of office) and NIMBY (not in my backyard). I was the first mayor to put the environment front and center on the New Bedford agenda. I stood up for the people of New Bedford, proclaiming that we deserved clean water just as much as anyone else in America, and I worked to ensure we got it. I sent the message that New Bedford is no longer the place where you dump your trash, foul the waters, spoil the beaches, and pollute the air. This is our home. We live here. We will protect it.

My days as mayor were coming to an end. It was time for me to move on. Now, I just had to go and find a job.

In New Bedford's South End, the beach is virtually in everyone's backyard.

III. EXPANDING HORIZONS

Aleutian Islands, 1993

CHAPTER 7

Beyond Mayor and New Frontiers

Job Search

Paul Levy was the first to call with a job prospect. Head of the Massachusetts Water Resources Authority (MWRA), Levy had decided to retire from the stressful job of leading the Boston Harbor cleanup. He was looking for a few candidates to put before the MWRA board.

"John, you've done such a great job pissing off 100,000 people in New Bedford, how would you like to take a crack at two million?"

We talked about the position, and Paul was encouraging. He had brought Boston to the threshold of a million-dollar-a-day cleanup for one of the country's highest-profile environmental projects. He had fought the same battles I had, only on a bigger scale. It would be an exciting job. I thanked Paul for thinking of me and threw my hat in the ring.

At almost the same time, the executive director's job at the Massachusetts Municipal Association became available. My good friend Jim Segel was leaving the post. I had served on the organization's board and its Mayors Association, so I was familiar with the mission. The MMA represented towns and cities on Beacon Hill. I applied for that job as well. I was also interviewing at private companies, including Polaroid in Cambridge. I had been impressed with their operations in New Bedford and had gotten to know the company's executives during my time as mayor.

It turned out the folks in the South End did not have the last word on rejection for me.

Polaroid wasn't interested in a former politician from New Bedford, and the Mass Municipal Association went in a different direction, hiring Geoff Beckwith, a former state representative from Reading. It was a good fit, and Geoff has provided exceptional leadership with his Beacon Hill experience and his master's in business administration from MIT. Once again, I was turned down publicly. Because the MMA is a public body, news outlets reported on my application and rejection. I tried not to let it bother me and turned my attention to the MWRA post. You didn't just apply for this job; you campaigned for it.

Gloria Larsen, Governor Weld's secretary of Environmental Affairs, was leading the search for the new director. The 11-member MWRA Board would make the final selection, so I would need at least six votes. The governor controlled three votes. Boston Mayor Ray Flynn oversaw three votes. Quincy Mayor Jim Sheets had one delegate, and the town of Winthrop had one. Three other towns in the MWRA district also each had one vote.

In January, the *Boston Globe* and the *Boston Herald* ran big stories about this high-powered competition and the leading candidates. In addition to myself, Segel was one and reportedly Levy's favorite. Another was Bob Hutchinson, the well-respected head of the Registry of Motor Vehicles, who had significantly improved that beleaguered agency. Also in the mix was Doug MacDonald, a Palmer & Dodge lawyer who did a lot of environmental work. Doug had been New Bedford's consulting attorney working with our City Solicitor Armand Fernandes on our wastewater consent decree, and I considered him a friend. A few others were also vying for the post.

I knew I needed to be strategic. For this fight, I tapped into the mayors' network. I began with an old friend, Mayor Flynn. He promised that if I secured three votes on my own, he would throw his three votes my way. Halfway there.

I made my case to Mayor Sheets. Again, a good relationship forged when I was a mayor proved key, and I came away with his commitment. In Winthrop, the city-to-city bond worked again, and I had another vote in my favor. I just needed one more. I met with Joe Favaloro of the MWRA Advisory Board to get the lay of the land, and he gave me the names of the three members who represented towns in the MWRA district. I made a case to the Norwood delegate, and after a long conversation, he agreed to vote for me. I had my six. Everything was falling into place.

I also met with Governor Weld in his office. He was polite. He never said he wouldn't support me, but the word was out that, for him, it was "Anybody but Bullard." I tried to change his mind. I knew he had objected to my criticism of him and the Bush administration for not providing enough financial help to New Bedford to construct our treatment plant. When we met, I took pains to explain that I had been advocating for my city as its mayor. I said I hoped that he, as a lawyer, would understand my role as an advocate for New Bedford. I promised that if I got the MWRA job, I would be an advocate for the people served by the MWRA. He didn't buy it. Many people admire Weld. I'm not one of them. I think he views government as a game. And he is very good at it. The way he, as a Republican governor, interacted with the Democratically controlled legislature showed how good he was. Fundamentally, though, I don't think government is a game but a resource to help people who aren't in a position to look out for themselves. I think it is something one should take seriously.

To learn more about the MWRA, I toured the treatment plant under construction on Deer Island. I went down in the tunnel being drilled for the outfall pipe that would extend to the middle of Massachusetts Bay. A self-propelled tunnel boring machine with a drill bit 27 feet in diameter was busily digging. It was an incredible and costly piece of machinery. It was so huge and so specialized that I couldn't figure out how they would remove it from the tunnel and what they would do with it afterward.

"What happens to this when the tunnel is finished?" I asked.

"We will just keep drilling past the endpoint and leave it there," was the answer.

The MWRA vote was scheduled for a Wednesday, and I felt confident that I had the six votes I needed. At least, I did until the Friday before the meeting when I called Frank Doyle, Ray Flynn's assistant. I thought it would be a routine check-in.

"How do things look, Frank?"

"They don't look good, John."

"What do you mean? The mayor promised me his votes."

Frank explained that the political landscape had shifted.

"He promised you his three if you lined up your three, and you don't have your three."

This was news to me.

"I've got Winthrop, Quincy, and Norwood."

"Correction. You used to have Norwood. (Attorney General) Jim Shannon just called the guy and flipped him over to Doug MacDonald."

I stood in the library at our Irving Street home in New Bedford. I was crushed. Outmaneuvered by my friend Doug MacDonald, I was a loser one more time. And once again, for all to see.

"Former Mayor John K. Bullard still doesn't have a job," the story in the paper said.

Laurie consoled me and gently teased, reminding me not to take myself too seriously.

"Do you think the next time you apply for a job, if you don't get it, we won't have to read about it in the newspaper?" she said.

So many rejections in a row left me feeling pretty low. I don't know what I would have done if I had not had Laurie to talk to. Lexie, Toby, and Matthew cheered me up too, and my team from City Hall days also rallied round.

Organizing Fishermen

I tried to stay busy, involved, and visible, as much as that hurt. I needed to keep networking. I was at a New Bedford Chamber of Commerce meeting downtown when Jerry Wheeler approached me. Jerry was the CEO and executive vice president of the New Bedford Seafood Co-Op. He said the group was creating a new position to organize fishermen in New England, and he thought I might be good at it.

Intrigued, I visited Jerry the next day at the Seafood Co-Op headquarters on Pier 3. Members of the fishing industry owned the cooperative. Years ago, the organization had been a fish processing company, but now it sold fuel and oil products to the fleet. They had a couple of barges that fueled vessels in the harbor.

Jerry said the board, made up of the industry's major groundfish and scallop boat owners, wanted more influence with government regulators. The industry faced hard times and might need to make a case before Congress for economic assistance. It needed to be more organized, but fishermen are fiercely independent and notoriously difficult to organize. With its stature, the Seafood Co-Op thought it might be able to lead such an effort. Jerry said the board was willing to commit resources and add a staff position. Was I interested?

I talked it over with Laurie. This could be the third iteration of what I had laid out in my thesis so many years ago. I could continue to specialize in a place and modify my professional skill to meet the needs of the place. Strengthening an essential part of my hometown made the mission very attractive. I knew many of the players already, but I would have to learn about fish and fisheries management in much more detail. I told the Co-Op I would relish the opportunity. At the beginning of May, after four months of soul-searching unemployment, I stepped into my new office on Pier 3, directly across the highway from my old office at WHALE, where I had started nearly two decades earlier.

Co-Op Wharf, north of Piers 3 and 4

One of the directors was Rodney Avila, who owned the *Seven Seas* and the *Trident*. Rodney has a huge smile, a hearty laugh, and a bottomless seabag of stories. Well-known on the waterfront, he had done just about every kind of fishing—dragging for cod, haddock, flounder, fluke, and squid; harpooning for swordfish; catching lobsters and dredging for scallops. You name it, Rodney had done or was doing it. He knew fishermen up and down the coast. And they knew Rodney and respected him. Many members of his family fished and were part of a multigenerational family enterprise. He was on the New England Fishery

Rodney Avila

Management Council (NEFMC), so he played a role in managing the fisheries. He generously agreed to be my guide in these early days.

Rodney introduced me to dozens of people on the New Bedford and Fairhaven sides of the harbor. Many were involved in the Seafood Co-Op. John Rita was the group's president and owned several scallopers. Arne and John Isaksen were father and son Norwegians from Fairhaven and owned scallopers. Arne is married to Gail, in her own right a hi-liner in the industry and the daughter of New Bedford pioneer fisherman Leif Jacobsen. Tommy Vital was an offshore lobsterman. Bill and Jo Bomster fished for scallops out of Stonington, Connecticut, but were very active in the cooperative. Roy Enoksen, the owner of Eastern Fisheries and Dockside Repairs, had his fleet tied up north of the bridge. As with many Norwegians, you needed a crowbar to pry six words out of Roy. Ray Starvish and Malvin Kvilhaug were others. Reidar Bendiksen was an innovative gear manufacturer on the Co-Op board.

Rodney took me around the docks of New Bedford and Fairhaven, showing me the different kinds of boats and introducing me to captains, crew, lumpers, processors, and other characters found along the working waterfront. Among the many bits of wisdom Rodney shared was one that has stuck with me to this day.

"John, we harvest dollars. They may look like fish or scallops, but our business is harvesting dollars."

After the port of New Bedford, Rodney took me to Point Judith, Rhode Island, and introduced me to Jim O'Malley, Jake Dykstra, Fred Matterra, and Jim MacCawley. In an interesting dynamic, New Bedford tends to ally itself with Point Judith rather than Gloucester. The state boundary isn't as important as the dividing arm of Cape Cod that separates the cold waters of the Gulf of Maine from the warmer waters in Southern New England fed by the Gulf Stream. We drove north to the port of Gloucester, and then on to Portsmouth, NH, and Portland, Maine, to meet more people. In Gloucester, we sat down with Angela Sanfilippo, who heads the Gloucester Fishermen's Wives Association. We met with fishermen and state Representative Tony Verga, who had been a commercial fisherman. Gloucester shares similarities with New Bedford, but there are differences as well. Gloucester fishermen are primarily of Italian heritage, while New Bedford fishermen are mostly of Portuguese, Norwegian, and Newfoundland Irish descent. At this time, in the early 2000s, Gloucester landed mostly lobster, tuna, and groundfish, while New Bedford's primary value came from scallops and catches of the declining yellowtail flounder.

We sat down with Erik Anderson, Jon Williams, and small groundfish guys from Portsmouth. In Portland, we met with Maggie Raymond, Artie Odlin, his son Jimmy, Barbara Stevenson, and others operating large groundfish boats in Maine. During this time, Janice Plante wrote a front-page story for *Commercial Fisheries News* on my appointment, so the word was getting out around the industry about the effort I was leading for the New Bedford Seafood Co-Op.

During the meetings, I explained that the Co-Op wanted to strengthen the voice of the fishing industry. We wanted to hear what others had to say about the management measures being considered by the New England Fishery Management Council. We hoped to formulate consensus wherever possible and communicate those ideas to the council from a position of unity. I also said that I thought we could begin to assemble a case for economic assistance to Congress, given the precarious condition of both the groundfish and scallop industries. Members in every port heard us out. They had nothing to lose. We weren't asking them to pony up any money.

Shortly after I took the job, the New England Fishery Management Council hosted a Groundfish Committee meeting at the Seaport Inn in Fairhaven, the scene of the police riot when I was mayor. Even though fishermen had a reputation as a gregarious and volatile lot, this gathering was much more peaceful. I went to listen and learn. It was standing room only. This was my first management meeting, and the proceedings were foreign to me. I stood in the back and took it all in, trying to become familiar with the process and the people. I realized I had a lot to learn.

One fisherman talked passionately about what he felt was depleting the schools of cod and other groundfish.

"It's these damned conner ants. They are eating all the cod," he said, or at least, that's what I heard him say. "Conner ants are everywhere. We'll never have any cod again until we get rid of these pests. We ought to be able to shoot the buggers. Damned conner ants."

I had known I would have to learn new vocabulary for this job, but I was totally out of my depth here. I didn't know *what* he was talking about. What monsters was he describing? How had this horrible, cod-eating marine insect escaped my notice? Were they bigger than lobsters? What else were they devouring? What did they look like? I was aghast at the horror of it all.

The fisherman returned to his seat.

"Ah yes, cormorants. Thank you for your testimony," the chairman said. "Next speaker, please."

I released a deep sigh of relief. No nightmares tonight. Cormorants are coastal sea birds with voracious appetites, but they weren't sea monsters.

I started attending regular council meetings, learning the language and rules of managing fisheries up close and personal.

In the decades leading up to this time, several events and movements culminated in a wide range of environmental legislation. In the early 1960s, Rachel Carson published her watershed book *Silent Spring*, which raised public awareness of the vulnerability of nature. Later that decade, astronaut William Anders on the Apollo 8 spaceflight shared his now-iconic photograph, "Earthrise," taken from space of the Earth rising over the Moon's surface, showing us for the first time that we all shared the same small, fragile planet, or as Carl Sagan called it, "the pale blue dot." Anders's famous quote, "We came all this way to explore the Moon, and the most important thing is that we discovered the Earth," inspired environmentalists everywhere. In 1969, astronaut Neil Armstrong walked on the Moon during the Apollo 11 mission, the same year that the Cuyahoga River caught fire in Cleveland, Ohio, dramatizing the effects of rampant pollution.

People were clamoring for environmental action. The first Earth Day celebration was organized on April 22, 1970. The Clean Air Act was signed into law in 1970. Following closely were the Clean Water Act and the Marine Mammal Protection Act in 1972. The following year brought the Endangered Species Act. And who was president during this environmental watershed moment? None other than Richard Nixon! That's how powerful this moment was. He was no Teddy Roosevelt, but the movement took on such momentum that all this happened anyway.

In 1975, our Congressman Gerry Studds introduced HR 200, the Fishery Conservation and Management Act, into the House. It was introduced into the Senate by Warren Magnuson of Washington and signed into law by President Gerald Ford. This was revolutionary in several respects compared to the other natural resource legislation.

Its first goal was to Americanize the fishery by extending our Exclusive Economic Zone from 12 out to 200 miles, forcing foreign fleets off the continental shelves and more than doubling the territory under US control. States retained control over waters three miles from shore.

The second goal was to achieve maximum sustainable yield from the fishery. Unlike the many other pieces of legislation, the Magnuson Act, as it was eventually named, was decentralized. The law called for a bottom-up, customized approach to fisheries management rather than a top-down, one-size-fits-all approach led by the federal government. In many ways, the council system is profoundly democratic. The act set up eight regional fishery management councils and charged each with creating fishery management plans consistent with national standards for each species in their jurisdiction.

The New England Fishery Management Council manages 29 marine species and is made up of 18 voting members, which include a representative from the National Oceanic and Atmospheric Administration; five representatives from New England states Maine, New Hampshire, Massachusetts, Rhode Island, and Connecticut; and 12 representatives nominated by New England state governors and appointed by the secretary of Commerce for three-year terms. Four non-voting members also sit on the council, one each from the US Coast Guard, US Fish and Wildlife Service, US Department of State, and the Atlantic States Marine Fisheries Commission.

Council members must have knowledge of the fisheries, but this can come in many forms, including commercial, scientific, or environmental. While government officials have some of the spots, citizens outweigh government employees and play a critical role in writing regulations. With the variety of fisheries and the complexity of commerce, science, and hands-on fishing, the process is complicated, to say the least. But many voices have a say.

Council meetings go on for days to ensure people on the council and in the audience can speak their minds. As I watched the fishery rules being made in this messy, democratic fashion, I thought of Winston Churchill.

"Democracy is the worst form of Government except for all those other forms that have been tried from time to time," Churchill said.

It takes forever to get a rule written. Debate is endless. It is a study in inefficiency as everyone gets their points of view across. But what is happening is that the complexity of fishing is being taken into account by people who are closest to the fishery and who have very good bullshit meters. There are different seasons, boat sizes, and catch histories. These things and more have to be weighed before fashioning a rule that meets ten national standards and is fair to many different types of fishermen. Not a job for the faint of heart.

The process might be quicker if left to a group of professional federal employees in Washington, DC, or Silver Spring, Maryland. But I don't think we would get better plans. There are certainly several disadvantages to the complexity built into the process by both the nature of the fishery and the wide-ranging input required. One drawback is that the many aspects and details make it difficult for fishermen, regulators, and compliance officers to understand them fully. To top it off, the council modifies the plan every few years. Plans can reach several hundred pages with all the provisions that have to be met, such as those for the National Environmental Policy Act. Expecting anyone outside the government to read all that is a real stretch. I got a real-life lesson on a US Coast Guard fast boat in Virginia one afternoon when

I was regional administrator of NOAA Fisheries. Lieutenant Commander Patricia Bennett, who sat on the council, took a few of us out for a tour. She tossed me her seabag, which must have weighed 40 pounds.

"John, try climbing up the side of a fishing boat in 12-foot seas with that load. We are required to carry copies of every fishery management plan with us whenever we make a boarding," she said. "Couldn't you guys find a way to make them less than 400 pages?! Who reads this stuff?"

As an organizer for the Co-Op, I had several jobs while attending these meetings. I needed to familiarize myself with the fishermen and fishing communities up and down the coast. I also wanted to know the people on the New England Fishery Management Council and the staff that supported them.

Joe Brancaleone chaired the council. He had been a boat owner and captain out of Gloucester but retired to run a Wendy's franchise. He still had many family members in the business, and they had a stake in the council's actions. Joe's cousin, Tommy Brancaleone, was particularly hard on him since council decisions affected the money Tommy and other fishermen earned. Arguments were passionate and personal. I imagined that Thanksgiving meals with the Brancaleone family were strained as we went through a prolonged groundfish crisis.

There were other situations like this. Rodney Avila was on the council, and he and his many family members were very active in the industry. Their knowledge gave them unsurpassed insight into the regulations being considered, but it also put them in very uncomfortable positions when they had to vote. Conflict of interest rules ameliorated some of the pressure, but not much. They constantly had to balance protecting the fishery resource by restraining fishing with protecting their friends' and families' need to earn a living by catching more fish.

Also on the council at this time was Dick Roe, the regional administrator for the National Marine Fisheries Service (NMFS). He and his staff were headquartered in Gloucester. Alan Peterson, science director for the service, ran the main lab in Woods Hole and several other satellite labs in the region, which stretched from Cape Hatteras to the Canadian border. Alan was very smart, had a forceful personality, and he called things as he saw them. Wearing a patch over one eye, he had a commanding presence. Management rules were supposed to be based on the "best available science," so one would think Alan would be very influential. But other factors also came into play and diminished the role of science. Without strong leadership from the service or council, these dynamics generated currents that could be overpowering.

During one council meeting in Plymouth, Dr. Brad Barr from NOAA's National Ocean Service came to talk about a national marine sanctuary that his agency was proposing on Stellwagen Bank, just to the north of Provincetown off the tip of Cape Cod. Brad said the new sanctuary program was designed to promote education. He talked about the importance of the habitat on Stellwagen Bank, the whales that congregated there, and the historic shipwrecks that made it a significant archeological site. This sanctuary talk made the fishermen in the audience and the fishery managers very nervous. It seemed to them that Brad's plan to protect habitat and historic sites on the bank was a disguised bid to keep them from working these waters and an overstep toward regulating fishing. I sat behind Brad as he tried to reassure folks.

"The sanctuary program will *never* be in the business of managing fisheries," Brad told the audience.

He could not have been clearer, but there was still worry in the room. That worry persists, even though the program has stayed true to Brad's word. The Stellwagen Sanctuary was created, and fittingly, it was named in honor of Gerry Studds, who had worked on so many fishing-related and maritime issues. The first openly gay congressman, he was known for his love of the ocean, Cape Cod, and Provincetown.

The Water's Edge and Rotch's Wharf

While I was working in my Co-Op office, it was never far from my mind that I was steps from Rotch's Wharf, where my ancestor, Joseph Rotch, had brought his whale fishery from Nantucket in 1765. His counting house, where the proceeds of the Rotch Fleet were tallied and disbursed, had also been just steps away before it was torn down.

I didn't talk about this connection much, but it had great meaning for me personally. In some ways, it made me feel as if I belonged on the waterfront, but it also made it impossible for me not to wonder if I measured up to the family expectations. Perhaps it would have been healthier just to appreciate the continuity or wonder why, in seven generations, I hadn't been able to move more than 100 feet! Joseph and his sons, William and Francis, set New Bedford on the course of being a city and engaged for all intents and purposes in the first energy business. The central street in town, William Street, was named for William Jr., whose house was located at its foot. William Jr. was the first president of the New Bedford Abolitionist Society and a lifelong friend and business partner of marine merchant Captain Paul Cuffe.

They were a family intensely involved in the shaping of the city. From this pier, the Rotch fleet sailed the world's oceans, connecting New Bedford to almost every culture on the globe. One example of this was Edmund Gardner, buried in our family lot in Rural Cemetery. He was the first whaling captain to bring a whale ship into the Hawaiian Islands, forging a strong New Bedford relationship. As I thought about these connections and looked out at the edge of the pier, I could see why the water's edge is the most important place there is in a city. It is where cities begin. Water connects a city's people to opportunity through immigration, trade, work, or discovery. Every time I watch someone step onto a boat, I think of what people have been doing for thousands of years. In some cases, those steps were forced steps of slavery, for which there can be no atoning. Sometimes, those steps carried people into storms and tragedy, and they never returned. Some lost their lives, their fortunes, and their way.

View of Hazard's Wharf, north of Rotch's Wharf, where Co-Op Wharf would be located

Still, many found opportunity through sea voyages and continue to do so. Traders seek better goods, routes, and markets. Explorers seek new discoveries. Immigrants seek a better life. Fishermen seek rich fishing grounds. The water's edge takes them there and greets them on their return. Working in a seaport by this edge was invigorating for me. It defined both my hometown of New Bedford and shaped generation after generation in my family.

You could get a good sense of New Bedford on Pier 3. Fishermen were always working on the boats—mending nets, welding hulls, checking electronics. They work on deck under the hot summer sun or on boats covered in ice in the biting winter cold. These guys work hard when they are ashore, and they work three times as hard at sea. You can see the price they pay on their hands in calluses, scars, and broken or missing fingers. Tough begins to describe the life, but it goes beyond tough. These fishermen are resilient, clever, imaginative, resourceful, and very, very knowledgeable about the ways of the sea, the creatures of the sea, and *everything* that makes a boat run at sea. They miss birthdays, anniversaries, sporting events, and school plays so that they can make a better life for their families. Whether the crew is three or eleven souls on board, it is a tight-knit team. Everyone knows what everyone else is doing, and the coordination is fluid and flawless because the pressure and force on the cables, rigging, and crew are so great that one false move or mistake means someone goes overboard or loses a limb. While fishing draws people who love the independence of going to sea, it always requires extraordinary teamwork because the stakes are huge, and the confines of the boat are small.

From Pier 3, one can feel the heartbeat of New Bedford—in the euphoria of a good trip or the sorrow of a tragic one. At this site, every Memorial Day, the New Bedford Port Society holds its Fishermen's Memorial Service, tolling the bell for fishermen lost at sea. This is the site of the Wharfinger Building, where until the fishing strike, housed the public auction where fortunes could be made or destroyed.

The Port Society's Memorial Day ceremony held on Pier 3 honors fishermen lost at sea.

Working on the waterfront connected me to New Bedford's modern-day fleet, and being on this pier connected me to a continuity to my family history. Certainly, part of that continuity was a heritage of public service. There were many members of my family who had lived lives where public service was a major ingredient. While my grandfather Bullard had told me about the two Rotches who served as New Bedford mayors and about William W. Crapo who served as the US congressman from the New Bedford area, my earliest direct experience with public service was through my mother's father, Clarence Kilburn, from Malone, New York.

"Gup," as we called our grandfather, was an upstate New York banker in a small town 11 miles south of the Canadian border. He was appointed to Congress right after World War II and served for 25 years. A conservative Republican in a rural district, he once told me he eventually retired because he "was sick of the Kennedys!" We would visit him in Washington, where he and his wife Anne (we called her "Gommy") kept a small apartment at One Scott Circle.

Gup gave us tours of the Capitol. He showed us the infamous bullet holes in the tables, where, in 1954, four Puerto Rican nationalists demanding Puerto Rican independence fired shots in the House Chambers while he was sitting there, wounding five US representatives. He introduced us to Vice President Richard Nixon. And in a highlight of my ten-year-old life, he took us to the FBI, where J. Edgar Hoover fingerprinted me. Hoover then took me to the basement for target practice, where we used some kind of an automatic weapon to fire at paper targets shaped like human figures. Just what every ten-year-old needs!

What I remember most about my grandfather was that he was very proud that he helped to bring the St. Lawrence Seaway into existence. The seaway helped create jobs in that region of New York and Pennsylvania, which desperately needed them. (I didn't realize then how much opening the Great Lakes hurt the Port of Boston.)

I also remember that Gup didn't seem bothered by others' opinions.

"If they don't like the way I vote, they can throw me out," he would say.

It seemed natural to him to vote for what he thought was right, not for how he thought it would play back home or on the Hill.

While I have become as politically different as I could be from my grandfather, I respected his character and integrity and hope my approach to politics and people benefited from his example.

Gommy and Gup knew their way around DC, but they never became DC people or let DC get to them. They took the train back and forth to Malone on a regular basis. They were down-to-earth, small-town American people. That made an impression on me even though I was young at the time. Even though he was an important man, Gup never acted that way. He was very different from my New Bedford grandfather, who liked the pomp and circumstance of public life.

My parents were also committed to public service. Both were town meeting members in Dartmouth. In New England, town meeting is the way Norman Rockwell depicts local government. In Massachusetts, there are 39 cities and 312 towns. Mayors and councils run the cities, but most of the towns operate through Open

With Katharine and John C. Bullard

Town Meeting, which allows any citizen to come to town meetings and vote on your town's budget, zoning laws, personnel appointments, and everything that makes a town work. Literally, you need to stand up and be counted.

I would hear friends in Dartmouth say, "Boy, you always know where your mother stands on something. She doesn't mince words!" You didn't need a hearing aid to hear her either.

My father served on the town Board of Health after he retired from the hospital. I learned a very important lesson from him while they were debating whether to impose no-smoking rules on restaurants. No other town had done that yet, and the idea was controversial, with one side calling for health protections against secondhand smoke and the other side saying that Dartmouth restaurants would go out of business as people chose nearby restaurants in other towns that allowed smoking. The debate raged. The sides were dug in. My father believed the debate could not be resolved with any more data. He forced a vote. The Board of Health prohibited smoking in restaurants. People adjusted. Nobody went out of business, and other towns soon followed.

What I learned from my dad was that as long as you fail to make a decision, people will keep debating, and they will keep saying the world will end in order to make their point. As soon as you decide, people will get on with their lives. They will adjust as best they can. Maybe the world will end. Maybe not. It depends on the decision. But once the decision is made, the debate is over. So, make the decision. As I embarked on my new mission in the fishing industry and managing fisheries, where debate runs deep in the process and the personalities, I realized that sometimes this was easier said than done.

The Sad State of the Fishery in 1992

As I met with my board and fishermen in different ports, I came to understand the sorry condition of the fisheries in New England. Both scallops and groundfish were managed by restricting the effort necessary to harvest rather than by placing a direct quota on each species.

While it might seem simpler and more direct to have scientists assess how many fish could be safely removed from the "spawning stock biomass" and set a quota that could be harvested, nothing is simple in fishing. In the early 1990s, a great majority of the industry and, therefore, the fishery council was worried that a quota-based management system would lead to consolidation of the fleet and the disappearance of the small family fisherman.

So, instead of these direct "output controls," the council used indirect input controls. They regulated effort by limiting how many days people could fish. They limited the horsepower and length of vessels. They regulated the mesh size in groundfish nets and the ring size in scallop bags to control fish and scallops sizes brought aboard the vessels and those left in the water. They limited crew sizes. They prevented people from fishing in certain areas, sometimes to protect essential fish habitat, but other times to reduce fishing mortality. They had open and closed seasons. The result became a labyrinth of complex regulations.

Groundfish was still overfished to such an extent in the 90s that fishermen were fearful of going out of business and were talking to me about how to design a plan for emergency economic assistance. We felt we needed to make an organized case to the federal government that the groundfish rules were so onerous and the stocks were at such a low level that economic aid was needed in the same way aid to farmers is provided after natural disasters in the midsection of the country.

We had a good group of fishing representatives like Jim O'Malley from Rhode Island, Maggie Raymond from Maine, and Angela Sanfilippo from Massachusetts. These representatives were smart and very connected to their community and to Capitol Hill. Together, we kicked around ideas for assistance and how to build support in Washington. We met with Jeff Pike, Congressman Studds's top guy on the Merchant Marine and Fisheries Committee. Jeff was from Chatham and the owner of the *Molly B,* a small fishing boat. He knew our issues backward and forward, and he brought in a colleague, Jean Flemma, who was also hard-nosed and sharp as a tack, with a wicked laugh. We continued discussions and reached out to people in other parts of the country. I talked with Jerome Selby, who was the mayor of Kodiak, Alaska, an island off the Aleutian peninsula that, like New Bedford, has been a major fishing port. We enjoyed a friendly rivalry and a definite kinship.

We remained active at the council meetings, working with members to fashion rules that would achieve the delicate balance of bringing back the fishery while maintaining the ability of the fishing families to eke out a living.

We weren't the only ones paying close attention to the New England Fishery Management Council. At many meetings, I ran into Peter Shelley, a lawyer with the Conservation Law Foundation, the group that had sued me over the sewer issue when I was mayor. CLF was the first non-governmental organization (NGO) to really take an interest in ocean activities. They had been instrumental in the cleanup of Boston Harbor and certainly in New Bedford's waters. Earlier, they had worked with the fishing industry to protect Georges Bank from the threat of offshore oil and gas development. Now, they were here to urge the council to take stricter actions to rebuild groundfish stocks.

Haddock had been declining since the passage of the 200-mile limit in 1976 and was now essentially commercially extinct with only a 500-pound landing limit. The biomass for cod was slightly better but experiencing sharp decline. Yellowtail flounder in southern New England, which supported New Bedford and Point Judith, had had its ups and downs since 1980, but by 1992 had crashed to almost zero. These were our high-value fish stocks, and they had been overfished, not by the Russians, but by us.

During my stint with the Co-Op, the boundaries of the congressional districts changed, and New Bedford was removed from Gerry Studds's district. The folks on Beacon Hill handed this mother lode of Democratic votes to Barney Frank, whose district meandered all the way up to Newton. Some called it the Ivy League district, from Harvard to Dartmouth. Gerrymandering shouldn't come as a surprise to those of us in Massachusetts, the home of 19th-century Massachusetts Governor Elbridge Gerry, for whom it is named.

Congressman Frank called me after the redistricting.

"John, I need your help. I need to learn about fish. Before New Bedford was in my district, if there was a vote that concerned fishing, I just looked over to Gerry to see which way to vote. That was good enough because there weren't really any fishermen in my district. Now with New Bedford, I need to know everything there is. Can I come and talk with you and some of your members?"

We set up a meeting. If there is a smarter person in Washington than this former Harvard professor, I haven't met them. Barney is the quickest study you will find. He learned everything he could about his constituents in the port of New Bedford so he could represent them on Capitol Hill.

The scallop situation wasn't any better than groundfish. The New England Fishery Management Council struggled to find ways to limit the catches to allow scallops to rebound. Captains and crews spend much of their time at sea shucking scallops. They pry open the shells and remove the adductor muscles, which open and close the shells and are the part of the scallop that we eat. Everything else is thrown over the side. The council was trying several regulations to control scallop catches. It limited the number of days that boats could fish to about 220 days per year. It tried to regulate boats by restricting ring sizes and by setting meat per pound limits. It wasn't enough, and it wasn't working. At the time, the rule was that boats could bring in an average of 40 meats per pound, which meant more young scallops in the catches. If scallops are plucked from the sea too early, they do not have a chance to spawn and replenish the stock.

Some were calling for fewer fishing days, more restrictive ring sizes, and lower meat counts to give the scallop biomass time to rebuild and encourage the harvest of more mature scallops. But the charge from my bosses was to go to the council to "protect the 40-meat count" and keep boats fishing for at least 200 days. This was a recipe for the continued depletion of the resource. I also kept hearing my bosses gripe about how bad the science was. They told me there were plenty of scallops and that the scientists didn't know anything about scallops. My bosses had little respect for the NOAA science.

I asked Alan Peterson, who ran the Science Center, to meet with New Bedford scallop vessel owners about the condition of the fishery. Alan appreciated the invitation and said he would bring Dr. Steve Murawski, his top guy on scallops. We met with about 20 boat owners one evening at the Co-Op. I give Alan and Steve a lot of credit for venturing into the lion's den. They knew what the owners thought of them, but they forthrightly laid out the science, slide-by-slide and face-to-face. Steve used transparencies in his presentation to explain what the data was showing.

"If there are ten scallops on the sea floor, you guys are so efficient that you harvest eight of those ten. One dies a natural death. That leaves one to propagate, and that is not enough to maintain, let alone build the stock. And you catch those eight before they have had a chance to spawn. They are tiny, don't weigh much, and don't bring you the money they would if you harvested them a few years later," Steve said.

New Bedford scallopers

There were questions. Alan and Steve answered them. No one challenged them directly. Everyone was respectful, and the boat owners' understanding increased dramatically, as did their respect for the NOAA science. It didn't change the fact that they were still in a hole, and they didn't know how to get out of it. How could scallop stocks bounce back?

The answer occurred in what seemed to me an accidental way. The New England council was debating ways to bring back groundfish, specifically yellowtail flounder, which are often caught in scallop dredges as "bycatch," meaning anything not intentionally targeted by the crew. The council was taking testimony from the public on a motion to close an enormous part of Georges Bank that abutted the boundary with Canada.

Ray Starvish

As various groundfishermen got up to argue that the area should not be closed to groundfishermen, a scalloper raised his hand to speak. Ray Starvish was not like other scallopers. He owned a few boats like other guys, but unlike the others, Ray was colorful and loved to talk. He took the microphone.

"Mr. Chairman. My name is Ray Starvish, and I can catch 30,000 pounds of yellowtail flounder in my scallop dredge on Georges Bank."

I can't remember if the members of the council actually hit themselves on their foreheads with their hands, but the effect was the same. They were gobsmacked. They could ban groundfishing boats there, but it would have little effect if scallopers were still allowed.

"Thank you, Mr. Starvish, for your testimony. We had not considered that. In addition to closing this area to groundfish vessels, we should entertain a motion to close this area to scallop vessels as well," a council member said.

As Ray returned to his seat with a smile, I remember thinking that he had probably made a few enemies. *That is the single craziest thing I have ever heard a fisherman say. He just kicked the entire scallop industry off of Georges Bank. I hope he makes it home alive.*

The New England Fishery Management Council did kick the scallopers off the eastern portion of Georges Bank. The closure lasted from 1993 until 1998—five long years. Scallops were allowed to spawn. In that time, the tiny scallops that were previously being caught now remained in the sea to grow larger and reproduce. When the bank was finally opened to scallopers, their landings increased by $50 million in the first year alone. Because the scallops were bigger, the price per pound went through the roof. The scallopers, having been on the mat for so long and not wanting to return to the bad times, changed the way they managed themselves, opting for a rotational system that would hit an area hard when the scallops were large and then close it while the scallops recovered, the way farmers rotate their fields on land.

The scallopers lived through five very lean years resulting from a vicious overfishing cycle. This cycle allowed for small scallops to be caught, leading to a depletion of young scallops, low numbers of spawning scallops, and low abundance, which in turn led to the need to harvest small scallops. Rinse and repeat. But this was turned into a virtuous cycle of harvesting large scallops after they had spawned for several years, to seeing large amounts of new scallops come along, to protecting them while they grow, to harvesting year after year of large scallops at a very high price, to investing in your own research to head off threats. Keep on keeping on.

So, maybe Ray Starvish wasn't crazy. If he was, maybe he was crazy like a fox.

CHAPTER 8

Off to Washington and Seeing the Country

Few Things Are More Political Than Fish: Joining the Clinton Administration

In November 1992, Bill Clinton was elected president of the United States, and my Harvard classmate, Al Gore, became his vice president. Gore and I had both attended Harvard, although I had not known him in college. As mayor, I had met Clinton during a Democratic Leadership Council event when he was governor of Arkansas.

Gore founded the council after Walter Mondale lost 49 states to Ronald Reagan in the 1984 presidential election, and there was a contest over how the Democratic Party should present itself. The Democratic Leadership Council wanted to move the party more to the center in a bid to win Southern states and attract moderate and suburban voters. Gore, a senator from Tennessee at the time, and Clinton were council leaders, along with Senators Sam Nunn of Georgia and Joe Lieberman of Connecticut.

During the Democratic Leadership Council's early years, I attended a retreat that featured a train ride from Washington, DC, to Williamsburg, Virginia, for the attendees. I had been a supporter of the Democratic National Committee and wanted to check out this new group. For an hour or so, I stood in the aisle with Governor Clinton and two women from Hollywood as he told one entertaining story after another. There was no doubt he had incredible magnetism. He had the three of us mesmerized.

The Clinton-Gore ticket had emerged victorious over incumbent President George Bush by more than 200 electoral votes, including many from the South. Clinton had campaigned on

With Vice President Al Gore

centrist positions such as school choice, a balanced budget amendment, and restrictions against illegal immigration—positions that would have been anathema to the more progressive DNC.

In March 1993, as the new administration was filling posts, I got a call from Congressman Studds while I was at my Seafood Co-Op office.

"Hello, Congressman. What can I do for you?"

"Hi, John. We have a new administration. I think you should run the National Marine Fisheries Service."

This took me by surprise.

"Well, sure, Congressman. I've been working with the industry now for about eight months. I must know more than anybody else about fisheries management. With all due respect, sir, are you out of your mind?"

"I understand what you're saying, John, but the people who know everything have gotten our fisheries into a mess. What we need is someone who knows how to make difficult decisions. You have shown with the sewer plant that you have the courage to make tough decisions."

He said that was what was needed in Washington.

"I appreciate the compliment, Congressman, but I'm not sure I know enough. But I do know that no one has done more for the fishing industry in this country than you have, sir. I have known you a long time and have enormous respect for your knowledge on this topic and your judgment."

I knew I would need a lot of support to get this type of position.

"If you really think I should do this, I will seriously consider it. But I am going to need your help in a big way."

He said his staff would introduce me to the key players.

Jerry Wheeler was supportive. He understood that if I did end up running the National Marine Fisheries Service, he would have accomplished what he had set out to achieve in hiring me. I would certainly be aware of what was going on in New Bedford, and he knew he would always have my ear.

During this time, Studds managed to have Governor Weld submit my name as a candidate for one of the "at large" seats on the New England Fishery Management Council. Artie Odlin occupied this seat from Maine, and it seemed unlikely it would go to someone from Massachusetts. But it was technically an "at large" seat, and they needed nominations. My name was on the list, but I wasn't expecting much from it. I turned my attention to the National Marine Fisheries Service directorship.

The job running the service is a "political" job as opposed to a "career" job, so the hiring process is different. Political appointees, or "politicals," serve at the pleasure of the president. If you have political pull, or "juice," you can get in fairly quickly. By the same token, if you don't do the job or the president's pleasure changes for any reason, you can be dismissed just as quickly. There are not many political jobs. NMFS has about 4,200 employees, and only one of them is political. For career or civil service jobs, you apply through the civil service system run by the US Office of Personnel Management. It is bureaucracy at its finest, designed to keep politics out and focus on qualifications and merit, although hiring and firing can take forever.

The system has evolved with the country. In the 1880s, we professionalized government by creating a non-political bureaucracy based on merit. Before that, we didn't expect much from government employees except loyalty and work at the polls. Nor did we pay much. We had a patronage-based system until leaders recognized that the work quality and technical skills needed to improve. The bureaucracy raised standards and pay for workers and protected them from political demands. Professional qualifications and expectations began to rise.

The analogy I use to describe the federal government at its best is a car humming along in good working order. The engine runs smoothly. The brakes work. The air conditioning, heat, and sound systems give you the environment you want. The windows go up and down. The thousands of parts work to perfection. The car will take you anywhere you want to go quickly, safely, comfortably, and legally. The bureaucracy of government is a complicated, highly technical system. You don't have to understand it. You just want it to get you where you want it to go.

Every four or eight years, a national election ushers in a new political administration. That new administration has earned its way through an intense conversation with the American people. Based on that conversation, the administration knows where it wants to go. The one new variable added to the car is the driver, and that determines the car's direction, speed, and distance. The driver doesn't need technical knowledge. The driver doesn't need to know how the engine turns over or how the air conditioning system cools the air. The driver just needs to set the direction, determine when to speed up or slow down, and decide when to change course. The politicals are the drivers, and you don't need a lot of political people. You just need people who know how to steer. It's a good system. Drivers come and go. The car—the government—keeps chugging along.

Studds arranged for me to interview with Commerce Secretary Ron Brown. I knew Brown from the days when he headed up the DNC and I was mayor. A dynamic leader with an incredible presence, he had started out in Chicago. He was considering a few other candidates, including Dr. William Hogarth, who led the fisheries agency for North Carolina, and former Republican Washington state Senator Rollie Schmitten, the fisheries director for Washington State.

In March 1993, I arrived to meet with Brown at the Commerce Department, located in the Herbert Hoover Building, just a block away from the White House. I made my way to his office on the fifth floor. We exchanged pleasantries before moving to the topic at hand.

"John, I thought I had a lot of experience dealing with complicated international issues. I have never seen anything like *fish*!"

Dr. James Baker, Secretary Ron Brown, and Dr. Kathy Sullivan

Strange Dealings With Fish: NOAA's Back Story

Brown was probably not the first Commerce secretary to say that. It did seem strange that he had to deal with fish in the first place. Several bureaus and agencies fall under the Commerce Department. Most seem to logically belong there, such as the Bureau of Economic Analysis, the International Trade Administration, and the US Patent and Trademark Office. But fish? It was odd.

The back story is quintessential DC and illustrates how things often really work in Washington. Fisheries landed at Commerce in the rush after Earth Day, when lots of environmental legislation was being created. The National Oceanic and Atmospheric Administration (NOAA), which oversees the National Marine Fisheries Service, was created in 1970. One of the people involved in the commission to create NOAA told me that after doing all the hard work outlining NOAA's mission and objectives, the members gathered at a bar. Over drinks, they kicked around names for the new agency. They agreed that the first word had to be "national." The guy who told me the story was from Hawaii, and he helped with the next word.

"I'll buy a round of drinks if the second word is 'oceanic,'" he offered.

They accepted. Eventually, the third word became "atmospheric," and the National Oceanic and Atmospheric Administration was born.

Originally, NOAA was slated to live in the Department of Interior with the Fish and Wildlife Service, which would have made a lot of sense. However, before the relationship was finalized, Interior Secretary Walter Hickel wrote a letter to President Nixon, urging him to listen to the young people protesting the Vietnam War. The letter became public and was published all over the country. Nixon demanded that Hickel disavow his word. Hickel, a fiercely independent former governor of Alaska, refused. Nixon punished him by not assigning the newly created NOAA to the Interior Department. He asked Attorney General John Mitchell to find an alternative home for the new agency. Mitchell gave NOAA away at a cocktail party, where he offered the agency to Commerce Secretary Maurice Stans, who had been the treasurer of the Committee to Re-Elect the President (CREEP). As Commerce is the smallest of all federal departments and NOAA would double its size, the decision wasn't tough for Stans in a city where the size of your budget defines you. So, that was why, in the Commerce Department devoted to trade, tourism, and the census, Brown found himself learning about and in charge of fish.

He told me he was carefully considering the candidates.

"You have by far and away the best political credentials. And without question, the *worst* fishery credentials," Brown said bluntly.

He said New York City Mayor Dave Dinkins had called, urging him to hire me for the post.

"What does Dave even know about fish?"

I couldn't attest to Dave's fish knowledge, and I knew I still had lots to learn in the field, but I felt my background would bring a lot to the job.

"I admit, Mr. Secretary, that the other guys have more experience managing fish than I do, but I guess what you have to ask yourself is whether the problems you are having with fisheries have to do with science and management strategies or with political ability."

Dinkins's support was less about navigating fish and more about navigating politics.

"I think Dave called you about me because we have worked together on several issues at the Conference of Mayors, and I think he has a high regard for my political ability."

I also met with Commerce Undersecretary Dr. James Baker, a close friend of Gore's and head of NOAA. As an atmospheric scientist, he was more interested in the administration's "dry" side than in the "wet" fisheries side. With his Van Dyke beard and his sharp eyes, Jim was highly intelligent, curious, and optimistic. I took an instant liking to him. I asked him how long the process to choose would take. He thought it would be a matter of weeks.

Well, weeks dragged on into months. Jeff Pike and Jean Flemma from Studds's office had me make visits on the Hill, meeting members of Congress like Billy Tauzin from Mississippi, who was then a Democrat so that I could get familiar with issues in other parts of the country. Instead of courting people in the South End of New Bedford, I was courting Wilma Anderson from the Texas Shrimpers' Association and Pietro Parravano from the Pacific Coast Federation of Fishermen's Association.

With Laurie and Senator Ted Kennedy

I was honored that Senators Ted Kennedy and John Kerry co-signed a letter of support along with the entire Massachusetts delegation, which at the time was a powerhouse with Congressmen Barney Frank, Gerry Studds, Joseph Moakley, who chaired the Rules Committee, and Richie Neal on Ways and Means, whom I had met when he was mayor of Springfield.

While this was happening, I continued to do my job at the Seafood Co-Op, going to council meetings, advocating for fishermen from New England, and working on an economic assistance plan for the groundfish industry.

When August rolled around, Secretary Brown's office announced the nominations to the fisheries councils all over the country. Whether he knew it or not, he had appointed me to the at-large seat in New England. I was at the New England Fishery Management Council meeting and was duly sworn in by Regional Administrator Dick Roe, along with the other newly appointed or re-appointed council members. Even though I was replacing a person from Maine, I remember several Maine fishermen and representatives coming up to me, offering congratulations, saying they preferred me and thought I would do a better job. My phone rang during the mid-morning coffee break when I had been a council member for about 12 minutes. It was Jim Baker.

He had news that I had been rejected—and accepted.

"Hi, John. Look, you are not going to get the job at NMFS. We are going to go in another direction with that and hire Rollie Schmitten."

I understood, although I was disappointed. Rollie was a good choice for the National Marine Fisheries Service.

First Office of Sustainable Development

Baker did offer me another job, though, as his special assistant for Sustainable Development.

"This is a top priority of the administration. They have created a President's Council on Sustainable Development, and I want you to help me out on this."

I wanted to know more about the post. And what about my appointment to the council?

"Yes, about that, John, we would need you to resign your position from the council. Preferably this afternoon."

I hadn't even had a chance to warm this seat.

"This afternoon. I see. Let me get back to you on that in a little bit, Jim."

I collected my thoughts and called Laurie. I thought I knew what had happened.

"While all the folks from Maine who are at the meeting told me they are glad I was appointed, I'm guessing there is one person from Maine who is very unhappy. And it is too bad that George Mitchell is the majority leader of the Senate. I bet when he heard a Massachusetts guy took a Maine seat, he rattled some cages."

There are few things more political than fish, especially in New England. Another call was coming in.

"Sorry, doll, got to go. Someone is trying to call me."

I switched to the incoming call.

"Secretary Brown, how good to hear from you.... Yes, Mr. Secretary, Jim told me that.... Yes, Mr. Secretary Jim told me that it was a high priority.... Yes, Mr. Secretary, he did say I would need to resign this afternoon.... Yes, Mr. Secretary, you say it is very important that my resignation be this afternoon. I understand. I serve at the pleasure, Mr. Secretary.... Yes, I look forward to working with you, too, sir."

I tendered my resignation. I think my 90 minutes on the council still stands as a record for minimum time served. I don't think the council gives out pins for that. On Monday the following week, Jim Baker called me at home. He was excited. I would soon learn that Jim tended always to be excited. It was one of the many things I liked about him.

"John, I've got an idea for your office."

He certainly did.

"We have an Office of Education and Intergovernmental Affairs. It has ten people in it. I'm thinking of reconstituting it as the Office of Sustainable Development and Intergovernmental Affairs. So instead of just being my advisor, you would head this office," Jim said. "It would be the first federal Office of Sustainable Development. What do you think?"

"When do I start?"

I got off the phone and turned to Laurie in the kitchen, amazed at the turn of events.

"A few days ago, I was working for the Co-Op. Then, I got appointed to a very part-time position on the council, which ticked off the Senate majority leader. Then, I got offered a job to be Jim Baker's advisor. Then, a couple of days later, Jim wants me to head a ten-person office. I wonder what's next!"

What was next was that I had to learn what "sustainable development" was. I wasn't clear on exactly what it was but knew I had better be a quick study if I was going to head the first federal office devoted to the subject. So, off I went to the UMass Dartmouth Library. I learned the definition arrived at by the United Nations Brundtland Commission, which concluded, "Sustainable development is development that meets the needs of the present without compromising the ability of future generations to meet their own needs." The concept of intergenerational equity is fundamental to the concept. As I learned more about the field, I discovered there were Three E's integral to sustainable development: economy, environment, and equity. We needed to provide economic opportunity. We needed to restore the environment. We needed to achieve social equity—no small feat. And we needed to do it simultaneously.

As I researched the concept, I realized that sustainable development had been at the core of so much of my life and political philosophy. It was what my historic preservation work had been about. It was what I was working toward on so many levels as mayor. It was what my whole fight with the sewer plant had been about. New Bedford's economic future depended on clean water, and, of course, it was unjust for poor and working-class people to have to give up the goal of clean air and clean water. I think most mayors intuitively know that these Three E's of sustainable development are linked. Only in the silos of Washington do they get pulled apart.

A couple of weeks later, NOAA's Chief Scientist Dr. Kathryn Sullivan came to New Bedford to formally announce that I would be heading to Washington as head of the newly created Office of Sustainable Development. Kathy had been an astronaut and was the first woman to walk in space. She has the "right stuff" through and through. For her to welcome me into the ranks at NOAA was an honor.

Assembling a Team

While I was preparing to go to Washington, Ris LaCoste called me one day at the Co-Op. Ris is a great chef from DC with local roots in Southeastern Massachusetts. Her mom, Yvonne, was a librarian for New Bedford while I was mayor, and her dad, Rene, was a firefighter. Once, before I was heading to DC for a Conference of Mayors meeting, Yvonne came to see me. She told me I should look Ris up at her restaurant called 21 Federal. I thought that was a great idea. When I arrived at National Airport in DC, I hailed a cab.

"Please, take me to 21 Federal Street."

Puzzled, the cabbie told me there was no such street.

Now, I was the one who was puzzled.

"What? Do you mean there is no Federal Street in the center of the federal government?"

I wasn't sure where to go if there was no such street.

"I'm supposed to go to 21 Federal Street."

The cabbie thought for a moment.

"Oh, you mean the restaurant."

I swear, I shouldn't be allowed near sharp instruments! The cab dropped me off. Ris gave me a big hug and an even bigger meal. The restaurant was named for the very successful restaurant that she and Bob Kinkead had run on Nantucket, where there is a Federal Street.

Later, when I was back in New Bedford, Ris called to say she and Bob were starting a new restaurant called Kinkead's that would be located next to George Washington University. She wanted to know where she could get good scallops. We talked about several processors, and I told her about Bill and Jo Bomster's new system of vacuum packing and flash freezing fresh scallops at sea so that they retained their natural color variation. She loved the idea, and I put her in touch with them.

Then I broached a sensitive topic.

"Ris, my daughter, Lexie, has just graduated from Cambridge Culinary School. She is looking for work in a restaurant. Are you hiring?"

"We certainly are, John. Send her down."

Lexie and I headed out soon after, but Laurie would be staying in New Bedford for several months while she finished her degree at UMass Dartmouth. She had taken 20 years off between her sophomore and junior years to raise her kids. For a while, after I left the mayor's office, all three kids and Laurie were in college at the same time.

In September, Lexie and I packed our stuff into a U-Haul truck and drove to Washington. With the help of a cabbie on an earlier exploratory visit, I found an apartment at 13th and Massachusetts Avenue, NW. It was a ten-minute walk to my office. Lexie had found an apartment in Falls Church, Virginia. We went to her new home first, unpacked, and got her settled. Then we unpacked mine. We were ready for our new adventures.

Lexie started as a line chef for Ris and Bob at Kinkead's. She couldn't have found two better teachers in the restaurant business. The menu

Laurie sends off Lexie and me to Washington

featured seafood, and the kitchen pioneered dishes with underutilized species. The restaurant had a premier location and was always packed with important people. Lexie worked hard, learned a lot, and enjoyed the experience.

It took me little time to get situated. On my first day, I showed up at the Commerce Building and wandered the maze of hallways. The building is seven floors tall and shaped like a ladder, with two outside corridors and eight rungs of corridors that connect them with courtyards in between. My office was Room 5222 on the fifth floor, which was the floor with the "blue carpet," also known for its rarefied air because of its proximity to the secretary and undersecretary of Commerce. My office was on the second corridor or halfway between the two. As I looked for my office, I was dropping breadcrumbs, knowing I was going to get lost, walking very slowly, looking at all the pictures of marine creatures, when I heard a voice call out from one of the rooms with a very Boston accent.

"Mistah Mayah."

"I must be home."

"You are. You are. Right in here, Mistah Mayah. This here is your office suite. My name is Tommy McDonough. I work across the way in Legislative Affairs, but I'm camping out here for a little while until your team gets settled in."

"Tommy McDonough. A pleasure to meet you. Thanks for making me feel so welcome."

Out of another office stepped a man in a white uniform.

"Hi, Mayor Bullard. I'm Don Winter from the NOAA Corps. I'm the acting director of the Office of External Affairs. I've been using your office, but it is now yours. Welcome aboard!"

I started to get the lay of the land. Don was a commander in the NOAA Corps, a little-known uniformed branch of the armed services. It operates NOAA's ships and planes and numbers only about 300 members. He never talked about it to me, but I heard from someone else that Don had once flown a helicopter in Alaska searching for a lost fisherman in dense fog. He was running on empty, trying to find the way back to his ship. With seconds to go before having to ditch into the frigid waters, he radioed the ship to blow its stacks. When it did, Don could just make out the dark smoke through the fog and safely brought everyone home. He was a very cool customer, and I had enormous respect for him. He had also worked on Capitol Hill for Louisiana Senator John Breaux, which would come in very handy.

Across the hall, Legislative Affairs was run by another Massachusetts political appointee, Sally Yozell, who had been sponsored by Senator John Kerry, for whom she had once worked. We had a Massachusetts connection because I knew Kerry well.

Next door to my office was International Affairs, headed by Will Martin, an attorney from Nashville. Will is very close to Al Gore, who also lives in Nashville. Will's wife, Jeanie Nelson, became the lead attorney for the Environmental Protection Agency. Laurie and I became friends with Will and Jeanie and have kept in touch through the years.

At the end of the hall was one of the longitudinal corridors, where Assistant Secretary Doug Hall had his office. He had been a vice president at The Nature Conservancy and dealt with the fish issues. At the end of the corridor, Baker's office looked out onto the National Mall, Washington Monument, Jefferson Memorial, and Lincoln Memorial.

I began to meet and assemble my team. The new Office of Sustainable Development and Intergovernmental Affairs (SDIA) had about ten positions, and, extraordinarily, about half of them were political and high level. Under its umbrella, NOAA has large "line" offices like the National Marine Fisheries Service and the National Weather Service that carry out missions with people located around the country. NOAA also has smaller offices based in DC that just provide policy. Our office was a policy office.

I inherited several employees from the former Office of Education and Intergovernmental Affairs. My team included a secretary (as administrative assistants were called at the time) and a half dozen or so mid-level staffers. I learned that we needed to change the reputation of the office, which had not been regarded as important or high-performing but as a place to park people.

Roan Conrad   Lance Simmens

Our leadership team was made up of myself and three assistant directors, all "politicals."

Rick Podgorny was a career guy with a high Government Schedule rank of 15, a top-level civil service bureaucrat in the word's best sense. He had been at NOAA for decades and knew all the ins and outs. He was very friendly, thoroughly professional, and good friends with John Carey, the top career administrative officer we would need for personnel and budget help.

Roan Conrad was a political SES, or Senior Executive Service, like me. That's the highest level without requiring Senate confirmation, akin to a general or an admiral in the military. Roan joined the Clinton administration because his brother, Kent, was a senator from North Dakota and a member of the Budget Committee. Although Roan grew up in North Dakota, he was pure Manhattan. A gay rights activist who had worked for NBC-TV as a producer, he traveled the country to attend more than 50 operas a year. Highly intelligent, opinionated, and charming, he had a laugh that could put you immediately at ease. I knew that we would work well together.

My old friend Lance Simmens also joined us at the same rank as Rick. Lance came in courtesy of his former boss, Senator Jim Sasser from Tennessee. Sasser was the senior senator to Gore and was the chairman of the Budget Committee. Lance brought to our team his knowledge of Capitol Hill, his great familiarity with the nation's mayors, his optimism, and what I always described as his "irresolute idealism."

Our foursome became a brain trust for this new office that Jim Baker had invented out of a low-performing backwater. Every morning, we would gather in my office for half an hour to an hour. I would sit behind my desk. There was one chair off to the side, and there was an oversized couch that held two. Our discussions were no holds barred. There wasn't a "yes man" in that group. The door was shut, and we would argue through whatever issue was on the table, sometimes at high volume—no shrinking violets. But when we reached a decision, *everybody* backed it. And everybody had each other's back. We lacked diversity, which was a big problem throughout NOAA, but we had a great core team. We needed to define our mission and build capacity.

We knew that Jim Baker was excited about the President's Council on Sustainable Development and wanted us to support his work on that. Roan was interested in that issue, so we decided that would be his focus. We also knew there would be a lot of pressure from fishing interests in New England and probably other parts of the country for disaster relief due to depleted stocks. Because this would involve working with Capitol Hill and state and local governments, it was a natural for Lance. Rick was going to help us increase the horsepower of our ten-person shop by finding good hires and connecting us to other departments in Commerce, such as the Economic Development Administration (EDA).

I would be involved in everything with their support. As our work became more complex and demanding, I realized I needed strong support staff. Rick set out to find me a top-notch secretary. He handed me a resume to look over. I took it home and read about Helen Westbrook, originally from Chicopee.

"OK, somebody from Massachusetts. That's a great start," I said as I looked at her information.

Helen was working for NOAA Fisheries. I glanced at where her career had begun, and my eyes opened wide. With Senator John F. Kennedy! Then, she moved to the White House and worked for President Kennedy. After the assassination, she worked for Mrs. Kennedy. My jaw dropped. *Mrs. Westbrook, do you think you can handle the pressure here at the Office of Sustainable Development?* How was I going to interview this lady? She would be interviewing me.

When she came into the office the next day, I was dumbfounded. She didn't look even close to retirement. It made me realize how young the Kennedy administration had been. I agreed to hire Helen, or, more likely, she decided to take a chance on me. At any rate, we worked together for five years and stayed in touch until she died in 2021. She called me "Jack" once, and my feet didn't touch the ground for a week. A few years ago, when I was in Washington, I brought Helen together with my pal Peter Fenn, whose dad had worked for JFK. Peter didn't know Helen, but Helen had known Peter's dad. I just sat back and listened as the two of them told JFK stories. It was an unforgettable evening.

Rick also helped swell our ranks by getting us a few presidential interns and other young staffers. They were intelligent, energetic, and added to the office. Christine Eustis was one of the presidential interns. She was tall and shy with big eyes. She was incredibly intelligent and worked with Roan on sustainable development. I ran into her years later when she was doing an excellent job as the assistant director at the Fish and Wildlife Service in Massachusetts.

Fernando Leyva joined us as a policy analyst. He had a science background and helped with analysis and speechwriting. I remember giving a speech that Fernando and I had worked on to a scientific audience in Florida. There were several hundred in the audience, and I had taken his scientifically oriented speech and added more humor and implications for action. I felt strongly that it wasn't enough to know something—you had to do something with what you knew. "If you act without information, you are dangerous. If you have information but don't act, you are irrelevant," I would often say.

As Fernando and I walked out of the meeting, I mentioned that the audience had seemed subdued, even bored.

"John, they are scientists. They expect boring lectures. That is their culture."

If you want to know why we aren't addressing climate change, you can look at what Fernando said and understand the uncomfortable truth: scientists, by and large, have been horrible at communicating to the general public. There are very serious consequences for that failure. It doesn't devalue your science to be able to explain it to a general audience. We need more Carl Sagans, not fewer.

Fernando is now a doctor for the Navy in San Diego. I bet he does ***not*** give a boring lecture!

Lance found a way to bring in Eric Dolin, a young man from NOAA Fisheries. Ever the self-promoter, Lance wanted someone to chronicle the work of disaster relief. Eric worked with us for a year or so. He continued developing his writing skills and eventually left NOAA to write books on New England history, from whaling to lighthouses to pirates. He remains a good friend.

One day, Secretary Brown's Chief of Staff Rob Stein called.

"John, how would you like to have David Cruise in your office?"

"Rob, I am here to serve. Does he come with his own FTE (full-time equivalent position)?"

"Yes, he won't cost you a dime. You would just be doing the secretary a favor."

"As I said, Rob, I am here to serve."

David Cruise had worked for Governor Bruce Sundlun of Rhode Island, so he was another high-level political, but I guess he did not fit in with Secretary Brown's office. He joined our group, and the morning shoutabouts became even more animated. David knew his way around and was politically savvy, so he added capacity to our team. When the North Cape oil spill happened off the shore of Rhode Island, Jim Baker and Doug Hall could have made great use of David's local knowledge of the state and local officials, but they didn't, which was a missed opportunity on their part.

Baker organized NOAA by having agency and policy-shop heads meet Monday afternoons at the big NOAA complex in Silver Spring, Maryland. We would share current news and issues we were confronting. Every quarter, we would have a two-day meeting to go over budget and objective milestones so everyone would know how we were doing against our approved work plans. There was a very high level of accountability and transparency, information that was all available to Congress, which was paying the bills.

In the Commerce building downtown, we had much shorter meetings on Tuesday and Thursday mornings to go over the "Plan of the Day." These POD meetings involved the policy offices and kept everyone up to date on fast-breaking issues. It helped ensure we were an integrated team where the right hand knew what the left hand was doing. It was a good way to run a railroad. I learned an awful lot about managing large organizations from my experience in DC.

President's Council on Sustainable Development

President George Bush (the father) actually started the President's Council on Sustainable Development (PCSD) before leaving the White House in 1993. It comprised about two dozen leaders: a third from industry, a third from the environmental community, and a third from offices of cabinet secretaries or heads of significant social organizations. The group was very powerful, representing environmental, economic, and societal interests—the three legs of the sustainable development stool.

Jonathan Lash, president of the World Resources Institute, co-chaired on behalf of the big environmental NGOs, including the Environmental Defense Fund, The Nature Conservancy, the Sierra Club, and the Natural Resource Defense Council. It is a delightful turn of events that Jonathan and his wife, Ellie, now retired, lived just a few miles away from us on the coast of Buzzards Bay. Dave Buzzelli, vice president of Dow Chemical, co-chaired on behalf of major industries such as General Motors, Chevron, Enron, and Georgia Pacific. My boss, Commerce Secretary Brown, was a member along with the Agriculture and Energy secretaries and the EPA administrator. We also had the retired president of the AFL-CIO, the head of the Columbia River Inter-Tribal Fish Commission, and the head of the National African American Leadership Summit.

When Clinton and Gore took office, they energized and populated the sustainable development council. They also added four ex-officio members: Baker from NOAA; former Vermont Governor Madeleine Kunin, who was then the deputy secretary of Education; Richard Rominger, the deputy secretary of Agriculture; and Undersecretary of State Tim Wirth, the former Colorado senator.

The President's Council on Sustainable Development had a staff of about 25, led by Molly Olsen. Members were busy CEOs and heads of large organizations. To make sure work continued along at a steady pace, each appointed one liaison to represent them. I was Jim Baker's liaison, and Jeffrey Hunker, who had come from the Boston Consulting Group to Commerce, was Brown's. The liaisons and staff became the "worker bees," taking direction from the members. We researched, prepared the briefing memos, and wrote the reports.

The goal of Chairs Lash and Buzzelli and the administration was to find national policies to achieve sustainable development. How could America achieve economic growth, environmental protection, and social equity all at the same time? As this was a president's council, everybody was thinking about federal leadership and a top-down approach.

We had many interesting discussions and debates. We could have spent eight years debating whether economic growth was a valid goal. Some believed it was, while others argued it was the source of our problems and that we needed to halt growth to achieve balance on the planet. This debate went on for months as the group met every quarter, alternating between Washington and various communities around the country. Our conversations reminded me of one of those beer commercials where everyone in the stadium says either "tastes great" or "less filling," with no resolution possible.

Finally, after too much time had been consumed, someone, it might have been Tom Donahue from the AFL-CIO, broke the logjam.

"Look, we are never going to resolve this if we just use the word growth," the person told the group. "It has too much baggage. We have to break it down. I think we can agree that we want job opportunities to grow. I think we can agree that we want average income to grow. I think we can agree that we want educational attainment to grow. Birth weight to grow. I think we want dropout rates to decrease. Pollution to decrease. Commuter time to decrease. You get my point. There are parts of economic growth that should grow. There are parts that should shrink. If we disaggregate it, a lot of the disagreements will go away."

That was one of many breakthroughs we had, and it led to a focus on indicators. You get what you measure.

Moving Around the Country

I hadn't been in the office for more than a couple of weeks when I was directed to represent NOAA at a meeting of Alaskan municipalities in Dutch Harbor in the Aleutian Islands. I got on a plane, and after a day's travel, I arrived in the port that I had always heard about as a competitor with New Bedford for the country's top port title.

Being on the nation's "last frontier" was an amazing experience, and I had to keep pinching myself that I was being paid to learn so much about America. I stayed in a small two-story hotel that looked as if it might have been from a Wild West film set. The road outside was dirt. Everything was owned by the one company in the one-company town. Their business was pollock. Across the street from the hotel was the factory where perfectly good fish were run through the "slime line" of machinery and came out the other end as pure white meat protein the consistency of mashed potatoes. The stuff had no smell or taste and was transformed into imitation crabmeat. Many of the workers were seasonal workers from the Philippines.

On my first morning, I was greeted by a familiar accent as I came down the hotel stairs into the lobby.

"Mr. Mayor, how are you?" a fisherman said.

I asked how he knew me, and he said he was a transplanted scalloper from Fairhaven.

"There aren't any scallops back East," he said.

Dutch Harbor is also home to the king crab fishery that became the basis for the popular TV show, "The Deadliest Catch."

During the meeting of the municipal association, we visited a number of the islands, traveling by Grumman floatplane. We even got out to St. Paul and St. George Islands in the middle of the Bering Sea, where I met the colorful "mayor" Max Malovansky. The Aleut people populate these Pribilof Islands, but many have Russian names since Russia owned the region before "Seward's Folly" transferred Alaska to the US in 1867. As we looked at some of the 500,000 northern fur seals around the islands, one of the Aleuts told me that since hunting bans on seals were enacted, there are almost no jobs on the islands for native people. He asked what I thought of that. He told me the young male fur seals serve no biological purpose and could be hunted for fur and meat while not allowing hunting on other seals, just as his people had done for centuries. I had no good answer and confessed to him that my ancestors had hunted whales and seals in these waters centuries ago.

I also met the state senator from this district. He told me it was the first time he had been to Dutch Harbor. Given the town's fishing prominence, I was surprised and asked how big his district was.

"It's two thousand miles long."

That was my first lesson in Alaska geography but not my last. If you overlay Alaska on the lower 48, Ketchikan would cover Savannah, Barrow would be in North Dakota, and Atka would be in San Diego. As they say in Alaska, "We could cut ourselves in two and make Texas the third largest state!" I returned with a much greater appreciation of our "last frontier."

On Tour with the President's Council on Sustainable Development

We held one of our early meetings in Seattle. A group called Sustainable Seattle had spent several years developing indicators of sustainability. They began with many meetings to ask their citizens what they thought was valuable about their community. From this, they built a list of over a thousand attributes.

They asked the citizens to winnow down this list by combining and prioritizing. They relied on the concept of what an "indicator" is. For example, "community gardens" made the final list, not because they are an important source of local food, though they can be that, but because they are an indicator that you have a neighborhood where people help each other out.

With this process, Sustainable Seattle got the list down to 40. The planners decided the list was still too long for people to absorb, so they reduced the list further based on what they could already measure versus what they would have to develop new measurements for. With this strategy, they got down to 20 indicators. The list was quite varied and included such items as the number of miles of pedestrian-friendly sidewalks, economic diversity (Seattle was the home of Boeing), salmon in the river, and community gardens.

I was friends with Seattle Mayor Norm Rice from my mayor days, so I went to see him. A Black man elected in an almost all-White city, Norm is a remarkable guy. He is very smart and a formidable politician. After catching up, I asked him about the indicator project. He was enthusiastic. Because I worked for NOAA, which regulates salmon, I asked him about the salmon indicator.

"Is the salmon fishery a big part of your economy, Norm?"

"Hell no, John. It's minuscule. It's cultural. The Pacific Northwest is defined as wherever a salmon swims. It is who we are. It's water quality. It's our history. It's our relations with the tribes. And yes, for fishermen, those jobs are important, but it is so much more important than that."

Another community where we met was Chattanooga, Tennessee, which has a wonderful story to tell. In 1969, Chattanooga was named the "worst-polluted city in America." They were an industrial city with air so dirty they needed the streetlights on in the middle of the day. But they had managed to turn the tide. In 1984, after a study identified social isolation as a problem, the city invited every citizen to participate in shaping a vision for the future. More than 1,700 people joined in Vision 2000, designing a "commitment portfolio" of 40 goals for the year 2000.

By the time the President's Council on Sustainable Development had arrived on the scene, 85 percent of the goals had been achieved through 220 programs, creating 1,300 jobs and an investment of $793 million. They started Revision 2020 with an additional 27 goals. Some of their ideas and accomplishments were remarkable.

During the process, a 7-year-old girl suggested an aquarium. The "experts" dismissed her idea, saying that an aquarium focused on the freshwater Tennessee River was bound to fail because you needed to have sharks to attract people. But the idea made it through the screening process and was modified to include the entire river system down to the Gulf of Mexico (where they have sharks). It is now a very popular attraction. How do you think people feel when a 7-year-old is taken seriously? That is empowering.

Because their air was so dirty, Chattanooga wanted electric buses. But they couldn't find anyone to manufacture them, so they formed a company to build the buses themselves. After outfitting their own city, they started selling buses to other cities, like Atlanta. Riding the buses was free, paid for by the parking fees at the major parking garage downtown.

With guidance from architect Bill McDonough, one of the nation's top thinkers on sustainable design, and his partner Michael Braungart, a chemist, Chattanooga developed an eco-industrial park based on matching material flows to eliminate waste and, therefore, pollution. Every industry requires an inflow of materials, such as metal, plastic, water, and electricity, to manufacture its products. The industry ships its products for sale and is left with waste, which can be leftover materials or heat or dirty water or chemicals. Normally, the company pays to remove that waste, or it fouls the air, water, or landfill with the pollution. In an eco-industrial park, material flows are mapped so one company's waste or outflow can line up with another company's needs or inflow. If you have only two companies in your park, this is very hard. But if you have many companies, it gets easier. The goal is to get a closed loop where there is no waste. This is called "eco-efficiency."

They had many other projects going on in Chattanooga, including re-purposing an old bridge that was no longer strong enough to carry trucks and automobiles. While some people wanted to remove the bridge, the community voted to restore it for pedestrian use only. The restored bridge became one of the most popular parks in the city.

There were several lessons from the Chattanooga story. One was that action on sustainable development was happening at the community level without waiting for permission or leadership from Washington. If anything, the leadership was coming from the bottom up. The second

Walnut Street Bridge, Chattanooga, before cleanup and restoration, 1980

Dave Crockett

Restored Walnut Street Bridge, Chattanooga, 2022

lesson was that it is possible to achieve the "Three E's." Chattanooga was rebuilding its economy and adding jobs. It was cleaning the air, water, and habitat. And the way it was doing all of that was profoundly empowering to its citizens. This was not the false choice of either/or. The Three E's of economy, environment, and equity reinforced one another, turning a vicious circle into a virtuous one.

On my trips to Chattanooga, I met many people and leaders there. One of the most memorable was David Crockett, who worked for IBM when I first met him and later became a city council member. David was a great-nephew of the hero of the Alamo and an impressive and colorful man. We were having dinner one evening at the Old Ebbitt in Washington and talking about fishing. The topic turned to catch and release. David asked if I hunted. I told him I did some duck hunting when I was a kid.

"Did you do shoot and release? That's what I do."

"Dave, if my name were Dave Crockett, I wouldn't even pick up a gun. What the heck is shoot and release?"

"Well, I was duck hunting with a friend, and some ducks came into our blind. My friend stood up and flushed them. He fired twice. Two ducks fell into the water. I said, 'Too bad.' He said, 'What do you mean? I got two ducks with two shots. I think that's pretty good.' I told him I do shoot and release. The next time a flock came into our blind, I stood up. I fired twice. Two ducks lost some tail feathers. 'See, *that's* shoot and release.'"

The President's Council on Sustainable Development met in San Francisco in 1994 at the newly created Presidio National Park, which overlooks the Golden Gate Bridge. I stood there gazing out over San Francisco Bay and the bridge, marveling at the view, when somebody from the Park Service approached.

"As a general rule, you can say that all of man's creations take away from the beauty found in nature. But you have to make an exception for the Golden Gate Bridge."

I couldn't agree more. At any time of day, in any weather, from any point of view, this feat of human engineering stands transcendent, enhancing what is already an awe-inspiring land and seascape. "Breathtaking" is deserved in this case.

Congresswoman Nancy Pelosi welcomed us to our deliberations in San Francisco, but our discussions would be fractious. Newt Gingrich had taken over as speaker, and there was an all-out assault in the new Republican House to gut all environmental legislation. At lunch, during the second day of the meeting, one of the NGO presidents stood up in anger and started wagging his finger at the corporate CEOs.

Golden Gate National Recreation Area, Presidio of San Francisco

"We have spent two years working together to build consensus for policies that achieve sustainable development. This work has required that we trust each other so that we can bridge the gaps that have existed. And now, at the very moment, while we are here in San Francisco continuing to negotiate these policies, you have instructed your lobbyists back in DC to flood the halls of Congress to undo everything we have worked for. How can we ever trust you again?"

It looked like the President's Council on Sustainable Development might come to an end. Angry looks and angry words were exchanged. Tom Donahue from the AFL-CIO stepped into the breach.

"Trust is overrated," he said. "I've negotiated hundreds of contracts. I didn't have to trust the people I was negotiating with in order to get a fair contract. It was about the words on paper. Could we reach agreement? That's what was important. You didn't have to trust someone to reach agreement."

With that, we could go on.

Pete Correll, the president of Georgia-Pacific (who often wore socks with Harley-Davidsons on them), said something I found very interesting. Georgia-Pacific was in the lumber business and clear-cut a lot of forests. It had more than its fair share of lawsuits with the EPA. He addressed EPA Administrator Carol Browner with surprising candor.

"Regulate us. Do your job. We might scream and protest, but, in the end, if your regulations are fair, we will find a way to compete successfully and make money. Ignore the noise and do your job."

This was the kind of honest dialogue possible when you gathered a small number of former antagonists around a table enough times. Trust or no trust.

We had another meeting outside of Washington. I can't remember the city—it might have been Chicago—where Mayor Richie Daley, who did not have the reputation as a tree hugger, was actually doing an awful lot to advance sustainable development. But the meeting's highlight, or lowlight, was when Vice President Gore addressed us remotely on the advantages of technology. We were gathered around our tables at lunch when he appeared on a large screen before these titans of industry, environment, and the cabinet. His talk, though, ended up being one technical glitch after another. The video wouldn't display correctly. The sound wouldn't sync with the video. We repeatedly lost the connection. After 15 frustrating minutes, they gave up. That presentation did not really underline the message that technology could provide the answer!

Hiking the Appalachian Trail with Laurie, Tipper Gore, and Jeanie Nelson

Giving the Secret Service the Slip with Tipper Gore

When not on the road or in the office, I was enjoying getting to know the area and people. Laurie and I had another interesting time with a Gore, this time with Mrs. Gore. One Saturday, my friend and colleague Will Martin asked Laurie and me to join him and his wife, Jeanie Nelson, to hike on the Appalachian Trail. As we left DC for Virginia, Will and Jeanie jumped in the back of the car, and so did a surprise guest—Tipper Gore.

"John and Laurie, Tipper is going to join us for the hike. Hope you don't mind," Will said. "John, don't be nervous driving. Tipper snuck out of the house, and the Secret Service doesn't know she's with us. That way, she can have some privacy."

"Sure, Will, I won't be nervous at all, knowing the Secret Service could pull me over at any time."

Before we got to the trail, we stopped at a general store for snacks and water. All five of us went in, Tipper with her ball cap pulled low over her eyes. There were a bunch of guys in camo gear who had been out looking for morel mushrooms. We got our provisions without anyone recognizing Tipper.

"So why the camo gear? How fast do morel mushrooms run?" I said, getting back in the car.

When we got onto the trail, we found out how fast Tipper ran. Well, she didn't run, but she and Jeanie took off at a pace that had Will, Laurie, and me gasping. We had a great day on the trail and returned Tipper to DC with none the wiser.

Judging Leadership

At a President's Council on Sustainable Development meeting in Colorado, a man gave me a copy of a book, *New Technologies for Buildings*, that he had written with Amory Lovins of the Rocky Mountain Institute, one of the best thinkers on energy policy, about how technology could help us achieve sustainability. The book wasn't long, perhaps 150 pages. I slipped it into my briefcase, meaning to read it at some point. At our next meeting, I ran into the man. Sheepishly, I confessed I hadn't yet found the time to read the book.

He said Amory had given it to President Clinton too, and that night the president had stayed up until 2 a.m. reading it. Then, he called his environmental advisor, Katie McGinty, and talked to her for an hour about the book. At 3 a.m., he called Amory to discuss it for another hour. I was too busy, but the president of the United States found the time.

This is one of the reasons I am proud to have worked for Bill Clinton. He had an insatiable appetite for knowledge. The press made a big deal about his appetite for hamburgers and women because that sells papers. They didn't focus as much attention on his incredible hunger for ideas and information that would keep him up until four in the morning, learning about something new. Curiosity to learn takes humility; you must realize you don't know it all and that someone else can teach you something. It takes the ability to listen and learn and then to change the way you think and act. It is an *essential* quality of leadership.

Bill Clinton is a flawed person. There is no excusing his affair with Monica Lewinsky. There is no excuse for his lying about it. But looking back, I believe history will see him as a good president. That is the dilemma we face when judging leaders like Thomas Jefferson, John Kennedy, Winston Churchill, and others. You have to look at the complete person. You can't just take the good parts. Nor can you let the bad parts erase the good. We are all frail, vulnerable human beings. So, I look at what President Clinton achieved in office when I judge his leadership.

Stewardship: It Takes Us All and It Takes Forever

Buzzelli moved on from the President's Council on Sustainable Development and was succeeded as co-chair by Ray Anderson, CEO of Interface Carpet of Atlanta. This $4 billion company manufactured industrial carpet tiles. Ray had a great story that illustrated the concept of "product stewardship," where you are responsible for what you manufacture—forever.

Ray had read Paul Hawken's book, *The Ecology of Commerce*. He realized he would be judged harshly by his grandchildren because his business of making carpets relied on taking petroleum out of the earth, and his product ended up in landfills as waste. He was determined to change the "take, make, waste" paradigm to one that took nothing from the earth and did no harm to the biosphere. He challenged himself and the other engineers at Interface Carpet to find a way.

The breakthrough was in re-imagining his company from one that manufactured durable goods to a company in the service business. Face it. Nobody wants to "own" carpet. It provides a service. Several, in fact. It is comfortable and beautiful. It muffles sound. But when it gets worn out, the last thing you want is to own it because you have to get rid of it, which usually costs you money. Ray changed the way the molecules used to manufacture carpet tiles were assembled, so the company could take the carpets back from their customers and remanufacture them repeatedly. They provided a service, and they could sell those molecules many times. The petroleum they once took out of the earth stayed in the earth. In the first 12 years of implementation, the company's greenhouse gas emissions decreased by 82 percent, while its profits doubled.

Here's another way to think of product stewardship: if you were going to make a TV or a computer or an automobile and knew you had to take it back, you would make it differently. You would manufacture it knowing you had to de-manufacture it. All the expensive and rare materials that go into complex technologies would be recovered and reused. They wouldn't end up in landfills or at the bottom of some poor community's harbor.

My time with the President's Council on Sustainable Development taught me many lessons. The biggest was that with enough time together among the leaders of big business and top environmental and governmental officials, you could see that there could be common ground behind the posturing. These leaders shared respect for science and the task at hand to control pollution. There was also an appreciation by business that pollution is waste, and waste is inefficiency. If there are ways to become more efficient, we can restore the environment, increase profits, and share wealth. These goals don't have to be mutually exclusive.

Another lesson is that business can act much more quickly than government. Generally, it is driven by data and can respond efficiently. When a challenge needs to be met, things happen quickly if business can be motivated to act. The challenge is making sure that change is in the public's interest. That is not an easy challenge.

The biggest lesson, though, was that sustainable development was not a top-down concept but a bottom-up one. We discovered by meeting in various communities that the fundamental building block of sustainability is an active, informed citizenry. Informed, because if you act without information, you are dangerous. Active, because if you have information but don't act, you are irrelevant. I have said that before, but I repeat it here because I have learned the truth of it. Citizens can gather in communities large and small. They do not have to wait for permission from Washington to create jobs, restore the earth, and do it in a way that involves everyone.

Dave Crockett was once asked who needed to get involved and how long it would take to make change. His answer remains true.

"It takes us all, and it takes forever."

Leadership at the local level was and is critical. When you have that, you can generate a lot of energy around the concepts the President's Council on Sustainable Development was advocating. Our office tried to nurture that everywhere we found it. And there were amazing examples.

I spoke at a meeting in San Luis Obispo, California, where 1,000 people turned out to chart a course for their future. They were very afraid that they might become Los Angeles, which I guess is a fate worse than death, and they wanted to do everything they could to avoid that. I have found that people often define what they want by giving examples of what they don't want. It is a helpful city-planning tool—the process of elimination.

On the other coast, we went to the much smaller and poorer community of Cape Charles, Virginia, on the Outer Banks. A mecca for bird watchers, Cape Charles is incredibly scenic, with the Chesapeake Bay to the west and the Atlantic to the east. It also had the highest percentage of homes with outdoor plumbing and other poverty indicators.

On the beach at Cape Charles, Virginia—a birdwatcher's paradise

Roan Conrad and I organized a federal roundtable of every agency we thought could play a role in assisting Cape Charles. We included state, county, and local agencies. We heard about the town's plan for itself, and then I chaired a meeting to extract from each agency what they could do to bring the plan to life. As we went around the room, there was both a sense of pressure to do something and a sense that if one's agency did something, its impact would be multiplied by every other agency's actions, so there would be great leverage. But the work started with a local plan born of local consensus and leadership.

The only problem from my standpoint was that after taking a short flight from DC to Norfolk, I had to rent a car to get there. I was running a little late for the evening meeting, and there was no traffic on the Chesapeake Bay Bridge, which is a straight shot that goes on forever. The tolls have long since paid for the bridge itself, but they still pay for a bridge police force that hangs out at the end of the bridge. They got me, which made me even later. When I arrived, I apologized to the local officials and explained the delay. The mayor was understanding.

"Oh, that's a notorious speed trap. Don't worry about it. Give me the ticket. I'll take care of it in the morning."

Being respectful of local customs, I gave him the ticket.

The next morning, after what I thought was a very successful meeting, the mayor thanked me for doing such a good job and gave me an update on my citation.

"Oh, by the way, I took care of your ticket. You are due in court in three months!"

A clever way to get return visitors. When I returned home, I told Laurie to plan for a getaway in a few months.

"Cape Charles is a beautiful town. There is a B&B right on Chesapeake Bay. You are going to love it!"

Roan found another place with an amazing mayor. Tom Suozzi was elected mayor of Glen Cove, New York, in 1993. Both his father and uncle had been mayors before him. While Glen Cove was on the "Gold Coast" of Long Island next to wealthy towns like Oyster Bay, Glen Cove itself was working class and industrial. It had two polluted Superfund sites on the waterfront, as well as a garbage dump and an unfinished housing project. The young mayor felt a familial ownership for the condition of the city, and he was determined to right all the wrongs.

Roan unearthed a small grant to convene federal, state, county, and local partners, and we met in the Glen Cove firehouse at the head of the harbor. Mayor Suozzi, who chaired the meeting, was amazing to watch. He began with a history of the community. He told us how we got to where we were today. He painted a picture of the future and what the harbor we were looking at would look like with clean water, economic activity, and housing. He laid out what each official needed to do to get us to that future. The plan made sense. He wasn't asking the impossible of anyone.

One by one, he put each of us on the spot.

"OK, Army Corps, you're going to dredge the harbor? Good! When? Two years? Not good enough. Can you do it in 18 months? You need EPA to remove PCBs? OK, EPA, how long is that going to take?"

Around and around the room he went. No one was spared. Everyone was on the hot seat. Everyone understood they had to be accountable to the group. They understood that they played just a part, but their contribution made a much larger picture possible. They needed to give a little to get a lot.

The plan worked. Leadership at the local level is critical. It is no accident that mayors are trusted more than other elected officials. Tom Suozzi became a Nassau County executive, a big deal in New York. He is now a congressman. But he left his mark on his hometown.

It takes us all. And it takes forever.

Tracking Down the Old Family Farm

My travels for the President's Council on Sustainable Development took me to many places, even to the past. Dave Buzzelli asked me to give a talk to the Chamber of Commerce, where Dow was headquartered in Midland, Michigan. After the 7 a.m. meeting, I had some time to kill before catching a flight back. I headed to nearby Flint to track down some personal history.

My ancestor Henry Crapo left New Bedford before the Civil War for Michigan to manage forestland bought with whaling money. Before long, he had been elected mayor of Flint. Jim Sharp, mayor of Flint when I was first elected in New Bedford, told me he had a picture of Henry Crapo in his office. Later, Henry Crapo was elected governor of Michigan and served two terms. He died at

Henry H. Crapo

65. His great nephew William Crapo Durant created General Motors in Flint. Durant built the company and lost it twice, ending his roller-coaster career broke and selling hamburgers in a Flint bowling alley.

I wanted to track down the Crapo Farm where Henry had been buried and where the famous Crapo herd of Hereford cattle had been raised. I had managed what was left of this herd when I returned to New Bedford after graduate school, and I was curious to see its origin. I knew my great uncle William Crapo had sold the Flint farm to the Teamsters for a housing development, but I figured I would give it a shot.

*Harlow Curtice, president of General Motors, and Charles Mott
at the dedication of the Durant Plaza in the Flint Cultural Center*

I drove around Flint until I found a grain store. I parked my rental car and walked in.

"Anybody here know of Crapo Farm?" I said in a loud voice.

A voice from the back of the store yelled back.

"Yeah, I used to work there."

We introduced ourselves, and the man agreed to take me there. All that was left of the farm were two silos whose tops were missing. He showed me a field with a contraption that he said was the remains of what Henry Crapo had used to drain the marshes to create pasture.

Stanford Tappan Crapo with Hereford cattle

I had heard from my grandmother, who was a Crapo, that Henry brought in Herefords from Canada. Because there was a lot of malaria in Michigan, he wanted to eliminate the mosquitoes' breeding grounds. The Crapo herd won many prizes. At the time, it was the oldest herd of registered Herefords continuously owned by one family in North and South America. I remember my Uncle Bill explaining why he had sold off such a famous herd.

"It's a lot easier to be the oldest than it is to be the best."

I understood. They used to be the best. Then, they became just the oldest.

I did locate Henry's gravesite, and then l spent some time looking around Flint. I saw that it, too, was no longer the best. GM's travails had left Flint in a sorry state. Its high-flying days of Billy Durant were long gone, and Flint was suffering as a community does when the one industry in a one-industry town leaves.

The Crapo farmhouse, called "Grassmoor"

CHAPTER 9

Turning Wild Ideas into Federal Programs

Fisheries Crises

While we were working with the President's Council for Sustainable Development, our office was also charged with developing a response to the fisheries crisis in New England. There were several reasons for this assignment. One was that as the former mayor of New Bedford and organizer of the fishing industry in New England, I was familiar with the issues and the people. I had a lot of valuable support on Capitol Hill, and the New England delegation was particularly powerful. Another reason was that the National Marine Fisheries Service, sometimes called NOAA Fisheries for short, had the job of regulating the groundfish industry, which was the industry most in crisis. As the regulator, NOAA Fisheries was not liked, to say the least. Having me lead the disaster assistance might make it more palatable.

I met with Rollie Schmitten, who had gotten the top NOAA Fisheries job I had competed for earlier. We had a good talk and developed an excellent relationship that never soured. He assigned me a person from the Sustainable Fisheries Division named Bruce Morehead. Bruce didn't know what he was in for when he met with Lance and me. The culture of the National Marine Fisheries Service and the culture of our office could not have been more different. Lance and I were wide-open thinkers. I had on my desk a framed gift from Senator Ted Kennedy of his brother Bobby's famous quote, "Some men see things as they are and ask why. I dream of things that never were and ask why not."

Bruce lived in the land of rules, regulations, and small, incremental change. In addition to our being political appointees and newcomers and Bruce being a career professional lifer, there was something else that could have made this relationship difficult. The fact that we were working on a disaster in New England was in itself an indictment of a failure to properly manage a fishery. Our work was a walking criticism of the National Marine Fisheries Service itself. Or at least it could be seen that way. But Rollie and Bruce never did.

Bruce, Lance, and I developed one of the best relationships we could ever have. Lance or I might throw out a wild idea, and Bruce, instead of saying, "That's crazy, you can't do that. You guys should be committed," would say something like, "OK, we might be able to get something like that accomplished if we did it this way. What do you think of that approach?" With that kind of back and forth, our goals would get implemented, and our wild-ass ideas could be turned into federal programs.

We started meeting with fishermen. We had one meeting to begin assessing needs in Portland, Maine, with about 25 people. Lance and I drove up with a young man from our office, Ruben Yui, who was also a political appointee. As we talked about the needs of fishing families at the meeting, I found myself saying, "What do we need?" I was thinking back to my recent past when I had been working for these same people as part of the Co-Op. After a few minutes, Barbara Stevenson, a formidable woman who owned several boats in Portland, looked me coldly in the eye.

"John, you're not 'we' anymore."

With that barrier established, we continued to work, and we identified 11 needs that fishermen, their families, and their communities would need if they were to get through the crisis. The list included grants, loans, health care, industry involved in research, and a novel idea to reduce the fleet's capacity by buying out boats.

We started developing each of these ideas, often with help from industry members. Jim O'Malley from Point Judith led a small group looking at reducing fishing capacity. He reviewed programs in Scotland and other places and talked with industry members, bankers, brokers, and others.

He came up with a simple, fair, and very intelligent plan. The premise was that a fishing vessel was worth about what it grossed in sales. Jim's team created a formula for an auction where the government would ask for bid prices from people who wanted to sell their boats. That would be the numerator. The average gross over the last three years would be the denominator. If a vessel owner wanted to sell his boat for $1.0 million and it grossed $1.0 million, its score would be 1.0/1.0 or 1. If the boat had grossed $2.0 million, the score would have been 1.0/2.0 or 0.5. The government would pick the lowest scores until it ran out of money. Simple, fair, accurate, transparent—and designed by industry.

Now, all we needed was the funding.

Apropos of Approps: Finding the Funding

One day when I was in my office, Commander Don Winter asked about the fishing disaster work. I told him we were surveying needs in New England and trying to finance the relief.

"You know, John, there is $65 million salted away for fishery resource disasters in a Defense Appropriations Bill?"

I could not believe what he was saying.

"What did you just say, Don? Why hasn't anyone told me about this? Does anybody know about it?"

"I do."

"How do you know about it?"

"I put it there when I worked on the Hill for Senator John Breaux of Louisiana. It's for fishery resource disasters caused by natural disasters like hurricanes Iniki, Hugo, and Andrew."

This might work.

"How much did you say again?"

"$65 million. In a Defense Approps bill."

"I owe you big time, Don."

I went across the hall to Legislative Affairs to talk to Sally Yozell. I asked her if she knew about the funds. She told me it didn't exist.

I went down the hall to John Carey in the deputy undersecretary's office. Same answer. Didn't exist. I saw Doug Hall, the assistant secretary. He didn't know about it either.

Maybe this wasn't going to work.

I was losing confidence. I went back to Don. He insisted the funds were there.

"Remember, I said it was in a Defense bill? These guys aren't used to looking in Defense bills," he said.

A little while later, Don brought me the language. There it was in black and white—$65 million for fishery resource disasters caused by natural disasters.

Making the Case for Assistance

Excited again, I walked down the hall to see Terry Garcia, NOAA's chief lawyer. I told him the situation and said we had a fishery resource disaster in New England. I told him Secretary Brown wanted us to address it, and there was tremendous support on the Hill for us to do something quickly. I told him we had met with fishing families and had a report with needs. Terry was a very sharp lawyer from California. He read the language.

"John, there is no question with groundfish that you have a 'fishery resource disaster.' The resource is in the toilet and has been for quite a while."

But it wasn't going to be that easy.

"Correct me if I'm wrong. Isn't the cause overfishing? That's not a natural disaster. I don't think you meet the second clause of the law. I'm not sure we can do this."

He wasn't wrong that overfishing was a big part of the problem.

Terry Garcia   *Doug Hall*

"Terry, you are correct that the primary cause is overfishing. But that is human nature. What is more natural than that?!"

He laughed, but he didn't bite at that argument. I tried another tack.

"Terry, there are a lot of families who are hurting up in New England because there aren't enough groundfish. If we provide economic assistance to these families, that helps them in the short term while taking steps to protect the long term, so we would be doing the right thing. And everyone would support this help, and no one would oppose this help, so it is highly unlikely that anyone is going to challenge your legal opinion because we are doing what everyone wants us to do."

Terry thought for a minute.

"Well then, John, we are going to need a very aggressive legal opinion."

That is why Terry is a good lawyer and an even better public servant. He keeps his eye on the ball and doesn't get distracted.

I went back to Assistant Secretary Doug Hall. He had a nice Southern accent and a wonderful sense of humor. Doug turned to me on one of our walks down the hall to see Secretary Brown.

"They must hate to see us walk down the hall. They're doing economic development, trade, and tourism, minority business development, and all we bring them is fish shit."

Doug was most certainly right. I have found that with fish, there are no win-win solutions and very few win-lose solutions. Mostly, it is lose-lose and all about the apportionment of pain.

On another occasion, Doug and I were walking up the block for a meeting at the White House, probably with a young White House staffer.

"John, you know what I hate about these meetings. Every young kid who works in the White House thinks that as soon as they enter the building, their IQ goes up 50 points."

Oh, I know an antidote for that.

One of the first times I entered the White House, I was dressed up in my darkest power suit and tie. My hair was slicked back, and I was certainly feeling full of myself as I approached the south security gate. Just as I was going through the gate, a bird crapped on my head! How perfect was that! Quite a humbling experience. It should be a mandatory part of White House orientation for all government workers as a way to let us know that in the eyes of everyone else, we are just, well, you get the idea.

At any rate, Doug and I had a great relationship. He supported the work of our office as much as he could. I told him we had identified the needs, the funding, and the legal basis. I told him we had a good team with Bruce Morehead from the National Marine Fisheries Service and our folks.

"John, you have to back it up with numbers. Make the case. Document it."

"OK, I'll start with the Census Department: they are down on the 3rd floor."

I went to Census and asked how many fishermen were in New Bedford. They came back in a few minutes and told me 300. *What?* I knew that number was way off.

"Thanks, you've been a big help."

I told Doug we wouldn't get any helpful information from the Census Bureau. Fishermen are notoriously hard to track, but 300 was ridiculously low.

"John, we are going to need you to guess, and when you guess, another word for that is 'estimate.' And you are a United States government official, so that will become an 'official government estimate.' Now get to work."

We got to work. Part of that work was a meeting with Secretary Brown and about 25 leaders on Capitol Hill, including such powerhouses as Senate Majority Leader George Mitchell, Senators Kennedy, Kerry, Cohen, Pell, and Representatives Moakley, Studds, Frank, and Markey. The New England delegation had some serious "juice." They pressed the point with Secretary Brown that the spotted owl in the Pacific Northwest wasn't the only national emergency. They pushed him to declare New England groundfish a fishery resource disaster and allocate funding. They also pressed him to name a point person they could communicate with on behalf of the administration.

Secretary Brown said he was seriously looking into a disaster declaration.

"John Bullard is my point person on this issue. He has my full confidence and acts with my authority."

On the short drive back to Commerce, I rode with Jonathan Sallett, Ron Brown's chief policy advisor.

"Jonathan, what does it mean to be the secretary's 'point person?'"

"John, it means when all this is over, the points of all the arrows will be sticking in your back, not the secretary's. Understand?"

"Completely."

The next day, Secretary Brown led a meeting with Jim Baker, Doug Hall, Rollie Schmitten, and Will Ginsberg, the assistant secretary of the Economic Development Administration, another Commerce agency that could be helpful. Others also were in the group, including Dr. Andy Rosenberg, who had taken over as the regional administrator of the Northeast region of the National Marine Fisheries Service.

Andy gave a concise briefing about the status of groundfish and the underlying cause of overfishing. While he didn't question the economic pain, he was concerned about what would be done to rebuild the resource. There was a proposed plan amendment under consideration by the New England Fishery Management Council, called Amendment 5, that was being vigorously opposed by the industry. Andy felt the plan was needed, at a minimum. As usual, the industry was questioning the science behind it, NOAA's science.

Secretary Brown took all this in. He was a very quick study, and he didn't waste time.

"Look, we are going to help these people out. They need the help, and we have the resources. We have legal justification and congressional backing. John Bullard is on point. You guys talk to Congress."

He directed me to form a federal interagency task force with assistance from Labor, Small Business Administration, Health and Human Services, and others. He emphasized the urgency.

"Keep talking to the industry and fishing families and local leaders about what they need. And do it in a way that responds to what Andy is saying, that protects the long term. And remember, this is a national emergency. So, act like it. People are hurting. Don't waste time."

Lance and I walked down Pennsylvania Avenue to the Labor Department, where we met with Tom Glynn, deputy secretary to Secretary Robert Reich. Both Reich and Glynn were from Massachusetts, so they knew the situation.

The *Boston Globe* had done a story about the dozen or so people from Massachusetts that had gone down to join the Clinton administration, promoting the idea of our state's influence. We were all on the list. So was Jane Garvey, who had run Public Works and then Logan Airport for Mike Dukakis. Clinton had appointed her to run his Federal Highway Administration and then to become the first female head of the Federal Aviation Administration. She was another Massachusetts transplant living in the Lansburgh, just off Pennsylvania, where Laurie and I lived before moving to Capitol Hill.

A beautifully restored former department store, the Lansburgh reminded me of New Bedford's old Star Store with huge plate glass display windows. We lived on the third floor with views up and down Pennsylvania Avenue. The restaurant Jaleo's was on the ground level, where we would often eat. It was something new, a tapas restaurant started by Chef Jose Andreas before anyone had heard of the man. He rocketed to fame as a celebrity chef and then turned his fame to good works such as making 3.5 million meals for people in Puerto Rico after Hurricane Maria. Interesting people lived in the Lansburgh. We could run into Janet Reno or Betty Frieden in the fitness center or see the guards making sure no one set foot on the fourth floor, where Jean-Bertrand Aristide waited in exile to be reinstated as president of Haiti.

The Lansburgh was in a transitional neighborhood. Half the buildings were gentrified, but porn shops and vacant buildings were still nearby. It was a ten-minute walk down Pennsylvania Avenue for me to work. Laurie worked at the National Archives for a while, almost right across the street. The Navy Memorial was nearby, as were Metro stops and the shops at Union Station. We could see the classical architecture of the Portrait Gallery out one of our windows, and a few blocks away was the modern white marble edge of IM Pei's East Wing of the National Gallery. During our stay in the Lansburgh, the Portrait Gallery had a show of Albert Pinkham Ryder, while the East Wing featured the magnificent landscapes of Albert Bierstadt.

"Imagine that," I said to Laurie. "These two world-famous painters dominating Washington, and they are buried within 100 yards of each other in Rural Cemetery in New Bedford."

The Lansburgh Apartments complex was a renovated department store off Pennsylvania Avenue.

Setting Up Fishing Family Assistance Centers

I explained to Tom Glynn that fishermen are technically self-employed, so even though they may not be fishing, they never get laid off. This means they don't qualify for unemployment compensation. When a factory closed in New Bedford, the Labor Department would set up a dislocated worker assistance center, counsel workers on how to file for benefits, and help them get training for new jobs. They would help them apply for extended health and unemployment benefits. It was not the workers' fault that the factory shut down, and it was in society's best interest to get each person back to work as soon as possible so they could again be fully contributing members of society.

"Tom, fishermen don't want more than other workers. But they don't see why they should get less."

I made the case that we needed his assistance.

"Now, I know you have every right to sit here and say, 'John, you guys in Commerce made this mess by not managing this fishery, so you go and fix it.' And, Tom, you would have a good point, and we have got some resources, which we are going to use to help these people. But we could use your help. We are a small agency. You can help a lot more than we can."

To his credit, Tom brought the Department of Labor all in. He said Labor would see that fishermen were eligible for unemployment benefits as if they were factory workers. He would instruct people at the unemployment offices.

We got that set up but heard fishermen weren't taking advantage of the program because they didn't feel comfortable. We decided to use $12 million of the emergency funding for this crisis. We proposed to Secretary Brown that we use $2 million for a pilot buyout program to reduce fishing capacity. We would use $1 million to set up six Fishing Family Assistance Centers and $9 million for grants. He listened to what we had in mind, approved our plan, and said he wanted the centers set up and staffed within two months. He would travel to open the first one. We were going to open centers in Point Judith, New Bedford, Gloucester, and Portland. We were also opening two mobile units.

We found sites near the waterfront in each city and staffed them with people known and trusted by the industry. We trained these people to be outreach workers so they could recruit and counsel fishermen on unemployment, health benefits, job training, and whatever else they might need. As an example of the kind of person we wanted, we hired Rodney Avila in New Bedford, and he was excellent. Fishermen were comfortable talking with him. Rodney is a compassionate, intelligent person—precisely the kind of person you want to help someone get back on their feet.

Tom Glynn steered us to two of his best people in New England. Sean King from Massachusetts was the son of Jim King, the renowned head of the Office of Personnel Management and advisor to many Democratic presidents. A literal and figurative giant of a man, Jim King had sworn me in as a member of the Senior Executive Service when I joined the administration. Partnering with Sean was Tom Davis, son of former Vermont Governor Dean Davis. Cutting the red tape back in DC was Eddie Flynn, son of my friend Boston Mayor Ray Flynn. Eddie is now president of the Boston City Council.

Lance, Tom, Sean, and I drove thousands of miles over New England to meet with fishermen and local and state officials. We always relied on Tom to get us where we needed to go, and invariably, in those days before Waze and Google maps, we would get lost. Getting lost with these guys was always entertaining, so we never took the assignment away from Tom. There was never a shortage of stories among four people with this amount of politics in their blood.

Sean is considerably younger than I am, but I learned a lesson from him that I have repeated more times than I can count.

"With all due deference to Tip O'Neill, all politics is *not* local," he said during one of our drives. "All politics is personal."

All politics is personal. It may seem obvious, but so many don't understand it. It is LBJ with his arm around his next victim. It is Ronald Reagan telling stories. It is Teddy Kennedy singing patriotic songs to Orrin Hatch to get his support for a children's health care bill. It was what the four of us did all the time. We built, maintained, and nurtured personal relationships, realizing they are two-way streets. Listen. Laugh. Empathize. Remember.

A FIG Leaf: The Fishing Industry Does Science and Other Grants

With great help from Bruce Morehead and Harry Mears at the National Marine Fisheries Service, we also set up a $9 million Fishing Industry Grant (FIG) program. There already was a grant program called Saltonstall/Kennedy, named for two Massachusetts senators, but the S/K program had a reputation for being a bureaucratic nightmare inaccessible to working fishermen. We wanted the FIG program to be simple, fair, and transparent. We wanted the emphasis to be on involving fishermen, but we wanted the goal to be advancing science while helping fishermen.

I remember a meeting in Doug Hall's office to discuss the program's design. Gary Matlock, a senior National Marine Fisheries Service official, balked at the goal.

"Fishermen can't do science; they aren't qualified," he said.

For me, this sentiment embodied an attitude at the National Marine Fisheries Service that was the cause of a lot of our problems and was the reason so many fishermen hated the agency.

"Gary, Vice President Gore has a NOAA program that is encouraging sixth graders to collect samples for our weather service. Are you telling me that sixth graders can do science, but fishermen can't?"

"Well, John, if you don't call it science but just call it data collection, I guess I could live with it."

So, the FIG program was born. It went out in two phases of $4.5 million each. Fishermen wrote proposals that involved partnerships with universities or scientific groups, marrying short-term economic relief with long-term benefit to the resource.

We got several interesting proposals. One thing that surprised me was that half the money ended up going to wild harvest fishermen who wanted to explore aquaculture ventures. Investing $4.5 million in aquaculture in the mid-1990s was a considerable investment, and there was a tremendous variety from shellfish to seaweed. I talked to several fishermen making this switch. Their motives varied but basically fell into two categories. Some wanted to do it temporarily until groundfish recovered, and then they hoped to return to wild harvest. Others said aquaculture work showed them a new path.

Senator John Kerry

"Before, I felt badly every time I pulled a fish out of the sea, knowing I was depleting the resource. Now, I know I am reaping what I sow," one fisherman told me. "I have a much better feeling about what I'm doing at the end of the day."

One fisherman was particularly inventive, growing a seaweed called nori and using it to wrap sushi. Nori is an invasive seaweed and can be grown only in eastern Maine, where the cold water kills it each winter, so it doesn't take over. The fisherman/entrepreneur would set out seed in the spring to harvest later, employing out-of-work fishermen who worked machines that looked like big upside-down underwater lawnmowers. After, they pressed the seaweed into very thin paper-like sheets. When I visited to see how it was going, the fisherman/aquaculturist had just taken delivery of a paper press the size of a shipping container. It was in his garage with instructions on how to install it—in Korean. Undeterred, he was busy putting all the pieces together.

Not everyone embraced changing their lifestyle. At a big meeting in New Bedford with Senator Kerry, the attitude of many fishermen seemed to be, "Just leave the money in a wheelbarrow at the end of a pier. We know what to do with it. We don't want to change the way we fish. We want to keep doing what we have always done and have you subsidize our losses."

I give Senator Kerry great credit for standing up in front of that angry crowd on the top floor of the Bourne Counting House and saying directly to them that the groundfish crisis meant they would have to catch fewer fish. It is a very rare politician who is willing to say that even though they know it to be true. The ones who know the issues the best, Gerry Studds, John Kerry, and Ed Markey, have had the courage to speak truth to fishermen. Most others take a convenient pass when it comes time to say that quotas must be reduced.

We gave a $200,000 grant to Eric Dawicki from Fairhaven to start up a marine training school in the old YWCA building in New Bedford. He wanted to train out-of-work fishermen for other marine trades like driving tugboats. The program successfully helped many fishermen keep their careers on the water. The school is now the Northeast Maritime Institute. It has several campuses and offers a degree-granting program. We gave Eric an early boost.

That grant also illustrated the politics of grant-making. We would give our list of grants to Sally Yozell across the hall. She had to be very careful about notifying members of Congress and senators at *exactly* the same time so no one would have an advantage to call recipients or the press with the news. It was a bit of a blood sport. I'm sure that Kennedy's and Kerry's offices got the news of Eric's grant simultaneously. But as in every such contest, Kennedy's office notified Eric, the press, and everybody else so far in advance of Kerry's office that you would have thought he was the only one responsible. He was a master at this. For those of us who actually did the work, it was fun to watch and admire! When Senator Kennedy ate everyone's lunch, he didn't leave any crumbs on the table. His staff was always the best.

Managing Fisheries: Not So Simple and a Demo Boat Buyout

With the $2 million, we ran a demonstration buyout program in New England and bought 11 boats to reduce the fleet. Almost all of them were steel, so we retired their permits and scrapped the vessels at no cost. Fewer boats fishing gave a break to the fish. Everyone seemed pleased, a rarity for a government program.

I attended nearly every New England Fishery Management Council meeting, and Andy Rosenberg and I acted as a team. Andy pushed for tougher regulations to bring the groundfish stocks back. When fishermen and their advocates complained about the economic impact, Andy did not sugarcoat the situation.

"You are absolutely right. This is going to hurt," he told them. "You need to go talk to John Bullard about that. He is going to help you. But my job is to bring back the resource."

This teamwork was one way we worked toward long-term benefits along with the buyouts and grants. And finally, we had opened lines of communication between fishing families, the council, NOAA, Capitol Hill, NGOs, and the press. People were talking and listening to each other. Something approaching trust was building.

I was leading a federal interagency team in DC that was leveraging resources from NOAA, EDA, Labor, SBA, and HHS. We coordinated with the governors' offices in five New England states and kept the powerful and very interested New England congressional delegation engaged and supportive. Our team earned the Commerce Department Gold Medal for its work. That award was nice, but it would have been better if we could have brought groundfish back.

Groundfish management is more complicated than it looks. One day, Deputy Secretary of Commerce Dave Barram stopped me in the hall. Dave came from Silicon Valley, where he was a chief financial officer at Apple. He was a sharp cookie. He was also a very good and regular guy.

"John, I don't get it," he said. "Why don't we just set a quota based on science for how much groundfish can be caught and then have a few big factory ships go catch them? That's the way we would solve the problem in the valley."

He wasn't the only one who thought that way, but it was not that simple.

"Dave, that certainly makes a lot of sense on the face of it," I told him and took the opportunity to issue an invitation.

"If you have a day to spare, I would love it if you would be willing to meet with some fishermen in New Hampshire who could talk to you about that question."

To his great credit, Dave agreed. One day, I picked him up at Logan Airport in Boston and drove him to the Forestry Center just past the famous Yokem's Restaurant, off the circle in Portsmouth, New Hampshire. Erik Anderson, John Williams, and about six other fishermen talked to Dave about the advantages of a small boat fleet. They told him how small boats created more jobs for the same amount of quota. They explained how they were more resilient and could adapt to shifting stocks. After about three hours, I drove Dave back to Logan.

"John, those guys should be teaching at the London School of Economics."

"Well, Dave, I don't know how many of them have their college degrees let alone their PhDs, but they are a smart bunch. Otherwise, they wouldn't be successful fishermen."

His day in New Hampshire gave Dave an accurate vision of the strength of the small boat New England fishery and what we were trying to protect.

Great TV

The press was also interested in what we were doing. Roan Conrad got me an interview on the *Diane Rehm Show*. A friend of mine, Terry Schaefer, was a producer for the *Today Show* and set up an interview with Bryant Gumbel, who was doing a show from Boston. As I sat there waiting for him to turn to me, I marveled at how quickly he could change gears, swiftly moving from the fisheries disaster to another topic when my three minutes of fame were up.

Perhaps the most interesting press encounter was at a Town Hall Meeting in Gloucester. *CBS Sunday Morning* came to do a piece. As the camera crew set up, Lance sat at the front table with the producer. I was in my suit, standing in the middle of the room, when a fisherman named Pepe came up to me and started yelling. He was about six inches from my face. From the smell of alcohol, I thought perhaps he had just come back from a fishing trip and imbibed in the long-honored tradition of lifting a glass in thanks for a safe return. He may have been thankful for that, but he was irate with me. His voice boomed angrily through the hall. His language was colorful. His hands gestured wildly.

Spotting drama, the cameraman came over and stood about one foot from us, shooting away. Even with the fisherman's volume, I could hear Lance and the producer talking in the background.

"I think this guy is going to slug Bullard," the producer said.

Ever my wingman, Lance calmly answered.

"Yeah, great TV, isn't it?!"

I listened to the man's complaints. His rant went on and on. I let him wear himself out. Fortunately, he didn't hit me.

My feeling on situations like this is that people have a right to be angry. It doesn't cost the taxpayer any money to let them blow off steam as long as nobody gets hurt. I don't take it personally. The great majority of fishermen I have dealt with are incredibly respectful, even during very difficult times. There are a few jerks, just like anywhere else. Actually, fewer jerks in fishing than anywhere else.

How to Not Catch Fish: Federal Relief for a Troubled Industry

"It will be a natural disaster if Senator Breaux doesn't get any of the 'Breaux money,'" Doug Hall told me as we discussed the requests we had gotten from the delegations in the Gulf of Mexico, the Pacific Northwest, and again from New England. What we had done in New England with the grants, the buyouts, and the centers had proved so popular that other fishing communities were asking us for similar help.

We took an immediate look at the cases in each region. There was still no question that New England had a "fishery resource disaster," but questionable whether a "natural disaster" caused it. However, we had made that call once, and no one had objected, so we could do it again. In the Gulf of Mexico, they had had one natural disaster after another, starting with Hurricane Andrew, which was mentioned specifically in the bill. The only problem was that the harvest of oysters and shrimp didn't seem to be affected by this kind of event, so it was hard to prove a fishery resource disaster. Only in the Pacific Northwest, with El Nino causing drought that reduced the flow in rivers and depleted salmon stocks, did we have an ironclad case to answer both components of the bill.

We went to Secretary Brown with a two-part strategy. First, we proposed allocating funds from the "Breaux money" to all three sections of the country. Second, we should allocate *all* of it so there wouldn't be any scraps to fight over. He agreed.

We decided that $15 million should go to the Pacific Northwest. Then, Senator Kerry had a conversation with his friend Senator John Breaux on the floor of the Senate. Out of that came an agreement that New England would get $25 million for boat buyouts, and the Gulf would get $13 million to be worked out by the states. I don't know how Kerry got that agreement for New England, just that he did. Now, we had all the coastal delegations supporting the release of the remaining funds in the disaster pool.

On August 3, 1995, the White House announced to news outlets the award of $53 million to fishermen in the Northeast, Northwest, and Gulf of Mexico. We had to announce the same with the delegations virtually simultaneously.

Secretary Brown, Doug Hall, and I went to the central portion of the Capitol, where Senator Kennedy had made his "hideaway office" available to us with its breathtaking view down the Mall to the Washington Monument and the Lincoln Memorial.

Secretary Ron Brown announces $53 million in aid to fishing communities.

Outside the office, staffers assembled the New England delegation with the New England press. We marched out, and Secretary Brown addressed the group, announcing that $25 million would be made available for a vessel buyout program as soon as the New England Fishery Management Council voted to approve Amendment 5, which Andy had been championing. Everybody smiled, shook hands, and posed for pictures. It took about 15 minutes tops, and then people were shown the door. We returned to the hideaway while the delegation from the Gulf came in. Secretary Brown repeated the same process, although he made no condition on this announcement. Wash, rinse, and repeat for the Pacific Northwest. It all took less than an hour, and we were back in the car to the Commerce building at the other end of Pennsylvania Avenue.

As tricky as all that was to navigate, we still had our work cut out for us. We had to translate these intentions into real programs. For New England, it was straightforward; we knew we were going to do a much larger version of the buyout program we had already run. We just had to wait for the New England Fishery Management Council to pass Amendment 5. The industry wanted the buyout, so it was a real incentive to support a plan that hadn't been too popular. Amendment 5 was going to significantly restrict the number of days that fishermen could fish. As usual during debates like this, when the science clearly showed that the restrictions were needed—and the Magnuson Act required we act based on the "best available science"—the industry countered with the argument that the science was not strong enough and charged that the restrictions would put them out of business.

It put New England council members in a tough spot. But the $25 million buyout made it easier. Ultimately, the council passed Amendment 5. I remember Jim O'Malley, who, more than anyone, had guided the design of the buyout program and was responsible for the industry support for it, casting his vote.

"I vote yes on Amendment 5 and the $25 million buyout," he said.

Of course, the motion was only about Amendment 5, but Jim felt the only way he could go back to Point Judith and face his constituency was if he paired the two.

The Gulf of Mexico was more complicated. We had to design programs that all five states wanted. I was talking to Lance and Bruce about how we could possibly get an agreement between the state directors when Larry Simpson, at the time the executive director of the Gulf States Marine Fisheries Commission, called. In his Mississippi drawl, Larry extended an invitation.

"John, I have an idea for how we can reach agreement on how to spend the disaster money."

He wanted us to come fishing in the Gulf with the directors.

"We'll catch some fish, we'll tell stories, we'll drink some bourbon and eat good food, and we won't come back until we have a plan everyone can agree to. What do you think?"

"Larry, that sounds like the best idea I've heard in a long time."

Bruce and I boarded a nice sport fishing boat with Larry and the state directors and headed out into the middle of the Gulf of Mexico. As there were nine of us (Texas brought two guys), we took turns fishing and telling stories while also throwing out ideas about programs that would meet each state's needs.

One of the best storytellers was Corky Perret, who was working for Louisiana at the time. He later got fired by a new governor and moved over to Mississippi. A proud Cajun who can bust your chops with the best of them, Corky is entertaining, very smart, and a legend in the South and beyond. After I left the government the first time, I wanted to give Matthew and Toby a taste of this culture, so I asked Corky if we could go fishing with him for a week. We stayed in Venice for a week and fished with Corky and one of his friends. Corky dubbed me "Big Bull," Matthew "Tall Bull," and Toby "Little Bull." As Corky had become like a family member, we all called him "Fulla Bull." He's a friend for life.

During the fishing trip with the state directors, the Gulf plan gradually came together. There was some horse trading, and Larry was masterful at keeping us moving forward toward agreement. After two nights at sea, we returned with a lot of fish and an agreement that addressed shrimpers, oyster farmers, gillnetters, recreational fishermen, and processors. Each state felt it got a fair share. That is to say, they all complained equally. Well, that isn't true. No one could complain like Corky, but that was a given.

For the Pacific, it took longer. Lance and I scheduled about a dozen town hall meetings in fishing communities from San Francisco to Seattle, which we would do in two trips. We alerted Dr. Steve Freese from the National Marine Fisheries Service West Coast Regional Office about our schedule, and he helped us to meet key players along the way. We invited congressional delegation members to attend the meetings with us and federal agencies like SBA, Labor, and EDA. We coordinated our work and travel plans with the governors' offices in the three states. It was a busy, ambitious itinerary, and we were going to hear from a lot of people about the needs of the region.

There was going to be a lot of driving and long days. But Lance always found a way to fit in fun whenever we could squeeze it in. At the San Francisco International Airport, he finagled us a red convertible for the same price as the economy car we had booked. There just *happened* to be an afternoon baseball game at Giants Stadium on our way into the city. Our first appointment wasn't until dinner that night, so we waited until the second inning when scalped tickets were 75 percent off. We watched the rest of the game. Lance had played college ball at Georgia Southern University, and our son Toby had played at Gettysburg College, so we both loved baseball. Lance even caught a foul ball.

After the game, we had dinner with Nat Bingham, a salmon fisherman who headed the American Seafood Harvester Association and fished on a boat called *Elliot M*. Nat was a gentle soul. He had started the salmon stamp program in California and was one of the nicest people I had ever met. While we ate, he laid out another great idea.

Will Stelle, the regional administrator for the Pacific Northwest, once explained that to understand salmon, I had to understand the Four H's. I had known Will from his early career

Corky Perret, aka "fulla Bull," an honorary member of our family

as a staffer for Gerry Studds on the East Coast. Smart and funny, he is a lawyer and sailor. He had one of the toughest, most complicated jobs in government. He was Andy's counterpart out West. The Four H's are harvest, hydropower, hatcheries, and habitat. These issues are complex, politically charged, and affect how many salmon live. Salmon are an anadromous species that hatch in the fresh headwaters of rivers and then make their way hundreds of miles downstream to the saltwater ocean, where they take a right turn north toward Canadian waters. They might be caught or find their way back to their home river several years later to spawn and die. The riverbed habitat is critical for this to work.

Nat told us about the salmon fishermen who were basically out of work in California. The fleet that once numbered 300 in northern California was down to 15. The unemployment rate for fishermen was 75 percent. He said one of the problems for salmon originated in stream habitats where ranchers let cattle walk down the riverbanks to get water. The dirt from the eroding banks was causing siltation over the gravel in the riverbeds, preventing the salmon from spawning. He suggested we hire salmon fishermen to build fences along the river edges. It was brilliant.

Sadly, in 1998, Nat died tragically at 59, much too young. His contributions to salmon fishing and saving salmon habitat in the West live on. He left the world and salmon in a better place.

We got many more ideas, but Nat's was a keeper, and we implemented it. I will never forget inspecting a site 200 miles from the ocean and seeing about six salmon fishermen in their yellow foul weather gear erecting cedar posts and barbed wire fencing along a salmon stream where the bank had eroded. An added benefit was that the program connected fishermen to ranchers, who, being so far from the ocean, hadn't been aware that their practices were impacting out-of-work salmon fishermen. It showed these two constituencies how their fates were tied. Salmon were an integral part of the region's commercial and environmental ecosystems.

When salmon finish spawning, they die. Their rotting bodies fertilize the soil. One of the state officials gave me a green tee shirt with an MC Escher-like drawing of salmon at the bottom morphing into a big pine tree. The caption read, "It's a little-known fact that salmon grow on trees." They certainly help grow trees. Our life systems are connected.

The morning after our dinner with Nat, we had breakfast with Zeke Grader, the executive director of the Pacific Coast Federation of Fishermen's Associations. Zeke and Nat worked together on many projects, and he made many of the same points Nat did. His organization was one of the largest in the country, and he was well connected politically.

After breakfast, we drove north, deciding to take the scenic Route 101. It didn't look that far on the map to our 1 p.m. meeting. We didn't realize how winding the road was. Lance was driving and enjoying the scenery, so we weren't moving too fast, and it became clear we were running behind schedule. Halfway there, I took over the wheel. The rest of the way, there were screeching tires. We arrived only a little late, and Congressman Dan Hamburg was only mildly miffed.

I opened the meeting by explaining that the Clinton administration and my boss had sent us to listen and act. We wanted to hear what fishermen and their families had to say about the state of the fishery and what they needed from the federal government. I introduced representatives from several federal agencies and told the audience that California fishing families were a high priority. I told them we would stay until the last person had a chance to speak, but I encouraged them to keep their remarks under three minutes so everyone would have a chance. There were over 200 people in the room. I thanked Congressman Dan Hamburg for supporting the disaster aid and invited him to make remarks.

The second meeting in Eureka went about the same. But the third meeting in Crescent City was unforgettable. When we got to the public library, we found about 300 fishermen and their families in a big hall overlooking the Pacific Ocean. The hall was separated from the entrance lobby by a partition. We had a table at the front of the hall where about six other federal officials and I sat. I think there was probably a member of Republican Governor Pete Wilson's staff there as well. The chairs were divided into two sections, with a microphone on a stand next to our table.

I gave my introductory remarks and introduced the members of the panel. When the first man got up to speak, I could tell he was worked up. He was upset that there weren't any fish. He was under tremendous economic strain. He had tried to get help from the Small Business Administration, but they had not been responsive. He started to look at the woman from SBA, who was sitting to my right. He was so angry that his eyes were boring holes in her. His face was getting alarmingly red.

"This guy is going to pop a blood vessel," I whispered to Lance.

When the man finished, I thanked him for his testimony, and as the next person came to the microphone, he moved around the partition toward the front door to leave. The crowd could no longer see him, but I could. He collapsed to the lobby floor. I knew the SBA woman was also an EMT and alerted her to the situation. She quietly got up from the table and walked to the lobby so as not to panic or inflame the crowd, which was already pretty hot. The rest of us continued listening.

She gave the man CPR while the library staff dialed 911. I kept an eye on both her and the audience. An ambulance transported the man to the hospital, and after the meeting, we learned he had suffered a heart attack but was all right. The SBA had rendered him more assistance that day in the form of their representative's lifesaving work than they had done in the months leading up to the hearing.

We returned to DC with our notes to begin formulating a plan. A few weeks later, Lance and I were back on the plane to Seattle, where we picked up Dr. Freese for another series of town hall meetings. Of course, we had to take in the obligatory ball game, this time at the Kingdome, and I think Lance even got another foul ball.

We held our first meeting in Sequim, Washington, and continued farther out the Olympic Peninsula to Port Angeles. As we traveled, our nostrils met with the pungent odor of paper mills, another struggling industry, and a reminder that salmon is indeed connected to trees. This part of the country faced the dual threat of no salmon and a halt to timber cutting because of the spotted owl crisis. We were joined by Congressman Norm Dicks, a member of the powerful Appropriations Committee and a very good person to have as a supporter of our mission.

Bill Clinton had once gotten a lot of credit for resolving the impasse between the loggers and the environmentalists by locking them in a room with nothing but pizza until they reached an agreement, then sweetening the deal with disaster assistance of $3 billion. We weren't sure pizza would do it this time, and we only had $15 million, with an "M," for disaster relief.

Before heading south, we went to the far northwest tip of the lower 48 to Neah Bay. There is a reservation there for the Makah Tribe. We visited and met with about two dozen members. Historically, the Makah hunted gray whales but gave it up decades ago when the stocks were down. As a tribe, they pre-existed the formation of the United States and did not feel they were subject to the Marine Mammal Protection Act, which was a US federal law. They told us they wanted to begin a small hunt because the size of the stock had greatly increased. They had sacrificed to rebuild the stocks, and the hunt was part of their culture.

As a federal government representative and descendant of whalers, I was conflicted. I sympathized with their argument as I did with the position of native Alaskans about sealing. But it was not NOAA policy to allow whale hunting, so I just listened. I noticed as they talked that there seemed to be a generational divide. The elders were pressing for the hunt, the younger generation less so. To me, it didn't seem to be a biological question. They wanted to go out in small boats

Members of the Makah tribe celebrate the killing of a gray whale in Neah Bay, Washington.

and take fewer than five whales from a population of over 20,000. NOAA never did give them permission. In 1999, they illegally shot one whale, which sank. Whaling is no longer part of the Makah culture.

From Neah Bay, we drove to Westport for our next meeting, passing through Forks, a timber town laid flat on its back by the halt in logging. While we saw the clear-cutting that had taken place, there was no question that the landscape was some of the most beautiful Lance and I had ever seen. We wondered how long it would take for tourists to find these gorgeous places and breathe some life into the towns we were driving through.

Congresswoman Jolene Unsoeld and her DC staffer Jay Sterne met us in Westport. Jolene was a strong supporter of the program and acted as a great connection between us and her constituents. Governor Mike Lowry was also very supportive of what we were doing, and we got great cooperation from Washington State.

While we were holding these meetings, Tim Egan, a journalist for the *New York Times* stationed in Seattle, got wind of what we were doing and called for an interview. During our conversation, I found out he had written a book on the Northwest called *The Good Rain*. I bought a copy and read it. He had been hiking and discovered Winthrop Glacier near Mount Rainier. Researching why a glacier out there would be named for a descendant of a Massachusetts colonial governor, he found an 1853 journal of a trip to the area by Theodore Winthrop. Egan retraced his steps, chronicling the changes over 150 years. I was fascinated by the book and immediately sent it to my nephew Peter McNaull, who lives in Seattle. It turns out I was too late.

"Uncle John, thank you so much for sending me the book. It's great. But I already have a copy. You can't live out here without this book. It's like the Bible."

We kept driving south in Washington, going through the logging town of Raymond, whose welcome sign proclaimed it, "The Town Too Tough to Die." That seemed to sum up the attitude of a lot of the places and people we met, as loggers, fishermen, and the businesspeople who depended on them struggled to survive as the underpinnings of their way of life were swept away with no sense of what was going to take its place. This region depended on the sustainability of natural resources, and those resources had run out.

Meeting in Astoria: The Willow Burches of the World

From Ilwaco, a once-thriving salmon port, we crossed over the mighty Columbia River to the picturesque town of Astoria, Oregon, on a hillside overlooking the river. We also had meetings scheduled in Newport and Coos Bay. The Astoria meeting was representative of what we heard and saw. And felt.

Author Carl Safina

The gathering was in a church hall and started at 5 p.m. As usual, we let representatives of the congresspeople and senators speak first, and they did their best to convey support for the fishing families in the room. Then, people got up one at a time and told their stories.

These stories were why Lance, Steve, and I came to these meetings on behalf of Commerce Secretary Ron Brown. "This is a national emergency. Act like it," he had said. All politics is personal could be felt here. As we listened to the people in Astoria and all the other places we visited, people told us their lives were crumbling. We listened to people who had struggled all their lives in the difficult job of salmon fishing, only to realize that salmon might not come back. The powerful interests of Bonneville Power might never allow the dams to be removed to give salmon greater access to the streams where they spawn. The Northwest is addicted to cheap power, and the salmon fishery is a small player against Bonneville, Boeing, and the like.

A woman named Willow Burch nervously approached the microphone. She looked me in the eye and said she used to fish but could no longer afford a permit.

"I hear people who are afraid they will lose their houses. Well…I lost my house."

As I listened to her, I could see she was proud. She was looking at me, and I was looking at her, and we were both trying to keep our composure. She told me how she had turned to mending nets.

"I've heard people here are asking to be bought out. The only thing I have to be bought out are dreams. I've lost everything. I have nothing left."

She asked us not to lose sight of her plight.

"Please go back to Washington and tell them I'm out here. I didn't cause these problems. Don't let them forget about me. Please don't let them forget that I'm here. I'm not a number. Please don't let them forget my name."

After hours of heart-wrenching testimony, we were emotionally drained. We looked for any open place to get a bite to eat. We found a Chinese restaurant. We ran into Carl Safina, who had been at the meeting. Carl is from Long Island and is a scientist who has specialized in birds. He was in the process of writing his first book, *Song for the Blue Ocean*, which looked at three natural resource issues: giant bluefin tuna in the Northeast, salmon in the Northwest, and corals in the Western Pacific. The meeting in Astoria would become a scene in this excellent book.

Over the course of our quarter century of friendship, where Carl has visited with Laurie and me and I have visited with him at his house in Lazy Point, he has found times to criticize me for decisions he didn't think met his standards. But we remain friends, and we both enjoy a good meal when we get together or, failing that, Chinese food in Astoria if that is all that is open. Because of Carl's excellent book, we can never forget Willow Burch's name or her story. Willow represents the plight of so many fishermen and women and their families when managers fail to make the tough decisions necessary to manage stocks. The managers think they are doing fishermen a favor, but it is the Willow Burches of the world who lose their houses. And their dreams.

Salmon Connect to Everything: Defining a Sustainable World

We took the testimony from these meetings, including suggestions for buyouts, loans, and habitat programs, back to DC. In partnership with the states, we designed programs tailored to the needs of New England, the Gulf of Mexico, and the Pacific Northwest. Bruce Morehead translated Lance's and my ideas into programs in New England and the Gulf. Steve Freese did the same in the Northwest. Secretary Brown supported us wholeheartedly.

As we worked, we were buttressed by Secretary Brown's instructions, a philosophy he later memorialized into an "Empowerment Permission Slip." It read: Ask yourself: 1) Is it right for my customers? 2) Is it legal and ethical? 3) Is it something I am willing to be accountable for? 4) Is it consistent with my agency's mission? 5) Am I using my time wisely? 6) Is the answer *yes* to all of those questions? 7) If so, don't ask permission. You already have it. Just do it.

Secretary Brown empowered us, which is one mark of a great leader. He didn't micromanage us. He knew what we were doing; he gave us a sense of urgency. He supported us and recognized our work. I frequently described his approach to these situations as "Courage and Compassion." Secretary Brown dared to support management measures needed to bring back the resources that would provide economic benefit in the long term. When regional administrators like Andy Rosenberg or Will Stelle made tough decisions, fishermen and their advocates would go to Congress, who would put pressure on Brown. He always backed up his people. That took courage. But it was also smart. He knew if he overturned one fishery decision, he would become the "Secretary of Fish," and he would have to make every fish decision. That was the last thing he wanted to do. But he knew these decisions caused real pain, and that is where the compassion came in. He forcefully supported our work to make sure we addressed the needs of fishermen and their families quickly, creatively, and with all the resources the federal government could muster. He did not want the Willow Burches forgotten.

The challenge we all felt was how to connect the immediate, compelling need of so many people like Willow Burch to resources that were clearly not enough and to a bureaucracy that took forever, all while the forces that had put the resource in trouble in the first place were still at work and continuing to create pain. We tried our hardest. For example, the large buyout we did in New England removed 72 percent of the active capacity of the groundfish fleet. At a meeting of the New England Fishery Management Council in Providence, I testified that this buyout would significantly benefit the resource over the long term, but *only if* the council acted to eliminate latent capacity that might be activated. They refused to do so, and the latent capacity was activated, so the benefit of our program was short-lived.

Congress passed a law to restore the Elwha River, just west of Port Angeles in the Northwest. This would involve the removal of two relatively small dams. It was a long, drawn-out battle, but in 2011, the Elwha Dam started to come down. A year later, the Glines Canyon Dam came down. Chinook salmon and steelhead trout had free run to the headwaters near Mount Olympus.

When the President's Council on Sustainable Development finished its report, I suggested to Co-Chair Jonathan Lash that we put a salmon on its cover.

"Jonathan, salmon connect to everything. They are jobs for hard-working people. They are the culture of the tribes who were here first. They are indicators of a healthy habitat. They must co-exist with forestry, hydropower, and agriculture. They cross international boundaries. They are hardy and fragile at the same time. Their very death brings life to others. There is no better symbol of the interconnections that define a sustainable world."

In the end, the best economic assistance and disaster relief is management that makes responsible decisions to avoid disasters in the first place. Of course, natural disasters are unavoidable. But over-fishing is avoidable. Dams are avoidable. Global warming is avoidable. Well, perhaps not avoidable, but we can reduce how bad it will be. Survival is about the decisions we are willing to make.

Senator Ted Kennedy and Congressman Barney Frank

One day, when another of many irate phone calls from Congressman Frank on some topic had everyone on the fifth floor hopping, Doug Hall made an interesting observation.

"John, why is it we work our butts off for people who are assholes, and we don't do anything for the ones who are gentlemen?"

It got me thinking about the most effective members of the House and Senate and what made them so. Our work concerned the coast, which left out the interior states, but even so, I had dealings with about half the country. I concluded that the two most effective leaders, by far, were Barney Frank and Ted Kennedy. I admit they come from

Barney Frank and Ted Kennedy

my district and state, but I still think it is true. Let me give a few examples.

At the early stage of the fishing disaster, Senator Kennedy wanted to motivate us. I knew the senator from my days as mayor. Once, when he had a few stops to make in New Bedford, he stayed at our house as a resting place between events. He used Toby's bathtub to soak his bad back and relieve the constant pain he had suffered since a plane crash in 1964. I was at the office for most of the day, and Laurie was home with him. We had dinner together in our dining room with his long-time staffer Barbara Souliotis. After dinner, Barbara drove him to his home on the Cape.

"John, you wouldn't believe it," Laurie said after they left. "Our phone didn't stop ringing (this was long before cell phones). Calls were coming in for Senator Kennedy from South Africa, from dissidents in the Soviet Union, from Hungary, from all over the world. They didn't stop."

"Laur, Senator Kennedy isn't just the senator from Massachusetts. He is a beacon for people all over the world."

As I did my work for Commerce, I was aware that he had a long relationship with Secretary Brown, who had been chief counsel to the Senate Judiciary Committee when Kennedy was chair. He was smart, and he attracted very smart staff. He and Brown were good friends.

One day, Secretary Brown summoned about five of us to discuss the pace of work needed to implement the disaster plan. Doug Hall, Lance, Sally Yozell, and Rollie Schmitten squeezed onto an overstuffed sofa in an antechamber outside the secretary's office. I sat in a chair to the side. The room had a high ceiling with dark wood paneling and a large fireplace with a mantle. Secretary Brown came into the antechamber from his office. It felt as if we had gathered for a coming storm.

Senator Kennedy entered from the visitor's entrance. The introductions were very brief. Kennedy lit into Brown. His arms were waving. His voice was loud. His face was red. His message was clear. There was an emergency in New England. People were in danger of losing their boats, businesses, homes, and families. And we were acting like we didn't understand that. Like we didn't care. He was fed up. Kennedy only looked at the rest of us in passing, waving his arm at us like we were a bunch of incompetent, uncaring people who couldn't get out of our own way.

The tongue-lashing took about five minutes. Then, Secretary Brown looked at us.

"Get the message," he said. "I expect things to happen a lot faster. Now, get back to work."

I was the last to go. I saw Kennedy and Brown standing by the mantle as I rose to leave. They were about six inches apart, laughing. Kennedy had his hand on Brown's shoulder in a sign of affection. I had witnessed great political theatre, and I hadn't even paid for my ticket.

Another example of Kennedy's skill concerned health care. Nick Littlefield told me how Ted Kennedy gathered his staff together after the Clinton national health care initiative failed in

Congress. He told his staff that they had fought the good fight. He said it hurt to lose, but he and they would *never* give up. Health care for all was a core value for him. If he had to enroll people one at a time, that was what he would do. He reached across the aisle to Senator Nancy Kassebaum to get transferable health care. And he and Nick serenaded his good friend and political opposite Orrin Hatch to co-sponsor health care for children paid for by a tax on tobacco. Hatch was a Mormon who loved kids and hated tobacco.

One day, Senator Kennedy called me to have lunch with him and Catholic Archbishop Cardinal Bernard Law in Boston. Kennedy expressed how important it was that fishermen, who have the most dangerous job there is, should have access to health care. He pointed out that paying insurance premiums is one of the first things to go during difficult times. He lamented that fishermen were no longer protected by unions. All of this I knew. All of this, he knew I knew. He wanted to emphasize it anyway, and I respected him for that. He was sincere, and he spoke from the heart.

"John, I want you to develop a health care program for fishermen," he said.

"Sure, Senator. Health care is one of the things NOAA specializes in," I deadpanned.

Kennedy was not put off. In fact, he had a plan.

"I understand," he said. "That's why we are having lunch with Cardinal Law. The Catholic Church owns a number of hospitals. They also have a social service non-profit arm called Caritas Christi. And as you know, many fishermen are Catholic. I've talked to Gerry Studds and Senator Kerry, and I think we can move $2 million from the $25 million targeted for the buyout, and you can design a health care program using Caritas Christi as a partner."

One of the things that made Senator Kennedy so effective was that he didn't just bring you a problem, which everyone on Capitol Hill knew how to do. He also was good at bringing you ideas and resources to solve the problem. Fewer people on Capitol Hill knew how to do that.

Out of that lunch, a team from Caritas Christi, along with Lance and me, designed a health care program for fishermen that was initially run out of NOAA. We then shipped it over to Health and Human Services, which was a more appropriate agency. To guide the fishermen in utilizing the benefits, in 1997, JJ Bartlett formed Fishing Partnership Support Services with community leaders like Angela Sanfilippo of Gloucester. The partnership is still going strong.

Barney Frank was effective for some of the same reasons. Like Kennedy, he had been a strong supporter of Clinton and had campaigned all over the country. Frank could draw crowds and raise money everywhere. His endorsement carried a lot of weight.

When Clinton first took office, one of the first controversies he got into concerned gays in the military. Barney Frank came to his aid and stood by him with a strong defense. Nobody on Capitol Hill wanted to get into an argument with Barney Frank. Barney is smarter, funnier, and can use a scalpel better than any opponent. When you have Congressman Frank defending you on an issue, it is almost, by definition, not a fair fight.

One of the first interactions Barney had with the National Oceanic and Atmospheric Administration was about the Superfund Trust Fund being used to rectify damage from the PCBs that Aerovox and Cornell Dubilier had disposed of in the New Bedford Harbor. NOAA was the lead of three trustees. A staffer from the National Marine Fisheries Service had the $21 million in a non-interest-bearing account. Frank was upset that no restoration projects had been funded several years after the fund had been established. He voiced his anger to Jim Baker, emphasizing that the fund's purpose was to restore New Bedford Harbor and that NOAA should get off its rear end and do its job. He suggested they needed a new trustee to shake things up. Jim Baker made me the NOAA trustee. We put the funds where they drew interest, and we rapidly accelerated the disbursement of money for projects so that the focus would be on restoration, not on having money in the bank.

I thought about the traits that made Barney Frank and Ted Kennedy effective. One was the loyalty they showed to the president. The second was that they had short memories. It didn't matter what you had done for them yesterday. They didn't care. If you didn't help them today with today's problem, they would go nuclear, meaning a call to the White House. As Doug Hall said, they were colossal pains in the butt. But they made you work for their constituents, and that is, of course, the point. We in the administration have a fixed amount of time. When Barney Frank is on your case, you will work for him and the people he represents.

It is also worth noting that they both had strong, unwavering core principles. They believed the government was there to help people who needed a hand up. It was there to help people who had been knocked down and needed something from the government to get back on their feet. Their philosophy was not about personal enrichment, special interests, or helping those already well-off. It was easy for me to go the extra mile for them.

Secretary Ron Brown: A Portrait in Courage and Compassion

On April 3, 1996, I was on the phone with Peter Kovar, Barney's chief of staff. Suddenly, Peter interrupted what we were talking about and asked if I had a television. Practically everybody had a TV in their office to track what was happening on the Hill via C-Span.

"Turn it on. Right now! I think your boss has been killed in a plane crash."

I flipped on the set and yelled out to Helen to get everyone into my office. Though no news outlets were at the accident site yet, they were reporting that Ron Brown's plane had crashed into a mountain near Dubrovnik, Croatia, with 34 others aboard, many of them Commerce colleagues.

I couldn't breathe. By now, Lance was in the room with Roan, Rick, and Helen. We tried to absorb what had happened. Ron Brown had brought us all in. He had inspired us. We would have run through walls for him. We knew he was leading a mission of business leaders to this war-torn region. He hoped they would invest and bring jobs that might replace centuries-old ethnic grudges with a uniting force of economic opportunity. It was a long shot, but it wouldn't have been Ron Brown's first long shot. We were so proud that he was using the Commerce Department as a force for good in the world. And now this.

That evening, President Clinton addressed Commerce staff at a gathering and used his considerable powers of empathy to soothe our souls and touch our hearts. My friend Laurie Payne, my sometimes squash partner, was on that plane. Clinton talked of young Adam Darling, who had biked across the country during the campaign asking people to vote Democrat. In the months after the crash, whenever I needed to be in Monterey, I would stay with Adam's parents, who still kept his room made up for him.

Ron Brown, always the best-dressed man in the room, with his handsome face, confident smile, and voice that made you think you could do anything, returned in a casket with the other crash victims to a solemn ceremony at Dover Air Force Base in Delaware. I sat in the audience next to Mayor Dave Dinkins for one last chance to say goodbye.

The Masks of Real People

In 1997, after an interim secretary who really didn't want the job, we got a new boss from Chicago. Bill Daley, brother of my former colleague, Mayor Richie Daley, took the reins as Commerce secretary. He had some things in common with Ron Brown. Both were from Chicago, schooled in insider politics, and very well connected. But the differences were many. Bill Daley was White, shorter, and wore Sears Roebuck without the pocket squares. He was quiet and understated. No one would call him charismatic. But like Ron Brown, he knew how to get things done, and he knew how to relate to people.

Barney Frank didn't take long to get Bill Daley to New Bedford to meet with the fishing industry and hear their complaints. I sat next to him in a meeting hall with a few hundred fishermen who peppered him with requests, complaints, and demands. Bill had been briefed on the issues before coming. He had Andy Rosenberg and me to fend off most of the questions. But he proved he could relate to the people in the room, and Barney Frank was very satisfied that he had come up to hear his constituents out.

In August 1997, Alaska Governor Tony Knowles requested disaster aid for the salmon fishery in the Bristol Bay and Kuskokwim River Valley. Sockeye and chum salmon runs were off 78 percent to the lowest catch since 1978. Alaska estimated the economic loss at about $100 million. While the exact cause was unknown, it was suspected to be the unusually warm weather and high temperatures in the river. Governor Knowles was a Democrat, unusual in Alaska, but fisheries are traditionally a strongly bi-partisan issue. Senator Ted Stevens, who had little sympathy for the hardship in New England because the region didn't manage its fisheries as well as Alaska did, was quick to find $7 million in a "rescission" from the Justice Department (meaning he took money away from Justice to give to Alaska), which he transferred to the National Marine Fisheries Service to get help to his people.

The money was approved in early November. In mid-December, Bruce Morehead and I planned to leave for Alaska to meet with affected fishermen and officials. Our itinerary was Seattle and then Anchorage, where we would meet Governor Knowles and some of his cabinet. We planned to spend the night and, in the morning, take a small plane to Bethel, a town of 5,000 that is the hub of the Kuskokwim River Valley. We scheduled a town hall meeting and figured we would spend the night, then take a small plane with skis to Tuluksak, 60 miles to the north on the river, for a morning meeting. We would get back on the plane and visit Tuntutuliak, 60 miles to the south of Bethel, for an afternoon meeting, returning to Bethel for the night. We would retrace our steps to DC. We thought we could do it in a week. When we laid out our plan to some experienced Alaska travelers, they laughed.

"A week! Are you kidding? You'll never make it in a week. Throw the itinerary out the door. You'll fly when the weather says you'll fly. You'll be lucky to get back by Christmas."

Bruce and I got to Anchorage on time. We met with the governor's secretary of Communities and Development, who would accompany us on our trip. He commended us for coming in the winter season.

"Most federal officials visit us in July and August so they can go fishing. You guys are here in December when it is cold and dark. You must be serious."

We explained that there was a 25 percent state matching share requirement and noted that Alaska was running a significant budget surplus that year, implying they should be helping their people more.

The next day we took a small plane northwest to Bethel. There aren't many roads in Alaska, and the distances are great. Everything is big in Alaska. Many people have small floatplanes. We took one that was equipped to land on snow. It was cold, and there were not many daylight hours this far north. We got a short tour of the small town and met with fishermen and town leaders who made real the statistics we had read about.

The people were primarily native Yup'ik, which means "real people." They ate what they caught or shot. That night, we had a meal where our hosts wanted to show us salmon in its many forms. They laid out a feast for us. After eating a lot of salmon, it was time for dessert. They brought out something that looked like very thick whipped cream and blueberries. It was so good that I had a second helping. As we walked to our small hotel, the secretary commented on how much I had liked the dish.

"John, I think you had your fat quotient for the year."

"Why? What was the dessert made of?"

"That was Crisco!"

"Wow! That was good. I'll have to try that again!" I smiled.

The next day, we wedged ourselves into the plane and flew north to Tuluksak. About 200 Yup'ik lived there. They had a small community building where we met, sitting in a circle facing each other. Scattered about the village were tiny homes, where the people lived, and some shacks, where meat was left to cure. At the center of town, there was a general store. A big tin of coffee cost $20, but no one in town could afford to buy it. The average annual wage was about $3,000, and about a third of that was the income stipend every Alaskan got from oil revenues.

At the meeting, everyone was outfitted with headphones so a translator could translate the Yup'ik languages into English and English into the Yup'ik languages. There was no heat in the building. The residents told us that because there was no salmon, there was no money to pay the heating bill. Everything was closely connected in Tuluksak.

The Yup'ik were covered in fur-seal boots, pants, coats, gloves, and hats. I looked at their weathered faces. I saw people I had read about in books but had never met before. I knew these people were tough, but I wondered why at the end of the 20th century in America, was it necessary for people to suffer like this? The trite phrase, "I'm from the government, and I'm here to help you," ran through my mind. On this very cold December day that was already dark at 2 p.m., I wondered if we could help them in time.

We listened to every story. We took notes and said we would work with the people in Washington and Governor Knowles to speed relief. We flew back to Bethel. On the way, I lamented to the secretary about our powerlessness.

"John, don't beat yourself up, these people are used to having nothing."

I again raised the issue of why a state as rich as Alaska wasn't providing immediate help. As always, there were complicated reasons, but it all meant that help was not getting to the Yup'ik.

Subsistence living in Tuluksak

The next morning, we headed south to Tuntutuliak, a similar distance south along the Kuskokwim as Tuluksak was north. The scene was similar. It was a town of 200 Yup'ik whose livelihoods relied on salmon that had disappeared. We listened. The stories penetrated as deeply as the cold and the dark. These places were as far away from Washington, DC, as you could get. How could Bruce and I bridge the gap and make the bureaucracy move? It wasn't just Willow Burch whose name needed to be remembered.

I went to the general store and bought a sealskin hat, which is the warmest hat I have ever owned. It reminds me every time I wear it of the tough people and the hard lives that are lived in the last frontier of our United States.

We made all our flights, which I gathered was some kind of miracle, and were back in DC in about a week or so. We set to work designing financial assistance for the Yup'ik and others in the Kuskokwim and Bristol Bay region. But we knew that as fast as we could make the bureaucracy work, the money still wouldn't get there until June. By then, they wouldn't need the heat turned on.

In January, Laurie and I were enjoying a walk on the National Mall from our apartment on Capitol Hill behind the Supreme Court. We loved living in Washington. It is America's hometown where the front page of the local newspaper carries headlines that are important the world over. We never stopped pinching ourselves that this was where the world's oldest experiment in democracy was happening.

In the mornings, I would commute on my bike and pedal past the Supreme Court. Then, I would go right by the north side of the Capitol before they erected any protective barriers that came later. I would continue my bike ride on Madison Drive along the Mall and, finally, cross the only street I had to cross, Constitution Avenue, to get to work. A ten-minute bike ride by all three branches of government, seeing amazing monumental architecture and downhill to boot! As I rode the elevator to the fifth floor with colleagues who had spent an hour in their car commuting seven miles from Rosslyn, I felt very fortunate.

Laurie had several jobs while we were in DC, all of which she really liked. She worked in the cause related marketing division at the headquarters of the Nature Conservancy for several years. She also ran several fashion stores at Union Station, which built on her experience in New Bedford. During the week, we were both busy with our work.

On weekends, Laurie and I might ride our bikes on the C&O Canal or the bikeway to Mount Vernon. Or we might take advantage of Rock Creek Park for tennis. When we decided we'd like to live in a neighborhood instead of the Lansburgh, many people suggested the northwest section of DC, steering us away from Capitol Hill and saying it was dangerous. But our friends who lived on the Hill loved it, so that's where we ended up. And we loved it, too.

We lived in a three-decker on 3rd Street, NE. We had some Hill staffers on one side of us and Florida Senator Bob Graham and his wife Adele on the other. At the end of the street was the Baptist Church that Frederick Douglass had attended. What a coincidence that we had lived a few blocks from his home in New Bedford, and now we lived in his first neighborhood when he moved to Washington.

There were more museums within easy walking distance than we could ever visit, but we certainly tried. And the memorials aren't just for school field trips. They have the power to move adults as well, and we liked visiting them.

Matthew had given me a remote-controlled model sailboat about three feet tall. On weekends now and then, I would take it down to the reflecting pool in front of the Capitol, launch it, and sail for an hour or two. One day, something straight out of a Charles Addams cartoon happened. As I was happily sailing my sloop from one side of the reflecting pool, I saw a guy pull up in his van on the other. He unloaded a wooden crate about four feet long, one foot high, and one foot deep. He brought it over to the pool's edge and opened the box. Inside was a black, sinister-looking submarine, which he launched into the 2½-foot-deep pool. I thought back to what my friend, Jim Mathes in New Bedford, used to say. He had been a submariner.

"There are two types of boats in the world: submarines and targets!"

No wonder I felt so nervous!

While we were in DC, we maintained our house in New Bedford. We were letting the minister of our Unitarian Church, Reverend Roger Fritts, who had married us, stay in the house. On the occasional weekend that we traveled back to New Bedford, Roger would find another place to stay. There was no question we still considered New Bedford home. That wasn't true of many people who move to the nation's capital. When I was first looking for a place in DC five years earlier, I had talked to Ginny Glover, a long-time DC resident and a close friend of my parents. I was hoping there would be many rentals on the market.

"At a change of administration, there must be a lot of turnover? People come in with the new administration and leave with the old one, don't they?"

"Well, John, you are partially right. New people come in. No one seems to leave."

And that is why the official bird of Washington seems to be the crane. At least heavy equipment cranes seem to be perched all over the city. There is a perpetual building boom powered by a government that expands under every administration, Republican or Democratic.

When I started work in the Clinton administration in 1993, construction workers were at the bottom of a deep hole across 14th Street from the Commerce Building. Every morning and every evening, I would check the progress of this new federal building. As I fashioned programs to assist distressed fishing families, I wondered who was making more headway. Sometimes, it was difficult to see if I was moving forward. These construction workers had the advantage of seeing their progress each day. It was there in steel, concrete, and stone, which would last hundreds of years. *What was I doing?* As 1998 dawned, I could see the building they were constructing take place. It would be named the Ronald Reagan Building. What irony! The largest federal building other than the Pentagon was named for a Republican who wanted to shrink government. I worked for a Democratic president who actually did shrink the size of government while bringing the budget into surplus and reducing the deficit—all while presiding over a surging economy.

Laurie and I continued our January walk on the Mall with these thoughts and others on our minds. As we strolled, we looked up at the National Gallery of Art. There, hanging from the rooftop, was a banner advertising the newest exhibit: "Yup'ik Masks."

It crystallized something for me. I turned to Laurie.

"I know we love living here in DC. My value to the administration has been that we come from a real place—New Bedford. Having been mayor and dealing with people 24/7 is the biggest asset I bring to the job. The first thing I noticed at NOAA was all the pictures on the walls; *none* had any people in them! And as wonderful a place as DC is, it is *not* a real place. In the parts of DC where we interact, there aren't real people. It is just like the banner up there says, Washington has only the masks of real people. It's time to go home."

I submitted my resignation to Jim Baker the next day.

I am forever grateful for the opportunity to have served our country. I am proud to have been a part of the Clinton-Gore administration. When your bosses are as smart as Bill Clinton, Al Gore, Ron Brown, and Jim Baker, they push you to your limit every day. When their motivations are to help those most in need, you know you are working for the right reasons. When their approach is to be guided by science and work collaboratively and with humility, you know you can be effective and true. And we were. But now, it was time to go home.

Within two weeks, we had departed DC and returned to New Bedford.

IV. Home Waters

Sailing Captiva *in New Bedford Harbor*

CHAPTER 10

Back to Massachusetts

Kennedy School Days

Before we drove home, I walked to the Russell Building to say goodbye to Senator Kennedy.

A supporter and friend since my days as mayor, he had backed me in joining the Clinton administration, and he had forcefully advocated for the people we were trying to help with disaster assistance. I had learned so much from him. He had known defeat as a presidential candidate in 1980 but, through hard work, had become arguably the most effective senator in the history of the Senate. While he was respected and comfortable working on the international stage, he epitomized my belief that "all politics is personal."

We reminisced, and he asked about my plans. I told him I wasn't sure. He suggested I consider the Kennedy School, explaining that its Institute for Politics sought people fresh out of government to teach undergraduates about the real world of public service. I said I would check it out.

Senator Kennedy loved sailing and had a beautiful blue schooner named *Mya* built in 1940 by Concordia, the same company that built our yawl in 1965.

"There is one thing I do know, John. You are going to get to spend a lot more time on the water than I am!" He gave me his broad toothy grin as I left his office.

I quickly applied to the Kennedy School and was accepted as a teaching fellow for the spring semester. Harvard paid a modest amount, covering housing in Cambridge with enough left over for Laurie and me to eat for the five months we would be there. I had a ground-floor office on John F. Kennedy Boulevard, a couple of blocks from Harvard Square.

For my non-credit seminar for undergraduates, I chose the topic of sustainable development. I lined up several guest speakers, including my former colleague Lance Simmens, who was then working for Health and Human Services, managing the fishermen's health care program, and supporting HHS Secretary Donna Shalala. I persuaded Peter Clavell, my good friend and former mayoral colleague from Burlington, Vermont, to come down. Peter called himself a progressive Democrat and had focused his administration and campaigns on making Burlington the most sustainable city in America. He had succeeded Social Democrat Bernie Sanders, who was mayor when I first became mayor.

About 30 undergraduates enrolled in my seminar. What is great about the Institute of Politics, which the Kennedy family endows, is that the focus is always on the students. We had great give-and-take conversations for a couple of hours twice a week. Because the class was not for credit, they came just to learn.

Sustainability was an issue in 1998, but climate change, while well known to scientists, had not really penetrated the public consciousness or conversation. Al Gore's book and movie, *An Inconvenient Truth*, wouldn't come out for another eight years. Still, these students knew things were out of whack, and they knew that in a case of intergenerational injustice, it was their generation that was being screwed by mine. They wanted to learn how and why that had happened and what they could do about it. They wanted their hands on the levers of power. And when you go to Harvard, you feel you are close to the levers of power.

The institute director was new that year. Senator Alan Simpson, a tall, thin, conservative man from Cody, Wyoming, had recently retired from the Senate and had come with his wife, Adele, to Kennedy country to share his wisdom and considerable wit.

Alan was a great friend of Ted Kennedy. Politically, they were as far apart as you could get, but they had high respect for one another. They enjoyed each other's company and couldn't go more than a minute or two without cracking each other up with a joke at the other's expense. They believed in government. They believed that politics is the art of the possible. They believed it was their duty to improve things and make tough choices. And they believed that government was an honorable profession, which is why it was so good to have Alan inspiring young people to consider government as a career instead of looking for high-paying consulting gigs.

Laurie and I found an apartment in a two-decker on Brattle Street toward Fresh Pond, about a ten-minute walk from Harvard Square. During our five months in Cambridge, Laurie took full advantage of our university identification cards to audit several Harvard courses and visit campus and city museums. We also stayed connected with New Bedford, just over an hour's drive away.

There were many benefits to being at the Kennedy School. Interesting people surrounded us. The small class of fellows was a fascinating group. Across the hall from me was John Perry Barlow, lyricist for the Grateful Dead and co-founder of the Electronic Frontier Foundation (EFF). JP had a friend, Annie Hayes, from New Bedford, so he was familiar with my hometown. He was from Pinedale, Wyoming, and was a libertarian and good friend of Alan Simpson's. He told me about when Pinedale officials decided the town needed a traffic light at the main intersection. After the first night, they discovered 30 bullet holes in the light and reconsidered their decision. Pinedale was a libertarian kind of town. People didn't like the government telling them when to stop and go.

When our son, Matthew, a serious Dead Head, found out I would spend the semester hanging out with JP, I went up a couple of rungs on the coolness ladder.

JP and I had many discussions about what constitutes "community" and issues surrounding internet regulation. That was, in fact, the subject of his course. He and Mitch Kapor had founded the foundation to protect civil liberties on the internet. JP was very suspicious of any regulation. He felt those who hacked the internet were akin to the Kilroy-Was-Here taggers— mostly innocent technical wizards just trying to show off. He didn't think they were malicious. I thought that was a bit naïve.

He also thought there was a generational divide. As he put it, the older generation had to learn about the internet as if it were a second language. It was not second nature. For the young, the web was like their first language, coming to them intuitively and naturally. He thought it was unfair to have the older generation write the rules for something they didn't understand. I thought he had a point on that score. This was like being back in college. Well, we *were* back in college. We could while away the hours just talking about things. It was great!

Strangely, all the fellows except me were Republicans the year I was there. I was the only Democrat among seven. Well, there was General William Nash, who had just returned from commanding Task Force Eagle, a multi-national division organized to implement the Dayton Peace Accord in Bosnia-Herzegovina. Party wasn't relevant with General Nash. What was

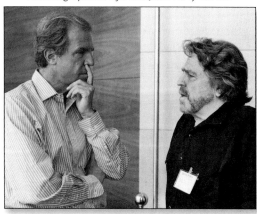

Nick Negroponte, left, and John Perry Barlow

relevant with Bill was his leadership style and his teaching of how the military could take the most diverse group of Americans and mold them into a highly professional, technically competent force with very high morale. There were lessons to be learned here.

Another person I spent time with was a young man from California, Dan Schnur. Dan had worked for Governor Pete Wilson. While we had wildly different political views, we got along very well. An expert in communications, he went on to work at an institute like KSG in California. It didn't surprise me to learn that he had joined John McCain's straight talk express because straight talk is what Dan was about.

When we started, there was a vacant office right behind JP and across from mine. Halfway through the semester, Oscar Arias stepped into it. The former president of Costa Rico spent a few months with us, talking with students in small groups and giving lectures to larger crowds. It was an honor to spend time with this man who had won the Nobel Peace Prize in 1987 for bringing peace to Central America—a region our country had been militarily enmeshed in for many years. I won't forget one evening when we all went to a spring Red Sox game and shared the enjoyment of baseball, hotdogs, and beer in Fenway Park.

You can't talk about the Kennedy School without talking about food. There were lunches and dinners daily with speakers that Harvard attracted from around the world. The pipe-line between the Kennedy School and Washington was especially fluid. It was as if there was one of those vacuum tubes you see in bank drive-up windows, whisking people back and forth between our nation's capital and the Kennedy School. The stay might be as short as an evening lecture or as long as a return to power. There was never a shortage of captivating people coming through, and as fellows, we always got to share a delicious lunch or dinner with them.

One evening, Laurie and I were going to listen to author and historian Doris Kearns Goodwin. We asked our longtime friend Beppie Huidekoper to join us. Beppie is tall, athletic, good-looking, single, and was Harvard's Chief Financial Officer (CFO) at the time. In other words, pretty damn intimidating. I asked Bill Nash to join us as well, figuring there couldn't be much that would intimidate a tank commander! As it happened, we sat at a table with Doris and her husband Richard and had a great conversation. Doris gave a talk about her book, *Wait Till Next Year,* a memoir about growing up in Brooklyn and rooting for the Dodgers before they moved to Los Angeles. The next day, I asked Beppie about dinner, and she said she had difficulty concentrating on Doris's talk because she felt a few tank squadrons were advancing on her!

Another lecturer I will never forget was a woman who survived the Holocaust. I cannot recall her name or the details of her story, but I remember the tone of her voice, which was soft, high-pitched, and gentle. There wasn't an ounce of bitterness. I thought back to Viktor Frankl's book, *Man's Search for Meaning,* where he said the Nazis could take everything except one's attitude. Attitude you determined yourself.

A certain attitude can be found in the way people talk about forgiveness benefiting not the one being forgiven but the one doing the forgiving. It lifts a weight off your soul. This woman, who had seen so much, suffered so much, and lost so much, did not seem to be bitter. How could that be? How could she smile? How could she have joy in her voice? If she could find happiness, then couldn't we all find our way there?

Many others taught and spoke while we were at the Kennedy School, and Laurie and I tried to soak up everything we could. I sat in on an instructive course taught by Ron Heifetz. Its focus was leadership without authority. It is hard enough to lead when you do have authority, but when you don't have authority and you have to influence those above you, it is even more challenging. Most of us find ourselves in that position much of the time, so learning to lead despite the hierarchy is a great skill to have. I took a course from Marshall Ganz, a community organizer in the Saul Alinsky mold. He later was instrumental in the campaign of a young Chicago community organizer named Barack Obama who would rise to become president of the United States.

Robert Putnam taught at the institute about social capital. He had published an essay, "Bowling Alone," in 1995 about how there were fewer bowling leagues, meaning people were finding fewer ways to get together in groups. This would become a famous book in 2000.

Roger Porter was also there. He had developed strategies for cities to focus on their own niche. They make movies in Hollywood because movies are made in Hollywood. That applies to New Bedford because our strategic advantage is that we are dominant in fishing. We have all the infrastructure. When other ports weaken, fishing operations will naturally gravitate to New Bedford. The strong will get stronger. Invest in what makes you strong.

Speaking as a Fellow

While I was a fellow at the Kennedy School, I was asked to speak a couple of times at public events. Pearl Houghteling, a daughter of a friend of mine growing up, was an undergraduate at the college. A member of an environmental club, she asked me to give a talk at Elliot House, where my father had lived when he attended Harvard.

Pearl posted signs around the campus, and about 20 students came. We talked about sustainable development and what it was like to work for the government at the federal and local levels. I thought back to how I had pretty much wasted my time at Harvard and realized these students were smarter, more focused, and going to achieve greater things than I had. I was very encouraged. No question, there were big challenges facing them, but there was talent and commitment to meet them.

Professor Alan Altshuler also asked me to give a faculty talk at the Taubman Center for State and Local Government over lunch. About 20 people gathered for the discussion. I began by complimenting them on what a tremendous resource they had created at the Kennedy School and describing what a rejuvenating experience it was for me to be there to partake in everything the school offers. I told them I shared their passion for public service and was grateful to the Kennedy family for endowing the institute with its focus on undergraduate participation. Then I got down to business. I said the focus of the Kennedy School was wrongly placed on steering students to the federal government or international postings. I said even the language describing levels of government as higher and lower was pejorative.

I mentioned what San Antonio Mayor Henry Cisneros, a graduate of the Kennedy School, had said—that the problems most important to Americans are not nuclear throw-weights but the quality of schools for their kids, the safety of their streets, whether the water that comes out of their taps is fit to drink, and how quickly firefighters and paramedics will arrive in an emergency. These may be local problems dealt with by "lower" levels of city and town governments, but life is lived at the local level.

Smart students should be encouraged to make a difference on those levels.

I pointed out that poor communities like my own, New Bedford, faced challenging problem, including that young creative people often left for bigger cities. Washington, New York, and Boston are not lacking for brains. People flock to those centers. But New Bedford, Fall River, Lynn, Lawrence, Gardner, Fitchburg, and a host of other Massachusetts cities near Harvard struggle to keep promising young people and would benefit from bright young people setting up residences in their communities.

We had a good discussion. The faculty mentioned that they were more concerned that graduates were sidestepping government altogether and instead were heading off to lucrative consulting jobs at firms like McKinsey & Company. They did not seem persuaded by my argument, which was a long shot, given that this was the Kennedy School at Harvard.

Job Hunting Again

The other reason to be an Institute of Politics fellow was to use the time, the office space, and the prestigious letterhead to find a new job. Having these provided a great advantage over trying to find a job while unemployed. Peter Fenn's dad, Kennedy School Professor Dan Fenn, had a suggestion for me. Dan knew my father at Harvard and worked for John Kennedy in the White House. He was a close aide and the founding director of the Kennedy Presidential Library in Boston after the assassination. Dan said the library was looking for a new director and encouraged me to apply. I wasn't sure, but I applied. That Dan Fenn had confidence in me when I didn't was enough. I trusted his judgment more than mine. Obviously, he knew what the job entailed. He had founded the place. And he knew me pretty well through all the work Peter and I had done together.

Still, I was surprised when I got called for a finalist interview. I went to the library to meet with Caroline Kennedy, Paul Kirk, and Jill Ker Conway. I knew Paul because he had been head of the Democratic National Convention (DNC). He was very close to Scott Lang and, of course, to the Kennedy family. Jill Ker Conway was an author, scholar, and former president of Smith College. I had never met Caroline Kennedy, and I was starstruck. She is beautiful, and she is…Caroline Kennedy.

A week went by, and I hadn't heard anything. Pete Zimmerman, a top administrator at the Kennedy School, and I were talking, and I asked what I should do. We went to Harvard together and played football on the undefeated Leverett House football team, so we had a long history.

"Well, John, I think the next move is that you have to make up your mind if you really want this job, and if you do, then you really have to go after it and tell them how much you want it."

Pete got me thinking. How much do I want this job? Certainly, it was high profile and glamorous. But the more I thought about it, the more it didn't fit in with what I had set out to do—fix up my hometown. My work in Washington fit because it had had an effect on New Bedford, although the job had not been confined to New Bedford. The work encompassed a broader definition of "hometown." But the Kennedy Library really had no bearing at all. Everything I had done so far had a general direction of making my hometown a better place. The Kennedy Library had no connection to that. As I thought it through, I realized that the answer to Pete's question was that I didn't really want that job. It wasn't for me. I called and withdrew.

I shifted direction. I called my friend Peter Cressy, the chancellor of UMass Dartmouth, and asked if he had time for a visit. Peter is a former Navy admiral, and he had brought SMAST to New Bedford. He went to Yale and was the president of Massachusetts Maritime Academy before taking over UMass Dartmouth. As someone familiar with boats, he knew you couldn't steer with a rudder unless you were moving, so he was always on the go. He is smart, forthright, and decisive. I like Peter a lot. I went to campus and met with him in his office, explaining that my time at the Kennedy School would be over in a month.

"I'd like to return home to work to make my hometown a better place. New Bedford is only going as far as UMass Dartmouth takes it. The same can be said for Fall River and Taunton, for that matter. The problems are in New Bedford and the other cities. The answers are here on this campus. I want to work here. Is there any way you can put me to work?"

Peter thought for a minute.

"You're hired."

UMass Dartmouth: All in the Family Business

"I'm hired. Fantastic! What do you want me to do?"

Peter thought another minute.

"I'll have you run our Family Business Center, which we are just starting. And you can help us raise money. You'll have an office right near my office."

I hadn't heard about the new center.

"That's great, Peter. What the heck is a Family Business Center? I don't know anything about that."

"You'll pick it up. You're pretty smart, even for a Harvard guy."

Peter could never resist busting my chops.

We negotiated salary, and he explained my duties. The Family Business Center was the idea of Bob Karam, an insurance man from Fall River and a close friend of Fall River Mayor Carlton Viveiros. Bob came from a very successful family. His brother Skip was the winningest basketball coach in Fall River's history and gave New Bedford teams fits year after year as they competed for state championships. Their brother Jim is a successful real estate developer and, at the time, was the chair of the UMass system's board of trustees. Bob was very influential and wasn't afraid to use his influence. He was also a generous and loyal supporter.

It turns out family businesses are quite interesting. When they work, they are the economic expression of a family's value system. That can be a very beautiful thing. When the first generation creates a successful family business, the family's wealth is usually tied up in the business. Kids are encouraged to enter the company to keep it going and partake in the wealth generated. That is where the problems can start. Some kids are talented and interested. Some are interested but not talented. And some aren't interested. And the founding generation can also be torn. Mom and Dad want to treat their kids fairly and equitably, but they also want to run the business profitably. They know some of their kids might not be equal to the task. How they resolve those issues can tear apart families and destroy businesses if not handled well.

That is why Family Business Centers have been created around the country—to give families a safe space to discuss problems that only they face and to have experts offer answers that might assist their families and their businesses. It is a rare family business that makes it to the third generation. "Shirtsleeves to shirtsleeves in three generations" is an axiom for a reason. There had been a well-known family business center at Northeastern University but none in Southeastern Massachusetts, so Bob Karam had suggested starting one at UMass Dartmouth.

He promoted the idea of a Family Business Center to Peter because one of the answers to solving the problem parents faced turned out to be setting up insurance policies for the kids who would not be involved in the business. Bob figured if the university established a center and recruited members, he might be able to help by selling insurance. It was a good idea because several important family businesses in the region could use this help. It was also a good idea for the university because that was the logical place to provide the service, and it would create supporters for the university. And it was a good idea for Bob Karam as an insurance man. Potential winners all around.

Raising the Bar and Raising the Funds

As for fundraising, the head of the UMass Dartmouth Advancement Office was Donald Ramsbottom. Don was a retired CEO from Fall River who was well connected in that city. He was a close friend of Chuck Charlton, a major university benefactor. Don was a consummate gentleman and very welcoming to me. I knew New Bedford well, so we would be a good complementary team. My sister-in-law, Tia Bullard, also worked in the Advancement Office. Tia had worked at Swain School of Design and came over to UMass in the merger. She and my brother,

Peter, hosted Friday evening dinners for the most influential people in the region, a fact that seemed to escape the good people at the university, who usually failed to take advantage of her incredible connections. Tia, being the polite person she is, did not force herself upon the higher-ups, so the university missed out.

I wanted to be at UMass Dartmouth because I regarded it as the locomotive that would haul the region as far as it would go. The biggest drawback New Bedford had, and Fall River too, was educational attainment. Ten percent of New Bedford's population had college degrees versus a national average of 25 percent and a statewide average of 33 percent. That might have been okay in the time of textiles, but it was a death threat in the modern information age. If we didn't change, our people would be flipping burgers until machines took even those jobs away.

While a few of our students would graduate high school and head to Boston colleges and beyond, to move the education numbers, we needed a good percentage of our high school graduates to get to UMass Dartmouth or Bristol Community College, which had a "2 plus 2" program where students could transfer to UMass Dartmouth after completing two years at the community college. Because of its location, tuition, and financial aid, UMass Dartmouth was far more accessible to New Bedford and Fall River students than other colleges.

There was also an understanding, almost a "contract," between the university and the region. UMass Dartmouth understood the area depended on the university for its economic future. Boston didn't really need UMass Boston. Lowell had other assets to rely on. And the Amherst area certainly had many universities and institutions besides the UMass flagship. No, the relationship between Southeastern Massachusetts and UMass Dartmouth was, and is, unique.

State Senator Biff MacLean

University Chancellor Cressy understood this fundamentally. While not from here, he "got" this relationship intuitively and knew it was a major strength of the university. Many of the faculty, but not all, understood this. There are, of course, some who prefer to teach in the "Ivory Tower." That, I guess, will always be the case. But there are enough who relish the connection to community that the links are there.

William Bulger, former president of the state Senate and head of all the UMass campuses, understood this connection. He grew up in a poor community in South Boston and valued education enough to learn Greek and Latin. And while Bulger didn't need help understanding this vital relationship, he was very close to Senator William "Biff" MacLean of Fairhaven, who would have explained it to him.

Biff MacLean is a complicated man. A five-sport athlete at Fairhaven High School, Biff sold insurance and went to Beacon Hill, first as a state representative and then as a state senator. He was an "old time" politician. He did favors, and he kept track. If he did a favor for you, he expected you to do one for him. Maybe two.

He was a master politician. He told me one of the first things he did when he got to the Massachusetts State House was to go around to all the offices at the Registry of Motor Vehicles, Veterans Affairs, and other places where he knew he would eventually have to go on behalf of constituents. He introduced himself—not to the heads of the offices but to the clerks. And he made sure he remembered their names. This way, when he needed something straightened out, he knew exactly who to call. And he knew the name of the person he was talking to. It was personal, and he knew it.

Over the years, Biff piled up many favors. And he helped many people get elected. He could sell plenty of tickets if you were having a fundraiser. He certainly helped me. After, there would be the phone call.

"John, would you look at this guy for this job?"

And I would. If the person was the best candidate, I hired them. A few times, the person Biff recommended was a superstar, and I was very glad Biff sent them to me. If the person wasn't the best, I would tell Biff I gave them a look. You had to be careful with Biff. You didn't want to get too entwined. But he was influential and could be of great assistance. I remember once when the *Ernestina* was in trouble. I don't remember the exact circumstances, but the schooner needed money for something.

"Well, how are we going to fix this?" Biff said to me as I sat in his Boston office.

Immediately, it wasn't *my* problem—it was *our* problem. That lifted a weight off my shoulders.

"Let's call Ed Fish," he said and picked up the phone.

There was no way I was going to call the head of Suffolk Construction, but Biff could. And for the next hour, he raised funds, working the phone with a little help from me. He was amazing.

Biff had a number of causes close to his heart, but if I had to guess the one closest, I would say it was UMass Dartmouth. If not the closest, it was pretty close. He loved the university and appreciated what it meant for the region. He also knew how Greater Boston tended to forget about us folks down here. He fought like hell for funding for the university's operating account and capital expenditures. Being a five-sport star athlete, when Biff fought, he usually won.

One expression of the special relationship was the SouthCoast Development Partnership. The CEOs of all the major businesses in the region would meet in the conference room next to the chancellor's office. Paul Vigeant, a special assistant to the chancellor like me, was the staff for this group of power brokers. The chancellor chaired it. While there were turf battles off campus, *everybody* loved and supported *their* university. It was wonderful the way that worked. Only the university could pull all those people together. They all knew that when the university advanced, so did they. They worked hard to advocate for resources, people, and policies. And the chancellor and university did everything to showcase what the school meant to the region.

To begin the Family Business Center, I talked with Bobby Karam about his ideas. He told me we could get sponsors from industries that might benefit, such as insurance firms like his, financial advisors, law firms, and other businesses that traditionally supported the university. We could recruit members from the many family businesses in the region. We could offer them expert speakers and a chance to discuss problems with other family businesses going through similar circumstances. We could help them avoid mistakes that could wreck not only a family business but also Thanksgiving dinners. Bob said we wouldn't want too many sponsors from any sector. It sounded like a good plan.

I went to see Paul Karofsky in Newton, who had started the Northeastern Center for Family Business. He was generous with his advice, sharing tips on how to run a center and his list of experts around the country who could be speakers. After seeing how Karofsky had done it and knowing Bobby Karam would be a strong supporter, I felt more comfortable about a way forward.

I put together a business plan with a budget. I recruited about eight sponsors and a few dozen members. We met about six times a year at White's of Westport, which is owned by the LaFrance family, one of our members. Everybody seemed to benefit from the sessions. Attendance was high, and the discussion was meaningful. These businesses are essential to our economy and our region's character. They are tied to the region more than other businesses, so helping them avoid the "shirtsleeves to shirtsleeves" dilemma is an important if often over-looked service.

Fred Dabney

Somewhat related to that was a request I got one day when a longtime friend of mine, Fred Dabney, showed up at my office with a fellow farmer, Jim Munger. Fred owned Quansett Nurseries and grew all manner of plants for the wholesale market. I had gone to college with him. Jim Munger grew the best tomatoes anywhere to be found. Fred started by saying how difficult it was to be in the farming business. Prices were low, especially for milk. Costs kept going up. It was harder to hold onto land. The next generation was reluctant to take over because animals don't take weekends off or have vacations. It was tempting to grow a last crop of houses and cash out, but they wanted to stay in farming. They could not afford to donate the land to a conservation trust. The list of issues went on.

It seemed there was not anyone or any group dedicated to helping the local farming community. Certainly, the Massachusetts Department of Agriculture is a resource, but there was nothing in the region. We decided we needed to start a new local group. If we were going to do this, we knew we needed to gather a few more people around the table.

We set up a second, larger meeting at the university, inviting about a dozen people, including Tony Vieira, who had been a Westport dairy farmer and now worked at the university; Bob and Carol Russell, who owned Westport River Vineyard; Sue Guiducci, who ran a vineyard in Dartmouth; and Jeff LaFleur of the Cape Cod Cranberry Growers Association in Wareham.

The meeting went well. There was a consensus that agriculture was important, in trouble, and needed an organization to support it. We turned our attention to a name. "Farmers" wouldn't work because it left out growers. For the opposite reason, we couldn't use "growers." "Business" or "entrepreneur" was put on the table.

"The problem we're dealing with is that many of us aren't businessmen or entrepreneurs. That's what we're trying to fix!" said Fred.

We finally settled on Southeastern Massachusetts Agricultural Partnership, and in 2000, SEMAP was born. We hired Moore and Isherwood, who designed the iconic deep blue and tomato red "Buy Fresh, Buy Local" bumper stickers that can still be seen today.

Our approach wasn't rocket science. We wanted to educate our members in ways they could increase revenues and decrease costs. Increasing revenues could happen by creating markets for local produce fresh from the farm through the creation of farmers markets, farm stands, and Community Supported Agriculture (CSAs), where families buy shares of a farm's produce and pick up a basket of produce every week.

This strategy had been developed with much success in the Berkshires. We were not averse to stealing and importing good ideas. We worked hard to get the message out that local food is fresh. It tastes better and is healthier for you. A local tomato is grown to be eaten, not shipped. You don't need a chain saw to slice it.

We worked with farmers to help them take advantage of farm property tax reductions. We assisted owners interested in selling deed restrictions to local land trusts, which would allow them to continue farming while protecting the land from development.

We also produced a directory of farms, so people could find local produce and know when it was available. We sponsored educational programs on subjects such as managing the amount of nitrogen used to fertilize. SEMAP has had some bumpy periods but still serves a valuable purpose 20 years later.

On the fundraising front, it was fun working with Peter Cressy, who was an Energizer bunny. He would gather the development team weekly and talk about prospects and strategies. He would include himself in the mix.

Chancellor Peter Cressy, right, with Assistant Chancellor Thomas Muliver, 1998

"Who do I need to have lunch with, and what is the ask?"

He kept the pressure on us. But it made us good fundraisers, and he was never afraid to ask people for money himself.

Asking people for money is a task almost nobody likes to do. I think this is because people associate it with personal begging as if you are asking for yourself. Asking makes you feel uncomfortable. But Peter understood what too few people understand—fundraising can be enjoyable and gratifying. First, you need to understand that you are asking for a cause, not for yourself. Usually, you are talking to someone you know and like, so there is mutual respect, and the conversation will probably be pleasant. Oftentimes, fundraising involves good food or drinks, making it even more rewarding! And here is the key: people give money to make an impact that makes them feel better. You are trying to put an opportunity in front of them that allows that. If you create the right opportunity, you and the donor feel better after the gift is made.

While at NOAA, I went to a Mid-Atlantic Fishery Management Council meeting in Philadelphia, where Dr. Brian Rothschild, a highly regarded fisheries scientist in southern Maryland, was also attending. He approached me during a break and asked what I thought about UMass Dartmouth. He had been asked to lead the Center for Marine Science and Technology (CMAST, later SMAST).

"Brian, I know it well. I don't know what moving there would mean for your career. Only you can be the judge of that. But I think UMass Dartmouth is the single most important institution in the Southeastern Massachusetts region. CMAST connects it to the ocean, which is the region's past, present, and future. If you came to CMAST, you would have an enormous impact on my hometown of New Bedford."

A month later, Brian and his wife Susan invited Laurie and me to dinner at their house in Solomons, Maryland. We drove four hours down Route 4 between the Chesapeake Bay and the Patuxent River to their part of paradise. When we arrived, we noticed a car with Massachusetts plates. We walked in the front door to find Peter Cressy almost literally twisting Brian's arm off! I guess we had been brought in for reinforcements. It must have worked because after a wonderful dinner, Brian and Susan decided to move to New Bedford, just around the corner from us. Brian became the founding director of CMAST.

Kevin Stokesbury at sea on a groundfishing vessel   *Sea scallops on the ocean floor*

Brian performed miracles. He was a wizard. He published more papers than any other member of the faculty. He secured more grants than anyone else. He filled up the original building, so they needed to bring in trailers for temporary offices. Then he filled up the trailers. And he drove the administration crazier than all the other professors and directors combined. Peter Cressy could manage him pretty well, but when Peter left and Jean MacCormack took over, if she were not an ex-nun, I'm sure the profanity coming out of her office about Brian would have turned us all blue. Still, Brian got things done.

There was another center director who could give Brian a run for his money in driving administrators nuts. That was Frank Sousa, who ran the Center for Portuguese Studies. Like Brian, Frank was a fundraiser and a super performer.

"Do you notice how the directors who give you the most heartburn are the ones who outperform everyone else?" I once said to Jean MacCormack.

There was a connection I wanted to make for Brian that I hoped might work. When I was a kid, one of my best friends was a boy named Peter Allatt. I spent a lot of time at his house on Smith Neck Road and, of course, had gotten to know his mom. His mother married a few times and was a Rinehart with wealth from Corning Glass. She had a serious interest in marine sciences and had been a major benefactor of the Woods Hole Oceanographic Institution. She had also supported the New Bedford Whaling Museum, but never the university. I introduced Gratia "Topsy" Montgomery to Brian, and they hit it off. A couple of months later, she endowed a chair at SMAST, and Brian became the Montgomery Charter Chair.

I wasn't as successful with Roy Enoksen. Brian and his protégé Kevin Stokesbury had done some fine underwater camera work showing a lot of scallops in the areas on Georges Bank that the New England Fishery Management Council had closed in 1994. They used the footage as part of a study to make the case to re-open the grounds, which the council did in 1998. That resulted in a $50 million increase in scallop landings in New Bedford. I approached Roy, one of my former bosses at the Co-Op, and made the case that he had made a lot of money because of the independent science at SMAST. I suggested that he could lead an effort to endow a chair to guarantee that independent science remain a part of SMAST in perpetuity.

"Now hold on, John. Don't go any farther. It sounds like you are about to ask me for $10,000."

"Roy, I'm going to ask you for a lot more than that!"

But Roy, one of the most generous people on the waterfront, wasn't buying. He didn't get to be as successful as he is by being a soft touch!

Star Store, SouthCoast Learning Network, and SouthCoast Signals

Another high-performing dean who could drive administrators around the bend was John Laughton, head of the College of Visual and Performing Arts and a renowned clarinetist. On top of his other responsibilities, John had the task of integrating the Star Store into a downtown campus for the arts. Thanks to heroic work by state Senator Mark Montigny, an alumnus of the university who followed Biff MacLean as our local state senator, this downtown landmark department store had been beautifully restored by developer Paul Downey and was being leased to UMass Dartmouth. Through the Swain School merger, UMass acquired the Boston University Program in Artisanry (PIA). With John's guidance, UMass moved the program to the Star Store and created two galleries on the ground floor. This relocation was significant for many reasons. The rebirth of New Bedford rested in large part on the energy and vision of artists. This move built upon that and was consistent with Roger Porter's advice of reinforcing strengths. The Star Store was diagonally across from the Zeiterion Theatre and in the heart of downtown.

A second advantage of the move was that it created another university anchor in the city along with SMAST, cementing the ties between the university and New Bedford. And third, the College of Visual and Performing Arts would bring many students into the heart of New Bedford at all hours of the day, which would be a boon for businesses in the downtown. Senator Mark Montigny and Chancellor Jean MacCormack deserve much credit for this project, which will benefit New Bedford far into the future. Also deserving of recognition is Dean John Laughton, who has become a lifetime friend of Laurie's and mine.

Side view of the Star Store, Purchase and Spring Streets, taken from the Zeiterion parking garage

Chancellor Jean MacCormack   Senator Mark Montigny   Attorney Mardee Xifaras

While we were living in New Bedford, Bart Nourse and Sandria Parsons came to me with an idea about education. Bart was a teacher at Tabor Academy. He was our son Matthew's crew coach, and Matthew thought very highly of him. It didn't take me long to see why. He was high energy and knowledgeable, it appeared, on every subject under the sun, most especially about how people learn. Bart and Sandria explained to me that "education is what you have to do; learning is what you want to do." They thought lifelong learning was one of the keys to a healthy community.

They also believed that there are people in the community who are masters of almost every topic: math, language, woodworking, ax throwing, hairdressing, you name it. They wanted to set up a network to connect people who had something to teach with people who wanted to learn. The program would increase the knowledge in the community, and since knowledge is like energy in that it feeds on itself, this would be the closest thing to a perpetual motion machine there is.

After an hour or so of listening to Bart and Sandria, well, mostly Bart, I was mentally exhausted and totally sold. They wanted to create the SouthCoast Learning Network. They needed a board of directors and asked me to be the founding chair. I agreed. We recruited other members and raised seed capital. We gathered a class of community teachers and put together a program of courses. I taught courses in "How to Chair a Meeting," "Public Speaking," and "Sustainable Communities." We ran about three semesters a year for several years before the university took it over and gave Bart and Sandria the boot, which was tremendously unfair.

We also engaged the Center for Policy Analysis, which had a couple of sharp researchers in Clyde Barrow and David Borges, to work with the community to develop 54 indicators of health, or "SouthCoast Signals." We did this in partnership with the Community Foundation and the *Standard-Times*. In 2002-2003, they measured the progress of the region's health using these 54 indicators and published a 95-page report. This broad-based indicator project evolved into a bi-annual report on community health needs that is more narrowly focused toward the health care community.

When I was at UMass Dartmouth, my friend Mardee Xifaras asked me to join the Southern New England School of Law board. I explained to Mardee that she had the wrong brother. I wasn't a lawyer. Of course, she knew this as she practiced law with my brother Peter.

"John, I want you on the board because you are at UMass and eventually, we are going to have to merge with the university. I think you can be a bridge between our two institutions and help bring us closer together."

Well, I never found a way to say no to Mardee, so I became the only non-lawyer on the board. The law school was having a tough time. It wasn't accredited yet, and the Boston law schools were doing their best to keep it that way. The requirements for accreditation—beefing up our library, tightening our admissions requirement, and so on—all negatively affected our bottom line. Our mission was to serve students from underserved populations, many of whom would pursue public interest careers. Our students tended to be older and work jobs while attending school. Our dean, Bob Ward, a very bright lawyer, navigated us through this period with skill, patience, and perseverance. He and Mardee made a great team. After I left, Mardee and Chancellor MacCormack, also a great team, successfully overcame the obstacles and achieved the merger. Accreditation quickly followed. UMass Law School at Dartmouth is now financially secure with growing enrollment, rising Bar passage rates, and the same public interest mission that drew me in the first place.

Travel Campaigning

In 2000, there was a presidential race between Al Gore and George W. Bush. In September and October, I took some time off to participate. Gore and the DNC asked Mardee to oversee Pennsylvania, always a key state, and she set up shop in Philadelphia. I told Mardee I could go for the campaign's last two weeks. When I mentioned my plans to my buddy Lance, who was from South Philly, he decided to come up from his house in Virginia and join us.

Mardee had this uncanny ability. She was important but not afraid to tackle the most menial job. She knew absolutely everybody in the country and had done every job she would ask anyone else to do. She was humble, which is rare in politics. She was a straight shooter without any hidden agenda. Her Midwestern roots gave her a warm, friendly, open-book personality. I knew her most of her life and never found an enemy.

Working among all the competing factions in Pennsylvania and Philly politics, Mardee stayed aware and above the fray, keeping everybody focused on the critical jobs at hand—identifying our votes and getting them out on Election Day. The strategy in Pennsylvania for Democrats is based on James Carville's description of the state: "It's Philadelphia on the east, Pittsburgh on the west and Alabama in the middle." We wanted to pile up huge margins in the two big cities and hoped they would be enough.

The afternoon of Election Day in headquarters, Mardee yelled over to me.

"Sam Waterston is yelling at his TV in New York. He feels powerless there and wants to help us out here. Can you drive him around to every police station in Philly and take him inside to meet the cops?"

Sam and I spent the late afternoon and evening until the polls closed, hitting every Philly police station. Police officers went nuts when one of America's most famous TV district attorneys walked into their station. It was awesome. I found out Sam's family had lived in Mattapoisett for 75 years, and he loved spending time on Buzzards Bay. Later, he generously did a short fundraising video for the Buzzards Bay Coalition from his home in Connecticut.

After the polls closed, Lance and I went to a bar for drinks and dinner with some campaign workers. We had pins showing the three critical states of Florida, Michigan, and Pennsylvania. Early that evening, it looked like we had won all three and the election. We were happy when we went to sleep in our hotel a little after midnight.

Sometime after 3 a.m., Lance woke to the news that we had lost Florida and the election. We were devastated. The race wouldn't ultimately be settled until the Supreme Court weighed in on the "hanging chads." Al Gore graciously, and for the good of the country, conceded, but we were heartbroken. Gore had garnered more votes, and we were convinced he had been robbed in Florida and by a stacked court.

CHAPTER 11

A SEA Change

Critical Mission, Challenging Environment

In the summer of 2002, Laurie and I were sailing our Concordia *Captiva* in a brisk wind toward Newport, Rhode Island, on a short passage from Block Island. It was a sunny day, and the southwest wind had us heeled over as we closed the shore off Castle Hill. My cell phone rang. It was Rick Burnes, my ocean sailing friend.

"John, we would like you to be the president of the Sea Education Association. When can you start?"

Dr. Ned Cabot

Rick and his friend Ned Cabot recruited me a few months before during the search process for the presidency of this unique Woods Hole academic institution. The Sea Education Association (SEA) was founded 30 years earlier to teach college students about the ocean. Founder Cory Cramer had served as its first president from 1971 to 1982. Rafe Parker took the helm for the next 20 years, and now they were looking for a third president.

I had been at the Family Business Center for a while and was ready for a change.

SEA is the only study-abroad program that teaches college students about the ocean, which is significant considering the ocean covers two-thirds of the planet. The first six weeks of study are spent in Woods Hole. The second six weeks are spent at sea on one of two 135-foot brigantines. Onboard, the students operate a 19th-century tall ship and 21st-century scientific equipment. The 20th century is pretty much omitted entirely. The founding academic partner was Boston University, which accredited the program so students could get a full semester's credit for their work.

When Rick approached me, I was drawn to the idea because the mission of teaching college students about ocean science is critically important. I couldn't believe this small institution on Cape Cod was the only place doing it. SEA's location in Woods Hole, where so much of the study of the oceans is located, was also attractive. And the ocean connection seemed consistent with my prior work at NOAA and my focus on my hometown, the seaport of New Bedford.

I wasn't sure what to think as I was interviewed for the job. Ned Cabot was a surgeon at Massachusetts General Hospital, a sailor, and a good friend of Rick's. He was chair of the board at SEA. I don't remember the interview questions, but I will never forget one of Ned's comments.

"You know, John, there isn't a very good history of washed-up politicians running academic institutions."

I was sitting at the head of the table in a chair with wheels. I used my feet to roll the chair back as if I'd been hit by a truck. Ned smiled.

"Dr. Cabot, I'm not sure that is accurate. I work now at UMass Dartmouth. The president of the UMass system is William Bulger. Though he is a former politician, he has been excellent as president, raising more money than his predecessors, supporting UMass on Beacon Hill, and understanding and supporting our unique mission. I wouldn't trade him for anyone. David Bartley was speaker of the House and then became president of Holyoke Community College, a post he has held for over 25 years. If he wasn't any good at it, they probably would have found a way to get rid of him by now. I don't know if any of you have served in public office or know what is involved in that line of work. I had to make some pretty tough decisions as mayor of New Bedford. But that, of course, is for you to judge."

Judge they did. And I made the cut.

The trustees were a great lot. I got along well with almost all of them. Many were sailors and members of the Cruising Club of America (CCA), a group that has done a considerable amount of ocean sailing. I had been a club member since 1988, so I knew many of these folks. Since the founding of SEA, there has been a great overlap with the club.

When I showed up for work at the Woods Hole campus, I took over from Don McLucas, a trustee who was serving as interim president. He had a sailing and business background and greeted me warmly. He vacated the office but said there was one unfinished piece of business. He had just let go the dean, Dr. Kevin Chu. Kevin was a whale biologist who worked for the NOAA Fisheries Science

SSV Robert C. Seamans, 2002

Center before joining the SEA faculty. But the faculty soured on him, so Don decided to let him go before I got there.

When I started, SEA had about 50 employees in five departments. There were 15 members of the faculty. Six taught nautical science and served as captains of the ships. Six taught oceanography and sailed as chief scientists. Three taught maritime history and rarely went to sea. After a reasonably straightforward search, we picked longtime faculty member Dr. Paul Joyce, an oceanographer, to be the new dean and head of the academic department.

The marine department was headed by Dr. Al Hickey, a long-time captain. Al is from Mattapoisett and is a doctor of chiropractic. The other captains answered to him, and he was responsible for keeping the ships in working order and up to the standards set by the US Coast Guard and the American Bureau of Shipping. Anything that went wrong, anywhere in the world, Al had to figure out how to fix it. Most importantly, parents sent us their kids and expected to get them back with all their fingers and toes. Al ensured that a culture of safety permeated everything on the ships, from maintenance to how we selected and trained the crew to where and when we sailed.

We recruited students from colleges and universities across the country. When I arrived, Brian Hopewell was the dean of enrollment. A charismatic musician and storyteller, Brian could charm anyone. The SEA Semester students praised the program highly. I figured Brian's main challenge would be how to turn away six applicants for every spot we had. Boy, was I wrong! I soon learned that filling the ships was a perpetual problem, putting major pressure on Brian's department since most of our $5 million-dollar budget came from tuition.

SEA's Finance and Administration Department was run by a congenial fellow and ably assisted by Sally Hampton. I learned early in running non-profit and government organizations that one aspect of financial management is accountability. WHALE's Treasurer, John Hodgson, told me to think of that as explaining the finances of your organization to your elderly aunt. It has to be simple enough to be understood without an excess of information. It must convey an accurate picture, so the audience understands the real strengths and vulnerabilities. And it has to

Rafe Parker   *Collecting data on the SSV* Corwith Cramer

be presented in a way that conveys trust and credibility. The more I dug into the finances at SEA, the less I saw any of those attributes. The difficulty wasn't just that we were in a weak financial posture but also that we couldn't even describe where we were financially.

The Development Department was headed in an acting capacity by Jan Wagner. Jan had lived on the Cape but moved to California. While SEA searched for a new development director, she was still holding down the fort. Our Annual Fund Drive was raising less than $500,000 a year. We had a modest endowment and were only part way through a capital campaign undertaken to build a new ship, the *Robert C. Seamans*. The ship, a brigantine, had just been completed by the Martinac Shipyard in Seattle and was supposed to extend our operations to the Pacific Ocean. There was a lawsuit over disputed change work orders, so all progress was at a standstill.

This was the staff that welcomed me. Well, welcome is really not the right word. SEA had built a very tight culture over its 30 years of existence. It was an insular organization, and I had come in from the outside. I hadn't risen through the ranks. I didn't come from the tall ship world. I wasn't an academic with a PhD. I didn't live in Woods Hole or even on the Cape. I didn't drive a Subaru. Everyone was perfectly nice to me, but there was not a day at SEA when I felt part of the organization. Of course, some individuals became my friends. They were wonderful, welcoming people. But the staff in the organization as a whole seemed unwelcoming.

Rafe Parker, my predecessor, tried to help. We embarked on several trips up and down the East Coast. Rafe introduced me to SEA's major supporters and did his best to convince them I was a fitting replacement. Rafe was and still is an inspirational figure to me. He was in England's Special Forces. On a training flight in Africa, Rafe was the last guy to jump out of a plane. As he exited, his parachute caught the fire extinguisher by the door and failed to open. Rafe fell to the ground, landed in a tree, and broke nearly every bone in his back. After a year in the hospital, he recovered. Though a decade or so older than I, he could outrun me for sure.

The more I learned about the difficulties of running SEA, the more amazed and impressed I was that Rafe had built two ships, engineered a campus housing 50 students and kept the place going for 20 years. As we visited supporters, I could understand their loyalty. Rafe was a gentleman who cared about people. He had empathy. He was sincere. He listened. When he asked, "How are you doing?" he **really** wanted to know. He invested time and attention in personal relationships.

All politics is personal.

Captain Beth Doxsee shoots Local Apparent Noon (LAN) to establish our latitude.

Students learn celestial navigation.

Experiential Learning

In addition, Rafe knew just how to explain the mission of SEA. We were the only institution where college students could study ocean science, history, and policy while spending enough time at sea to understand the ocean in all its moods and dimensions. And at a time of increasing environmental change, this has never been more important, especially considering how much of the planet is covered by water and how much of the earth's biomass is in the ocean.

But as Rafe would point out, the lessons don't stop there. SEA's form of experiential learning is the ideal form of leadership development. The six-week sea component is divided into three two-week periods. For the first two-week segment, students do what they are told. They literally "learn the ropes." In the second segment, they individually lead a certain operation in the lab or on deck under the guidance of a mate or assistant scientist. Finally, in the last two-week period, each student leads the deck or lab for a whole watch, essentially in command of the watch. This leadership training is hard to find elsewhere.

Spending so much time in the car with Rafe allowed me to probe about the culture of SEA. He described his relationship with the faculty as adversarial, which surprised me. Perhaps hostile is the natural relationship between any independent faculty and any administration that needs to manage an entire institution as a coherent entity. Though I was startled at Rafe's confession, I found it very comforting to know that even he, Rafe Parker, had experienced over his 20 years what I had felt in my first few weeks.

Early on, I decided one of the best ways to understand our program was to go to sea with the students. My first trip was aboard the new *Robert C. Seamans*, which was finally completed and delivered to us. I joined the ship in Puerto Vallarta, Mexico, and sailed the first leg across the Sea of Cortez to La Paz before it continued to Hawaii. This initial week-long period is when the class first meets the ocean. While on land, they have cell phones. The land is stable. They sleep at night (well, sort of) and are awake during the day. As soon as they step on board, a lot changes. We take their phones, so they are no longer in touch with the outside world. A watch system means they sleep and work at different times day and night because the ship operates 24 hours a day. The motion of the ocean is constant, meaning most students are seasick for the first three days. Sea sickness comes in three stages. First, you feel so bad you think you will die. Second, you hope you are going to die. Third, you get over it and know there is life after death. After about three days, you get your sea legs. You are no longer seasick. You become comfortable not having a shower every day. And importantly, you have stopped thinking about friends and family at home and are focused on your shipmates and the tasks at hand. You are in the moment. At that point, you feel as if you can go forever.

I sailed on portions of five trips, about 3,000 to 4,000 miles, in the ten years I was at SEA. I was always impressed with our faculty and crew and the power of our teaching model. Every trip left me with a deep respect for the importance of taking students to the deep ocean for an extended period so they could absorb this part of the world.

Captain Sean Bercaw

Mostly, I was awestruck by our students. When given a choice of study-abroad options— go to Italy or Australia and study the humanities and drink wine or go to sea and study science— they chose the more difficult course. They chose to travel outside their comfort zone to a place that literally would make them sick. These were tough kids who wanted to test themselves.

One of the trips I took with the students stands out. I met up with the *Corwith Cramer* under the command of Captain Sean Bercaw in Bermuda for the final leg to Lunenburg, Nova Scotia. Professor Joyce Chaplin of Harvard, who was writing a book on Ben Franklin, also joined us. When Franklin was head of the Postal Service, he noticed that mail transiting to England took less time than mail coming back. From that observation, he postulated and then verified the existence of the Gulf Stream, a great river in the Atlantic Ocean. Dr. Chaplin wanted to see for herself. We often took visiting scientists or historians like Professor Chaplin on our trips. How fortunate for our students to have the opportunity to converse and to pick the brains of some of the finest minds around.

A day or so out of Bermuda, dolphins started riding our bow wave during the mid-afternoon class period. It was the first time we had encountered them, so Captain Sean and Chief Scientist Chuck Lea let the students go up to the bow to marvel at these intelligent mammals. There was much screaming and joy from the humans on the ship, and one could only deduce that the dolphins were playing in our bow wake. When the dolphins appeared the next afternoon, Sean

Afternoon class on the quarterdeck

Rare bottlenose whales follow closely behind as we map the Gulley for the Canadian government.

and Chuck told the students they had to stay aft in class. Deprived of company at the bow, the dolphins came back to the stern, where they surfed on the stern quarter wake. Apparently, they loved an audience.

After crossing the Gulf Stream, where Joyce witnessed the abrupt change in temperature, color, salinity, wave pattern, sea life, and weather, we headed east to map a canyon known as "The Gulley." We had permission from Fisheries and Oceans Canada to help them map this canyon that is about 50 miles long and almost a mile deep. We had a Chirp Sub-bottom profiler, which mapped the geology of the bottom by sending a sharp noise—a *chirp*—through the water below. The signal bounced back to us, and we could map the bottom. We would also send the information to Canada's Department of Fisheries and Oceans.

As we made transects of the Gulley, I was puzzled to see about 50 rare bottlenose whales, each 20 feet long or so, following us. I had read that whales are disturbed by loud noises, and the chirp was loud. It annoyed everybody on board until we got used to it. These whales certainly didn't have to be near us, but here they were. They didn't seem bothered at all and tagged along during our mapping like a herd of horses.

After reaching the gulley's northern end, we headed west toward Sable Island, a long thin sandbar shaped like a smile located about a hundred miles south of Nova Scotia. It is unpopulated by humans except for four scientists—three meteorologists and one social scientist. About 400 wild horses have lived there for several hundred years, along with thousands of gray and harbor seals. Captain Sean had secured permission from National Parks Canada for us to land, but even with permission, you need perfect weather. We anchored to the north and were in luck with absolutely flat calm water and a sunny day. I was in the first shore group to board our inflatable rescue boat. Sean took about six of us, and all seemed perfect until we were about ten feet from the sandy beach.

"Watch out!" Sean suddenly yelled.

Out of nowhere came a 3-foot breaking wave, crashing over the boat and soaking all of us in chilly 45-degree water. We got to the beach, and Sean gunned the outboard in reverse and went back for the second group. Luckily, I had secured my camera in a watertight bag. Everything else was drenched. *Perhaps this is a sacred place. Before you set foot here, a baptism is required.*

After the class assembled, we marched to the meteorological station. We listened to a brief history of the island and were given instructions on where we could go. The herd of feral horses had been there since the American Revolution, descendants of horses confiscated from Acadians on the mainland by the British and brought to the island by John Hancock's uncle Thomas.

We spent the day exploring the island, wandering among dunes and along the beach, and looking at the horses with their long, rough hair. There were seals everywhere. Later, when I rejoined NOAA, I would hear people complain about the numbers of seals gathering on Cape Cod and attracting great white sharks. Besides the danger to humans, fishermen argued that the seals were causing the cod stocks to crash, something not supported by science. Some fishermen used these factors to argue for a "culling" of the Cape Cod seal herd. Killing seals is against the Marine Mammal Protection Act, but there is an even more fundamental problem: the Cape population of seals is part of this larger northern population, which would continually replenish whatever was "culled."

As we spent time on this spit of land so far from human settlements, I thought how fitting it was that scientists are often the first people to represent the human race in an unknown or little-known place. That is the case on Sable Island. It is the case on the Moon, the very deep ocean, and the two poles. It seems we humans put our best foot forward when we send scientists first to make an impression.

After getting back on board the *Corwith Cramer*, we sailed the last remaining leg to the seaport and World Heritage Site of Lunenburg, Nova Scotia, where the cruise ended for our students. While there, I could catch up with Captain Dan Moreland of the barque *Picton Castle*.

Laurie and I met Dan when he came to New Bedford to restore the schooner *Ernestina*. Dan did his first circumnavigation under sail on the Brigantine *Romance* in 1974-76. He had done several circumnavigations since. In other words, Captain Dan has seen and experienced a lot of ocean. He knows almost everyone there is in the tall ship world. He has much to teach.

Two of a herd of 400 wild horses that have occupied Sable Island for 250 years

Dan and I discussed the job at SEA. One concern he had was also a concern of mine—the insularity of the organization. Dan said everyone at SEA seemed confident that there was "a SEA way" to do things, and all other ways were inferior. This superiority complex bothered him. He told me how at the end of a circumnavigation, he gathered all those aboard for final words.

"I told everyone that they might find themselves on another tall ship someday. You have learned much about being a mariner in your sail around the world, and you might be tempted to advise this new ship on a better way to do something. Resist this temptation. For even on the worst run vessel, there will be things you can learn."

That was the essence of humility. There is always something you can learn. Somehow, that lesson had eluded SEA. I could understand how you need to have one way of doing things as you rotate different people on and off two ships over the years. For safety's sake, it must be very clear how every operation gets done. There cannot be any confusion about that. But one should always be willing to learn from others. SEA's safety record was, and is, superb, so there is reason to be proud. I still think humility keeps you on your toes and looking for how to get better.

As SEA's marine department, legal department, and board continued their dispute with Martinac Shipyard over the change order, there was a moment when a settlement could have been reached. But we were so convinced of our position that we could not visualize how Martinac could be right. This was very early in my tenure, so I was not deeply involved. SEA fought to the end and lost in court. The argument cost hundreds of thousands of dollars that SEA didn't have. The cost of hubris.

Keeping What's Good

As I got to understand what SEA was about, I started to form a picture in my own mind of what I thought was valuable and worth protecting and enhancing and what needed changing. That is the challenge for someone new entering an organization—to be able to tell the difference. The next question was whether I could effectively bring about change in a culture as strong as what existed at SEA. I knew we needed to preserve the mission—teaching college students about the science, policies, and history of human interactions with the ocean environment. I couldn't see anything more important, and SEA is the only organization attempting that mission.

Looking over SEA were the trustees. Under the leadership of Dr. Ned Cabot and Vice President Rick Burnes and with the calming wisdom of Treasurer Sam Gray, there were a little over two dozen very loyal board members. Because many were ocean sailors, they did not get rattled, and they had a camaraderie that was a great asset. I felt a bond of trust with most of them, along with support that I did not necessarily feel from the staff. That was important to me.

One of the trustees was Robert C. Seamans, for whom our Pacific ship was named. Bob had joined our board shortly after SEA was created, and he chaired the board from 1989 to 1993. But he gained fame as the number-two man at NASA. Bob told me the story: JFK wanted to respond to Russia being first in space. Robert McNamara proposed going to Mars. Bob proposed going to the Moon. I often wonder what it must have been like being in the room with only a few people while making that momentous decision.

Bob died in June of 2008 as he neared his 90th birthday. A year later, the family had a memorial service at Kresge Auditorium at MIT, where he taught. The family asked me to speak on behalf of SEA. I readily agreed and asked whom I would follow in the speaking program.

"Neil Armstrong."

"Great. OK, well, I guess someone has to do that."

I don't know how many speeches I've given, but I have never had to follow anyone like Neil Armstrong. What words could I possibly use that would do justice to Bob? I thought and thought and finally realized I was incapable. I asked our alumni director to comb through our files for a student who might have sailed on the *Seamans* and might be seeking a career in NASA or some related field.

We chose Zena Cardman, who wrote a very moving tribute, far better than anything I could have said, about her time on the *Robert C. Seamans*. At the service, I said what I needed to say about Bob and his contributions to young people, drawing comparisons between a relatively small ship on a hostile ocean and the lunar module. Then, I turned it over to Zena to have the last words:

Robert C. Seamans

> The interface between humans and technology fascinates me. Compared to many other creatures on Earth, we are fairly limited in our natural range of habitat. We can't fly, we can't breathe underwater, we don't do so well in extreme temperatures. We are exceptional, though, in that we create technologies which allow us to explore elements beyond the land—technologies like boats and rockets. What I grew to love about sailing was actually becoming a part of this technology that harnesses natural forces. We set the sails. We engage the engine.
>
> I have been asked a few times why people still bother with tall ships when technology has progressed so far beyond sails. We sail for the challenge, for the thrill, the accomplishment, or maybe simply because we want to go somewhere.
>
> In any case, the ocean is there, and we have something that floats. We went to the Moon for similar reasons in the 1960s. We have yet to go back, not exactly because we lack the technology, but because—some say—we haven't been able to muster that spirit again. Should you meet the students with whom I sailed on board the *Robert C. Seamans*, I think you will realize that our spirit for challenge, adventure, and intellectual gain still exists. For me, this is the legacy of Bob Seamans.
>
> At night on the *Seamans*, I couldn't help but look up at the stars. I delighted, too, in celestial navigation, an art which, these days, is more easily done with GPS units. That we can derive a point on the surface of our planet from a few pinpricks in the sky is impressive, I thought. But that we understand what those pinpricks are and where we are in relation to them is profound.
>
> Few things in sailing are as important as knowing where you came from, where you are, and where you are going. I maintain that the same holds true for anything I do in life. There is nothing more thrilling than knowing where you want to wind up and pointing your bow into the dark sky separating you from that goal. I will keep the legacy of Bob Seamans with me as I steer toward mine.

Bob Seamans wrote a great book, *Aiming at Targets*. Zena aimed at hers. She qualified for the Astronaut Group 22 in 2017.

The SEA campus itself gives the program an advantage. It is small and personal. There are two buildings for classrooms and offices and a reception area for gatherings. There are five small cabins where the 50 students live and share cooking duties. There is a modest amount of open space for throwing a frisbee or cookouts and such. But the big thing is that the campus is in Woods Hole and near a cluster of other scientific institutions, so students and faculty can take advantage of that. Right next door is Woods Hole Research Center, founded by the incomparable George Woodwell and now named for him. George was succeeded while I was there by John Holdren, who spent eight years as the chief science advisor to President Barack Obama. Down the road a bit are the Woods Hole Oceanographic Institute (WHOI) and the US Geological Survey (USGS), and nearby in the village are the NOAA Fisheries Science Center and the Marine Biological Lab (MBL). If you look at the lower 48 states, ocean science is concentrated in each corner. The University of Washington owns the Northwest. Scripps dominates the Southwest. Miami's Rosenstiel School is the power in the Southeast, although the University of South Florida is giving them a run for their money. In the Northeast, the tiny community of Woods Hole stands alone, perhaps in the world, as a research community united by ocean science. To have the students spend time here is very good for them.

Another thing SEA got right is the experiential way of teaching. Preliminary time in Woods Hole is followed by six weeks at sea. This is enough time to create a deep relationship with the ocean. Chris LeGault, an alumnus of SEA who went on to a distinguished career at NOAA's Science Center in Woods Hole, told me that in all his ocean research, he never again had a cruise that long. A senior administrator at WHOI, who was responsible for hiring people to staff its research ships, told me that SEA graduates were highly sought after.

"If someone comes to me from SEA, I just hire them. I know they know their way around scientific equipment. I know they can handle themselves at sea. I know they will make a good shipmate. I know they are a mariner. I know they are used to hard work in difficult conditions. That's all I need to know."

Our teaching model also taught leadership. It is no coincidence that so many countries use tall ships to train their naval officers. The deck of a ship is a great platform for learning and leading. We had some great teachers who were passionate about what they were teaching. Knowing your subject matter and knowing how to teach are two very different things. Most of our faculty were very good at both. The students sensed their passion and excitement for the subject matter and became excited as well.

This brings me to the most important element that needed to be protected and enhanced—our students. When I came to SEA, not being familiar with Study Abroad, I expected, for some

Woods Hole is the center of marine science in the northeast United States.

reason, that most of the students would be male. I was surprised that the first class I met was two-thirds female. I asked Brian Hopewell if that was unusual. He said it was the norm.

As I was talking with some students at lunch one day, I raised the topic. I mentioned that Larry Summers, the president of Harvard at the time, had made the controversial assertion that women were not as interested in science as men. I asked if their class indicated that he was off base. The young women I was talking with treated his assertion with contempt. As we chatted, one student explained why she thought women outnumbered men in the class.

"Study Abroad involves risk because you aren't sure about the credits toward your major. You are leaving your friends behind. You don't know what the experience is going to be like."

"But I associate risky behavior with guys."

"Well, you may be thinking of uncalculated risks like drinking or driving too fast. What I'm talking about are calculated risks. Guys have to see how all the dots connect from the courses they take to the career they are going to have. We are willing to say, 'I'm not sure where this leads, but I bet it leads somewhere.' That's a calculated risk."

Boy, the president of Harvard sure could learn a lot from our students!

Women or men, SEA students came with a sense of wonder and excitement for the adventure ahead. They worked hard and immediately got to know one another, realizing they would be spending six weeks in *very* close company. They were comfortable outside their comfort zones, which meant they learned quickly. They kept their egos in check and supported one another when support was needed.

I addressed each class on the first day they arrived for their campus portion of the program. Before they headed to sea for the ocean voyage, I gave them a send-off speech. Always ask yourselves two questions: *'What's going on here? What do I do about it?'* The first question involves your powers of observation, something that is critical in science but also in life. The second question is what you do with the information you have. Sometimes that will be obvious. Standing orders say if you see a vessel approaching within three miles, you are to notify the mate. Other times, it might not be so obvious. Whether what you observe are potential storm clouds, a gauge that is reading too hot, or a worried look in a shipmate's eyes, think about, 'What do I do with this information?' We are a science-based institution, and we believe that actions should be based on fact-based information. But we are also in the business of creating leaders. We think *you* are going to become leaders, and we believe with information comes the obligation to act.

Many of SEA's alumni do become leaders, especially in ocean-related fields. I have lost track of how many SEA alums I have run into in the halls of NOAA in Washington and in regional offices. They were doing science, forming policy, managing fisheries, enhancing aquaculture, and protecting marine mammals or habitats. Or they were working for NGOs or academic institutions. One way or another, they were impacting the world around them. Even just starting out at SEA, I could tell the students and student experience were critical and definitely deserved protection.

SEA has a culture of safety—another value worth protecting and enhancing. When parents dropped their kids off on the first day, I would tell them how seriously we took the responsibility. Our ships are designed to be safe. We maintain them to the highest standards. Our captains and crews go through rigorous safety training several times a year. The first three days of a voyage are devoted to safety drills for fire, person overboard, and abandon ship scenarios. One of our trustees, Ken Potter, was head of the Transportation Safety Board for Canada, which gave him incredible experience investigating marine accidents. He described a safety system as erecting a series of safety nets and told us that most accidents are a result of many of these nets all failing at once. His advice was invaluable to us as we developed our own Safety Management System.

One example of how this worked was when we got a call one morning in 2005 from Captain Steve Tarrant. We were in Woods Hole, and he was on the *Corwith Cramer* off the coast of Cuba. Captain Al Hickey was still the director of the Marine Department, and he called Paul Joyce and me to apprise us of the situation. The *Cramer* had spotted a small boat carrying refugees, and it was in trouble. It was morning on a calm day. The refugees had disabled their craft and were seeking to come on board. Al had contacted the Coast Guard. No other ships were nearby. It was up to us.

As Steve maneuvered the *Cramer* closer to get a better look, the SEA crew counted over 30 people, guessing they were from Haiti, which was several hundred miles away. We had many questions, but all revolved around safety. We were concerned about the safety of the refugees, and we were concerned about the safety of our students and crew. We consulted with our medical team, safety experts, and lawyers. Fred Carr, a lawyer with admiralty law experience, gave us important advice.

"Guys, don't worry about the law. Do what you think is right."

Fred is an excellent lawyer, and his advice let us all put our energy where it should be.

We consulted a couple of doctors, including Dr. John Cahill, an infectious disease specialist. We were concerned about the possibility that some of the refugees might be sick. The doctors advised us that if we decided to make the rescue, we should isolate the refugees on the foredeck, not allow contact with the crew, provide them with water and simple food, and proceed as quickly as possible to a port where we could let them disembark.

We considered our options. We had about 35 people on board, mostly students. We knew there were over 30 people on the refugee boat, but we weren't sure of their ages. One of our students spoke French, and when we sent her with a mate on a rescue boat to communicate with the group, they said they were looking for asylum in Jamaica, which would be about a day's travel. As they got closer, they could see some very young children onboard.

As Al, Paul, and I discussed this with Captain Steve, we understood we had an obligation to perform the rescue. It is an obligation that one ship has, if able, to come to the aid of another. And we were able. We also thought we should do it soon while it was light out and we had calm weather.

We didn't want their severely overcrowded vessel, aptly named *Delta*, a term scientists use for "change," to capsize or sink, which would make the rescue a much higher degree of difficulty. We also discussed the risk that, once aboard, the refugees might try to seize the *Cramer* to bring themselves to Florida or Cuba, or somewhere else. Captain Steve judged that to be a minimal risk. We trusted his judgment because he was there, and we weren't. After the captain had a chance to think about how the crew would set everything up, he briefed the crew and the students.

Crew of the Cramer *lift Haitian refugees to safety.*

They brought the *Delta* alongside the *Cramer* and deployed a boarding ladder. One by one, 51 Haitian refugees boarded the *Cramer* and were directed to the foredeck, where they were given water and simple refreshments. A temporary head was set up, and the foredeck was roped off to maintain separation. Besides getting an accurate count, we could see that ages ranged from a breastfeeding infant and his mother to several elders. There appeared to be no injuries. After all the refugees were safely aboard, our crew sank the *Delta,* so that it would not be a hazard to any other vessel that might run into it in the dark.

When everyone was settled, the *Cramer* set a course for Jamaica. When I knew everyone was safe, I notified my friend Terry Schaefer at *The Today Show,* which wanted Captain Steve and some students to come on the show when they landed in Port Antonio, Jamaica. After the cruise finished in Key West, Florida, and the students returned to their campuses, many were interviewed about their experiences.

As I listened to the interviews, I was struck that everyone from Steve to each of the students wanted only to talk about the plight of the refugees and the conditions in Haiti that had forced them into that dangerously overcrowded boat. None of them wanted to talk about their heroic rescue saving 51 lives, which earned them the Cruising Club of America's highest award for seamanship, the Rod Stephens Trophy. Did we teach that I wondered, or was this empathy and sense of goodness already in these young people when they came to SEA? Did it just need a situation like the plight of these refugees to reveal the quality of our captains and crew, the staff on shore, the experts on our board but, most importantly, the students themselves?

Diversity in Marine Sciences—The Oceans Connect Us

From my first day at SEA, it was inescapable not to notice how White the place was. We had one Black faculty member, who left after a year, only one minority on the trustees' board, and none on our board of overseers. Our student body, too, was overwhelmingly White.

Having come from Washington, where diversity was a common sight, and having fought successfully to bring diversity to city government while I was mayor of New Bedford, this Whiteness was unsettling. Our ships spent a lot of time in Polynesia and the Caribbean, and to have our program be so Caucasian was a shortcoming for students.

I had to find out more. First, I asked to meet with Dr. Ambrose Jearld, whom I had heard was very committed to diversity at the NOAA Science Center. Dr. Jearld said he would get back to me. After a week, he called and agreed. I went to his office.

He told me he had checked me out by calling Dr. Brad Brown, a White guy who worked for NOAA in Miami and was a long-time champion for diversity. Brad had told Ambrose that during my time at NOAA, I was a persistent advocate to the administration, pushing for greater effort toward diversity. Brad had given Ambrose his endorsement. Ambrose had also called some friends in New Bedford and found out I was a lifetime member of the NAACP and had been active for a long time in civil rights there. Knowing all that, Ambrose agreed to meet.

"Dr. Jearld, thank you for agreeing to meet. I have heard so much about you. I am new at SEA and new to the Woods Hole community. I couldn't help but notice that SEA is a mostly White organization. I wanted to ask you if we are the only organization that is not diverse or whether this is a problem others might suffer from as well?"

Ambrose leaned back in his chair and smiled. He gave a short, low laugh.

"No, John, you are not alone at SEA. Woods Hole is one of the Whitest places you are going to find, and that is the case with every institution here."

So began the first of many conversations. We discussed some of the causes of the lack of diversity. As Ambrose explained it to me, Woods Hole is a community focused on marine science, and minority students interested in sciences are not likely to be drawn to oceanography or related fields. They are more likely to go into medicine, in part so they can pay off their student debt. As far as their relationship with the ocean and ships goes, they tend to associate the sea and maritime history with forced passage on slave ships. SEA trustee and historian Jeff Bolster has written

Black Jacks, which tells how integral minorities are to maritime history. Anyone visiting the New Bedford Whaling Museum and looking at the photographs of whaling vessel crews can see the same thing. It is a shame that this history is not better known, but until it is, the association with slavery can be an obstacle to recruiting minorities to the marine sciences.

Dr. Ambrose Jearld

Another barrier, Ambrose pointed out, is that Woods Hole is in Massachusetts, a pretty White state, and the village is located on Cape Cod, which is as White as the beaches. We both acknowledged that homogeneity is a natural state. Diversity doesn't occur by itself. It is something you must work at. It is like pushing a rock uphill. If you push really hard, you can move the rock toward the mountaintop. If you relax for a second, the rock will slip downward. You can never rest. Gravity is on the side of homogeneity.

I asked Ambrose if he thought, given that all six scientific institutions suffered the same lack of diversity, whether it would make sense to approach this problem as a group or whether he thought I should just try to tackle this at SEA alone. He responded by saying that would depend on whether the other institutions thought the problem was serious enough to work on it. We agreed that I would approach the heads of the other organizations. I anticipated diversity would be an issue as basic as motherhood and apple pie. People would tell me they were all for it. The question would be the level of commitment they were prepared to make.

I started by meeting with Bob Gagosian, who was the CEO of WHOI. Bob was not physically large, but he carried enormous weight, not just in Woods Hole but in the country and the world. WHOI is the world powerhouse in ocean sciences, and everyone looks to it for leadership. Bob is a high-energy guy with a positive attitude. He is a quick thinker and brilliant. A conversation with him leaves you exhausted, in a good way. Bob was a fan of SEA and served on our board of overseers. He acknowledged the issue and conceded that all the organizations would be better served if we were more diverse. We talked about how we work to solve international issues and how the world is primarily a black, brown, and yellow place. We would be smarter if our population more reflected the world. He acknowledged the difficulties of recruiting and emphasized the mantra of always having to get the "best qualified people." When I pressed him on the need to form a joint initiative, he told me he had many priorities and would have to talk with his board, but he thought this was a reasonable approach.

This was a big first step.

Similarly, we went to George Woodwell, my neighbor at the Woods Hole Research Center, and Bill Schwab at US Geological Survey on the WHOI campus. In Woods Hole village, I met with Bill Speck at the Marine Biological Lab and Frank Almeida at NOAA's Science Center. All agreed to work together, although it was clear this was not a pressing need for any. It took us a year, but by 2004, we had negotiated the Woods Hole Scientific Community Diversity Initiative. It was the first agreement on any subject that all six institutions had signed, so having the promotion of diversity be the subject matter for the initial joint undertaking was in and of itself significant. We set out to create "pathways of opportunity" in the Woods Hole community to attract people from underrepresented groups beginning in primary education, leading to higher education, post-graduate work, research, and lifetime careers.

The Memorandum of Understanding (MOU) set three goals. The first was to advise the organizations on ways to promote diversity. The second was to support employees to reach their full potential, and the third was to develop programs to recruit, retain, and mentor people in a way that increases diversity. All the CEOs signed the MOU on July 27, 2004. We agreed to meet once or twice a year to monitor progress and assign one or two people to the Diversity Action Committee (DAC) to devise and carry out the work plan. While I chaired the Diversity Initiative Board for the first few years, Ambrose chaired the DAC, which I also attended. We were a great team. Ambrose also joined the SEA board so that we could incorporate the work of the DAC right into SEA.

The DAC started to plan various events to raise awareness and support the goals. Black History Month was already occurring, so we pitched in on that. We added a Juneteenth celebration in the summer that had every institution set up booths. There were music venues and food booths; for a day, Woods Hole looked more like the United Nations than Cape Cod.

Perhaps the biggest step was the invention in 2009 of a summer program by Ambrose and George Liles, a colleague of his at NOAA's Science Center. With support from Center Director Nancy Thompson and John Oliver down in Washington, Ambrose and George designed the Partnership in Education Program (PEP). Our academic partner was the University of Maryland Eastern Shore, a Minority-Serving Institution (MSI) with a special relationship with NOAA Fisheries.

PEP recruits 17 college juniors or seniors from MSIs to Woods Hole in the summer. They live on SEA's campus. They attend classes for four weeks taught by faculty drawn from all six institutions, and they may also do a short research voyage on the *Corwith Cramer*. They partner with a scientist to do a ten-week research internship. The goal was to excite these talented young scientists-to-be about careers in the ocean sciences and Woods Hole in particular. In 2022, PEP added a seventh institution, the Buzzards Bay Coalition.

Ambrose played a key role in all of this. When he described Woods Hole, he would say, "Everyone who works here is here because they knew someone." He would go on to describe the personal reference system that works in the scientific community. I would call it the Old Boy Network, except the gender barrier has been broken. So has the barrier of international boundaries. The barrier that remains is racial, and it is the hardest nut to crack. You can't really talk about diversity without talking about race.

With PEP students in New Bedford

When you look at the phrase "most qualified applicant," you have to think carefully about the implications of that phrase. If you are hiring someone you hope will be in your organization for several decades and one candidate is a little bit more qualified than another, but that other candidate started from further behind and had to travel a much greater distance to get to the same point, then whom do you want to put your money on five years down the road? Another way to find the "most qualified applicant" is to ask the question, "Who makes the team better?" Most teams are better if they have diversity. You don't want a band made up of just saxophone players. As Ambrose would say, "You want to make sure the person meets the qualifications. When you start getting into most qualified, that can be a slippery slope where biases come into play."

Another way that Ambrose was so valuable to the PEP program was that every student seemed to know who Ambrose was before they got here. Ambrose was well known to minority college students, acting as their North Star to guide them to this wonderful program where doors to the future in marine science and beyond would be unlocked and where they would support one another, not just during the 14 weeks but long after.

As Ambrose pointed out, "Everyone is in Woods Hole because they know someone." Well, in the case of the PEP students, that "someone" was Ambrose. He was determined to build a network of racial minorities that would work in the ocean sciences at Woods Hole. Seventeen students will not change the makeup of Woods Hole. But 17 students every year will have an impact, and NOAA Fisheries, upon Ambrose's retirement, assured everyone that the funding for PEP would always be there.

Now, there is a John K. Bullard Diversity Award that is given periodically to recognize leadership in promoting diversity in the Woods Hole scientific community. And there is an annual Ambrose Jearld Jr. Lecture each summer that invites scholars, scientists, authors, and others who challenge the status quo to bring perspective, knowledge, and expertise to the subject of building a more diverse and inclusive community. Every summer, 17 new young students take their place in the Woods Hole community, ready to learn, continue the struggle, and build on that network.

It takes us all, and it takes forever. Slowly, the rock moves uphill.

2021 Partnership Education Program (PEP) students aboard the Corwith Cramer

Changing What's Not

Figuring out what needed to change was easier than accomplishing those changes. We had to fill the ships. To do that, we had to boost enrollment. We determined we had to offer more course choices and needed to recruit differently.

As I was coming on board, one of our alumnae, Dr. Barbara Block, a professor at Stanford University and a world authority on bluefin tuna, proposed that she take her whole class on a trip. The shore component would be taught in Monterey. The sea component would be on the *Robert C. Seamans* in the Pacific, and the session would be condensed into ten rather than 12 weeks to match up with Stanford's quarter system. Barbara is brilliant, but she is her own weather system and can leave destruction in her wake. People who work with her sometimes don't like the experience. I spent a lot of time negotiating the agreement. We did a trip with Barb every other year, and she filled the ship each time. She showed us you *could* do it.

As I observed her teach a class, I watched the eyes of the students as they listened to Barb. She reached them with her passion and conveyed the *excitement* of science. She also persuaded Carl Safina to come along on the sea component. Carl informally taught the students about journaling. When I asked him why he participated in the entire sea component, he told me he never got five weeks in one place to think, and this was a great opportunity for him. Dr. Jan Witting from SEA went on these trips as our chief scientist, and after every trip, he swore he would never do it again. But he was again willing to do it when the next trip came along. Captain Phil Sacks, one our most senior captains, did the honors on board. The first year, Dr. Mary Malloy went to teach maritime history with a focus on John Steinbeck. She sent me a note and a picture of the view out her office window on the boat, which overlooked Monterey Bay.

"When the view out my window at SEA looks like this, I'll come back!"

I took it to Dean Paul Joyce.

"Paul, deploying faculty is like deploying scientific equipment. You hope you get them back, but you are never sure!"

We worked with the faculty to design new courses. We had six different programs instead of offering one course six times a year. Mary Malloy, Geoff Schell, and Captain Steve Tarrant designed a course called Colonization to Conservation in the Caribbean. Unlike other classes, it was taught in an integrated way with all three faculty in the room all the time. Naturally, this put a strain on them, both the time commitment and figuring out the new syllabus.

Halfway through the course, Steve came running down the corridor from his office to mine. He came inside and sat down. I thought there might be an emergency.

"What's up, Steve?"

"John, I'm having so much fun in this course. I am learning so much from Mary and Geoff. I can't believe it. It's awesome. I just had to tell you! That's all. Gotta run. Get back to class. See ya."

I wish everyone were like Steve. The faculty created other new courses and new cruise tracks to take students to new destinations. But the adage I had learned as mayor—everyone wants progress; no one wants change—was as much in effect at SEA among the faculty as anywhere else, and change was often slow.

Using the Stanford model, we also worked to forge relationships with other universities. We had one long-standing relationship with Williams College, where the shore component was at Mystic Seaport, and the *Corwith Cramer* took them to sea. But we needed to develop many more such programs.

On one of my many trips to Philadelphia, I persuaded the Wharton School of Business to design a short program focused on leadership training that would put their students on the

Students present their work every afternoon.

Deploying scientific gear under the
watchful eye of chief scientist Dr. Chuck Lea

Seamans for about two weeks. I went to a geology professor at the University of Chicago to get a course just for his students. I worked with the late Professor Jim McCarthy at Harvard to get a course for his students in the Caribbean. There was no question that the quality of our programs could attract the best institutions in the country. It was just a matter of working hard enough to fill the ships year after year.

One of our trustees, Dr. Jian Lin, a geophysicist at WHOI, suggested that China might offer us a tremendous market opportunity. Parents in China were allowed to have only one child, and there was intense competition to get letters of recommendation from American professors to get these special children into American graduate schools. He suggested we develop a partnership with the Ocean University of China in Qingdao. I was a trustee of Massachusetts Maritime Academy, which had a partnership with Shanghai Maritime, and I thought Jian's idea was brilliant.

Paul and I headed to Qingdao, a city that looks to be the size of Boston but has 20 million people. We signed an agreement, but the wheels of getting students on campus rolled very slowly.

We also had to change the way we recruited individual students. There was no question Brian Hopewell was charismatic, but he was a one-man band. It wasn't enough. We needed a team approach to flood the universities and colleges with SEA representatives. We needed a system, not a personality. Brian gave way to Katherine Enos who put together a team of recruiters. I told Paul that each faculty member needed to make one or two college trips. I let Katherine know that I would hit the road, and I wanted her to work with Jan Wagner in development to plan trips where I could visit colleges and talk to donors. Katherine also worked with Associate Deans Virginia McGuire and Erik Zettler to target a top 20 list of colleges that matched well with our credit transfer program, existing relationships, and financial aid. Katherine and her team streamlined a system to reach out to more programs, get SEA people on campuses more often, and use alumni better.

SEA also revamped its marketing materials to change outreach to students and their parents, polishing both the message and the medium. We moved away from almost total reliance on a staid four-color catalog that focused on the seriousness of science and emphasized our being in Woods Hole to more web-based, action-oriented messaging.

We had one debate in a trustee meeting that illuminated this shift. We were fortunate that one of our trustees, Linda Maguire, ran an educational consulting firm specializing in marketing, so we had some real expertise in the room. Katherine and I advocated using words like "adventure" and "discovery." There were audible gasps from some of the faculty and trustees who felt these words would diminish the seriousness of the science. I made the case.

"Let me see. The scientists here in Woods Hole spend their lives discovering things that have never been known before, traveling to parts of the ocean that no one has seen before, proving that what we all knew to be true isn't true at all, and fighting to be the first to publish what they learn. And you are telling me there is no adventure in that! What are you all doing it for? The money?"

We started using "adventure" and "discovery" in our material.

Rich Wilson was a trustee who had raced alone around the world. Twice. While doing that, he communicated with thousands of school kids, educating them about everything from the ocean environment and sailing to geography and the asthma he was battling. He suggested we might send a video report from each ship once a day. We took the idea to the maritime department. At first, we met resistance, but Rich was persuasive.

"The crew onboard is too busy. They don't have time to do the video, Rich."

"Really. I was alone on a 72-foot boat in the Southern Ocean in a gale. And I could do it. Are they busier than that?"

"Well, it would get them thinking about the outside world, and we want them thinking about the ship."

"Well, it would get the outside world thinking about the ship, and maybe that would help put a few more people on the ship."

We started doing short video reports. It didn't seem to harm the shipboard experience, and as far as I know, all the other work still got done. *Everyone wants progress. No one wants change.*

We had to change on many fronts to stay competitive. We revamped the way we reported on the financial implications of all of this. We hired a new CFO, Scott Branco, whose office was right next to mine. I was closer to Scott in more ways than one. I totally trusted him. We talked all the time. He and his assistant, Sally Hampton, straightened out the financial statements, and in no time, we could convey accurate and credible information to the board. Scott lived in Barnstable and had come from a non-profit. He, too, was an outsider to SEA, but he built good relationships with everyone and was trusted by everyone on the board and staff. He also built good relationships with our local banks, which would be necessary when the weather got rough.

We brought in a new development director, Dan Cooney, who had me excited. Dan is from Marion, and when we added his energy to Jan Wagner's experience and knowledge of SEA's contacts, I thought we would be off and running. And we were for a year or so. Jan moved to California but was happy to continue in a secondary role. Annual giving started to ramp up. We completed the $15 million capital campaign that built the *Seamans* and were working to develop a base for the future. One of the ways we did that was to host "Development Sails" in Tahiti on the *Robert C. Seamans*. Existing supporters or potential supporters would fly into Papeete airport, and we would sail for about a week, visiting Moorea and Huahine before returning. The trips were memorable for the remoteness, the beauty, the sailing, and the food. It was an excellent opportunity to showcase how we teach students about the ocean and show off the scientific equipment and the ship itself. You could not help but be impressed.

But it was also hot. These cruises were in January when the sun was at 23 degrees south latitude. Tahiti is just a bit north of that or closer to the equator. When you look down at noon, you don't see your shadow. When you are on deck, wind from the water wards off the heat, and frequent short rain showers cool you and rinse you off now and then. But below decks at night, the heat is oppressive.

On one trip, Laurie and I shared a bunk room with SEA donors Ned and Lillie Johnson of Fidelity. Ned and Lillie participated in every aspect of the daily routine, from sail handling to cleaning up after meals. We had small fans in our bunks to move the air around, but it seemed a losing battle.

"It may be really hot, but at least it's a moist heat," we joked as we were dripping in our bunks. Students would acclimate after a few days of this weather, but the first few days were definitely *not* New England!

Ned asked why we didn't have air conditioning. I told him the rationale. If we air-conditioned, the students might be tempted to spend a lot of time below decks. We wanted them topsides to experience all that this wonderful part of the world had to offer. That seemed to make sense to Ned. Needless to say, swim calls were welcome respites!

All these changes were paying dividends, and we were seeing progress, even if I didn't believe I was changing the culture of SEA. But soon our fortunes turned. Dan Cooney, who had made such great progress, decided he could not work as part of the development team, and we lost his outward perspective.

Then beginning in 2007, the housing bubble began to deflate and then it popped because it was floating on a whole bunch of bad loans that had been bundled together to magically sell to someone as a good investment. But the magic pixie dust blew away. The market crashed, and we entered a fierce recession. Parents did not want to spend money sending their kids to study abroad programs. Our enrollment plummeted. I cut my salary drastically and imposed a lesser salary cut on senior management. Scott and I went through the budget and trimmed everything we could.

We bought some time, but the recession was deep and long. We had to sell land. We had to borrow funds. We had to cut staff and reduce programs. The process was painful, and everyone felt it. To get through, we focused on teaching the students we had.

Robert C. Seamans *in Moorea, French Polynesia*

At SEA: Coming or Going?

As SEA tried to weather to financial crises, the executive committee called on Scott and me to present the latest financial plan. We met at Rick Burnes' office at Charles River Ventures in Waltham in the old Polaroid Building, the one I had helped build when I was in college. I remember it was a Friday afternoon.

Scott and I presented the numbers and the plan going forward, and we answered everyone's questions. At the end, we were asked to wait outside.

"Scott, how do you think that went?"

"I think it went as well as could be expected, John. I think they liked our plan. I think they support what we are doing. They know it's a tough time, but they support us."

After about ten minutes, Ned came out.

"John, can you come back in here."

I went back in. It was just Ned and Rick.

"John, we have to let you go."

My stomach felt as if it had disappeared. Ned was crying.

"You have worked so hard for SEA. You have done so many good things. Rick and I admire your leadership so much. We are so grateful for what you have done. It's just we are in a place now where we have to make a change. We have to go in a different direction."

He and Rick went on a bit. I didn't hear much. I was shattered. At some point, I responded.

"What would you like me to do?"

"Go home tonight. Come back Monday and Susan Humphris (a trustee and scientist from WHOI) will announce this to the staff and announce that Paul Horovitz will be the acting president. Then you can take the morning to remove your things."

I knew Paul Horovitz. He had been on the search committee. He was a headmaster in California. I had checked him out with friends, and I had been wary of him from day one. He was also very close to our development director. He was very smooth.

"That sounds fine, except I am going to SEA right now to tell senior management. They deserve to hear this from me. We've gone through a lot together, and I want to be the one that tells them."

We shook hands. I got in my car and called Scott, who was on his way home to the Cape.

"I guess it didn't go as well as we thought, Scott!"

I told him I had just been fired. He was shocked. He was sad, consoling, and supportive. It was late in the afternoon, but I asked him to assemble senior management in the conference room so I could tell them directly.

While Scott called the SEA folks, I called Laurie.

Laurie has always been my fiercest defender, and she didn't hold back. She didn't spare anyone her anger. No one has been more loyal than Laurie, and it was helpful to me to let her anger at SEA wash over me. We are so complementary that way. I hold my feelings back and keep them so far in check that even I can't find them. With Laurie, feelings are right there for all to see. We are good for each other that way. And now, when I was suffering, Laurie was emoting for both of us. Thank God for that.

At about six that evening, I arrived back on campus. Scott was waiting with Paul Joyce, Katherine Enos, and David Bank, a captain who had succeeded Al Hickey as director of the marine department. Jan Wagner was on the phone from California. I told them about the meeting with the executive committee and the meeting after that with Ned and Rick. I told them I had been fired. I told them that Paul Horovitz would be announced as acting president on Monday morning at an All Hands meeting. I would deliver the news and depart after wishing everyone well. They looked stunned.

I thanked them for their hard work and told them they and SEA would get through these tough times. I delivered the news matter-of-factly, and their reactions were perfunctory. After a short discussion, we adjourned. I loaded my car with as much stuff as possible and drove home. Over the weekend, I tried to process with Laurie what was happening to me. I guess it was an accelerated five stages of grief: denial, I got through that quickly; anger, Laurie helped me with that for sure; bargaining, what was I bargaining for; depression, I was probably entering that; and acceptance, that was a ways away.

Sunday evening, I got a call from Paul Joyce that there could be a problem with the trustees' plan. He told me that a couple of faculty members had entered a reception area at SEA to find Paul Horovitz drinking wine with

SEA students were always a great source of energy and hope.

the students on Saturday evening, which was against several of SEA's rules. Horovitz had already notified Burnes, Richard "Rick" that he would resign. The trustees were investigating and deciding what to do. The All Hands meeting was still scheduled for Monday morning.

I spent a lot of time preparing a farewell speech. It was reminiscent of the speeches I gave after losing political races. I tried to be gracious and wish people well as they moved on without me. I thanked them for the honor of working with them and emphasized the importance of their work.

When I arrived on Monday, Susan Humphris was there to deliver a message, and everyone knew *something* was up. I contacted Rick and Ned, who weren't there, and told them I was aware they had a problem on their hands. I let them know that if they wanted to change their minds and not fire me, I would be willing to swallow my pride and continue working as if Friday afternoon had not occurred. The board, which had been having many conference calls over the weekend, was now under the leadership of Linda Maguire, with Ned and Rick supporting her as vice chairs. It was obvious that they could not proceed as they had planned. Paul had shown a serious lack of judgment right off the bat. He had to go. They accepted my lifeline.

At 11:00 a.m., at the All Hands meeting, Susan Humphris walked into a room full of anxious people expecting some momentous news. She basically pulled a Gilda Radner "Never Mind." It was awkward, to say the least. People said different things. Everybody looked at each other, their eyes asking, "What the hell is going on here?" Finally, we all went back to work.

The mortgage meltdown didn't go away, and the recession gripped the country. My pay cut stayed in force, and we continued to struggle, as did the country. Gradually, the economy picked up. Katherine Enos and her team, with help from the faculty, began to rebuild enrollment, and we were starting to feel better. Our annual fund was now bringing in over $1 million a year, and we were planning another capital campaign that would focus on the endowment, which we knew we needed for a sound financial foundation.

In 2012, I had been at SEA for ten years. The benchmarks for beginning the new campaign kept moving. It seemed like the leaders on the board were a little nervous about taking the plunge. I was tired. I had enjoyed my relationship with the board, but I continued to feel like an outsider with the organization's staff. It was wearing on me. Laurie and I talked about it. A decade was enough. I was 65. I probably had another chapter in me if I left now. I had mixed feelings about leaving SEA. In one sense, leaving took a tremendous weight off my shoulders. But I still believed in the good parts of SEA. The mission is critical. The teaching method is genius. There is simply no better way to learn about the ocean. I had been up against a very strong culture. I had tried to change it but couldn't.

Getting Out the Vote

While at SEA, I continued to be involved in issues important to me. One of those was, of course, politics. I had worked in Pennsylvania and endured the heartbreaking loss of Al Gore to George Bush in 2000. Four years later, my senator John Kerry decided to challenge Bush for the presidential nomination. During the primaries, I went up to New Hampshire to work for him. When I told a class at SEA what I would do over the weekend, a student asked me what my job would be.

"Well, you need to keep in mind a few things. First of all, I was the mayor of a good-sized city in Senator Kerry's state. Secondly, I was a fairly high-ranking official in the Clinton-Gore administration. And third, I know John Kerry pretty well. Given all of that, I am going to drive up to the headquarters in Portsmouth and report to a 20-year-old who is going to be too busy to deal with me, so she is going to hand me over to an 18-year-old, and I am going to do whatever the 18-year-old tells me to do."

They looked at me with curiosity. I encouraged them to think about volunteering some time.

"This is the nature of political organizations, and this is why you students should think about getting involved. They are pure meritocracies run primarily by people your age who can work around the clock, living on pizza and Diet Coke. People who deliver results rocket up the organization chart. People who don't, don't. There isn't time for bureaucracy."

I explained why it was important to help out in other states.

"In strongly Democratic Massachusetts, it is hard to have an impact. But we are near to New Hampshire, and Maine, and Pennsylvania, which are states that always make a difference, where you can have an impact on who your next president will be."

That Sunday afternoon in New Hampshire, there was a big rally for Kerry in a farm field in the snow. There were many speakers, but they saved the headliner for the end. Senator Ted

John Kerry running for president in New Hampshire

Kennedy spoke just before Kerry. As Kennedy approached the mic, the crowd started to cheer. He almost didn't have to say anything. When he did speak, I thought for a moment that he must have reached into his wrong pocket for the speech because he started reading the directions that he had followed to get from Logan Airport to the farm field. And with every turn in the road, in his Kennedy accent, he would pause and look at the crowd, and the crowd would simply erupt. His directions drew them closer and closer to their destination.

"And do you know why I made that right turn onto Main Road and drove three-quarters of a mile down to where we are gathered?"

"YYYYEEEESSSS!!!!" screamed the crowd.

"YOU'RE RIGHT—TO ELECT THE NEXT PRESIDENT OF THE UNITED STATES. JOHN KERRY!"

The crowd went absolutely nuts.

I have heard a lot of great political speeches in my life. I have never heard one that was a set of Google map directions.

My political mentor Mardee Xifaras headed to Ohio to run Kerry's 2004 presidential campaign in this critical state. Laurie and I and some friends, Carolee Matsumoto, David Gilbertson, and Susan Peterson, went to Columbus to do whatever we could in the campaign's last weeks. The race was very close, and the Ohio electoral votes were the deciding factor in who would be president.

Ohio is reliably Democratic in the north, with cities like Cleveland, Akron, and Toledo being manufacturing centers close to Pittsburgh and Detroit. The southern part of the state, bordering Indiana and West Virginia, votes reliably Republican. Columbus is in the middle in more ways than one. The highway that rings Columbus is Route 270, and a headline in the *Columbus Dispatch,* while we were there, read, "Rt. 270, is the Road to 270," meaning whoever won Columbus would win the presidency.

As campaign volunteers, we made phone calls, knocked on doors, did literature drops, and stood on street corners holding campaign signs from early morning until late at night. The atmosphere was electric because we knew we were in the bullseye.

During one walk through a neighborhood, I learned the power of advancing technologies. Almost everyone had Caller ID, so it was very hard to get through to people on the telephone. They wouldn't pick up unless they recognized the number. The campaign figured a way around that. Knowing that the call would go to voice mail, they left a taped message. I found out how effective this was when an excited lady answered her door. I identified myself as a volunteer for John Kerry. Her face lit up.

"Oh, my God! You wouldn't believe it! President Clinton just called me! He left a message on my voicemail asking me to vote for Senator Kerry! Do you believe it?!?" I told her that her vote was very important and that she needed to make sure she got to the polls.

On the last night, Laurie and I worked security for a concert Bruce Springsteen put on for Senator Kerry at the Ohio State campus. Kerry was there along with 50,000 of his closest friends as we tried to keep people somewhat away from the stage. On Election Day, there were extremely long lines in many minority polling locations and accusations of irregularities in the disqualifications of provisional ballots. The Secretary of State Ken Blackwell was an acknowledged advocate for the Bush campaign, hardly the person one would want running an impartial election.

The results in Ohio were not determined until the following day when Kerry decided not to contest his narrow loss. He conceded to Bush. Once again, a gentleman Democrat put country over party. Once again, we had an agonizing loss to digest, up close and personal.

Two years before, in 2002, I spent a week in Pennsylvania with my friend Lance Simmens, working for Ed Rendell as he campaigned for governor. Ed became mayor of Philadelphia just as I left the mayor's office, so I only knew him a little, but Lance was close to him. At the start, Rendell was not favored to beat fellow Democrat Bob Casey in the primary, and it wasn't certain a Democrat could win in Pennsylvania anyway. Lance and I were there for Ed's first week. He took a bus starting in Pittsburgh, headed northeast to Scranton, and then traveled south to finish in Philadelphia several days later. Our job was to get to each city or town a few hours before the bus did and assemble a crowd.

One of the great things about getting involved in politics is that it is an opportunity to learn about America. From the dynamic, thriving metropolis of Pittsburgh to the small towns of Johnstown, the site of the Great Flood of 1889, and Hollidaysburg, where it looked like someone was waiting for the last person to turn off the lights, we could see the great variety of issues that people face, and the wide range of problems people encountered even when they live in close proximity to one another. As we went through State College, it amazed me that Beaver Football Stadium, with its capacity of 106,572, could comfortably hold the entire population of my hometown of New Bedford to watch the Nittany Lions on a Saturday.

To get the finances of Philadelphia under control, Mayor Rendell negotiated tough contracts with police officers, firefighters, and teachers. Lance and I found their representatives waiting for us at every stop with placards opposing Rendell. They called themselves the "Truth Squad."

We spent about a week on the bus tour. We visited Scranton, the home of President Joe Biden. We stopped in Bethlehem with the shell of the great Bethlehem Steel plant, once an industrial giant whose products helped build American cities and World War II warships. The company had declared bankruptcy the year before. We spent time in Allentown, which singer Billy Joel described as a place where "they are closing all the factories down" in his evocative song.

The bus tour was a great start for Ed's campaign. He beat Casey in the primary, won the governorship, and served from 2003 until 2011. Lance went to work for him as his liaison to all 2,561 municipalities in the state.

Lunch with Deval

In 2005, Deval Patrick called me to have lunch in Woods Hole. We met at the Captain Kidd and talked for two or three hours over our meal. Like me, Deval had joined the Clinton administration. He had been an assistant attorney general running the civil rights division. Afterward, he returned to Boston, joined a large law firm, and became in-house counsel to several major corporations. Now, Deval was interested in running for governor. Mardee was already on his team. When he met with me, he wanted more information about the players and issues. He asked my advice on the issues in Southeastern Massachusetts, particularly New Bedford, and how to campaign there. I was sure I wasn't the only person he was talking to, but I was flattered he was turning to me so early and spending so much time with me.

I told him that Southeastern Massachusetts was sick and tired of being left out of the conversation by the bigwigs in Boston. They loved Dukakis because Dukakis paid attention to the region, conducted cabinet meetings down there, learned about the issues important to the area, and spent time locally. Deval should do the same.

I said there were many issues, but the ones where he could make a real impact were higher education and getting the commuter rail from Boston to New Bedford and Fall River. I told him Southeastern Massachusetts would go as far as UMass Dartmouth would take us, and if he became a champion for that campus, he would get support without alienating anyone.

We were the only region in eastern Massachusetts without commuter rail connections to Boston, something we used to have. That rail connection needed to be restored to take traffic off Route 24 and the Southeast Expressway and provide service to this underserved region. Governor Weld had guaranteed it with the words, "or you can sue me," and then broke his promise. The region is sick and tired of getting nothing but broken promises from Boston.

I talked about many other issues—fishing, educational attainment, immigration, and economic development. It was a long list, but I wanted to give Deval the things that were very important and that, as governor, he could directly impact.

I liked Deval and said that I would be with him.

Deval is a very gifted politician. He has a perfect story to tell, similar to Barack Obama's. He grew up on the South Side of Chicago. With hard work and good people in his corner, coupled with his own intelligence and perseverance, he ended up at Harvard and Harvard Law. He is a very gifted speaker. He could develop a good rhythm, modulate his voice, turn a phrase, and mesmerize a crowd.

Deval won and became the first Black governor in Massachusetts history.

He asked me to serve on a 13-person transition team to pick his cabinet. We had about two months to find, persuade, and install about two dozen people who would determine whether Deval's administration would be successful. At our first meeting, John Isaacson, founder of the search firm Isaacson Miller, told us that while we didn't have much time, we still had to go through the four steps of an executive search.

"The first step is that every search is the answer to a problem, so you have to define the problem," Isaacson explained. The second step is you need to cast a very wide net identifying everyone who might be the answer. The third step is to find out more and more about less and less. The final step is vetting the final two or three for the governor to choose. You have about six weeks, and we are here to help you."

Deval Patrick in New Bedford

I was with attorney Mike Angelini on the transportation team. Mike and I now serve on the board of the Buzzards Bay Coalition and have become friends. It started with this trial-by-fire.

As we looked at our field, we understood that the Transportation secretary would have to manage the Port Authority, MBTA, Logan Airport, and Turnpike Authority and Highway Department. While the secretary managed these entities on behalf of the governor, many groups had independent boards appointed by previous governors. They didn't even have to return the secretary's phone calls. We thought about the almost inevitability of a roof panel in one of the Big Dig tunnels falling on a car as a typical problem that would face the secretary on any given day.

"Why would anyone want this job?" was our first reaction. We scoured the country and got down to three finalists to recommend to the governor. All have ended up serving.

Deval served eight years as governor and did a great job.

How to Talk About Climate Change

Besides politics, I was also very concerned with climate change. I had spent enough time in Washington and Woods Hole listening to scientists to know this was a serious issue with profound policy implications that were not being addressed. I remember a conversation with a NOAA colleague in a corridor in Washington. He was visiting DC from his office at the National Center for Atmospheric Research in Boulder. We were aghast at how the Newt Gingrich revolution was trying to eliminate the Commerce Department. Their arguments were so ignorant as to be embarrassing. They didn't think we needed a National Weather Service because we had the Weather Channel, not knowing that the Weather Channel gets all its information from the NOAA's Weather Service.

I asked my friend how the congresspeople and senators could be so ignorant. And why hadn't our scientists communicated better?

"Well, it is not our culture. We are brought up as we pursue our PhDs that if we do our work professionally, the grants will come based on merit. It is degrading and beneath us to lower ourselves intellectually to the level of those on Capitol Hill to explain why these services are needed."

That conversation took place in the mid-90s. It wouldn't take place today. Today there is much attention in the scientific community on how to better communicate science. It's late coming, and some scientists still haven't gotten the memo, but it is necessary and encouraging.

When I heard that Al Gore would conduct a training session on how to talk about climate change, I was excited and determined to sign up. While I had been drinking beer at Harvard, Gore had learned from Professor Roger Revelle about the increase in CO_2 emissions. Emissions are measured on top of Mauna Loa on the Big Island of Hawaii, a place I had visited while I was at NOAA. Those measurements showed that CO_2 in the atmosphere, which has varied between 180 and 280 parts per million for the last 800,000 years, is now over 400 PPM. We have never put this much of this greenhouse gas into the atmosphere in all of human history. And there are consequences.

Gore's *An Inconvenient Truth* was a powerful statement. It had what I considered the three essential elements of a great political speech. First, it defined the problem of climate change as an existential threat. If we don't meet this challenge, future generations of our species and almost every other species will perish. Second, while this challenge is momentous, we are up to it. We have faced other great challenges and met them. We have won world wars. We have gone to the Moon. We have advanced the cause of civil rights, women's rights, and LGBTQ rights. We have narrowed the ozone hole. There is a list of significant achievements of what we can do when we put our minds to it. We have the technologies to win this battle. Third, and this is the part left out of most political arguments, we need everyone to play a role. Some have said that putting a man on the Moon is the wrong analogy. That was accomplished with relatively few superstars in Houston. This is more like putting *everyone* on the Moon!

Gore had developed a great message. The movie based on the book showed him walking alone through hundreds of airports like the Lone Ranger. He then had another brilliant idea. He founded The Climate Project to train citizens to give the same talk he was giving and give it to their neighbors and friends. He would hold the training sessions in Nashville.

I called Lance.

"We have to sign up."

We enrolled in the second session Gore had. The first one enrolled 50 trainees. Ours had 200 from around the country. We arrived in Nashville on a late Friday afternoon in 2006. After settling in and enjoying a welcome barbecue, we were brought into a large room. Mr. Gore, as everyone called him, went through the slide show for the first time. He did it in real time, not lingering on any slides so that we would get a sense of the pace he wanted. There were about 300 slides, a lot with animation. The graphics were fantastic. Gore never read from the slides. He looked at us, not the screen. There was science, humor, and in the end, hope. The show went about an hour and 20 minutes.

We adjourned to the bar afterward, where Al and Tipper Gore joined us. The following day, Gore explained that by Sunday afternoon, we would be able to give his slide show, and we would leave with the presentation on our computers and a copy of his book in our hands. In return, all we had to do was commit to giving ten presentations over the course of the coming

Al Gore giving his presentation in 2007

year. The audiences could be our own choosing—neighbors, school groups, or advocacy organizations. If we weren't sure how to line up an audience, then The Climate Project could funnel requests they were getting for speakers to us. We couldn't accept speaker's fees, and, of course, we could do more than ten. Jenny Clad was the CEO of The Climate Project, and she was at the session getting to know everyone over the weekend.

Saturday morning, Gore went through the slide show a second time. This time, he spent a lot of time on every single slide, explaining the science behind each one, how it might be questioned or attacked, and what the rebuttal should be. He had a scientist with him to back him up on the tough stuff, but it was immediately clear that, unlike most politicians, Gore is a subject matter expert in his own right. He didn't need any help in anything from how to modify a slide's layout to the underlying science. The breadth and depth of his comprehension are breathtaking.

Going through the slide show in this manner took all morning. We broke for lunch and got to know each other better. Afterward, Andy Goodman, an expert in communications from Los Angeles, gave us an entertaining and compelling presentation on communicating with slides. We were all gathered around at tables of eight as Andy began. He put up a slide from a children's advocacy organization, pointing out that the slide had about ten bullet points and over 100 words. It was hard to read.

"Leaders of organizations like the one here, who do the Lord's work, think that gives them the right to give boring presentations. This is the first slide. It gets worse."

Andy advanced to another slide cluttered with even more bullet points. This one had some boxes, and the print was getting smaller.

"What makes this slide even worse is when the speaker turns away from the audience to read every single word. But it gets worse."

Andy put the third slide up. There were bullet points, boxes, triangles, circles, and arrows connecting everything. At this point, and I am not making this up, a person at one of the tables had a seizure and collapsed onto the floor.

Knowing his point had been made for him, Andy just stood and watched as a former EMT rushed over and helped the poor soul, who was stabilized and was fine after a few minutes.

For about 90 minutes, Andy gave us great advice on crafting a slide presentation. Each slide should have very few words. There should be interesting graphics and pictures. Use animation. Never talk to the slide. The slides illustrate your talk, not the other way around.

I have always thought slides are overused in science. There is no question that to communicate science, which relies on graphs, charts, and images, you need to use slides. But in my opinion, they can too easily become a crutch that takes away from the most effective tool one has to communicate. And that is your face. In the highest stakes arenas—before the Supreme Court, in Congress, on a jury in a murder trial—advocates want the audience looking in their faces whenever possible. Why? Because they don't know how to use PowerPoint or Keynote? No. Because they want to persuade someone to believe something or take an action.

After Andy's presentation and a break, Gore gave the talk for the third time. Like the first time, he ran through it at normal speed. By now, many of us felt we could say the words along with him. After he finished, we headed to downtown Nashville for dinner and a show at the Grand Ole Opry.

On Sunday morning, Mr. Gore told us that the most difficult presentation is always the first. Everyone gets nervous about public speaking. Everyone gets butterflies standing up in front of a crowd. He told us the second presentation would be much easier. So, we were all going to get the first one out of the way right now!

He had the staff divide us into four groups of 50 people in separate rooms, each with a slide projector and a screen. A staffer asked us one at a time to stand up as the staffer started advancing the slides. We took turns, each presenting five slides at a time. We were nervous. We stumbled. Still, we got them mostly right. It went quickly, and there was time for about four rounds. We got better with each round. We could see each other begin to feel more comfortable, stand a little straighter, speak a little louder, and smile a little more.

By Sunday noon, as we were heading to the airport, I told Lance I had never been more impressed with a training session. The 58 hours had been packed with information. Gore had been personally involved in every aspect, giving the talk three times himself. Conceptually, from this weekend, he was sending 200 people out to give his speech to different audiences. While we would not give it as well as he would, we would make up for it by reaching audiences he couldn't reach by presenting to groups where we might be trusted in ways he wouldn't be because we were locally known.

Confessions of a Unitarian

After I got back, Jenny Clad called and asked if I would do a favor for Mr. Gore. He was going to give a presentation to a New Baptist Covenant Celebration in Atlanta in January 2008. It was a different kind of audience, and he was worried about it. He wanted to speak more in Biblical terms. Gore wanted me to talk to a man named Paul Gorman in Amherst, Massachusetts, whom he knew from the United Nations and thought could give him great advice. Paul is the executive director of the National Religious Partnership for the Environment. Jenny asked me to talk to him, get his ideas, take notes, and send them to Gore.

"Jenny, I'm a Unitarian. I don't know anything about religion!"

"You'll do fine."

I drove out to Amherst and met Paul. I confessed I was a Unitarian, and Paul gave me my first surprise.

"Great, that's the way I started."

We talked for about three hours about climate change as sin and about Genesis as man's responsibility for stewardship over all God's creatures instead of dominion. I filled a pad of paper and sent my notes to Jenny. After Mr. Gore gave his speech, I called her to ask how it had gone.

"He hit it out of the park."

I didn't give ten talks. I gave about 70—to audiences in the US and Canada, ranging from groups of a dozen to almost a thousand. I talked to first graders and senior citizens. To scientists and graduate students. To high schoolers and vacationers. I always tried to customize my talk based on who was listening. I always tried to understand where my audience was coming from, what they wanted to hear, and what they needed to hear.

I tried to remember Mr. Gore's advice about budgets: "You have a time budget, a complexity budget, a fear budget, a humor budget, a hope budget."

I always ended with a picture of a local sports team celebrating a victory.

"Look at the smiles on those faces. You know how you get to wear those smiles? You set high goals. You work hard as a team to achieve those goals. You overcome adversity and the naysayers. And when you achieve victory in the arena, *then* you wear those smiles! You know who doesn't wear those smiles? The people who sit in the audience and don't participate. If you aren't in the arena, you don't ever get to wear those smiles. Well, we are going to overcome adversity and meet the challenge of climate change if we are all in the arena together.

"And then, we will wear those smiles."

V. TURNING TIDES

With Carlton Viveiros aboard the Ernestina

Chapter 12

Regional Administrator for GARFO at NOAA

A Fisheries Fixer-upper?

As I was getting ready to retire from SEA, I was asked to moderate a panel on fishing at the New Bedford Whaling Museum. Eric Schwaab was the new head of NOAA Fisheries under President Obama, and he was coming to New Bedford at the invitation of Congressman Barney Frank. The meeting was bound to be contentious, and people hoped I could keep it under control.

I was standing outside in the sunshine during the lunch break when Dick Allen approached me. Dick was a lobsterman from Rhode Island whom I knew from my Seafood Co-Op days. He served on the New England Fishery Management Council and was smart, intellectual, and independent. He often took positions different from the rest of the industry. Like many fishermen, he was a unique character, and I liked him.

We got to talking, and he suggested I should take the job as regional administrator of the Northeast Regional Fisheries Office headquartered in Gloucester, whose region covers marine ecosystems from Maine to North Carolina.

He said fisheries management was a disaster. He thought I could "fix it up."

"Dick, I thought you were a friend of mine."

It caught my attention, though. I hadn't known the job was open.

"What is Pat Kurkel doing?"

"She is retiring. The place is a mess. They need someone like you."

"Jeez, Dick, I was thinking of retiring."

"Well, think about it."

I finished moderating the session, and a few days later, I was at my desk at SEA in Woods Hole when the phone rang.

"Hi, John, it's Barney."

"Good morning, Congressman."

"John, will you join the growing consensus that you should be the next RA for NOAA?"

Gloucester's outer harbor

Although Barney is a powerful force, I wasn't sure his backing for the job would be a welcome reference.

"Congressman, I'm sure with your help, I'd be a cinch. They love you down there."

Barney had been ruthless in his criticism of NOAA Fisheries, the regional office, and especially Dr. Jane Lubchenco, who in 2009 President Obama appointed as head of NOAA. And believe me, nobody could criticize like Barney Frank. Barney could turn words into weapons better than anyone, and you did *not* want to be on the receiving end.

A few days later, Johanna Thomas called me. She worked for the Environmental Defense Fund. I had become familiar with EDF and its CEO Fred Krupp during my time at the President's Council on Sustainable Development.

NOAA chief Dr. Jane Lubchenco confers with President Barack Obama and Science Advisor Dr. John Holdren about the Deepwater Horizon disaster, 2010.

EDF's strategy often was to achieve environmental solutions through market mechanisms. I wasn't aware they were interested in the oceans or fisheries, though. Johanna had recently relocated from the Pacific Northwest to Maine to engage EDF in fisheries issues in the Northeast. She wanted to meet, and I agreed. She came to our house, and we had a long talk. As we chatted, a lightbulb went off in my head, reminding me that Dick Allen had done some work with EDF. Perhaps my meeting with Dick wasn't as accidental as it appeared.

EDF was concerned that groundfish stocks were in real jeopardy because NOAA was not making difficult decisions. Johanna described relations between NOAA and every constituency as being at an all-time low. Industry, environmentalists, Capitol Hill—nobody thought they could trust what was coming out of the regional office. Communication was non-existent. That was the case for the management arm, the science center, and the enforcement branch.

Johanna painted a very bleak picture. Dick was right. It was a mess. As a result, good management could not happen, fish stocks would suffer, and so would the jobs that depend on them. Johanna told me that Dr. Lubchenco recognized the need for significant change in the regional office and would support a candidate like me. The NOAA head had a distinguished career at Oregon State University and had served on the EDF board. But by 2012, she was coming under fire from a number of quarters.

I had once attended a field hearing in Boston that Senator John Kerry held. Dr. Lubchenco arrived late, making people wait. She gave her testimony to the senators, answered a few questions, and departed for a meeting with the *Boston Globe* editorial board, not staying to listen to testimony from members of the fishing industry. The message to those working in the industry was, "I don't care about your troubles." That was duly noted by the senators present.

Richard Gaines, a formidable reporter for the *Gloucester Daily Times*, unearthed an email from Senator Kerry to his brother Cam, who was serving as general counsel at the Commerce Department. The senator expressed exasperation that Lubchenco would leave his hearing early. He was livid. His brother replied that people at headquarters were just as frustrated. You can imagine the conversations behind closed doors when Gaines published that bombshell.

Representative Don Young of Alaska   Karen Hyun, NOAA Policy Advisor

Ocean Planning

Shortly after that hearing, I was asked to testify on ocean planning before the House Committee on Resources, the committee that Gerry Studds used to chair but which was now chaired by his long-time colleague from Alaska, Don Young. I was serving on the Massachusetts Ocean Commission, and we had produced the first Ocean Plan in the country. The plan proposed planning for uses of the ocean, similar to how we planned for land uses. The idea was to anticipate and recognize that increasing uses are being proposed for the ocean, with an increasing potential for conflict. To minimize these conflicts, the plan called for gathering all the science we could and all the users we could to increase communication and rationally plan for the future so society could benefit.

One obvious example is the potential for conflict between offshore wind generation and the historic use of fishing. But there are many others. For a comparison with governing that goes on on land, you might consider this issue akin to zoning. Still, for some reason, people advocating ocean planning thought "zoning" was a loaded term and advised staying away from it. As a former mayor, I didn't see anything controversial about zoning. It told a developer that if they wanted to build something consistent with the stated zoning, the path would be easy. If they wanted to build a factory in a residential neighborhood, they would have problems.

In preparation for my testimony, I called Karen Hyun, a staffer for the Democratic side. She started our conversation with a warning.

"John, you need to understand. Chairman Don Young hates ocean planning. The other panelists are the US Chamber of Commerce, who will say this is anti-business, and the farm lobby, which will claim this will end all agriculture in the Mississippi basin."

Karen said they would not go easy on me.

"They are planning to have you for lunch."

I thanked her for the heads up. With help from John Weber, one of the two main staffers for the Massachusetts Ocean Plan, I prepared my testimony and delivered it to Congress. I commended the Chamber of Commerce for recognizing there was an ocean to be interested in and tried my best to refute their outrageous claims that the sky would fall if we planned for different uses in the ocean as we did on land.

While at the hearing, I had a chance to catch up with Dave Whalley, senior staff to Chairman Young and on the committee for decades. Because Young and Studds had worked so closely together, Dave and I had a good relationship. I talked to him about ocean planning. He could see my point, but in the Wild West mentality of Alaska, it really wasn't going to fly. I was very cognizant of the importance of the institutional knowledge and the personal relationships of people like Dave. Staffers like Dave, Jeff Pike, and Jean Flemma don't get their names on bills, but over the years, they have done more for fisheries management than many members of Congress.

Qualification and Application

While in DC, I asked for an appointment with Dr. Lubchenco. She agreed. It was good to get back in my old office neighborhood, and I was warmly greeted by her assistants Linda Brown and Pat Thorne, two very effective gatekeepers.

During our meeting, I told Dr. Lubchenco that, while I had never met her, she was a hero of mine for the address she gave upon accepting the presidency of the American Association of the Academy of Science. She talked about the "compact" between scientists and society. She said, in this relationship, society encourages scientists to pursue their degrees and attain knowledge. But she noted that this should not be a one-way street. Scientists owe society in return. The compact calls on them to use that science to better society. The pursuit of science is not an idle pursuit; it is for a purpose.

I told her of my strong conviction of the need to combine knowledge with action and how I admired her for that. And I told her how many young women at SEA looked up to her as a role model. She made it clear that women can and do excel in science, despite what Harvard President Larry Summers had said. I let her know I was interested in the regional administrator position in Gloucester and offered only one qualification: I had the support of both EDF and Barney Frank, two entities that "don't agree on what day of the week it is" but could agree that I would be good for this post. I said if she offered me the job, I would take it on two conditions. The first was that she would be committed to change, and the second was that she would empower the regional administrator with minimal interference from above.

She said she would think about it, and we concluded our meeting. Then began a process that can exist only in the federal government. As this job is a "career" job as opposed to the "political" job I had had before, I had to apply, like every other applicant, through USA Jobs. And as the level of the job is Senior Executive Service (SES), the level I had at in my first posting at NOAA, there is a rigorous review process. While I submitted a resume, the main part of the application involved five written Executive Core Qualification (ECQ) statements, covering my core competencies backed up by experience in only the last ten years.

To help me in this task, I consulted frequently with Paul Doremus, an assistant administrator at NOAA Fisheries. Paul is one of the most competent administrators I have ever met. He earned the Presidential Rank Award, the highest award you can earn, when he was working at the National Institute for Standards and Technology (NIST), a sister agency to NOAA.

I found writing the ECQs frustrating. I had already been SES for NOAA and didn't know why I had to qualify again. It seemed ridiculous that I couldn't reach back more than ten years to draw on my years as mayor. Why couldn't I talk about running a city with 3000 employees and a budget of $100 million to demonstrate I knew something about financial management.

"It's not recent enough," Paul said.

"What, do they think I'd forget something like that?!"

Not only that, but I had to write the ECQ statements without acknowledging the roles of others. As any manager or leader knows, one person doesn't do things; it is always a group effort.

"No more *we's*, John. Just use the word, *I*."

"Paul, you know that's not the way it works in real life."

"No, but that's the way they want you to write it. Like you did everything by yourself."

As I was rewriting everything for the fourth or fifth time with Paul generously helping me along, I became exasperated.

"You know, Paul, one of the most important tasks an executive does is to allocate resources. Any executive who spends this much time on this task should be disqualified from the job."

"John, everybody goes through this. It's an awful process. Some people hire folks to write their ECQs. Just persevere."

"Paul, this is like legalized fraternity hazing. Except I bet, there is no beer at the end."

The Executive Core Qualifications statements seemed a waste of time to me, and even worse, a deterrent to many who might consider working for the government.

"You know the first time I was here, Jim King was head of OPM. I can't believe he would have stood for such BS," I told Paul. "I was talking to Bill Karp in Woods Hole while he was going through the same ordeal to lead the Science Center. He almost gave up. This process costs the government good people. This is no way to hire anyone."

During the protracted application process, I was also meeting with fishing groups. Many knew me from my time as mayor, working for the fishing industry at the Co-Op and my previous stint at NOAA, designing economic assistance programs for the fishing industry. Up and down the coast, they were very supportive of my candidacy.

I met with environmental groups. They knew I had made the difficult decision to bring New Bedford into compliance with the Clean Water Act when I was mayor and that it had cost me my job. That conferred significant credibility. After the end of a long meeting, my friend Peter Shelley and I were walking down a sidewalk in Boston when he turned to me.

"John, the only thing that bothers me is that you might not agree with me on every issue."

He smiled.

"Peter, what you should worry about is whether I will agree with you on any issue."

I smiled back.

I also went up to tour the Gloucester facility. Acting Regional Administrator Dan Morris set up a meeting with senior staff in the fourth-floor conference room. I only knew two of the dozen or so people gathered. Harry Mears ran the grants program and had worked closely with me on the economic assistance programs in New England. And Gene Martin ran the general counsel's office. Gene was at all the council meetings, so I had gotten to know him pretty well over the years. I liked them both, so that was a good start.

Dan had everyone explain what they did, and I gave something of my background. I talked about how I thought conditions at the regional office could improve in that they all did very important work, but their relationships with the outside world seemed strained. I said I hoped I could help with that. But there was no question they saw me as an outsider who would bring change, and change is always anxiety-producing.

The formal hiring process methodically and painfully was grinding its way to a conclusion. And here is the kicker. While the job was seen as a very difficult task and drew only a couple of applicants, several years later, I was talking to NOAA's chief of staff, who had been sent over by the White House to try to keep Dr. Lubchenco from causing any more brushfires. This chief of staff told me over coffee that when she came over, she had been given a memo with about ten crises that NOAA was facing. She said each crisis had a plan of attack. One problem was that weather satellites were over budget and behind schedule. That crisis had a long plan on how to put out that brush fire.

"Every crisis had a long plan except for one. The crisis labeled Groundfish Collapse just had three words: Hire John Bullard."

It appeared there were two tracks. The White House had a very short track, but the bureaucratic process needed to grind through all the gears. They ended up in the same place, and I was offered the job.

Intentions: Meeting My Team and Expectations

My intention was to stay at the regional office long enough to straighten out relationships and get things on track, and, optimistically, I thought that would take a couple of years. And that's what I told Laurie. Laurie knows me very well, and when she heard that, I think she understood this was like me saying I would be home from work in 30 minutes. It was my sincere intention, but it was never going to happen in a million years.

I couldn't find an apartment in Gloucester, but I did find a nice place on South Street in Rockport, about a ten-minute drive to the office. My plan was to drive up on Monday mornings, stay through the week and drive back after work on Friday afternoons. I knew there was no way I was going to commute 90 miles every day through Boston traffic, keep my sanity and have any energy left for the job.

I arrived to work early on my first day, August 6, 2012, and greeted the two office assistants outside my office, Susan Oliver and Megan Ryan. I walked into my deputy's office. Dan Morris, a former commander in the NOAA Corps, stood up to greet me. He had served as acting regional administrator for the six months since Pat Kurkels' retirement. The way this office runs, the deputy is the chief administrative officer. All employees report to the deputy, and the deputy reports to the regional administrator. The bond between Dan and me would be critical. I was coming in essentially to take over for him. I was an outsider from New Bedford, which didn't have a great reputation at NOAA, and I had been in politics. I wasn't a scientist or a fishery manager. I was a wild card with a mandate for change. I figured Dan was going to be very cautious around me. Building a bond was going to take a long time.

I told Dan that it was important that I get out on the road quickly for a listening tour to meet with our constituents up and down the coast. But before that, I wanted to address all our employees on my first morning. Dan agreed that would be a good idea and said he could put that together in an hour.

Dan Morris, schooner Adventure, *and the 400-year-old fishing port of Gloucester*

"Dan, you know, I come in here because we have to make some changes to the way we relate to the outside world. Before I talk with everyone, I want to know what people are worried about."

"They are worried about you, John."

"Thank you, Dan, for being honest. I need you to always tell me what you think I need to hear. We will be a great team if you do that. If you shield me from the truth, we will fail."

"Roger that."

I put some thoughts on paper and addressed the roughly 200 people for the first time. I thanked them for their dedication under fire. I told them that congressional reviews, lawsuits, and administrative reviews all called for significant change in the way we do our job, and so, change was going to happen. I told them that my task during this time of change was to protect what is good, change what needs changing and be wise enough to tell the difference. I told them I respected them and counted on them to do things right. My job was to make sure we did the right things. I said it was ok to make small mistakes, and I would try to keep us from making big ones. I told them that I tended to be very direct with people in terms of telling them what I thought and that I hoped and expected them to be direct with me. I wanted vigorous debate about the best way to solve a problem. If people disagreed with me, I wanted them to tell me. Only then would we get the best solutions. But after a solution was arrived at, I hoped everyone could support it.

I told people that I understood that we were a regulatory agency that deals with laws, but we needed to understand that we were also dealing with people's lives. In the case of the groundfish crisis, this was a potential national emergency. While we think about laws, we should be guided by doing the right thing. Figuring out the right thing was most important. Then we could figure out the laws for how to do that. Lastly, I told them I needed to get out of our building, meet the people we served, and listen to them. I hoped that for the next month

The rocky coast of Cape Ann

or so on this listening tour, I could get an idea of what the top ten or so issues were and what success might look like on each of these issues.

With help from NOAA staff Allison Ferreira and Maggie Mooney-Seus, we started scheduling the first of 17 town hall meetings from Ellsworth, Maine, to Manteo, North Carolina. These would be attended by 550 fishermen. I needed to hear from them what they thought were the most pressing concerns. From these meetings, I wanted to achieve several goals. I wanted everyone to know who I was, that I was accessible, and that I cared about them enough to come to their home territory in my first weeks on the job. I also wanted to develop a Top Ten list, so I could start to understand what our major priorities needed to be and make my own assessments of what the biggest issues were. Also, I knew we had a real problem in the trust department, and we were only going to rebuild it with lots of face-to-face communications, follow-through, and open, honest dialogue.

During my first week, I met with Richard Gaines of the *Gloucester Daily Times* for a three-hour interview on the rocks overlooking the Atlantic. People at NOAA advised against it because Richard had written so many negative stories about NOAA. They thought he was extremely biased against the agency. I thought perhaps he wrote negative stories because nobody ever talked with him.

My relationship with the press is like my relationship with everyone else. I am careful about what I say. I tell the truth. If I don't know the answer, I tell them I don't know and will try to find out. But I am pretty open with the press. Much more open than most in government. I understand that they have a right to ask anything, and we have a right not to answer. I know that we are mutually dependent, yet we have, in a sense, adversarial roles. I also knew that the trust relationship had to be rebuilt with the press.

Richard wrote a very favorable article. We would always have very pleasant conversations following that. He would usually rip me in his articles or columns for decisions I made, but he was accurate, fair, and we had a good relationship.

Making a List

From the 17 meetings, a list of issues emerged. At the top was the New England groundfish crisis. This had been a crisis for decades, so it was no surprise. At a gathering in our office building in Gloucester, fisherman Joe Orlando was sitting six feet from me. Near the end of the meeting, he spoke to me in a voice that reached into my soul.

"John, am I going to make it?"

"Joe, I wish with all my heart I could say, 'Yes,' but the truth is we don't know. This is a very serious situation with cod. We know the economic impact that this has on the families of Gloucester and other ports that depend on groundfish. All I can tell you is we are going to work as hard as we can to rebuild cod stocks and to do it in a way that addresses the economic harm that the collapse has caused you and others in this fishery."

Another hot button issue involved harbor porpoise. These marine mammals were sometimes caught in gillnets, and the National Marine Fisheries Service had been working hard with gillnet fishermen to find ways to eliminate the catch of this protected species. But deaths had spiked, Senator Kerry's office was involved, and there was a real battle between the environmental community and the gillnet fishermen, with NMFS stuck in the middle, being screamed at from all sides.

River herring made the list as another endangered species. River herring encountered dams, which blocked their passage from spawning grounds at the heads of rivers to the sea, and then, if they reached the sea, they were caught in the huge nets of the herring factory trawlers.

When I attended an Atlantic States Marine Fisheries Commission meeting, I added another item to my Top Ten list, courtesy of their chairman, Dr. Louis Daniel from North Carolina. He buttonholed me on my first day and, after welcoming me and introducing himself, proceeded to burst my left eardrum about how the National Marine Fisheries Service was crazy to list sturgeon as an endangered species now that they were rebounding. After a half hour of high volume on the consequences of our collective stupidity, I added sturgeon to our list.

Then Louis took me to dinner and introduced me to the leaders of the Atlantic States Marine Fisheries Commission, where he regaled us with his abundant storytelling. Over my years at NOAA, Louis became a close friend. He was funny, knowledgeable, committed to sustainable use of natural resources, and a leader respected by his fellow state directors.

I went to a meeting on Cape Cod attended by many fishermen and more than the usual number of regular citizens. In the front row was a radio news person with her tape recorder and microphone and her station's call letters clearly visible. Much of the discussion centered around the thousands of gray seals that gathered on Monomoy Island and the beaches of Cape Cod. Protected by the Marine Mammal Protection Act, they were enjoying a resurgence. Fishermen blamed them for depletion of cod stocks and other species, although stomach analysis was not conclusive about that. Citizens were concerned because the herds were getting so large that they were attracting great white sharks, which were scaring people away from the beaches and threatening the Cape Cod economy

A very nice older lady sitting next to the radio reporter raised her hand to ask me a question.

"Mr. Bullard, would you be in favor of allowing us to kill enough seals to reduce the population so the beaches would be safe, and we could save the cod?"

I looked at her. I looked at the reporter sitting next to her, now very interested in what I would say. I looked at the audience, now very interested in the conversation. I looked back at her.

"You seem like a very nice lady. I've only been on the job for about a week. I took an oath to uphold the law. One of the laws is the Marine Mammal Protection Act, which protects those seals. So, if I were to answer your question affirmatively and this reporter sitting next to you

Seals sun bathing on Monomoy Island, Cape Cod

were to put it on the news, I would be out of a job before my first week was over. Is that what you want?"

But she had made her point. Seals made my Top Ten.

North Atlantic right whales, which ended up consuming my last year at NOAA, did not make my Top Ten because they were coming back at the time, and people felt good about the progress we were making.

Another species that made the list was dogfish, a type of shark considered overabundant. Everywhere I went, I heard about fishermen hauling up thousands of pounds of dogfish, which had no American market and a very low price. The fish tore up the nets and required very special handling because they produced uric acid, essentially digesting themselves if you didn't process the fish right away. Dogfish made the list so we could improve the handling of the fish at sea and develop markets at home, including different ways to cook it and perhaps what to call it.

I added our budget to the list because there were threats in Congress of budget shutdowns and budget cuts. Like most agencies in government, we had a budget that was almost entirely personnel. Also, I had found out from Dan that I was not the only issue in our Office of Personnel Management making life difficult for the agency. Where OPM had budget authority, it had routinely made it very difficult for Dan and our assistant regional administrators to fill vacant positions. As a result, we routinely operated with about 20 percent of our workforce vacant. I thought this was a tremendous vulnerability because it meant our current staff members were doing other people's jobs, and it meant that Congress could, at any moment, swoop in and remove that 20 percent. Our budget became the seventh and final member of our Top Ten club.

I should have added an eighth item after a meeting in Ellsworth, Maine, where a fisherman expressed concerns about climate.

"Mr. Bullard, you know we follow temperature very carefully up here. It tells us everything we need to know—from where the fish are going to be, to when the lobsters are going to molt, to what the shrimp season is going to be like. Temperature is something every one of us watches *very* closely."

He said the community had noticed concerning changes.

"The temperature has been rising in the Gulf of Maine. You can notice it a little bit each year. But this past year (2012) was something else! This past year, where we are in the eastern Gulf of Maine, increased 12 degrees. And at the bottom of the Gulf, it increased 5 degrees."

I heard a lot of different testimony, and my memory might not be exact on what he said. I remember thinking as we drove back to where we were staying that night how some people tend to exaggerate. But then, months later, I read a study, I think from the Gulf of Maine Research Institute, that 2012 was an anomaly as an exceptionally warm year for the Gulf of Maine. It's not surprising that I heard it from a fisherman first.

So, looking back, I should have added Global Warming to my Top Ten list, especially given all the talks I had given. It wasn't long before it became evident that warming oceans were causing all kinds of management headaches as fish stocks started to move.

But after two months of travel and 17 town hall meetings, I had a list of what the 550 constituents thought was most important for us to focus on. I kept that handwritten list on a bulletin board next to my desk where I could see it every day and where every member of my staff who came in to see me could see it. We certainly added things to it, like right whales and deep-sea corals and climate change and summer flounder, but it gave a good picture of what was important, and it was a reminder that the picture was created by listening to people.

I also went down to Washington to meet with members of the House and Senate and their staff. The National Marine Fisheries Service had a staff member from its congressional affairs office support my visits. Stephanie Hunt set up the meetings, distributed briefing materials, had background material on everyone, and, if there was follow-up needed, made sure we delivered it. She was excellent, knowing everything from all the issues to the fastest way to get from one office through basement corridors to the next office. She was invaluable.

Again, the purpose of the congressional visits was to rebuild trust, which was non-existent. I knew practically all the members from previous work, so there was a base to build on. I told them what my goals were. I was determined to rebuild fisheries, but I was very aware of the economic implications of my decisions. I reminded them that when I had been at NOAA before, when there had been a crisis, we had worked in partnership with Congress to deliver economic assistance. I told them that assistance might be called for again with New England groundfish. I told them I would be in frequent touch with them, and they should feel free to contact me whenever needed.

Governor Deval Patrick was also concerned about our office. He was very close to President Obama and Valerie Jarrett in the White House and prevailed upon them to set up weekly calls with Eric Schwaab at NOAA and the regional administrator in Gloucester. I had been told before I took the job that the level of distrust by the National Marine Fisheries Service of the Gloucester office was so bad that Dan had one full-time staffer just responding to "taskers" from headquarters—requests about what we were doing. The weekly calls with Governor Patrick's representative and Eric Schwaab's representative were another case of distrust, causing people to want to look over our shoulders constantly.

Fortunately, I had an excellent relationship with Governor Patrick. The weekly call started on a friendly note as I was a known quantity. Gradually, the one-hour calls became half-hour calls. Then the weekly calls became every other week. Then, Governor Patrick's person stopped calling in. Finally, Eric Schwaab's representative determined that we didn't need to have the calls anymore because they trusted us.

And the taskers from headquarters got fewer and fewer as the folks downtown realized the same thing. We were grownups, we knew what we were doing, and we didn't need supervision all the time.

And members of Congress started to use us. Senators Sheldon Whitehouse and Jack Reed from Rhode Island had a meeting in Galilee on a fishing issue. It involved some contention where the industry disagreed with what NOAA was doing. I drove down. I have the highest respect for both of these senators. They are highly intelligent and very effective for Rhode Island. There is no one more well-spoken on the topic of global warming than Sheldon Whitehouse. And Jack Reed, who sits on the Appropriations Committee, is as humble as he is powerful and delivers the goods time and time again for his state, never seeking the limelight, always deferring to others.

My role in a setting like this is to explain the federal position to the fishing community, let the senators defend their constituents, and listen as the fishermen tell me why what we are doing is hurting them.

Fishing is hard work. I have tremendous respect for practically all fishermen. And I know that the regulations we promulgate can cause serious short-term pain. And life is lived in the short term. I also understand that if someone wants to express that pain by raising his voice or describing the regulations or the government or even me in colorful language, then it might make them feel a little better. What is the harm? And it doesn't cost the taxpayer any money.

I will get my back up if someone criticizes my staff or impugns my motives or honesty. But if someone wants to call me an SOB, then I think that is part of my role at a public hearing. Most fishermen I have found, despite the pain they suffer, are unfailingly polite.

Well, at this hearing, a few people did get out of hand. Colorful language was used. I stood and listened as the senators looked on, not sure what to make of this new regional administrator. After that, at every event where I appeared with Senator Whitehouse, he would spot me in the crowd, point me out and introduce me.

"I want to introduce John Bullard, who is the regional administrator for NOAA Fisheries. He is a very good man. I have never seen anyone better at being yelled at by angry fishermen than John!"

On Matters of the Media

As any public official can tell you, dealing with the press can be complicated. Over the years, I have listened to and considered a lot of advice on the subject. During a 1985 executive education course for newly minted mayors, Marty Linsky, who had worked for Governor Weld and was an expert in press relations, described the mutually dependent but adversarial relationship between leaders and the press and how that functioned.

"Always be friendly, never be friends," Marty cautioned.

That may be good advice, and I take Marty's point, but I have violated that on several occasions and fortunately have not been burned.

Marty pointed out that our agendas are not always the same, although government leaders and the media need each other. We need the press to get our message out to the public, and they need us so they can write and report complete stories. Marty told us that members of the press are not our public relations department. Their job is to hold us accountable and represent the public interest. If journalists are good, they will ask tough questions and sometimes make us feel uncomfortable. Importantly, Marty emphasized that the press has a right to ask any question, but we do not have to answer every question asked.

He advised going into interviews with an objective of what message we wanted to convey. I always tried to take that advice, preparing ahead of time to consider the issues to be covered. As mayor or as a NOAA official, I faced many high-profile, complicated, and controversial issues. Usually, before an interview, I would spend time with my press person and issues experts so I would be up to speed about the issue at hand, the journalist, and their reporting. It was helpful to know what a journalist was interested in and what they had written about in the past.

We would also put together some talking points and discuss what we wanted to get across. I would number these from the most important on down and make a list of reminders to keep handy. As the interview took place, I would try to get my list covered. If a reporter didn't ask me about what I wanted to say, I would "bridge," meaning I would answer quickly the question posed and then move to the point I wanted to make.

Ideally, once you have given the reporter your top talking points, you should stop the interview because the reporter has the information you want them to have. But I was and am miserable at this rule because although I followed his "be prepared" rule, I tended to violate Marty's "never-be-friends" rule. It's a good rule in many ways because it recognizes that you have different jobs to do, and following it keeps your relationship strictly professional. Friendships can get in the way of that. But they can also make for better communication, connection, and understanding.

Over the years, I have worked with excellent people advising me on media relations. When I became regional administrator for NOAA's Northeast Regional Fisheries Office, I was lucky to have excellent press support, first with Maggie Mooney-Seus and then Jen Goebel. They made a very difficult task look easy. Some days, I didn't make their job any easier. NOAA tends to be a very buttoned-up organization, where the less you say, the better. NOAA also believes in asking permission, while I am more the "ask forgiveness" type.

Typically, Maggie or Jen fielded requests from the press if news outlets called us, or they would initiate the contact if we had news we wanted to get out. They prepared me with information on the issue and the reporter. They anticipated the questions and advised on the best answers. They sat through interviews if possible. If a follow-up was needed, they made sure we followed up. After the interview, they made sure headquarters or anybody else who needed to know learned what I had said from us—before anyone in headquarters could read, watch, or hear about it from another source.

I tend to be a very open person. I believe in transparency. I believe that if I am telling people the truth, then I never have to worry about remembering what I said. I have worked for government and non-profits, and I think transparency is in the public interest. I think many public officials are afraid to reveal what they are doing or planning because they think it will be harder to achieve their goals if people know. Usually, the opposite is true. If people know what you are doing, they trust you, and you have a chance to win their support.

Another communications expert, political consultant Tad Devine, also had some important advice. Tad was a chief strategist for Vermont Senator Bernie Sanders and a senior advisor for Al Gore and John Kerry. Once, during a talk in Westport that I attended when I was regional administrator, he said that to be effective, one must be authentic, reach people on an emotional level, and tell stories.

After Tad's talk, I returned to Gloucester and gathered the people who had the most contact with the press and outside constituencies. I went over what Tad had said. What is fortunate for us, I said, is that the people at NOAA *are* authentic. We don't have to worry about that. We are mission-driven. We care about what we are doing and the impact it has on people. There is nothing phony about us. But connecting on an emotional level is harder because we are a science-based regulatory agency. The people who listen to us have their lives at stake, so they hear through an emotional lens. If we do not acknowledge that, we will not connect with our audience, and we are just wasting everybody's time. One way to make that connection can be to tell a story. It doesn't have to be long, but it does have to have a point and illustrate a message in a human way. It is the way humans have communicated for thousands of years.

This isn't just a Democratic principle. George Shultz was secretary of State to President Ronald Reagan. When he turned 100, he wrote an op-ed in the *Washington Post* about a speech he wrote for Reagan:

> I brought a draft foreign policy speech to the Oval Office for Reagan to review. He read the speech and said, "That's fine," but then began marking it up. In the margin on one page, he wrote "story." I asked what he meant.
>
> "That's the most important point," he said. Adding a relevant story will "engage your readers. That way, you'll appeal not only to their minds but to their emotions...." A story builds an emotional bond, and emotional bonds build trust.

As Sean King said, "All politics is personal." Like so many things, press relations are about personal relationships, which means getting to know people and investing in a relationship. Sometimes, I had time to build a relationship with a reporter. When I was mayor, the local paper always had two or three reporters who covered City Hall. I would see them several times a week. They knew the issues. They knew the personalities. They knew my family. They knew the history of the city. While their questions could be adversarial, they were almost like family in that we knew each other very well and saw each other all the time.

With the press, there are complicated rules. You can speak on the record, which means they can quote you. You can also speak on the record but not for attribution, which means they can use what you say but do not attribute it to your name. They may identify you more vaguely, something like a "government official." You can be off the record, which means you can tell them something, but they can't use it unless they get it from another source. You can also talk on background, giving context that can be helpful to their understanding of an issue but usually not attributable to you. Or you can give them information and embargo it until a certain time when they can release it. This gives them time to research other information pertaining to that news.

If you know a reporter well enough to have a relationship of trust, it is much easier to go back and forth between these situations, which is important. I always think it serves everybody well if a reporter understands an issue in depth. If a reporter is willing to put in the time to understand what can be complex, and fishing or sewer treatment or police relations are always complex, then I am going to take the time to explain at least my view of the issue in as much detail as the reporter wants. It just won't all be on the record.

I have heard many people complain that they were misquoted by reporters. I've been quoted plenty of times over 50 years of being covered. I'm sure there has been a time when somebody got a quote wrong, but I honestly don't remember a single one. The closest perhaps was when Bryant Gumbel was interviewing me on the *Today Show*, and I was identified at the bottom of the screen as working for the US Chamber of Commerce instead of the US Department of Commerce. But that is being *really* picky. I find reporters in all media do a great job of getting things right. The more common occurrence is a person who sees what they said written up in the paper accurately and regrets what they said. Then, the reporter becomes the handy scapegoat.

A few interviews and relationships stand out in my mind.

My good friend Bob Vanasse runs a site called Saving Seafood. It pulls together fishing news from around the country each morning and delivers to your computer inbox at six in the morning, East Coast time. Bob is originally from Fairhaven, and even though he is a Republican, he worked on my mayoral campaigns. He knows the fishing industry well and is always looking for ways to promote it. Bob had been talking to Fox News for a long time, trying to get them to cover the industry, and finally, a national reporter came to my office in Gloucester to cover the groundfish crisis. We talked about Bob's effort to get recognition for the industry. The reporter drew a rough map of the US on a piece of paper and looked at me.

"I keep telling Bob that they care about fishing here and here and here and here (pointing to New England, the Gulf of Mexico, the Pacific Northwest, and Alaska), and they don't give a shit about fishing *here!*" His hand washed over all the US except the coasts.

He told me he had come as a favor to Bob. I tried to get him excited about the story.

"This is a perfect story for you. It practically writes itself. You have some wonderful fishermen down on the Gloucester docks who are very hardworking and very photogenic. And they are being put out of business by the evil federal bureaucrat up on the hill. That's me. This is a perfect story for FOX. You can tell it in 30 seconds."

"You're right, John. That should be a perfect story. But it seems more complicated than the way you tell it. Because you see, I've already been down on the docks. And everybody down there likes you."

We got into the details of the issue. As we talked, he discovered what everybody who wades into fishing issues finds out—fishermen are wonderful people, and the issues are complicated.

Sean Horgan covers fishing for the *Gloucester Daily Times,* so I often find myself on the other end of the phone with him. I love those calls. Why? Not because of the fishing issues—Sean's questions could be as tough as anybody's. No. Sean used to be a sports reporter, and we both love sports. We could kill a half hour talking sports—about how the Red Sox were doing, or he would regale me with stories of covering Bill Parcells or stump me with endless sports history questions—before we even touched on fishing.

It isn't easy being a reporter today. The pay sucks. News conglomerates are eviscerating newsrooms, so morale is in the toilet. My conversations with Sean, I think, did us both some good. They were a break in my day when I got to smile and kick back for a while. And Sean got information out to the public that they deserved to know because it affects their families and livelihoods.

One day, Jen Goebel fielded a call from the producer for Michelle Miller of *CBS Evening News.* They wanted to do a story on the groundfish crisis in New England. The logistics were going to be difficult because I was at a Mid-Atlantic Fishery Management Council meeting in New Jersey. While that was close to CBS's New York studio, it wasn't close to any commercial fishing boats.

We settled on a waterfront marina that had a bunch of high-end sport fishing boats tied up. I met her during a break in my meeting, and we set up where the sport fishing boats were in the background. We each sat on bar stool-like seats on the marina dock with a lot of lights shining on our faces and several cameras running. After sound checks and getting my name and title, Michelle began with her first question. She hit me right between the eyes.

"Mr. Bullard, why do you insist on using questionable science to put the historic fishing fleet from New England out of business, a fleet that has been fishing for cod out of Gloucester for 400 years?"

Suddenly, the lights seemed hotter, and the cameras seemed like they were one inch from my face. The bar stool seemed to be 50 feet in the air and teetering. So many issues to address in that one question. Where even to begin? Later, back at the council meeting, I saw Bill Karp, head of the Science Center, and I told him about Michelle's question.

"Well, John, you should have replied, 'Because it is the mission of our agency!'"

I wasn't as clever or as daring as Bill.

I began with Michelle by saying that the science about the cod collapse is some of the best in the world and has been peer-reviewed many times. The collapse occurred over decades and is caused by overfishing because we have failed to constrain fishing effort sufficiently. I told her that NOAA and the councils were working to address that because the long-term health of the fishing families of New England depends on rebuilding cod and other depleted species. In the short term, we need economic assistance help from Congress. The interview continued for a while, but I felt like the first question had put me in a six-foot hole, and I had been digging out from the beginning.

David Abel

After the cameras were turned off, Michelle noted that I had been mayor of New Bedford. She asked me if I knew Dutch Morial, the former mayor of New Orleans.

"Well, of course, I knew him, but I knew his son Marc better."

Dutch had stopped being mayor the first year I became mayor. Marc was mayor when I was in Washington, and I would interact with him on issues that he took a great interest in.

"Well, Marc is my husband."

Under my breath, I said, "Oh Lord, please let that help me in the editing room."

To Michelle, I said, "Is Marc still with the National Urban League?"

We talked a while longer, and the groundfish crisis got more exposure.

David Abel is another example of a reporter where "always be friendly, never be friends" flew out the window. David reports for the *Boston Globe*. I got to know him because his beat is the environment, so he covers fish and whales. But the *Globe* is smart, and they know what they have in this Pulitzer Prize winner, so you can also find his byline on the front page above stories on poverty or COVID-19 or race relations. Or even on off-beat stories like guys going magnet fishing and pulling up old guns. And because David finds himself with so much free time—what with all these stories, a wife, and young kids—he also produces award-winning films. He covered the last airboat guy in the Everglades and has done a trifecta in New England, covering the groundfish crisis in *Sacred Cod*, the dispute of lobster territory with Canada in *Lobster War*, and the potential extinction of the North Atlantic right whale in *Entangled*. Now he is working on how Boston's Seaport District will be underwater.

During our many interviews, what stands out is his willingness to learn the intricacies of issues. He is not afraid of hard work or complicated topics. He interviews lots and lots of people, not just the minimum. He doesn't just want both sides of an issue—he wants *all* sides and all shadings. And he wants to bring out the personalities behind the policies—to make the stories human. With me, and I'm sure with others, he would persist and cajole and wait to get you to say a little more than you intended. One time, I was sailing with Laurie off Block Island while we were on vacation. I was on the phone with David, who asked about the summer flounder issue and the interference by the Trump Commerce secretary's office in decisions that rightfully should be made regionally. While the situation was unprecedented, I didn't want to discuss it. I figured it could get me fired, but David could tell I was angry.

"John, you really need to go on the record with this."

"Let me think about it, David. Call me back in the morning."

He did, and I went on the record saying that the secretary's office was meddling in fisheries decisions that the regional administrator should make. I said that was inappropriate and would hurt the Atlantic States Marine Fisheries Commission.

The next time I was in Virginia at an ASMFC meeting, I walked into a room where my bosses Sam Rauch and Chris Oliver were. I could feel a chill from the group, but they didn't fire me, for which I will always be grateful. I am sure they took some heat back at headquarters, but David Abel was doing his job as a good reporter in getting the whole story out to the public.

CHAPTER 13

A Reckoning and a Deepening

The Cod Crisis and Working Waterfronts

When I worked for NOAA in the 1990s, the groundfish crisis was serious enough that Congress and NOAA distributed over a hundred million dollars of federal aid to address the economic hardships suffered by the fishing families. When I returned in 2012 to NOAA Fisheries, it didn't take long to realize that the crisis, if anything, had only deepened. There had been an assessment in 2008 that had given people some hope that cod stocks were rebuilding, but those hopes were dashed in 2012. At a New England Fishery Management Council meeting in Portsmouth, New Hampshire, in January 2013, it was time for a reckoning.

"We are headed slowly, seemingly inexorably, to oblivion," I said to the council and the audience of worried and angry fishermen and concerned environmentalists. "I do not deny the costs that are going to be paid by fishermen, families, communities. They are real. They will hurt. There are not enough cod for people to make a decent living."

The facts at the time were that the cod stocks in the Gulf of Maine were at 18 percent of what scientists thought a healthy population should be. Out on Georges Bank, the stocks were only at 7 percent. Recruitment was very low, which is to say the adult cod weren't having much success adding baby cod to the population. The newest cod generations were dangerously low, spelling disaster for future populations. To set a quota in light of these facts, the New England council was considering reducing Gulf of Maine fishing quotas by 77 percent in the Gulf of Maine and by 61 percent in Georges Bank. While these limits would be devasting for the industry, there was a serious question of whether the cuts would even be enough to help the cod stocks bounce back.

As the council members debated these motions, a parade of witnesses gave public testimony. The testimony from fishermen was heartfelt and generally made the point that the economic pain would be catastrophic. David Goethel, a fisherman from New Hampshire who served the maximum nine years on the New England Fishery Management Council and never succeeded in rebuilding groundfish, said, according to the four reporters from the *New York Times* covering the meeting, that the regulations would be ruinous.

"Right now, what we've got is a plan that guarantees the fishermen's extinction and does nothing to ameliorate it."

He voted against the cuts as he always did. He only recently retired in New Hampshire after a long career.

Carlos Rafael of New Bedford also said that regulation would be doom.

"I'm leaving here in a coffin. With all these cuts, I won't be able to keep half my fleet working. I'll have to cut down from 20 groundfish boats to maybe five or six."

Carlos went on to build his groundfish fleet to over 40 boats before being hauled off to jail for misreporting his catch. Known as the "Codfather," he was the biggest crook in the nation's fishing industry. Thanks to good work by NOAA's enforcement division and other federal agencies, he has been permanently barred from commercial fishing.

This is the dilemma that has put groundfish in the place it is. Fishermen, often eloquently and persuasively, talk about the uncertainty of the science, describe the unpredictable natural cycles of fish stocks, proclaim that they have never exceeded the quotas set by the councils, and declare the economic harm that they will suffer. They offer up this fishermen's stew of arguments for higher risk tolerances, higher quotas, and more fish to catch. They have great political power, and they bring all of it to bear. And when their high quotas result in low stocks, they stand back and say, "Well, we never exceeded the quotas," as if their hands are clean. They pretend they had no hand in making the mess they are living with. It is so much easier and more convenient to blame the government. It is like watching a car crash in slow motion. You know there is going to be agony. You know it can be avoided. But the dynamics are such that everyone seems powerless to avoid the tragedy. It is a real tragedy with real economic consequences.

Carlos Rafael, aka the Codfather.

As Angela Sanfilipo explained to me in Gloucester 20 years before, lower fish stocks mean more alcohol abuse, more drug abuse, and more domestic abuse to go along with fewer jobs and more poverty. As the mayor of Gloucester at the time explained to me, when a fish plant turns into a condo, that waterfront use is gone forever. The condo never turns back to a fish plant. The soul of a city dies one bad management decision at a time.

Because ground fishermen are hurting, and they must think about maximizing today's catch, they walk up to the microphone and plead their case for higher quotas. Meanwhile, the New England Fishery Management Council has made some great decisions and managed other stocks very well. Scallops, for example, are one of the best-managed species on the planet. But regulating groundfish as a whole, and cod and flounder, in particular, has left us with a legacy of doing the wrong thing, and no excuses change the result that there aren't any fish for fishermen to catch.

And so, we weep.

Some of Carlos Rafael's fleet tied up in New Bedford

Making Difficult Decisions

At this critical meeting, a majority stepped up to the plate and did the right thing, voting to cut the quota by 77 percent. It wasn't an easy decision, and it wasn't an easy pill to swallow. Think about that for a moment—what it would be like to have the resource that makes you money and provides you with a living cut by 77 percent. How would you deal with that?

Vito Giacalone   *Jackie Odell*

The industry decided they would have a rally to support the groundfish industry on the Boston Fish Pier to get support from Congress for disaster assistance. It was organized by Jackie Odell and Vito Giacalone of the Northeast Seafood Coalition in Gloucester. Both Jackie and Vito are very smart and hard-working. I had open lines of communication with them, and we shared feelings of mutual respect.

One of the first controversies I had to deal with concerned harbor porpoise and an impending closure on the gillnet fishery about to be triggered by too many porpoise deaths. Jackie and Vito brought me an alternative that was initially opposed by the environmental community. Jackie and Vito insisted it would achieve the same reduction in porpoise deaths but allow the gillnet fishermen more time to fish. I asked our scientists to evaluate the proposal and told our guys I would follow the science. It turned out the fishermen's proposal was just as good or better, so we went with it. That earned trust with their group.

When I asked Jackie about attending the rally because I, too, supported fishermen, she advised against it, saying there was too much anger against me for leading the fight for the cuts. I asked Allison Ferreira in my office if she thought I should attend. She advised against, saying it would be dangerous.

Despite that, I wanted to attend, and I thought it would be okay. I knew fishermen could get hot and yell, but I found them to be respectful. I wasn't worried. I thought if I didn't go, the message would be that I didn't care. If I did go, then it showed I cared, and if any of the speakers wanted to criticize me, they would have to do it to my face, as I was sure they would see me in the audience since I tend to stand out because of my height.

On Monday, April 28, 2013, a large crowd gathered on Boston Fish Pier. Attorney General Martha Coakley, Senators Elizabeth Warren and Mo Cowan, who had been appointed after John Kerry resigned to become secretary of State, criticized me and called on me to delay the cuts with an "interim rule." Congressmen John Tierney and Bill Keating did the same. All also said they would support disaster relief. Every politician criticized NOAA and me for putting the fishermen in the position they were in. The speakers could see me from the stage and made sure they directed their ire personally at me. But they probably also toned it down a bit because I was there.

No one called for rebuilding the stocks so they could support more fishing. Blame the science. Blame the government. But never, never blame the fishermen who influence the decisions that lead to years of overfishing.

And so, we watch the car crash.

One result of my being there was to get NOAA's side of the story out to the public. After the press interviewed the politicians, they turned to me, and I could explain the rationale behind the decisions.

The response to the cuts was swift. Massachusetts Attorney General Martha Coakley sued us on behalf of the fishermen, saying our action was much too tough. A few days later, CLF sued us, saying our action was too weak.

On Saturday evening, I was having dinner at the Back Eddy near our house in Westport and joked with Laurie.

"Well, we haven't been sued in a couple of days. I love weekends!"

A couple of weeks later, the *Boston Globe* ran an editorial that looked at both lawsuits:

> But in the case of cod, in particular, there's a reason to believe it's the industry, not the government, that's in denial. Indeed, the new Northeast Fisheries Regional Administrator, John Bullard, a former mayor of New Bedford who sympathizes with fishermen, stands by the limits announced earlier in the spring.
>
> In fact, one day after Coakley filed suit, NOAA got sued from the environmental side of the debate, as the Conservation Law Foundation said the agency was still not doing enough to preserve cod stocks. No one wants to see a single fisherman go out of business. But if there are no fish, there is no business.

If life were fair, the 77 percent cut would have begun a slow but steady rebuilding of the cod stocks in the Gulf of Maine and on Georges Bank. But life isn't fair. And while scallops and haddock enjoyed one banner year after another, cod and yellowtail flounder could not buy a year with good recruitment. Nature wasn't helping us by making baby fish. In 2015, we went back to the New England Fishery Management Council saying, "As tough and as painful as your past cuts were, they didn't do the job. The cod stocks are not growing, and you have to do more."

The council could see the science. While many fishermen would argue with it, the council didn't. But they also didn't want to make any more cuts. They made motion after motion, all resulting in tie votes. So many tie votes. No plan could get a majority. After about eight failed motions, they gave up. It seemed as if their plan of action was inaction designed for them not to act but to get me to act. They weren't at all reluctant to dump this in my lap.

Earlier, at a three-day meeting in Washington of all three Atlantic councils and the Atlantic States Marine Fisheries Commission on the subject of the impact of climate change on the management of fish stocks, I listened to a couple of fisheries managers from the Canadian Maritimes. They told me of a lesson they had learned when their cod stocks crashed 20 years earlier.

When cod stocks decline, cod tend to aggregate in tight bunches. Because fishermen are hunters and can find those aggregations, they perceive fish in high density and think there are lots of fish. Scientists survey the whole area and see vast stretches with no cod and conclude low biomass. At council meetings, you have scientists saying one thing and fishermen saying another, both passionately believing their "truth." The Canadian managers told me their biggest regret was that they had not protected the last aggregations of cod and that failure had caused a 20-year delay in rebuilding their cod stocks.

Groundfish management plans are, in the words of one judge who reviewed them in a lawsuit, "exceedingly complex." They can run 400 pages. They take lawyers, biologists, policy analysts, and managers to put together. When I first came to NOAA Fisheries, my assistant regional administrator for fisheries was George Darcy. George had been with the National Marine Fisheries Service for so long that he helped write the Magnuson Stevens Act. George would often sit next to me at council meetings to guide me on how to vote on certain issues. At other times, one of the policy analysts for a certain species would be by both of our sides to guide us through the complex issues of a certain management plan as the council debated. George had recruited incredibly smart young people to staff his office. He had a great team, and he led them well.

I had total trust in George, and one day I made a confession to him.

"George, I just don't understand what's in this part of this plan that is being debated before us."

"John, I don't understand everything in the plan either. That's why we have staff. To make sure all the many details are consistent with law, will conform to all the regulations and will do the best job at rebuilding stocks. Don't worry!"

With that comment, he removed a great weight from my shoulders.

With George Darcy

During the many briefing sessions with our staff, it was fun trying to keep up with them because they were so very smart. By the end of the day, my brain was tired.

As good leaders, George and Dan groomed a succession of leaders to follow. When George retired, Mike Pentony followed and eventually succeeded me. Some might say fisheries management isn't rocket science, but Mike was a rocket scientist before he was a fisheries manager.

Leading the difficult groundfish team and following Mike was Sarah Bland, who at a young age exhibited remarkable leadership capabilities, among them the ability to motivate her team and to engage with the outside world. I got more information from Sarah about what was going on in the industry than from everyone else combined. I stressed engagement as part of our culture at the regional office. Sarah epitomized it.

What was perilous in our situation was that the last aggregations of cod in the Gulf of Maine were right outside Gloucester Harbor, so the fishermen in Gloucester were convinced there were plenty of cod. That was one reason the council was not going to act. To protect the cod, I directed our team to come up with a plan of rolling closures that would close areas where the cod aggregations were and would move those areas as the cod moved. We imposed those closures by emergency action. We could do this for a year with a six-month extension, which would give the New England Fishery Management Council time to do its job. If they weren't going to act, then I was. After I activated the emergency measures, the council passed a slightly weaker variation of our emergency action, but again it was too little, too late.

There are two other issues of importance to the sustainability of the groundfish industry. One concerns the concentration of fishing power, which was addressed under Amendment 18. The question here was the vision of the fishery. Did the council want to protect small independent owners or allow a few operators to concentrate quota into a limited number of private commercial fleets? Already some owners like Carlos Rafael had accumulated sizable amounts of quota by buying out boat quotas from others. The economists the council hired advised that, despite this accumulation, no one had acquired enough to affect the market. Using this, council members like Dr. Libby Etrie argued that the council should not require any boat owners to give up any quota that they already owned.

Therefore, the plan that the New England Fishery Management Council passed preserved the status quo in terms of fleet diversity and was considered by many to be very weak. Later, when Carlos was required to sell his fleet, these same people complained that he had been allowed to acquire too many boats. The hypocrisy was so thick you could fillet it with a knife.

Another key issue concerns having official observers on boats. Fishermen are required to report their catch. They are also required to keep all legal-sized fish. When a human observer is onboard, this almost always happens. Problems can arise when an observer is not on board, which is the case on four out of five trips.

The quotas for cod and some of the flounder are so low that they become "choke species." That is, when you harvest your quota of cod, you must stop fishing even though you may have plenty of quota left for haddock, pollock, redfish, and other species. So, fishermen often don't want to catch cod because it means a shortened, unproductive trip. To get around this, the unethical do not record or land cod if they do catch them.

If they have an observer on board, they must follow the rules and suffer a loss. When there isn't an observer on board, they catch cod with their haddock and then they discard the cod overboard, some of which dies from coming out and being dumped back into the sea. Then they whisper about it in the hallways, what a terrible system we have and how the science is terrible because we don't know how many cod are out there. The science relies on accurate landings reports, and fishermen who cheat are sabotaging the system they are criticizing.

The New England Fishery Management Council is addressing this issue with Amendment 23. But the question is whether the council and the industry really want to know the truth or whether they want to maintain the status quo.

Before I retired, I described two pictures. I called the first the status quo picture, or the "Carlos option." It is one where fishermen discard fish, scientists never know how many cod are killed, stock assessments are therefore inaccurate, everybody whispers about who is doing what, nobody trusts anybody, fishermen say there are plenty of cod, scientists say there aren't, and quotas get set very low but not low enough to bring back the stock. I asked, why would anybody defend this option?

Then I described a second option. I said we could put cameras on most every boat to measure only if people are discarding and require fishermen to land everything except marine mammals and dogfish. Species would be identified at the dock, where it is efficient and accurate. No human observers needed to be on board, except for those required for biological sampling, which is a very small percentage. There would be no observers to feed or get in the way. Other fisheries do this routinely without complaint. This option means we would know every fish that is landed, so the science takes a quantum leap forward. There is *No Discarding*. If fishermen are correct that there are a lot of cod out there, then we will find out right away. This option turns fishermen from being scofflaws to being part of the science program. It builds trust instead of eroding it. It would dramatically increase the landing of cod, which had been illegally discarded so the management would have to allow for that to avoid the whole fishery from being shut down. That would take cooperation from the NGOs and innovative legal work. But it could be done.

Finally, in 2022, after much procrastination, the council passed Amendment 23, requiring observers on 100 percent of trips and allowing for electronic monitoring. But they made this contingent on 100 percent funding from Congress, so the cost to industry would be zero. If not, the coverage rate would revert back to 40 percent. Now, it is up to Congress to support an industry that is on its last legs. Congress can do this. It isn't a lot of money to spend for an industry that, in many ways, defines New England and the beginnings of our country. It is the right thing to do. But Congress has shown it has a very hard time doing the right thing. Until it does so on a consistent basis, we will continue to observe the car crash.

Scallops: The Making of an Industry

After Carlos Rafael was hauled off to jail and forced to sell his fleet, Keith Decker, the head of Blue Harvest fisheries, called me. I had retired from NOAA, and he wanted my advice. Blue Harvest was in the scallop business and had moved into New Bedford in a big way. He had bought a couple of Jim Odlin's groundfish boats and was thinking about buying Carlos's groundfish fleet. He wanted to know what I thought about groundfish.

"Keith, you are in the scallop fishery. It is the best-managed fishery in the world. The stock is abundant. The price is obscenely high. You have developed a system of rotational closures that works and is relatively easy on the boats and crews. You put ten to fifteen million dollars of industry-funded research into identifying long-term threats. You actually act like an industry, thinking twenty to thirty years ahead, planning for the future. You are certified by the Marine Stewardship Council. You have a very good relationship with federal scientists and managers and work together cooperatively."

Then I laid out the situation with groundfish.

"Everything I just said positive about the scallop industry—the industry you are already in—doesn't exist in groundfish. It is the polar opposite. A total basket case. You need to have your head examined wanting to get into that industry."

This is why I will never be a consultant. Keith was way ahead of me, though. He knew how horrible the fishery was.

"John, there is more groundfish biomass than ever," he correctly pointed out. "It is all haddock, pollock, and redfish. We have the ability to catch those fish and create good markets for those species. And if we could get the council to properly manage the fishery, we could bring back cod and flounder." Getting the council to properly manage groundfish was the sticking point.

"So, you are willing to get engaged in the council process?"

"Thinking about it."

That was the most optimistic I had been about groundfish in a long while. If someone like Blue Harvest wanted to be in it for the long haul and could influence decisions for the long haul, then perhaps the council could protect groundfish.

It turns out I was naïve about Blue Harvest. As the New Bedford Light, a non-profit digital news site I helped start after I left NOAA, pointed out in a 2022 story, Blue Harvest is owned by a hedge fund controlled by a foreign billionaire. It used the catch share system to accumulate market share and used its vertical integration to exploit its workers. It operates in a way that can be good for fisheries management of the resource, but not good for those whose jobs depend on it. That is an evolving story. As far as laws go, there is the Magnuson Act; then there is the law of unintended consequences.

Back to my conversation with Keith. How did sea scallops become the success story they are?

It's necessary to go back to the 1950s when scallops were selling for under 50 cents a pound. Nobody ate scallops, and the market was small. But New Bedford fishermen were catching lots of them. Twenty million pounds were landed in the US in 1952.

The Norwegians and Newfoundlanders, who comprised much of the industry, decided they needed to create a market out of nothing. Leaders like Leif Jacobsen, one of the great highliners of

Blue Harvest Seafoods in New Bedford's North Terminal

the fleet, along with Jim Costakes, Jacob Ostensen, and others started a scallop festival. They got celebrity chefs like Julia Child to feature scallops, and, after a while, scallops were starting to become center of the plate delicacies at white tablecloth restaurants. By 1976 and the Magnuson Act passage, scallop prices off the boat had almost quadrupled to nearly $2 a pound. In a fish market, they were $3.50 a pound. While landings held steady at 20 million pounds, consumption doubled to over 40 million

Signage at the New Bedford Scallop Festival on Pope's Island in 1959 boasts, "All You Can Eat..." for 99 cents.

pounds, requiring imports to meet demand. The leaders of the scallop fishery had, in essence, created an industry where one had not existed before.

While the fishing industry had created a market, by the early 1990s when I was working at the Seafood Co-Op, landings had been driven into the ground, and the industry was destroying the product by harvesting baby scallops at 40 meats per pound. In order to increase the weight, and therefore the price they were getting for their product, they were soaking these meats at sea in a salty brine solution which caused the meats to retain water and plump up. It was one thing to sell scallops for $3.50 a pound. If you could sell water for $3.50 a pound, that was even better!

Fishing industry leader Gail Isaksen (third from right) helps serve up New Bedford's newest delicacy at the Scallop Festival at Marine Park on Pope's Island, August 1960. Next right are Synnøve Risvik (with hat) and Solveig Knutsen.

The Virginia Institute of Marine Sciences did a study for the industry, looking at scallops from the time they came onto the boat until they were consumed by the customer. The result of the study was that customers preferred the "soaked" scallops! Rather than feeling ripped off, customers found the soaked scallops moister and a bit saltier in taste, and they preferred that product to the natural one. Soaked scallops turned a uniform white, while natural scallops came in various shades of whites and off-whites. While it was not legal to soak scallops, the customers didn't seem to mind.

After Ray Starvish's infamous testimony in 1993 caused the New England Fishery Management Council to close a substantial part of Georges Bank to the scallop industry for five years, the biological advantage of the scallop took over, and scallops began to grow and multiply. Now, five years might seem to some like a short time, but as Albert Einstein said, "You put your hand on a hot stove for a minute, and it can seem like an hour." Scallop boat owners and crew were already hurting, and the closed area was like holding onto a hot stove. The time didn't pass very quickly.

In 1998, scientists from UMass Dartmouth and the Science Center in Woods Hole both identified mature scallops in the closed area and informed the council of their findings. UMass professors Dr. Brian Rothschild and Dr. Kevin Stokesbury received much of the credit for this discovery, but others too reported on the large increase of scallop biomass.

The New England Fishery Management Council, having taken the courageous step of closing the area, now took the far easier step of opening the area. Landings in New Bedford increased by $50 million in the first year alone. What was more, the scallops being harvested were much bigger. Instead of 40 meats per pound, they were selling scallops of under ten meats per pound, or "U-10s." The significance of this was twofold. First and most importantly, these scallops now had several years to spawn before being harvested, so they were replenishing the stock. Second, the larger scallops were commanding a far higher price.

The industry, possessed of instant wealth and remembering what the hard times were like, took steps with the council not to return to those days. They wanted to preserve the stocks for years to come. They instituted a system of rotational closures. Working with stock assessment scientists, they identified where there were high concentrations of large scallops. Then they allowed vessels

Part of the New Bedford fishing fleet in front of the Cannon Street power plant

a very limited amount of days inside those grounds where they could turn a profit. Scallopers would hit that area hard for a year and then close it down for a couple of years so scallops could rebound. This is similar to what farmers do with their fields.

Because they were making very good money, scallopers also decided to invest in their own research and development. They put aside 3 percent of the catch in pounds, which were sold for a Research Set Aside (RFA). This could amount to over $10 million for scallop vessels and universities to conduct research related to the industry. It might enhance stock assessments. It might test gear that would reduce the bycatch of species like yellowtail flounder, a "choke species" with the power to shut down the fishery. It might look at turtle excluder devices or figure out what was causing some meats to turn gray and thus become unmarketable. All of this RSA research is beyond the scope of NOAA, and it became a very valuable complement to the long-term health of the

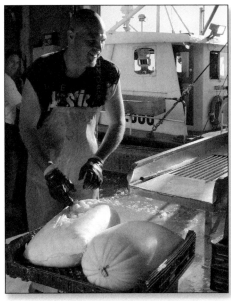

Unloading 40-pound bags of scallops, fresh off the boat at Eastern Fisheries

industry. It is conducted by a partnership of scallopers and scientists, a great model for how science can be done so that the results are accepted at the end.

In these and other ways, scallopers worked and continue to work to earn the name "industry." Other members of the fishing industry don't do anything like this.

Scallopers have a tight organization, the Fisheries Survival Fund, with lawyers in Washington. Drew Minkiewicz is one of them. Drew, who happens to be an alumnus and former crew of SEA, is a very smart lawyer. He does his homework and is not afraid to get way down into the weeds on fisheries regulations. He has been at it a while and is an expert on the regulations. He

knows the regulators, scientists, and everyone in the industry and on Capitol Hill. He keeps his word and has a good relationship earned through hard work and unrivalled persistence. When he is on your case, he is like a bull mastiff who won't let go of your leg.

The Survival Fund also supports scientists who testify on their behalf and bring credibility to the positions they take. With these methods, the industry forms cohesive views and has the ability to take positions, negotiate, reach consensus, and stick to the agreement. Industry leaders think longterm, as in 20 to 30 years down the road. If they discover a spot rich young scallops, they alert NOAA and urge officials to close the area to protect it for future use. They don't mind taking an economic hit for a few years if it will pay off three or four years down the road. They also guard the integrity of the product. For instance, if they notice some scallops are infected with a nematode-like worm, they work together to put measures in place to ensure vessels do not land the infected shellfish, which, while not considered a serious health hazard, could turn off consumers and endanger the market.

The scallop industry has earned the seal of approval from the Marine Stewardship Council, which is the gold standard for a sustainably harvested resource. And nature rewards this responsible management. The abundant resource seems to crank out one large year class after another, which the industry and the New England Fishery Management Council work together to shepherd to adulthood.

The economic result of this is a price off the boat that can exceed $15 a pound at times and total value in the neighborhood of $500 million a year. As most of the scallops are harvested out of New Bedford, this has caused my hometown to be ranked as the top dollar port for the last two decades running.

In October 2015, NOAA Administrator Kathy Sullivan visited New Bedford to meet with fishermen to hear their concerns. It was part of a one-day trip to our region. She began with a visit to our regional office in Gloucester, where she addressed all hands. I have known Kathy from my first tour at NOAA. She is a rock star. While she is an oceanographer and recently became the first woman to dive to the deepest part of the ocean in the Mariana Trench, she is also a former astronaut and the first woman to walk in space. She also helped launch the Hubble Space Telescope.

We have a lot of young women working at our NOAA regional office in Gloucester, and to have Kathy come was a great motivator. When she was selected by *Time* magazine for its Top 100 list, I sent the page down to her office so she could sign it for my granddaughter, Maddie, as inspiration for what girls can become in science.

After leaving our office in a buzz (obvious question: "What's it like to walk in space?" Kathy's answer: "Well, you don't really walk. Actually, your feet are pretty useless. You use your hands a lot."), we went to the New England Aquarium in Boston, the venue for a fisheries meeting. As I drove, I briefed her on fishing issues, various players in the region, and questions she would likely face. I dropped her off at the aquarium and went to park. By the time I got to the meeting room, she was in full discussion with most of the environmental nongovernmental organizations (NGOs) in New England. They were pressing her on the need for tougher action to rebuild groundfish, specifically cod, and the need for greater observer coverage and to get cameras on boats to eliminate the illegal discarding of fish. There was discussion of climate change, warming waters, ocean acidification—and the impact on fisheries and habitat. We also talked about deep-sea corals and North Atlantic right whales. While there were some private conversations, as we had lunch and discussed these issues around the table, I got the sense that the leaders of the NGOs were satisfied with the leadership I was providing, understanding that I had to balance a number of competing interests.

After lunch, I drove Kathy down to New Bedford. We took a tour of the harbor with Mayor Jon Mitchell and Director of the Port Ed Anthes-Washburn, so Kathy could see the harbor, the fleet, and the city from the water, which is the best way to experience a seaport. As we went under the 1899 Fairhaven Bridge, the mayor gave me a gentle jab, telling Kathy he wanted very much to replace the historic bridge to open up the northern section of the harbor.

"Can you believe, Dr. Sullivan, that your regional administrator wants to keep this relic in place just because it's historic?!?"

After the tour, we were hosted by Roy Enoksen at Eastern Fisheries. Roy is one of the most successful scallopers in the world with operations in China, Japan, and Europe. He is also a very quiet person. He is generous, relative to other members of the fishing industry and has been a loyal supporter of the Seamen's

Kathy Sullivan: oceanographer, astronaut, boss

Bethel, among many other causes. Roy had hired a great chef, George Karousos, who prepared several large plates of scallops for a mid-afternoon snack.

The mayor had invited about a dozen members of the fishing industry to the private meeting. Scallop leaders were there as well as a few groundfishermen. John Williams was there to talk about red crab. There may have been someone from the nearby surf clam operation. Members of Kathy's traveling team were there. Bill Karp, the director of the Science Center, came over from Woods Hole, and we made up the team from NOAA. No press was in the room. Mayor Mitchell asked Kathy to start by introducing herself, and then said we would go around the table.

"Kathy Sullivan, NOAA administrator. Former astronaut."

When everyone had introduced themselves, and it was back to the mayor, he looked at Kathy with a huge smile.

"I just can't get over how you can just say when you introduce yourself, 'Former astronaut.'"

Kathy looked at him deadpan.

"If you got it, use it."

A great start to a meeting with a bunch of tough fishermen!

For an hour, they peppered her with complaints about how bad the science was, how tough the regulations were, how observers cost way too much, and how they were honest folks and didn't need observers anyway. Practically all the complaining was coming from the groundfish folks.

Kathy was answering some of the questions and letting Bill and me respond to some of the issues. Bill was taking most of the heat. It was clear that they all had a good relationship with me, even if they didn't like some of my decisions. I was a local guy. They trusted me and knew how to get hold of me whenever they needed to talk. After a little more than an hour, Kathy had to get on to a meeting in Rhode Island, so we parted ways. I stayed with the group for a bit longer to determine what needed follow up. The next day when Kathy was back in DC and I was driving home from Gloucester, I got a call from Paul Doremus.

"John I'm sorry to bother you, but I'm afraid you are going to have to fill out some more paperwork."

"What is it this time, Paul?"

No one likes paperwork.

"Dr. Sullivan came back from her meeting in New Bedford, and she has decided to nominate you for a Presidential Rank Award. It is the highest award a government worker can earn. You are not guaranteed to get it, but it is an honor just to be nominated. But you do have to fill out a narrative, which we will help you with."

I was honored.

"Paul, they must have put something in the scallops. Is Kathy not well? All the people Kathy met with did was complain. I feel lucky I still have a job!"

Well, she did nominate me, and I did *not* get the award, but for a hero like Kathy Sullivan to give me a pat on the back had me walking on air. I have been in the position of leading organizations, and my responsibility is to find every way I can to motivate people to achieve to the best of their capabilities. That means putting them in positions where they can succeed. It means noticing when they do succeed and acknowledging it. I don't know anyone who doesn't want to be told they have done a good job. To be on the receiving end of it from Kathy Sullivan, well, I would have run through a brick wall for her.

While the scallop industry remains strong, it is not to say it has nothing to worry about. I met with a scallop boat owner several years ago, and he wanted my take on how the industry was managed.

"John, I'm about to invest $7 million in a new boat (most of that is the cost of the limited access permit), and I want to get your opinion on the future."

I spent 20 minutes or so on all the virtues I saw in scallop management, concluding that I think it is the best-managed fishery in the world. But I had one warning for this fisherman.

"Captain, have you ever heard of ocean acidification?"

"No, what is that?"

"You should Google it. It is going to affect the future of your industry, and before you invest $7 million, I would learn everything I could about it."

To be fair, there are a number of members in the industry who now know a lot about ocean acidification, or OA. And scallops may not be as vulnerable as some other shellfish like oysters or mussels. But as we pump carbon dioxide into the atmosphere about half of it gets absorbed by the oceans. This is a good thing for global warming because if the oceans did not do this, the planet would now be a lot warmer than it is already. But the carbon dioxide in the ocean becomes carbonic acid, and that makes it more difficult for any shellfish to take carbon and make a shell out of calcium carbonate. The shell dissolves as the creature tries to make it, the way chalk dissolves in vinegar. Whether it is a pteropod at the base of the food chain or an oyster or a scallop, the more energy you spend making shells, the less energy left for things like reproduction.

As pH levels decrease and the waters become more acidic, the oceans become a more hostile environment for scallops. And while fish or lobsters can move to adapt to temperature changes, it is harder to understand how a creature like a scallop adapts to ocean acidification. The first thing to do is to understand this potential threat while the resource is strong, and the industry is wealthy and has the resources to mobilize.

Aquaculture may play a large role here where you can culture large amounts of scallops in confined spaces where the pH can be adjusted in affordable ways. The scallop industry has already undertaken field trips to Japan to learn how this can be done. Looking ahead and investing in solutions—this is how a strong industry stays strong.

Beyond Fish: Living Marine Resources

During my first couple of weeks back at NOAA, I was talking to Dave Gouveia and some others in the Protected Resources Division. In our mission to protect all living marine resources, our responsibilities extend beyond fish. We also protect sea turtles and marine mammals like seals and whales.

I told Dave about an encounter that Laurie and I had with a harbor seal off Tenants Harbor in Maine on our 40-foot Concordia yawl. As we approached the harbor late one afternoon, we saw a seal tangled up in lobster gear. The buoy line was wrapped tightly around his neck several times. We approached slowly and tried to unwrap the line with a boat hook, but it was deeply embedded. I'm still not sure how I did this, but I grabbed hold of the line and hoisted the five-foot seal over our bow and onto our deck. For some reason, he was very calm as he stood there. I asked Laurie to sit on his back as if she was riding a horse while I worked on the lines around his neck with a knife. There were at least three wraps, and they pierced the skin. We cut them away, and unfortunately, as we did so, the line slipped away before I could reattach it to the buoy. This meant there would be one angry lobsterman out there.

After I had cut away all the lines, I looked at Laurie sitting on the seal.

"Stay right there!"

"Are you crazy!"

But she did. I got my camera. The seal didn't budge. After I took a picture of Laurie astride the seal, she got off, and we stepped away and looked at the now freed seal. Now what?

"How are we going to get him off the boat?" Laurie asked.

"I think he is going to figure that part out by himself."

After a few seconds of looking around, he ducked under the lifelines and over the side without so much as a thank you. At the end of the story, I turned to Dave.

"Dave, how many laws did I break?"

"Well, John, I'm glad we found out about this after you got the job and not before," he smiled.

He didn't recommend this kind of rescue.

Laurie rescues seal

"Just don't go doing that again. If you find yourself in that position, what you are supposed to do, is call the stranding hotline number (866-755-6622) and let trained professionals handle the job. Those seals bite, and it could have had a nasty outcome. You were lucky."

A few months later, the shoe was on the other foot, and it was Dave coming to me with an unsanctioned rescue story. Dave came into my office and said there was a news report that Bobby Kennedy and his brother Max, sons of the late Senator Robert F. Kennedy, had jumped into the water to disentangle a 700-pound leatherback turtle in Nantucket Sound. It was all over the news. The concern was that, while they were successful, what they had done was both dangerous and a violation of the Endangered Species Act. He wanted to talk over what our approach should be.

"What do you want to achieve, Dave?"

He was worried others might follow suit, thinking this was the way to deal with such situations.

"If we could get Mr. Kennedy to issue a public statement saying what he did was wrong and discouraging others from trying the same thing, that would be great."

Dave also thought the situation might yield some good intelligence that might help in marine mammal protection.

"If we could get any equipment they might have recovered, it would be helpful in letting us know what kind of gear entangled the turtle and where it may have come from."

He worried that the high-profile rescue might inadvertently lead to tragedy.

"We don't want to assess any penalties or anything like that. It's just the Kennedys are

Leatherback turtle entangled in fishing line

very influential. We don't want to have every Tom, Dick and Harry jumping in the water trying to disentangle large turtles. It's very easy for a swimmer to get caught in the line and get pulled under by a 700-pound turtle. And those turtles can hold their breath a lot longer than we can. You can end up with a fatality pretty easily. If you can believe it, some guy tried to swim alongside a whale off of Virginia to remove some rope. It's the best of intentions, but these people are going to get themselves killed."

I thought I might be able to help by reaching out to the Kennedys.

"Dave, I've known Bobby for a number of years. Why don't I give him a call and see what we can do? Would that be OK with you?"

I first met Bobby when he was giving a talk on why we should save the environment. I was and remain incredibly impressed with his intellect, except for the craziness he expresses on the subject of vaccines and autism. We have bumped into each other several times over the years and admire each other's work. Bobby co-founded the Hudson Riverkeeper Program. The program became a national movement, and we joined it while I was on the Buzzards Bay Coalition Board, so we are an official riverkeeper. It is a significant environmental watchdog group, and Bobby deserves a lot of credit for its inception. He was teaching at Pace Law School then and used his students to help bring lawsuits against polluters like GE. While some say, "the solution to pollution is dilution," others say, "the solution to pollution is prosecution." Certainly, the Buzzards Bay Coalition has used that tool when others fail, and Bobby Kennedy helped us put it in our toolbox.

I called the Kennedy compound, and a woman's voice rang out loudly, "Hello!"

"Ethel, is that you? It's John Bullard. I met you when you visited New Bedford while I was mayor. Is Bobby there? I need to talk to him about the turtle."

"Oh yeah! He's here. Wasn't that something! Aren't they great?"

"Yes, Ethel, you must be very proud of your boys. Can I speak to Bobby?"

I explained the situation to Bobby. I told him that, while what he had done had worked out OK and was done with the best of intentions, it was a violation of the Endangered Species Act. It was dangerous, and we didn't want others, less experienced than he and Max, copying the Kennedys and endangering themselves.

Bobby understood immediately. He asked what he could do. I asked if he would put out a public statement and told him we would be happy to draft one. He agreed. I asked him if they had recovered any gear. They had, and Max had it. He said to send someone over, and Max would give them a tour of the compound. I thanked Bobby for his cooperation, sent over a brief statement which he okayed, and we released it. We sent someone over to get the gear, and I thought everything was buttoned up.

I forgot I was dealing with the Kennedys. The fact that I, a mere federal administrator, had busted Bobby Kennedy made international news. It was in everything from the *National Enquirer* to England's *Daily Mail*. At the next All Hands meeting in Gloucester, I apologized to all our employees for getting NOAA mentioned in media where NOAA had never been seen before!

Three years later, in 2016, we had another incident that garnered a lot of attention. We had had a lot of success rebuilding humpback whale populations in the North Atlantic. The population had increased to about 20,000, which was great news. More whales, however, meant more interactions with people, and sometimes those interactions had bad outcomes.

Just before Thanksgiving, a young humpback found its way into Moriches Bay on the south coast of Long Island on a king tide, which is an abnormally high tide. Moriches Bay is built a little like a lobster trap. The entrance has a narrow winding channel surrounded by shallow sandbars. The entrance opens up to a large bay with deeper water. It is easier to get into than to get out of. Many local boaters have run aground on the sandbars.

Well, this whale, probably chasing small bait fish such as menhaden, sometimes called "bunker," found its way into Moriches Bay during this very high tide and spent a pleasant few days there, drawing the attention of many people who became its fans. A few days before Thanksgiving, the whale decided to leave. No one is clear whether it acted on its own or if it was being pursued by boaters. In any case, the whale ended up stranded on one of the sandbars next to the channel. In a matter of minutes, the whole town was up in arms.

Because strandings happen up and down the coast and can involve whales, injured seals, porpoises or cold-stunned turtles, NOAA has set up a stranding network of trained non-profit organizations that can quickly respond and take appropriate action. The stranding response organization near Moriches Bay at the time was the Riverhead Foundation for Marine Research and Preservation. Unfortunately, a few months earlier, they had a staff upheaval, losing a key person. I had signed a letter to them then, warning of de-certification due to lack of capacity. When Mendy Garron, our stranding coordinator, put the letter in my hands and I read it, I dropped it on my desk as if it were hot to the touch.

"Wow, Mendy, are you sure we want to be this tough on them?"

Humpback stranded in Moriches Bay, 2016

"Yea, John, they really don't have any capability now to handle a stranding and don't appear to be moving in a direction to build capacity. We need to shake them up."

We sent the letter.

Then the whale stranded. And we found out Mendy was right.

But we also had a problem as I saw it with our protocols. There's a Catch-22 in responding to a large live stranded whale. The best chance for success is for the whale to remove itself in the first 24 hours. And this often happens with a rising tide. We know from experience that towing a large animal, which is not easy to do with a lively and possibly uncooperative whale, can lead to internal damage and injuries like broken bones, so trying to help a whale is risky business. Here's the catch. Our science also says that animals that don't get off the beach in 24 hours suffer so much internal damage from their own weight that risk of mortality goes through the roof. As it seemed to me, our protocol seemed to be that it's too risky to help a stranded whale in the first 24 hours, but then they are too injured to do anything but euthanize them after 24 hours.

We sent a couple of people to the site to assist Riverhead and keep people away from the whale. Biologists from Riverhead, along with state marine police and the Coast Guard, tried the only thing they could at several high tide cycles—they used their boats to try to create enough wake around the whale to rock it off the sandbar, where it was stuck. It wasn't working. Our hopes for a speedy rescue were fading fast.

We started to assemble a team that might have to euthanize the whale if it didn't free itself. We located Dr. Craig Harms at the North Carolina State College of Aquatic Veterinary Medicine, where he is a professor of Aquatics, Wildlife, and Zoo Medicine and the director of the Marine Health Program.

From California, the team acquired a pole syringe long enough to reach into the whale's heart. We secured the proper sedatives and analgesics from our stranding partner, the International Fund for Animal Welfare on Cape Cod. New York had the proper unit for euthanasia. We flew them all to Riverhead on the busiest travel day of the year, the day before Thanksgiving, which was a logistical miracle.

As Craig was examining the whale, I was on the phone with Governor Andrew Cuomo in his Manhattan office. Tony DiLernia is a friend of the governor and had paved the way a bit for me. And I had met Cuomo when he was HUD secretary for President Bill Clinton. Naturally, the governor was concerned with the whale's health and all the people in the Moriches Bay area who had become fans of the whale. He wanted to know what we could do to save it.

I told him we had one of the foremost whale health scientists examining the whale as we spoke to assess whether the whale could be moved. I expected a report in a few hours.

"John, I want you to know—anything you need from the state of New York, just call me. If you need heavy lift helicopters or large bulldozers, whatever you need, we will get them to you. Just ask."

"I appreciate your offer, Governor, but it depends on the health of the whale. I'll call you as soon as I know."

He gave me his private number and we hung up.

A couple of hours later, we had a conference call with Dr. Harms and a few others from NOAA and Riverhead. As we feared, the whale had suffered too much internal damage to be able to be moved to sea. In Dr. Harms' opinion, it needed to be euthanized, which he was prepared to do first thing the next morning.

I called the governor and explained the situation.

"John, it's the day before Thanksgiving. You can't do this. Everyone is going to go crazy. Just tow it out to sea."

"Governor, believe me, I understand. This is not a pretty picture."

Logistically, euthanizing a whale is not a simple procedure, and it wouldn't be easy to do or to watch in the bay. Dr. Harms would have to approach the whale from the side. He needed to insert a six-foot needle into the heart—a bullseye—for a quick death so the animal wouldn't suffer. While the process of paralyzing the heart is painless to the whale, it causes the nerves to make the tail and flippers move, which will make those on shore think the whale is trying to escape. Anyone who has watched this is moved to tears. As difficult as it would be to watch, I explained to the governor that we needed to do it in the bay, and in many ways, it was the better option.

"We have to do a necropsy, and this is an ideal, safe place for the necropsy. If we tow the animal out to sea, then we will injure the whale, probably break its back in so doing. It will die a painful death and eventually wash up on one of your beaches in a December storm where our guys will endanger themselves doing the required necropsy. No, this is what we have to do, and we have to do it tomorrow."

The governor understood.

"John, the way you explain it, I fully support your decision. I ask only that whenever you issue a press announcement that you say that the state of New York offered all resources available."

"Governor, I appreciate your support, and there is no question we will state that."

The next morning, Dr. Harms and some others went out to the whale. With hundreds on shore watching, he gently approached the animal from the side, and, with the help of the team, was able to carefully inject the giant syringe directly into the suffering animal's heart. He did it perfectly, and a short while later, the humpback passed away peacefully. It had reflexively moved its tail and flippers, which brought gasps and shouts of anger from the crowd.

Then a towrope was tied to the tail, and the team towed the whale across the channel to a secluded beach and performed the necropsy. Afterward, using heavy equipment, they buried the whale. Because there was so much anger in the community, we promised the local leaders and Congressman Lee Zeldin that we would return after the holidays for a community meeting to discuss what had happened and the lessons learned going forward.

We held that meeting on February 6, 2017. Any thoughts that the passage of time might have diminished the passion people felt over the incident were blown away when we found about 300 people filling the hall to capacity. Congressman Zeldin's local staffer made some introductory remarks, and, while he could have taken the easy road by bashing NOAA, he was very fair in setting the stage.

I moderated the meeting and said we would stay as long as people had questions. While there were a number of presentations, the star of the show was Dr. Craig Harms. I have mentioned to folks at NOAA on many occasions the advice given by political consultant Tad Devine, that effective communication must be authentic, reach people emotionally, and tell a story. That is hard to do when you work in a scientific or regulatory agency, but it isn't impossible. And it is critical because that is the way people *hear* you. And that is what communication is about. Do people *hear* you?

The audience came into the room believing that the NOAA team was a bunch of uncaring, unprofessional bureaucrats. Dr. Harms told a story about getting up on the whale, about feeling and listening to its heartbeat. He talked about looking the whale in the eye. He talked about how many whales he had had to euthanize for various reasons and why you come to that conclusion. He used statistics, but he also talked about his feeling toward the animals that were his life's work. He talked about how dangerous it can be for a person, an amateur, to get near a stranded whale. Getting hit by a flipper or a tail can kill a person not familiar with the incredible force that whales, even injured, weak whales, possess.

As Dr. Harms was telling his story, my eyes were on the audience. They were transfixed. As he got to the part where he drove the syringe into the heart of the whale, there were very few dry eyes in the house. I don't think many listeners thought we didn't care or that Craig didn't know what he was doing.

Besides having Craig describe the analysis of what went into our decision to euthanize the whale and the results of the necropsy, we also reported that we felt that the stranding network as it existed during the time of the incident needed improvement. And we announced that the Riverhead Foundation would henceforth handle small marine mammals like seals and porpoises and turtles, but that large marine mammals would now be covered by a new organization run by Rob DiGiovanni, who had been dismissed by Riverhead despite his excellent leadership and technical skills. It was essential from our perspective to have Rob running the large whale stranding network in that region again. It was unfortunate that while he was off the case, we had this one tragic incident. A painful lesson.

As painful as that lesson was, losing one humpback whale when there are over 20,000 doesn't threaten the species. The same cannot be said for North Atlantic right whales. These whales now number only about 350, and their population is declining. Of greater concern is that the population of breeding females is under 100, and only they can build the population back.

When I returned to NOAA, the right whales seemed to be a success story that everyone could be proud of, but they are now endangered. North Atlantic right whales got their name because they swam close to shore, they produced high quantities of whale oil and baleen, and, because of their huge quantities of blubber, they floated when killed. They were an ideal whale to hunt.

The whalers out of New Bedford, including my ancestors, hunted the right whale to the brink of extinction with their hand-thrown harpoons and Nantucket sleigh rides. Even with the Marine Mammal Protection Act (MMPA), recovery was slow. By 1990, the population was about 280 animals.

MMPA prohibited whaling in the 1970s, and international treaties stopped the hunting by all countries except a few. In the US, in 1996, we created the Atlantic Large Whale Take Reduction Team to find ways to reduce the mortality of large whales. Like the fishery management

Her calf clinging to her side, a right whale succumbs to entanglement in fishing gear off the Georgia coast.

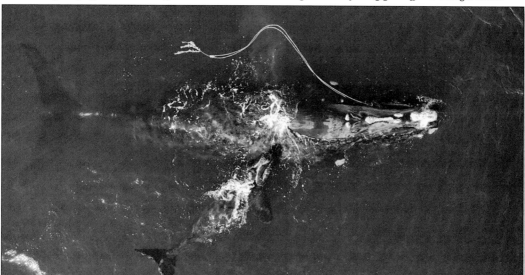

council process, the team is made up of lots of stakeholders. It has lobstermen and gillnetters, whose lines endanger whales. It has scientists from NOAA, academia, and organizations like the New England Aquarium and Woods Hole Oceanographic Institute. It has environmental NGOs to advocate on behalf of the whales. It has representatives from Canada who have attended recent meetings because right whales now spend more time in Canadian waters. With the waters warming, Canada is where they need to go to get their food. The Large Whale Take Reduction Team also has a bunch of folks from NOAA, whose responsibility it is to manage the whales.

As with the council system, this setup is very democratic and therefore has all the advantages and disadvantages of democracy. With 60 or more people in a room trying to reach agreement on contentious issues, the debate takes a long time. People's nerves get frayed. And consensus is elusive. But if agreement is reached, the buy-in from having everyone at the table is a tremendous advantage.

The first steps we took involved looking at shipping lanes and data on whale sightings. We then recommended small adjustments to shipping lanes. Adjustments to the entrance to Boston Harbor added about ten minutes to travel times but reduced ship strikes by about 85 percent.

We also worked with the US lobster industry to reduce the amount of line the whales would encounter in the water. We asked lobstermen to stop using floating lines between their traps. This meant that the sinking line was more likely to snag on rocks, but it wouldn't be in the way of a diving whale the way the floating line was. We also got most lobstermen to increase the number of traps they put on the strings of traps attached to each buoy. If there used to be four traps and two end buoys, now there might be eight traps and two end buoys. That would come close to cutting in half the number of vertical lines in the water. Together those two provisions removed about 20,000 miles of rope from the path of right whales.

We also worked with the Commonwealth of Massachusetts and the Massachusetts Lobstermen's Association to close large areas in Massachusetts Bay and the Great South Channel where right whales gather in the spring. This closed about 25,000 square miles to lobstering and other trap pot fisheries, as well as similar gillnet closure areas.

These provisions represented real sacrifices by the lobster and shipping industries, but they had a positive impact. The right whale population started to grow, and by 2010, it was nearing 500. That is not a lot of animals, and the growth wasn't fast, but people were encouraged.

I believe that it is important to know if trends are moving in the right direction or the wrong direction. If they are moving in the right direction, then time is on your side. If things are getting worse, then time is your enemy. In 2010, we felt things were improving and time was on our side. Actually, because stock assessments do not produce instantaneous results, we still felt that way up through 2015.

But then the science started to reflect a downturn. There is always a lag in the data, making it hard to detect a downturn, which at first was gradual. And then, in 2017, all hell broke loose. A total of 17 right whales died that year, 12 in Canada and 5 in the US. It was an unmitigated disaster.

Ecosystem changes caused by warming oceans meant that right whales were traveling further and further north in search of food. A scouting trip in 2015 detected three right whale carcasses in the Gulf of St. Lawrence, suggesting a need for Gulf-wide surveys. And in 2017, it was clear that much of the whale population had turned the corner into the Gulf of St. Lawrence. This Canadian body of water, where I had sailed with my friend Ned Cabot about a decade earlier, is fairly enclosed. It borders Quebec and Newfoundland on the north and Nova Scotia and New Brunswick on the south. The St. Lawrence River is a major shipping channel to Montreal and the Great Lakes, so there is a lot of marine traffic, and there is a snow crab fishery that uses stronger buoy lines tied to pots that are a lot larger than the US lobster traps. The same kind of dangers exist for the whales as they moved north. The problem in 2017 was that whales hadn't been documented in large numbers in these waters, so the government of Canada was totally unprepared for their presence.

My boss Sam Rauch made sure I was named the point person for the US as we opened discussions with Canada. This made sense. Right whales traveled up and down the East Coast of the US. This was my territory and I had a close relationship with most of the affected parties.

The staff on the management side, led by Mike Asaro, worked in our office. The scientists worked in Woods Hole. Sam knew we wanted to shorten the communication lines. And I had plenty of experience working with Canadians. On the New England Fishery Management Council, we jointly managed with Canada stocks of cod, haddock, and yellowtail flounder that crossed our boundaries as part of a group with the cumbersome name of Transboundary Resource Steering Committee. We met twice a year and had gotten to know each other well. One of my Canadian counterparts, Morley Knight, and I still correspond years after we both have retired, and I consider him a good friend.

I also became friends with the Canadian delegation at the Northwest Atlantic Fisheries Organization (NAFO). That organization regulates fishing in international waters off Canada, primarily on the Grand Banks. There are 13 members or "contracting parties," as close as Canada and the US and as far away as Russia, Ukraine, Japan, and South Korea. At our first meeting, Kevin Stringer, the head of the Canadian delegation, brought me, the head of the US delegation, two coffee mugs. One was a Boston Bruins mug. One was a Montreal mug. He suggested that as a show of friendship for our first meeting, we place the mug of the other country on our table. We did this for the first day or so. One of his assistants, I found out, was a rabid Bruins fan, so we had a lot of fun with those mugs.

A few years later, when I was at a meeting in Montreal, I happened to meet the minister of Fisheries and Oceans for all of Canada (the equivalent of a US cabinet secretary), Dominic LeBlanc. I went up to him after he gave a great speech, all without notes, in French and English. He was informed, passionate, and eloquent. I knew from his biography that he had gone to Harvard Law School. I thought about President Donald Trump, who was barely fluent in one language, and I confessed to myself some envy. I introduced myself.

"Oh, you are the Bruins fan!"

"Minister LeBlanc, you have been well briefed!"

The *Ernestina* Connection

Morley and I carried on an email correspondence for months. We had a NAFO prep meeting in St. John's, Newfoundland, and Morley called me beforehand. At an earlier meeting in New Bedford, I had given every delegation member ceramic tiles of the *Ernestina-Morrissey* because the schooner had sailed under both US and Canadian flags and was important and revered in both countries. Its most famous captain, Bob Bartlett, had a home in Brigus, Newfoundland. I had once mentioned to Morley that my friend Captain Dan Moreland had sailed the *Ernestina* into Brigus in the 1970s.

"I know that, John. You see, there is only one pier in Brigus, and only one side has enough draft for the *Morrissey*. I was tied up to that side in my boat, so I had to move when your friend sailed in."

"You're kidding me, Morley. You were there. What a small world this is."

During his call, Morley proposed we go on a side trip while I was around.

"John, you know Brigus is about a 90-minute drive from where we are meeting in St. John's. If we get our business done in the morning, we could go out and see Captain Bob's home. What do you think?"

"Sounds like a great plan, Morley."

We finished our business, and we drove out to the Bartlett homestead in Brigus. After spending an hour there, I suggested we try to find where Captain Bartlett was buried, so we asked for directions to the local cemetery, and off we went. For almost an hour, we looked to no avail. As we searched, a Canadian official approached me.

"Mr. Bullard, do you know that none of us can get to see Mr. Stringer for even a couple of minutes back in Ottawa because he is so busy, but you have him wandering around a cemetery here for an hour."

"Well, this hour may be just what Kevin needs."

Schooner Effie M. Morrissey *leaves Brigus Harbor for the Arctic, 1928.*

We piled back into our cars, feeling like our search was unsuccessful, but unexpectedly the lead car drove about a hundred yards and screeched to a halt. There, on the left, was a small cemetery with an elaborate wrought iron entrance gate that spelled out "Bartlett Family Cemetery."

We were able to pay our respects and resume our trip back.

All politics is personal. It is very hard to negotiate with people if you don't know them or share some basis of understanding. Trust isn't essential, but it certainly helps. Friendship helps.

Trying to Right the Right Whale

At our first of many meetings between the US and Canada over the right whale crisis, we had about six folks from NOAA and an equal number from Canada. Eventually, their delegation was led by Adam Burns from Ottawa, and he and I developed a close and trusting relationship. They had fisheries managers and scientists as well as Coast Guard and Transport officials. We had our protected resource experts led by Mike Asaro and Science Center population experts led by Pete Corkeron and Sean Hayes.

While our Atlantic Large Whale Take Reduction Team based decisions on the consensus system, Canada's was different. In Canada, the central government would listen to their stakeholders, but after they listened, they could issue an edict. Their process was much more top-down. They could act faster.

The facts of the crisis were not in dispute. These new whale deaths were in Canadian waters. The Gulf of St. Lawrence is like a big bathtub with only a few ways in or out. NOAA planes were surveying the gulf to conduct population surveys, spotting dead whales, entangled whales, and whales washing up on deserted shorelines. No one was in denial. Canadian biologists were conducting necropsies on the whales they could reach and ascertaining that ship strikes and crab pot entanglements were the cause. It wasn't a big mystery.

After the facts were established, I made several points in laying out the American position. The first was that the extinction of the North Atlantic right whale was not something that was going to happen on our watch. It was an unacceptable outcome, and we hoped the Canadians agreed. Second, we felt that to reverse the current trend and rebuild this iconic species, we needed to work together, sharing ideas, research, resources, and sacrifice. I told my counterparts that we had a long history of working together on both coasts, which provided a solid foundation for this effort.

I explained some of our efforts, such as shifting shipping lanes, removing 20,000 miles of lobster line, and closing 25,000 square miles of lobster ground to rebuild the population. That very real sacrifice had produced results for a while, bringing the population from 280 to almost 500. I knew that I would have to go back to my industry and ask for more sacrifice on their part, but before I did so, Canada and their industry would have to take actions equivalent to ours.

I told them that our Reduction Team process seems to show that our fishing industry is willing to sacrifice if two issues can be addressed: they need to be confident in the science about whale mortality and its causes, they need to feel that the sacrifices we are asking of them are fair relative to others who may also be contributing to mortality. I pointed out that at that moment, almost all the deaths were in Canada, and Canada had yet to take any actions on either shipping or fishing.

Adam Burns and the Canadian delegation accepted the facts and shared our goals. They understood our position and realized they needed to act. We had a long discussion about what joint research could be undertaken and what management measures might reduce ship strikes and gear entanglements. They were particularly interested in our Dynamic Management Areas (DMA). When we locate right whales, we immediately set up a management area around them. Through NOAA and the Coast Guard, we let everyone know speeds were required to be below ten knots in these area. The Canadians anticipated they would get a lot of resistance to a blanket speed reduction, and they wanted to contemplate the pros and cons of requiring a reduction in speed only when whales were spotted. After discussing this and other issues at length, we adjourned the meeting.

Minister LeBlanc held a listening session in his native New Brunswick, signaling how seriously the administration of Justin Trudeau was taking the crisis. And in short order, the government-imposed rules that would be effective for the season of 2018. They took a lot of heat, but they acted quickly, decisively, and with force equivalent to the situation.

The result was immediate. There were no recorded right whale deaths in Canadian waters in 2018 and only three in the US. Unfortunately, for the first time, no births were recorded, so we still lost ground—ground that we did not have to lose. Because of the success of their regulations and the backlash they faced, Canadian officials backed off on their regulations, with predictable results. In 2019, nine dead whales were stranded in Canada and one in the US. This outpaced the seven young whales born that year. We are still moving in the wrong direction. More than 80 percent of right whales show signs of entanglement, about half of those more than once. Dragging around ropes and gear takes energy that would otherwise be used to gain weight, so whales that are alive are much thinner. That contributes to much higher intervals between calving. Instead of recording 20 calves a year, we are now seeing perhaps three to five.

In his book *We Are All Whalers*, Dr. Michael Moore of the Woods Hole Oceanographic Institute, who has probably performed more necropsies on right whales than anyone else, describes the agonizing death by starvation that a right whale endures over a period of a half year or more as it slowly starves to death. Lobstermen say they don't see any floating corpses, but by this time, the whales can be so emaciated that they sink to the bottom. If this were happening to animals on land, no one would stand for it. The population models say that we can afford to lose less than one whale a year. We are headed to extinction.

Before retiring, I had a model of a right whale on my desk and thought about extinction every day. *How could we let this happen?*

I formed two working groups of the Reduction Team to look at solutions. One would focus on weak rope. Could we go back to using rope that breaks at 1,700 pounds instead of 3,500 pounds? That way, when a whale does get entangled, it can more easily break free. Amy Knowlton of the

New England Aquarium and her team estimated that using weaker rope would reduce mortality by over 80 percent and could be implemented within a year or two at a very moderate cost. The Massachusetts Lobstermen's Association is currently working on a pilot project with this rope.

Dr. Michael Moore of WHOI

The second working group we set up involves research into ropeless traps. Instead of having a lobster pot buoy attached to a line that floats on top of the ocean, you have a trap or a string of traps at the bottom with a radio-controlled inflatable float attached to a line. When the lobsterman gets in the vicinity and pings the float, it inflates and comes to the surface, where the lobsterman gathers it in like a regular buoy. The line is only vertical for as long as it takes to gather the traps. Ultimately, the ropeless trap gets all the lines out of the water, meaning there is no need for closed areas. But there is a myriad of problems, from very high cost to how you would keep scallopers and groundfishermen from dragging over your lobster traps.

The point is there *has* to be an answer. The best people to come up with the answer are the fishermen and scientists on the Reduction Team. They are closest to the problem, smart as all get out, and they have the biggest stake in the game. Well, almost the biggest stake in the game. The right whale, after all, is facing extinction. Stakes do not get higher than that.

Where We Make Fish

While I was at NOAA, there were more than enough opportunities to get discouraged as we worked to rebuild stocks of marine mammals or fish. While we certainly had our success stories like humpback whales or gray seals on the mammal side or haddock and scallops on the fish side, we spent much of our energy on what seemed like the intractable problems of species that were low and declining. They took our time and consumed our optimism. It was harder to have a spring in your step when you realized that wild Atlantic salmon might vanish forever from the rivers of New England, or that there might never be cod in Cape Cod Bay, or that right whales might vanish.

A chance to work on habitat restoration was always just what the doctor ordered, and we did that on land and at sea. On land, we worked to improve fish passage along rivers by removing dams or finding ways around them. At sea, we worked to protect essential fish habitats. In both cases, these efforts relied on science and partnerships among many governmental and non-governmental entities.

I'm not sure what the first dam removal project was that I went to, but John Catena from our Restoration Center came into my office and asked if I would like to attend the ceremony. Technically, he didn't have to do that because John reported directly to Silver Spring, Maryland, even though he was located in our building in Gloucester. But I had worked with him from my earlier tour at NOAA, and he wanted to involve the regional office. I jumped at the chance.

It was a small dam in Taunton, and NOAA had provided the bulk of the funding for its removal. Old dams can be dangerous because if they fail during floods, they are a threat to life and property. But they can be tricky to remove because the lake created by the dam is often loved by those who live next to it. They enjoy boating and fishing and don't want the lake replaced with a river and wetlands, as beautiful as that environment can become in a few short years. The known is frequently favored over the unknown.

But John's assistant, Jim Turek, had helped stitch the financial partnership together and built community support for removal. We were there to celebrate clear fish passage on this part of the Taunton River. The statistics of what happens when you remove dams in terms of increases in river herring counts are staggering, giving more credence to the proposition that if you remove an injury to nature, it doesn't take her long to heal herself.

I was asked to make a few remarks at the ceremony.

"People have asked me, 'How is your job going?' and I have replied, 'Well, it would be a lot easier if somebody told me how to make fish!' Well, this is where we make fish."

I mentioned how these projects ripple their way through to the survival of fisheries.

"With the removal of this dam, you will see dramatically increased numbers of river herring and shad. They will spend part of their time here in the Taunton River and part of their time out in the Atlantic Ocean ecosystem, where they are prey for many important species, from birds to whales. While we are many miles from the fishing grounds that support ports like New Bedford and Gloucester, this river, with this dam removed, connects us to the sea and to everything the sea represents."

Congressman Frank was also there. He was nearing retirement, and everywhere he went, citizens were finding ways to thank him for his years of effective service. On this day, Steve Smith, executive director of the Regional Planning Agency, introduced Barney and presented him with a plaque. The plaque was about two by three feet and made of aluminum. As Steve, a longtime friend of mine, was reading from it, I turned to the congressman.

"Good luck, Barney, getting that through security."

He received the plaque in his typical style.

"Thank you, Steve. I make it a practice never to throw away any plaques within a half mile of where people give them to me." That is Barney in a nutshell. Rude. Funny. And I can't remember anything else he said. But he supported the people in his district, and he made public servants like me work hard for constituents. He was as tough on me as anyone. But we remain good friends.

In the St. Croix and Penobscot Rivers in Maine, the dams are bigger, the issues are bigger, and the stakes are bigger. In addition to river herring and shad, you can find the very last of endangered wild Atlantic salmon. These fish spawn in the cold waters of eastern Maine, make their way to the Atlantic and turn north, where they must survive the commercial Greenland salmon harvest before returning several years later to their home river, where they can be counted one by one because their numbers are so low.

The partnerships to ease fish passage for all these fish is awe inspiring. It includes several federal agencies, active participation by the state of Maine, the Passamaquoddy and Penobscot Nations, and a whole host of environmental organizations who bring financial, technical, and community organizing skills to the table. The result of this cooperation is that while NOAA might be the largest grantor of funds, we feel that every dollar put into a project is multiplied many times over by everyone else at the table.

The biggest removal project we supported was the Veazie Dam on the Penobscot River in Maine. In July 2013, two big bucket loaders took the first bites out of the historic dam, and water began to flow, exciting the hundreds of people gathered downstream and reporters from the *New York Times* to the *Boston Globe* to dozens of Maine papers and journals. NOAA invested $21 million in this ten-year effort, which cost $60 million. It was one of 60 projects we funded that year from Maine to Virginia and out to the Great Lakes. Most dam removals weren't as big as this, but they all required partnerships and intensive planning and produced impressive results.

At the Veazie Dam, Kirk Francis, chief of the Penobscot Nation, spoke about how the removal of the dam healed a wound for the Indian Nation that for thousands of years had as an important part of its culture the unfettered passage of salmon, shad, and other species up and down the river.

Acknowledging the broad partnership necessary for dam removal

In my remarks, I emphasized how dam removals connected salmon and other species to their spawning grounds, just as they connected all stakeholders in the effort to save a river. They connected the deep ocean to the interior reaches of the forest. They connected different communities to each other, and, as Chief Francis pointed out, through the Penobscot, they connected us to thousands of years of our history here. This was a profound healing.

Mike Michaud, the Maine congressman from the second district, talked about his early life working in a paper mill in Millinocket, further north on a branch of the Penobscot, and what the dams meant to mills and mill towns and the passage of time and the passage of fish. It was a moving speech from a humble man who had a very strong connection to the river.

About three years later, I returned to the site of the Veazie Dam. I looked around and wasn't exactly sure where it had stood. I was amazed because it had been such a huge dam, dominating the landscape, and now the Penobscot flowed in its winding way, with a natural rocky shore leading up to woods on each side. Standing at the water's edge, a fly fisherman cast into the river. Overhead flew a bald eagle, both man and bird on the lookout for fish. It was as if the dam had never been there, and we had taken the way back machine to a couple of centuries earlier. Nature heals.

We also worked with Brookfield Power Company, which owned 38 dams in Maine and produced almost half of the state's 760 megawatts of hydroelectric power. These dams operated on the Kennebec, Androscoggin, and Union Rivers, and we wanted to see if we could reach an agreement with Brookfield that would be good for salmon and other anadromous fish. They were interested in exploring this, and we set up a series of meetings with Brookfield, NOAA, the state of Maine, and The Nature Conservancy.

Demolition begins on the Veazie Dam, Penobscot River, Maine.

As usual, I had a great team. Rory Saunders worked out of our office in Orono, Maine, and knew the territory, people, and issues in depth. Everyone from all sides had a lot of respect and trust in Rory's work and his word, which is critical. Kim Damon Randall headed our Protected Resource Division, which covered endangered species like salmon. She was so good that we selected her to replace Dan Morris as my deputy before I left. Maine was, and is, represented by Pat Keliher, who heads their Division of Marine Resources. Pat has earned the respect of all constituencies, serving governors as different as the far right-wing Republican Paul LePage and the Democrat Janet Mills. I was also careful to keep the Penobscot Tribe aware of what we were doing, as they were also key stakeholders in this issue.

Brookfield had already invested millions of dollars in building some impressive fish ladders, including some natural fish ladders that were state-of-the-art. But their local executive Todd Wynn made clear at one meeting as he returned from a visit to the parent company in Canada that their middle name is "Power" not "Fish," and they needed to be in the business of generating power. Our request to eliminate a number of dams was going to be very difficult to achieve.

All dams operate under licenses under the Federal Energy Regulatory Commission (FERC), and these licenses have expiration dates. One strategy was to wait for relicensing and fight Brookfield in that process, but we were hoping to work out a master agreement where their investment in dam improvements would garner them enough community goodwill for saving salmon and other fish and bird species that they would see this as in their long-term interest.

When I retired in 2018, these discussions were still ongoing.

Closer to home, NOAA worked with the Buzzards Bay Coalition to remove a dam that had long served the Acushnet Sawmills at the head of the Acushnet River. Downstream from the dam, the Acushnet River is a Superfund site where the EPA is spending millions of dollars to remove PCBs embedded in the river bottom and shoreline. The Coalition has led many restoration projects along the shore with grants awarded by trustees from the Superfund settlement. All of this effort is to try to make the harbor and river "fishable and swimmable," according to the Clean Water Act. It is also consistent with what I had laid out decades earlier as mayor—the people of New Bedford deserved clean water just like everyone else.

But with the dam in place, that wasn't going to work for anadromous species like herring and shad. The Coalition, led by the remarkable Mark Rasmussen, approached the Hawes family, who owned thousands of acres that serviced the sawmills. The Hawes family had been stewards of this land for 150 years and were excited about the vision Mark painted. The mills had not operated in decades. While the old mill and the dam were in Acushnet, right across the street is New Bedford's densely populated North End. Mark explained that with the dam removed, the retention pond would revert to a naturally flowing river and wetland environment. The Coalition could then build nature trails that would

With the dam removed, people and fish enjoy a free-flowing Acushnet River.

link to nearby cranberry bogs. This environment with the flowers, berries, birds, butterflies, fish, sights, smells, and sounds would be accessible to some of the poorest children in New Bedford, who would ordinarily not have a chance to experience a river or estuarine environment in a city whose fortunes were built by its connection to the sea.

Mary Ellen and Peter Hawes were enthralled by the vision, and all the pieces were put in place, including NOAA's. In November of 2015, a ceremony celebrated the opening of the river and the surrounding park to the public. The dam had been replaced by a natural fishway several years before, and the retention pond had reverted to a river and natural wetlands. River herring, which had numbered 200 to 300 with the dam and an old fish ladder, now routinely numbered 10 to 20 times that, reaching over 16,000 fish in 2019!

Over 500 people a week visit the trails, seeing the headwaters of the Acushnet River, a natural oasis in the heart of the industrial North End. Especially notable, as the coronavirus hit in 2020 and restricted people's movements, folks were able to venture out to trails like those at the Acushnet Sawmills. People could enjoy the outdoors in a socially distanced and responsible way and see that, while their whole world had turned upside down, the river still flowed, the flowers still bloomed, the butterflies still danced among the marsh flowers, and birds still swooped down to catch insects. One ecosystem seemed at peace anyway.

Our habitat restoration biologist Eric Hutchins also worked with the town of Plymouth as it carried out a remarkable 16-year project on Town Brook. Spearheading this has been Dave Gould, the town's director of Marine and Environmental Affairs. Dave is like the pied piper for river herring. He put together a sustained partnership with NOAA, the US Fish and Wildlife Service, and the Commonwealth of Massachusetts. Over 16 years, we removed four dams, lowered another dam, and improved two fish ladders. This gave river herring unimpeded access to an additional 269 acres of spawning habitat. Halfway through the project, I participated in a community effort of carrying fish up the river by bucket. Now they can make it on their own. Where once only 150,000 herring could reach the spawning grounds, now we expect upwards of 500,000. As I said, this is how we make fish.

Sea Mounts and Monuments

We also worked to protect habitat at sea. The biggest effort was launched unsurprisingly by the Mid-Atlantic Fishery Management Council (MAFMC). Under the leadership of Chairman Rick Robins of Virginia and Executive Director Dr. Chris Moore, the council looked at the 15 canyons along the edge of the continental shelf near the boundary of America's Exclusive Economic Zone, or 200-mile limit. These canyons formed over 10,000 years ago during the last ice age when the continental shelf was above water and sea level was 120 meters lower than it is now. Rivers like the Hudson ran all the way out to the edge and the silt they carried carved deep canyons bigger than the Grand Canyon as they ran over the edge of the shelf, leaving us what is now known as Hudson Canyon and 14 others in the area managed by the council. And into these canyons grew a vast and diverse ecosystem of hard and soft deep-sea corals, as beautiful as anything you could see in the tropics.

Under their mackerel, squid, and butterfish management plan, the Mid-Atlantic council felt they had the authority to manage these corals in what would be a first in the nation effort. They also set out to establish a process that would try to build consensus from the start instead of the usual tug of war between fishing folk and the environmental NGOs. Key to this was laying a base of good science.

Kiley Dancy, one of the many crack staffers that Chris Moore employed, started gathering reams of data on where the coral lived. What depths were critical? She also started to compile trip data from various fisheries to see which industries were likely to be most impacted by canyon regulations. Her research showed that squid fishermen and the red crab fishery were about the only two that interacted with the coral. The red crab fishery out of New Bedford was just two boats and fished a very narrow depth band in the canyons where red crab live. You really couldn't tell the boats to fish somewhere else. The squid boats stayed on the shelf but occasionally "flew" their nets over the edge. Their nets are delicate, and it is not in their interest to get hung up on the canyon walls.

Chairman Robins entrusted this consensus approach to Warren Elliott of Pennsylvania. Warren is a recreational fisherman and a consummate diplomat. One of his ancestors served a short term as mayor of Philadelphia, so I think there are definitely political skills in Warren's DNA. It didn't take him long to show his genius. Warren set up a workshop for April 29 and 30, 2015 in the Doubletree Hotel at the Baltimore Washington Airport. About 100 of us gathered for two days of intensive negotiations on the boundaries of what we would protect in the "discrete zones" of the 15 canyons and the "broad zones" in between the canyons.

Greg DiDomenico was executive of the Garden State Seafood Association of New Jersey. Greg lives in Virginia, but he is one of the most effective advocates for fishermen I have met. His board chair was Ernie Panacek, who runs Viking Village in Barnegat Light, New Jersey. I met Ernie during my first few weeks on the job and took an immediate liking to him. He took a tremendous hit during Superstorm Sandy but is the definition of a resilient personality. You cannot keep Ernie down. Greg was there to represent all the fishing interests. Ordinarily this would be an impossible task, but Greg is not an ordinary person. Quietly in the background was Eric Reid from Rhode Island, who was on the New England Fishery Management Council and worked for a major squid harvesting and processing firm. Hank Lackner was also a key player. He is a squid fisherman out of Montauk, New York, with a deep body of knowledge.

Chris very smartly hired a Geographic Information Systems mapping expert, Dr. Lucas Marxen, from Rutgers University to come to the workshop. He set up the maps with proposed boundary lines. Whenever someone proposed moving a line, he could instantly redraw the map so that everyone in the room could see the impact.

On the NGO side, Jay Odell of the Nature Conservancy and Brad Sewell of the Natural Resource Defense Council represented all the environmental groups. They met before the meeting and established their objectives and goals, which Jay and Brad brought to the table. They worked out a "good cop, bad cop" routine. Jay was the good cop, and Brad was the bad cop. Thus, the stage was set.

Warren laid out the plan for the two days and provided some background information. Then we got down to business. The fishing industry put its map up on the screen, and the NGOs put up theirs, so everyone could see the differences, which were mainly a matter of depth along the canyon walls. While those differences might have seemed huge at first with the NGOs pushing for up to 1,000 meters and the fishermen saying they wanted 100 meters, I was thinking that we were talking about canyon walls that are almost vertical. Enforcement has to be described horizontally, so the difference between a depth of 100 and a depth of 1,000 meters may only be a few boat lengths on the surface. But still we had a gap to close.

The first issue was whose map to use. Warren resolved that. The NGO maps were the only ones that would work with the Rutgers software, so we used those for the base and kept the industry maps projected on a nearby screen for reference. Jay made the first move by saying that the NGOs were not wedded to their lines. They were willing to move them. Then Hank stepped forward and did something very brave.

"I'll show you where I fish."

Fishermen would sooner drop their drawers and run around the room in their skivvies than tell you where they fish. When Lucas mapped Hank's fishing history, it became real where the boats fished and where they didn't. Trust began to build.

We started with the first canyon and its proposed boundaries. Back and forth the sides went moving "fence posts" here and there, arguing about depth, presence of corals, frequency of fishing, and so on. Finally, when agreement was reached, Jay and Greg walked from each side of the room to the midpoint in front of the screen and shook hands. The room applauded.

We went on to the next canyon. Some canyons took an hour. Some took ten minutes. But in two days, we negotiated the boundaries of all 15 canyons and the broad area that connected them on the shelf and the edge of the shelf. By the time what we had agreed to in this room had passed through the rule-making process in 2017, we had successfully protected 38,000 square miles from bottom-tending gear, an area the size of Virginia. This is 20 times larger than Grand Canyon National Park!

The Urban Coastal Institute of Monmouth University gave the council, the Garden State Seafood Association, and the Nature Conservancy their Regional Ocean Champions Award for their leadership with deep sea corals. They gave the National Champions Award to my former NOAA colleague, Terry Garcia of National Geographic, and Dr. Sylvia Earle, who is generally regarded as the leading environmental spokesperson for the health of the ocean. To see a picture of Greg and Sylvia smiling with their arms around each other is to witness the impossible become possible—the fiercest environmentalist who won't even eat fish, applauding the work of the staunchest defender of the fishing industry for work to save deep sea corals. This showed what is possible when the stars align as they did with deep sea corals.

With the model set by the Mid-Atlantic Fishery Management Council, the New England Fishery Management Council took up the same issue with the 21 canyons on the edge of the continental shelf that extended from the northern edge of the mid-Atlantic boundary to the Canadian boundary and out to the 200-mile limit. In this area are four seamounts, which are old volcanoes that rise up from the deep and are not subject to fishing.

Council Chairman John Quinn ran a workshop similar to the one in the mid-Atantic council. He held it in his (and my) homeport of New Bedford in the Waypoint Event Center at the local Marriott in the historic Baker Whale Oil Works on the waterfront. Because so many of the issues had been identified in the earlier session and fishermen like Eric Reid and representatives from the NGOs brought that experience, the negotiations went more quickly. It was also true that because the New England Fishery Management Council tends to be more industry-friendly, they set the depth at a level of 600 meters, lower but still significant for the protection of deep-sea corals.

This amendment, which protects 25,153 square miles, including 21 canyons and four seamounts, was passed by the council as I was retiring from federal service in January 2018. It was a wonderful last action to be involved in as a member of the NOAA team. The amendment finally went into effect after clearing all the regulatory hurdles in November 2019 when NOAA gave final approval.

Together, the actions protected a marine area greater in size than all the land included in New England. That remains quite an achievement but not the only achievement in the protection of habitat by the New England council. They wrestled for ten years on a habitat amendment as well.

In earlier years, the council had closed large swaths of bottom as a way to control the amount of fish harvested. This was when they managed fish through "effort controls." But when they moved to directly limiting the harvest through fishing quotas, they needed to separate the areas of bottom that had been closed to reduce catch from the areas that had been closed to protect "essential fish habitat." And defining that habitat is easier said than done, which is why it took ten years.

Council members listened to scientists, and they watched the video feeds from submersibles that showed the corals and the other habitats necessary to protect spawning and young fish. They drew lines. And more lines. They argued over the lines and moved them back and forth. Eventually, they came to agreement and protected amazing places like Cashes Ledge in the Gulf of Maine from gear that drags across the bottom. This is the way the Magnuson Act is supposed to work.

Into this scene, President Barack Obama came with a desire to create marine monuments in the same way Teddy Roosevelt had created monuments on land like Devil's Tower, the Petrified Forest, and the Grand Canyon. Obama's strategy was to expand a marine monument in the Pacific and create a new one somewhere in the east. He homed in on New England.

He was clearly being pressured by Conservation Law Foundation and other NGOs who wanted Cashes Ledge as a National Monument as well as the canyons and seamounts. I was getting calls from NOAA Fisheries headquarters as this was very political, and pretty quickly, the White House stopped going through channels. Christy Goldfuss was head of the Council on Environmental Quality, which was the White House's policy shop for the environment. She and her assistant started calling me frequently about what the boundaries of the monument should be, who the different players were, what their interests were, and how best to proceed.

We were devoting lots of staff time to getting her all kinds of data on fishing effort, natural resources, endangered species, critical habitat, all while under orders to keep everything very secret. That was a joke because the fishermen most concerned with this, my Westport neighbors Grant Moore and Dave Borden, both offshore lobstermen, were meeting in Washington with Christy, and knew just as much or more than I did. My friend Eric Reid from Rhode Island, who had concerns over the squid fishery and was talking to Christy all the time, also knew everything that was going on. He was even preparing his own set of maps, which he was taking to lobby within DC.

The two councils and NAFO protected about three dozen canyons and seamounts on the edge of the Continental Shelf and beyond along with their extraordinary habitats

Northeastern U.S.
Submarine Canyons & Seamounts

The White House effort to keep the process quiet was laughable and counterproductive. I moderated one large briefing in Rhode Island where the industry folks basically said the Magnuson Act provides for a transparent way to protect habitat, and the White House should let that work.

I argued strenuously to Christy that the New England Fishery Management Council had done the right thing by protecting Cashes Ledge. It was a tough vote for them to take. It took courage, and they had done the right thing. If the White House came in after that and slapped a monument on Cashes Ledge, the council would never again take another tough vote. They would just say, "Let the White House protect the habitat or the fish." The White House should reward the council by backing off. They listened and, much to the chagrin of CLF, decided not to make Cashes Ledge a monument.

But the White House still wanted a monument, so they drew a boundary around the then unprotected seamounts and three nearby canyons on the shelf edge. This was less controversial. No one fished the seamounts. They gave the offshore lobster and red crab guys a seven-year grace period and drew the boundaries where almost no one else was affected. They made one decision that was really inconsistent, allowing recreational fishermen to keep fishing for highly migratory species like tuna, swordfish, and marlin in the monument, but prohibiting commercial fishermen from doing so. I tried to tell them that that would create enforcement issues as well as be unfair, but I had won my one battle. I wasn't going to win another.

Later, to curry favor with Maine lobstermen, President Trump announced he was overturning the Obama designation. Trump thought Maine fishermen would be overjoyed, and perhaps they were. Fishermen, being the fiercely independent people they are, tend to vote Republican, but the monument is southeast of Nantucket, so it is pretty far away from the lobstermen Trump was trying to impress.

The seamounts are a fascinating part of our marine geology. The New England Seamounts are a chain of about 30 extinct volcanoes that rise from the seafloor about 12,000 feet. The western edge is what President Obama protected with his monument declaration. They extend eastward into international waters past the Bermuda rise, the longest mountain range in the North Atlantic.

The Northwest Atlantic Fisheries Organization manages fisheries in this part of international waters by bringing together twelve "contracting parties" to agree on the underlying science and then set quotas for stocks such as cod and haddock and so forth. The parties are countries that have historically fished these grounds like the US, Canada, Russia, Japan, Cuba, and also the European Union.

NAFO had protected many of the eastern seamounts in earlier actions. I was the leader of the US delegation, and at our annual meeting in Cuba in 2016, I saw an opportunity to bridge the gap by extending protection on seamounts from what President Obama was proposing to what NAFO had already done. I quietly circulated a letter backed up by an earlier scientific paper that had supported this idea. Countries agreed that protection was a good idea. There was minimal to no fishing on the tops of the seamounts. But they wanted some time to think about it. All international agreements take time. When we convened again in September 2017 in Montreal, I had already let everyone know this was going to be my last meeting before I retired. In recognition of my work, they unanimously voted to protect the four seamounts in between the US Monument and the existing NAFO-protected area.

I told our staff the lesson of this is that we had just accomplished something similar in impact to what the president had done but with no fuss, no headlines, and no controversy. I said you always have to look for opportunities to act, and when they present themselves, then go for it.

Chapter 14

On Stirring Kettles of Fish

Stopping the Phone From Ringing

Presidents and secretaries of Commerce are usually wise enough to know they don't want to get into the middle of managing fish. In June 2013, President Obama appointed Penny Pritzker to be secretary of Commerce. She is a member of a very wealthy and politically connected family in Chicago and raised a lot of money for the Democratic Party. This kind of background is a traditional pathway to becoming a secretary of Commerce. She is a very smart lady in her own right.

Secretary Penny Pritzker

My friend Karen Hyun moved over from House Resources Committee staff to Secretary Pritzker's office and called me during the secretary's first week.

"John, the secretary has a letter from the entire Massachusetts delegation wanting to meet with her to talk about groundfish. She doesn't want to do it. What should she do?"

"Karen, she should tell them she has already met with me. She is totally up to speed on the issue. She has full confidence in me, and she doesn't need to meet with them. Of course, she would have to meet with me."

"OK, I'll run that by her. Don't go far."

Karen called back a few hours later.

"Get your butt down here. You have half an hour to brief her on groundfish."

"OK, Karen, but I need to know a couple of things first. Does she know NOAA is in her department?"

NOAA makes up about one half of the Department of Commerce.

"Yes."

"Does she know what the National Marine Fisheries Service is?"

"She will by the time you get here."

"OK. Good to go."

My staff got me a flight to National Airport. In the time before the meeting, I was fending off calls from my various bosses who wanted to know if they could be part of the meeting. I told the heads of NOAA and NOAA Fisheries that, as far as I was concerned, of course, they could. They were my bosses. But it wasn't really my meeting. They ended up attending.

I was ushered into the office that I hadn't been in since Ron Brown was secretary, and I took a seat next to Secretary Pritzker. I told her I had studied architecture in graduate school, and it was an honor to meet a member of the family whose name adorned the highest prize in architecture. I began by saying that I knew she had a request from the Massachusetts delegation to talk to her about groundfish.

"Madame Secretary, the thing about New England groundfish as opposed to, say fish in Alaska, is that there are more congressmen than there are fish."

I laid out the landscape, or more accurately, the seascape.

"The nature of fisheries management is there are no win-win solutions. Not even win-lose. It is mostly lose-lose or the apportionment of pain. I and my colleagues make difficult decisions that people don't like, and then the aggrieved parties go up the food chain to get our decisions reversed. That is what is happening now with the Massachusetts delegation."

From Karen, I already knew that the secretary was not keen on getting tangled up in fish.

"Secretary, my job is to make your phone stop ringing. I had that job for Secretary Ron Brown and Secretary Bill Daley, both from Chicago like you. While you obviously can't talk to Ron Brown, who was a hero of mine, you can certainly talk to Bill Daley about how well I did my job."

I explained how I could be valuable to her.

"The way your phone stops ringing is that when people call you up, you say, 'John Bullard speaks for me,' and they will stop calling you. And you can get on with the important business of trade missions and increasing business opportunities for the American people."

She was amenable.

"Sounds like a good plan, John. Let's do it."

"Thank you, Secretary. I am always here to be of service."

Secretary Pritzker was true to her word. She backed me up on every decision. And so did President Obama. I found out later that my friend Massachusetts Governor Patrick was not pleased with the restrictions I was placing on the groundfish industry and called the White House to have them overturned. When he explained the situation to Obama Senior Advisor Valerie Jarrett, she listened to him, checked out the situation, and he got nowhere.

One characteristic of good leaders is they back up their people in the field unless they have very good reason not to. There are a couple of reasons for this. One is that, of course, it builds loyalty and morale when the troops like me know that the folks above have your back.

The second, less obvious reason is that as soon as a secretary of Commerce overturns a regional administrator's decision, then everyone knows that the secretary is willing to make fishery management decisions, and he or she becomes the "Secretary of Fish." And as I mentioned to Secretary Pritzker, that is not a fun job to have. You can't make just one decision; you are going to have to make all of them.

Fluke: The Over/Under on Undermining and Overturning

One secretary who didn't understand that concept was Wilbur Ross, the last secretary I worked under who was appointed by Donald Trump. While I was a career employee at NOAA Fisheries, I certainly have a political philosophy, and it is diametrically opposed to Donald Trump. Still, I wanted to work well with Wilbur Ross, who was a businessman who turned around companies. During his confirmation hearing, he pledged to honor the integrity of NOAA's science and respect its mission. I was looking for hope wherever I could find it.

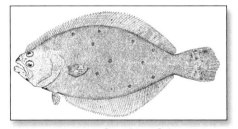

Summer flounder or fluke

Our first meeting in DC with Timothy Gallaudet, a rear admiral in the US Navy and the highest political appointee at NOAA, was encouraging as he pledged not to retreat at all on NOAA's work on climate change. And the administration appointed Chris Oliver, who was the longtime director of the North Pacific Fishery Management Council, to head NOAA Fisheries. Alaska's fisheries are very well managed and show a healthy respect for science, and Chris, having spent the early part of his career in Texas, knew just about everybody he needed to know.

As the Trump administration took over, I watched as the EPA and the Department of Interior got decimated. We pulled out of the Paris Climate Accords, and every environmental rule seemed under attack. Scientists in other agencies were shown the door or quit or were muzzled, but NOAA seemed to operate under the radar. I thanked my lucky stars for that, while growing angrier and angrier at the larger picture.

Finally, though, too good to be true was too good to be true, and it happened to me with summer flounder, or fluke, as it is colloquially known. Fluke are caught primarily from Massachusetts to Cape Hatteras. The fluke fishery is very important for New York and New Jersey. Like a lot of species in warming waters, they are moving north, and nowadays, more and more fishermen in Massachusetts and Rhode Island are catching this fish.

Fluke are caught in state waters and federal waters, so they are managed by both the states through the Atlantic States Marine Fisheries Commission and the Mid-Atlantic Fishery Management Council. Fluke was a healthy stock until about 2012 when, like a number of flounder species, it started to decline for reasons that have eluded scientists. As is the case with fishery management, it takes a few years for science to realize that a stock that is growing has started to shrink. And then, it takes a couple of years to react to that science by formulating a new management plan. And then, it takes some time for the fish to react to the plan. Under the best of circumstances, you don't get instant results. "Nipping a problem in the bud" is not in the fishery manager's lexicon.

After Trump took office and installed his administration, we were wrestling with a decline in this very important stock. For the Mid-Atlantic Fishery Management Council, this was the only stock they managed that was in decline. They were very proud that every stock they managed was healthy, so they were determined to bring this one back into good shape. You do that by reducing fishing. The Atlantic States Marine Fisheries Commission (ASMFC) was facing the same choice. The commission is made up of the state fishing directors from the 15 states from Maine to Florida plus a few other bodies. NOAA gets a vote as does the Fish and Wildlife Service. The state directors had lots of experience bringing back stocks, and they knew that what was needed was the courage to reduce fishing effort.

But *that* causes real anger. Fishermen get really upset and start holding rallies and start calling on their elected leaders to do something about it. And like every fisherman in this situation, they start questioning the science.

I was working from home one Friday when I got a call.

"Hi John, this is Bob Martin. I'm the commissioner of New Jersey's Department of Environmental Protection. Got a minute?"

"Hi, Bob. For you, sure. What's on your mind?"

"You know, John, I think we have a lot in common. I spent a lot of time in Massachusetts. I went to Boston College. Went to BC Law. You know, I still root for the Patriots."

"I bet we do have a lot in common, Bob. You know, my wife is from New Jersey. My first wife is from New Jersey. Bob, all my wives are from New Jersey. So, you see we do have a lot in common. What's on your mind?"

Summer flounder was on his mind.

"I know you think that summer flounder is in decline, but the science is really wrong on this, John. The trends are good. And we simply cannot impose any cuts on this fishery. It is way too important to New Jersey."

"Bob, believe me, I know this is a big fishery in New Jersey. And in New York. I know a lot of jobs and families depend on this. And I know a lot of people are up in arms about the proposed cuts. But what I also know is that since 2012—four years ago—this fishery, which used to be so robust, has been in decline. There have been 15 state surveys taken, and 13 of them, including yours, Bob, including your surveys, Bob, show summer flounder in decline. This is supposed to be science-based decision making."

He insisted that regulators must be mistaken.

"But the science is wrong, John. It is horribly wrong," he said his voice rising on the phone.

"Look, Bob, this is going to be one of those phone calls where you tell your staff, 'Don't ever let me talk to that guy Bullard again.' OK, Bob, it's not going to go well. Now we have a meeting next week in Alexandria at the ASMFC. I expect you will be there. I'm going to be there. We can talk in person. Perhaps you can get the other 14 state directors to see it your way. I'm only one vote."

The following week, I was in Alexandria for the meeting. To accommodate the three representatives from each of the 15 states plus the two federal agencies and a couple of other parties, there needed to be a *large* room with many tables set up in a rectangle so everyone could face each other. There also had to be room at the table for the scientists and other experts, as well as a seat for members of the public who were going to testify. Then there was room behind this large table for the many members of the public and everyone's staff to sit. All in all, several hundred people sat in the main room of the hotel for the meeting, which usually lasted several days. Everyone went out at night to different restaurants where relationships formed that were the foundation of trust needed for tough management decisions. Many of the people in the room had been working together for decades.

Not so, Bob Martin. This was the first meeting I had seen him at.

Before the meeting started, I was sitting outside the big room with my team as people were gathering. Mike Ruccio was our lead on summer flounder. Mike is a big athletic guy who played goalkeeper on his college soccer team and then worked in fisheries in Alaska before coming to the regional office. Allie Murphy was there. She was the lead on Jonah crab, which was moving into the lobster territory in southern New England. We were trying to develop a management plan for this new fishery that might take the place of the shrinking southern New England lobster fishery. Allie was as slight as Mike was robust, but she, too, was an athlete, a long-distance runner. She had also come down from Gloucester. So had Chip Lynch of the General Counsel's office. Chip handled ASMFC matters for us, among other duties. And coming over from headquarters was Kelly Denit. She was a multi-sport star at Yale, and you could tell by the way she carried herself that she didn't take any guff.

As we were talking about how summer flounder would go that day, I saw a person that I assumed had to be Bob Martin walk up the stairs with a determined look. I went over to him and introduced myself.

"Bob, welcome to ASMFC. Glad you made it. We talked on Friday about having a chat about fluke. There will be some time during the break this morning to do that, or we can meet right now. There is a room right over there that we can use. I see you have your team with you. Do you want to meet with our respective teams, or do you want to meet just you and me?"

If I had been holding a glass of water, it would have turned to ice.

"Just you and me, and I'll be there in a couple of minutes."

I returned to my team.

"Bob wants to meet with just me in a couple of minutes. What do you guys think is the over/under on how long it takes him to threaten to have me fired?"

That drew smiles and some laughter and lessened the tension. We joked about it and ended up at seven minutes for the over/under. I went into a side room and sat in a chair by a table. Bob came in a few minutes later and sat down. No pleasantries. He started in with how he thought the surveys on fluke weren't any good. I repeated that his own state survey and 12 other surveys showed fluke biomass was declining. He said he wanted an exception to the Magnuson Stevens Act, and he thought it was unreasonable that we wouldn't support him.

Left to right, Sam Rauch from headquarters, Mid-Atlantic Fishery Management Council Vice Chair Warren Elliott, and Chair Mike Luisi

Dr. Jon Hare, left, heads the Northeast Fisheries Science Center in Woods Hole. Regional Administrator Mike Pentony is now leading GARFO in Gloucester.

"Bob, I don't have in my pocket a one-day only, good on Tuesday, exemption from the Magnuson-Stevens Act."

I explained that he could take his cause to the other members.

"You know, Bob, I am only one vote anyway. There are 15 states. You should offer your motion to Chairman Mike Luisi from Maryland and see what happens. He may rule you out of order for trying to force them to go against Magnuson Stevens. He may allow it to go to a vote. But you should make your best pitch to Chairman Luisi. I'm only one vote."

"You are not being reasonable, Bullard. Do you know who my boss is? Do you know how close he is to the president?"

Bob's eyes were cold and unblinking. He let the question hang there. I looked at my watch. Five minutes. Under.

I certainly knew who Chris Christie was. And as tempted as I was to be a wiseass and make some snide comments—*Oh whatever happened to Governor Christie? Is he the attorney general? Or did he make secretary of Defense? I can't remember what part of the cabinet he ended up in.*—I just kept those thoughts to myself.

"Well, Bob, I think we've made our positions clear. I'll see you out in the main hall."

After telling the team about the meeting, I sought out Chairman Mike Luisi. Mike, besides chairing the Summer Flounder Board for the Atlantic States Marine Fisheries Commission, is the chair of the Mid-Atlantic Fishery Management Council. He is a very good guy, and we have a good relationship. While he represents Maryland, he is from Philadelphia, and he is a diehard Philadelphia Eagles fan. He hadn't got over the time in 2005 when the Patriots beat the Eagles 24-21 in the Superbowl. To say that he hates the Patriots is a gross understatement.

I found Mike and went up to him.

"Mike, Bob Martin is going to introduce a motion asking for a waiver from Magnuson Stevens for New Jersey so they can exceed the fluke quota. Now, when you are deciding whether or not to rule this motion out of order or not, I just want you to keep one thing in mind. While Bob represents New Jersey, he grew up and went to school in Boston, and he is a die-hard Patriots fan. Just one thing to factor into the equation."

Mike laughed. Of course, he would never let anything like that enter his mind. Of course not.

During all the back-and-forth negotiations that took place over this issue, our team, led by Mike Pentony, crafted a solution that would comply with Magnuson Stevens, would rebuild the fluke populations, and was fair to all the states. Mike, besides being trained as an actual rocket scientist, is from South Jersey, so he knew the territory here. We were fashioning and building a solution the way it is supposed to be done under the law. It was based on the science. It involved all of the states in the ASFMC. It would have strengthened the fishery. And it would have strengthened the fishery management process. No one would have been "happy." No one would have "won." That is the way it is with fisheries management almost all of the time.

Secretary Wilbur Ross and Earl Comstock

Then Wilbur Ross decided he wanted to be "Secretary of Fish." On the advice of his aide, Earl Comstock, who had done some fisheries work in Alaska and gave the impression that he thought he was smarter than everyone else, the secretary's office overruled us and decided to give New Jersey an outright win at the expense of the fish, the process, and their own agency. While I was technically a career employee and was not supposed to be "political," I am capable of political thought, and I could never figure out whose bright idea it was to make one state happy while pissing off 14 other states.

Earl Comstock was eventually shown the door, but only after he did tremendous harm to two fisheries: the fluke fishery in our area and the red snapper fishery down in the Gulf of Mexico, to name two.

For most of the 20th century, New Bedford was the nation's #1 port in flounder landings. Here, fish lumpers remove pens of summer flounder and yellowtail from the dragger Commodore *to be processed at Pilgrim Fish filet house.*

Chapter 15

Morale, Sea Monkeys, and Racehorses

Performance Reviews

As I have mentioned, the federal government does a horrible job hiring people. The process takes too long. It discourages applicants from completing the process. It is not successful in diversifying the workforce. It results in a permanent vacancy of a quarter of the funded positions, which means that people are doing the work of those who are not there on a regular basis. This leads to stress and burnout.

But the federal government, at least at our part of NOAA, does do an important job once people are employed, investing in that workforce through performance evaluation and training. And we took that job seriously. When I started at the Northeast Regional Office in 2012, morale was low. That should affect performance, but everyone was still doing their jobs very well; they just were not feeling appreciated.

Everyone had a job description, and once a year, every manager reviewed performance through a process called Commerce Alternative Personnel System (CAPS). It starts with the person's job description and their plan of work for that year. Then each employee assesses their own performance against their plan of work. Then every employee meets with their supervisor, who goes over their performance and gives written feedback, both positive and negative.

At the end, there is a place for professional development, so that both the employee and the supervisor can discuss what kind of training or other kinds of opportunities could lead the employee to further develop their skills and abilities. Then a work plan for the following year is discussed and agreed upon by both the employee and the manager, so the employee's goals are not imposed from above but mutually agreed upon. This meeting usually takes an hour.

At the midpoint of the year, a check-in meeting takes place that is much shorter and is designed to touch base to see if there are any major issues or if things seem to be on course. The reason this system is so good is that, in my experience, problems arise when there is no meaningful communication between managers and employees about performance. It can be a difficult topic and thus easy to put off. And when it is put off, expectations may start to differ between what the employee thinks and what the manager thinks. Neither party is aware there is a difference of opinion until something happens that causes a shock. And then it is very unpleasant and difficult to deal with.

"You were supposed to have that project on my desk this week, and you are only halfway done. How can I review it and give it to my boss next week, when it's going to take you another month? Now I'm going to look bad."

"I thought you said sometime this fall. I didn't know you meant this week. You weren't specific enough."

Scheduled conversations and specific goals can avoid misunderstandings that lead to situations where correcting the problem takes a lot more time than avoiding it in the first place. Once these meetings take place, then all the managers report to their managers and so on up the food chain. Finally, Dan Morris looks at every single one of the evaluations to see if they are graded fairly and the scores produce an average that evens out by department.

Our region at Gloucester should be about the same as others in the country so individual scores will have some meaning. In other words, Dan guards against grade inflation.

As important as CAPS is, it is like going to the dentist. *Nobody* wants to do this. Dan cajoled, encouraged, and bribed with ice cream, which he and I dished out at the end, and he used his considerable sense of humor to get people through the process. He also educated, funded, and encouraged managers to get their employees to take advantage of professional development. He did this because he knew that when people come to work for us, they are going to be with us for a career. It makes a lot of sense for us to invest in making them more skilled, more experienced, more connected, and better trained in any way we can.

Dan and I also wanted to make sure we had a strategic plan that looked down the road. We set up a process including employees at every level, beginning with identifying our core values and then composing our vision, mission, goals, and objectives. We wanted this process to flow from within our organization and not to be imposed from the top down. The worst thing in the world would be if Dan and I said, "These are the values that govern us."

The values that came out of this process included such characteristics as integrity, collaboration, trust, hard work, and professionalism. Our vision was described as "a future in which the American people continue to benefit from healthy oceans and coastal ecosystems in the Greater Atlantic Region." And stepping down to the next level, we set our mission as "stewardship of living marine and diadromous resources through science-based conservation and management."

We then set three organizational goals to achieve this mission:
- Amplify the economic value of sustainable commercial and recreational fisheries.
- Conserve and recover protected species while supporting responsible fishing and resource development.
- Improve organizational excellence and regulatory efficiency.

In increasing granularity, we set achievable objectives to fit under each of those goals. One of my directives to the team was that every employee had to be able to see where they fit into the picture, so they would know their work was important. The team that led this effort was headed up by Harry Mears, who directed the division that covered finance, administration, and grants. Harry was a wizard and was one of the two or three people I had known from my earlier stint at NOAA, when I was delivering economic assistance. We had worked very closely together on the vessel buyout program and the fishing industry grant (FIG) program in the 1990s.

We wanted to coordinate closely with our colleagues at the Science Center in Woods Hole. Harry's counterpart there was Jack Moakley. Jack was a very interesting guy. While, like Dan Morris, he came to the Science Center through the NOAA Corps, his uncle was Joe Moakley, the famous chairman of the House Rules Committee in DC. I had gotten to know his uncle, who was a very quiet man but one of the most powerful men in Washington because every bill had to go through his committee. Jack and I spent a lot of time talking Boston and Washington politics.

Jack and Harry were very close, so it made it much easier for our respective strategic plans to fit together, important because they were going to have to merge into one in the near future. The two of them had one other thing in common, although neither knew it at the time. Both would die way too soon. Harry did not get to enjoy even a year of his retirement, which left everyone at NOAA devastated. And Jack fought brain cancer from his workstation until it finally claimed him.

Two finer public servants and friends would be very hard to find.

Budget Woes: Watering Plants and Feeding Sea Monkeys

While we were working as hard as we could to build up our workforce in Gloucester, events in Washington sometimes made our efforts more difficult. One was the government shutdown that occurred from October 1 until October 17, 2013. President Obama was trying to get health care passed, and the Republican-controlled House was fighting him at every turn. That included blocking a budget for the fiscal year beginning October 1. Encouraged by far-right Senator Ted Cruz, the House refused every compromise that the Obama administration and the Democratic-controlled Senate offered.

Seeing this coming, we had developed a plan with guidance from our bosses in Silver Spring. Everyone would go home before October 1 with orders not to work from home. We had identified about a dozen "essential workers" who would come into the office in Gloucester to either maintain computer equipment, track fishing catches, or do the very few other jobs that simply had to be done without delay.

I was one of those workers. The fishery councils were funded by grant money, so they were not affected, and the Mid-Atlantic had a meeting scheduled in Philadelphia, so I purchased my tickets before October 1 for the meeting. But there would be no staff to help me and no lawyers to keep me out of trouble!

October 1 came, and the bluffing parties in Washington shut the government down. I entered our office building with about ten others. We decided we would meet for lunch in my conference room so we could touch base with each other once a day.

It was eerie being in a building almost entirely devoid of life. I wandered the halls. I had promised to water everyone's plants, so that whenever they returned, they would not be confronted by a dead plant in their office. Mark Grant had sea monkeys, and he had told me how to feed them, so I looked after them as well.

I checked in with headquarters and prepared for the council meeting.

When I arrived, I felt naked without staff to guide me through all the issues and motions. Sarah Bland called me part way through the meeting to check in on how I was doing, which was very thoughtful of her and meant a lot to me. At the end of the meeting, North Carolina member Dewey Hemilright took a moment just before adjournment to address me in his southern drawl.

"Well, John, I wasn't sure how you were going to do up there all by your lonesome, but I guess you muddled through well enough."

High praise from Dewey!

What was most troubling to me about the shutdown is the message it sent about our employees. Not only did it force us to label some people "non-essential," but it sent a message to the American people that devalued government and held all of us up to ridicule like the gang that couldn't shoot straight. We were having a hard enough time in Gloucester, where our jobs involved regulating people and telling them things they didn't want to hear. This was just another reason for our folks to feel bad about their jobs.

Finally, on Thursday, October 17, Congress passed a bill and Obama signed it and everyone returned to work. We had an All Hands meeting in the first-floor conference room, and it was magical to watch. Everyone was smiling and talking with each other, hugging and catching up, and sharing how they had gone through the past two weeks. I could see that this wasn't just *work*. This was a community that cared for each other. They were happy to be back in each other's company. There was nothing forced about the energy in the room.

That afternoon I participated in a call with leadership in Silver Spring and my counterparts around the country. Jim Balsiger, who holds my position in Alaska, warned Sam Rauch and the others that we needed to be on guard for very low employee morale because of the shutdown based on what he was seeing about employees returning. I realized that we had a very special group here in Gloucester.

GARFO: Portuguese for Fork

The federal government tries to measure everything, and their own employees are no exception. The Federal Employee Viewpoint Survey (FEVS) was born. Dan and I thought this was another opportunity to make lemonade out of lemons. I was taking a page from a captain on a SEA ship who instructed the students before their first dawn watch cleanup—an arduous hour before breakfast of scrubbing down every inch of the boat to make it shine, and, importantly, make it disease resistant—"If you can't get out of it, get into it."

That was Dan's and my philosophy. We were going to get into it. And we had just the guy to lead this effort. Dan, in one of his patented acts of wizardry, had brought on board Dr. Kevin Chu, who is a remarkable human being. I had known Kevin when he was a dean at SEA until the faculty there got him fired just before I arrived. He is a scientist with expertise in large marine mammals and had been the number two person in a West Coast science center that NOAA closed in a consolidation, leaving Kevin without a seat.

Dan called up Paul Doremus and proposed a way to solve several problems at once. Senator Barbara Mikulski of Maryland was the chair of the Senate Appropriations Committee. While she was diminutive in stature, she was a titan in other ways. And she had gotten it into her head that our office, the Northeast Regional Office, did not pay enough attention to her state or region. She wanted to move our whole office to Maryland, and as chair of Appropriations, she could do that. Everything headquarters did seemed to annoy her.

Dan and I proposed to Paul Doremus and headquarters that they assign Kevin to us. That is, they would pay him, but he would work for us. We would have him set up a small office in Annapolis, where his daughter lived, and we would move a half dozen of our people who already worked in that region to that office to create critical mass.

I asked Rick Robins and Chris Moore, the leadership of the Mid-Atlantic Fishery Management Council, to write letters to Senator Mikulski saying that we gave them exemplary service, second to none. And I spent a lot of time in the senator's office. I found that her chief of staff was a very good friend of a faculty member at SEA, Dr. John Jensen, and had an interest in Great Lakes marine archeology. Once again, all politics is personal. Instead of fighting the chairman as headquarters was doing, Dan and I were trying to court her. We described the office we were setting up. We described the relationship we had with the Mid-Atlantic council.

In the end, Chairwoman Mikulski wrote into her bill that we could stay in Gloucester as long as we changed our name to the Greater Atlantic Regional Fisheries Office, which is how we became GARFO for short. At an All Hands meeting to announce this decision and let everyone know they would not be faced with either having to move or losing their jobs, Wallace French, the head of our IT department, pointed out that GARFO is Portuguese for fork. And that became my new tag line.

"Hi, I'm John Bullard. Regional administrator of GARFO, Portuguese for fork."

Nobody forgot our name.

As Machiavelli wrote, a leader's first duty is to protect his or her people.

Kevin came over to work in our shop and was happy to locate in Annapolis near his daughter. He also had a home in Woods Hole, where he had worked at both our Science Center and at SEA. He could also spend some time in the Greater Atlantic Regional Fisheries Office. Kevin has a personality that is just made for getting people to work together. He can draw people out. He has a way of listening that has you say what you want to say and then he just sits there letting the silence fill the room, creating a vacuum, and then you say what perhaps you didn't at first intend to say but which is so important for people to hear. Kevin is such a gentle old soul that every space he is in is a safe space where even the most disempowered and voiceless are drawn out.

When the employee survey was sent out, we encouraged everyone to fill it out and communicated we were going to take the results very seriously as a way of working toward improving the work environment. We did everything we could to let our employees know their voices would be heard and respected. Kevin headed the team to process this.

What did we find out from several years of doing this? By and large, people were highly motivated about the mission we are engaged in, the quality of work being done, and the way they are treated and evaluated. They are proud of the place they work and the people they work with.

They didn't, however, think poor performers were disciplined enough, and they didn't see a lot of room for advancement. This last point was a difficult one because so many of our people were young, good, and in it for the long haul. Our budget wasn't expanding, so there just were not a lot of job openings. We have lots of talented, bright people, and it is natural they are also ambitious. Finding ways to advance everyone's career is a challenge. It was certainly one of the contributing factors to why I retired. I knew my departure opened up the top spot, and there would be a chain of openings from that one.

The other complaint about poor performers was harder to assess. Dan spent a lot of time on everyone's evaluations and guiding every manager. He worked especially hard with managers trying to identify early employees with problems and then focusing a lot of attention to either correct the problem through support, like training or progressive discipline, or to ease the person out of GARFO.

GARFO Magic

In our last couple of years at the Greater Atlantic Regional Fisheries Office, I remember talking with Dan about this process and listening as he told me with a relaxed smile how good he felt that for the first time, he didn't see a single problem employee in our over 200 people. This is a credit to our employees, our managers, and to Dan.

When we looked at our FEVS scores and compared them to other offices in NOAA Fisheries and all of NOAA and all of Commerce, we were at the top or near the top. When Sam Rauch came up to visit, I told him he should bring back some of the bottled water to headquarters because something was going on at the Greater Atlantic Regional Fisheries Office that he might want to spread around the agency. When Kathy Sullivan and Eileen Sobeck said good-bye to everyone at the change of administrations after the 2016 election, they pointed out the GARFO magic.

There are way too many employees to single out, but a few examples may suffice. First, of course, is Dan Morris. We are two very different people. I could tell when I first set foot in the office that he was very skeptical of me. And I am sure that my first steps did not decrease his skepticism. He is a NOAA Corps buttoned down, by the book, keep your cards close to your chest kind of guy. I am the opposite. But as we worked together, we saw how complementary we were. Our different skills matched up, and we built trust in each other and knew that we had each other's back. We became a great team. While our senses of humor are different, the humor became a bond. Dan was indispensable to our success.

Julie Crocker works in protected resources. In private life, she and her husband run Crocker's Boat Yard, which restores old wooden boats like the Concordia-built yawl that Laurie and

I owned. For the Greater Atlantic Regional Fisheries Office, Julie handles projects like the building of the Tappan Zee Bridge replacement, approving all the work being done in terms of environmental impact, especially with regard to the endangered sturgeon. This project was so important to New York Governor Cuomo that he was going to dedicate it to his father. It also had the attention of New York City Mayor Bill de Blasio. And Senate Minority Leader Chuck Schumer was interested in the project. And President Trump also came from New York City. None of these people are shrinking violets unwilling to pick up the phone at the slightest hint of bureaucratic delay.

In order to avoid killing sturgeon, the supply boats that went from shore out to the construction site in the Hudson needed to stay under five knots. The boats didn't want to do that because it slowed down the work. The state kept changing its plans, so Julie had to keep reviewing different plans, always under impossible timeframes and intense political pressure. But she did her job. She was always professional, and the folks from New York, who were making these impossible demands throughout the project, respected her and, therefore, the Greater Atlantic Regional Fisheries Office.

The same can be said for Mike Asaro and Colleen Coogan during the right whale efforts. As an animal such as the North Atlantic right whale is going extinct, passions legitimately run hot. And wherever people gather, the people who represent the federal government are going to be on the hot seat. Mike is a scientist and Colleen a communicator, although those descriptors sell them both short, as they have devoted their lives to protecting living marine resources. When people start yelling at them from all sides, they stay composed and focused—focused on what gets us to a solution that avoids extinction.

Susan Olsen worked for NOAA for 47 years. I knew her as the person who administered the Saltonstall-Kennedy Grant program. This national program created by Massachusetts Senators Leverett Saltonstall and John Kennedy awarded funds to partnerships of fishermen and academic scientists for projects that furthered the long-term interests of the fishing industry. The application process was opaque to say the least, and most fishermen did not even apply because it was so intimidating. But Susan was undeterred. She reached out, and in her persistent, friendly manner encouraged people from our region to apply. She helped them through the process, guiding them through every step and, year after year, our region's fishermen submitted more applications than any other. While I argued to headquarters that as both Saltonstall and Kennedy were from Massachusetts, we should get all the money, that argument was not persuasive, and we got only our fair share. But Susan's personality and professionalism made this program accessible and gave people a shot that they wouldn't ordinarily have.

Joanne Pellegrino was one of our port agents who represented us in different ports in the region. Joanne was stationed in New Jersey. She put a human face on NOAA, and her task was to listen to what was going on in the different ports and to communicate information we were trying to get to people about new regulations or other matters. When Superstorm Sandy hit Barnegat Bay on Monday night, October 29, 2012, it wiped out fishing boats, piers, processing plants, and people's homes and cars, including Joanne's. Devastation was everywhere. But somehow, there was Joanne, checking in with people, making sure they were OK, assessing damage, and inventorying losses so we could start the process of getting emergency funding. It was Joanne's reassurance and the knowledge that she was there to help even though she had suffered loss as well that reinforced the bond between the fishing industry and NOAA.

Sarah Bland is cut from the same mold and epitomizes many of the values I tried to champion at the Greater Atlantic Regional Fisheries Office. While she is one of the youngest in

Sustainable Fisheries, her managers kept giving her tough assignments, like groundfish, which she excelled at. As she started to head her own teams, her leadership abilities started to shine. But a couple of things stood out for me. One is that she has a way of getting people in the industry to talk to her, so she knows more about what is happening in the outside world than anyone else. Sarah is the person I think of when I think "engagement." She makes us a smarter organization because she knows what everyone else is thinking. She brings a lot of information to the table. The other thing is that she is unafraid to walk into my office with an idea. She would often stop by, stick her smiling face in and say, "Got a minute?" An open-door policy only works if people actually walk through it. Mike Pentony recognizes her talent. After I left, he promoted her first to head of Sustainable Fisheries and then to be his assistant regional administrator.

Two guys I have a ton of respect for are Dave Gouveia and Willie Whitmore. Dave was on the senior level of Protected Resources and helped me out with harbor porpoise issues and large whale issues. He is incredibly bright, works hard, and built a great record. When the top job at protected resources opened, he was a strong candidate, but we chose Kim Damon Randall, another very strong candidate, and Dave was very disappointed. In the same way, Dr. William Whitmore saw all the talented people in Sustainable Fisheries and almost no opening that would allow for his advancement. He has a PhD and a lot of talent and ambition. He had successfully run for selectman in Ipswich. He, too, knew he had more to offer.

Both Dave and Willie realized the way up the organization is often not straight up but back and forth. Dave applied for and was selected to lead our largest division, Analysis and Program Support, which deals with statistics and permits. It is a very different skill set that required Dave to broaden his reach, which will enhance his abilities and growth potential in the future. Willie took a job in Operations and Budget, which like Dave's move, will require learning how the Greater Atlantic Regional Fisheries Office operates and could open doors in the future.

While I could go on and on, I will end this section with Mike Pentony. Mike is taller than me, younger than me, smarter than me, and way more knowledgeable about fisheries regulations than me. At council meetings, members, out of politeness, would direct their questions to me, knowing I would say a sentence or two before turning it over to Mike for the details they were really interested in. He led his division, which had the difficult task of managing people in a way that morale stayed high, regulations got out on time, training was completed, everyone was treated fairly, and occasionally, there was even fun! There was no hesitancy on anyone's part that Mike should take my place when I retired.

When I met with my staff for the final time, besides reviewing all the progress we had made, I told them how they had challenged me. They are so smart. They weren't all rocket scientists like Mike, but they all, without exception, bring their "A" game to work every day. They believe in the mission, they work hard, and they go about their business in a professional, inspired manner. The result of being surrounded by people like that, coming at me every hour on different issues, is that my brain got tired just trying to keep up with these young wizards. I would go home at the end of a long day, collapse in a chair with a glass of bourbon, and review the workday. *Today, I got to run with racehorses.*

Gone Fishing—Tony, Tim, and Terry

My boss Sam Rauch was a great guy to work for. Before I got to Gloucester in 2012, he had been hands-on, overseeing every decision, looking over everyone's shoulder, requiring frequent reports of our activities, and basically showing everyone that the level of trust in our abilities wasn't that great. As the weeks went by and I instituted a new way of engaging the outside world, he saw that things on his end were calming down. The phone calls were less frequent, and the reports tapered off and stopped. He started to trust our judgment and leave us alone.

Sam has many admirable qualities. He is a lawyer and knows fisheries regulations and their complex permutations and impacts in great detail. He knows the players on Capitol Hill and the politics in fisheries. He knows when to be patient and when not to be patient. Most political appointees who come in to run NOAA Fisheries are smart enough to stand back and let Sam run the show while they grab the spotlight, which Sam is very happy with. In every conversation I had with Sam, I knew he had more experience, knowledge, and smarts than I did. When it came time for me to participate in some professional development, I decided to propose something a little unorthodox.

"Sam, I've taken a bunch of those courses at the Kennedy School. They are good. But they're expensive. They would be wasted on someone like me, who is at the tail-end of his career. Save them for someone starting out. I'm not doing them."

"You have to do something, John. What do you have in mind?"

I wanted to go to sea and learn meditation.

"Tell you what, Sam. I'd like to learn what it is like to fish on a commercial fishing boat by going out on a commercial trip. And I would like to learn mindfulness-based stress reduction. They have a program at Omega Institute. It is approved by the Defense Department. What do you say?"

Being the good boss he is, he approved my alternative plan. I spent five days in Rhinebeck, New York, and meditation has been part of my life ever since.

I called up Captain Terry Alexander and asked him if he would allow me to go fishing with him to learn what he does. And he agreed. Terry fishes for groundfish on his steel-hulled 70-foot *Jocka*. He had a crew of two, Guido Carlton and Rodney Hoverson, who had fished with him for a long time. Terry is on the New England Fishery Management Council, and he invited Council Chair John Quinn to come along as well. We also had cameraman Steve Liss with us. The *Boston Globe* reporter David Abel was making a film, "Sacred Cod," about the groundfish crisis, and Steve was his cameraman. This was a great opportunity to get footage at sea with several key players.

In late August 2015, we all boarded the *Jocka* in Provincetown for a three-day trip. The skies were sunny, and the seas were like a mirror. There wasn't a breath of air. Steve asked Captain Terry a strange question as we cast off the lines and got underway.

"How big would you say the seas are right now?"

We all looked at each other. There were no seas. It was like a parking lot.

It turned out that Steve, who had about 50 *TIME* magazine covers to his credit, is one of those unfortunate souls who gets seasick very easily. Some people think seasickness is related to how much time you spend at sea, but I think it is about how your middle ear is constructed. If you are lucky, like I am, you aren't affected by the motion of the ocean. If your ear is constructed differently, you get seasick no matter how much time you spend at sea. It goes away after you get your "sea legs" and your body acclimates to the motions, but that can take three days. And during those three days, it is a very unpleasant experience, and it is very difficult to function. Steve Liss, to his great credit, as bad as he felt for three days, filmed everything we did, interviewed everybody at all times of day or night, and he never let the fact that he felt like hell get in the way of his getting the job done.

On the first day out, we did an hour tow. I was standing on the deck when they emptied the cod end and out poured 2,000 pounds of cod onto my boots. Terry smiled at me.

"See, John, I told you there are a lot of cod out here!"

"Wow, Terry, that is impressive. By the way, Terry, do you have quota for that many cod?"

"Nope."

"What are you paying to lease cod from somebody else?"

"$2.50 a pound."

"And what are you going to sell them for?"

"Two bucks."

"I see. So that was an expensive lesson you just taught the regional administrator."

"Yea, John. I wasn't counting on catching that much cod!"

It was fascinating to watch Terry, Guido, and Rodney operate. When you set the gear, especially when you haul back, the forces on the cables are fierce. You put your hand in the wrong place for a split second, and you are missing a hand or a finger, or your arm is broken. The work is dangerous and unforgiving, and the nearest emergency room is hours away by helicopter airlift. I saw Terry, Guido, and Rodney acting as one body. They didn't need to talk to one another. They had performed these operations together so many times that it was like ballet, albeit ballet in heavy foul weather gear. There was a gracefulness in seeing actions that had evolved a smoothness through the gradual elimination of all wasted motions. The net would be hauled back, the cod-end raised, and the catch disgorged onto the deck. Then Rodney and Guido would each take a two-foot stick with a nail in the end of it and start picking fish. Fish that were too small or the wrong species would get thrown overboard alive. Legal-sized fish would deftly get tossed into heavy plastic totes that separated the fish by species and size. The men's aim was flawless. In a matter of minutes, all the fish had either been returned to the sea or separated and sent below deck on ice. The net was back in the water for another tow. Tows lasted about 45 minutes, and we worked around the clock.

We caught three large halibut, but because we were only allowed to keep one, two of them were tossed over. Halibut are a very large flounder-type fish that are starting to rebound, which is an encouraging sign. They are delicious eating. More challenging to eat are the many dogfish we caught. They are a type of shark, and most fishermen consider them a pain in the neck. They command a very low price and are difficult to handle both on the boat and in the net.

We also dragged up a beautifully preserved absolutely white whale vertebra about two feet in each dimension. Terry ordered it tossed over because we were not allowed to have marine mammal parts on board. After I had returned to the office, Dave Gouveia told me a simple phone call would have allowed us to bring it in to give to a museum. It was certainly museum quality.

There were brief interludes for cigarette breaks or conversation. I would visit Terry in the pilothouse. There he sat in his comfortable captain's chair surrounded by wire. The wires went to radios and every imaginable electronic device that would tell him the depth of water, the temperature, the location of the vessel, the track the vessel was making, and the weather. All of these were in duplicate or triplicate. All were sophisticated, so the device to measure depth, for example, showed layers of the water column all the way to the bottom. The device relaying the track of the vessel could show the vessel's history, so Terry could tell exactly where he had fished back through the years. And so on.

I learned a lot from Captain Terry. He could take apart and fix every piece of equipment, knew where all the different species of fish were at every season, and knew all the management rules and Coast Guard regulations. He also knew how to cook and tell more stories than you could remember. If there is someone you want to go to sea with, it is Captain Terry Alexander. Oh, and he runs a hair salon on the side. And he may be the funniest guy who isn't on late-night TV.

We all shared duties in the galley, cooking up three or four meals a day and cleaning up afterward. The watch system allowed people to grab some sleep, but the fishing continued day and night.

I have sailed tens of thousands of miles and spent a lot of time at sea. There is something about the time before dawn when it is quiet except for the noise of the engine, and you feel the enormity of space as you gaze at what seems like an infinite number of stars. It seems as if you and your shipmates are the only people on the planet. Then dawn slowly creeps up on you, with the sky very gradually lightening in the east, teasing you. The air seems to get colder as the sky turns from black to deep blue to lighter blue to green to orange to yellow, and then the top rim of the sun peeks out to announce a new day. You feel you have just received a magnificent gift as the heat touches your face and you start to notice all the birds that have always been there.

Terry's leadership style was very different from mine in one important respect. Most important, he knew how to do everyone's job on the boat. At NOAA, I didn't know how to do anyone's job except my own. Observing Terry was very humbling. After several days, Terry put John, Steve, and me back on shore at Provincetown and went back out to complete his trip. I had learned a tremendous amount about what it takes to operate a commercial fishing boat, and I thanked them all for sharing their time with me.

I was excited and elated to tell folks back at the office about my trip and was still feeling high when Terry called me a couple of days later, after they had put in and unloaded in Boston. Guido and Rodney were driving back home to Maine when the pickup truck Rodney was driving went off the road and rolled over. Rodney wasn't wearing a seatbelt and was ejected

With, left to right, Guido Carleton, Capt. Terry Alexander, Rodney Huverson, and John Quinn aboard F/V Jocka

from the truck and killed. Guido was in a hospital in Portsmouth, New Hampshire, with serious injuries that would keep him from fishing for a long time.

The shock made the room go dark.

I had just been with these guys in close quarters for several days. You think the danger is being at sea on a fishing boat. You sigh with relief when the trip is over, and you step foot on dry land. And then, this. No more sunrises for Rodney. Ever. No matter how often I tell myself that every day is a gift not to be taken for granted, I need to remember. And I have a picture of our *Jocka* crew in my office to remind me.

The year after I went fishing with Terry, to fulfill a requirement for professional development, I told Sam I wanted to see what recreational fishing was like. I requested to go out with Tim Tower from Maine.

Sam said that wasn't allowed.

"Not allowed! Why the hell not?" I politely asked.

"Because it is recreational, not commercial. And recreational means you would be having fun. And we cannot be spending money for you to enjoy yourself. That is a conflict of interest."

"Sam, I know you are legally correct, as you always are. But that is patently ridiculous. Recreational fishing is big business. The patrons who go out on the boats may enjoy themselves, but it is **work** for the guys who run the charter boats. They work just as hard as the commercial guys. We summarize their contribution to the economy in our State of the Fisheries Annual Report. How can I learn about what they do if you won't let me experience what they do? Besides, I promise not to have any fun!"

Sam, being the great boss that he is, agreed to let me go—as long as I didn't have any fun.

I had met Tim Tower several years before when he came down to Gloucester's office. He is tall and lean with hands that look like barn doors. He is strong and well-spoken, and what I really like about him is that he isn't one of the chronic complainers. He is a smart businessman, and he figures out how to make money.

I headed up the night before to Ogunquit, Maine, to go fishing on his boat, the *Bunny Clark*. I had dinner in his restaurant, Barnacle Billy's, right above the dock. It was the freshest fish, and it was delicious.

The next morning, I parked in his lot ($10) and got on the boat. I think there was a charge for something else. I know the impression I got was that Tim was finding ways to get a little bit of money from lots of steps along the way, besides just collecting the basic charter fee.

We headed out with a full boat, including about four Black kids from New York City who had never fished before. Tim's approach to charter fishing is to make every trip special. He writes a newsletter, and in it, you can see that his priority is to make every experience unique and wonderful for his passengers, regardless of what they catch. He and his mate attend to everyone on board with consummate patience and humor. With two dozen people with lines overboard, there are bound to be tangled lines, and Tim is quick to shout, "Tangled lines are what put the 'party' in party boats." He or the mate expertly untangles the lines, and the guests get to know each other better.

As I watched all this and got a little fishing in on the side, I concluded that Tim and his mate perhaps worked harder than his commercial counterparts. One, they had to show up every day, no matter how badly they felt, because there would be two dozen customers on the dock waiting for them. Two, they weren't allowed to be in a foul mood. They had to humor the customers and always wear their happy faces.

It was a nice day out on the water. Some of the guests were old hands who had come to put food on the table. Others were there for a rare day on the ocean, and if they caught a fish, that was icing on the cake. The kids from New York had never been on a boat before, so everything was new to them. They approached every detail with a sense of wonder. It was so cool to see that they had Captain Tim Tower and his mate as their ambassadors to this foreign part of our planet, explaining what was a new world to these wide-eyed kids. They were not going to forget this day.

I managed to interview Tim in a few slow moments during the day to learn his history and what his business was like. Like Captain Terry, he knew every aspect of it, from the life story of the waitress who had served me dinner the evening before to every nut and bolt that kept the *Bunny Clark* humming. And like Captain Terry, he knew where the fish were at every hour of each day of every week of the year.

On the steam home, the mate filleted all the fish we had caught so the guests could take their catch home to cook. And Tim started handing out awards. He had prizes for the biggest fish of every species. He had them for the prettiest fish. He even had one for the person who had the worst time that day because he had been seasick. That award winner smiled a big grin for the first time since getting on the boat. Captain Tim made sure *everyone* left smiling. Except for me, of course. Because under the terms of my agreement with Sam, I didn't have any fun.

I did a few other recreational trips. One of the most successful skippers is my very good friend from New York Captain Tony DiLernia. I met Tony in the mid-90s when I first worked for NOAA, and he was on the Mid-Atlantic Fishery Management Council. Tony has a long history in fishing, and he knows everybody. He is well respected because of his knowledge, outsized personality, honesty, intellect, and storytelling. And he loves a good meal and a good cigar. People just like being around Tony.

Senator Chuck Schumer relies on Tony for advice on fishing issues that pertain to New York and on which people are helpful or getting in the way. He was good friends with Governor Mario Cuomo and had even taught him how to fish. Tony has friends in high places, which can be helpful when necessary. When I was working on economic assistance plans for the Clinton administration and needed to learn about the various players in the councils, I met Tony over a long lunch in Queens. It was the first of many, many meals with Tony that were substantive and enjoyable, and long.

Tony's business is the only charter business on the East River side of Manhattan. Rocket Charters is located on a pier where East 23rd Street intersects FDR Drive. To say this is prime real estate is an understatement. Tony's clientele come up from Wall Street at the end of the day to enjoy good fishing, good cigars, good bourbon, and good storytelling. It has been fully booked for decades.

Laurie and I joined him one day at a fundraiser for Wounded Warriors, where Milt and June Rosko also joined us. Milt literally wrote the book on fishing. His *The Complete Book of Saltwater Fishing* is the bible for recreational fishermen. We departed mid-morning from a pier on the Hudson with a hundred other boats for a fundraiser contest for a worthwhile cause. Tony had dozens of spots from the Hudson out to the Statue of Liberty around the Brooklyn Bridge and up the East River to Roosevelt Island. We would anchor, fish for a while, and if, after ten minutes or so, Tony didn't think the striped bass were there, his mate brought the anchor up, and we were off to another spot. I asked Tony about the pace.

"Tony, I thought fishing was supposed to be relaxing. We are never in a spot more than ten minutes."

"I live or die depending on whether my clients catch fish. So, we are going to keep moving until we find them."

Charter boat guests have fun. The captains and mates sweat it out like everyone else who goes to work. But with Tony, as with Tim, he makes everything look like fun through the force of his personality. I caught a nice-sized striper, and by mid-afternoon, we were back at the dock.

On a personal trip to New York, Laurie and I visited with Tony and LuAnn for dinner and a show. We started off at the original Palm Restaurant on 2nd and 45th. Tony explained that when the restaurant opened in 1926, it was frequented by big shots and newspaper reporters and illustrators from the nearby papers. As the papers didn't pay their people that well, they frequently ran up tabs they couldn't pay. At that point, the owners had the illustrators draw pictures on the walls of their important clients. The tradition of famous people having their caricatures on the walls was born. Captain Tony was very proud that he was recently put up on the wall. The Palm Restaurant was a speakeasy during bootleg days and eventually gave birth to franchises all over the country. Sadly, the original closed due to a family fight in 2015. After dinner, we went to see *Spiderman* on Broadway, and then Tony and LuAnn took us to several after-theatre venues, from quiet jazz to coffee and dessert. While I think of New York as a very large and impersonal city, everywhere we went, Tony was greeted as a member of the family by the establishment's owner. When it came time for the bill, the owner insisted, "No bill, no bill!" I knew that Tony brought these people a lot of business and that Tony treated everybody the way he treated Laurie and me. He treated people like they were members of his family. We have remained good friends with Tony and LuAnn and on our way to and from Florida each year we try to see them in Tampa, where they now spend the winters.

Tony was a dean at CUNY Kingsborough Community College in Brooklyn, and he invited Woods Hole Science Center Director Bill Karp and me to give a lecture to students on climate change. We went down there, and Tony assembled about 400 high school and community college students to hear us talk. These students were in the bullseye of Superstorm Sandy, so global warming was not some intellectual concept. I showed the slideshow I had updated from Al Gore's Climate Project, complete with a riveting video of news coverage of the hurricane hitting New York and their neighborhood. I watched their faces as they relived the horror.

Tony had put the right people in the room to hear the right message. Young people like Greta Thunberg and Alexandria Ocasio-Cortez will lead the fight against climate change because the issue is one of intergenerational injustice.

VI. Windward

Eighty degrees north on the S/V Cielita

CHAPTER 16

Passing of a Generation

My parents died within a few years of each other, my father in 2002 and my mother in 2005.

My father, Dr. John Crapo Bullard, died on December 26, 2002, of bone-marrow failure. A few days before, we had had our traditional Christmas Eve family dinner at 19 Irving Street. That had been going on since my grandparents had lived in the house. Dad had been very sick for a while, but he rallied for the family gathering and was seated next to Lexie. He made one of his usual great toasts. After dinner, some of us went to Christmas Eve service at the Unitarian Church, and Mom and Dad went home.

The following day, Dad's health worsened, and he headed to St. Luke's Hospital, where he had worked for over 40 years. With all the family gathered around him except Matthew, who was in Boise, we got to say our goodbyes on Christmas Day. Mom and I stayed with him overnight and played his beloved Bach as he dozed.

On the day after Christmas, family gathered again at the hospital. Sister Annie, who is a nurse practitioner, and my Harvard dorm mate Dr. Mike Egan, who had shepherded Dad through his last agonizing years, looked at his vitals and told us it was time for Dad to move on. And just the way he lived, quietly, he took his leave.

I wanted so much to be like my father. As a child, I found his signature at the bottom of a letter, and I copied my name over his, over and over and over again, to see if I could sign my name exactly the way he signed his, changing only the "C" for a "K." I could never measure up to my father, but I tried. He was smart, athletic, and funny. He worked so hard. I knew that I didn't want to be a doctor because he worked all day, and then, after dinner, he went to his study to read medical journals all evening, cut out the articles, and staple them together to file the next morning. He worked on Saturdays. I didn't see him much.

I had and still have asthma. Every week, he would give me shots in the arm. I dreaded it. The needles were bigger back then—the size of ice picks, it seemed. He would hold my arm and show me the needle.

"Johnny, this is going to hurt you more than it hurts me."

I don't think he ever raised his voice or showed emotion. He was a master of damning with faint praise.

"Well, those grades are pretty good, I guess."

I would feel six inches tall.

Dad taught me how to sail and how to love sailing. He would unfold a big old paper chart of Buzzards Bay and spread it out on the table in the cabin of whatever boat we were on. Then he would bring out the parallel rules, a plastic triangle, and the yellow Eldridge tide table book. Together we would chart the course for that day, accounting for the set and drift of the tide. All this would be plotted neatly in pencil on the chart. We did this over and over, and it became second nature to me. And even though, in many ways, he didn't let you close to him, in these times, I felt like we were one, that he was passing down his love for something important. Whenever I am on a boat, he is with me. I always kept a few of his things on our boat: the chronometer, a few tools, some rolls of electrical tape, and a marlin spike. They are treasures I hold very close.

I remember Dad sailing the family's Concordia yawl in the days before Laurie and I bought the boat from my parents. On a close reach, Dad liked to sit to leeward, one hand on the tiller

Mom and Dad were married October 1, 1946, in Malone, NY, on a day with three feet of snow.

and one hand on the lifeline, looking forward under the jib so he could see and feel the curl at the luff of the jib as you sail right on the edge of the wind. After the boat became ours, it was the place I liked to sit. With my hand on the smooth end of the tiller that he had held for so many thousands of hours, I felt like he was holding my hand.

On my first overnight trip, I was with Mom and Dad on our Yankee sailboat named *Tempest* in Hadley Harbor. We were sailing with their friends the Underwoods. Evening descended.

"Dad, I can't see the mainsail furled on the boom."

"No, Johnny. It seems to be covered with mosquitoes."

We got the screens up as fast as we could, and I got in my sleeping bag as quickly as possible, but it was too late. I spent the night in a bag full of mosquitoes. How could you not learn to love sailing with experiences like that!

The contradiction was that even though my father worked so hard I hardly ever saw him, he and Mom put on these experiences that formed indelible memories. We would go on what Dad would call "exPOtitions," after Winnie-the-Pooh. It might be a canoe trip with eight other families, all close friends. Or a ski week to Black Mountain, taking over Charlie Lovett's Inn. Or sailing on another sea.

"It's my 25th reunion at Harvard. We can either spend a week at Harvard or go cruising in Norway on an old 12-meter. Let's vote on it." Mom voted for Harvard. We spent an amazing ten days on *Zinita*, a classic 12-meter in Norway and Sweden.

Dad was a great doctor. He went through Harvard in three years because of the War and then after that to Harvard Medical School. A captain in the Army Medical Corps, he worked for the Veterans Administration after the war. He worked at Columbia Presbyterian in New York, where he met Mom, a nurse. He spilled an enema bowl and asked her to clean it up. She told him he should go get the mop. One of the great pick-up lines in all of history. I still can't fathom what it takes for a female nurse in the 1940s to say that to a doctor. That's my Mom.

Dad was in private practice as an internist/gastroenterologist with three other doctors from 1953 to 1973 on Orchard Street in New Bedford, next door to where my brother now practices law. There is an old joke: "Internists know everything and do nothing; surgeons do everything and know nothing, and pathologists know everything and do everything but too late." Well, jokes aside, Dad was a doctor who did what needed to be done. He was fantastic at understanding what was going on with people and figuring out how to help them.

He told me that he and his classmates were frustrated in med school because they were taught how the body worked, while at other med schools, students were taught what to prescribe for certain symptoms. Dad and his classmates thought the other schools were giving more practical schooling. But he learned that what he was taught was timeless and would be a foundation to build on.

When Dad had his first heart issue at age 52, he decided to give up private practice to work more reasonable hours as the medical director at St. Luke's Hospital. His father, John Morgan Bullard, had been president of the trustees at St. Luke's, and there were Crapos that had been heavily involved as well, so the ties between the hospital and Dad went deep.

I asked Dad why he was going to work at the hospital.

"Well, John, I think the hospital is being run for the doctors. It needs to be run for the patients. We have to change some things, and because I have worked alongside all these doctors, I might be able to bring about that change."

A few years later, I asked him how it was going.

"When I was in private practice and making house calls, everyone thought I was Jesus Christ. Now I hear the Lord's name a lot, but it's usually taken in vain at the changes in hospital practices that I have recommended. It seems administrators are not a well-loved class of people!"

Dad had a great memory. When I was 16, I learned how to drive in his old VW bug in a back cornfield on our cattle farm in Dartmouth. On New Year's Eve, I was driving into Padanaram Village to go to a party at my best friend Cary Francis' house. Approaching the bridge, the road bends to the left, and I hit a patch of ice. I was speeding. I thought of my father as I left the roadway and the car headed for a telephone pole. *Dad is going to kill me.*

Somehow, the telephone pole removed both left fenders but missed me. The car traveled quite a way off the road and over some rocks. I was OK, but the car was totaled. The police came, and so did my father. He looked at how far I had gone off the road.

"Looks like you might have been moving a little bit."

I wished the telephone pole had killed me.

Twenty-three years later, in 1986, I was in my first year as mayor. I was driving the city car reserved for the mayor, and Lexie was driving my old VW bug. She was coming home one night from an errand in the North End and thought someone was following her. She ran a stop sign, and a car hit her. Fortunately, she was fine, but the car was totaled. As I was telling Dad the story, his first concern was for Lexie's welfare. When he found out she was fine, I told him my old VW bug had been totaled.

"Serves you right."

He had a long memory.

A year later, I was having lunch at Freestones with Dad around my 40th birthday. I'm not sure what we talked about. He used to say that small minds talked about people, medium minds talked about events, and great minds talked about ideas. I'm guessing we were talking about events. He was an insatiable reader—Virginia Woolf, Tolstoy, Solzhenitsyn—nothing light. He was certainly out of my league.

I do remember one thing my father said that day.

"John, it was about this time in my life when you asked me, 'Dad, when did you start to realize you were losing it all?'"

"Wow, Dad, you've been holding that in a long time. I said that? That's so cruel. I'm sorry."

One of the lessons Mom and Dad taught us was to live an outer-directed life. Dad showed us that having a fulfilling career takes hard work and serious commitment. He and Mom showed us that commitment to family is about setting an example to follow. It is about working hard to provide opportunities for growth and development. It is about nurturing with love, laughter,

A chat with dad in his later years

integrity, forgiveness, coaching, discipline, high expectations, encouragement, and support. But they also showed us that living for yourself and your family *is not enough*.

They were Dartmouth Town Meeting members. They won far more elections than I did. Dad also served on the Dartmouth Board of Health, and he boiled the role down this way.

"There are three fundamental rules which define this position: 1) Solid waste is bad. 2) Water runs downhill. 3) The Board of Health is sacrosanct unless it vetoes the plans of individual property owners or developers."

Besides public service, he served on many other kinds of boards. Despite the time he spent practicing medicine, he gave time and money to Friends Academy, the Whaling Museum, the Rotch-Jones-Duff House, St. George's School, and the Unitarian Church. In my experience, the medical community is notoriously difficult to approach for money. Many in that group seem to believe that their work is their contribution. Dad, Drs. Greer McBratney, Gail Davidson, and Gil Shapiro were exceptions to that rule.

A few months before Dad died, I was sitting with him in his living room at Nonquitt. It was just the two of us, and I asked him if he believed in life after death.

"No way."

"Any doubt in your mind on that score?"

Ever the scientist who needed data to believe something, he didn't hesitate.

"Nope."

"Well, you may be right, Dad. I think it will be like entering a fog bank. First, there is nothing, as you say. Can't see a damned thing. And then, like a fog bank, at some point, light and shapes vaguely appear and eventually get sharper, and you emerge out the other side."

I had the same conversation with my Mom a couple of years later, sitting in the same chairs. She had cancer, and it was getting worse.

"Mom, you believe in life after death?"

She smiled, and her eyes grew wistful.

"Oh, sure, Johnny. I do. I know I'm going to see your Dad on the other side."

Their answers were as different as they were. While they were both tall, Dad was thin-boned, and Mom was big-boned. In the pictures during the war, you could tell she was a knock-out. Absolutely beautiful. But growing up in Malone, New York, just south of the Canadian border, with a gay older brother and a younger brother, she did her share of protecting her siblings. I'm sure "knock-out" had more than one meaning.

While Dad spoke as if there was wartime rationing on words, he was soft-spoken with the ones he did use. With Mom, you always knew exactly what she thought. Her laugh was genuine and could be heard several houses away.

With Dad away so much, she had to do a lot of what it took to raise us. While living on the farm on Gulf Road, my friends and I would walk to Gulf Hill Dairy and buy Raleigh cigarettes out of the machine. I was collecting the coupons on the back so that I could get an Air Force jacket. One Saturday, when I was ten or so, I was on the seesaw with my friend Jeep Walsh from New Bedford, when Mom confronted us.

"So, I understand you guys are smoking cigarettes now. Is that true?"

I gave a panicked look at Jeep and back to my Mom. I confessed.

"OK, then, you're such a big guy smoking cigarettes. Why don't you smoke one of mine?"

She handed me a lit unfiltered Camel. I had been smoking filtered cigarettes, and I never inhaled. I don't know what possessed me, but I stuck the Camel in my mouth. I drew in the smoke, inhaling for the first time in my life. I couldn't see myself, but I must have turned eight shades of green. I started coughing and fell off the seesaw, which dumped Jeep onto the ground.

"You don't look so smart now. That better be the last cigarette you ever smoke, buster."

It wasn't, but it was Mom's unforgettable form of discipline, and it made an impression.

Born Katharine Kilburn, she was the daughter of an influential New York congressman. She attended Cornell University and Columbia Presbyterian School of Nursing. Important, intelligent, independent, and talented in her own right, she was strong-willed enough to tell Dr. Bullard to "get your own mop."

She nevertheless followed him to Boston and then to Dartmouth. Mom learned to sail because Dad loved to sail, and she became a great sailor. She learned how to play tennis because Dad loved tennis, and she became a great tennis player.

Kay Bullard, as she was known, was a Dartmouth Town Meeting member for 47 years, and she and Dad routinely were top vote-getters. She made an indelible impression at Town Meeting, where she never needed a microphone, and nobody ever wondered on what side of an issue she stood.

My mother worked hard on all my campaigns. And she recruited many of her friends out of their comfort zones and into the neighborhoods of New Bedford to join what, for many, was their first mayoral campaign. Before running for mayor, when I was figuring out how to save the Rotch-Jones-Duff House, I went to Mom and told her about the historic gardens. With her help, we got the Buzzards Bay Garden Club involved, a partnership that still exists.

Like other mothers, Mom doled out advice, some of which I took.

On public speaking: Stand up straight. Speak clearly. E…nun…ci…ate.

On tennis: Placement before power. Whack! Don't hit the ball so hard! WHACK!

On marriage: Separate checkbooks. Marriage isn't a 50/50 proposition. It's 100/100. You give 100 percent, 100 percent of the time.

On personal behavior: A place for everything, and everything in its place. Say please and thank you. Pleaseandthankyou. Stop your bellyachin'.

On clothing: Don't you want a jacket? It's going to get cold. Remember, it's easier to stay warm than to get warm. Boating variation: It's easier to stay dry than to get dry.

While Dad showed no emotion toward us, Mom more than made up for it. She smothered us with emotion. I got the impression that a New England man should have no emotion; if he did, he certainly shouldn't show it. No hugs. No "I love you's," not until the very end. Mom was the opposite, and it was disconcerting to me. One seemed too little, and the other seemed too much, at least when I was growing up. After Dad died, Laurie asked Mom if she might be less lonely if she had a cat around to keep her company. Mom initially resisted but then started talking about a Siamese cat she had liked before. Laurie got her to consider the idea.

"Why don't we just go to the shelter and see what they have? You don't have to get a cat unless you find one you really like."

"Well, OK. I guess I could do that."

Laurie and Mom went to the shelter, and as soon as Mom saw the orphan cats lined up in cages along the walls, she wanted to adopt them all. She came home with one black cat named Beau. A few days later, she figured Beau needed a friend, so they returned, found another black, brought her home, and named her Belle. As Mom walked around her yard looking at the gardens and the water, Beau and Belle followed her, which isn't what cats usually do. They were incredibly devoted to her.

Mom got sicker and sicker from cancer, and again, my sister Annie, a nurse practitioner, was so helpful as we made more frequent trips to St. Luke's.

I remember once when Mom was being admitted to the hospital, and the nurse was taking her medical history.

"Have you ever smoked?"

"Well, yes, when I was younger, I smoked."

"How much would you say you smoked?"

"Well, I was a nurse in a hospital, and they discouraged smoking, so I would say only two packs a day."

I grew to be 6'5" tall. I don't know what I would have been if my mother hadn't smoked during pregnancy. And given up alcohol during pregnancy? Are you kidding me!

In the summer of 2005, Mom was fading. Sally spent a lot of time coming down from Maine. Peter took care of all the estate issues. Annie was serving as a go-between with the hospital.

On a sunny Sunday, July 17, Laurie and I were visiting Mom. Toby, Jen, and great-granddaughter Maddie were visiting as well. It was a beautiful day. Mom was in her hospital bed in her bedroom, where she could look onto Buzzards Bay. She could see her cutting garden and the vegetable garden, where Dad spent so much time. In the distance, she could see the red nun buoy #4 that marked Lone Rock, where she had helped us spread Dad's ashes. We sat with her for a few hours. Then, it was just the two of us, and I was crying. Mom looked at me with her warm smile.

"Everything is going to be fine, Johnny."

One of the hospice nurses came and suggested I go outside for a while. We sat on the back deck in the sunshine. After a few minutes, the nurse motioned us back into Mom's room. We walked in, and Belle was at her feet on the bed.

Mom's eyes were closed, and she was gone.

Kay and Dr. John were icons in the community. They set high standards and filled them in every area of life—professional, family, community service, friendships, character, sports, travel, and philanthropy. It was a long and daunting list. When they died, they left a gaping hole in my life. As the eldest son and namesake, I have felt pressure to perform since I was old enough to understand. There is no question that my parents made me a better person with their guidance and support. There is also no question that they laid out a path, but the choice to follow it was mine. How much of my life is what I designed and how much is their influence is impossible to answer and probably irrelevant.

I am thankful for so many things that any complaints along the way seem petty. I am fortunate beyond my rights. On the Fourth of July, just a few weeks before Mom died, I asked her what lesson she most wanted to pass on to her grandchildren and great-grandchildren.

"Speak the truth."

She lived by these words. Seems like a foreign language today.

A Toast to 40-Year-Old Eggnog

What binds us together from generation to generation is often what we pass on. Some of that—inheritance, secrets, wisdom, histories—can be pretty weighty. Some of it is just delicious.

Back at the beginning of my career in 1974, my boss, cousin, mentor, and friend Sarah Delano, passed on a family recipe to me. She and I were both Rotches. I wish now that I had asked her how many generations the recipe went back, but I do know how it has moved forward and outward. The recipe was for eggnog, and she gave it to me as we were preparing for the WHALE Holiday Party.

Sarah Delano is served eggnog from her recipe. At right is Peggi Medeiros, and in the background is Captain Dan Moreland of the Ernestina.

The recipe called for fresh eggs, milk, cream, and many different liquors. What intrigued me was that the recipe said I should put away some of the eggnog in the refrigerator and keep it for the following year as a starter, the same way you would use a starter for sourdough bread. The recipe was for a gallon, but we were having about 40 people to the WHALE party, so I octupled it and made eight gallons. It covered the party, and I had enough left over for family during the holidays.

The eggnog was a big hit, and after Christmas, I put a container of it in an antique refrigerator we had in the pantry on Irving Street, where it sat until the following December. As I made the second year's batch for WHALE's Holiday Party, I made it exactly the way I did the first year, except I added about a quarter cup of the first year's batch to each gallon. The party was a success, and the story of the eggnog took hold.

Twelve years later, after I became mayor, the party moved to City Hall and got bigger. I had to spend more time in the kitchen watching Sunday football while whipping up batches of 14 or so gallons. It had acquired the name "Walk-a-Block-and-Fall Eggnog" because of its potency, so we strictly limited rations because we wanted people to get all the way home.

It all went along smoothly for a few years, but disaster struck. I cannot recall why, but one summer, we lost electric power at Irving Street for almost a week. When it came back on, I took the container of eggnog out of the icebox. It looked okay, and I knew there was a lot of liquor in it along with the milk and cream, but it was too risky, even for me. Down the toilet, it went—15 years down the tubes. We would have to start over.

And then, fortune smiled. Our nephew Peter McNaull, living in Vermont then, mentioned that he had some of our eggnog in his fridge. We were ecstatic! We had shared it with family but didn't think anyone had any of it left. Peter kindly drove the starter down to Massachusetts to keep our streak alive.

When we moved to Washington, the "mother" came with us, as did the tradition of eggnog at holiday parties. Fortunately, I didn't have to make as much as when I was mayor. But it played as well in DC as it did back home.

When I returned to NOAA in 2012, I ran into Alan Risenhoover, who in the 90s had worked in Legislative Affairs across the hall from me when I was in Sustainable Development. He had moved to Silver Spring, managing highly migratory species like swordfish, tuna, and marlin. We reminisced about old times.

"The one thing I most remember, John, is the eggnog."

I still make the eggnog and give it out to a few friends, but now that I'm retired, the volume has gone way down. It is fun to think that some of the eggnog molecules are now almost 50 years old. Pretty soon, they will be eligible for listing on the National Register of Historic Places!

If you want to start your own family tradition, here, courtesy of Cousin Sarah, is how to make one gallon, with my embellishments.

Walk-a-Block-and-Fall Eggnog

1 quart whole milk	½ pint brandy
2 cups sugar	½ pint light rum
1 quart whipping cream	¼ pint dark rum
6 large eggs	1½ pint bourbon
Dash of vanilla	¼ cup of last year's eggnog
Dash of nutmeg	

Combine milk and sugar until sugar dissolves. Whip cream. Separate eggs. Beat yolks well using low speed. Add brandy very slowly to yolks. Add rum slowly. Add bourbon. Pour yolk and liquor mixture into milk and sugar. Stir. Add a dash of vanilla. Beat whites until they hold peaks. Fold whipped cream into liquor mixture. Lightly fold in egg whites. Serve chilled and garnish with nutmeg. When you let it sit, the mixture separates, with the thickest parts rising to the top and the alcohol sinking to the bottom. Before you serve, mix it again with an eggbeater or whisk.

Moving House

Laurie and I decided it was time to move out of "The Family House" on Irving Street. It was time to simplify and downsize. Knowing the significance of the house having always been in the Rotch, Crapo, and Bullard families, I reached out to see if anyone was interested in continuing the stewardship that we had done for almost 40 years. No takers. We decided to sell. This was the house where I taught Matthew how to ride a bicycle. Where Toby and I shot hoops in the back driveway, and he worked on his pitching as I tried to handle his curveball. It is the house where Lexie occupied the room with the Oriel window that inspired Sarah Tappan Crapo to write a poem. We all knew Sarah still inhabited the house as a friendly ghost and loved Lexie's room (really Sarah's room) more than any other.

This was the house where we mapped out political strategies for our campaigns, just as Congressman William W. Crapo and mayors William J. Rotch and Morgan Rotch had done. It was the house where Toby and his New Bedford High School baseball team friends played Nerf basketball in the front hall while being chaperoned by Walter Ramos, who didn't notice that they had drunk all my beer after their game. It was the scene of endless four-square games, flashlight tag, and tennis balls hit by baseball bats over Esther Chalfin's hedges, which, for some reason, never made her angry. It was summer evening discussions over cocktails and cigars with Ken and Helena Hartnett, proof that people of Irish and English descent really could get along.

It was mowing the lawn on Saturday morning and catching up on all the news as neighbors walked by and stopped to chat. It was living in an incredibly diverse neighborhood with people of Polish, Irish, Cape Verdean, Russian, Swiss, French, English, Portuguese, and Canadian descent, all within a house or two of ours. It was living in a house whose spaces ennoble you with their grace and whose leaky windows and constant maintenance drive you to your wit's end.

It was a large house, and we had filled it with stuff. Two big floors we lived on. A full basement. A third floor that wasn't heated and an attic. And a garage. All full of stuff. We needed to downsize big time. The kids wanted some things but not a lot. We had a nice model of the *Charles W. Morgan,* and Matthew wanted that. It is about four feet long and three feet high—and delicate. The shipping cost was equal to the model's value, so Laurie and I decided it was time to drive to Boise. We rented a small van, put in the model and some other things Matt wanted, and drove to Idaho. We took an extra-long weekend, driving down and flying back in about five days. It was a great way to see the country, and we thought we might even do it again.

We sold a lot of stuff. We had to get into a special frame of mind to do this, but once we did it, we felt much lighter. We began selling through a high-end auction house, worked our way to yard sales, and then resorted to a dumpster. When the house was cleared out and cleaned, we sold it to a couple who lived two blocks away. Now, they have the pleasure that the house and the neighborhood gave us.

And we have the fresh start. For this, Laurie and I looked from the Cape Cod Canal to Mount Hope Bay. We wanted something smaller and easier to maintain. One day, after about two-dozen showings, we drove into Westport and were greeted by a sign that read, "Welcome to Westport, a Right to Farm Community."

As you drive around Westport, you notice the farms and the fields and the miles and miles of stone walls. If you think about those stone walls, you realize that every stone was first placed in the ground by the glacier that had scraped it along the surface as it moved along the ground and then retreated 10,000 years ago. Each stone had to be dug up out of that unforgiving dirt one at a time by a farmer 250 years ago, lugged over, and heaved up on top of another stone to form a wall that would outline a field that would keep the farmer's livestock from wandering. This, after the farmers had cut down the first growth of forest and removed the roots. They did all this without power tools, except for the kind you fed. Gradually, some of those fields have returned to forest, which is why you see some stone walls running through second growth forest today. "Right to Farm" was earned with centuries of skinned knuckles and long days, and it isn't to be taken lightly.

We found a very simple, partially finished house at the end of a driveway in the dunes of Westport Point. It is a plain box with cedar shingles. Three floors. No basement. We added a boatshed and a smaller shed for storage. Laurie brought in architect and friend Pam Donnelly, to help finish the house, and together they worked wonders. We came to terms with the idea that we no longer lived in an architectural monument that was on the cover of architectural textbooks and where busloads of tourists would gather round to take pictures. No, we lived in a box that looked like some other house came in it. It was quite a change. But it was Westport simple, and everything worked, which meant that on weekends, I didn't have to fix anything.

Cousin Peter Bullard did the landscaping, and we moved in. Instead of a dense, diverse neighborhood, we had one family next door whom we really liked. And lots of deer, turkeys, and toads in our nearby vernal pool. Instead of hearing the constant traffic on Hawthorne Street as cars go back and forth to the hospital, we hear the waves of the ocean crash onto the beach just on the other side of the dunes. We can't see the ocean, but as my friend and the founder of Maine's Island Institute, Philip Conkling, told me, "If you can see the ocean, the ocean can see you."

Instead of New Bedford's top fishing fleet in the country at the foot of the hill, we see at the foot of our drive about 20 small fishing boats that go out lobstering. I do worry that we built at an elevation of 14 feet, and I ask myself if I forgot the part of Al Gore's speech that had to do with sea level rise. But in the summer, it amazes Laurie and me that as we drive the 11 miles south from Route 88 to our house, the temperature drops a degree for every mile. We will take the cooler temperatures as a trade-off for the risk of flooding.

Despite these differences, there are similarities between Westport and New Bedford that attracted us to this place. Chief among them is that both are authentic. Nothing phony about either place. New Bedford is a gritty, industrial, working class, diverse, working waterfront, in-your-face city. Westport is a gritty, agricultural, right-to-farm, in-your-face town. Politics is a contact sport in both places.

A good place for a new beginning.

Retiring and Readjusting

In January 2018, I retired from NOAA and from working for pay. There were many going-away parties, many kind words, and many jokes. David Abel wrote a nice front-page story about me in the *Boston Globe*. My brother was impressed.

"John, I thought you had to die to get a story like that!"

I said goodbye to colleagues at work, which was difficult because we had been through many battles together and had grown very close. I have never worked with smarter, more idealistic people. As I looked out at their mostly young faces, I felt very good for our country despite the mess that Trump was visiting upon us every day of the week. Laurie and I packed up my little apartment in Rockport in December before our Captiva vacation in Florida. When I returned in January, I stayed in the nearby Rockport Inn for the last few weeks at NOAA.

My buddy and deputy, without whom I could never have succeeded, Dan Morris, had retired a few months earlier. Harry Mears, who had been there the longest, had retired and then died before being able to enjoy his retirement, which sent a shock throughout the building. I knew that with Mike Pentony succeeding me and Kim Damon Randall succeeding Dan, GARFO would be in good hands, and the torch would be passed to a younger generation, as it should. But I miss the mission and the people every day. There is no finer governmental organization at the federal level than NOAA.

Laurie and I talked about life after my career. Laurie has worked her whole life and wasn't retiring. More than once, I heard the adage, "I married you for better or worse but not for lunch." But there is no question that my career has taken a toll. There have been way too many nights and evenings away from home. I have been focused and passionate about my work, and that has sometimes called into question where the family fits in my priorities. It was time to readjust the work-life balance.

Laurie has been committed to her work on the board of the Immigrants' Assistance Center (IAC) in the South End of New Bedford. New Bedford has always been a "gateway city." We welcome immigrants to America and help them as they transition to a new country. There is an unwritten mutual compact that immigrants come to this Gateway City to build their lives and their versions of the American Dream, and in so doing, they help build a better New Bedford. This compact has been in force from New Bedford's beginning.

The IAC, under the leadership of its dynamic director, Helena DaSilva Hughes, runs several programs to facilitate those transitions. After Trump was elected, immigrants were demonized and terrorized, and the workload of the IAC went through the roof. Laurie worked with Helena on the board and staff to handle the increased load. Laurie was on the phone and at meetings daily, working with Helena and other staff and board members to raise money, build capacity, and improve governance. In these and other ways, she works to ensure that immigrants in New Bedford know they have someone making the road to the American Dream a little easier to travel.

With her deep background in retail, Laurie also ran the Front Room store at the Shattuck Gallery in Westport. She has owned and managed stores in Washington and elsewhere. She is also an artist and has exhibited her photographs in several galleries.

While I was away, Laurie took care of the house, solving all the problems that came up. She knew all the contractors much better than I did. When I got home on a full-time basis, we discussed what our new life would be like. She would continue her commitments because they were fulfilling. I would take more responsibility around the house. I had managed to do some tasks on weekends, but now I was here all the time and could shoulder more. We were looking forward to traveling together more.

"From now on, I want to get on a plane only if you are also on it, and we are going someplace fun," I told Laurie.

We told the kids that we would take them all anywhere they could agree on as a retirement present for putting up with my absences. With five grandchildren with different school and sports schedules, that proved surprisingly difficult, but we ended up in August 2018 at Three Bars Ranch in British Columbia.

There, under the guidance of three generations of the Beckley family, we rode horses every day, did some flyfishing, shooting, river rafting, bow and arrow target practice, hiking, and all kinds of games. The food was great. The horses were good to us, and the wranglers were some of the nicest young people you will ever meet from Canada, the States, England, and Australia. We had a blast. Our entire family very rarely gets together, so to have everyone in the same place for a week with no TV and the air filled with laughter and the smell of horses was a great way to cap off a career.

Someplace fun

Laurie and I also took a cruise, beginning in Barcelona and ending in Venice. To see the works of architects and artists like Antoni Gaudi and Michelangelo up close and in person was breathtaking. I had studied architectural history and art in college and had read an entire book on the *Laocoon*. To see that piece a few feet away from me in the Vatican was simply divine. As much agony as there is in *Laocoon*, you can also find grace and eternal peace in the *Pieta*. We were so glad to have seen these works in person. How could Michelangelo find such beauty in a piece of stone?

We went to Italy, Greece, and Croatia, stopping for a while in Dubrovnik for a bus tour. Our bus climbed out of the old town and paused at a place high up for us to get out and take pictures looking down on the beautiful ancient walled city. While everyone was looking down at the view, I approached the tour guide.

"I am from the United States and used to work in the US Commerce Department for Secretary Ron Brown. Could you tell me if the location of where his plane crashed is anywhere near here?"

"Turn around and look up the hill. That is where Secretary Brown's plane crashed."

I wasn't ready for the immediacy of his response or the closeness. Fortunately, Laurie was standing nearby because I lost my composure and started to tear up. I just stood there, not able to talk or move. The kind guide quickly looked through his phone, and in a few seconds, he was showing me photographs of the stainless-steel cross his country had erected at the site as a memorial to Secretary Brown and the 34 others on the plane. The guide's quick reaction reinforced in me the impact Secretary Brown had had on the world with his policy of engagement.

Family reunion at Three Bars Ranch in British Columbia, 2018

CHAPTER 17

Causes Close to Heart and Home

Buzzards Bay Coalition

At home, there were two efforts that I immediately wanted to get back into, and Laurie was fully supportive. One was the Buzzards Bay Coalition, and the other was the schooner *Ernestina-Morrissey*.

The Buzzards Bay Coalition (BBC) formed in July 1987 to save Buzzards Bay. My mother was one of the founding members. At the time, it was clear that the major threat was the City of New Bedford and its outdated wastewater treatment plant. This single-point source of pollution made it comfortable for some suburbanites to get all self-righteous and indignant with their finger-pointing about who was to blame for the poor water quality in the bay.

The Coalition formed as a broad group of people from Westport and all the towns around the watershed to Wareham, then over the bridge onto the Cape and to the other side of the bay onto the Elizabeth Islands. It started small and grew in members and effectiveness. I chaired its board of directors for a number of years after I returned from Washington.

When I, as mayor, modernized the New Bedford sewer plant, pollution lessened, but it did not disappear. Everyone was forced to find a new enemy to focus attention on. Instead of a single-point source of pollution, we realized there were hundreds, really thousands, of non-point sources of pollution. Instead of pointing fingers at someone else, we realized the enemy was often ourselves with our polluting septic systems or our overly fertilized lawns.

We were very fortunate to have a young man from Fairhaven as our executive director. His name is Mark Rasmussen, and he grew up on the bay. Mark pushed us as a board. He is very ambitious, aggressively setting worthwhile goals for himself and the organization. If you were on the board, you had to run to keep up with Mark. He is an out-sized talent, and he would invariably mobilize the staff and board resources to achieve and surpass the goals. A visionary thinker, he not only can see the picture from 30,000 feet but can get down in the weeds and discuss technical details with scientists and engineers. And he can fund-raise like nobody's business. Once, when evaluating Mark's performance, I remember concluding that the Coalition needed to keep pace with Mark.

"We are going to have to be as aggressive and ambitious as Mark is and grow as an organization as fast as Mark wants to grow, or we will lose Mark. And that may make some board members uncomfortable, but that is our choice."

Fortunately, we have always had great board members, so we strap on our seatbelts and enjoy the ride. This is not to say the board members are passengers because they are anything but. We took our mission to "Save Buzzards Bay" very seriously and knew it had to be based on science. Under Director of Monitoring Tony Williams, we recruited a cadre of over 100 citizen scientists, who test the waters every five days from May through September. I am one of these baywatchers. Tony equips us all and trains us in how to take samples, test, and record for temperature, salinity, turbidity, and dissolved oxygen in the estuaries around the bay. He also goes out several times a year to test for nitrogen and checks the deeper waters that we volunteers can't reach with our equipment. We have been doing the Baywatchers Program for nearly three decades, making it one of the nation's longest research projects on water quality. The data acquired is analyzed at the Marine Biological Lab in Woods Hole, allowing us to assess the bay's health in all of the rivers and coves. That information helps us to form and advocate policy positions, advocated by Coalition lawyer Korrin Petersen.

One big step occurred when we discovered high nutrient loading near Hix Bridge on the East Branch of the Westport River. We traced the source to the Pimental Farm, which operated an industrial feedlot, cramming nearly 700 cattle on packed dirt right next to the river's edge. When our pleadings to the state to enforce the laws went unheeded, we debated what to do.

We had never brought a lawsuit before. We knew that if we did, especially against a Westport farm, we would make some enemies. When we talked with the Westport River Watershed Alliance, they were not interested in joining us in a lawsuit for that very reason. But the Westport Fishermen's Association, led by the late Jack Reynolds, whose members were most familiar with the costs of polluted water, told us they would be enthusiastic partners. And Jack was on our board, so he could help make the argument that sometimes you cannot persuade people. Sometimes, you have to litigate. There is an adage, "The solution to pollution is dilution." We were coming to the realization that in the case of the East Branch of the Westport River, "The solution to pollution is prosecution."

Attorney Phil Beauregard was also on our board. He secured pro bono legal counsel from Boston to bring the case against the landowner under old English "common law," treating pollution as trespassing, and against the Commonwealth of Massachusetts for failure to enforce their own laws. We won the case, with Mark Rasmussen and Jack Reynolds appearing in court for us. The feedlot was closed down, and the water quality downriver immediately improved.

The Buzzards Bay Coalition protects the watershed of Buzzards Bay and Vineyard Sound.

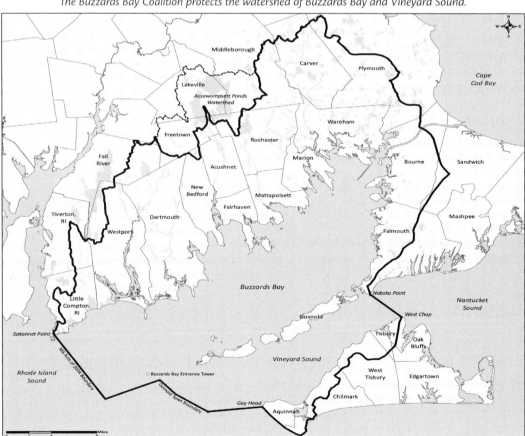

What also improved was our standing in the region. Finally, everyone knew that the Coalition meant business and was not afraid to take serious action in defense of the rivers and bay. Our membership started to climb dramatically into the thousands.

We also realized that to save the waters of the bay, we would have to save the lands in the watershed that drained into the bay. After returning from Washington, I chaired a task force of representatives of all the communities of Southeastern Massachusetts focused on preparing for the reestablishment of train service from Boston to New Bedford and Fall River. Part of the task force's work was to develop plans for Priority Development Areas and Priority Protection Areas in each of the roughly 40 communities. This part of Massachusetts is the fastest growing in the state, even without the train, and I would often describe "the race for space" between the developers and the preservationists. One-quarter of the land had already been developed. One quarter had already been protected as either parkland or with conservation restrictions of some form. Half of the region was up for grabs.

In the early 2000s, the Buzzards Bay Coalition partnered with the Trustees of Reservations on an ambitious $30 million campaign to acquire land in the watershed. It wasn't long before we realized that the two organizations had different cultures. The Trustees of Reservations were more conservative, and we were more entrepreneurial. After a short while, we had an amicable split and cut the baby in half. While we are a much smaller organization, we took half the goal and half the projects and set off to raise $15 million, about five times more than we had ever raised before.

Laurie worked on the campaign as part of the development team, and toward the end, we brought in John Vasconcellos. He came from a large New Bedford family and would rise to become our development director and later the head of the SouthCoast Community Foundation. But the center of energy was always Mark, and the campaign exceeded our goals and expectations. We had a headquarters in a restored mill building in the North End of New Bedford across from Joseph Abboud's manufacturing headquarters. There, we brought on amazing professional staff like Korrin Petersen to lead our advocacy efforts and Brendan Annett to lead the team that put together all the complex land deals. Mark has an amazing way of attracting top talent, getting them to work together as a team and keeping them for long periods. That is another sign of his leadership ability.

When I was away in Gloucester, attorney Laura Ryan Shachoy from Marion became board chair, and she and Mark recruited even more talent to the board. We thought we were moving at a fast pace, yet the pace picked up even more under Laura's leadership. She was followed as chair by Mike Angelini from Falmouth but remains a board member.

While I was chair, we decided to open a small office in Woods Hole. It was a remote location and a bit of a logistical headache, but we thought it might be worthwhile to have a presence on the Cape side of the bay. Mark brought the issue to the board as a question of whether we should do it, but as with most questions Mark posed, he had done his homework, and behind the question was a very good idea. The issue really wasn't a question at all. It was just nice that he posed it that way, making us think we were making a decision! After we had operated in Woods Hole for several years, the Wheeler family donated a critical property to us, complete with a house. There was also an endowment. It was a multi-million-dollar gift, which turned out to be a pretty good return on the investment that sprang from Mark's question.

The chairs between Laura and myself were John Ross and Tom Gidwitz. During their terms, the Coalition ran another capital campaign that acquired more land and built a new headquarters. We decided to move into an old bar in New Bedford's waterfront historic district, two buildings away from where I had started work in 1974 on Front Street. This historic building had every environmental technology possible, from a green roof to waterless urinals.

The capital campaign raised more than $50 million. Besides the Wheeler property in Woods Hole, we also built, thanks in large part to board member David Croll, a lab and field station in Marion, equidistant between our headquarters and our Woods Hole property. We store our scientific equipment and the boats used in the summer at the field station.

We also built an educational program facility in Onset Village in Wareham, which could serve the significant minority population there and the region as a whole. Unfortunately, just as we completed the facility, the COVID-19 pandemic shut down the world, so practically all the programming we had planned, including our grand opening, got deferred. As we come out of the pandemic, programs and events continue to be added. While there were many land deals as part of this $50 million campaign, one of the biggest and most exciting was the opportunity to acquire, and thereby save, roughly half the island of Cuttyhunk.

The Coalition works simultaneously on so many projects that it is very hard to track them all. Land acquisition, often in partnership with various local land trusts but just as often Coalition-led, remains a priority. Working with towns to improve wastewater systems is another priority and is as varied and technically complex as the different situations in each town or combinations of towns. The Coalition supports local health boards and conservation commissions as they enforce existing laws and regulations or create new ones. Other focuses are restoring natural resources through dam removals, protecting salt marshes, or maintaining our considerable protected spaces. Public access and education are important because we know that if people understand the natural environment where they live, they will protect it. As the environmentalist Baba Dioum said in 1968, "In the end, we will conserve only what we love; we will love only what we understand, and we will understand only what we are taught." And finally, we know everything we do needs to be

Board and staff of the Coalition at new headquarters in the Waterfront Historic District

based on science, so that remains our foundation. As the Coalition's work grows, so does its reputation and influence. Now people on Martha's Vineyard ask us for help, and our work extends all the way to Sakonnet Point in Little Compton, Rhode Island. Even as we stretch the boundaries of Buzzards Bay, we try to remain a local group because that is what gives us credibility. Buzzards Bay faces several serious threats ranging from climate change to outdated wastewater systems to occasional oil spills. But for the many people who love the bay, the Buzzards Bay Coalition is the greatest hope for a bay that can support abundant life in all forms.

Lovely *Ernestina*

The other effort I wanted to get back to was the *Ernestina-Morrissey*. Built as the *Effie M. Morrissey* by the James and Tarr shipyard in Essex, Massachusetts in 1894, the ship had a distinguished career as a Gloucester Grand Banks fishing schooner under Captain William Morrissey, who named it after his daughter Effie. On the third trip, William's son (and Effie's brother) Clayton took over at age 19 and went on to fame as a Gloucester schooner man. Many think that Clayton served as the model for the iconic Gloucester statue of the Fishermen's Memorial's man at the wheel. As one of the last Gloucester fishing schooners, the *Ernestina-Morrissey* is historically significant and worth saving.

That is just the beginning of a remarkable story. The schooner fished out of Digby, Nova Scotia, and then worked as a coal freighter out of Brigus, Newfoundland, for a brief time when owned by Harold Bartlett. In 1926, he sold the schooner for $6,000 to his nephew, famed Arctic explorer Captain Bob Bartlett. Captain Bob sailed her on summer voyages to the Arctic for almost 20 years. He would take young boys with him, who became known as "Bartlett Boys," in an early example of ocean experiential education. Their parents paid a very good "tuition" for this experience. They

Schooner Effie M. Morrissey *at berth in Gloucester Harbor during her fishing career*

Schooner Ernestina *sailed as a packet ship in Cabo Verde, bringing people and supplies to and from New England.*

would bring back polar bears and wildlife for the Smithsonian, the Bronx Zoo, and other institutions. Captain Bob was known by many for his appearances on newsreels and features in the pages of the *National Geographic*. His "Little *Morrissey*" was a key to his story.

During World War II, the *Morrissey*, now leased by the government and jointly commanded by Alexander Forbes and Captain Bartlett, charted the west coast of Greenland for locations for air supply bases and then charted the supply route to Murmansk, Russia. The schooner sailed north of 80 degrees north latitude–within 600 miles of the North Pole. If this had been all that the schooner had done, the *Morrissey* would be an internationally significant vessel, undoubtedly worth saving, but the schooner had even more stories to tell.

After the war, some ex-Navy men bought the schooner and re-outfitted it as a pleasure yacht. They painted her white and set sail for the Pacific. They got as far as Bermuda, changed their minds, and returned to New York. There the ship caught fire, sank to the bottom, and eventually was raised and towed to Rowayton, Connecticut. That could have been the last port of call except for a Cape Verdean, Captain Henrique Mendes, whose business was to buy old fishing schooners and squeeze a few more years out of them to bring people and cargo from Cabo Verde to America. The schooners would be cast aside when they could no longer make the trip. He bought the *Morrissey* and made enough repairs to get her sailing again.

From 1948 to 1965, he brought immigrants and supplies under sail from Cabo Verde to America. It didn't take long for a flaw to appear in his business plan. He fell in love with this particular schooner as everyone involved before and since has done. After a year or so, he changed the name to *Ernestina* in honor of his daughter. The *Ernestina* was part of a fleet of Cape Verdean-owned packet ships, which meant that unlike most immigrant groups, Cape Verdeans had control of their own means of passage to the United States.

Gloucester fishing schooner, sailing freighter, Arctic exploration vessel, US Naval Supply Vessel, the last sailing vessel to bring immigrants voluntarily to America—if you can find a more important sailing vessel that isn't associated with some naval battle, then let's hear it. Yes, this is a big story.

Oh, I wish I knew this in 1969 when, by happenstance, we tied *Adele* to the dock right behind the *Ernestina*. We had stopped in Mindelo, Sao Vicente in Cabo Verde on our way back across the Atlantic. While our skipper, Bunny Burnes, was off trying to fix our refrigeration, I had time to introduce myself to the man on board the *Ernestina*. I went aboard and overcame the language barrier to introduce myself and tell the captain, Alberto Lopes, that I was from New Bedford, at which point his eyes lit up. He showed me around. I could tell the schooner was in bad shape. Instead of rising up at the bow and stern, both ends sagged off. It's called "hogged" when a vessel can no longer hold the lines she was built to because the strength of the wood has finally given up

The *Ernestina* wasn't even allowed to make trips to other islands, let alone to other countries. It looked like she would die, tied up to that dock. I took a few pictures and didn't think much because I didn't know her history then. Or how much I would become involved with her later.

The next time I encountered the *Ernestina*, I was chairman of New Bedford's Bicentennial Commission in 1975. A group from Philadelphia approached me saying they wanted to restore the *Effie M. Morrissey*, which was still located in Cabo Verde. They were former Bartlett Boys, and they were focused on that segment of her history. They seemed uninterested in the Cape Verdean history but wanted my backing to persuade the Cape Verdean community in New Bedford to help them financially. I wished them luck.

A Gift from Cabo Verde, Saving the *Ernestina*, Sailing to the Statue of Liberty

Later though, when Cabo Verde achieved its independence in 1975, the country decided it would rebuild the *Ernestina* and make the schooner a gift to the people of America. This was a monumental effort as no trees grow in that country, which is an extension of the Sahara Desert and was in the midst of a prolonged drought. With some support from American friends, the government of Cabo Verde made an extraordinary investment over several years in rebuilding the *Ernestina*. It is hard to imagine the magnitude of their gift, but it is estimated to be the equivalent of one day's income for every single person living in Cabo Verde at that time. Extraordinary.

In 1982, a Cape Verdean American crew under the command of Captain Marcos Lopes sailed the restored schooner with sand ballast, no engine, and no electronic navigation, but with pigs and plenty of chickens to New England. They presented the schooner as a gift to the Commonwealth of Massachusetts, requesting that the *Ernestina* be used for educational purposes.

Once Massachusetts received this gift, it did what the state has periodically done—let the *Ernestina* sit and deteriorate. This went on for a year with basically no one in charge. Schooner supporters expressed concern, but had no authority over a state vessel.

A crowd greets Ernestina *at her homecoming in New Bedford, August 24, 1982.*

Captain Dan

Captain Daniel D. Moreland heard about the schooner's plight and wanted to help. He knew about the ship from his father's time in Africa. Captain Moreland was only 29 years old but had much to offer. An experienced schooner man, he was the perfect person to follow in the footsteps of Captains Morrissey, Bartlett, and Mendes. Dan had already sailed around the world once on the brigantine *Romance,* skippered the *Pride of Baltimore,* and spent four years as bosun on the Danish training ship *Danmark.* He had experience working in wooden shipyards and held the rarest license issued to Merchant Marine officers today: Master of Steam, Motor, or Auxiliary Sail, Vessels of Any Gross Tons upon Oceans.

The schooner supporters met with Dan and picked his brains for advice on the ship. He visited the schooner in Gloucester and saw a vessel wasting away. No one wanted to take on the responsibility of being her captain. The ship was in such bad shape that most thought she should be scuttled.

My good friend Mardee Xifaras was working for Governor Michael Dukakis at the time. When she heard about the problems, she set out to fix things as she often did. She met with Dan in her home. Dan described Mardee as a "smart, persuasive lady." She told him he was to do anything "that was not completely nuts. A little nuts was all right." The schooner's home port moved to New Bedford, and the state appointed Dan as captain of the *Ernestina,* perhaps saving the ship from ending up at the bottom of the ocean or in a scrapyard.

Laurie and I became very good friends with Captain Dan as he went about his work in New Bedford. The funding for upkeep and restoration came in fits and starts, so the work took time but slowly moved forward. Dan used the time to conduct extensive oral and forensic research, getting to know the schooner, the community, and the history. He wanted to understand how everything fit together. Dan paid attention to detail. He drew the logo that is still used today on the letterhead. He recruited and trained crew and shipbuilders. He planned and implemented an operating plan. Young as he was, Dan could train young crew in everything: how to splice wire, how to navigate by the stars, how to scarf a wooden joint, and how to drive a trunnel.

Laurie worked with Dan some in the office, and I provided Dan support when I was at WHALE and later when I was mayor. Laurie got her mom, Anne Dunbar, to donate funds in

Captain Dan Moreland

388

honor of her late husband, Chic, to pay for new masts. After Dan had the *Ernestina* restored and operating, I went on a few trips with him.

For the Centennial of the Statue of Liberty in 1986, Laurie, Lexie, Toby, Matt, and I joined Captain Dan and the crew. We sailed from New Bedford to South Street Seaport in lower Manhattan. As we approached the dock, the East River was pushing us at close to seven knots, making docking very tricky. The *Ernestina* is a heavy boat, and to my knowledge, Dan had not taken any boat into this particular dock before. We were looking at an irresistible force and an immovable object. But Dan gauged it perfectly and brought the schooner alongside so smoothly that if the bumpers were covered in Kleenex, they would not have torn.

We arrived on Friday, and the Parade of Sail was Sunday. On Saturday, Dan thought it would be good to take everyone, including guests from New York, for a sail. We headed south around the tip of Manhattan, paid our respects to Lady Liberty, and headed north up the Hudson. It was a spectacular day with a brisk wind, and the views of New York and the Jersey shore were astonishing. After a few hours, we tacked and started close-hauled southerly back around. The afternoon breeze picked up, and the Hudson's current was pushing us into it. We were heeling over, and the *Ernestina* was really charging along with a "bone in her teeth," meaning there was a good-sized wave off her lee bow. It was an exciting ride that got more exciting when we heard a loud "CRACK," and all eyes looked aloft.

We saw the main gaff snap in half. The gaff is about a ten-inch diameter piece of wood that projects from the mast and holds up the largest sail that flies on the tallest and aft-most mast. The gaff was flopping around in the strong wind and threatening to rip the sail or worse. Dan immediately ordered the crew to lower the mainsail and moved all guests forward, so the broken gaff couldn't hit them as it came down. Once the gaff was down and secured, Dan instructed the crew to detach the sail and remove all fittings from it and the jaws that help attach the gaff to the mast. By the time we reached the dock, we had the broken gaff removed from the sail and all its hardware off. It was now just two pieces of wood. Our challenge was to replace it with one piece of wood.

So, off we all went looking around South Street Seaport. After about 30 minutes, one in our intrepid band returned to Dan smiling. We went over to look at the discovery. Lying in the dirt under a big pile of staging was what looked like an old forgotten mast. Dan got out a tape and measured. The old mast was big enough. It would even have to be cut down some. He got out his pocketknife and probed the wood in several places. Solid as rock.

"This piece of wood does not look very happy right here," said Captain Dan. "I think this old mast would prefer to be sailing again, and I think we are the ones to make her dreams come true."

With that, we moved all the staging and carted the mast on our many shoulders to the *Ernestina*. Out came the saws and drills, and in three hours, we had a new gaff. About this time, Peter Neill, the president of South Street Seaport, came toward us full tilt with smoke coming out of his ears.

"What do you think you are doing, taking property of South Street without permission?" he bellowed.

"It didn't look like you were using it, and we need a gaff for the Parade of Sail tomorrow," Dan calmly told him.

Peter was not mollified until many years later, but there was no getting around the fact that his discarded mast was now our gaff and would sail in the parade. I think if the mast had feelings, it would have rejoiced at being bailed out of jail.

On Sunday, we again headed south. The parade would be many rows of Class A boats with smaller boats on each side. Class A boats are the big square-rigged ships that draw all the attention.

Celebrating the Centennial of the Statue of Liberty, July 1986

The US Coast Guard training ship *Eagle* would lead the parade. We would be in the third row, flanking Denmark's *Danmark*. We were there because of Dan's relationship to that ship. But it was also fitting to be near the front of this very long parade as we were the only vessel in the parade that had actually brought immigrants to America, which was, after all, what we were celebrating.

That voyage and the pictures of the *Ernestina-Morrissey* with the Statue of Liberty in the background were important on many levels. We showed that the *Ernestina* could represent New Bedford on the national stage. And we showed the people of Cabo Verde that we were honoring their gift.

I got a chance the following year, in 1987, to personally express that when Laurie and I visited many of our sister cities. It was a whirlwind trip to Fayal in the Azores and several other cities, including Funchal in Madeira and Mindelo on the island of Sao Vicente. In Cabo Verde (as well as Lisbon), we met with government officials, got to know family members of New Bedford citizens, visited cultural institutions, and did what we could to strengthen the already strong ties that New Bedford's whaleships had established.

In Sao Vicente one evening, we listened to people sing about their beloved *Ernestina*. They sang about how they were sad they could not see her. They sang about how they longed for her to return. As we listened to people talk to us about the *Ernestina* and about relatives in New Bedford, Laurie and I appreciated how strong the bonds are between the immigrants in New Bedford and their homelands. The songs were of longing, which in Portuguese translates as "Saudade." One of New Bedford's branch libraries is named Casa de Saudade. It is located in the same building as the Immigrants Assistance Center, the building where Laurie has spent so much time. I knew that night that if we were ever to sail the *Ernestina* back to Cabo Verde, the nation would explode with jubilation.

After our time in Mindelo, we joined our good friend Ambassador Vern Penner in Praia, the capital of the island of Santiago. I also met with Aristides Pereira, the first president of the independent nation of Cabo Verde. Called Cape Verde in the past, the country has recently adopted the name, Cabo Verde. I was in awe of President Pereira.

"I never got to meet George Washington or Thomas Jefferson, the men who helped make my country independent. It is an honor to meet you, sir, and congratulate you on bringing independence to your country in 1975. In my city of New Bedford, which has about 15,000 people who trace their origins to these islands, we celebrate our Independence Day, which is July 4, as a part of our Cape Verdean Independence Day celebration on July 5, and we have a *huge* parade in honor of your country's independence. It is miles long!"

I described to him how our city cherished its ties to Cabo Verde.

"The relationship between America and Africa is characterized by ignorance and exploitation. The relationship between New Bedford and Cape Verde, which goes back over 100 years, is characterized by family ties, deep understanding, and mutual benefit. That relationship is symbolized by the extraordinary gift your country made to our people when you sent *Ernestina* to our shores."

I told him about the thrill of sailing the *Ernestina* into New York Harbor.

"President Pereira, I wish you could have been aboard her as we sailed by our Statue of Liberty last year, which is our nation's symbol welcoming all immigrants to America. You would have been so proud. We will do our best to see that your gift is well taken care of and continues to represent the bond between our two countries."

The Campaign Schooner

In 1988, Michael Dukakis was running for president. He was also head of the National Governors' Association, which was having its annual summer meeting in Travers City, Michigan. As a close aide and friend to Dukakis, Mardee Xifaras, as usual, was in the thick of everything and heavily involved in his campaign.

Mardee was such a champion of the *Ernestina* that in the governor's office, the schooner was nicknamed "Mardee's boat." When the call came for Dan to sail the *Ernestina* to Travers City, Michigan, for the governors' conference, you didn't need to be a math whiz to put 2 and 2 together to figure out where that idea had come from. There would be a budget for the trip, and Dan understood that in operating tall ships, it is about "chasing the money." The *Ernestina* sailed up around Nova Scotia and the Gaspe, into the St. Lawrence River, and through the Great Lakes to Travers City. During the stay, 3,000 people boarded the ship every single day. The *Ernestina* was a hit in the heartland. When Dan returned, he told me, "John, it would have been easier to sail to Cape Verde."

Dan Moreland stepped forward to captain the schooner when no one else would. He bailed the state out and returned the Cape Verdean gift to a condition that did Massachusetts proud. He had done the impossible. He restored the *Ernestina* and won the highest award possible from the National Trust for Historic Preservation for the quality of his work. He developed an operating program of a little less than a million dollars a year that worked, where revenues supported expenses. He made the *Ernestina* a going concern. Dan worked with community help from members of the local

Ernestina-Morrissey *under full sail in the Mayor's Cup Race off the Gloucester coast in September 2002*

Cape Verdean community, including Robert Alves, Gene Monteiro, Joli Gonsalves, Tom Lopes, Marcie Haddocks, Carl Brown, and Tommy Grace. He reached out to the various constituencies linked to the *Ernestina-Morrissey* and connected to them.

He sailed the schooner back to Brigus, Newfoundland, with a largely Cape Verdean crew and the name *Ernestina* on the stern. The schooner tied up to the same dock Captain Bartlett had tied up to years before. More than 3,000 people came to see the ship. That might not seem remarkable until you realize only 700 people live in Brigus. The crew took every person in Brigus, Captain Bob Bartlett's hometown, out sailing. Some went two or three times. When the ship first sailed in, the people of Brigus called the schooner the "Old *Morrissey*." By the time the schooner left, people had started calling her *Ernestina*.

Disgrace of State

Instead of giving Dan a medal for putting over ten years of his young life into this project, the state sent a pack of stickler accountants down to see if he had done all the work according to state accounting standards. When they found he hadn't followed every rule, they ran him out of town in one of the greatest injustices associated with this schooner. Dan had not misspent any funds. He just had not accounted for them the way state accountants do. It still makes me angry. Dan is a captain and a ship restorer. The state gave Dan almost no help; they just got in his way. Then, they threw him under the bus.

Heartbroken and bitter, Dan left and went on with his life. He found an old freighter in Norway and transformed her into a handsome sailing bark called the *Picton Castle*, which he sails out of the World Heritage Site port of Lunenburg, Nova Scotia. He has completed seven circumnavigations on the bark, more than any other captain has done on one sailing ship in the history of sail. Remarkable!

There have been many able seamen who have skippered the *Ernestina-Morrissey*, Dan stands alongside those iconic captains who have poured their hearts and souls into the schooner: Captains Clayton Morrissey, Bob Bartlett, Henrique Mendes, and Dan Moreland.

After Dan left, the *Ernestina* continued its ups and downs with the state. Sometimes, the commonwealth paid attention to the schooner and adequately funded it. Sometimes, it didn't. On one occasion, the ship sprang a bad leak near Greenport on the north fork of Long Island and almost sank. Maintenance was sporadic. Eventually, the schooner lost her Coast Guard certification to carry passengers and lay tied to the dock in New Bedford.

Despite the state's failure to always care for the *Ernestina* properly, the ship has had some good captains and some good experiences. The Schooner *Ernestina-Morrissey* Association was formed to support her. As with old buildings, you have to win the battle every day. You can only lose it once.

I remember a trip in 1997 off Marblehead for the annual turnaround of the *USS Constitution*. The harbor was, of course, very crowded that summer day, with many small boats out to see "Old Ironsides" make its yearly voyage. Jeff Stone was the *Ernestina's* captain at the time, and he was steering our 135-foot schooner carefully through the spectator fleet, so those aboard could take it all in. Because the *Ernestina* is a large, heavy vessel, she does not turn on a dime.

Some novice brought his 25-foot sailboat right under our bow and then decided to turn sharply back in front of us, thinking, I guess, that we could just slam on the brakes or quickly change course. Our bowsprit hit his rig and broke his mast in two. As he fled the scene, he yelled back at us, "You big black bully boat." On board at the time was Jim Bean, a chantey man. One of my favorite chanteys came out of that encounter, "Lovely Ernestina."

Over the years, as a supporter of the schooner, I learned a few things about old ships. Laurie and I had gotten to know Waldo Howland, who created the Concordia yawl sailboat class. We saw Waldo every winter in Captiva and were very good friends. Waldo had overseen restoring the whaleship *Charles W. Morgan* when Mystic Seaport decided to raise her out of her bed in the sand and keep her in sailing condition, a major change in philosophy. Waldo offered me some sage advice one day as we were walking out of the New Bedford Whaling Museum down Centre Street.

"John, you either put a ship in a little bit better condition today than she was in yesterday, or she will put herself in a little bit worse."

Aside from the fact that this philosophy could be said about many things, including my own body(!), it is very wise when it comes to boats. If you follow it to a conclusion, it means you need to operate a vessel all the time because if you are operating a vessel, then you have crew constantly chipping and painting, regularly oiling machinery, and continually fighting the intrusion of water and the resulting mold. And so on. That approach is manageable and incremental; nothing gets out of hand because maintenance is ongoing.

Another thing I learned is that a vessel like the *Ernestina* makes news entering or leaving a port. But as soon as the schooner is tied to a dock for three days, the ship becomes part of the furniture and becomes invisible. Motion is essential to keep the schooner in the people's eye. And, of course, to keep the *Ernestina* educating.

A Band of Angels

When I returned from Washington and worked at SEA in Woods Hole, I reconnected with the *Ernestina*. I saw how far the ship had deteriorated. Then, I got lucky. And the *Ernestina* got lucky. I was in Philadelphia for a few days recruiting students, teaching a class at University of Pennsylvania on climate change and meeting with some of our trustees and overseers. One of them, Peter Gibbons-Neff, was a good friend. I was staying with him and his wife, Debbie. An excellent sailor, Peter had invited me to race with him on Chesapeake Bay. Peter and Debbie suggested I meet with Gerry Lenfest to get him interested in SEA, and they made an introduction. Gerry

Captain Moreland returns Ernestina *to port in New Bedford.*

393

was a lawyer who had packaged a group of small cable TV stations and sold them to Comcast for $7 billion. He had set up the Lenfest Foundation to fund ocean research. Peter and Debbie said he loved sailing and all things Philadelphia.

Gerry and I hit it off as soon as I walked into his office in Conshohocken, just north of Philadelphia. He had big bushy eyebrows, a broad smile, and an inquisitive mind, interested in all kinds of things—climate change, education, sailing. Gerry's office had several pieces by the famous American woodworker and furniture maker George Nakashima. Laurie and I had one chair by this artist, considered a father of the American craft movement in the 20th century. We talked about Nakashima and several other topics, and an hour and a half flew by. As I was preparing to leave, Gerry said he had a question.

Gerry Lenfest at Bristol Marine with Ernestina-Morrissey *under restoration in background*

"Is the *Morrissey* still in New Bedford?"

"Why yes, Gerry, she is. Why do you ask?"

"Well, when I was 12 years old, Captain Bob Bartlett asked me to go sailing with him to the Arctic."

I tried to catch my jaw before it hit the floor. I don't remember if I was successful. What are the chances?

"Did you go, Gerry?"

"No, the war got in the way. And then there weren't any more opportunities."

Every year after that on my trips to Philadelphia, I would stop by to see Gerry, and we would continue our conversations. He made modest contributions to SEA.

One summer, Gerry brought his boat, *Beau Geste*, to Woods Hole, and I helped him get a space at WHOI's dock. He and Marguerite invited Laurie and me for drinks and dinner with his captain, Andy Tyska. We had cocktails and a delicious dinner. We were well into stingers as it neared midnight. I asked Gerry if he would make a major gift to SEA. I thought the timing was perfect. He didn't.

"No."

"Gerry, why not? You care about the ocean. You care about teaching young people. You care about climate change. We have a great relationship."

"True on all counts. Just not my thing."

What I loved about Gerry was that he was so down-to-earth and plain-spoken. He never put on airs. He never thought making a lot of money made him better than anyone else. He was a straight shooter and never pulled any punches.

"OK, Gerry. I understand. I appreciate you hearing me out, and I really appreciate the amazing evening Laurie and I have spent with you and Marguerite. I hope it is still OK if when I'm in Philadelphia I might still stop by for a visit."

"Oh yes, that would be fine, I look forward to those."

The following year when I went down, I figured I would press my luck on SEA's behalf again.

"Look, John, I'll give SEA $150,000 if you promise never to ask me for another dime."

I thought a bit and smiled.

"OK, Gerry, that is very generous, and I promise not to ask you for another dime—for SEA."

Gerry wanted an update on the *Ernestina.*

"So, John, what is it going to take to get the *Morrissey* fixed up?"

Gerry knew the ship was now called the *Ernestina,* but his association was through Captain Bartlett, so to him, his beloved schooner was always going to be the "Little *Morrissey.*"

"Gerry, I think what needs to happen is for it to be transferred from the Department of Conservation and Recreation to the Massachusetts Maritime Academy. DCR has more mission than resources, and they don't really know how to take care of a historic ship. When a problem occurs, to them, she is a pain in the ass. Mass Maritime uses ships for teaching purposes. They know ships. If there is a problem, they look at it as a teaching opportunity. A transfer turns everything 180 degrees in the right direction."

As a trustee of Massachusetts Maritime, I anticipated there would be resistance. And I told him that.

"What's that going to take, John?"

"The marine department sees her as a cost center. I think she is going to have to come with a dowry for them to be interested."

"How much?"

"Jeez, I don't know, Gerry! People are going to have to spend some time figuring that out. If I had to take a wild stab at it, I would guess somewhere in the neighborhood of $10 million, but that is a total shot in the dark."

Gerry offered the schooner a lifeline.

"OK, John. I want you to reach out to Mass Maritime and tell them someone is interested in providing funds to facilitate such a transfer. Don't tell them it is me. Just somebody serious. See if you can get a figure from them. If you can, then we should meet with them."

"OK, Gerry, I'll get to work."

Bristol Marine crew carefully dismantles Ernestina-Morrissey's *hull.*

Caulking the seams using traditional methods and materials　　　　　*The finished product glistens.*

With that, Gerry Lenfest launched his efforts to bring the *Ernestina-Morrissey* to Mass Maritime.

These efforts took many years and were quite involved. The transfer required so many meetings that everybody's patience was sorely tested. But we kept making progress because the *Ernestina-Morrissey* had such loyal supporters. Chief among them were Mary Anne McQuillan and Julius Britto of the Schooner *Ernestina-Morrissey* Association (SEMA).

Mary Anne and Julius led a band of volunteers that never gave up. Julius was the first chairman of the Schooner *Ernestina* Commission, having been appointed in 1982 by Governor Michael Dukakis to receive the gift. The group is not a fundraising powerhouse like the Whaling Museum or the Buzzards Bay Coalition, but its members are persistent. They keep plugging along, doing whatever is necessary. That might be organizing workdays. Or it might be gathering archival documents and making sure they are protected. Or it might be generating interest in the schooner by getting magazine or book writers involved in the schooner's story. Or it might be raising money to buy sails, masts, or whatever else is needed. Or it might be applying constant pressure on the various branches of state government to take care of the official ship of the commonwealth. There are several people about whom you can say the schooner would not be here were it not for them. You certainly must put Mary Anne and Julius near the top of that list.

Another of the *Ernestina*'s angels is Bob Hildreth. A successful investor with interests in South America, he has a passion for educational advancement for those who get left out of the mainstream. He has a tiny office across the street from Trinity Church in Boston. Like Gerry, he is a down-to-earth guy with a twinkle in his eye. Like Gerry, he fell hard for this little schooner. And we are lucky he did. While I have never been a businessman—outside of a minor episode with Laurie, Scott Lang, and a few others running an ice cream store after I lost my first mayor's race—when I got to know Bob and Gerry, I saw that they didn't shy away from a few setbacks. They were determined, goal-oriented, and focused on success. Neither one was going to be deterred. Having both on the side of the *Ernestina-Morrissey* was a formidable combination.

I approached Mass Maritime first through Admiral Rick Gurnon, and then, when he retired, I worked with Admiral Fran MacDonald. By the time things got serious, I was no longer a trustee, but I knew the people there, and we had a basis of trust. The academy was willing to accept the schooner if the ship was restored to Coast Guard specifications and their budget was increased enough to cover operating costs.

Simultaneously, we talked with the Department of Conservation and Recreation (DCR). They would oversee the restoration and hand the finished product over to MMA. DCR Commissioner Leo Roy, whose ancestor by marriage, Alexander Forbes, had been the official captain of the *Morrissey* during World War II, thought the transfer was a good plan. He realized his department's limitations in caring properly for the ship.

We talked with our delegation in the state Senate and the House of Representatives. State Senator Mark Montigny has always been a strong supporter of the *Ernestina* and has managed to help the schooner get funding on several occasions. Mark was a neighbor when Laurie and I lived in New Bedford and is a close friend. Mark delivers, whether it is funding or needed legislation. Tony Cabral, also a New Bedford neighbor and friend, worked to support the effort in the House.

We worked with the governor's office, first with Deval Patrick and then with Charlie Baker. While I was close to Deval Patrick, I didn't know Baker, and we are of different parties. When it came time to get Governor Baker's support for legislation transferring responsibility for the *Ernestina-Morrissey* from DCR to MMA and approving a $500,000 increase in MMA's budget, we set up a meeting with Governor Baker, the secretaries of Education and Environment, Leo Roy and Fran MacDonald, as well as Bob Hildreth and myself. Rick Lopes, an excellent Cape Verdean filmmaker, had been working on a feature-length documentary on the project funded by Gerry. He put together a seven-minute video summarizing the project. We began the meeting with that. I was the narrator. Governor Baker instantly saw what we were trying to do. He asked some good questions for clarification and needed almost no persuasion.

"I'll put $500,000 in House 1 (the governor's budget bill). This project is going to be successful, and the legislature likes success, so they will support it. I don't see a problem."

Boothbay Harbor Shipyard had done the restoration work's first phase for about $6 million. The commonwealth had put up $2.5 million. Gerry and Bob matched that with their donations, and the Schooner *Ernestina-Morrissey* Association had promised to raise another $1 million, which for them was like climbing Mount Everest.

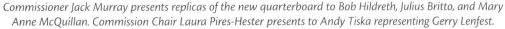

Commissioner Jack Murray presents replicas of the new quarterboard to Bob Hildreth, Julius Britto, and Mary Anne McQuillan. Commission Chair Laura Pires-Hester presents to Andy Tiska representing Gerry Lenfest.

Halfway through the work, the shipyard faced financial troubles and was poised to sell out to a condominium developer. Again, Gerry stepped in to save the day, buying the shipyard and putting Andy Tyska in charge. Gerry already owned a boatyard in Rhode Island and one in Massachusetts, both of which Andy ran for him. Andy was not just Gerry's boat captain. Andy was a naval architect and, I sensed, someone in whom Gerry saw a little of himself at a younger age.

Harold Burnham was the supervising restoration architect. His family had been building schooners like the *Morrissey* for seven generations out of their small yard on the Essex River. Wendy Pearl of the Department of Conservation and Recreation oversaw the work.

Captain Dan Moreland never lost sight of the *Ernestina*. During this time, he was out of the country, but he still knew what was going on and still cared about the schooner he had restored more than 30 years earlier. He would email me and call periodically with suggestions and concerns.

The restoration was "aggressive" as there was almost no original wood and few original parts. That is what happens with a working ship. Pieces get replaced one at a time, over time. But the *Ernestina-Morrissey* remains, having been lovingly rebuilt to the highest standard.

When Phase One was coming to an end, on February 27, 2018, Gerry wrote an email to Andy offering to fund the completion of the restoration by the shipyard. This was conditioned on the maritime academy operating the vessel as a school training ship in its educational curriculum, with the state providing funding for that purpose. He also required that MMA work with New Bedford schools and those in other areas so children could learn seamanship and the history of the vessel's ties to Cabo Verde and the Captain Morrissey years.

These conditions were agreed to, and the restoration of the ship was completed in 2023. Mass Maritime now uses the ship for education programming.

As I was getting ready to retire from NOAA in the summer of 2017, I attended a meeting of the Mid-Atlantic Fishery Council in Philadelphia. Gerry invited me to dinner at his apartment in Rittenhouse Square. I arrived and found Gerry, Marguerite, and their granddaughter, Olivia,

Julius Britto and Bob Hildreth hold christening waters collected from ports visited by Ernestina-Morrissey.

who was about to go to college. Gerry was now using a walker to get around, but his smile was the same. Andy had shipped down some mussels from Maine, and Gerry was boiling them up with linguine. Before dinner, Gerry and I sat at a small table in the living room overlooking the square.

"John, Andy tells me you are going to retire at the end of the year."

I nodded.

"Any plans?"

I told him I wanted to spend more time with Laurie and work more on the *Ernestina-Morrissey* and the Buzzards Bay Coalition. And I wanted to get on a plane only if Laurie was with me.

"Those are good plans, John. How would you like to work for me? That way, it would be a little easier for you to spend time on the *Morrissey*."

"Gerry, first of all, thank you so much for the offer. That means so much coming from you. But what retirement means to me is that when I get up in the morning, I don't have to think about who I am working for. And I actually think I will be more effective if I am *not* working for you. I know I am going to be asking people for money for the *Ernestina-Morrissey* or to support the schooner in other ways. I don't want anybody thinking I am doing that for any reason other than that I believe in the vessel."

"Are you sure I can't change your mind?"

At this point, Marguerite piped in.

"Gerry, John wants to be retired. Can't you understand that!"

I thanked Marguerite under my breath. Gerry agreed to move on.

"You are an honorable man, John. Let's go have dinner."

Then, he winked.

"But if you ever need anything, you call."

Gerry died on August 5, 2018, before we could finish the project and give him a chance to sail on the schooner he so lovingly helped save. *Gerry, I wish I could call you and say, "What I need, Gerry, is for you not to die so that you could see what you made possible."*

Ernestina-Morrissey *returns to New Bedford, November 29, 2022.*

The *New Bedford Light*

It didn't take long into my retirement for two projects to turn into more.

When I retired and returned home, my former New Bedford neighbor Ken Hartnett called. Ken had been the editor of the *Standard-Times* and was an old-school reporter. He had worked for the Associated Press in Wisconsin, covering the great football coach Vince Lombardi during the years that the Green Bay Packers dominated football. He had worked at the *Boston Phoenix* and the *Boston Globe* and had covered Mayor Kevin White. He is Irish Catholic and has become a great friend.

Our conversations usually started as we saw each other on the sidewalk, and he would yell over, "Hey, John, what's going on?" like any good reporter. From there, the conversation meandered to neighborhood news or events. I never thought it possible that an Irishman and a person of English descent could get along so well, but we do.

Ken talked to me about the sorry state of the local newspaper. And a sorry state it is. I was tempted to chalk this up as a former editor complaining about the paper going downhill after he had left. But the decline was evident. When I was mayor, the *Standard-Times* had two or three reporters covering City Hall alone and dozens of others to cover important beats such as education, health, police, courts, schools, business, and the waterfront. The newspaper also had reporters assigned to nearby towns. They had a political cartoonist and so many great photographers. The paper took thoughtful editorial positions on issues important to the region, and it was a *force* that mattered.

Now the newspaper is one among hundreds in a large chain that cares not a whit about New Bedford. Three or four reporters are spread thin and cannot cover much. They have one excellent photojournalist, Peter Pereira, whose photographs capture your attention on page one. His photos also appear in the *New York Times*, *National Geographic*, and other national and international

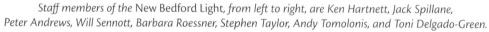

Staff members of the New Bedford Light, *from left to right, are Ken Hartnett, Jack Spillane, Peter Andrews, Will Sennott, Barbara Roessner, Stephen Taylor, Andy Tomolonis, and Toni Delgado-Green.*

media. He is bigger than the *Standard-Times*. Fortunately, he loves our city and continues to turn his lens on New Bedford and the region.

Ken described this "ghost" newspaper and how we would inevitably become a city without a paper. He pointed out that without journalists, there is no accountability. There is no democracy. He told me we could not let that happen. We needed to do something. I enlisted on the spot. One by one, we grew our little band of individuals committed to community journalism, and the *New Bedford Light* was created. We recruited a diverse group of community activists, some with backgrounds in journalism, law, non-profit governance, education, and politics. No one said we were barking up the wrong tree.

We received encouragement from the SouthCoast Community Foundation and the GroundTruth Project. We secured major financial support at the outset from Irwin and Joan Jacobs and then Mary and Jim Ottaway. The Crapo Foundation stepped up with a major grant at the onset. We exceeded our fund-raising targets for the first year ahead of schedule. We have attracted several Pulitzer Prize-winning journalists to our team. We recruited Steve Taylor, who started Boston.com for the *Boston Globe,* to be our founding publisher, and Bobbie Roessner, who won a Pulitzer Prize for her work with the *Hartford Courant*, as our founding editor. We began publication as a non-profit news site on June 7, 2021. A little over a year later, our news staff numbered more than the *Standard-Times*. The *New Bedford Light* is already having a major impact on the community and is drawing interest nationwide as an example of community journalism.

The first journalist we hired, Will Sennott, earned one of eight Pro Publica grants given out in the country over very stiff competition, which allows him to delve deeply into the complexities of the fishing industry. His blockbuster story about a foreign-owned hedge fund exploiting American fishermen immediately had US senators calling for investigations and the Justice Department combing the docks. In the first week, we delved into the issue of how COVID-19 impacted New Bedford. It was a combination of data-driven analysis and human stories not found anywhere else. Other stories have zeroed in on the impact of rising housing costs, the complexities and promise of the offshore wind industry, and the story of a domestic violence case resulting in the resignation of the CEO of the region's largest hospital group.

In addition to the news, the *Light* brings our readers a more complete picture of the nuances and intricacies of New Bedford, from daily fish prices and street fashion styles to the most complete cultural calendar, community voices, and a fine arts auction for emerging artists.

Having been on one side of the relationship with the press, I never thought I would be working on the other side. But the time is right for the *New Bedford Light*. It is already shining and serving the community of greater New Bedford.

Westport Calling

Westport, our new home, also came calling after I retired. The Westport Select Board asked me to serve on the town's Planning Board to fill a vacancy. I thought this would be a way to give back to our new community while also learning about it. After a few years of service, I ran for election to the board and won a three-year term unopposed, something I never experienced in New Bedford!

One of the most significant issues we face on Tuesday evenings is farmers, in this "Right to Farm" community, coming to us with proposals from solar developers. The developers want to erect solar farms, usually by clear-cutting forests behind their fields. The issues are complicated, but the net result is that we have permitted enough projects so that Westport generates electricity through solar to power 150 percent of our own needs. Not bad for a fairly conservative town. And we have added revenue for farms that may not have to resort to growing a last crop of houses.

I am also now chairing Westport's Climate Resilience Committee. We will try to identify the potential impacts to Westport from climate change, the risks to the community, who will be affected, and what steps we might take to adapt. We have set up committees on agriculture, health, water, infrastructure and safety, and engagement and fundraising. It is a huge task, but as my friend Dave Crockett in Chattanooga said, "It takes us all, and it takes forever."

New Bedford Ocean Cluster

New Bedford Mayor Jon Mitchell also asked me to get involved and lead the New Bedford Ocean Cluster, a new non-profit organization formed to create economic opportunity in the New Bedford region. I agreed to become president of the board. The organization is focused on four "pillars:" commercial fishing, offshore wind, aquaculture, and marine technology. I told him I was excited to go to work for my hometown and grateful for the invitation.

New Bedford has been the nation's top commercial fishing port for more than 20 years, so there is no question about the opportunity in the fishing industry. Even though we are number one, we can still improve.

Offshore wind is poised to have the same generational impact on New Bedford as whaling and textiles did more than a century ago. Not only is the creation of renewable energy necessary for our survival, but hundreds, perhaps thousands of jobs will be created. But this is a new, highly technical industry. So, we have to prepare our people for these jobs. And that is Ocean Cluster's most immediate task.

As was the case when I entered City Hall and when I worked at NOAA, I understand that the easiest path is not the right one. This is a European industry, and it is White. What is easy is

Mayor Jon Mitchell hosts a delegation from the United Kingdom to the Massachusetts Clean Energy Center at the Marine Commerce Terminal, April 2022. They visited, seeking opportunities in the growing field of offshore wind.

for the Europeans to move their effort over here. What we have to do is build a work force that involves *our* people and reflects *our* diversity. We need to reach out into the minority community and get people of color interested, trained, and involved in offshore wind. We need to get the commercial fishing industry, which sees offshore wind as a threat to remember Rodney Avila's adage that, "We harvest dollars. They may look like fish, but we harvest dollars." Offshore wind is a great way for commercial fishing to harvest dollars.

I learned at NOAA that aquaculture is the fastest-growing form of fish protein production. New Bedford has much of the infrastructure already in place. We need to capitalize on that and be part of that growth. And marine technology is what ties it together and makes us smarter. Instruments on fishing boats, wind turbines, and aquaculture farms all collect data about the marine environment we depend on.

As I lead this effort with a brilliant board of directors, whose knowledge of these fields is deep and thoughtful, and a new energetic, smart executive director in Jen Downing, I am enthusiastic about our prospects. We were recently visited by three foreign delegations in a month's time. When speaking to a delegation from the northern United Kingdom, Mayor Mitchell spoke of our optimism and challenges in meeting this moment.

"Those of us from New Bedford who visited the areas in Europe where offshore wind has taken off have an advantage of a glimpse to the future. We have witnessed how fast this industry grows. People here look around and don't see much happening. They don't know what is about to hit us. We don't have much time to prepare."

I think how fortunate I am to be part of this movement. It will be like riding a very large fast-moving wave. Having done that in boats, I know how exciting that can be. This will be very good for New Bedford, but we have a lot of work to do to prepare and make it happen.

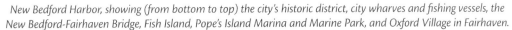

New Bedford Harbor, showing (from bottom to top) the city's historic district, city wharves and fishing vessels, the New Bedford-Fairhaven Bridge, Fish Island, Pope's Island Marina and Marine Park, and Oxford Village in Fairhaven.

CHAPTER 18

Sunrises and Sunsets

Family

At the beginning of my career, I set out to "save the world" by making my hometown a better place. Deeper inside that quest lay another question—for whom are we saving the world?

Following the stories and spiderwebs my grandparents spun for us at 19 Irving Street, I learned about the city I came from, its contributions, and generations past. Preservation work, politics, and sustainable development across America taught me about the debt we owe to future generations. Why keep trying to make our world a better place? We do it not only to honor the past but also to celebrate the promise of the future. We do it for our children and their children.

Forever shipmates

When I started out as a young man, hometown meant two words: New Bedford. As time passed and experience provided me with greater perspective, my definition of hometown broadened to a much wider community. As I have gotten older, my sense of family, too, has taken on a more expansive meaning.

Family is spiderwebs. It is childhood, tradition, and community. It is parents, children, and grandchildren, my own and those of the people I love. Friends have become family. Family have become friends. Family is sailing seas and climbing mountains. It is the fight to create a better world and the people who fight alongside you. There is no question that what has held me together in my life is my literal, immediate family. Laurie, the kids, and our grandkids have provided support, encouragement, nourishment, motivation, and release.

I have spent hundreds of days with Laurie on our boat, traveling thousands of miles in all kinds of weather. We have sailed leisurely across Buzzards Bay, with one of us napping along the way, comfortable in the sunshine. We have beat into 55 knots of wind under jib and jigger with the engine on, clawing our way to refuge offered by a Maine harbor. We have spent a week of vacation hauled out on a Travelift while a sheared propellor shaft was replaced, using our inflatable dinghy each evening for a cocktail cruise around the harbor. We have raced with other classic yachts to Newport, once with the boat leaking so badly that we hand pumped the whole way. Laurie is so good at sea. She never gets rattled. She always knows what to do, and we have perfectly complementary skills. Going out sailing or cruising on a sail or powerboat is a great way to get away from everything and just be together. With the motion of the ocean. And the sound of the waves against the hull. And the birds. And the sunrises and the sunsets. And the stars, especially the first star we see at night. I've often thought that problems seem infinite when you are on land, coming at you from every direction. As soon as you cast off the lines, life becomes much simpler. You are just trying to get from here to there. Everything you have is right on the boat. If it isn't, well, you just do without.

We had one sail where we got up with the sun in Nantucket Harbor and made our way out of Nantucket Sound and east around Monomoy and the elbow of the Cape for breakfast.

404

With a light wind from the southwest, we reached along the beach of the National Seashore, staying about 200 yards offshore. As the Cape has a gentle curve to it, it always looks like you are about to round the corner, but the corner never comes. Just endless, endless beach. For hours and hours, we sat in our cockpit and took in the sand, the dunes, and, eventually, the people. Mid-afternoon brought a freshening breeze and our speed picked up and *Captiva* was frolicking with 20 knots of breeze and no waves in the lee of the land. Finally, as the sun started to set, we did round the corner at Race Point, for a short beat into Provincetown and dinner. Thoreau had his walk on the beach; we had our sail along the beach. He did it alone. We shared the experience. To each his own.

Laurie and I are complementary in many ways. I tend to be idealistic and very positive about people. Someone has to work hard to get on my bad side. Laurie is skeptical about most things and is a tough judge of people. She has a sharp eye. For me, she is very good to have around. I have a short memory when it comes to people who have crossed me. Laurie's memory is indelible. She is as loyal as they come. To have her by my side is formidable. For anyone to have Laurie as a friend is to have a force by your side.

Laurie is my best sounding board in politics. She can size up people quickly, which I find very instructive. I always listen carefully to her opinions on those we meet. Laurie has developed an on-the-mark intuition and an expert's eye.

As with all political junkies, politics has become a full-contact sport. Our response is interactive as we read the paper in the morning or listen to the news at night. We can't just read a story. We have to talk about it. We have to do something about it. That might be something local like protesting for gay marriage on City Hall steps or against our White supremacist former sheriff of Bristol County Tom Hodgson, a Trump fanboy whose policies have terrorized our local immigrant population. It might be national in scope, such as spending time in Columbus, Ohio, during the final weeks of John Kerry's presidential campaign or heading to Laurie's home congressional district in New Jersey for a couple of weeks in 2018 to help elect Mikie Sherrill as the first Democrat in over 100 years, part of the Blue Wave.

Laurie and I do our best each day to practice the words of Angela Davis: "I am no longer accepting the things I cannot change. I am changing the things I cannot accept."

We have tried to set an example for our kids by showing them that our responsibilities go beyond family. We have always worked. We have done our best to provide for our children's education and development; certainly, Laurie carried much more of the load here than I did. One of the outstanding accomplishments of Laurie's life before I knew her was that she got a job at a fantastic private elementary school, Friends Academy in Dartmouth, as a single mom in a new place. This allowed her to educate Toby and Lexie while also being with them. I sent Matthew to Friends as well because I had gone there, as had my siblings and my father. The kids were already in the same school when Laurie and I got together.

As Lexie, Toby, and Matt grew up, their lives were shaped by the Irving Street neighborhood and the many facets of New Bedford and the

Smiles all around as Mikie Sherrill is elected to Congress in Laurie's New Jersey home district.

region. My nearest friend lived three miles away when I grew up in Dartmouth. On Irving Street, dozens of friends were within a few blocks. Few people drove on the street, so we painted a four-square for the neighborhood. The kids spent hours playing four-square, whiffle ball, flashlight tag, or some other game that parents probably never knew about.

Just as Sarah Tappan Crapo fondly watched out the Oriel window for friends in the 1870s, so Lexie watched her friends approach our house on Irving Street. While architectural historians thought the house was museum-quality, we lived in it as a family home. Toby or Matthew and their friends would set up a Nerf basketball hoop on one of the four gothic doors in the octagonal front hall, and fierce games would go on all night. A museum, it was not! Irving Street was our family home base. As our kids got older and went to college, they took something of this home with them as they created their own homes and lives.

Following her maternal grandmother's passion for gourmet foods, Lexie enrolled and graduated from Cambridge Culinary Institute with a chef's degree. Laurie and I reaped the benefits of her homework assignments! Twenty years later, like her mother, Lexie received her bachelor's degree at UMass Amherst. Toby went to Gettysburg University, where he played very serious baseball and decided on a career in financial services. Matthew went to Rutgers University, where he rowed crew and majored in atmospheric sciences, which evolved into a career in technology. He also enjoyed some serious ocean sailing.

Lexie's first job was as a line chef in DC. Career moves included restaurant jobs in Manhattan, Saratoga Springs, Buffalo, and Boston. She became a food broker in western Massachusetts, where she married and gave birth to Caroline, a daughter who is passionate about horseback riding and gymnastics. A seasoned professional in the food service industry, Lexie is living as a single mom with a strong network of friends in the Pittsfield area. What amazes me is that she and Laurie talk three or four times a week, drawing laughter, strength, and support from each other. For a while, I called it the "two-generation slumber party" because they reminded me of girls at a sleepover, relaxed in their pajamas, sharing their stories and thoughts late into the evening. Now, Caroline gets involved too, so it's a three-generation slumber party. We are fortunate that our family has this closeness.

Toby comes to cheer Matthew at Rutgers rowing competition.

Toby decided at Gettysburg that he wanted to make money. He spent a summer selling Ricoh copiers in Roxbury, learning that you have to make many hundreds of calls to get one appointment and arrange dozens of appointments to get one sale. In other words, success in sales means you will suffer a *lot* of people saying "No!" to you. But if you are willing to work hard and have a positive attitude, you can build on your successes. That is Toby. Nobody works harder, nobody is more positive. He is the person who sees a pile of manure and says, "There has to be a pony here somewhere."

When we vacation in Captiva, you can always spot Toby. He is the one with the kids following him on some adventure. He has a fun-loving, magnetic personality. He is a natural leader. This is partly because he is a kid himself and partly because he is so positive and radiates fun, joy, and

Laurie, Lexie, and Caroline—
the three generation slumber party

Matthew, Toby, and Lexie

enthusiasm. I emphasize, though, that he works harder than anyone I know. He graduated from college, joined a financial services firm, and started selling and learning. In a business where you eat what you kill, he is a killer. He married a terrific woman, Jen Coakley, and they have two dynamo kids, Maddie and Wyatt. Maddie has been a standout athlete at Cohasset High School and now attends University of Miami. Wyatt matches high grades with his father's love of baseball. They value friendships and their lives are full. In a world of chaos, Jen is the one who amazingly keeps everyone on course. Jen gave up a career in financial management to focus on the family and that decision has meant the world to Maddie, Wyatt, and Toby.

Matthew worked for a weather services firm in Billerica, installing software for TV stations, airlines, and others who needed good weather forecasting tools. For a while, when Laurie and I were in DC, Matthew and Toby lived in Charlestown together, and Lexie lived nearby. We returned home thrilled that we'd be near all our kids. But it didn't turn out that way. Toby married Jen and got transferred to Charlotte, North Carolina. Matthew chased a love interest out to Boise, Idaho, and started work at Micron Technology. Lexie also left the area. Laurie and I looked at each other and said, "Maybe we should change our breath mints!"

Matt shifted away from weather and into the world of IT. He also moved away from the ocean and our little New England mountains, or hills, and into the foothills of the Rockies, where mountains rise to 14,000 feet instead of the paltry 3,000 feet that we are used to. He met Jody Thatcher, a physical therapist, and they set down roots in Boise's North End, one of the nicest neighborhoods you will find in America. Jody had started as a physical therapist working for someone else until she decided to start her own practice. Now she runs a very successful small business, Thrive, whose name says it all. And it is located just a bike ride from their house! Jody is as athletic as Matt and their outdoor adventures take our breath away. Oliver and Bibi followed, so now we have five grandchildren with very different identities, and we love watching them grow up.

We visited Boise in 2017 and participated as a family in the downtown Women's March the day after Trump's inauguration. About 5,000 marchers came out on a snowy day to protest the threat to reproductive, civil, and human rights. Boise is an island of blue in a very red state, and everywhere in the crowd, you could see very creative signs and the march's signature pink "pussy-hats" with their perky cat ears, mostly homemade or handcrafted, worn in response to vulgar remarks Trump made about women during the campaign. Bibi was only two months old at the time. Matthew and Jody were starting her feminist activism early! We get examples of Oliver's writing and see a young man with unlimited imagination and wonder where that will take him.

We continue to plan adventures together. Sailing has been a big part of my life. It has forged a tremendous bond with Laurie, and it certainly connected me to my father.

I remember one unforgettable sailing trip when Toby and Matt joined Dad, my brother-in-law Lark, and me to deliver the family's Concordia yawl from Padanaram to Northeast Harbor, Maine. The boys were teenagers. It's an overnight trip that normally takes about 24 hours. You are usually going with the wind, and it can be a really nice sail. But something happened on this one. Maybe it was some bad food that my mother prepared, or maybe the ocean swells were just a bit off, but Matt and Toby got seasick just as we passed through the Cape Cod Canal and entered Massachusetts Bay, heading out to sea. Dad knew how to get us through the trip.

"We have to keep them topsides in the wind, so let's get them in their sleeping bags and lash them to the leeward rail, where we can keep an eye on them."

We did that. Toby and Matt lay in their bags feeling horrible as we made our way east. They slept when they could. They would periodically wake up, throw up into the sea, and go back to sleep. We tried to keep them hydrated and fed them saltines, which was about all they could get down. They were miserable. We sailed through some rough weather, but Lark, Dad, and I got the boat to Northeast Harbor the next morning. As soon as we moored and the boys set foot on dry land, the transformation was instantaneous. It was as if Toby and Matt rose from the dead, none the worse for wear.

"Damn, that was fun! When can we do that again?" A sign of true sailors. I would go to sea with them anytime.

With, left to right, Dad, brother-in-law Lark Madden, Matthew, and Toby

Extended Family

My immediate and extended sailing family has enriched my life. Laurie and I have done lots of sailing and had our adventurous moments, but our cruising has largely been confined to New York and New England waters. We ventured further while I was at SEA. Laurie sailed with me on a few trips aboard the *Robert C. Seamans* to French Polynesia and Hawaii, where we encountered lots of big waves in the middle of the Pacific. We could understand why those islands are known for surfing.

But to sail in other parts of the world, I have had to join the OPYC – the "Other People's Yacht Club." It is a great yacht club. You don't have to own a boat or pay dues, but to be invited, you do have to know how to sail well. In the 1960s and 70s, I joined the Burnes family for three Atlantic crossings as well as cruises in Ireland, Europe, and the Caribbean. They were my second family for almost a year.

In the mid-70s, George Lewis asked me to join his crew in Newport as we campaigned his One Tonner *Lively*. Back then, One Tonners were the hottest boats to race internationally, like Formula One racecars. We set out in the fall of 1974 to compete in the World Championships that would take place in Newport the following year. That fall, we were the fastest boat in the world, beating boats 30 feet longer than our 38-foot length. George's two sons, George Jr. and Cam, were on board as crew too. Cam was a real hot shot, who went on to become a professional sailor, racing multi-hulls around the world for a living. Also on board were a young Australian named Lee and my cousin Peter Bullard, who acted as navigator.

Lively was designed by Doug Peterson, who had set the sailing world on fire the previous year in Sardinia with his breakthrough *Ganbare*. This young San Diego designer was beating all the established designers, and in 1974, we had his latest design. The problem was that by the time 1975 rolled around, *Lively* was no longer the latest Peterson craft out there, and we were competing with more modern designs.

George rented a house in Newport, and we practiced hard for a year. We got to be very good, but then we had to be because we would be competing against the best in North America in

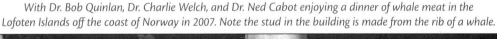

With Dr. Bob Quinlan, Dr. Charlie Welch, and Dr. Ned Cabot enjoying a dinner of whale meat in the Lofoten Islands off the coast of Norway in 2007. Note the stud in the building is made from the rib of a whale.

August. The qualifying contest included a week of races: three of 24 miles, one of 150 miles, and one of 360 miles. Famous sailmakers Ted Hood and Lowell North had boats entered. Ted Turner of America's Cup fame (well, that wasn't the only thing he was famous for!) was there along with 20 other skippers.

Cam did most of the driving, although I split the sections upwind with him because I had a knack for beating into the wind, where you get into a rhythm with the Newport winds that shift through about 20 degrees every 12 minutes or so. If you time your tacks right, you can put a lot of distance on other boats. But it became clear that the newer boats could head much closer to the wind than we could because we were made of wood, and they were made of aluminum. It was discouraging coming to the starting line, knowing that the only way we could win was by taking huge risks. After the five races were over, we finished seventh, qualifying to race in the World Championships that September.

More weeks of practice were ahead of us. We would have the best international skippers against us when the races started. Boats came from all over, including Japan, Germany, England, Ireland, Italy, Australia, and New Zealand. While the cast had changed, the results stayed the same. Lowell North dominated with his yellow *Pied Piper*, and we finished seventh in the world out of 24.

After, I decided I wasn't going to compete seriously anymore. There were a couple of reasons for this. One was the time commitment. I had a young son and a wife and was just beginning my career in New Bedford. I couldn't keep devoting the time I had taken over the past year to continue competing at that level. Second, I had noticed that boats had become so light in the quest for speed that they were getting dangerous. It didn't really matter on a day race, but when you are sailing 360 miles far out to sea, you don't want to worry about whether your boat will hold up. I am forever thankful to George Lewis for allowing me to see what it is like to test myself against the best, but it would be cruising for me after that.

The Arctic Circle and Nearing the North Pole

In a similar way, I am thankful to Ned Cabot for the cruising equivalent. I met Ned when he was the board chair of SEA. While he was an excellent surgeon, he loved high-latitude sailing and had a modified J-46, *Cielita*, built for sailing in those waters.

In 2005, Ned invited me to join him in the Bras D'Or lakes on the northern part of Nova Scotia for a sail across the Cabot Straits—named for Ned's ancestor, the Italian navigator John Cabot, who explored the area in the 15th century—and into the Gulf of St. Lawrence. Dr. Bob Quinlan and Dr. Charlie Welch joined us. When I boarded, I looked at the three docs and figured I had the best medical plan!

We spent ten days in the Gulf of St. Lawrence, stopping at Les Îles-de-la-Madeleine, where the water temperature was quite warm due to the surrounding shallow sandy bottom. We proceeded up the northern edge of the Gaspé Peninsula and across to the southern shore of Quebec and the Mingan Islands, where I got off. We saw only one other sailing vessel. Little did I know that 12 years later, when I was working at NOAA, this area would be the place where so many North Atlantic right whales would be killed by ship strikes or entanglements with crab pot gear.

Two years after that sail, Ned gathered the same crew for another trip. By this time, he had sailed the *Cielita* up to the Shetland Islands on the northern edge of Scotland at 60 degrees north latitude. This is about the same latitude as the southern tip of Greenland or Anchorage, Alaska. I met the boat in Lerwick, and we headed north for Svalbard but encountered strong headwinds, so we put into the Lofoten Islands on the northwest coast of Norway. It is hard to find a more picturesque harbor with its brightly colored houses and wooden fishing boats with hulls varnished on the bottom half and white on the top. After filling our fuel tanks and taking what Ned called a "walkabout" past the cod drying on racks outside, we gathered for dinner in a tiny restaurant, where every other stud was made from the rib of a whale.

Seeing whale meat on the menu, I asked the waitstaff what kind.

"Sperm."

I told Ned, Charlie, and Bob that I doubted that statement as the Norwegians whaled mostly for minke whales, which were abundant. I ordered the whale meat anyway and was surprised at how similar to steak it looked and tasted—not fishy at all.

We departed in light airs and quite warm temperatures. As we were now well above the Arctic Circle, the sun never set. We sailed in daylight 24 hours a day until we reached Svalbard. This large island hadn't been owned by any nation until relatively recent, when all the nations doing business there agreed that Norway should possess it as long as other countries were permitted to keep doing what they had been doing—like Russia continuing its mining.

We pulled into Bellsund and proceeded to the head of the fjord, dodging the car-sized "bergy bits" that had broken off from the glacier at the head of the deep and narrow inlet. Ned had had the *Cielita* reinforced with extra fiberglass against ice. Avoiding ice altogether was impossible, but we still didn't want to hit any of these bigger ice chunks.

Our instrumentation revealed one of many surprises that we discovered while sailing these northern latitudes. Surrounded by melting ice, we expected the water to be cold and relatively fresh. Instead, we found it was almost 50 degrees Fahrenheit and about 33 percent saline, comparable to the Gulf of Maine. What explained those readings was a map of the Gulf Stream, which showed a thin finger running up the west coast of Svalbard. The stream, a warm-water river in the ocean that starts south of Florida and travels north, brings tropical heat close to the coast

The Cielita *at anchor in Svalbard, Norway*

of southern New England, which gives us our mild winters. The Gulf Stream then crosses the Atlantic and warms northwest Europe. But a sliver shoots north, and we could see its power here.

We continued our northward sail. Svalbard is in a polar high-pressure zone, so there is little wind and little precipitation. Its landscape is a desert of ice and rock. You won't find much living or growing here unless you look very carefully to see lichen gripped to the rocks. The only wood is driftwood carried by the currents from Siberia. The sky is cloudy much of the time, and the mountains are covered in snow and ice. When the ocean is calm, which it frequently is, the water reflects the clouds, snow, ice, and rock. Many of my photographs look monochromatic, with variations of silvers and grays occasionally broken by a patch of blue sky or a swatch of color from someone's yellow foul weather gear or red sweatshirt.

As barren as it is above the surface of the water, the environment changes dramatically once you go underwater. You encounter a jungle of almost impenetrable strands of kelp, lush and rich like a rain forest. When we hauled up anchor, hundreds of feet of kelp would be attached. The difference felt surreal, as did living in constant sunlight. It was disconcerting not to have twilight or nighttime to give you a sense of the rhythm of the day. Because of the long, bright days, we had to watch the clock for our cues on when to turn in.

A helicopter landed nearby as we approached a landing in the sound between the mainland and the island Prins Karls Forland. It looked like a scene from a James Bond movie. Two government representatives—sysselmannen—got out and approached the *Cielita*. Ned received them with the boat's papers. These women were in uniform, armed, about 30 years old, and beautiful.

Small icebergs calving off of a glacier

"Do you have a gun?" was their first question. "How big is your gun? May we see it?"

Svalbard has 3,500 people and 5,000 polar bears, and it is clear which species tops the food chain. For safety, humans are not allowed on land without a gun that can kill a polar bear. From our boat earlier, we had seen a mother and her two cubs feeding on a caribou on a section of ice. It was a magnificent scene. You definitely do not want to encounter a bear. They can outrun you and outswim you, and there is no place to hide. Ned showed the two officials our rifle, so we were allowed ashore for our "walkabout." We did not run into any polar bears.

We sailed north to Ny-Alesund, a scientific village in an old mining town. It is the northernmost village in the world. Its population is about 30 in the winter and grows to about 130 in the summer when several countries set up their Arctic research stations. Eight countries have territorial access to the Arctic and can set up their own research centers: Canada, Denmark, Iceland, Norway, Sweden, Finland, Russia, and the United States. Other countries wanting to do Arctic research usually maintain research centers in Ny-Alesund. After walking around the former mining town, we set sail north until we reached the northernmost edge of Svalbard, near where the Dutch had had a whaling station in the 16th century. By this time, we had gotten to 79 degrees, 30 minutes north latitude.

"Ned, we are only 30 miles from 80 degrees north," I said. "We should keep sailing."

"John, that would just be a stunt."

Ned smiled from under his ski goggles. I smiled back from under my goggles.

"Of course, it's a stunt. So is going to the North Pole. But we're up here. It's a beautiful day. We might as well venture north of 80 degrees. Not many people sail this far north."

Off we went, straight into about 30 knots of wind. Sailing up here requires special clothing. I wore a thin layer of thermal socks under a thick layer of thermal socks. Same with long underwear and long-sleeved tees–a thin layer under a thick layer designed to wick away moisture. Over that, I put on work pants and a work shirt. On top of that, I put on heavy-duty foul weather gear and thermal boots that I had gotten from New Bedford Ship Supply. On my hands, I wore a layer of thin thermal gloves under thicker thermal gloves. A ski hat and ski goggles completed the

Momma bear and cubs in Svalbard look cute. They think we look delicious.

outfit, along with a harness that allowed us to always be hooked to the boat. If a wave or a sudden movement caused us to go overboard, we would still be attached to the boat and could be brought back aboard quickly. The sea is so unpredictable, unbuckling even for a few moments, which at times you have to do, could cost a life.

We beat into the north wind for several hours until the GPS read 80 degrees. We were now within 600 miles of the North Pole. We still couldn't see any pack ice. We all took pictures of ourselves at the helm and the GPS reading and then reluctantly turned the boat and headed south. We didn't quite reach the North Pole, true, but we achieved a milestone few ever reach.

Eventually, we put into the main city of Longyearbyen, which would be my departure point. Longyearbyen was named for John Munro Longyear, who 100 years ago came from Boston, of all places, to establish a mining company. It has about 2,400 residents and a colorful downtown. A global seed vault was being built in an abandoned mine, sort of a Noah's Ark of seeds to safeguard seed varieties from across the globe. Longyearbyen was chosen because even if the power went off, the seeds would stay frozen in the permafrost of the mine. In this way, should disaster strike, humanity could rebuild our agriculture from what was stored in the vault.

Before we parted ways, we shared a final meal of reindeer and seal. I was surprised that the seal did not taste fishy but was tender and delicious. As I greeted the on-coming crew the next morning before heading to the airport, they asked what we had been eating during our visits ashore. I mentioned a diet of whale, reindeer, and seal. One of them shot off a snappy one-liner.

"So let me get this straight, if it appeared in a Disney movie, you ate it?"

While that may not make my NOAA colleagues happy, when we were in foreign countries, we wanted to experience the local diet and learn from the people there.

Five years later, Ned had completed his long northern latitude voyage and was finally returning home to Boston. He was looking forward to seeing his grandchildren and could smell home waters as he departed Labrador to cross the Cabot Strait one more time. The weather report was ominous, and he was shorthanded. But this was the last short leg, and he was anxious to get home.

Ned Cabot poses with three options for dealing with polar bears: high-powered rifle, shack for shelter, or getaway boat.

I wasn't with him on this trip but heard what happened to my friend and shipmate. He unclipped his harness to go to the helm to relieve the person steering the boat, where he would clip his harness in again. Ned was unclipped for only a couple of seconds. During those few moments, a rogue wave crashed over the stern and washed both Ned and the helmsman, Fin Perry, overboard. The force of the wave broke the steering mechanism. Fin had been clipped and somehow got himself back on board. He had Ned's hand in his own for a moment, but the force of the ocean was too great and separated them. *Cielita* had her sails up and was traveling downwind with no way to steer. My dear friend Ned Cabot, the ultimate seaman, was lost in the Cabot Strait.

It is a nightmare that haunts all who go to sea, seeing your boat travel away from you. The ocean exerts powerful forces over us. Most of them are so positive and are why we are drawn to the sea. It is endlessly beguiling and can appeal to all our senses. But the ocean can be ruthless and unforgiving. Ironically, as powerful as it can be over humans, humans can also bring it to its knees. Global warming and acidification show its fragility. So many contradictions. I have learned so many lessons from my time on the ocean and from friends like Ned.

From Ocean Currents to Moving Mountains

There are similarities I find between oceans and mountains, and while I haven't spent anywhere as much time in mountainous environments, I have relished the challenges they present. The biggest similarity between a mountain and the ocean is that both are in charge—you get to do only what they will allow. You approach both with knowledge, training, humility, and respect, often with the help of family and friends.

The first mountain I tried to climb was Glacier Peak in the Cascade Range in Washington in 1999. It was a joint effort with sons Matthew and Toby. As my nephew Peter McNaull lived in Seattle, he joined our group, along with two other nephews, Gussy and Charlie Koven. Gussy lived in LA and Charlie in San Francisco. Like Matthew, they had both been rowers in college. Glacier Peak is a little over 10,000 feet high, which is unremarkable for the West but dwarfs anything on the East Coast. All five young men are phenomenal athletes in superb condition, but I was over 50. As soon as we made the plan, I began training, working on my leg strength and endurance, visualizing what the climb would be like.

We got to the base of the mountain and spent a couple of days training with our guides on how to climb with a "rest step," how to climb in snow or on ice, how to descend using a "plunge step," and how to use a pickax to self-arrest during a fall on an ice glacier. We learned rope work and the different knots you use in mountaineering. A few were like ones we knew from sailing, but most were different.

After training, we began the long trek in and up. Here, too, clothing mattered. As hikers say, "cotton kills," so they avoid it because it absorbs moisture and leaves you vulnerable to the cold. What you want are lots of layers of thin wicking polymer material that absorb your sweat as you burn calories and transport the moisture away from your body to keep you dry and warm.

After a long day's hike, we made camp on the glacier and were ready for an early start for the summit the next morning. We woke at 3 a.m. and had coffee and breakfast. We got our gear on, including headlamps attached to our helmets. The excitement was palpable. We could see it in each other's faces. It was so cool to share this moment with Toby, Matt, PJ, and the Koven boys. As we were ready to strike our tents, our head guide, Dale, broke the bad news. It had begun raining, creating weather ideal for hypothermia. We would get soaking wet on the summit climb, and our body temperatures could hit dangerously low levels with the cold. He could not responsibly let us climb. So, down we went. In more ways than one. The mountain had prevailed. We got to the bottom and went into Seattle to spend a day at the REI climbing wall instead.

Over lunch, it became clear that Matthew wasn't giving up on the idea of a summit climb.

"I know a mountain in Idaho where there won't be any rain in August. Let's plan a trip for next year."

PJ, Toby, and I joined Matthew the next year in Boise. We drove Matt's Ford Explorer to Stanley in central Idaho to attempt to conquer Castle Peak in the White Cloud Wilderness. As we bumped along down a very long and rough dirt road, we got a flat tire. We didn't let that deter us. After a short delay to change the tire, we kept on. Then, disaster happened. We got a *second* flat tire. We had one spare tire but not two. Matt and PJ hitchhiked back to Stanley, but by the time they returned with a new tire, we had lost a day. Toby and I had fixed dates to return east, so we had to abandon our climb.

Again, the mountain had prevailed. We switched gears and spent a relaxing couple of days backpacking and flyfishing in the Boulder Chain Lakes.

The summit kept calling, though. A couple of years later, Laurie and I visited our good friends and neighbors Bob Bowen and Wendy Bauer, who lived near us in New Bedford on Arnold Place. Their next-door neighbors and good friends, David Gilbertson and Carolee Matsumoto, were there too. Mountain climbing came up, and Bob suggested we climb the Grand Teton in Jackson Hole, Wyoming. David and Carolee have a place out there, and they were enthusiastic about that idea, though they did not necessarily want to climb. Bob, a few years younger than me and a serious swimmer in college, was game for the climb.

Over drinks, a plan emerged. Bob discovered Exum Guides, considered among the best guides on the globe. He said Exum didn't have to pay their summer guides much since the job was so sought after. Once you had been an Exum guide, you could write your ticket for trips pretty much anywhere else in the world.

I contacted Matt and Toby. We set a date for August 2003. This time, Laurie and Lexie would join us for the trip, although not the climb. Jen wanted to do the climb. We rented a house in Jackson Hole for a big family gathering. PJ said he was in. When we contacted Charlie and Gus Koven, we got a surprise indicating that maybe this time, the stars would align.

Charlie and Gus told us that their grandfather Gustav Koven and his brother Theodore had made the third ascent of the Grand Teton with Paul Petzoldt, who had founded Exum Guides with Glenn Exum. Exum had made the first ascent on July 15, 1931, solo, and Petzoldt had made the second ascent, also solo, later that day. The Koven brothers had joined Petzoldt for the third trip. When Exum Guides found out a couple of Kovens would be in our party, they were as excited as we were!

On one of our climbs with sons Matthew and Toby, nephews Peter McNaull and Gus Koven, and friends

By the time we traveled to Wyoming, Bob Bowen, the instigator, had dropped out, so it was just family. I remember looking out the plane's window as we approached the airport and looking up, way up, at the Teton Ridge in the sunlight. I stared up at the Grand, with its crooked top, the tallest of Tetons, commanding all around it. *What have I gotten myself into?* This wasn't a 10,000-foot peak. The Grand reached almost 14,000 feet. I definitely had a lump in my throat. It was hard to swallow.

Laurie and Lexie enjoyed all the attractions of Jackson Hole while the guys and Jen spent two days of rigorous training with the guides. Four hours in the morning. Four hours after lunch. We did drills and learned skills, including technical climbing on how to go up a rock face, belay with rope and rappel down without burning your hands as the rope raced through the belay device.

Midway through the second day, I asked one of our guides a couple of questions.

"Is the training harder than the actual climb?"

"Well, John, we would be pretty stupid guides if we made the training easier than the climb."

"OK, that makes me feel better," I said, sweat pouring from my forehead. "Last question. Do you think I can do this climb?"

"John, we wouldn't let you go up if we didn't think you could do it. And yes, we think you're good to go."

For the first time, I felt a shred of confidence. My nerves steadied just a bit.

This feeling on the edge of dread has not been uncommon in my life. Sometimes, it occurs during adventures like this mountain climb or crossing an ocean in a storm when you test yourself and the outcome is in doubt. Sometimes, you're standing in front of a crowd, not knowing exactly what you are going to say but knowing you have to be good, you have to move them, and you aren't sure it will happen this time. Sometimes, you're leading by being the first to say

Sunset with Matthew on the saddle of the Tetons, looking into Idaho

something or do something and wondering if anyone will follow or if you will just be out there by your lonesome. Sometimes, you're fashioning a career where there isn't a path, wondering if the future leads anywhere at all when you have a family who depends on you. *Am I good enough? Do I have this? Can I do this?*

After our two days of training, we had a great family dinner and packed up our gear in our backpacks. Jen wasn't feeling well, so she had to give up the climb, which disappointed her greatly after acing the training. Early the next morning, our crew and about 20 other hikers started a long trek from the trail head up a beautiful valley on a slow sunny climb. Our destination for the end of the day was ten miles away and at an elevation of 11,000 feet, at the "saddle" between the Grand and an adjacent mountain. Gradually, fields gave way to hills, and hills gave way to boulders. The sides of the mountain grew steeper and steeper.

By mid-afternoon, we were walking on snow and ice. Our pace slowed as the air got thinner. We tired more quickly, and the footing became more difficult. Before sunset, we reached the saddle, where there was a large cabin. The guides started preparing dinner. We claimed spaces inside the cabin for our sleeping bags and milled around, taking in the view. I took advantage of the lone outhouse out behind the cabin. I don't know if there is a rating system for outhouses, but this one would definitely be at the top for the view from its window, overlooking all of eastern Idaho as the sun set. It doesn't get better.

We ate, drank water, and bedded down. Altitude sickness affects everybody in different ways, but one common symptom was summed up in an article in *Outside* magazine a few months later featuring an 18-year-old girl from Worcester who was doing the climb with her dad. She was in our group, and the story described the night she spent in the cabin with "17 flatulent strangers."

That was us! We were famous! Flatulent strangers. I told the family and said I wanted to get t-shirts printed up.

"There we are, written up in *Outside* magazine! It sounds like the name of a rock band."

On a serious note, in the middle of the night, the base camp called to relay that Jen had a health issue and was going to the local hospital. Toby immediately headed down the mountain in the dark with a guide. After the planning, training, and making it to the saddle, the mountain would deny Toby. But Toby is all about family and has his priorities right where they should be. He did not hesitate to go back. He conquers mountains his own way.

At 4 a.m., we got up, dressed, and packed for the summit. We left whatever gear wasn't necessary because we would be returning to the camp on our way down. We took ropes, water, and snacks. I brought my knee brace for a torn meniscus I suffered a few years before while playing tennis.

The climb now was all rock and technical for the most part. At one point, there was a choice of paths. PJ and the Kovens chose the more challenging route. I chose the easier, the Owens-Spaulding route, and Matthew, bless his heart, stayed with me. All I remember from this "easy" route is one passage called "The Belly Roll," where we had to shimmy along a ridge for about 25 feet. It had a knife-edge, and each of us straddled it with our hands out front, pulling us along, and feet draped over each side. Easy enough. The mountain was on my right. On my left, the drop was straight down about as far as I could see. It wasn't really difficult. It's just that when you looked down, there was no bottom, so that raised the stakes somewhat.

The air was thin. Every step I took up was exhausting. Every step was a straight-up climb or lift. Everything hurt. My quads. My knees. My biceps and shoulders. With every foot toward the 13,770-foot peak, I thought about the summit picture I wanted of my family and me to keep as a reminder that I could overcome challenges. With every step, I thought about the smiles that would be on our faces. Up and up, we went. I looked at the rock in front of my face or what was ahead above me.

Alaska trip in 2022 with Matthew,
Bibi, Lexie, Jody, Oliver, Laurie, and Caroline

Maddie is joined by Wyatt, Jen, and
Toby on her 2022 study abroad in Italy.

It seemed we had every kind of weather as we went. The sun rose and came out. It rained for a while. It hailed, and it snowed. We kept climbing. We got to the summit just before noon, and PJ, Charlie, and Gussy were waiting for us.

Today, 18 years later, Laurie and I are here in Westport, where snow covers the ground most winters. This year, it hasn't been above freezing for several days. As I do every day, I look at the summit picture on top of the Grand with our helmets and ropes and smiles on our faces.

Hometown is where your family is. And making it a better place is a challenge for sure. No question, the outcome is uncertain, the terrain rocky, and the climb steep. But doing it for future generations, with future generations, why, that will definitely put a smile on your face.

Reaching the summit of the Grand with Matthew, Gussy, PJ, and Charlie

Acknowledgments

I have never written a book before, and you have probably guessed that already. The first people I turned to were writers who are also friends of mine. I have written a lot—letters, memos, speeches, op-eds, articles—but I had never attempted a book. So I wanted the advice of real writers, and having completed a book after five years of effort, I am more impressed by their abilities than ever. And I was impressed before.

My neighbor Ken Hartnett—author, editor, and friend—looked at the first few chapters and gave me invaluable advice about the two characters in the book, myself and my hometown. He said that I would have to open up about myself more than I was comfortable with and let people inside because both characters needed to come alive on the page so the reader could get to know them. I hope I have followed Ken's wise counsel well. You are the judge.

My schoolmate Tim Phelps, also an author and journalist, took an independent look and gave me similar advice to Ken's, reinforcing the message. Both were also encouraging, which was important to me, as was Sam Allis, another in the line of journalist, author, and friend who urged me on. So did Sam's fellow *Boston Globe* reporter David Abel who is an excellent writer and filmmaker.

John Spooner is a financial advisor by day and a wicked good author by night. And a friend all the time. He read what I had written and kept coaxing me forward. He was particularly helpful with the title. Without early encouragement from these folks, I would not have pressed on.

During the writing of this book, I drew from a number of sources to assist my memory. While the book is not intended to be a footnoted history book, I didn't want to make egregious errors.

Authors and lovers of local history, Marsha McCabe, Joe Thomas, and Arthur Bennett produced a wonderful book called *Not Just Anywhere* that records the story of how we revitalized the waterfront historic district. Barbara Clayton and Kathleen Whitley's *Guide to New Bedford* as well as *New Bedford Mansions* by Peggi Medeiros were both good references. And I still pull out my grandfather John M. Bullard's *The Rotches*, which is the go-to book on this pre-eminent family. I referred to many clippings of the *Standard-Times*, once the paper of record, to bolster my memories of my mayoral days.

And then there were many people who talked over old times and refreshed my memory, and for whose time I am very grateful, including Phil Beauregard, Ken Alves, Rodney Avila, Lance Simmens, Bruce Morehead, Steve Freese, Sean King, Corky Perret, Carl Safina, John Laughton, Al Hickey, Carolee Matsumoto, Greg DiDomenico, Warren Elliott, Kim Damon Randall, Jen Goebel, Colleen Coogan, Mike Simpkins, and Mark Rasmussen, among others too numerous to be named but also instrumental to the process. While these people and sources certainly improved my recollections and the accuracy of the stories told in this book, the book remains my version of events.

After I completed my first draft, I sent it to several friends whose writing I really respect. Nat Philbrick, Eric Dolin, and poet Everett Hoagland all took the time to read my offering, which in itself is a gift I can never repay. They called me or wrote me or visited with me to express their views that the story was worth telling and worth reading. Such comments from giants mean so much to a first-time book author and left me floating for a while.

Then I learned that writing is just a part of the life of a book. Then comes editing, rewriting, and publishing. And here again, I am grateful for the help I got. I have known and worked with Joe Thomas at Spinner Publications since its inception, and I have an enormous amount of respect for Spinner as a publishing house of local and regional history. I feel honored to be part of the Spinner team. Joe walked me through the publishing process, and we talked about the next step, which would be getting me an editor.

Clara Stites took the first stab at this. I have known Clara since we were both young. She is an accomplished author herself, and she also worked on my mayoral campaigns in the marketing area. She and her late husband, Clay, are among Laurie's and my very closest friends. Clara knows me. If anyone can take an ax to my writing or bring out the "bullshit" meter, it is Clara.

She read the entire manuscript and made significant first-level improvements.

We needed to get to the next level of editing, and after a couple of false starts, I was fortunate to have Natalie White enter the picture. Natalie is an associate editor at Spinner and works closely with publishers Joe Thomas and Jay Avila. I had known Natalie when she was a reporter for the *Standard-Times* covering the waterfront and some City Hall events when I was mayor. Natalie went over every word, checking for duplications (I've been known to tell the same story twice), correcting spelling of names and logical ordering. And cutting, cutting, cutting. The book kept getting thinner and better. I wish I could do that.

While that was happening, Joe and Jay were going through pictures I had given them as well as their incredible trove of photographs to illustrate the text and design a layout that would please you. Other Spinner editorial resources at work include Susan Grace, Zachary White, Claire Nemes, and Corey Nuffer. We hope the result achieves the goal.

The last acknowledgment is about the subject matter, my life and its purpose—fixing up my hometown. I could not have led this life without Laurie. Laurie always had my back. No matter how many people might be attacking me, Laurie was there defending me. If there was a success, she was there to share it. And she is fighting her battles, too, so there is always a sense of shared purpose that we are in this together. I can't imagine doing this alone. Doing this with Laurie is just so much fun! My greatest acknowledgment and blessing is that I get to share this life with her.

As I finish this book, I have been reflecting on the question of "Why?" And that is my last acknowledgment. As I wrote about my grandparents' spider web games and the concept of "future generations" inherent in sustainability, I was reminded of the Native American saying, "We do not inherit the earth from our ancestors; we borrow it from our children."

As my children Lexie, Toby, and Matthew were growing up, I worried about that debt, which motivated me to work to help protect the future. Now that we have grandchildren, I worry about the world we are leaving them and how they will judge us—and me. That continues to motivate me in my life and, in part, inspired me to write this book. I want them to share my stories and know who their Poppy is, but in these pages I also hope they might discover inspiration and perhaps find some tools to take and make their own as they live out their lives and impact the future. I thank you, Maddie and Wyatt, Caroline and Oliver, and Bibi, for what you have brought to my life and what you will bring to your world.

– John K. Bullard

INDEX

On June 14, 1986, Maki Mandela, daughter of Nelson Mandela, was a featured speaker at an anti-apartheid rally held in her honor in New Bedford. The mayor announced that on the following day, the City's retirement fund would sell the last remaining bond associated with South Africa.

An important day for New Bedford: The magnificent statue of Lewis Temple—former slave, blacksmith, and inventor of the toggle harpoon—designed by dear friend and sculptor Jim Toatley, is unveiled posthumously on the lawn of the New Bedford Free Public Library. Unveiling the monument from atop the ladder is Toatley's son, Gordon.

Mindelo Mayor Nelson Santos and his wife join the Cape Verdean Independence Day Parade. Nelson had many friends in the crowd.

I

Police Department finally gets four new Harley Davidsons

Chief Benoit and the mayor square off for a race when Ringling Bros. and Barnum & Bailey Circus comes to town.

*In pursuit of salmon, Kodiak Island, Alaska, 1993—
photograph by Kodiak Island Borough Mayor Jerome Selby*

In March 2023, under the command of Mass Maritime's Captain Tiffany Krihwan and after its $11 million restoration, the *Ernestina-Morrissey* joins a parade of sail off St. Petersburg, Florida.

Andy Burnes on the Adele *during the 1969 Trans-Atlantic Race graces the cover of* Sail *magazine, December 1971. Photograph by John K. Bullard.*

Photography Credits

Number refers to page number; letter refers to the image's position on the page clockwise from left to right.

John K. Bullard & Family Collection

John K. Bullard Photographs: 9, 11a, 11b, 19, 99, 101, 151, 193, 208 , 212, 214, 224, 239, 255, 284, 307, 322, 331, 365, 369, 371b, 373, 380a–b, 402, 404, 405, 406, 407a–b, 408, 409, 411, 412, 413, 414, 416, 417, 419a–c, 425, 441, 444

Spinner Publications Archives

Milton Silvia Collection: 13b, 16a–b, 17a–b, 18d, 28a–b, 34–b, 35a, 38, 43a, 44, 47, 49b, 50, 53, 55, 59, 61a, 63, 75a, 76, 77b, 79a–b, 85, 104, 105a–b, 106a–b, 109a, 110a–b, 117a, 117c, 118, 121, 130, 147b, 152, 174, 179, 202,

Jay Avila photographs: 14, 158, 189, 190, 267, 324, 326–327, 344,

John K. Robson photographs: 60, 65a–b, 71, 93a–b, 100, 191, 295, 327, 384, 403, 426, 429, 439

Joseph D. Thomas photographs: 18e, 64c, 83a, 122, 125, 129, 135a–d, 138b, 139, 154, 163, 196, 355, 387

Richard Fortin Collection: 23a, 28–29, 64a, 72–73

Spinner Collection: 22, 32, 39d , 41b, 42b, 57, 58a 66, 67, 69, 77a, 87a, 94b,–c, 95b–c, 97a, 201, 264b, 339, 351, 371a

Standard–Times Collections

Standard–Times Archives: iv, 15, 18a–c, 23a–b, 27a–b, 28a–b, 31b, 33b, 34c–e, 35b, 37, 39a–c, 41a, 41,c, 42a, 43b, 49a, 49c–d, 58b, 61b, 62, 64b, 68, 74, 75b, 78a–b, 79c–d, 80, 81, 82a, 83b, 84, 86a–b, 87b–c, 89c, 90, 92a–b, 103, 106c, 107, 109b, 111, 113, 114, 117b, 119, 120, 123, 124, 126, 128a–c, 132, 133, 134, 138a, 140a–b, 141, 142, 144, 147c, 148, 149, 155, 165, 166, 167, 181a–b, 183, 186, 187, 197, 203, 206, 207, 236, 262, 268b–c, 301, 325a–b, 376, 386a–b, 388, 390, 393, 432

Gannett Archives: 264a, 319a–b, 399

Ronald Rolo: 147a, 159, 160,

Others

Boston Globe: 317

Boston Public Library: Leslie Jones Collection: 385

Buzzards Bay Coalition: 382,

Carl Safina: 245

Cyber–physical Architecture #2: 21

David Crockett: 222a

Frank Leslie's Illustrated Newspaper: 36

Fred Leblanc: 391

Hauck Family: 51

Historic American Buildings Survey: 96a–b; 234

Kettereing University Archives: 228a–b, 229a–b,

Kevin Smith/Alaska Stock: 251

Maine.gov: 343a–b,

Massachusetts Institute of Technology: 24, 25

National Aeronautics and Space Administration (NASA): 278, 329

National Oceanic and Atmospheric Administration (NOAA): 210, 216b, 232a–b, 266a–b, 303, 304b, 333, 336, 348, 354a–b

New Bedford Light: 400

New Bedford Whaling Museum: 31a, 89a, 94a, 95a, 97b, 102

New York City Municipal Archives: 171

Newsroom Ink: 241

Northeast Seafood Coalition: 320a–b

Preservation & Rehabilitation of a Historic Commercial Area: 45

Roan Conrad: 216a

Richard Paull Family: 33a

Rick Lopes: 443

Rotch Jones Duff & Garden Museum: 89b

Schooner *Ernestina–Morrissey* Association: 394, 395, 396a–b, 397, 398

Sea Education Association (SEA): 270, 271, 272a–b, 273a–b, 274a–b, 275, 276, 281, 285, 287a–b, 289, 291

South Carolina Educational Television (SCETV): 172

The Nature Conservancy: 226

Turner Construction: 13a

UMass Dartmouth: 265, 268a; SMAST: 169

Waterfront Historic Area League: 30, 40, 82b

Wiener Zeitung: 175

Wikimedia Commons: 221, 222b, 223, 244, 247, 257, 292, 297, 302, 304a, 308–309, 311, 332, 350, 355a–b

Woods Hole Oceanographic Institute: 279, 283, 341